On Higher Education

On Higher Education

Selected Writings, 1956–2006

BURTON R. CLARK

With the Collaboration of Adele Clark

Foreword by Patricia J. Gumport

The Johns Hopkins University Press

Baltimore

The Johns Hopkins University Press
2715 North Charles Street
Baltimore, Maryland 21218-4363
www.press.jhu.edu

Library of Congress Control Number: 2008930596

ISBN 13: 978-0-8018-9020-8 (hc)
ISBN 10: 0-8018-9020-9 (hc)
ISBN 13: 978-0-8018-9021-5 (pbk)
ISBN 10: 0-8018-9021-7 (pbk)

A catalog record for this book is available from the British Library.

Special discounts are available for bulk purchases of this book. For more information, please contact Special Sales at 410-516-6936 or specialsales@press.jhu.edu.

Happy he who came to know the causes of things.—Virgil

CONTENTS

FOREWORD

This volume is a gift, and the opportunity to write the foreword an honor. *On Higher Education* is a fitting capstone to Burton R. Clark's distinguished scholarly career. The essays in this volume span a half-century, and they reflect both the enormous range of topics that captured his analytical interest and the originality of insights from his field research—work that excavated and created a rich body of literature on higher education systems and organizations.

When Professor Clark enthusiastically accepted the invitation to assemble this collection, I knew it would be crafted with the same consistently high quality as each individual work. Adele Clark, his wife and creative partner, worked very closely with him in choosing the selections and in scrupulously editing the introductions to each part and the commentaries to each essay. To my mind the book is even more impressive than initially imagined: Professor and Mrs. Clark tackled a year-long task with their typical tireless effort, choosing from a lifetime of materials and deciding among a number of approaches. The result is a remarkable achievement written with parsimonious clarity.

It is not hyperbole to say that the works of Burton R. Clark helped lay the foundation for the study of higher education. They have defined the field for the many academic generations that preceded and will succeed ours. I know my colleagues join me in highest regard for this impressive scholarship. Professor Clark will long be known for the originality, breadth, and depth of his intellectual contributions to our field—from micro- to meso- to macro-level insights. To give just one example, I recently used the ideas in his 1973 article as an organizing framework for an entire edited volume, *Sociology of Higher Education,* to depict the evolution of the field over the past thirty years. There was good reason to dedicate the volume to him.

The reader will understand how the present selection of essays represents an opportunity for Professor Clark to contemplate his own scholarly achievements over the past fifty years. The collection is organized in four major parts arranged chronologically and thematically. It begins with an excerpt from a doctoral dissertation that reflected training at a time when sociologists were immersed in structural-functionalism, and extends, over decades, to the cross-national studies he continued to investigate well into his eighties. The collection thus follows Professor Clark's journey from his early field research on organizational adaptation, to his analysis of the U.S. system, then on to his expansive writing comparing the complex dynamics of national systems, and finally to his later fieldwork on entrepreneurial universities. It also makes apparent how, along the way, he moved beyond his formative beginnings as a sociologist, drawing upon the other social sciences to become more fully interdisciplinary.

The introductions to each part and each essay are new commentaries that locate each selection within the context of Professor Clark's broader agenda and career. With characteristic humility, these reflections make clear his perspective on the distinctive aims and contributions of each piece. His self-awareness also reveals how a scholar forges ahead propelled by intellectual curiosity, and translates that energy into focused projects that yield valuable insights for others to consider. In this way, Professor Clark teaches what is possible by his own example. The reflections are written in a genuine voice, characteristically direct and sparse, but sprinkled with biographical details that reveal much about his circumstances at each stage, including his great care in wielding his skills as a researcher and his words as an author. These reflections are quintessential Clark—speaking always as both teacher and student of higher education. His ever-engaging voice captures the broad significance of the work while illuminating details that bring the circumstances fully to life.

This collection is indispensable for faculty who teach about higher education, and will help graduate students understand the scholarly legacies that define the major currents of thinking about higher education as a complex enterprise. Professor Clark shows us how to draw original conceptual insights from field research. His conceptual contributions resonate so deeply that many are taken for granted by the younger generations who may not have read his original works. The concepts of "saga" and "cooling-out" function, e.g., are central to our understanding of how colleges operate. His work on the academic profession reveals how faculty inhabit small and different worlds. And his most recent research, on entrepreneurial universities, uncovers the workings of their steering cores; i.e., how leaders see the necessity of sharpening their institutional missions and priorities. I have chosen these examples of his many original contributions; our colleagues and members of the profession at large will each have their own favorites.

Indeed, Professor Clark's work ignited my own interest in studying higher education. He helped me to define not only my academic career but also my habits of mind. I was fortunate to work directly with him as a postdoctoral researcher upon completion of my PhD. Both interpersonally and from his writings he has continued to shape my thinking about the core issues in higher education, and to elucidate the dynamic interplay among academic structures, values, and contexts. His work has also fueled my ongoing interest in studying the persistent tension between imperatives for continuity and change. His publications frame several of my own studies, and they structure syllabi for my graduate courses—introductory work and advanced seminars.

Highest honor must be accorded to a scholar whose collective work changes how people think. Such work is all the more laudable when it stands the test of time. To his students, Professor Clark's advice in both word and deed will be heard for years to come: do fieldwork; study comparatively (cross-nationally); connect with practitioners; and write vividly, yet crisply. As a special aside to those who undertake major research projects: he has long advised us to write books—for they stand up by themselves on the shelf. Indeed, this volume will stand proudly in all of our libraries. Vintage Clark in substance and style, it may well improve with age.

Patricia J. Gumport
Stanford University

INTRODUCTION

The work in this volume, a half-century of research, arches from a dissertation account of adult education in a school system to an explanation of how some modern universities throughout the world have managed to deliberately change their traditional character to a more adaptive posture.

Throughout, we first seek to expose the complexity and nuance of how core features of higher education operate. We emphasize the concrete realities of actual practice and reveal how one scholar built perspectives and concepts in a cumulative fashion from research studies carried out over a long period of time. The selections show how I got started, how I built momentum in my work over decades, and, in the concluding part, how I focused on the way instruments of change can be purposefully instilled in universities and colleges.

The thirty-three selections gathered here are from published articles, chapters of key books, and public lectures and addresses from the beginning of my career through my postretirement years. The selections are arranged in four parts that follow a chronological flow. Because I savored writing in book format, an unusual number of lengthy choices are key book chapters from the 1980s.

Part I, Fashioning an Analytical Mode, sets forth the findings of three successive research studies, beginning with my doctoral dissertation. Each study was thoroughly grounded in field research. The dissertation was a case study of a peripheral program—adult education—in a school district. It highlighted concepts of organizational marginality and precarious values. The next venture in the field was a case study of a community college, which produced the twin constructs of open-door colleges and the cooling-out function. The third involved studying three leading, highly selective liberal arts colleges over five years; this led to the notion of organizational saga.

By the end of these three studies dating from the mid-1950s to mid-1960s, I had settled on a useful research style: to develop clarifying concepts *inductively* from the realities reported in qualitative case studies. These investigations focused on the institutional level of development. We hope the selections are particularly helpful to graduate students and young academics now making early, hard choices about how to become productive scholars.

Part II, Probing the American National System, offers a melange of additional pieces written in the late 1960s and early 1970s: student culture, faculty professionalization, flexible interorganizational relations, university reaction to deep crisis, and an early definition (1973) of the sociology of higher education. These essays pointed to a system level of development as well as to the institutional. They also veer from topic to topic, with little of the interconnections seen in part I. Conference-type topics will often do that.

Part III, Cultivating Cross-National Insight, is the largest of the four parts. Articles, speeches, and particularly book chapters from the late 1970s, 1980s, and 1990s, following a career-shaping decision to "go international," are included. This dominant section offers a case study of an entire European national system, the opaque Italian structure. It points to the key book in my career, *The Higher Education System: Academic Organization in Cross-National Perspective*, published in 1983. I drew on its concluding chapter to make an early strong statement—based on comparative analysis—of the best way to organize universities for the future.

In 1985 I wrote the resolute article, "What Went Wrong in America," based on a cross-national understanding of the relation between secondary and higher education. Farther along, a 1993 essay stressed the fast-growing complexity of modern universities, which follows upon the explosive growth of knowledge. In a lecture that same year, I explained how the core of the research university changed dramatically from its beginnings in nineteenth-century German universities to its later development in departments and research centers of late twentieth-century American universities. Part III concludes with a major address in 1998—the Comenius Lecture—presented to a large audience of university administrators at a UNESCO World Congress on Higher Education in Paris. By that point I was well into the pursuit of specific elements of university change; these comprise the essays in part IV.

Those were exciting years. The terrain of cross-national comparison of national systems and their many universities is vast. The challenges, then and now, include how best to shake countries out of their national tunnel visions and how best to convey the news that universities simultaneously do many different things, some patently antagonistic to each other. The question "What is the university?" is always the wrong one. Journalistic simplicities have to give way—if truth be told—to complex stories that escape contextual confinements even as they remain based in specific settings.

Part IV, Revealing the Armature of University Change, focuses entirely on how some modern universities develop an infrastructure and culture that connect them primarily to change rather than to the status quo or the status quo ante. While doing field research in five European universities, I advanced the idea of "entrepreneurial university" as an enveloping concept, which could be used to frame institution case studies. This concept and the case studies were reported in a 1998 book, *Creating Entrepreneurial Universities: Organizational Pathways of Transformation.*

The idea of entrepreneurial universities seemed applicable to a wider, international arena, and from 2000 to 2003 I added nine more widely distributed cases to my original five. At the same time I pushed beyond the ideas of transformation to features of sustained change. Complex institutional accounts are offered in *Sustaining Change in Universities: Continuities in Case Studies and Concepts* (2004). Part IV ends with normative statements, published and unpublished, which vigorously argue for the advantages of focusing on interrelations among elements of change as they interact with one another in specified contexts. I argue strongly that the abstraction of variables from their contexts loses crucial interactions.

A transition from a disciplinary perspective to an interdisciplinary one is evident in parts III and IV. As I went international, I simply had to understand the rudiments of history, politics, and economics of each country and how they shaped the framework of its university system. My new colleagues in other countries were also, more often than not, historians or political scientists; rarely were they institutional sociologists. My early post-docs and faculty associates in the Yale group were mainly historians, who brought to the table an exacting regard for factual reality. "Isms" such as postmodernism did not make much headway in such circles. I gained more than I lost as I gradually cut my once-a-year ties to sociology and increased my participation in interdisciplinary national and international associations centered on the study of higher education.

The primary audience for this collection of my writing surely will be professors and graduate students in the social sciences, especially those who study universities. If the book accomplishes the two goals set forth at the outset, students can find much rooted knowledge about the workings of higher education. By reading these essays from beginning to end, they also can acquire insight into the making of a career—through unhappy as well as fortuitous appointments, failures as well as successes—from an account of one researcher's half-century of effort and achievement.

Comments on each piece place each essay in its own context of time and circumstance. Sometimes we highlight the occasion, as in the 1998 Comenius Lecture. Sometimes we emphasize the state of knowledge at the time, as, for example, the statements on faculty governance and culture in the early 1960s, when the literature was thin. We sought to minimize repetition, but recurrent themes do occur. Overlapping is inherent in a body of work that throughout followed certain analytical approaches. Such repetition ensured that basic points were highlighted, not lost, in the shuffle of shifting specific topics.

I have tried to weave a research tapestry with a complicated design. Vertical threads, representing ethnographic and historical perspectives lead, one by one, to the realities of practice. Horizontal threads are the cross-national cases that specify what is unique and what is common about each national system. Thus, they combine international comparisons with a pursuit of observable reality. Both types of threads make a striking pattern of intense color and richness. Taken together, we hope they constitute a major advance in grappling with the vast complexities of modern universities and their enabling systems.

A note about terminology: Please understand that when I wrote a piece before the 1970s, *man* and *men* were terms used to refer inclusively to both men and women. The shift to more careful delineation of the female gender took place gradually after that time.

PART ONE

Fashioning an Analytical Mode

These earliest essays served to develop a personal analytical style. That style is qualitative; it is based on institutional case studies; and it insists on reasoning inductively from observed practice rather than deductively from prior theorizing that prejudges reality. I would return to this mode four decades later, in the essays that constitute part IV.

From the hindsight of a half-century of research (and old age) I believe that training graduate students by means of theory-defined hypotheses takes them precisely in the wrong direction—at least when they tackle the character of such complicated social systems as universities and colleges. As these fledgling researchers abstract variables from particular contexts, they move away from interactions among basic features that propel actual decision-making. They assume that all other factors embedded in certain local settings play out elsewhere. They do not. No wonder researcher knowledge is so different from practitioner knowledge! It is often useless to the people running things.

The comments introducing the following essays describe further how each came about in a certain sequence, and why by the end of my first dozen years I thought I had a useful analytical mode in hand.

INTRODUCTION TO CHAPTER 1

At the close of World War II in Europe in the spring of 1945, my regiment (part of the 42nd Infantry Division) ended its eastern advance in the small Austrian town of Anif-bei-Salzburg. Several months later, when the U.S. government dropped two atomic bombs on Japanese cities, thus hastening the Japanese surrender, a transfer to the Pacific Theater to take part in the storming of the Japanese beaches was no longer a possibility. I needed to make a decision about life after the army. Old hands in my unit who had been to college convinced me that the upcoming GI Bill, just announced, was too good a deal to overlook. The government's promised financial assistance—in my case fifty months of college tuition plus a monthly stipend—prompted me to apply to several universities. UCLA sent back an early favorable reply. I requested and gained admittance to the September 1946 entering class.

At twenty-five, I was very happy to have survived the war in one piece, jubilant to be safely alive, wearing civilian garb, in the bright sunlight of Southern California. However, like so many other veterans, I was conscious of years lost in getting to an education and moving into a career. We were very grateful that we could count on that marvelous boon for vets—the GI Bill. In my case, it got me to college at last some eight years after graduation from high school.

Once there, I was highly motivated to graduate and attended summer sessions as well as winter terms. While moving rapidly to a bachelor's degree in 1949, I sampled engineering, political science, economics, psychology, and sociology along the way. During my senior year I decided to pursue graduate training in the widespread possibilities of sociology. Why sociology? It was a young discipline that was just spreading its wings. I was taken with the possibilities of new insightful analyses that could illuminate the workings of entire sectors of society. I also married Adele Halitsky, an undergraduate who was majoring in zoology. (She dissected dogfish at home and even stored them in a bathtub filled with formalde-hyde.) We decided I should remain at UCLA in the new, small, sociology segment of a combined department of anthropology and sociology, rather than chance a move to one of the heartland sociology departments, then at Columbia, Harvard, and Chicago.

Two years of graduate coursework convinced me to become an analyst of purposeful formal organizations, an approach modeled by Robert K. Merton at Columbia. His brilliant essays on latent functions and unan-ticipated consequences in organizations and the work of a remarkable group of his students—Philip Selznick, Seymour Martin Lipset, Peter Blau, Alvin Gouldner, for example—convinced me of the richness of an organizational approach. Other academics of my generation trained to pursue the ways of formal organizations sought to specialize in study-ing business firms, public agencies, hospitals, and prisons. I decided to concentrate on schools and colleges, a sphere that had caught little atten-tion.

After bringing my newly acquired "Mertonian" point of view to bear on the organization of schools and colleges, my first choice for a disserta-tion topic was to study leadership in the huge Los Angeles school district. A faculty committee assembled by Philip Selznick and Leonard Broom, the department chair, accepted my proposal. With their assistance the proposal won financial support for one year in the form of a Social Sci-ence Research Council Award. So off I went to the district's downtown headquarters to gain access, interview, observe, and gather armfuls of documents.

Within thirty days it was clear that I was in over my head: what I had aimed to do would take five years at least, not one. And there was always the chance of eliciting superficial findings as I attempted to make my way through multiple screens of opaque bureaucracy. I decided then to study one branch of the system, a set of twenty-five adult schools trying to survive as best they could among major system divisions devoted to elementary education, to secondary education, and to an emerging one: "junior colleges." My dissertation committee agreed.

I found that the strength of any particular educational purpose or "value" depended on its organizational underpinnings. Everyone might agree in public opinion polls that adult education is a good idea. But its support becomes problematic when its organizational location throws it into competition with the education of the young in public schools and colleges, and with the core purposes of such other locales as unions, libraries, and museums. I wrote up my dissertation around the ideas of organizational marginality and precarious values. Here I was much influenced by Selznick's classic volume, *Leadership in Administration: A Sociological Interpretation*, published by Harper & Row in 1957. (A paperback edition was made available by the University of California Press in 1984.)

The manuscript was accepted by the University of California Press for publication (*Adult Education in Transition: A Study of Organizational Insecurity*, 1956), and I followed up by publishing two articles on the subject. One went directly to the *American Sociological Review* (ASR), the central journal in sociology (a pleasing location for scholarly repute). The other went to the Center for the Study of Liberal Education for Adults in Chicago because I wanted to bring my interpretations to the attention of relevant "practitioners." We have included only the first article here. One article tells the story well enough, especially because adult education plays a minor role in the ongoing study of higher education. The articles in chapters 4 and 5 are better, more relevant examples of how to publish simultaneously for scholarship and practitioner audiences.

Publishing articles in two places after having written a book foreshadowed inclinations developed more fully later in my career, particularly after I took on an interdisciplinary stance and became interested in attracting the attention of practicing administrators. During the 1980s, 1990s, and between 2001 and 2004, e.g., I published five articles in the small new journal, *Tertiary Education and Management* issued by the European Association for Institutional Research. By then, I had purposively strayed far from the mainstream sociology journals in my original discipline.

Early publications from my dissertation bolstered my confidence. I felt validated as a scholar who could do organizational case studies and publish results in qualitative narratives. That confidence included my willingness to concentrate not on publishing articles year by year about findings that surfaced early on, but to write a book every five years or so in which I would incorporate them. For me, the dogma became: for each field study, write a book and develop at least one major concept in a derivative article. When I later became a mentor, I touted this line of thinking to several generations of graduate students. I was pleased when a major sociological reader, *Complex Organizations* (1961), edited by Amitai Etzioni, chose to include my ASR article. This reader contained the work of such iconic figures as Max Weber, Chester I. Barnard, Talcott Parsons, Robert K. Merton, James G. March, and Herbert A. Simon. It was a pleasure to be included in a section on organizational goals, just a few years after my first article was published. Appearing here is a slightly abridged version of the original paper as it appeared in the highly useful Etzioni reader. Later validation came my way when *Adult Education in Transition* was reprinted in 1980 by Arno Press (a New York *Times* company) after it was selected by Harriet Zuckerman and Robert K. Merton as one of the fifty best dissertations in sociology during the past half-century.

After this period of concentrating on adult education, another sector, "junior colleges," as they were then called, caught my eye. I gradually began to focus on this level of public education at the same time I accepted a three-year teaching stint at Stanford.

CHAPTER I

Organizational Adaptation and Precarious Values

WITH THE PROLIFERATION of formal organizations in modern bureaucratic society it is apparent that the fate of various social values may be affected by the action of administrative agencies. Organizational analysis has shown that rationally contrived structures may transform their initial values in the process of adjusting to emergent problems. Where a number of organizations undergo a similar value transformation, the change may shape a value system of the larger society. The processes by which organizations shape values, however, are only dimly understood and difficult to discern. It is proposed that such effects can be seen most clearly by studying organizations that are tied to weakly established values. The purpose of this essay is, first, to identify some of the conditions of weakness in social values, and second, to present a case study of one type of value modification. The case materials have been taken from research on the adult education movement in California.

Precarious Values

Social values may be defined as conceptions of the desirable that are distinctive of some human group.[1] These conceptions are usually voiced in goals and standards of action—in relatively specific notions of *what* should be obtained and *how*. The aspect of values that concerns us here is the degree to which they are secure. The degree of security will, of course, be determined by many conditions of the social and cultural context. The

Based on "Organizational Adaptation and Precarious Values: A Case Study," *American Sociological Review* 21, no. 3 (1956): 327–36. As abridged in *Complex Organizations: A Sociological Reader,* edited by Amitai Etzioni, 157–67. New York: Holt, Rinehart and Winston, 1961.

following are several general grounds for value insecurity that are identifiable in a wide range of situations.

1. *Social values tend to be precarious when they are undefined.* This concerns the link between general value conceptions and a proximate set of goals and norms. Values are *undefined* when they are not embodied in existing goals and standards of committed groups. They lack specific normative reference and no one knows what various symbols really mean. Values may be precarious, then, when there is a strong need for definition of behavioral cues, for identification of what is proper in the name of given symbols. This may be referred to as content weakness, or weakness in the normative system.

2. *Social values tend to be precarious when the position of functionaries[2] is not fully legitimized.* This concerns the grounding of a value in a firm social base. A surrounding population may be so hostile to the value conceptions of a smaller group that the group must struggle even to gain a position within the relevant arenas from which to work. In such extreme cases, e.g., the Jehovah Witnesses, the right to act must be won. A search for legitimacy in this sense is a central tactical problem for highly deviant political groups, such as the Communist Party of the United States. The point is that in specific organizations or in the general society, values may be precarious because of the weak position of custodians in the social structure.

3. *Social values tend to be precarious when they are unacceptable to a "host" population.* This condition, the most apparent source of weakness, is usually related to the second factor above. Groups supporting a new set of values, for instance, are likely to obtain a legitimate status only as their goals and practices become minimally accepted, i.e., seen as in general accordance with the value systems of the larger society. But to some degree these two conditions are separable. Pluralistic societies "tolerate" minority values. Thus functionaries may have a legitimate status even when their values are somewhat disliked by other groups. Then value weakness stems solely from lack of support by the general membership of the larger social system. Hence, the unacceptability of certain values to a host population can be taken as an analytically distinct factor in the precariousness of those values.

Secure values, then, are those that are clearly defined in behavior and strongly established in the minds of many. Such values literally take care of themselves. Precarious values, on the other hand, need deliberately intentioned agents, for they must be normatively defined, or socially established, or both.

This poses the general problem of how groups attempt to implement their values when they are precarious, and what changes in meaning and acceptance are incurred. The case in point concerns adult education administrators in a state school system. While adult education has had some acceptance in the American society as a general conception, functionaries have generally found themselves working with a weakly established set of values. As will be seen below, the goals and standards of this field have been somewhat undefined for several decades. In addition, adult education has had a marginal existence within the public schools, with its administrative agencies forced to search diligently for a secure operational base. An organizational adaptation has ensued that involves a transformation in values. This adaptation may be understood by recapitulating the core problems of adult education departments and the general response they have made.

The Case of the Adult School

CONDITIONS OF ADMINISTRATIVE ACTION

Adult education emerged as a movement in the United States in the 1920s with newly acquired organizations and a corps of spokesmen. Within the public schools the movement meant a changed conception of adult participation. Before 1925 "night school" was emphasized, with programs restricted mainly to elementary and high school work, vocational training, and Americanization-Citizenship classes. The schools were heavily "remedial" in orientation, based originally on an extended-day definition.

Since 1925 there has been a steady drift away from these characteristics, with a trend toward diversification of effort and broadening of clientele.

1. *The manifest ends of action.* The philosophy that became prevalent in the late 1920s with the emergence of an adult education movement had, in retrospect, two sharply divergent aspects: first, as an outgrowth of the Americanization effort, purpose was frequently voiced in the language of "enlightenment." This connoted a commitment to liberal education and a sense of educational mission. But the attempt to tie adult education to the ideals of liberal education did not prove viable. Grassroots administra-

tors were not in step with this doctrine but increasingly stressed a tenet related to the means of administration—that a proper conception of adult education could be implemented only by breaking away from formal patterns and clientele restrictions. For a quarter of a century this liberation theme has been growing within administrative circles, with the result that administrative units have increasingly worked with diffuse purpose. The program should be extremely diversified in order to meet a host of present individual, group, and societal problems. Such "purposes" hardly constitute directives, however, and officials are under pressure to establish more specific aims. The specific objectives of adult education in California are stated as follows:

1. To make adults aware of their civic responsibilities to one another and to the community
2. To make them economically more efficient
3. To develop an understanding of the attitudes and personal adjustments required for successful home life and family relationships
4. To promote health and physical fitness
5. To provide an opportunity for cultural development
6. To supplement and broaden education backgrounds
7. To provide for the development of avocational interests through opportunities for self-expression

Generality of purpose remains, however, with "cultural development," "self-expression," etc., covering a wide range of possibilities. Also, the different objectives do not receive priority or emphasis, since a selective approach would reflect the tendency toward restriction and formalization from which adult education officials have sought to escape. Selective aims have not been forthcoming, and statements about specific objectives merely reaffirm that purpose is to be as broad as possible. Open-ended purpose is a basic characteristic of California adult schools.

The more indefinite purpose becomes, however, the less can ends intervene in administrative choice. For goals to influence decision-making, they must provide cues for what should be done. When the administrator is confronted with the recurrent question of what courses to add to his program, his diffuse aims leave him without criteria. He works within a milieu where there is no *educational* reason for the administrator to favor one subject over another. Thus, stated objectives are likely to become simply a rationale for a program broadly conceived and flexible in administration. The manifest ends of action function to widen administrative discretion.

2. *Organizational marginality.*[3] Since the basic purposes of the public schools center on the training of the young, various levels of education have become legitimized by relevance to this concern. Elementary schools, high schools, and junior colleges form an educational ladder in the public schools, and in California they all come under the doctrine of free public education. It is with these major units, comparatively well established within the school hierarchy and in the public image of education, that adult schools compete for position, budget, and support.

Within this organizational complex, adult education resides as an activity that is disconnected from the primary endeavor. It is not a part of the sequence of grade, its "students" exist completely outside of the range of compulsory attendance and have other occupations. These attributes leave adult education as a peripheral, non-mandatory effort of the schools, and its officials typically find themselves organizationally marginal. This marginality stems from the program's comparatively low degree of legitimacy as an important school activity and charge on public funds. A school program needs acceptance from various groups—its own personnel, other school units, the state legislature, politically potent interest groups, and the unorganized public. Only in the eyes of its own administrators and some of its teachers has the adult education activity had the level of acceptance that would guarantee its stability. The California Congress of Parents and Teachers, e.g., is a strong supporter of adult education and is closely tied to adult schools through co-sponsorship arrangements, but when pressed PTA will maintain that the "compulsory education program" should not be jeopardized by "volunteer programs in which category we place adult education."[4]

The marginality of the program may thus be seen as the *basic source of insecurity for administrative units.* Without a firmly legitimized status, the adult schools have little control over the conditions of their existence. Their position as "low man on the totem pole" is dangerous not only in times of depression, but whenever school finances are under pressure, for they stand to be "cut the first and the most severely when financial support runs low."[5] To win a permanently secure niche, administrative strategy needs to be oriented toward ultimately achieving a "peer" status (the ideal), or a fixed partial parity of status that is clearly defined and respected by all. Short-run tactics, however, must be oriented to the problem of justifying peripheral activity. The schools need "results." Thus, marginality within the larger, host educational systems heightens the effect of the following conditions.

3. *Operating pressures.* The most important pressures bearing upon these schools in day-to-day administration arise from *the enrollment economy.* First, school income is largely set by student attendance. Financial support from the state is figured by the hours of attendance logged the previous year, producing a direct relation between student turnout and level of state aid.[6] Unless a school maintains and preferably increases attendance, future support is likely to stagnate, and a major slump in attendance constitutes a serious threat to organizational welfare. The closeness of this relationship depends upon the degree of *local* support, i.e., whether local authorities will back the program out of their own tax levy if state aid decreases.[7] The less likely this guarantee, the more budget and support rests on a quantity-of-clientele basis.[8] Since marginality is the common condition, *the appropriations process sets incentives for action in the direction of building attendance.* There are no dependable sources of financial support independent of student turnout. Therefore, everything is staked on the search for clientele.

A second important aspect of the enrollment economy is the tenuous tie of student participants. The student body is part-time, voluntary, and highly susceptible to casual attendance and easy termination. Participation is sharply affected by outside events beyond the control of the organization, e.g., warm weather, holiday seasons, and community events. Of all student groups, part-time adult students are surely the most difficult to maintain, and any adult education agency, public or private, has to solve the problem of sustaining a non-captive student body. The point is that the enrollment economy becomes a double-barreled pressure for adaptation to outside interests. On the one hand, administrators are faced with an uncommitted clientele, on the other, with the fact that students are the rationale for existence, and in California their attendance the basis for appropriations. These conditions converge to define the prime short-run problem to be that of creating and sustaining a clientele base. An adaptation is called for that will reasonably guarantee the attraction, retention, and replacement of students. The needs of the enrollment economy generate persistent pressures to which administrators and teachers must make a number of adaptive responses.

These pressures cannot be ignored, for they are reflected in policies set by school boards and top professional staffs. For example, minimum size requirements for both the introduction and the continuation of classes are widespread throughout the state. Their effect is to make enrollment *the* criterion by which courses are initiated and continued.

The organizational adaptation. These conditions of an organized system induce the following tendencies. Irrespective of intent, *the enrollment economy* renders the adult school highly sensitive to public likes and dislikes. Since "the public" is quite heterogeneous in both educational background and part-time interest, ready adjustment to it entails a conglomerate, "cafeteria" program. At the same time, the *manifest ends of action* are permissive and allow the school to adapt freely. Stated ends interpose no objection to the tendency that follows from practical pressures; in fact, they favor an effort to do all things for all men. There is an absence of specific missions from which standards and professional authority might flow. In addition, *marginality* deepens the need for administrators to assume an "other-directed" orientation. Insecurity fastens attention on building support by means at hand.

With these conditions lying behind administration, the cumulative effect of decision-making is to adjust the program rapidly to expressed interests of the population. The adult education program that has developed in California may therefore be characterized as dominantly *a service enterprise,* for the key feature of this adaptation is the attempt of the schools to service consumers in an immediate way. Here several features of the schools may be adduced as evidence of a normatively unrestricted activity. (1) The main instruments of program building have become "the sign-up list" and "the group petition." These devices are simply objective ways of gauging demand. If demand is of the magnitude where the survival of a proposed class becomes probable, then its initiation is feasible. If the number of recruits increases, then more classes can be added and that part of the course assortment will grow. Thus, the schools have an extreme version of what is known elsewhere in education as the elective system, and the relatively unlimited play of student choice determines the evolution of the collection of courses. (2) The structure of the teaching force is accommodated to the requirements of a service enterprise. Such a high degree of staff flexibility is needed that full-time work and guaranteed employment become administratively undesirable. Adaptation to a heterogeneous clientele involves considerable specialization in subject matter and the hiring of the part-time specialist, e.g., a welder, a gardnener, a dental technician, a housewife skilled in lampshade-making. In Los Angeles in 1952, e.g., over 90 percent of the adult teachers were part-time, with one-fourth working four hours a week or less.[9] Less than 20 percent had tenure in adult education and less than 5 percent possessed tenure at a full-time level of employment.[10]

Building programs by consumer preference, however, produces an administrative dilemma. Located within school systems, adult education officials find their practices scrutinized by others in the light of school norms that are professional or "inner-directed" in kind, i.e., that educators should plan, initiate, and control changes on the basis of research and the assessment of experts. When laymen challenge school practices, for instance, the administrator ordinarily rests his case on expert opinion. Moreover, the drive for higher professional status on the part of teachers and administrators reinforces these sentiments. Thus, there are school values, central to the self-image of the educator, that are against ready adjustment to student demands.

When this professional orientation is brought to bear upon the adult activity, the administrators do not fare well. They are judged to be in a posture of expediency, with much of their work seen as having little relationship to "education." From outside the school system, state legislators and economy-minded interest groups repeatedly challenge the propriety of what is done. Cake-decorating, rug-making, and square dancing are some of the classes that bring the adult schools under fire. In one recent case of opposition, the entire state program underwent a hostile, sustained scrutiny by an investigating committee of the state Senate.[11] The current program was challenged as one saturated with frills, with 55 percent of total enrollment placed in the frill category.[12] This investigation resulted in unfavorable publicity and restrictive legislation.

Thus in many ways a service enterprise, uncontrolled by school norms, sorely tries the educational respectability of the agencies involved. But the service tendency cannot be turned off easily since it is impelled by basic pressures of an organizational system. Classes of a questionable nature continually crop up when field administrators work with ad hoc demand, under pressure for an enrollment payoff. The crux of the matter is that the adult schools labor under incompatible needs. Their central dilemma is that the short-run need for clientele, set by the enrollment economy, strains against the long-run need for educational respectability as the basis for legitimacy. The adult schools are torn between being a service facility and a school enterprise.

Notes

1. Clyde Kluckhohn, "Values and Value-Orientations in the Theory of Action," in Talcott Parsons and Edward A. Shils, eds., *Toward a General Theory of Action* (Cambridge, Mass.: Harvard University Press, 1952), 395 and 417.

2. A term used by Hertzler in describing those chiefly responsible for the "active implementation" of institutions. Used in this way, *functionary* refers to activists outside of organizations as well as organizational agents. Joyce O. Hertzler, *Society in Action* (New York: The Dryden Press, 1954), 200–201.

3. The "organizations" under analysis are adult schools, units of school systems that have adult education as their only program commitment. Multi-program organizations that may include adult education (e.g., junior colleges) are here excluded.

4. Testimony of PTA representative in *Partial Report of the Senate Interim Committee on Adult Education,* The Senate, State of California, March 1953, 461.

5. Bureau of Adult Education, *Report and Proceedings of the Montecito Workshop in Adult Education,* California State Department of Education, 1952, 85–86.

6. Five hundred and twenty-five hours of student time are equal to one unit of "average daily attendance," the basic unit in state apportionments.

7. State apportionments and local tax levies are the two main sources of school revenue. Thus there is an inverse relationship between the proportion of costs covered by one source as compared to the other. Local boards of education and professional administrators tend to view "cost" as the share of total outlay that is shouldered by the local tax levy, for which they are directly responsible.

8. Some adult education officials are allowed only as much money as their enrollment brings into the local school system from state aid, i.e., *no* support from local tax funds.

9. Adult Education Branch Files, Los Angeles School System.

10. Personnel Division Files, Los Angeles School System.

11. See Partial Report of the Senate Interim Committee on Adult Education, The Senate, State of California, March 1953, *passim.*

12. Ibid., 171–74.

INTRODUCTION TO CHAPTERS 2 AND 3

I accepted a position in the sociology wing of a joint department of anthropology and sociology at Stanford in 1953. It was my first academic appointment. At the time, Stanford was, as declared by its president, still "land rich and money poor." The small sociology faculty was operating in difficult circumstances (in effect, in receivership) as the administration and senior faculty from other departments attempted to entice leading sociologists such as Paul Lazarsfeld to come out to "the farm" and build a major sociology department. As a disposable junior faculty member, I was kept on one-year appointments for three years. I also had to learn how to teach. The closest I have come to a stomach ulcer was during the first half of the first year. I was attempting to finish my UCLA dissertation against a mid-winter deadline while at the same time spending five hours preparing for each hour in the classroom. To make matters worse, I recall teaching a course in social disorganization, a subject for which I had no background and little regard. The assignment to give four additional courses that year added to my angst.

But I was also thinking about research. While working in the field in Los Angeles, I became intrigued with the rising prominence of two-year junior or community colleges, which are structurally located between high schools and four-year colleges. After exploring the possibilities of studying examples of these colleges located within commuting range of Stanford, I selected a relatively new one in San Jose. I then set out during my last two years at Stanford (and the following two years at Harvard) to identify a latent problem lurking in the local college that could possibly hold true for two-year colleges throughout California and the nation.

It gradually became clear to me, while interviewing teachers and counselors and studying student records, that the open-door admissions policy (California junior colleges did not even require high school graduation) created major challenges within the college. A wide discrepancy existed between the hopes of a large number of students and their hobbled personal ability to realize those wishes. To elucidate this problem, I turned to "the cooling-out function," a fascinating construct originally voiced by Erving Goffman in the early 1950s for other domains in society.

Unfortunately, the meaning of the concept became distorted during the next two decades. As I originally formulated it in some detail, it pointed to a "soft landing" for disappointed students in alternative programs within the college—a better alternative than dismissal from the college. But as used by many critics of community colleges, it referred to a hard termination of students, preventing them from further pursuit of a college career. The concept also led to a range of alternative conceptions such as cooling-in and warming-up. Wishing to make clear my original thinking about the matter, I took advantage of an opportunity that arose to do so. The results were published in the article "The 'Cooling-Out' Function Revisited," which follows in chapter 3.

Community colleges have flourished since the 1960s. They now serve as the channel for almost one-half of all students entering American higher education. Still, considering the great importance of this pathway, they continue to be understudied and poorly understood. I am glad that my book *The Open Door College: A Case Study* and the article I wrote in 1960 ("The 'Cooling Out' Function in Higher Education") established both "the open door" and "the 'cooling-out' function" as baseline concepts. George B. Vaughan, the editor of the book in which my revisited article appeared, pointed out "that every writer discussed in this introductory chapter draws upon Clark's work . . . , for without an awareness of his writing it would be difficult to understand much of the literature" (3).

CHAPTER 2

The "Cooling-Out" Function in Higher Education

A MAJOR PROBLEM OF democratic society is inconsistency between encouragement to achieve and the realities of limited opportunity. Democracy asks individuals to act as if social mobility were universally possible; status is to be won by individual effort, and rewards are to accrue to those who try. But democratic societies also need selective training institutions, and hierarchical work organizations permit increasingly fewer persons to succeed at ascending levels. Situations of opportunity are also situations of denial and failure. Thus, democratic societies need not only to motivate achievement but also to mollify those denied it in order to sustain motivation in the face of disappointment and to deflect resentment. In the modern mass democracy, with its large-scale organization, elaborated ideologies of equal access and participation, and minimal commitment to social origin as a basis for status, the task becomes critical.

The problem of blocked opportunity has been approached sociologically through means-ends analysis. Merton and others have called attention to the phenomenon of dissociation between culturally instilled goals and institutionally provided means of realization; discrepancy between ends and means is seen as a basic social source of individual frustration and recalcitrance.[1] We shall here extend means-ends analysis in another direction, to the responses of organized groups to means-ends disparities, in particular focusing attention on ameliorative processes that lessen the strains of dissociation. We shall do so by analyzing the most prevalent type of dissociation between aspirations and avenues in American educa-

"The 'Cooling-Out' Function in Higher Education," *American Journal of Sociology* 65, no. 6 (May 1960): 596–78.

tion, specifying the structure and processes that reduce the stress of structural disparity and individual denial. Certain components of American higher education perform what may be called the cooling-out function,[2] and it is to these that attention will be drawn.

The Ends-Means Disjuncture

In American higher education the aspirations of the multitude are encouraged by "open-door" admission to public-supported colleges. The means of moving upward in status and of maintaining high status now include some years in college, and a college education is a prerequisite of the better positions in business and the professions. The trend is toward an ever tighter connection between higher education and higher occupations, as increased specialization and professionalization ensure that more persons will need more preparation. The high-school graduate, seeing college as essential to success, will seek to enter some college, regardless of his record in high school.

A second and allied source of public interest in unlimited entry into college is the ideology of equal opportunity.[3] Strictly interpreted, equality of opportunity means selection according to ability, without regard to extraneous considerations. Popularly interpreted, however, equal opportunity in obtaining a college education is widely taken to mean unlimited access to some form of college: in California, for example, state education authorities maintain that high school graduates who cannot qualify for the state university or state college should still have the "opportunity of attending a publicly supported institution of higher education," this being "an essential part of the state's goal of guaranteeing equal educational opportunities to all its citizens."[4] To deny access to college is then to deny equal opportunity. Higher education should make a seat available without judgment on past performance.

Many other features of current American life encourage college-going. School officials are reluctant to establish early critical hurdles for the young, as is done in Europe. With little enforced screening in the precollege years, vocational choice and educational selection are postponed to the college years or later. In addition, the United States, a wealthy country, is readily supporting a large complex of colleges, and its expanding economy requires more specialists. Recently, a national concern that manpower be fully utilized has encouraged the extending of college training to more and different kinds of students. Going to college is also in some segments of society the thing to do; as a last resort, it is more attractive than the army or a job. Thus ethical and practical urges together encourage the high school graduate to believe that college is both a necessity and a right; similarly, parents and elected officials incline toward legislation and admission practices that ensure entry for large numbers; and educational authorities find the need and justification for easy admission.

Even where pressures have been decisive in widening admission policy, however, the system of higher education has continued to be shaped partly by other interests. The practices of public colleges are influenced by the academic personnel, the organizational requirements of colleges, and external pressures other than those behind the open door. Standards of performance and graduation are maintained. A commitment to standards is encouraged by a set of values in which the status of a college, as defined by academicians and a large body of educated laymen, is closely linked to the perceived quality of faculty, student body, and curriculum. The raising of standards is supported by the faculty's desire to work with promising students and to enjoy membership in an enterprise of reputed quality— college authorities find low standards and poor students a handicap in competing with other colleges for such resources as able faculty as well as for academic status. The wish is widespread that college education be of the highest quality for the preparation of leaders in public affairs, business, and the professions. In brief, the institutional means of the students' progress toward college graduation and subsequent goals are shaped in large part by a commitment to quality embodied in college staffs, traditions, and images.

The conflict between open-door admission and performance of high quality often means a wide discrepancy between the hopes of entering students and the means of their realization. Students who pursue ends for which a college education is required but who have little academic ability gain admission into colleges only to encounter standards of performance they cannot meet. As a result, while some students of low promise are successful, for large numbers failure is inevitable and *structured*. The denial is delayed, taking place within the college instead of at the edge of the system. It requires that many colleges handle the student who intends to complete college, and allows such student, whose destiny is to fail, to become involved.

Responses to Disjuncture

What is done with the student whose destiny will normally be early termination? One answer is unequivocal dismissal. This "hard" response is found in the state university that bows to pressure for broad admission but then protects standards by heavy dropout. In the first year it weeds out many of the incompetent, who may number a third or more of the entering class.[5] The response of the college is hard in that failure is clearly defined as such. Failure is public; the student often returns home. This abrupt change in status and in access to the means of achievement may occur simultaneously in a large college or university for hundreds, and sometimes thousands, of students after the first semester and at the end of the freshman year. The delayed denial is often viewed on the outside as heartless, a slaughter of the innocents.[6] This excites public pressure and anxiety, and apparently the practice cannot be extended indefinitely as the demand for admission to college increases.

A second answer is to sidetrack unpromising students rather than have them fail. This is the "soft" response: never to dismiss a student but to provide him with an alternative. One form of it in some state universities is the detour to an extension division or a general college, which has the advantage of appearing not very different from the main road. Sometimes "easy" fields of study, such as education, business administration, and social science, are used as alternatives to dismissal.[7] The major form of the soft response is not found in the four-year college or university, however, but in the college that specializes in handling students who will soon be leaving—typically, the two-year public junior college.

In most states where the two-year college is a part of higher education, the students likely to be caught in the means-ends disjuncture are assigned to it in large numbers. In California, where there are over sixty public two-year colleges in a diversified system that includes the state university and numerous four-year state colleges, the junior college is unselective in admissions and by law, custom, and self-conception accepts all who wish to enter.[8] It is tuition-free, local, and under local control. Most of its entering students want to try for the baccalaureate degree, transferring to a "senior" college after one or two years. About two-thirds of the students in junior colleges of the state are in programs that permit transferring; but, of these, only about one-third actually transfer to a four-year college.[9] The remainder, or two out of three of the professed transfer students, are "latent terminal students": their announced intention and program of study entails four years of college, but in reality their work terminates in the junior college. Constituting about half of all the students in the California junior colleges, and somewhere between one-third and one-half of junior college students nationally,[10] these students cannot be ignored by the colleges. Understanding their careers is important to understanding modern higher education.

The Reorienting Process

This type of student in the junior college is handled by being moved out of a transfer major to a one- or two-year program of vocational, business, or semiprofessional training. This calls for the relinquishing of his original intention, and he is induced to accept a substitute that has lower status in both the college and society in general.

In one junior college[11] the initial move in a cooling-out process is pre-entrance testing: low scores on achievement tests lead poorly qualified students into remedial classes. Assignment to remedial work casts doubt and slows the student's movement into bona fide transfer courses. The remedial courses are, in effect, a subcollege. The student's achievement scores are made part of a counseling folder that will become increasingly significant to him. An objective record of ability and performance begins to accumulate.

A second step is a counseling interview before the beginning of the first semester, and before all subsequent semesters for returning students. "At this interview the counselor assists the student to choose the proper courses in light of his objective, his test scores, the high school record and test records from his previous schools."[12] Assistance in choosing "the proper courses" is gentle at first. Of the common case of the student who wants to be an engineer but who is not a promising candidate, a counselor said: "I never openly countermand his choice, but edge him toward a terminal program by gradually laying out the facts of life." Counselors may become more severe later when grades provide a talking point and when the student knows he is in trouble. In the earlier counseling the desire of the student has much weight; the counselor limits himself to giving advice and stating the probability of success. The advice is entered in the counseling record that shadows the student.

A third and major step in reorienting the latent terminal student is a special course entitled "Orientation to College," mandatory for entering students. All sections of it are taught by teacher-counselors who comprise the counseling staff, and one of its purposes is "to assist students in evaluating their own abilities, interests, and aptitudes; in assaying their vocational choices in light of this evaluation; and in making educational plans to implement their choices." A major section of it takes up vocational planning; vocational tests are given at a time when opportunities and requirements in various fields of work are discussed. The tests include the "Lee Thorpe Interest Inventory" ("given to all students for motivating a self-appraisal of vocational choice") and the "Strong Interest Inventory" ("for all who are undecided about choice or who show disparity between accomplishment and vocational choice"). Mechanical and clerical aptitude tests are taken by all. The aptitudes are directly related to the college's terminal programs, with special tests, such as a pre-engineering ability test, being given according to need. Then an "occupational paper is required of all students for their chosen occupation"; in it the student writes on the required training and education and makes a "self-appraisal of fitness."

Tests and papers are then used in class discussion and counseling interviews, in which the students themselves arrange and work with a counselor's folder and a student test profile and, in doing so, are repeatedly confronted by the accumulating evidence—the test scores, course grades, recommendations of teachers and counselors. This procedure is intended to heighten self-awareness of capacity in relation to choice and hence to strike particularly at the latent terminal student. The teacher-counselors are urged constantly to "be alert to the problem of unrealistic vocational goals" and to "help students to accept their limitations and strive for success in other worthwhile objectives that are within their grasp." The orientation class was considered a good place "to talk tough," to explain in an *impersonal* way the facts of life for the overambitious student. Talking tough to a whole group is part of a soft treatment of the individual.

Following the vocational counseling, the orientation course turns to "building an educational program," to study of the requirements for graduation of the college in transfer and terminal curriculum, and to planning of a four-semester program. The students also become acquainted with the requirements of the colleges to which they hope to transfer, here contemplating additional hurdles such as the entrance examinations of other colleges. Again, the hard facts of the road ahead are brought to bear on self-appraisal.

If he wishes, the latent terminal student may ignore the counselor's advice and the test scores. While in the counseling class, he is also in other courses, and he can wait to see what happens. Adverse counseling advice and poor test scores may not shut off his hope of completing college; when this is the case, the deterrent will be encountered in the regular classes. Here the student is divested of expectations, lingering from high school, that he will automatically pass and, hopefully, automatically be transferred. Then, receiving low grades, he is thrown back into the counseling orbit, a fourth step in his reorientation and a move justified by his actual accomplishment. The following indicates the nature of the referral system:

> *Need for Improvement Notices* are issued by instructors to students who are doing unsatisfactory work. The carbon copy of the notice is given to the counselor who will be available for conference with the student. The responsibility lies with the student to see his counselor. However, experience shows that some counselees are unable to be sufficiently self-directive to seek aid. The counselor should, in such cases, send for the student, using the Request for Conference blank. If the student fails to respond to the Request for Conference slip, this may become a disciplinary matter and should be referred to the deans.
>
> After a conference has been held, the Need for Improvement notices are filed in the student's folder. *This may be important* in case of a complaint concerning the fairness of a final grade.[13]

This directs the student to more advice and self-assessment, as soon and as often as he has classroom difficulty. The carbon-copy routine makes it certain that, if he does not seek advice, advice will seek him. The paperwork and bureaucratic procedure have the purpose of recording referral and advice in black and white, where they may later be appealed to impersonally. As put in an unpublished report of the college, the overaspiring student and the one who seems to be in the wrong program require "skillful and delicate handling. An accumulation of pertinent factual information may serve to fortify the objectivity of the student-counselor relationship." While the counselor advises delicately and patiently, but persistently, the student is confronted with the record with increasing frequency.

A fifth step, one necessary for many in the throes of discouragement, is probation: "Students [whose] grade point averages fall below 2.0 [C] in any semester will, upon recommendation by the Scholarship Committee, be placed on probationary standing." A second failure places the student on second probation, and a third may mean that he will be advised to withdraw from the college altogether. The procedure is not designed to rid the college of a large number of students, for they may continue on probation for three consecutive semesters; its purpose is not to provide a status halfway out of the college but to "assist the student to seek an objective (major field) at a level on which he can succeed."[14] An important effect of probation is its slow killing-off of the lingering hopes of the most stubborn latent terminal students. A "transfer student" must have a C average to receive the associate in arts (a two-year degree) offered by the junior college, but no minimum average is set for terminal students. More important, four-year colleges require a C average or higher for the transfer student. Thus probationary status is the final blow to hopes of transferring and, indeed, even to graduating from the junior college under a transfer-student label. The point is reached where the student must permit himself to be reclassified or else drop out. In this college, 30 percent of the students enrolled at the end of the spring semester, 1955–56, who returned the following fall were on probation; three out of four of these were transfer students in name.[15]

This sequence of procedures is a specific process of cooling-out;[16] its effect, at the best, is to let down hopes gently and unexplosively. Through it students who are failing or barely passing find their occupational and academic future being redefined. Along the way, teacher-counselors urge the latent terminal student to give up his plan of transferring and stand ready to console him in accepting a terminal curriculum. The drawn-out denials when it is effective is in place of a personal, hard "No"; instead, the student is brought to realize, finally, that it is best to ease himself out of the competition to transfer.

Cooling-Out Features

In the cooling-out process in the junior college are several features that are likely to be found in other settings where failure or denial is the effect of a structured discrepancy between ends and means, the responsible operatives or "coolers" cannot leave the scene or hide their identities, and the disappointment is threatening in some way to those responsible for it. At work and in training institutions this is common. The features are:

1. *Alternative achievement.* Substitute avenues may be made to appear not too different from what is given up, particularly as to status. The person destined to be denied or who fails is invited to interpret the second effort as more appropriate to his particular talent and is made to see that it will be the less frustrating. Here one does not fail but rectifies a mistake. The substitute status reflects less unfavorably on personal capacity than does being dismissed and forced to leave the scene. The terminal student in the junior college may appear not very different from the transfer student—an "engineering aide," for example, instead of an "engineer"—and to be proceeding to something with a status of its own. Failure in college can be treated as if it did not happen; so, too, can poor performance in industry.[17]

2. *Gradual disengagement.* By a gradual series of steps, movement to a goal may be stalled, self-assessment encouraged, and evidence produced of performance. This leads toward the available alternatives at little cost. It also keeps the person in a counseling milieu in which advice is furnished, whether actively sought or not. Compared with the original hopes, however, it is a deteriorating situation. If the individual does not give up peacefully, he will be in trouble.

3. *Objective denial.* Reorientation is, finally, confrontation by the facts. A record of poor performance helps to detach the organization and its agents from the emotional aspects of the cooling-out work. In a sense, the overaspiring student in the junior college confronts himself, as he lives with the accumulating evidence, instead of the organization. The college offers opportunity; it is the record that forces denial. Record-keeping and other bureaucratic procedures appeal to universal criteria and reduce the influence of personal ties, and the personnel are thereby protected. Modern personnel record-keeping, in general, has the function of documenting denial.

4. *Agents of consolation.* Counselors are available who are patient with the overambitious and who work to change their intentions. They believe in the value of the alternative careers, though of lower social status, and are practiced in consoling. In college and other settings counseling is to reduce aspiration as well to define and to help fulfill it. The teacher-counselor in the "soft" junior college is in contrast to the scholar in the "hard" college who simply gives a low grade to the failing student.

5. *Avoidance of standards.* A cooling-out process avoids appealing to standards that are ambiguous to begin with. While a "hard" attitude toward failure generally allows a single set of criteria, a "soft" treatment assumes that many kinds of ability are valuable, each in its place. Proper classification and placement are then paramount, while standards become relative.

Importance of Concealment

For an organization and its agents one dilemma of a cooling-out role is that it must be kept reasonably away from public scrutiny and not clearly perceived or understood by prospective clientele. Should it become obvious, the organization's ability to perform it would be impaired. If high school seniors and their families were to define the junior college as a place that diverts college-bound students, a probable consequence would be a turning-away from the junior college and increased pressure for admission to the four-year colleges and universities that are otherwise protected to some degree. This would, of course, render superfluous the part now played by the junior college in the division of labor among colleges.

The cooling-out function of the junior college is kept hidden, for one thing, as other functions are highlighted. The junior college stresses "the transfer function," "the terminal function," etc., not that of transforming transfer into terminal students; indeed, it is widely identified as principally a transfer station. The other side of cooling-out is the successful performance in junior college of students who did poorly in high school or who have overcome socioeconomic handicaps, for they are drawn into higher education rather than taken out of it. Advocates of the junior college point to this salvaging of talented manpower, otherwise lost to the community and nation. It is indeed a function of the open door to let hidden talent be uncovered.

Then, too, cooling-out itself is reinterpreted so as to appeal widely. The junior college may be viewed as a place where all high school graduates have the opportunity to explore possible careers and find the type of education appropriate to their individual ability; in short, as a place where everyone is admitted and everyone succeeds. As described by the former president of the University of California:

> A prime virtue of the junior college, I think, is that most of its students succeed in what they set out to accomplish, and cross the finish line before they grow weary of the race. After two years in a course that they have chosen, they can go out prepared for activities that satisfy them, instead of being branded as failures. Thus the broadest possible opportunity may be provided for the largest number to make an honest try at further education with some possibility of success and with no route to a desired goal completely barred to them.[18]

The students themselves help to keep this function concealed by wishful unawareness. Those who cannot enter other colleges but still hope to complete four years will be motivated at first not to admit the cooling-out process to consciousness. Once exposed to it, they again will be led not to acknowledge it, and so they are saved insult to their self-image.

In summary, the cooling-out process in higher education is one whereby systematic discrepancy between aspiration and avenue is covered over and stress for the individual and the system is minimized. The provision of readily available alternative achievements in itself is an important device for alleviating the stress consequent on failure and so preventing anomic and deviant behavior. The general result of cooling-out processes is that society can continue to encourage maximum effort without major disturbance from unfulfilled promises and expectations.

Notes

I am indebted to Erving Goffman and Martin A. Trow for criticism and to Sheldon Messinger for extended conceptual and editorial comment.

1. "Aberrant behavior may be regarded sociologically as a symptom of dissociation between culturally prescribed aspirations and socially structured av-

enues for realizing these aspirations" (Robert K. Merton, "Social Structure and Anomie," in *Social Theory and Social Structure* [rev. ed.; Glencoe, Ill.: Free Press, 1957], 134). See also Herbert H. Hyman, "The Value Systems of Different Classes: A Social Psychological Contribution to the Analysis of Stratification," in Reinhard Bendix and Seymour M. Lipset, eds., *Class, Status and Power: A Reader in Social Stratification* (Glencoe, Ill.: Free Press, 1953), 462–42; and the papers by Robert Dubin, Richard A. Cloward, Robert K. Merton, Dorothy L. Meier, and Wendell Bell, in *American Sociological Review* 24 (April 1959).

2. I am indebted to Erving Goffman's original statement of the cooling-out conception. See his "Cooling the Mark Out: Some Aspects of Adaptation to Failure," *Psychiatry* 15 (November 1952): 451–63. Sheldon Messinger called the relevance of this concept to my attention.

3. Seymour Martin Lipset and Reinhard Bendix, *Social Mobility in Industrial Society* (Berkeley: University of California Press, 1959), 78–101.

4. *A Study of the Need for Additional Centers of Public Higher Education in California* (Sacramento: California State Department of Education, 1957), 128. For somewhat similar interpretations by educators and laymen nationally, see Francis J. Brown, ed., *Approaching Equality of Opportunity in Higher Education* (Washington, D.C.: American Council on Education, 1955), and the President's Committee on Education beyond the High School, *Second Report to the President* (Washington, D.C.: U.S. Government Printing Office, 1957).

5. One national report showed that one out of eight entering students (12.5 percent) in publicly controlled colleges does not remain beyond the first term or semester; one out of three (31 percent) is out by the end of the first year; and about one out of two (46.6 percent) leaves within the first two years. In state universities alone, about one out of four withdraws in the first year and 40 percent in two years (Robert E. Iffert, *Retention and Withdrawal of College Students* [Washington, D.C.: U.S. Department of Health, Education, and Welfare, 1958], 15–20). Students withdraw for many reasons, but scholastic aptitude is related to their staying power: "A sizeable number of students of medium ability enter college, but . . . few if any of them remain longer than two years" (*A Restudy of the Needs of California in Higher Education* [Sacramento: California State Department of Education, 1955], 120).

6. Robert L. Kelly, *The American Colleges and the Social Order* (New York: Macmillan Co., 1940), 220–21.

7. One study has noted that on many campuses the business school serves "as a dumping ground for students who cannot make the grade in engineering or some branch of the liberal arts," this being a consequence of lower promotion standards than are found in most other branches of the university (Frank C. Pierson, *The Education of American Businessmen* [New York: McGraw-Hill Book

Co., 1959], 63). Pierson also summarizes data on intelligence of students by field of study, which indicate that education, business, and social science rank near the bottom in quality of students (65–72).

8. Burton R. Clark, *The Open Door College: A Case Study* (New York: McGraw-Hill Book Co., 1960), 44–45.

9. Ibid., 116.

10. Leland L. Medsker, *The Junior College: Progress and Prospect* (New York: McGraw-Hill Book Co., 1960), chap. iv.

11. San Jose City College, San Jose, Calif. For the larger study see Clark, *The Open Door College*.

12. San Jose Junior College, Handbook for Counselors, 1957–58, 2. Statements in quotation marks in the next few paragraphs are cited from this.

13. Ibid., 20.

14. Statement taken from unpublished material.

15. San Jose Junior College, "Digest of Analysis of the Records of 468 Students Placed on Probation for the Fall Semester, 1956," September 3, 1956.

16. Goffman's original statement of the concept of cooling-out referred to how the disappointing of expectations is handled by the disappointed person and especially by those responsible for the disappointment. Although his main illustration was the confidence game, where facts and potential achievement are deliberately misrepresented to the "mark" (the victim) by operators of the game, Goffman also applied the concept to failure in which those responsible act in good faith ("Cooling the Mark Out," *passim*). Cooling-out is a widely useful idea when used to refer to a function that may vary in deliberateness.

17. Ibid., 457; cf. Perrin Stryker, "How to Fire an Executive," *Fortune* 50 (October 1954): 116–17 and 178–92.

18. Robert Gordon Sproul, "Many Millions More," *Educational Record* 39 (April 1958): 102.

CHAPTER 3

The "Cooling-Out" Function Revisited

The cooling-out function—like democracy—is not very attractive until you consider its alternatives. It is likely to remain an important part of what American community colleges do.

IN THE MID-1950s, after finishing a dissertation on the character of adult schools (Clark, 1956), I became interested in doing a similar analysis of community colleges. While teaching at Stanford, I spent a summer visiting a number of colleges in the San Francisco Bay Area to explore the feasibility of such research, particularly to weigh the advantages and disadvantages of a case study rather than a comparative analysis of several colleges. I decided to take my chances by concentrating on the college and getting to know it well, looking for connections among the parts of the organization in order to characterize it as a whole. The college I selected was a relatively new one in San Jose that offered entrée and was within easy commuting of Palo Alto. The fieldwork of the study and manuscript preparation during a period of three years or so led to a book and an article published at the end of the decade (Clark, 1960a, 1960b). The book covered the emergence and development of the college. It attended to unique features, but emphasized characteristics that, on the basis of available comparative data, a few side glances, and some reasoning, seemed to be shared with most other public two-year institutions and hence could be generalized—something to lay on the table that could be checked by others elsewhere and might, in explanatory power, be worth their time and effort. I spoke of the character of the community college in such terms as diffuse commitment and dependency on an unselected external social

"The 'Cooling-Out' Function Revisited," in *Questioning the Community College Role,* edited by George B. Vaughn, 15–32. San Francisco: Jossey-Bass, 1980. Reprinted with permission of John Wiley & Sons, Inc.

base; pointed to roles it played in the larger educational structure in acting as a screening agent for other colleges at the same time that it opened wider the door to higher education; and suggested that such colleges have particularly sharp problems of identity, status, and autonomy.

Foremost among the generalizations was the "cooling-out" function, a conception that clearly has also been seen by others as the most important conclusion of the study. My purpose in this essay is to review the concept twenty years later. In retrospect, was it appropriate in 1960? Does it still pertain? How has it been used by others? Since its crucial features are often overlooked, I begin by reviewing the original idea. I then explore the possible alternatives to this particular function as a way of understanding the reasons for its existence. In light of the experiences of our own and other countries during the past two decades, we can better understand the alternatives now than we could twenty years ago. Finally, I take up some ways that the idea has been used by others and conclude with a judgment on the value of the concept.

Original Conception

At the outset of the research, cooling-out was not on my mind, either as a phenomenon or as a term. As I proceeded in my observations, interviews, and readings of available documents and data, I was struck with the discrepancy between formal statements of purpose and everyday reality. A poignant part of reality was the clear fact that most students who were in the transfer track did not go on to four-year colleges and universities. What happened to them? It turned out that the college was concerned about them, both as individuals, and, in the aggregate, as a persistent administrative problem that would not go away. Emerging procedures could be observed that were designed to channel many such students out of transfer programs and into curricula that terminated in the community college. As I observed teachers and students, and especially counselors who seemed central to what was going on, it became clear that such reassignment of students was not easy.

It involved actions that, no matter how helpful, would be felt by many involved to be the dirty work of the organization. This effort to rechannel students could have been called "the counseling process" or "the redirection-of-aspirations process" or "the alternative-career process" or by some other similarly ambiguous term so heavily used in education and sociology. I played with the terms then readily available but all seemed to have the analytical bite of warmed-over potatoes. While I was stewing about how to point a concept, a friend called my attention to an article by Goffman (1952) in which, for various sectors of society, the need to let down the hopes of people was analyzed brilliantly. Goffman used terms from the confidence game in which the aspirations of the "mark" to get rich quick are out of line with the reality of what is happening to him or her, and someone on the confidence team is assigned the duty of helping the victim face the harsh reality without blowing his mind or calling the police. Now there was a concept with a cutting edge! So I adopted and adapted it, aware that it would not make many friends in community college administrative circles.

How did cooling-out appear to happen in educational settings? Moore has summarized well the argument that I originally put forth.

> The process as described by Clark entails a student's following a structured sequence of guidance efforts involving mandatory courses in career planning and self-evaluation, which results in "reorientation" of the student rather than dismissal. The process begins with preentrance testing, which identifies low-achieving students and assigns them to remedial classes. The process is completed when the "overaspiring student" is rechanneled out of a transfer program and into a terminal curriculum. Throughout the process the student is kept in contact with guidance personnel, who keep careful track of the student's "progress."
>
> The generalizable qualities of cooling out as Clark saw them involve *offering substitutes or alternatives* to the desired goal (here a transfer program); *encouraging gradual disengagement* by having the student try out other courses of study; *amassing objective data* against the preference in terms of grades, aptitude tests, and interest tests; *consoling and counseling* the student through personal though "objective" contacts; and *stressing the relative values of many kinds* of persons and many kinds of talents rather than the preferred choice. (Moore, 1975, 578–79)

Crucial components of the process that were stressed in the original statement and that I would want to emphasize even more now are that

(1) alternatives are provided—the person who is to be denied a desired goal is offered a substitute; and (2) aspiration is reduced in a "soft" consoling way, easing the pain and frustration of not being able to achieve one's first goal and the difficulties involved in switching to and learning to value the offered alternative education and career.

Once I had virtually "seen" the process in operation in one community college it was easy to generalize. After all, the community colleges in general embraced the open-door philosophy and hence were unselective on the input side, while necessarily facing the standards of four-year colleges and universities and being somewhat selective on the transfer/output side. Figures were readily available for all community colleges in California and the nation as a whole that showed how many students entered the transfer track and how many came out of it. And, there was no evidence that community colleges anywhere in the country took the traditional stern approach that students who could not for one reason or another do the transfer work were failures who should be sent away. To the contrary, the attitude expressed everywhere was a generous and open one that the community college should not label students as failures; instead, students should be helped as much as possible "to find themselves" and to find courses and career objectives appropriate to their abilities.

Hence a general assertion was warranted: its specific steps might vary, and colleges might or might not be effective in carrying it out, but the cooling-out process would be insistently operative in the vast majority of American public two-year colleges. This was necessary given the position of the two-year units in the general educational structure and the institutional roles that had emerged around that position.

Alternatives

One way to enlarge our understanding of this phenomenon is to place it in the context of alternatives. Can it be subordinated or replaced by other ways of proceeding? How could the roles of community colleges be so altered that the process would be unnecessary? Indeed, what has been done at other times and is presently done in other places that reduces greatly the play of this process? Six alternatives come to mind, a set that comes close to exhausting the broad possibilities. As backdrop for these alternatives, let us keep in mind that the cooling-out process in community colleges is rooted in (1) open-door admissions, a policy of non-selection; (2) the maintenance of transfer standards, an attitude that those who transfer should be able to do coursework in four-year colleges and universities; and (3) the probable need to deny some aspirants the transfer possibility and to face the problem of what to do with them.

PRE-SELECTION. One clear alternative is pre-selection, either in earlier schooling or at the doors of the colleges. National systems of education continue to select students at the secondary level, indeed to have specialized schools that are terminal. This form of selection remains the model pattern in Europe and around the world, despite the efforts to "democratize" and universalize secondary education in so many countries in the past two decades. The secondary school graduates who qualified for higher education, in the most generous estimates, were still no higher in the early and mid-1970s than 30 percent of the age group in West Germany, 35 percent in Italy, and 45 percent in France (Furth, 1978). Of course, in the United States, automatic or social promotion of students during the secondary schooling has been the opposite of selection, amounting to mass sponsorship. Some selection still takes place, particularly through assignments to curricular tracks within the comprehensive school, but it is minor compared to the dominant international mode. Current efforts to stiffen standards of secondary school graduation in the United States will, if effective, tend to increase pre-selection.

Naturally, selection can also take place at the doors of community colleges, no matter what the extent of selection at the secondary level. Some minor amount of selection perhaps takes place in some community colleges in certain regions, particularly in the Northeast, where the long dominance of private higher education has left a legacy of selection for quality and low regard for the more open-door public institutions.

The greater the selection in the secondary school or at the doors of the colleges, the less the need to select within the doors. The gap between aspirations and scholastic ability is narrowed, since a higher threshold of ability is established. Every increase in selectivity reduces the conditions that generate the cooling-out process.

This alternative runs against the grain of American populist interpretations of educational justice that equate equity with open doors. The reestablishing of sharp secondary school selection or the closing of the open door is not what most critics and reformers have in mind. But we need to keep pre-selection in view if we want to understand why most countries in the world currently have considerably less need for a cooling-out function than the American system of the past quarter-century and the foreseeable future. The traditional injunction is a simple one: if you want to reduce cooling-out, keep out the candidates for cooling-out.

TRANSFER-TRACK SELECTION. All right, community college personnel can say, we have an open door but we certainly do not have to let every Tom, Dick, and Harry—and their female counterparts—declare himself or herself to be a four-year college student and set sail in the courses that give credit for later transferring. We will stop the "nonsense" of everyone having a chance and, instead, openly select at the doors to the transfer program. Those who appear likely to be latent terminals, if we do not select, will now be manifest terminals from the outset, and hence the need for the cooling-out process will be drastically reduced.

This alternative is logical enough, certainly to the academic mind or the conservative critic, and it surely occurs to a minor degree in many community colleges. A quick and honest no at the outset, proponents would say, is better for the student, the faculty, and the institution than a drawn-out, ambiguous, and manipulative denial in the style of cooling-out. But, logical or not, this alternative is also not likely to carry the day in American reform. The open-door philosophy is too ingrained; community colleges evermore define their boundaries loosely; almost anyone, part- or full-time, can enroll in courses offering transfer credit; and, besides, students are now in short supply and colleges generally for the foreseeable future will be less rather than more particular.

OPEN FAILURE. Perhaps the basic alternative to cooling-out is unequivocal dismissal or withdrawal. This response is a classic one, found in the United States in the recent past in the state universities that felt it was politically necessary to have virtually open-door admission but then proceeded to allow the faculty to protect standards and slim the flow of students by weeding out in the first year those "who cannot do the work." Processes of admit-and-dismiss are widely operative in other countries, particularly where the forces pressing for more access are able to block sharp selection at the doors of the system but, at the same time, faculties remain free to flunk or discourage to the point of self-dismissal as many students as they wish in the first year or two.

As pointed out in my original formulation, this alternative is a hard response in the sense that failure is clearly defined as such: it is public, with the student required to remove himself from the premises. It is a rather harsh form of delayed denial—"we have to let them in but we do not have to keep them"—and can be viewed from inside or outside the system as heartless, a slaughter of the innocent. One role of the community college, as the most open segment in the American differentiated system, has been to lessen the need for this response in the state universities and public four-year colleges. The academically marginal and less promising students have been protected from the open-failure form of response by removing them from the settings where it was most likely to occur. Cooling-out has been the "softer" response of never dismissing a student but instead providing him or her with an alternative.

This open-failure alternative is also one not likely to carry the day in the United States. Those who are most critical of community colleges do not seem to have it in mind and nowhere does it appear on the agenda of reform. Old-fashioned toughness—"You have failed, so get out of here!"—is not about to be reestablished as a general mode, either in two-year or most four-year colleges.

GUARANTEED GRADUATION. In this alternative we take the social or automatic promotion of students that has characterized much of American secondary education in recent decades and apply it to postsecondary education. As an ideal type, the formulation reads: let everyone in who wishes to come and let all who persist graduate. In the transfer part of the two-year college, this means let all complete the two years of work, receive the associate in arts or associate in science degree, and transfer to whatever four-year colleges will accept them. Standards are then not directly a problem since students will be allowed to graduate and transfer without regard to scholastic achievement or academic merit. The cooling-out effort is no longer required.

This alternative is attractive for many participants and observers, especially those for whom equality is the primary value in higher education to the point of moving beyond equality of access and opportunity to equality of results. It surely is operative to some degree in numerous unselective four-year as well as two-year colleges: once the student is in, the college has a strong interest in seeing that he or she receives a degree. However, this alternative does not serve competence very well and debases the value of degrees, threatening the credibility and legitimacy of postsecondary institutions. It contributes to the inflation of educational credentials whereby individuals must have longer schooling to obtain a certificate of some value. It is a risky road, one of which the dangers have already been spelled out by the experience of the American secondary school and the value of the high school diploma. One may even think of this alternative as a cheating form of equality: Everyone is equally entitled to credentials that have lost their value. Guaranteed college graduation does not solve the paradox—the search for equality defeating its own purpose when it is carried to the point of equal results and statuses (Dahrendorf, 1980). Much of the thrust of the search for equality is to enable people to be freer to choose, which means that institutions and programs must offer a wide range of choices while reducing the barriers that prevent people from having those choices. But equal results, in such forms as automatic passage and uniform certification for all, restrict the opportunities for choice.

REDUCTION OF THE TRANSFER-TERMINAL DISTINCTION. Another alternative is to reduce the distinction between transfer and terminal as much as possible. Here there are the two possibilities. One is to narrow the status gap by enhancing the status of the terminal programs. Community college personnel have worked long and hard at this solution, helped considerably by the specific short-term programs that have high practical returns in well-paying and interesting job placements, e.g., fashion designer in New York City or electronic technician in a Massachusetts or California technological complex. Those "life chances" do not look bad, compared to the perceivable returns from a bachelor's degree in English or sociology. But the bulk of terminal programs—centered more at the level of secretarial and mechanical training—are nowhere near that attractive and it remains hard to give them a parity of esteem with what people think a full college education will bring. Prestige ranking of occupations by the general population continues to give sociologists something to analyze, setting limits on how much one can realistically rank the middle-status ones with those of high status.

The second possibility is to blur the distinction, reducing as much as possible the labeling of courses and curricula as transfer and non-transfer, and hence the parallel official and self-labeling of students as on one track or the other. Community colleges have long had courses that serve the double purpose and students who mix the two. There are natural administrative interests within comprehensive schools and colleges to reduce the internal distinctions that divide staff and students, and often raise havoc with morale. Then, too, community colleges have long had the self-interest of wanting to certify who is an appropriate candidate for further education without having clearly designated transfer programs in which the specific courses and course sequences are dictated by the programs and the requirements of the four-year institutions.

The transfer-terminal distinction and the meaning of the transfer track have blurred somewhat during the past two decades. Some community colleges manipulate the labeling of courses in order to increase their attractiveness and especially to bolster financial support based on student headcounts in degree-credit courses (Cohen and Lombardi, 1979). Part-time students who come to a college just to take a single course, with no intention of getting credit for it let alone using it toward transferring, are found in transfer courses. "The transfer courses have become discrete. Many students already have baccalaureate degrees and are taking the 'transfer' course in photography to gain access to the darkroom, the 'transfer' course in art to have their paintings criticized, the 'transfer' course in a language so they can travel abroad" (25). In general, an increasingly diffuse approach to transfer programs has been encouraged by basic trends of the past decade: more part-time, occasional, "non-credit" students; more poorly prepared students—as high as 50 percent of enrollment—with the college staff then having to concentrate on the six Rs of higher education—remedial reading, remedial writing, and remedial arithmetic; more student occupational interest; and a "non-collegiate" drift in community college philosophy toward the organization serving as a community center or even a "community-based" legal entity operating without campuses, full-time faculty, or formal curriculum.

But the blurring of distinctions and meanings has limits beyond which lies a loss of legitimacy of the community college *qua* college. The definitions of college held by the four-year institutions and by the general public still set boundaries and insist on distinctions (that auto repairing is not on a par with history or calculus as a college course). Again we face an alternative with self-defeating tendencies, one sure to arouse much hostility and stimulate countertrends. The community college will still have to pick and choose among courses as to what is bona fide transfer work and worry about course sequences and the progression of students through them. To eliminate the transfer operations would be to give up a hard-won place in the higher education stream (Cohen and Lombardi, 1979, 27).

MOVE THE PROBLEM TO ANOTHER TYPE OF COLLEGE. There remains the most general structural alternative: eliminate the transfer part of the two-year college, or do away with the community college entirely, or convert two-year into four-year institutions. Then the cooling-out function, or one of the above alternatives (slightly modified), would have to occur in a four-year context. After all, most four-year colleges in the U.S. system have relatively open admission, and it need not strain them to open the doors still wider. Some of these institutions have had and still have two-year programs and offer two-year degrees, either terminal or allowing entry to the junior and senior years. Also, two-year programs on the main campus and two years of coursework available in extension centers have given even major universities an internal "junior college" operation. And now the increasing competition for students is causing four-year colleges to lower admission barriers and to build the two-year segments.

It is easy to imagine some move in this direction and, amid the bewildering variety of U.S. postsecondary education, this alternative is surely operative today. But, again it is not an alternative likely to dominate: the two-year entity is institutionalized and here to stay for the foreseeable future. Then, too, the problems that follow from this alternative are sufficient to block any major development. High among the problems is the reluctance of four-year college and university faculties to support two-year programs and to give them esteem. The evidence has long been in on this point, in the form of the marginal status accorded university extension in the family of university programs and AA degrees in BA-centered institutions. At the same time the need for short-cycle programs does not lessen. As other advanced industrial societies have been finding out the hard way, in their expansion into mass higher education since 1960, the need steadily grows, from both consumer demands and labor market demands, for a greater differentiation of degree levels rather than a de-differentiation. Thus other countries have been moving toward short-cycle education. They too are impelled to devise more stopping points, as well as more educational avenues. The crucial structural decision is then whether to put the short-cycle programs within institutions committed to longer programs of higher esteem or to give them to a separate set of institutions. There is no evidence that the first choice is the superior one. In fact, if successful programs depend upon faculty commitment, there is a strong argument for separate short-cycle colleges.

In short, the problem that causes colleges to respond with the cooling-out effort is not going to go away by moving it inside of other types of colleges. *Somebody* has to make that effort, or pursue its alternatives.

Use and Abuse of the Idea

The idea of cooling-out has received considerable attention in the past twenty years. The original journal article, "The 'Cooling-Out' Function in Higher Education" (Clark, 1960a), has been widely reprinted in books of reading in sociology, social psychology, and education. The term used to name the concept undoubtedly has been eye-catching.

Beyond this direct absorption of the idea there have been interesting efforts to extend or revise its use, including the construction of counter or opposite concepts. If students can be cooled out, what about faculty? In an important case study of a new community college in a white ethnic part of Boston, London (1978) argued that the faculty suffered a great gap between their expectations and their reality and had to find ways to console themselves and otherwise handle disappointment. The particular college he studied provided a setting likely to magnify this phenomenon, but, even so, what is starkly revealed in an extreme case can be usefully explored in other cases where it may be more muted and shielded from view. As community college experts know well, the gap between expectations and reality is wide wherever the recruited faculty come from traditional sources and have traditional values and then have to face first-generation college-going students who not only have poor scholastic preparation but want to remain attached to their own traditional values of family and neighborhood.

Then, what about cooling-out as applied to particular social categories or students? Moore (1975) interviewed over sixty women in three community colleges and focused attention not on their rechanneling from transfer to terminal curricula but rather on a rechanneling of nontraditional career aspirations for women into traditional choices. In most cases, she reported, the two rechannelings coincided. But not in all, since some original choices were for fields such as data processing that were in the terminal track. Hence she skillfully broadened the use of the idea: "The general concept of cooling out, namely the amelioratory process of lowering and rechanneling aspirations, suits women's career choices as well as it does the transfer process" (580). Her focus on women caused her to explore the role of parents and high school counselors, as well as college counselors and the two-year institutions overall, in pressuring women to move away from choices of nontraditional careers.

Then there is the possible development of reverse concepts; is there a "cooling-in" or "warming-up" function? There surely is, as community college spokesmen have long maintained. There clearly are students who perform better scholastically than they did in high school and who raise rather than lower their aspirations. They may even begin in a terminal program and are moved by observant personnel or by their own efforts to transfer courses. Baird (1971) explored the aspirations of community college students over time, using survey questionnaire data from twenty-seven colleges, and divided the students into *coolers* (lowered aspirations) *warmers* (increased aspirations), and *stayers* (retained original aspirations). He concluded that, "contrary to expectation, cooling out occurred seldom, while warming up was relatively common" (163). He pointed to an interplay between high school and college experiences: that coolers (really "coolees"!) had been encouraged by their high school successes to plan for higher degrees, then ran into academic difficulties in the community college and revised their ambitions downward; that warmers had been led by background and high school experiences to plan lower, then succeeded academically in the community college and revised expectations upward. His research had the advantage of a survey covering a large number of colleges and students (over 2,500). But the differences between the groups were small; the results were confusing and hard to integrate; the data centered on self-reported aspirations; the processes of colleges and the actual experiences of students were not observed; and those who were gone by the end of two years were out of the sample.

Without doubt, the most prevalent abuse of the concept of cooling-out has been its confusion with casting-out. This abuse is not apparent in the serious research literature. Those who have written on the topic have typically observed most of the essential characteristics of the original conception, but I have personally been exposed to it in dozens of conversations and meetings during the years, in such remarks as "she was cooled out" or "don't cool me out" that are meant to refer to a quiet, even devious, effort to simply get rid of or rail someone. Most social science conceptions are liable to a stretching that becomes distorted as they are popularized. One of the major drawbacks to the cooling-out terminology is that its catchiness encourages such distortion, all the more readily allowing the idea to slide toward "pop" usage.

Finally, we have the use and potential abuse of the cooling-out process in which it is picked up and used in more general analyses of stratification and inequality in society. Here the community college nearly always comes out as a villain, discriminating against the dispossessed, keeping the poor and the minorities away from four-year colleges and universities by letting them in and cooling them out. If this is so, the argument goes, such colleges are then operating objectively as instrumentalities by which the upper classes dominate and maintain privilege. One then need only add a little suspiciousness and the community college is linked to capitalism—at least to American capitalism—with a strong suggestion of a conspiracy in which capitalists construct community colleges to serve their own interests.

In the most carefully constructed argument of this genre, Karabel (1972) has emphasized the large proportions of lower-income and minority students in community colleges. Hence there is a social class difference in who is subjected to the cooling-out process, with the community colleges seen as generally operating to maintain the social class system as it is. Karabel points out at the beginning of his essay that this effect is not necessarily intentional; that the two-year college "*has* been critical in providing upward mobility for many individuals" (526) and that measured academic ability is more important than class background in the United States in predicting where one goes to college. The main thrust of the argument goes in a different direction. College standards are seen as a covert mechanism for excluding the poor and minorities, serving to justify universities and colleges "as a means of distributing privilege and of legitimating inequality" (539). The community college is essentially a tracking system that is "class-based," (*passim*)—with all the ambiguity of "based." The effort to promote one- and two-year terminal programs is yet another instance of "submerged class conflict" (548–52), since officials want it while the students do not. And the whiff of conspiracy is strong: "This push toward vocational training in the community college has been sponsored by a national educational planning elite whose social composition, outlook, and policy proposals are reflective of the interests of the more privileged strata of our society" (552). The cooling-out process is implicated in all of this, particularly in helping to legitimate inequality by using academic standards in hidden ways to block the upward mobility of the poor and the minorities.

Since Karabel was interested in reform, he concluded with the question of what to do. He suggests that investing more money would not make much difference; that transforming community colleges into four-year institutions would still leave them at the bottom of the prestige hierarchy; and that making the colleges into vocational training centers alone would simply accentuate tracking. The solution he proposes is the grand one of a socialist reconstruction of the entire society: "The problems of inequality and inequality of opportunity are, in short, best dealt with not through educational reform but rather by the wider changes in economic and political life that would help build a socialist society" (558). However, the experiences of socialist societies around the world have hardly been encouraging in their capacity to improve national systems of higher education, including the provision of equal opportunity.

The other major effort in the inequality context, one less carefully constructed, is Zwerling's book, *Second Best: The Crisis of the Community College* (1976). At the time he wrote the book, Zwerling was a teacher at Staten Island Community College in New York City. He was angry at virtually every aspect of the community college, especially the one at which he worked, other than the special programs and approaches in which he and a few colleagues invested their efforts. He portrayed the community college as "just one more barrier put between the poor and the disenfranchised and the decent and respectable stake in the social system which they seek" (xvii). He took note of cooling-out, devoting a chapter to it as the main role of counseling, and concluded that it helps the college maintain the existing system of social stratification. By means of cooling-out, the college "takes students whose parents are characterized primarily by low income and low educational achievement and slots them into the lower ranks of the industrial and commercial hierarchy. The community college is in fact a social defense mechanism that resists basic changes in the social structure" (xix). In helping to maintain inequality, cooling-out, as he portrays it, works all too well.

Again, what to do? In a mishmash of new directions, Zwerling proposes consciousness-raising, in which students are taught more about what is happening to them, thus making them angry and leading them into a process of heating-up that will replace cooling-out. In addition, they should be given more experience in the real world that will help them choose a career. Then, too, they can be helped over "the transfer trauma" by visits to Yale and similar classy institutions. In short, a "student-centered approach . . . offers the possibility that the old cooling out may at last be replaced by a new heating up" (206). But in his final chapter, Zwerling leaves behind such tinkering and moves to the sweeping structural conclusion that if we want a less hierarchical society, we have to restructure the entire system of higher education, beginning with the elimination of the community colleges: "At the very least this would mean *the elimination* of junior or community colleges since they are the most class-serving of educational institutions" (251). All students would enter directly into a BA-granting school. In addition, state systems should award a system-wide BA, instead of allowing individual colleges and universities to award their own degrees of widely different prestige. All this would eliminate "second best," as everyone moved through equated institutions and obtained equal results.

Arguments of this nature have helped fuel an attack on community colleges by those who singe-mindedly pursue the value of equality. Those who speak for minority groups are bound to take a dim view of community colleges and demand direct and open access for whole segments of the population to four-year colleges and universities, when they come to believe that "educational equity means nothing if it does not mean equality of educational attainment" (Winkler, 1977, 8). They then argue that the concern with equality in higher education should shift from getting minority students into colleges to getting them out as graduates holding bachelor's, doctoral, and professional degrees. Any elimination along the way by means of cooling-out, dropping-out, or flunking-out, is then suspect as discriminatory, unless it happens in equal portions across social categories.

This shift in the inequality line of reasoning in the United States has been little informed by the experiences of national systems elsewhere. Some other nations, particularly France and Italy, have long tried to achieve equal results by means of equated institutions, nationally mandated core and common curricula, and the awarding of degrees by a system-at-large rather than the individual institution. Many systems have long held out against short-cycle institutions and programs, as second best to the traditional universities. But the problems thereby created, as systems moved from elite to mass higher education, have been immense, dwarfing our own in magnitude and making us appear fortunate in comparison. Thus the general drift of painful reform in other advanced systems is toward greater differentiation of types of institutions and degree levels, the introduction of short-cycle programs and degrees, more screening in the first year or two, and the breakup of the system-wide degree. The dilemma is still there: either you keep some aspirants out by selection, or you admit everyone and then take your choice between seeing them all through, or flunking out some, or cooling out some. The more other systems get involved in mass entry, the more their problems become similar to ours, including the problem of gap between aspiration and scholastic ability, and the more they must get involved in cooling-out or opt for one or more of the alternatives I have presented.

Conclusion

In the hindsight of two decades, what would I change in the original analysis if I had to do it over again? The most important change would be to have distinguished more clearly between effort and effectiveness in the cooling-out process. It is one thing to observe the procedures constructed by colleges and the work they put into cooling-out operations, and another to ascertain their effect on students, essentially answering the question whether the effort was effective or not. The distinction was a part of my thinking and writing—appearing in such phrases as "when it is effective"—but should have been clearer. Since I was doing an organizational analysis, I concentrated on the effort side. I had a less clear grasp of the effects, since I was not essentially doing an "impact" analysis, spent much less time with students than with counselors and teachers, and did not systematically interview or survey the students for their reactions. A clearer distinction at the outset could have saved some later confusion about the state of the process. I could also have emphasized a point that naturally follows: the process, no matter how well constructed and operated, is not likely to work smoothly. It tends to become problematic, as individuals and groups react to it. This heavily problematic nature has been caught by some later researchers, such as Baird (1971) and London (1978). My own writings undoubtedly contributed to it, since social actors can learn from the results of social science and adjust behavior accordingly.

Then, too, it probably would have helped to have carried the cooling-out process one step farther: after students move from transfer to terminal programs, or while they are being asked to do so, they often quickly move from college to a job or some other form of withdrawal. This would have hooked cooling-out to the enormous attrition of community colleges and suggested a major two- or three-step flow in the denial of hope, lowering of aspirations, and disengagement. But all this would have blurred the sharp focus of the original argument, and I did not have good data on the process of complete withdrawal. You have to stop somewhere, if you want to keep guesses from overwhelming limited information.

One change that I would make if I were doing the research now instead of twenty years ago would be to either do research on, or introduce a major caveat about, regional and state differences. We should not expect one-thousand community colleges to operate closely alike in the U.S. system, since our decentralized structure has given primacy to local and state control for community colleges and hence has subjected them more to local and state variations than to national administered uniformity. Then, too, the American system of higher education overall is the most market oriented of the world's advanced systems, with competition a prime element that causes colleges to be uncommonly sensitive to different clienteles, labor markets, and the actions of other colleges. Thus, research today on community college operations ought to take seriously the possibility of considerable variation. At the least, regional differences should be studied, since among informed observers it is well known that New England is a long way from California. The East remains relatively transfer oriented and standards oriented—a setting where tradition, resources, and vested interests have given primacy to private higher education and a resulting institutional hierarchy in which the community college often appears as fifth best, let alone second best. It is then hard for researchers in Boston, New Haven, or New York to imagine the "California model," which has developed in a context where public higher education has long been dominant, community colleges won legitimacy before World War

II, and virtually everybody in the hometown, or on the block—including Grandma—has gone by the college to take a course. In that type of setting, the colleges have had middle-class as well as lower-class clienteles, suburban as well as downtown locations, and students who qualified for selective institutions as well as those who did not. Now, during the 1970s, the California-type college has moved another step down the road of openness, toward becoming such a diffuse enterprise that its legitimacy as a college, as earlier indicated, may soon become problematic. In this evolution, sequential transfer work has become a minor item, as a share of the whole, buried under huge enrollments of "singe-course" students. The California model is more widespread and influential in the nation than that exemplified in the Northeast.

The change in approach that I would *not* make if I had to do the study over again, then or now, would be to extrapolate from my internal analysis of the community college to grand theories about the role of education in society. This is too easy as armchair sociology and too lacking in detailed analysis of connecting links. We especially lack the information and the capacity in the state of the art to compare situations in which the cooling-out process operates and those in which it does not, the latter then offering one of the alternatives set forth above. The trouble with the leap to grand theory is that, poorly grounded in empirical research, it is particularly vulnerable to ideology of various persuasions. It also tempts Large Solutions, by others if not the researcher, that have a wide gamut of unanticipated and often undesired effects, outcomes that may do major damage to the less knowing and less powerful actors who cannot get out of the way. Witness the way that problematic research by James Coleman and Christopher Jencks has been used by political forces against U.S. public schools. Contemporary social science has grave weaknesses in application to social policy, and nowhere more so than in educational matters. One has to tread gently, even upon the cooling-out process and its obviously unattractive features.

This side of utopia, academic systems, whether in a socialist or capitalist country, will be, in Erving Goffman's large phrase, a graveyard of hope. The graveyard may be large or small, busy or infrequently used, but it will be present. Only the naive do not recognize that with hope there is disappointment, with success, failure. The settings that lead toward the cooling-out effort remain, all the more so as democracies open doors that were formerly closed. Any system of higher education that has to reconcile such conflicting values as equity, competence, and individual choice—and the advanced democracies are so committed—has to effect compromise procedures that allow for some of each. The cooling-out process is one of the possible compromises, perhaps even a necessary one.

References

Baird, L. L. "Cooling Out and Warming Up in the Junior College." *Measurement and Evaluation in Guidance* 4, no. 3 (1971): 160–71.

Clark, B. R. *Adult Education in Transition: A Study of Institutional Insecurity.* Berkeley: University of California Press, 1956.

———. "The 'Cooling-Out' Function in Higher Education." *The American Journal of Sociology* 65, no. 6 (1960a): 569–76.

———. *The Open Door College: A Case Study.* New York: McGraw-Hill, 1960b.

Cohen, A. M., and J. Lombardi, "Can the Community Colleges Survive Success?" *Change* 11, no. 8 (1979): 24–27.

Coleman, J. S. *Equality of Educational Opportunity.* Washington, D.C.: U.S. Government Printing Office, 1966.

Dahrendorf, R. *Life Chances: Approaches to Social and Political Theory.* Chicago: University of Chicago Press, 1980.

Furth, D. "Selection and Equity: An International Viewpoint." *Comparative Education Review* 22, no. 2 (1978): 259–77.

Goffman, E. "On Cooling the Mark Out: Some Aspects of Adaptation to Failure." *Psychiatry* 15, no. 4 (1952): 451–63.

Jencks, C., et al. *Inequality.* New York: Basic Books, 1972.

Karabel, J. "Community Colleges and Social Stratification." *Harvard Educational Review* 42, no. 4 (1972): 521–62.

London, H. B. *The Culture of a Community College.* New York: Praeger, 1978.

Moore, K. M. "The Cooling Out of Two-Year College Women." *Personnel and Guidance Journal* 53, no. 8 (1975): 578–83.

Winkler, K. J. "Graduation, Not Admissions, Urged as Desegregation Focus." *Chronicle of Higher Education,* March 21, 1977, 8.

Zwerling, L. S. *Second Best: The Crisis of the Community College.* New York: McGraw-Hill, 1976.

INTRODUCTION TO CHAPTERS 4 AND 5

It took me almost all of my three years at Stanford and the two at Harvard to draft a book on open-door colleges. I learned a great deal during those five years about the peculiar compromises and bargains that can be fashioned in leading research universities. The Harvard appointment allowed me to leave Stanford (before it fired me!) with my head held high ("He went *where?*"). The move to the East Coast and the appointment to a small, dedicated faculty in a foundation-subsidized administrative career program put me in touch with bright, upward bound K–12 teachers and junior administrators, often older than myself, who joshed that only my intense enthusiasm for my subject overcame my pedagogical weaknesses. We were part of a larger, closely knit group even though the program veered in one direction and my higher education research interests went in another. All this ended when, after just two years at Harvard (on a five-year contract), a perfect offer to pursue my interests came my way. I readily accepted a full-time research post at the new Center for the Study of Higher Education in Berkeley, which soon morphed into a new position, a half-research, half-teaching arrangement that led to tenure.

After so much time and effort studying nonselective institutions, I was ready to try my hand at studying institutions that fell into the opposite end of the continuum: highly selective colleges. At Berkeley the main project centered on following students through four undergraduate years in three leading liberal arts colleges, Antioch, Reed, and Swarthmore. Findings were contrasted with those at San Francisco State and the University of California, Berkeley, a state college and a state university, respectively. I was in the field making ten-day to two-week visits over several years (1958–63). When a team effort to write an integrated volume faltered, I turned to writing my own book, *The Distinctive College,* and I submitted "The Organizational Saga in Higher Education" to the *Administrative Science Quarterly* (ASQ), a journal for both scholars and practitioners.

50

"Belief and Loyalty in College Organization" went to the *Journal of Higher Education*, a venue intended for researchers.

Even as similar private institutions, Antioch, Reed, and Swarthmore were different in many ways: they had different curricula, administrative structures, historical lines of development, constituencies, faculties, and students. I struggled to capture what they had in common. Late in the writing, it dawned on me that what was singular to all was the intense belief each had in its own character. How to conceptualize this intangible phenomenon? For several months, I weighed such words as *purpose, mission, doctrine, belief, story, legend*; in the end I decided that *saga* seemed to most aptly describe the phenomenon.

Taking this concept to the organizational-theory literature was a more fruitful stroke than I could have imagined. The ASQ 1972 article turned out to play a leading role in the emergence of the idea that organizations have their own special culture. A citation analysis, done in the early 1980s, of thirty-two articles on organizational culture showed that my article was among the most frequently cited sources. Mine was the only cited source directly based on case studies. The others referred to Clifford Geertz's 1973 classic, *The Interpretation of Culture,* and noted books by William G. Ouchi (*Theory Z,* 1981) and Terence Deal and A. Kennedy (*Corporate Cultures,* 1982). The concept of organizational saga, developed from doing research on just three small colleges, helped to place me in the fast-growing literature on organizations. At the time, the focus was overwhelmingly centered on business firms, and articles on organizational culture became a veritable industry by the 1990s.

The notion of an organizational saga endures in the twenty-first century. My ASQ article was reprinted in full as part of a 1998 collection of papers on qualitative analysis of organizations. The well-regarded editor of that volume commented that it "served as an inspiration to many students trying to understand how a sense of unity and devotion, uniqueness and purpose comes to members of formally established organizations . . . the article has had enormous influence. . . . In the context of its time and place of publication, Clark's writing is a classic of experimental, evocative, almost musical prose" (Van Maanen, 1998, 194). If musical, I hope my prose had a clear melodic line with only a few dissonant chords and little fugue-like repetition.

The wide, enduring use of "saga" on top of the extensive play of "cooling-out," has validated for me the old claim in scholarship that there is nothing more useful than a good idea. A really good idea in the social sciences, however, comes not from idle speculation, which can be blown away, but from research rooted in closely observed practice. The notion of an organizational saga is all the more valuable when young scholars find inspiration in an approach to studying organizations that focuses on values and meaning.

The second article, "Belief and Loyalty in College Organization," drawn from the saga inquiry, appeared in a journal devoted to the study of higher education. It emphasizes the role of belief in one's own college, thus promoting loyalty to it. For organizations generally, this line of thinking received a brilliant statement by Albert O. Hirschman in his classic *Exit, Voice, and Loyalty* (1970).

Reference

Van Maanen, John, ed. *Qualitative Studies of Organizations*. Thousand Oaks, Calif.: Sage Publications, 1998.

CHAPTER 4

The Organizational Saga in Higher Education

SAGA, ORIGINALLY referring to a medieval Icelandic or Norse account of achievements and events in the history of a person or group, has come to mean a narrative of heroic exploits, of a unique development that has deeply stirred the emotions of participants and descendants. Thus a saga is not simply a story but a story that at some time has had a particular base of believers. The term often refers also to the actual history itself, thereby including a stream of events, the participants, and the written or spoken interpretation. The element of belief is crucial, for without the credible story, the events and persons become history; with the development of belief, a particular bit of history becomes a definition full of pride and identity for the group.

Introduction

An *organizational saga* is a collective understanding of unique accomplishment in a formally established group. The group's definition of the accomplishment, intrinsically historical but embellished through retelling and rewriting, links stages of organizational development. The participants have added affect, an emotional loading, which places their conception between the coolness of rational purpose and the warmth of sentiment found in religion and magic. An organizational saga presents some rational explanation of how certain means led to certain ends, but it also includes affect that turns a formal place into a beloved institu-

Reprinted from "The Organizational Saga in Higher Education," *Administrative Science Quarterly* 17 (June 1972): 178–84, by permission of vol. 17. © Johnson Graduate School of Management, Cornell University.

tion, to which participants may be passionately devoted. Encountering such devotion, the observer may become unsure of his own analytical detachment as he tests the overtones of the institutional spirit or spirit of place.

The study of organizational sagas highlights nonstructural and nonrational dimensions of organizational life and achievement. Macro-organizational theory has concentrated on the role of structure and technology in organizational effectiveness (Gross, 1964; Litterer, 1965; March, 1965; Thompson, 1967; Price, 1968; Perrow, 1970). A needed corrective is more research on the cultural and expressive aspects of organizations, particularly on the role of belief and sentiment at broad levels of organization. The human-relations approach in organizational analysis, centered largely on group interaction, showed some awareness of the role of organization symbols (Whyte, 1948, chap. 23), but this conceptual lead has not been taken as a serious basis for research. Also, in the literature on organizations and purposive communities, *ideology* refers to unified and shared belief (Selznick, 1949; Bendix, 1956; Price, 1968, 104–10; Carden, 1969); but the concept of ideology has lost denotative power, having been stretched by varying cases. For the phenomenon discussed in this essay, *saga* seems to provide the appropriate denotation. With a general emphasis on normative bonds, *organizational saga* refers to a unified set of publicly expressed beliefs about the formal group that (a) is rooted in history, (b) claims unique accomplishment, and (c) is held with sentiment by the group.

To develop the concept in this essay, extreme cases and exaggerations of the ideal type are used; but the concept will be close to reality and widely applicable when the phenomenon is examined in weak as well as strong expression. In many organizations, even some highly utilitarian ones, some segment of their personnel probably develop in time at least a weak saga. Those who have persisted together for some years in one place will have had, at minimum, a thin stream of shared experience, which they elaborate into a plausible account of group uniqueness. Whether developed primarily by management or by employees, the story helps rationalize for the individual his commitment of time and energy for years, perhaps for a lifetime, to a particular enterprise. Even when weak, the belief can compensate in part for the loss of meaning in much modern work, giving some drama and some cultural identity to one's otherwise entirely instrumental efforts. At the other end of the continuum, a saga engages one so intensely as to make his immediate place overwhelmingly valuable. It can even produce a striking distortion, with the organization becoming the only reality, the outside world becoming illusion. Generally, the almost complete capture of affect and perception is associated with only a few utopian communities, fanatical political factions, and religious sects. But some formal rationalized organizations, as, e.g., business and education, can also become utopian, fanatical, or sectarian.

Organizational sagas vary in durability. They can arise quickly in relatively unstructured social settings, as in professional sports organizations that operate in the volatile context of contact with large spectator audiences through the mass media. A professional baseball or football team may create a rags-to-riches legend in a few months' time that excites millions of people. But such a saga is also very fragile as an ongoing definition of the organization. The story can be removed quickly from the collective understanding of the present and future, for successful performance is often unstable, and the events that set the direction of belief can be readily reversed, with the great winners quickly becoming habitual losers. In such cases, there seems to be an unstable structural connection between the organization and the base of believers. The base of belief is not anchored within the organization nor in personal ties between insiders and outsiders, but is mediated by mass media, away from the control of the organization. Such sagas continue only as the organization keeps repeating its earlier success and also keeps the detached followers from straying to other sources of excitement and identification.

In contrast, organizational sagas show high durability when built slowly in structured social contexts; e.g., the educational system, specifically for the purposes of this essay, three liberal arts colleges in the United States. In the many small private colleges, the story of special performance emerges not in a few months but over a decade or two. When the saga is firmly developed, it is embodied in many components of the organization, affecting the definition and performance of the organization and finding protection in the webbing of the institutional parts. It is not volatile and can be relegated to the past only by years of attenuation or organizational decline.

Since the concept of organizational saga was developed from research on Reed, Antioch, and Swarthmore, three distinctive and highly regarded colleges (Clark, 1970), material and categories from their developmental histories are used to illustrate the development of a saga, and its positive effects on organizational participation and effectiveness are then considered.[1]

Development of Saga

Two stages can be distinguished in the development of an organizational saga, initiation and fulfillment. Initiation takes place under varying conditions and occurs within a relatively short period of time; fulfillment is related to features of the organization that are enduring and more predictable.

INITIATION

Strong sagas do not develop in passive organizations tuned to adaptive servicing of demand or to the fulfilling of roles dictated by higher authorities (Clark, 1956, 1960). The saga is initially a strong purpose, conceived and enunciated by a single man or a small cadre (Selznick, 1957) whose first task is to find a setting that is open, or can be opened, to a special effort. The most obvious setting is the autonomous new organization, where there is no established structure, no rigid custom, especially if a deliberate effort has been made to establish initial autonomy and bordering outsiders are preoccupied. There a leader may also have the advantage of building from the top down, appointing lieutenants and picking up recruits in accord with his ideas.

Reed College is strongly characterized by a saga, and its story of hard-won excellence and nonconformity began as a strong purpose in a new organization. Its first president, William T. Foster, a thirty-year-old, high-minded reformer, from the sophisticated East of Harvard and Bowdoin went to the untutored Northwest, to an unbuilt campus in suburban Portland in 1910, precisely because he did not want to be limited by established institutions, all of which were, to his mind, corrupt in practice. The projected college in Oregon was clear ground, intellectually as well as physically, and he could there assemble the people and devise the practices that would finally give the United States an academically pure college, a Balliol for America.

The second setting for initiation is the established organization in a crisis of decay. Those in charge, after years of attempting incremental adjustments (Lindblom, 1959), realize finally that they must either give up established ways or have the organization fail. Preferring that it survive, they may relinquish the leadership to one proposing a plan that promises revival and later strength, or they may even accept a man of utopian intent. Deep crisis in the established organization thus creates some of the conditions of a new organization. It suspends past practice, forces some bordering groups to stand back or even to turn their backs on failure of the organization, and tends to catch the attention of the reformer looking for an opportunity.

Antioch College is a dramatic example of such a setting. Started in the 1860s, its first sixty years were characterized by little money, weak staff, few students, and obscurity. Conditions worsened in the 1910s under the inflation and other strains of World War I. In 1919 a charismatic utopian reformer, Arthur E. Morgan, decided it was more advantageous to take over an old college with buildings and a charter than to start a new one. First as trustee and then as president, he began in the early 1920s an institutional renovation that overturned everything. As president he found it easy to push aside old, weak organizational structures and usages. He elaborated a plan of general education involving an unusual combination of work, study, and community participation; and he set about to devise the implementing tool. Crisis and charisma made possible a radical transformation out of which came a second Antioch, a college soon characterized by a sense of exciting history, unique practice, and exceptional performance.

The third context for initiation is the established organization that is not in crisis, not collapsing from long decline, yet ready for evolutionary change. This is the most difficult situation to predict, having to do with degree of rigidity. In both ideology and structure, institutionalized colleges vary in openness to change. In those under church control, e.g., the colleges of the more liberal Protestant denominations have been more hospitable than Catholic colleges, at least until recently, to educational experimentation. A college with a tradition of presidential power is more open to change than one where the trustees and the professors exert control over the president. Particularly promising is the college with a self-defined need for educational leadership. This is the opening for which some reformers watch, the sound place that has some ambition to increase its academic stature, as, e.g., Swarthmore College.

Swarthmore began in the 1860s, and had become by 1920 a secure and stable college, prudently managed by Quaker trustees and administrators and solidly based on traditional support from nearby Quaker families in Pennsylvania, New Jersey, and Maryland. Such an organization would not usually be thought promising for reform, but Frank Aydelotte, who became its president in 1920, judged it ready for change. Magnetic in personality, highly placed within the elite circle of former Rhodes scholars, personally liked by important foundation officials, and recommended as a scholarly leader, he was offered other college presidencies, but he chose Swarthmore as a place open to change through a combination of financial health, liberal Quaker ethos, and some institutional ambition. His judgment proved correct, although the tolerance for his changes in the 1920s and 1930s was narrow at times. He began the gradual introduction of a modified Oxford honors program and related changes, which resulted in noteworthy achievements that supporters were to identify later as "the Swarthmore saga" (Swarthmore College Faculty, 1941).

FULFILLMENT

Although the conditions of initiation of a saga vary, the means of fulfillment are more predictable. There are many ways in which a unified sense of a special history is expressed; e.g., even a patch of sidewalk or a coffee room may evoke emotion among the believers; but one can delimit the components at the center of the development of a saga. These may center, in colleges, on the personnel, the program, the external social base, the student subculture, and the imagery of the saga.

PERSONNEL. In a college, the key group of believers is the senior faculty. When they are hostile to a new idea, its attenuation is likely; when they are passive, its success is weak; and when they are devoted to it, a saga is probable. A single leader, a college president, can initiate the change, but the organizational idea will not be expanded over the years and expressed in performance unless ranking and powerful members of the faculty become committed to it and remain committed even after the initiator is gone. In committing themselves deeply, taking some credit for the change and seeking to ensure its perpetuation, they routinize the charisma of the leader in collegial authority. The faculty cadre of believers helps to effect the legend, then to protect it against later leaders and other new participants who, less pure in belief, might turn the organization in some other direction.

Such faculty cadres were well developed at Reed by 1925, after the time of its first two presidents; at Antioch, by the early 1930s, after Morgan, disappointed with his followers, left for the board of directors of the new Tennessee Valley Authority; and at Swarthmore, by the 1930s, and particularly by 1940, after Aydelotte's twenty years of persistent effort. In all three colleges, after the departure of the change agent(s), the senior faculty with the succeeding president, a man appropriate for consolidation, undertook the full working out of the experiment. The faculty believers also replaced themselves through socialization and selective recruitment and retention in the 1940s and 1950s. Meanwhile, new potential innovators had sometimes to be stopped. In such instances, the faculty was able to exert influence to shield the distinctive effort from erosion or deflection. At Reed, for example, major clashes between president and faculty in the late 1930s and the early 1950s were precipitated by a new change-oriented president, coming in from the outside, disagreeing with a faculty proud of what had been done, attached deeply to what the college had become, and determined to maintain what was for them the distinctive Reed style. From the standpoint of constructing a regional and national model of purity and severity in undergraduate education, the Reed faculty did on those occasions act to create while acting to conserve.

PROGRAM. For a college to transform purpose into a credible story of unique accomplishment, there must be visible practices with which claims of distinctiveness can be supported; i.e., unusual courses, noteworthy requirements, or special methods of teaching. On the basis of seemingly unique practices, the program becomes a set of communal symbols and rituals, invested with meaning. Not reporting grades to the students becomes a symbol, as at Reed, that the college cares about learning for learning's sake; thus mere technique becomes part of a saga.

In all three colleges, the program was seen as distinctive by both insiders and outsiders. At Swarthmore it was the special seminars and other practices of the honors program, capped by written and oral examination by teams of visiting outsiders in the final days of the senior year. At Antioch it was the work-study cycle, the special set of general education requirements, community government, and community involvement. At Reed it was the required freshman lecture-and-seminar courses, the junior qualifying examination, and the thesis in the senior year. Such practices became central to a belief that things had been done so differently, and so much against the mainstream, and often against imposing odds, that the group had generated a saga.

SOCIAL BASE. The saga also becomes fixed in the minds of outside believers devoted to the organization, usually the alumni. The alumni are the best located to hold beliefs enduringly pure, since they can be as strongly identified with a special organizational history as the older faculty and administrators and yet do not have to face directly the new problems generated by a changing environment or students. Their thoughts can remain centered on the past, rooted in the days when, as students, they participated intimately in the unique ways and accomplishments of the campus.

Liberal alumni, such as those of Reed, Antioch, and Swarthmore, seek to conserve what they believe to be a unique liberal institution and to protect it from the conservative forces of society that might change it—i.e., to make it like other colleges. At Reed, e.g., dropouts as well as graduates were struck by the intellectual excellence of their small college, convinced that college life there had been unlike college life anywhere else, and they were ready to conserve the practices that seemed to sustain that excellence. Here, too, conserving acts can be seen for a time as contributing to an innovation, protecting the full working out of a distinctive effort.

STUDENT SUBCULTURE. The student body is the third group of believers, not overwhelmingly important but still a necessary support for the saga. To become and remain a saga, a change must be supported by the student subculture over decades, and the ideology of the subculture must integrate with the central ideas of the believing administrators and faculty. When the students define themselves as personally responsible for upholding the image of the college, then a design or plan has become an organizational saga.

At Antioch, Reed, and Swarthmore, the student subcultures were powerful mechanisms for carrying a developing saga from one generation to another. Reed students, almost from the beginning and extending at least to the early 1960s, were great believers in the uniqueness of their college, constantly on the alert for any action that would alter it, ever fearful that administration or faculty might succumb to pressures that would make Reed just like other colleges. Students at Antioch and Swarthmore also offered unstinting support for the ideology of their institution. All three student bodies steadily and dependably transferred the ideology from one generation to another. Often socializing deeply, they helped produce the graduate who never quite rid himself of the wish to go back to the campus.

IMAGERY OF SAGA. Upheld by faculty, alumni, and students, expressed in teaching practices, the saga is even more widely expressed as a generalized tradition in statues and ceremonies, written histories and current catalogues, even in an "air about the place" felt by participants and some outsiders. The more unique the history and the more forceful the claim to a place in history, the more intensely cultivated the ways of sharing memory and symbolizing the institution. The saga is a strong self-fulfilling belief; working through institutional self-image and public image, it is indeed a switchman (Weber, 1946), helping to determine the tracks along which action is pushed by men's self-defined interests. The early belief of one stage brings about the actions that warrant a stronger version of the same belief in a later period. As the account develops, believers come to sense its many constituent symbols as inextricably bound together, and the part takes its meaning from the whole. For example, at Antioch a deep attachment developed in the 1930s and 1940s to Morgan's philosophy of the whole man and to its expression in a unique combination of work, study, community participation, and many practices thought to embody freedom and nonconformity. Some of the faculty of those years who remained in the 1940s and 1950s had many memories and impressions that seemed to form a symbolic whole: personnel counselors, folk dancing in Red Square, Morgan's towering physique, the battles of community government, the pacifism of the late 1930s, the frequent dash of students to off-campus jobs, the dedicated deans who personified central values. Public image also grew strong and sharp, directing liberals and radicals to the college and conservatives to other places. The symbolic expressions themselves were a strong perpetuating force.

Conclusion

An organizational saga is a powerful means of unity in the formal place. It makes links across internal divisions and organizational boundaries as internal and external groups share their common belief. With deep emotional commitment, believers define themselves by their organizational affiliation, and in their bond to other believers they share an intense sense of the unique. In an organization defined by a strong saga, there is a feeling that there is the small world of the lucky few and the large routine one of the rest of the world. Such an emotional bond turns the membership into a community, even a cult.

An organizational saga is thus a valuable resource, created over a number of years out of the social components of the formal enterprise. As participants become ideologues, their common definition becomes a foundation for trust and for extreme loyalty. Such bonds give the organization a competitive edge in recruiting and maintaining personnel and helps it to avoid the vicious circle in which some actual or anticipated erosion of organizational strength leads to the loss of some personnel, which leads to further decline and loss. Loyalty causes individuals to stay with a system, to save and improve it rather than to leave to serve their self-interest elsewhere (Hirschman, 1970). The genesis and persistence of loyalty is a key organizational and analytical problem. Enduring loyalty follows from a collective belief of participants that their organization is distinctive. Such a belief comes from a credible story of uncommon effort, achievement, and form.

Pride in the organized group and pride in one's identity as taken from the group are personal returns that are uncommon in modern social involvement. The development of sagas is one way in which men in organizations increase such returns, reducing their sense of isolation and increasing their personal pride and pleasure in organizational life. Studying the evocative narratives and devotional ties of formal systems leads to a better understanding of the fundamental capacities of organizations to enhance or diminish the lives of participants. The organization possessing a saga is a place in which participants for a time at least happily accept their bond.

Notes

I wish to thank Wendell Bell, Maren L. Carden, Kai Erikson, and Stanley Udy for discussion and comment. Parts of an early draft of this essay have been used to connect organizational belief to problems of governance in colleges and universities (Clark, 1971).

1. For some discussion of the risks and tensions associated with organizational sagas, particularly that of success in one period leading to later rigidity and stagnation, see Clark (1970, 258–61). Hale (1970) gives an illuminating discussion of various effects of a persistent saga in a theological seminary.

References

Bendix, R. *Work and Authority in Industry.* New York: John Wiley, 1956.

Carden, M. L. *Oneida: Utopian Community to Modern Corporation.* Baltimore: Johns Hopkins Press, 1969.

Clark, B. R. *Adult Education in Transition: A Study of Institutional Insecurity.* Berkeley: University of California Press, 1956.

———. *The Open Door College: A Case Study.* New York: McGraw-Hill, 1960.

———. *The Distinctive College: Antioch, Reed, and Swarthmore.* Chicago, Aldine, 1970.

———. "Belief and Loyalty in College Organization." *Journal of Higher Education* 42, no. 6 (1971): 499–515.

Gross, B. M. *The Managing of Organizations.* 2 vols. New York: Free Press, 1964.

Hale, J. R. "The Making and Testing of an Organizational Saga: A Case-Study of the Lutheran Theological Seminary at Gettysburg, Pennsylvania, with Special Reference to the Problem of Merger, 1959–1969." Unpublished EdD dissertation, Columbia University, 1970.

Hirschman, A. O. *Exit, Voice, and Loyalty.* Cambridge, Mass.: Harvard University Press, 1970.

Lindblom, C. E. "The Science of 'Muddling Through.'" *Public Administration Review* 19 (1959): 79–88.

Litterer, J. A. *The Analysis of Organizations.* New York: John Wiley, 1965.

March, J. G., ed. *Handbook of Organizations.* Chicago: Rand McNally, 1965.

Perrow, C. *Organizational Analysis.* Belmont, Calif.: Wadsworth, 1970.

Price, J. L. *Organizational Effectiveness: An Inventory of Propositions.* Homewood, Ill.: Richard D. Irwin, 1968.

Selznick, P. *TVA and the Grass Roots*. Berkeley: University of California Press, 1949.

———. *Leadership in Administration*. New York: Harper & Row, 1957.

Swarthmore College Faculty. *An Adventure in Education: Swarthmore College Under Frank Aydelotte*. New York: Macmillan, 1941.

Thompson, J. D. *Organizations in Action*. New York: McGraw-Hill, 1967.

Weber, M. *From Max Weber: Essays in Sociology*. Translated and edited by H. H. Gerth and C. Wright Mills. New York: Oxford, 1946.

Whyte, W. F. *Human Relations in the Restaurant Industry*. New York: McGraw-Hill, 1948.

CHAPTER 5

Belief and Loyalty in College Organization

MY PREMISE IS that there are ideational elements in complex organizations that do not lie outside of matters of governance but rather exist as basic sentiments that help determine the structures of governance and how they work.[1] In this approach, problems of governance are seen to vary with the quality of institutional self-conception. The key mediating elements in this relationship are loyalty and trust. In the causal flow, the organizational self-conception heavily determines the degree of loyalty and trust, which in turn affects in a major way the problems and forms of governance.

Sociologists commonly conceive of two broad dimensions of social bonding: the structural, consisting of patterns of relation and interaction of persons and groups, and the normative, consisting of shared beliefs, attitudes, and values. The two dimensions appear in complex organizations as organizational structure, including informal patterns and "organizational culture." When we approach issues of governance in colleges and universities, we have an overwhelming tendency to fix on the dimension of structure. We look to see how much authority is located in the position of the president, how authority is delegated and otherwise caused to be located in various subunits, and how the committee system operates. We seek the mechanisms that allow faculty and administrative authority to exist simultaneously and provide a reasonable degree of peaceful effectiveness most of the time. When we want to improve things, we ask how to "restructure" the organization. My purpose here is to fix on the other dimension, that of organizational culture. I wish to dramatize the

First published in *The Journal of Higher Education* 42, no. 6 (June 1971): 449–515, used by permission of The Ohio State University Press.

importance of normative bonding in the formal organization, so that we will always ask about its fundamental beliefs as well as its fundamental structures. This means that when we want to improve things, specifically governance, we will ask how to "re-norm" the organization or how to alter the basic beliefs of the personnel and other participants about the nature of the enterprise.

How does normative bonding occur in formal organizations? There are undoubtedly many ways, of which we have thus far dimly sensed only a few. I will concentrate here on one fundamental route, that of development of an institutional story. I will refer to this phenomenon as an *organizational saga*. In the following pages, I first discuss the concept of a saga; then, drawing upon research on small colleges, describe the buildup of college sagas; and, third, emphasize the consequences of a saga for loyalty and trust.[2] The final section of the essay speculates on the nature of belief and loyalty in large universities, as compared with small colleges, and attempts to specify the matter of governance as problems of a sense of the whole and the social conditions of trust.

An organizational saga is a collective understanding of unique accomplishment in a formally established group. Based on past exploits, the formal group develops a unitary sense of highly valuable performance and place. The group's definition of the situation, intrinsically historical, links stages of organizational developments. The definition is also embellished: while based on a past reality, it has, over time, through retelling and rewriting, become rounded and sentimental. The participants have added affect, an emotional loading that places the understanding between the affective coolness of rational purpose and manipulative doctrine and the capitulation to sentiment found in religion and magic. An organizational saga presents some administrative logic, some rational explanation of how certain means led to certain ends, but it also contains a sense of romance and mystery that turns a formal place into a deeply beloved institution. Participants are passionate to the point where we say they partake of the gospel of the organization.

Most organizations probably develop in time at least a weak legend for some segment of their personnel. Those who have together persisted for some years in one formal place will have had, at minimum, a thin stream of shared experience into which neither they nor anyone else can ever step again. Sensing that flow of common fate, they find cause to elaborate a plausible account of uniqueness. The story helps rationalize for the individual his commitment of time and energy for years, perhaps for a lifetime, to a particular enterprise. Even when weak, the belief can compensate in part for the loss of meaning in much modern work. If labor itself does not provide direct satisfaction, there is all the more reason to clutch the pleasure of the story that gives some cultural identity to one's otherwise routine instrumental efforts. By this reasoning, the loss of craftsmanship heightens the tendency to add value to one's involvement by tooling and retooling a symbolic expression, a minor legend of some sort. At the other end of the continuum, among the deviant cases of extreme expression, a saga engages the mind and the heart so intensely as to make one's immediate place overwhelmingly valuable.

Organizational sagas also vary in durability. We seem to find fragility in organizational legends that bloom quickly in relatively unstructured social settings, as in the case of professional sports organizations that operate in the volatile context of contact with large spectator audiences through the mass media. For example, the New York Mets professional baseball team created a rags-to-riches legend in a few months' time in the summer of 1969, one that greatly excited millions of people. This instant saga, which gave so much life and unity and pride, was also highly fragile as an ongoing definition of the organization. For a variety of reasons, the story could be removed quickly from the collective understanding of the present (and future) and placed in memory of the concluded past. In such instances of the highly perishable organizational saga, "successful" performance is often unstable. The original events that set the direction of belief can be readily reversed by later opposite happenings, with the great winners becoming quickly just another bunch of habitual losers. The saga must then be seriously amended or replaced by a story of the fall from grace. Such cases, too, seem to entail an undependable structural connection between the organization and the base of believers. The large mass base is not anchored within the organization itself or in personal ties between insiders and outsiders, but rather floats at the end of the line of mass media mediation, away from firm control by the organization. Thus, in first approximation, such sagas continue to have direct effect only as the organization goes on repeating its earlier success and also keeps the mood of detached followers from straying to other sources of excitement and identification.

Belief and Loyalty in College Organization   67

In contrast, we observe high durability in organizational sagas when they are built relatively slowly in relatively stable, highly structured social contexts. One such arena is the educational system, specifically for our purposes here the realm of liberal arts colleges in American higher education. Within a cohort of hundreds of small private colleges, the exciting story of special performance emerges not in a few months but at a minimum over a number of years and more likely in a decade or two. When the saga is firmly in place, it is embodied in many steady components of the organization, affecting the definitions and performances of the future and finding protection in the webbing of the institutional parts. The exciting story will erode sooner or later, but it has a stubborn capacity to continue. It is not here today and gone tomorrow; it can be relegated to the shelves of history only by years of attenuation or organizational decline into crisis.

How do strong and durable organizational sagas develop? The possibilities in college organization are illuminated by developments in three distinctive and highly regarded American colleges, Reed, Antioch, and Swarthmore.

We distinguish two stages in the building of organizational saga, its initiation and its fulfillment. Initiation takes place under widely varying conditions and occurs within a relatively short period of time. Fulfillment converges on certain inescapable features of organization that are enduring and more predictable.

Sagas do not develop strongly in passive organizations, those tuned to adaptive servicing of demand or to the obedient filling of role dictated by higher authorities. The saga is initially strong purpose, born in an image of the future conceived and enunciated by a single man or a small cadre. The first task of the agents of change is to find a setting that is open, or can be opened, to a special effort. The most obvious setting is the autonomous new organization. In the new place, there is no established structure, no rigid custom. The environment may stand back for a while, especially if a deliberate effort has been made to establish initial autonomy and bordering outsiders are preoccupied with their old problems. A leader may also there have the notable advantage of building from the top down, appointing lieutenants and picking up recruits who like his banner and the sound of his drums.

Among liberal arts colleges, Reed College is strongly characterized by the phenomenon of a saga, and its embellished story of hard-won excellence and nonconformity began as strong purpose in a new organization. Its first president, William T. Foster, a thirty-year-old high-minded reformer, took himself from the sophisticated East of Harvard and Bowdoin to the untutored Northwest, to an unbuilt campus in suburban Portland in 1910 precisely because he did not want to be trapped in established institutions, all of which, including his alma mater Harvard, were to his mind corrupt in practice. The projected college in Oregon was clear ground, intellectually as well as physically, and he could there assemble the people and devise the practices that would finally give this country an academically pure college, a Balliol for America. The later saga was initiated by a man with a mission, one stubborn to a fault, who took a new organization as his means of creating a distinctive college.

The second setting for initiation is the established organization in a crisis of decay. The deep crisis born of sustained decline is the great eraser of prior commitments. Those in charge, after years of attempting to muddle through with incremental adjustment, realize finally that they must either give up established ways or give up the organization. Preferring to survive, they may relinquish the helm with grudging gratitude to the one proposing a plan that promises revival and later strength, or they may even accept a man of utopian intent. Deep crisis in the established organization thus re-creates some of the conditions of the new organization. It suspends past practice; it forces some bordering groups to stand back a pace, to give the victim air, or even causes them to turn their backs and flee at the sight of the organizational mess; and it tends to catch the attention of the reformer who is looking for a great opportunity. As we have long known, crisis is the natural condition for charisma, and the institutional call goes out for the unusual man "who can save us."

Antioch College is a dramatic case in American higher education of the revolutionary overturn that leads to a saga. Started in the 1850s, its first seventy years were characterized by little money, weak staff, few students, and obscurity. Never too strong, the condition of the college worsened in the 1910s under the inflation and other strains of World War I, and in 1919 Antioch tottered on the edge of the grave. At the time, a charismatic utopian reformer, Arthur E. Morgan, came in contact with the college. He decided it was more advantageous to take over an old college, available for the asking, with buildings and a charter, than to start a new one. He grabbed hold, first as a trustee and then as president, and took off in the early 1920s in a fantastic bit of institutional renovation, overturning everything from the trustees on down. As president, he found it easy to push aside old, badly debilitated structures and usages. He elaborated a grand plan of general education involving an unusual combination of work, study, and community participation, and he set about to devise the implementing tool. For a few years, even up to a decade, the place belonged to him. Crisis and charisma made possible a radical transformation out of which came "a second Antioch," a college soon characterized by a sense of exciting history, unique practice, and exceptional performance.

The third context of initiation is the established organization that is viable rather than in crisis, secure in person rather than collapsing from long decline, yet in a state of readiness for evolutionary change. This is the most difficult situation to illuminate and predict, having to do with degrees of rigidity in established successful organizations. In both ideology and structure, institutionalized colleges vary in openness to change. In those under church control, for example, the colleges of the more liberal Protestant denominations have been more hospitable than Catholic colleges, at least until recently, to educational experimentation. A college with a tradition of presidential power is more fertile ground than one where the trustees check the water fountains and the professors spin a tight collegial web over the president's office. Particularly promising is the college with a self-defined need for educational leadership: "We have just had for twenty years a good business-affairs man in the presidential chair, and now it is time for some leadership on the educational side." This is the opening for which some reformers watch. They seek neither the drama and danger of the new college nor the trauma of one deep in crisis, but the solid footing of the sound place that has some ambition to rise in academic stature.

Swarthmore is a case in point. Begun in the 1860s, it had become by 1920 a secure and stable college, prudently managed by Quaker trustees and administrators and solidly based in traditional support from nearby Quaker families in Pennsylvania, New Jersey, and Maryland. Such an organization would not usually be thought promising for reform, but Frank Aydelotte, who came to the presidency of Swarthmore in 1920, judged it ripe for change. At the time, Aydelotte was a promising, well-sponsored man in the marketplace of college administration. Magnetic in personality, highly placed within the elite circle of former Rhodes Scholars, personally liked by important foundation officials, and recommended as a scholarly leader, he was offered other college presidencies. He picked Swarthmore as a decent place appropriate for an effort to jump to the first rank, open to change through a combination of financial health, liberal Quaker ethos, and some institutional ambition. His judgment proved correct, although the tolerance for his gradual changes in the 1920s and 1930s was narrow at times and a less forceful man might not have squeezed through. The point is that he perceived openness in a traditional setting and moved in with his mission, his plan for change. He began the gradual introduction of a modified Oxford honors program and a host of related changes, setting in motion a stream of events and noteworthy achievements that supporters were to identify later as the Swarthmore saga.

While the conditions of initiation of a legend vary, the means of durable embodiment are more predictable, converging on certain inescapable features of organization. There are, of course, unique features in each case and a host of detailed ways in which a unified sense of a special history is expressed. In a liberal arts college, one may find a patch of sidewalk or a coffee room partaking of a legend, evoking emotion among the believers. But such bits and pieces can be grouped analytically in major and minor categories and we can seek to assert, for broad classes of organization, the components that are at the center of the development of a saga. As a beginning, we identify in American colleges the personnel core; the program core; the external social base; the student subculture; and the organizational ideology itself.

THE PERSONNEL CORE. We have spoken of a saga as a story of a development, a story believed by an organized group that becomes more united by sharing the belief. In a college, the key group of believers is the senior faculty. When the senior men are hostile to an emerging theme, however it was introduced, its attenuation is ensured; when they are passive, its success is anemic; and when they are devoted to the idea, the making of a saga is probable. A single leader, a college president, can initiate the change, but the organizational idea will not be expanded over the years and expressed in performance unless ranking and powerful members of the faculty swing into line and remain committed while the initiator is present and, especially, after he is gone. The leader is perishable; he is only one, and increasingly the implementing work is the work of others.

As they invest themselves deeply, taking some credit for the change and seeking to ensure its future, charisma is routinized in collegial authority. The faculty cadre of true believers, formed over years and potentially self-replacing for decades, helps to effect the legend, then to protect it against later presidents and other new participants who, less pure in belief, are ready to swing the organization in some other direction.

After ten to fifteen years of the effort to build distinctively, such faculty cadres were well developed at Reed, Antioch, and Swarthmore. In all cases, the senior faculty took over after the departure of the change agent or agents, with the succeeding president a man appropriate for consolidation or for the full working out of the experiment. The faculty believers also replaced themselves well, through socialization and selective recruitment and retention, passing the mantle in the 1940s and 1950s to a second generation. Meanwhile, new potential innovators had sometimes to be beaten back. In such instances, faculty power to protect faculty belief was the main means of shielding the distinctive effort against erosion or deflection. At Reed, e.g., major clashes between president and faculty in the late 1930s and the early 1950s were precipitated by a new change-minded president, coming in from the outside, squaring off with a faculty proud of what had been done, attached deeply to what the college had become, and determined to maintain what was for them, the students, the alumni, and many outsiders—friend and foe—the distinctive Reed style. From the standpoint of creating a regional and national model of purity and severity in undergraduate education, the Reed faculty did on those occasions, in its own stubborn way, serve creatively while acting conservatively.

THE PROGRAM CORE. For a college to transform purpose into an exciting story of accomplishment, there must be visible practices around which claims of distinctiveness can be elaborated. We find a celebration of innovative courses and requirements, special methods of teaching, and a climate of learning not duplicated elsewhere. On the basis of a few unique practices, the program becomes over time a set of communal symbols and rituals, rich with invested meaning. Academic men point to their decorated spears, their village totems, their bracelets signifying honor and beauty, as they speak proudly of the courses and curricula they have lovingly fashioned by hand and the trials they have devised for students to give great meaning to what otherwise would be only a paper credential. A simple thing like not reporting grades to the students becomes a symbol (as at

Reed) that the whole college cares about learning for learning's sake. Thus inflated, mere instructional technique becomes part of a general legend.

In the three colleges at hand, the program was seen by insiders and outsiders alike as the heart of distinctiveness, the center of the exciting story. At Swarthmore, it was the special seminars and other practices of the honors program, capped by written and oral examination at the hands of teams of visiting outsiders in the final days of the senior year. At Antioch, it was the work-study cycle, the special set of general education requirements, and the legitimating of community involvement as a form of education. At Reed, it was the required freshman lecture-and-seminar courses, the junior qualifying examination, and the thesis in the senior year. Such practices became the core content of a belief that here things had been done so differently and to such a degree, against the mainstream and often against imposing odds, that the group had been party to a saga.

THE SOCIAL BASE. The institutional story becomes fixed also in the minds of some outside believers, a segment external to the physical boundaries of the campus, who have become deeply devoted to the institution. Usually the core of the external social base is the alumni of the changed institution. When a college saga is strong, this extended family is second to none in sentimental attachment to the general visions and the specific symbols of what the college has become. The alumni are the best located to hold beliefs enduringly pure. They are of the institution, yet do not have to face directly the new problems generated by a changing environment or an evolving input of students. For them the embodied and exciting idea of the college can be everything, taking on the qualities of an untouchable saga.

The relatively liberal or radical alumni here become conservative, seeking to protect what they believe to be a unique liberal or radical institution from all the conservative forces of society that might change the college to pull it back in line, make it like other places. The alumni at Antioch, Reed, and Swarthmore all have exhibited this small paradox. At Reed, for example, dropouts as well as graduates constitute an alumni struck by the intellectual power of their small college, convinced that life on that tight little island has been unlike life anywhere else, and ready to conserve the practices that seem to sustain the mysterious power of the campus. Here, too, for a time, one might interpret conservative acts as contributing to an innovation, protecting a distinctive place while it attempts a full working out of the potential of a particular direction of effort.

THE STUDENT SUBCULTURE. The student body is the third group within which we find essential believers, not as overwhelmingly important as they in full pride are likely to think but still a necessary support for the legend. If the definitions of the dominant student subculture do not reflect the central theme of the institution, then that theme will weaken. To become and remain a legend, a change must be supported by the student subculture over decades, integrating significantly with the central ideas of the believing administrators and faculty. When the students define themselves as personally responsible for upholding what the college has become and are ready to take on enemies, real or imagined, then a design or plan has become to an important degree an organizational saga.

At Antioch, Reed, and Swarthmore, the student subcultures have been powerful mechanisms for carrying a developing legend from one generation to another over a long period. Reed students, almost from the beginning and extending at least to the early 1960s, were unexcelled believers in the uniqueness and power of their campus, constantly on the alert for any action that would alter the place, even fearful that some men in the administration and faculty might succumb to pressures of the day and seek to make Reed into a college that would be just like all the others. Students at Antioch and Swarthmore also have long offered unstinting support for the respective institutional idea. Each student body steadily and dependably transfers campus ideals from one generation to another. Often socializing deeply, they help produce the graduate who never quite rids himself of the wish to go home again, i.e., back to the campus. To marry such a graduate is to find that one has also married a college. A tiny place, of no account in the large affairs of society, observers might say, and yet there are clearly those who deeply love it.

THE IDEOLOGY. Finally, the invested institutional idea has self-sustaining capacity. Upheld by faculty, alumni, and students, expressed in the practices of the teaching encounter, the institutional theme is even more widely a generalized tradition expressed in statues and ceremonies, written histories and current catalogues, even in an "air about the place" felt by participants and some outsiders. The more special the empirical history and the more forceful the claim to a place in history, the more intensely cultivated are the ways of sharing memory and symbolizing the institution. The idea spills over everywhere, to be found on paper, in concrete, on the faces of men. Thus, so widely and deeply embodied, in so many linking parts, the legend is a strong self-fulfilling belief. Working through institutional self-image and public image, a saga is indeed a switchman, in Weber's famous phrase, helping to determine the tracks along which action is pushed by men's self-defined interests. In short, a developing ideology of a special history can help make a special history.

As a picture of the institution that is at once encompassing and sentimental, an organizational saga is an unparalleled means of unity. It forges links across internal divisions and organizational boundaries, as internal and external groups emotionally share their common belief. It binds together various operations of work and avenues of participation, emphasizing the whole over the parts, as the specific forms are seen to have contributed to the making and expressing of the story. Most important, the saga deeply commits the individual to the organization. With deep emotional engagement, some believers significantly define themselves by their organizational affiliation. Their bondage to other believers is like that of comrades in a cause: they share an intense sense of the unique, knowing a beautiful secret. A symptom of a powerful saga is a feeling that there are really two worlds—the small blessed one of the lucky few and the large routine one of the rest. An emotional bond of this quality turns the membership into a community, even a cult. It maximizes for the individual the satisfaction of being associated with the organization that far surpasses the rewards of money and skill in the job. The organization becomes a model in a sense of what the individual wants to be: a social being with clear identity, a proven ability to cope, and a social definition of success. At the least, the individual has the satisfaction of playing a small part in a successful group effort.

An organizational saga is thus a valuable resource, created over a number of years out of the social components of the formal enterprise. As participants become ideologues, their common institutional definition becomes a foundation for trust, easing communication and cooperation. With little regard for the clock, they extend and intensify their efforts in what others call work. They are uncommonly happy when the organization is well and unusually sad when it is not. We find them loyal beyond reason. Such bonding has effects beyond that of enlarged effort and enhanced morale by giving the organization a competitive edge in recruiting and maintaining personnel. It is capital against the vicious circle of organizational decline in which some actual or anticipated erosion of organizational strength leads to the exit of some personnel, which leads to further decline and more exit. A high degree of loyalty causes individuals to stay with a system, to save and improve it rather than to exit to serve self-interest elsewhere. The genesis and persistence of loyalty is a key organizational and analytical problem. Enduring loyalty follows from a collective belief of personnel and followers that their organization is special, that, at least for them, it is distinctive. That kind of belief comes from a credible story of uncommon effort, achievement, and form.

Pride in the organized group and pride in one's identity as taken from the group are personal returns that are in short supply in modern social involvement. The development of organizational legends is one way in which organizational man increases such rewards. The concept of the organizational saga, therefore, finally steers our attention to dimensions of pride and joy in organizational life. As we study the devotional ties of the formal institution we move closer to the fundamental differences among organizations in their capacity to enhance or diminish our lives. In the organization possessed by a saga, we find at least for a time a formal place in which men happily accept their bond and their condition. They would have it no other way.

Small colleges possessed by sagas can govern themselves somewhat differently from colleges of the same size that have only a weak self-belief. Among those sharing the deep emotional commitment in a saga-defined college, the felt commonality is the backbone of a sense of relationships firmly bridged. Differences and conflicts are seen as secondary, and solvable through informal exchange among comrades. Normative capital accumulates that can be spent in emergencies without incurring a normative deficit. With this source of linkage working overtime, the tendency lessens to seek new administrative structure as the solution to all problems. Those who are aggrieved argue the relevance of their actions for the institutional idea to which nearly all are committed. Due process and adjudicating procedure are given little weight. In contrast, the weaker normative bonding in the institutions of weak self-belief gives greater play to the factionalism and fragmentation inherent in the specialized commitments and orientations of the academic disciplines and the normal division of work into "administration" and "faculty" and "academic" and "business." As belief in the part ascends over belief in the whole, loyalty attaches to the part rather than the whole. Governance then calls for more mediation among the parts, with a tendency to explicate the mediation in quasi-formal and formal rules of procedure. As normative bonding weakens, even in systems of small scope, one or more internal groups will develop a self-interest in having informal relations replaced by more discernible structure. Surely almost all of us at one time or another have been agents of this bureaucratic tendency. We seek to ensure through rules what we feel is no longer reasonably provided through ties of sentiment and unified belief.

But in small educational systems, this tendency need not go very far. Administrators, faculty members, and students often encounter one another, spontaneously and informally—as well as deliberately and formally—as they enter the common mailroom, walk the paths between the few buildings, and share the tables in the cafeteria. So even if there is not much common belief, or the unified belief is only weak in expression, there is likely to be some capital of interpersonal trust on which to operate, some of which can be spent in handling the worst conflicts when they occur.

As we move from small colleges to modest-size universities and then to large multiversities, we not only tend toward formal structure but it also becomes exceedingly difficult to develop a credible story that embraces the whole. On ideational as well as structural grounds, belief in and loyalty to the whole will likely weaken. Moral or ideational capital will be in short supply and all too readily exhausted in time of conflict, crisis, or decline. The formal burdens of governance are thereby increased considerably, with little to resort to other than further elaboration of rules and due-process machinery of conflict resolution.

If the large campus becomes an administered political system of factions of divergent belief, solutions to problems of governance must tend basically in one of two directions: (1) to accept the general nature of the system and then seek to devise the best machinery for the formal representation of factions and the formal resolution of conflicts; or (2) to change the nature of the system in the direction of more unified belief and the reducing of factions. Most large campuses tend in the first direction. Sensing that they are evermore like vast industrial conglomerates, held together by an administrative framework, they seek new or enlarged formal patterns that will channel conflict into peaceful streams. Much attention must go to the legitimation of such patterns, since the social conditions of trust here take the form of participants coming to believe they can get fair treatment in processes due them. No one particularly expects to turn out to work for the common interest since it is hard to know what the common interest is. There is little to fall back on, normatively, in times of stress. The best way to prepare for governmental stress in such settings is to build up a capital of formal procedure. If the procedures are prepared in depth, securely interlocked, and coated with acceptance, they may, we hope, hold us together in the worst of times.

Some large campuses attempt to solve the problem of governance by moving in the second direction, toward more unified self-belief and a reduction rather than an explication and formalization of factions. We usually call this move "decentralization." We try to make certain components of the whole relatively self-contained and autonomous, to create a confederation of units each small enough and sufficiently limited in its concerns to develop its own mission, its own culture and community, and even its own saga to some degree. One's organizational end-in-view is to create units of a size and scope appropriate for developing over time a sense of a distinctive whole. The social conditions of trust here reside in shared belief as well as the intimacy of interaction. Down this road, we teach ourselves to rely in governance on shared belief, informal influence, satisfaction, and loyalty.

One can make a powerful case for moving in either of the two directions discussed above. The overall size of the American system of mass higher education alone argues persuasively that the first direction is the primary route. With that many students, many very large campuses seem a practical necessity, particularly as we take into account the business and economic models that have long informed the definitions of the situation held by legislators and state officials. The decentralization approach then seems excessively romantic. On the other hand, the feeling will not go down in nearly all campus circles that the first way is not the best way, that we must decentralize to create the units most conducive to education work. This route, too, at times seems a practical necessity, particularly as we take into account the collegial model that has long informed the faculty's definition of the situation and the expectations of students that they will be seen and treated as individuals. Decentralization may be the price of peace where these faculty and student definitions have not been met but remain enduringly strong.

The phenomenon of the organizational saga, observed in extreme form in Antioch, Reed, and Swarthmore, is a powerful argument for the second route. There are such rich personal and institutional returns from sagas as to argue strongly for those forms of academic organization that make them most likely. Even in modest strength, a saga adds much meaning to the work of administrators and faculty and the transitory participating of the students. When seen as a matter of degree, rather than all-or-nothing, we can encourage ourselves to create, even in adverse settings, those general conditions that are conducive to this and other forms of normative bonding. The normative buildup changes materially the nature of administration and governance.

Thus, as we trace the effects of an organizational saga on belief and trust and then on the problems of governance, we turn our attention away from such structural changes as bicameralism and altered representation on committees and focus instead on the size and scope and mission of the entity that is to be governed. We return to the embodiment of goals in the historical development of an organization and what meaning is thus available to those who give so much of their lives there. In raising explicitly the matter of whether and how academic groups come to have rewarding collective representations of themselves, we perhaps in the end can even link matters of governance to the quality of life within the modern college and university.

Notes

1. My formulation of a basic relation between institutional beliefs and institutional governance has been stimulated by verbal and written comments of Albert J. Cohen of the University of Connecticut.

2. These sections draw upon Burton R. Clark, *The Distinctive College: Antioch, Reed, and Swarthmore* (Chicago: Aldine Publishing Company, 1970) and Burton R. Clark, "The Saga of the Formal Place," the revised version of a paper presented at the annual meeting of the American Sociological Association in September 1970, in Washington, D.C.

PART TWO

Probing the American National System

We chose the following essays because they illustrate what the American higher education system looked like forty to fifty years ago, as seen through the eyes of one persistent observer. The essays range from student culture, faculty professionalization, and unusual administrative linkages, to universities under stress and a foundational essay on the sociology of higher education. Spanning the years spent on the faculties of Stanford (1953–56), Harvard (1956–58), Berkeley (1958–66), and onward to the early years at Yale, they were the outcomes of additional intellectual voyages I undertook while mainly focused on the research described in part I.

This section covers a variety of miscellaneous, passing topics written at a time when the related literature on those subjects was small. But the ideas they express exhibit a useful simplicity. For example, in one essay Martin A. Trow and I pursue a four-legged typology of student cultures. This simple framework turned out to have lasting influence. Another essay, "The Wesleyan Story," was part of a volume on universities and colleges operating under the stress of severe crisis in the late 1960s and early 1970s, creatively edited by David Riesman and Verne A. Stadtman. They pulled together empirical accounts of how those institutions variously coped—some poorly, some comparatively well—and still contain instructive lessons that give the work lasting value. What I wrote developed the concept of "moral capital" as an intangible force that could help hold together a campus and its outside supporters through difficult days. Colleges and universities without it were more battered by the strains of that historic period.

A discerning reader may note that the selections in part II are neither as coherently connected as those in part I, nor as animatedly expressed as those in parts III and IV of this volume. These essays offer commentary on one topic and then switch to another subject in the next. They do not follow from a connected flow of research. Like so many observers who write opinion pieces not rooted in a serious stream of research, I moved among conference-inspired disparate topics raised at the time.

In any event, we hope each selection in part II provides a useful avenue of thought for the reader, even when it stands as an outlier in the overall flow of my work over the past half-century.

INTRODUCTION TO CHAPTER 6

Early in my career I became interested in the power of public images of colleges. This essay, originally delivered as a paper at a conference in Berkeley in 1959, sets forth a framework contrary to customary views on the subject.

What provoked me at the time was the common approach taken by those who study how students change during their undergraduate years. They tended to treat student characteristics at the point of entry as "independent" variables, set by background and prior choices and untouched by the special qualities of individual institutions. This seemed invalid to me, since what is now called "brand" (then known more appropriately as "image") clearly plays a role. Colleges certainly have a "preentry" impact: in some cases, their public images powerfully attract particular students; in others, the images cast a wider net and all comers are selected.

Thus public image is a link in the ongoing interaction between the character of a college and the nature of its student body. Studying that linkage requires both historical analysis and comparisons among institutions. Realities become complicated, but as this early essay explains, they can be appropriately and readily probed.

CHAPTER 6

College Image and Student Selection

MUCH RESEARCH IN higher education now asks the question: what is the relative contribution of student qualities and institutional qualities to the achievement of students after college? This question has been stimulated by the work of Knapp and associates on the undergraduate origins of American scientists and scholars. Knapp and Greenbaum offered an hypothesis of institutional productivity, proposing that behind the superiority of some colleges in the production of scientists and scholars lay a "singular hospitality to intellectual values."[1] Some psychologists have recently argued for an opposed hypothesis, one of student quality and motivation. This hypothesis takes the view that "differential student populations among colleges appear as a more probable explanation of differences in productivity (of scientists and scholars) than the special qualities of individual institutions."[2] In brief, the view of these psychologists is that the institution is not the critical factor but that it is the kind of student that the college has.

Research that follows the distinction between student quality and institutional influence unfortunately tends to assume that the characteristics of entering students are independent of the specific nature of the college the students attend. Student characteristics not only are distinguished in analysis but also are essentially taken as given. Research begins with the attributes of entrants and goes forward from this baseline; little accounting is made of why a college has one particular group of entrants and not others. However, the entering student body is not accidentally determined, being shaped for the most part by characteristics of the college. The influence of a college, broadly speaking, includes the attracting

"College Image and Student Selection," in *The College Student and His Culture: An Analysis*, edited by Kaoru Hamamoto, 178–91. Boston: Houghton Mifflin, 1968.

of a particular student body out of a large pool of students. I will be concerned in this essay with this preentry impact of colleges, addressing in part the question of why the entering class of a college will have particular qualities and not others.

I will define a sequence in which a college's historical development is reflected in the composition of its current student body, which in turn affects its campus influence. One administrative problem I will highlight is the control of student self-selection; behind control lies the problem of building and projecting an image of the college.[3] I believe that a radical separation of student qualities from the special qualities of colleges is a distortion of reality that should be avoided. The caliber of entering students is an organizational characteristic, one that is shaped by the history of the college and by the roles it assumes in higher education and the larger society.

Selection by Image

A college may be said to select students directly and indirectly. Directly, it has an admission policy and selection machinery, although the policy may not be clearly stated and the machinery may be submerged in a dean of students office or in the work of faculty committees. Direct selection is through the process of official recruiting and selecting. Indirect "selection" is made through images held by outsiders, the images giving rise to student self-selection. Students make themselves available to a college according to their impression of it. Self-selection by students is, in large part, a selection by public impressions; it can be manipulated by affecting public images, as college presidents and admission officers well know.

A college that wants to upgrade itself can attempt to shift self-selection from one type of student to another by assuming a public posture of academic toughness. A college that is unable to draw students from its own state because it is considered too radical may attempt to increase local self-selection by dimming the "unfavorable" local image. However, the manipulation of public images in itself is not without limit; behind the image of a college lies its historically derived character, and with some distortion and lag images are influenced by current characteristics of the campus. The admission officer attempting to convince outsiders that his college is not really radical has a difficult time changing this belief when high school counselors visit the campus and observe bohemian dress and behavior. Perceived character is affected by operational character, past and present.

The chain of effects rapidly reviewed above is that (a) the characteristics of students entering a college are partly determined by (b) student self-selection, that self-selection stems from (c) public images, and that these images in turn are partly conditioned by (d) what the college has been and is like today.

Selection through the effect of public images substitutes for direct selection. Self-selection may bring the acceptable students to a college without its admission office doing more than marginally differentiating among the recruits and processing the necessary papers. Organizationally, selection through public image may be functionally equivalent to direct selection, functional in maintaining the college and in supporting a particular organization character. A clientele is supplied and frequently this is the student membership desired by the college. Functional equivalence may help to explain how some colleges have become places of academic excellence without, relatively, much of an admission apparatus. Reed College, which is discussed later, seems an example. Elaborate selection work may be dispensable if the public images of the college result in its recruiting the kinds of students it wants.

This functional equivalence holds, however, only if public images of a college coincide with the character that the college desires for itself. The "right" kind of student then makes himself available. If the images are opposite to desired character, of course, the "wrong" kind of student tries to be admitted. For example, if the image of a college as a "social club" persists while the college wants to be considered a serious place, the indirect selection produces the wrong kind of recruit and the work of admissions is made correspondingly more difficult.

Salience of Image

Even if the content of the images held by the public is all that a college desires, a situation in which insufficient students will appear is still possible. The number of applications depends in part on the academic market: in the worst of times, virtually all colleges may find students in short supply; in times of abundance, most colleges will be in favor. But the state of the market is a broadly indeterminate condition for any one college, and one that cannot be controlled by the organization in any case. More closely determinate—and also more within the reach of college authorities—is the power or potency of the public image. If the public image of a college is prominent and clear, the college will be likely to attract a considerable number of students and may be able to draw from this number a much larger proportion of desirable students than undesirable ones.

The history of Reed College illustrates the role of a strong public image. Apparently a very high degree of self-selection to Reed exists. The college has long obtained an academically promising student body without being able to exercise much direct selection; that is, without having a high ratio of applications to students accepted. For the fall of 1958, nearly four out of five applications were accepted (375 out of 475 completed applications, or 79 percent), leaving only narrow possibilities for purposeful selection by the college. But self-selection seems reasonably accurate; students who are not highly academic do not apply and relatively few applications have false expectations. Those who do apply have, on the average and in generous measure, many characteristics valued by college staffs. In the fall of 1958 beginning students at Reed scored very high in tests designed to measure complexity of outlook, concern with ideas, and psychological maturity.[4] These students also scored very high in cultural sophistication and in concern with world and national affairs. In addition, they have high scholastic ability. How does Reed College acquire its high-level students, with a relatively low ratio of applications to admitted and entering students?

I think it does so because of the distinctive Reed image, which comes through clear and strong to a national public or professional people as well as to the local population of the Pacific Northwest. People know about Reed and they think they know what it is like. Many liberal intellectuals on the Berkeley campus of the University of California, e.g., come close to defining Reed as the only liberal arts college on the West Coast that is suitable for their sons and daughters. High school counselors in the San Francisco area see it as one of the several places that they would frequently recommend to very intelligent seniors.[5] For many parents in the Pacific Northwest, on the other hand, Reed is among the very last places to which they would send their children. The college is typed by them as wild and woolly and possibly very dangerous. Impressions of the college go to extremes. With little grayness, the Reed images cut sharply through the vast pool of college applicants, rejecting very large numbers and attracting a special few who reasonably approximate what the college would like to have.

The saliency of Reed's public image is historically no accident. A particular, distinctive character and image have been deliberately cultivated by the college since the day it opened its doors in 1911. The early bulletins of the college asserted vigorously that Reed was to be a college without side shows, that students interested in sports or social life were not wanted. The first catalogue of the college stated:

> Intercollegiate athletics, fraternities, sororities and most of the diversions that men are pleased to call "college life," as distinguisht from college work, have no place in Reed College. Those whose dominant interests lie outside the courses of study should not apply for admission. Only those who want to work, and to work hard, and who are determined to gain the greatest possible benefits from their studies are welcomd.[6] Others will be disappointed, for the scholarship demands will leave little time for outside activities, other than those which are necessary for the maintenance of health.[7]

The Reed catalogue and public pronouncements maintained this severe, militant tone for a decade. By that time a public image with some momentum of its own was established. Nearly one-third of the students in the first five graduating classes has proceeded to graduate work. Fellowships had been awarded to Reed graduates by Oxford, Harvard, Princeton, and Columbia.[8] Such outcomes were duly publicized. Professors at Harvard and other eastern universities were, according to reports of the college, feeding favorable impressions of the scholarship of Reed graduates into the academic grapevine. Nationally the college became known as a serious, intellectual place. In the Pacific Northwest, Reed's "difference" became widely perceived and elicited there much *un*favorable comment. The college was seen as lacking athletics and social life, the president and the faculty were viewed as reformers, and on top of everything else the college could not even spell correctly—the first president insisting upon using a simplified spelling. Particular images of the college became widely and deeply established in public attitudes, and the substance of these images has persisted for forty years.

The national and local images of Reed have been continually reinforced since the first decade by the college's academic record, which has been publicized by articles in popular magazines as well as in scholarly publications. The college has been depicted in newspaper and popular magazine articles in the past few years, for example, as "an egghead paradise,"[9] "the college where Plato is fun,"[10] "a college where learning comes first,"[11] and a place that is "proud to be different."[12] These articles all stress intellectual commitment and academic results of the highest order. Typical of the detailed comments were these that appeared in a newspaper story: "[Reed] leads all colleges in turning out Rhodes scholars, with an average of one in eighty-two male graduates"; "the college turned out 132 successful scientists in every one thousand male graduates, compared to seventy in a thousand in the next-highest college"; "Reed and Stanford have the only nuclear reactors on West Coast campuses at present. A senior student built Reed's reactor."[13] With such public comment, the fact is of small wonder that Reed now tends to be defined, especially in the Pacific Northwest, as a place for very brainy boys who want to major in the natural sciences.

Images of Reed have also been reinforced by "headline" events. One such event was the visit of the Velde House Committee on un-American Activities to Portland in 1954 with several members of the faculty accused of being Communists. Another was Reed's being among the handful of colleges that refused outright to accept money for student loans under the 1958 National Defense Education Act because of loyalty oath provisions. Reported nationally—in *Time* magazine, e.g.—this action by the college undoubtedly was widely admired by liberal professionals and added to the college's standing as an avant-garde college. But in the Portland area this action may have confirmed for many what they already believed: that "the college is crazy." A Portland taxi driver spontaneously raised this issue with me in March 1959, knowing only that I was visiting the college. He knew that the college had turned down the federal money, that the decision entailed a conflict between principle and money, and that he and other normal people would have taken the money. He said that principles were all right, but only up to a point, the point where money enters.

Reed has tried to be different and has succeeded. Its perceived difference has influenced who applies and who considers applying when approached by admission officers. In addition, the images of the college held by its own staff and alumni have shaped the recruitment of faculty and students alike.

One way of studying the content and salience of public image of colleges is through students' impressions of the special qualities of their college on entrance. In the fall of 1958, entering freshmen at Antioch, Reed, Swarthmore, and San Francisco State College were asked the question: "Do you see this college as having some special quality that distinguishes it from other colleges and universities?" The students then checked one of two responses, "not greatly different from other colleges," or, "it has a special distinguishing quality." This was followed by: "If the latter, would you note briefly what you think this special quality is." No specific answers were offered the students; they answered as they pleased and these comments were later classified. Several general points are apparent in the data summarized in Table 6.1. First, the state college was the only one of the four that a number of the entering students, 55 percent, considered not greatly different from other colleges. That they considered it so is not unexpected in the case of a heterogeneous, public, four-year college, especially when it is part of a system of ten state colleges. In the case of each of the other three, opinion was virtually unanimous that it has a special distinguishing quality. Second, the three small private colleges were not simply perceived in common as good or small or avant-garde. The answers were discriminating and certain components of varied images stand out. One component, "academic rank and standards," or the general academic status of the college, was reported by 42 percent of the entering students at Swarthmore, 26 percent at Reed, and 6 percent at Antioch as a special quality of their college. Another component was serious intellectual atmosphere, a quite salient feature at Reed, where it was reported by 52 percent; less so at Swarthmore, 39 percent; and least at Antioch, 13 percent. A third component, however, the perceived liberalism and experimental nature of the campus, showed 31 percent reporting at Antioch, 17 percent at Reed, and 8 percent at Swarthmore.

An image syndrome of each of these colleges, as reported by *entering* students, can be summarized as follows:

ANTIOCH. Entering students listed its particular academic features, especially the cooperative work program; a liberal-progressive tone; individual and group responsibility, which includes the honor system and community government; and freedom for the individual. Alongside the

TABLE 6.1. Impressions of Entering Freshman Students as to Special Quality of Their College

Special Quality of the College	Respondents (in percent)[a]			
	Antioch	Reed	Swarthmore	SFSC
Not greatly different from other colleges	0	0	4	55
Academic features (honors program, co-op program, small classes, etc.)	51[b]	16	9	34
Academic rank and standards (including high ideals)	6	26	42	2
Intellectual atmosphere (intelligent students, serious attitude, intellectual freedom)	13	52	39	2
Liberalism (progressive, experimental, diversity of experiences)	31	17	8	2
Good student-faculty relations (individual treatment)	5	8	17	2
Friendly (not snobbish, mature social life, informality)	11	10	34	6
Individual and group responsibility (honor system, student participation in government, democratic)	35	15	1	0
Freedom for the individual (nonconformity, lack of restrictions, freedom unspecified)	25	33	13	0

[a] Respondents were permitted to make more than one answer and the percentages add to more than 100 percent for each college. Each figure is the percentage of students offering that particular impression.
[b] Underlined percentages are 25 percent or more.

special cooperative program, entering students found the freedom and the "civic" overtones of the Antioch student life quite important. The college is apparently defined by many entering students as a school for liberals, perhaps even as a school for responsible liberals. Less salient in these impressions is the academic rank of the college and the intellectual nature of the campus climate.

REED. Three components stand out in the impressions: serious, intellectual atmosphere; freedom for the individual; and academic standing. Reed is apparently seen as a place for the free intellectual. Not as prominent as in the Antioch image are special academic features, campus liberalism, and student responsibility.

SWARTHMORE. Entering students mentioned its general academic status, intellectual atmosphere, and "friendliness." Apparently Swarthmore is seen as an intellectual place of high socio-academic status. Not so prominent in the minds of entering students are particular academic features, liberalism, and freedom for the individual. Two points are especially interesting. First, the Swarthmore honors program, which has been and is today important in the academic status of the college, is little remarked by entering students as the college's most distinguishing quality. Second, the "friendly" category, which included lack of snobbishness, informality, and mature social life, had unexpectedly high prominence.

SAN FRANCISCO STATE COLLEGE. Students saw this college as not greatly different from other colleges with some mention of particular academic features. These included the general education program, a good department in a certain field, independent study, and the teacher training program. Few comments were made about anything other than academic features.

"Good student-faculty relations" had low salience at all the campuses; only at Swarthmore was it mentioned by more than 10 percent of the students.

The content of the images reported by entering students at these four colleges varies considerably. What about the differences in salience of the images? The sheer volume of comment in an open-end question partly exhibits this: the more prominent the image, the more likely the students have something to say about the college. The number of responses per respondent, for the question that asked for the special quality of the college, was as follows: Antioch, 1.8; Reed, 1.8; Swarthmore, 1.7; and San Francisco State College, 1.1. The three small colleges drew about the same volume of comment, and this at a level nearly twice that of the large state college. Saliency is also indicated by whether students commented that the college was different from other colleges. The percentages of students reporting that they thought their college was different from others were: Antioch, 100 percent; Reed, 100 percent; Swarthmore, 96 percent; and San Francisco State College, 45 percent.

These crude explanatory indicators support the notion that a comprehensive public college will have public images of relatively low salience, while some small, almost precious private colleges will have highly salient images. Philip Jacob, in his *Changing Values in College,* spoke of Antioch,

Reed, Swarthmore, and similar schools as colleges of peculiar potency in impact on students.[14] If they are, their potency may well prove to *begin* with potent public images. A close connection between image and impact is likely, as suggested in a 1957 Columbia University self-study. The Columbia study committee was "impressed by the importance of what may be called the identity and visibility of the Columbia undergraduate schools."[15] They proposed that "it is the college with an identifiable and exciting educational objective that draws its students most effectively into an intellectual community and has the most telling influence upon them. Such colleges are generally of moderate size, and have fixed themselves in the minds both of their students and of outside observers for some special quality or purpose that infuses all their activities."[16] The connection suggested is that the salience of overall images affects the impact of college on students. While this impact is mainly an on-campus effect, it spills over to the outside. The fact is that the images held by prospective students and other outsiders, as well as the images held by faculty and present students, may link the very identity of a college to the processes of attracting and admitting students. For one thing, the meaning of entry is likely to be greatly heightened when the college is seen as something special; a personal distinction attaches to matriculation itself at a noted school. Apparently for many students entering Swarthmore the sheer fact of acceptance is breath-taking and promotes a readiness to take on a new identification. These students believe the college is out of this world, a place to which, they well know, few are called. The Swarthmore public image, especially in the states of the Eastern Seaboard, seemingly has the kind of potency that works on students' feelings and loyalties even before they enter the door. Similarly, on the part of some new students at Antioch, there is an apparent willingness to become an Antiochian as fast as humanly possible. The salient image touches motivation, perhaps setting in motion an anticipatory socialization.

A relationship between image and type of student attracted to major types of colleges is suggested by work of the Cornell Values Study. Norman Miller[17] has shown that *entering* students at four Ivy League schools are more supportive of civil rights than freshmen at five state-supported colleges. A difference of this kind in political sentiment could *not* be accounted for by background factors; when religion, socioeconomic status, regional background, and size of hometown are held constant, Ivy League students remain consistently more liberal with regard to civil rights than their state college counterparts. The Ivy colleges clearly attract students whose values differ from those who attend state colleges and universities. With this, there is also evidence that the campus climate at the Ivy colleges is more pro–civil rights; the absolute and relative increases in liberality between freshmen and seniors are greater among Ivy League students. (From 45 to 68 percent, a 23 percent increase, compared to 31 to 44 percent, a 13 percent increase.) Miller found one important correlate in the Cornell data of the liberal political attitude, and that was educational values. Students were asked to choose from a number of alternative goals the one that, in their opinion, ought to be emphasized by the ideal college or university. Students in both the private and the public colleges who thought that college should emphasize "a basic general education and appreciation of ideas" were more pro–civil rights than those who believed it should "provide vocational training"—develop skills and techniques directly applicable to one's career—in the Ivy League schools 61 to 46 percent and in the state colleges 51 to 32 percent. The Ivy League schools simply had more students favorably disposed to the humanistic values of higher education. Among Ivy League freshmen the ratio of those holding general education values to those believing in the primacy of vocational training was 2 to 1 and this ratio increased to more than 8 to 1 for seniors. In contrast, state college students who chose the general education ideal were outnumbered 3 to 1 in the freshman year and only pulled up to a 1 to 1 ratio in the senior year.

Data collected in 1958 from freshman students at Antioch, Reed, Swarthmore, and San Francisco State College show a similar difference in educational ideals. On the same question used in the Cornell Values Study, 57 percent of the students entering the three private colleges chose general education as the most important purpose of a college education while 23 percent chose training for vocation, or a ratio of 2.5 to 1. Opinions were the reverse in the state college, with 23 percent stating the general education ideal and 67 percent the vocational purpose, a 3 to 1 ratio in favor of vocational training.

These data clearly suggest quite different campus climates and quite different attraction of students in terms of what Martin Trow has referred to as cultural sophistication.[18] The campus climates apparently reach prospective students in general, widely held images, with much self-selection as well as direct selection at work. The more culturally sophisticated student seeks—or is led by friends and advisors to—the more culturally sophisticated college, and the Ivy League colleges have this reputation.

Without this linkage of college character to public image to characteristics of entering students, many colleges would have difficulty in maintaining their characters. It is highly doubtful whether agents of a college could by conscious effort alone attract and recruit the kind of student who maintains the traditional campus ethos. Like attracts like through mediating images. One effect of public images for a variety of organizations is to attract new members with orientations and dispositions roughly similar to those on the scene or lost through graduation. Public images have a membership-replacing function.

The Rigidity of Image

While attraction by public image may be functionally equivalent to selection by an admissions office, it is inherently more resistant to change and hence is more conserving of the character of a college. Admission policy can be changed rather quickly by official directive, but, once public images are established, they are more difficult to affect and are likely to respond slowly. Public images, which are firm in the attitudes of outsiders and removed from direct control, may become largely a matter of community sentiment rather than of rational thought. This tendency, as much as faulty communication, will cause changes in image to lag behind changes in operations and in campus habits. For example, the definition of a college as radical may linger in a conservative neighborhood long after it ceases to be appropriate and may be only partly amenable to influence by rational argument.

An image is a constraint, and the stronger the image, the stronger the constraint.[19] We may see this as a dilemma of distinction. The college that strikes boldly for a highly distinctive character and a unique image is also making connections with the outside world that are not easily revoked. The highly distinctive college has a potent claim for attention, but it also brands itself in the eyes of the world as *that* kind of place. When the times change, image and ingrained character resist change in the college.

The dilemma of distinction may be clarified by pointing to colleges whose relatively indistinct character permits change more readily. Public colleges generally cannot be as sharply distinctive in characters as private colleges, since they react to heterogeneous interests and take on comprehensive, diffuse orientations. The locally controlled public junior college is currently the extreme case. It admits all applicants; it offers courses for transfer, terminal, and adult education students; and it is willing, as a "community college," to try to do something for almost anyone. Its broad, indeterminate orientation encourages a blurring of public image. But then it is not inherently committed to any one specialty or to a narrowly based clientele. As compared to the college of distinct character and image, it can change rapidly in a rapidly changing environment. More easily than the unique school, it can in any order of succession be primarily a vocational school, an adult center, or a lower division version of the four-year college. The multisided, blurred public image is cultivated in the administration of some junior colleges because it promotes a diffuse impression of functions and permits flexible adjustment to public pressures.

The distinctive private college generally does not want to become a service enterprise. When it does attempt or is forced to adjust to a mass market, its prior selective commitment, expressed in a salient image among other things, will delay the change. Alumni and other outsiders remain identified with the old institution, and the old channels of referral and self-recruitment persist. To have a history of distinction is to accumulate resistance to change.

Conditions of Weak Image

The foregoing discussion concludes that the building and communicating of an effective image is fundamental in recruiting students. Public impressions of a college are the foundation on which direct selection must build.

This conclusion, however, bears on the college that is, or wishes to be, selective. Where selection is an issue, the content and the strength of public images are important. The college that would be selective wishes to relate to a segment of the public, and public images help to cultivate a segment, although not always the one desired by the college. But what about colleges of little or no selectivity? In the public two- and four-year college of little selectivity—in what might be called *the mass college*[20]—a routinization of college-going takes place; students may routinely flow from the high school into such colleges, with few hurdles interposed. Entry is virtually a right of the high school graduate and the social base of the college is broad. In this case the self-selection of students is less directly and narrowly tailored by public image; the college has less chance to use images as a way of selecting. If by law or custom the doors of the college are open to all and the fact is widely known, then the images the college propagandizes matter relatively little. In any case, the image the college presents cannot be one that shows that it is only for certain kinds of students and not for others. It will likely move toward comprehensive, diffuse definitions of itself to rationalize its diverse operations.

Many students go to a college or university with hardly any image of it at all. Self-selection is shaped by features of society other than organization images and some choices are largely accidental. Some may regard even a leading college as just one among many. Swarthmore, for example, is a college with a nationally salient image. It has received much acclaim since Aydelotte revamped the college around an honors program in the 1920s; it now draws students from almost all the states (forty-two states in 1958 were represented in the student body) and has about seven applicants for every student admitted. Even so, a few students—eleven in the class entering in the fall of 1958—reported they saw it as not greatly different from other colleges. Too, a considerable proportion of high school counselors on the West Coast apparently know very little about the college. In a small group of counselors,[21] 75 percent did not know what state Swarthmore is in; 50 percent by their own self-rating knew nothing about it; and 13 percent had never heard of it. No one in this group of thirty-seven counselors considered Swarthmore to be among the three colleges and universities they would first recommend to very intelligent seniors. The same non-recognition was accorded Radcliffe, Oberlin, and Carleton. The colleges perceived were Harvard and MIT in the East, and Reed, Stanford, the California Institute of Technology, and the University of California in the West. Obviously, the fact is that the public images cultivated by the other colleges simply do not extend into the consciousness of many high school advisors who are geographically removed. This fact perhaps illustrates the channeling of communication regarding impressions of colleges. However, a college image does not need to reach many to do the recruiting job desired. Swarthmore's geographical distribution of students included eighteen from California in 1958, and for these students to have gone three thousand miles to that particular college solely to get away from home is highly unlikely. They or someone who influenced them had specific leads and meaningful impressions.

The non-image, as in the case of the image of weak distinction, is most likely to exist for complex public institutions, especially for those that are part of a system of colleges very similar in name and purpose, e.g., teachers' colleges or state colleges. In such cases accidental or incidental choice in the sense of control by image is quite likely. Part of the routinization of college-going is the increasing geographic availability of college, and with this, self-selection on the basis of neighborhood convenience.

Research Directives

This essay has suggested that a college's public image determines in large measure the kind of students that enter it. Images are characteristics of a college that shape student self-selections; they help to delimit a clientele or social base. Images vary in strength and identifiability, however, and the extent to which they delimit varies with their salience. In any case, the pool of potential students attracted by image conditions directs recruitment and selection.

The clientele-defining function of images is a consequence of the individual character of a college that is easily overlooked in research on higher education. It is a basic link, however, in the ongoing interaction between the character of a college and the nature of its student bodies and is a complex matter in the development of colleges. Research is needed to identify the public images of college, to show how these images were determined, and to trace their effects. How can this be done?

One necessary step is intensive historical analysis of a few colleges that have highly salient images of academic quality. The central matter is to identify the ways in which such colleges have constructed and communicated desired images, how they happen to initiate and maintain a "snowballing" effect of reputation and student quality. Contrary to expectations, colleges can and have achieved positions of prominence in the face of ghastly financial and administrative difficulties. Their achievement apparently entailed a commitment to an exciting and identifiable objective or style of life and a dissemination, intentional and unintentional, of the fact of this commitment. There are different, specific ways for a college to obtain high academic quality and status—various goals, programs, and patterns of organization—but probably common among these ways is a distinctive commitment that attracts the outsider and binds the participant. Historical analysis needs to show how the rise and persistence of distinct image can affect the recruitment patterns of a college over a period of time, as, e.g., in moving from a locally to a nationally based student body.

A second necessary research step is the description of current images of colleges. In addition to the impressions of entering students, those of school counselors, especially in "feeder" high schools, and of parents would also be helpful. The nature of these impressions may be examined through interviews and questionnaires. The images of particular colleges presented in the mass media and in professional literature are also relevant and, since they tend to run to a pattern, they may be readily approached through a simple analysis of documents.

A third step is to link different impressions of entering students to the ways that they define their college participation and are affected by their college years. Students holding different images of a college, perhaps because of different backgrounds, may well expect different things to happen and want different outcomes. One example is the very seriousness with which they approach the academic life of the college. Differences in entering impressions are likely to give rise to differences in dropout, in avenues of participation, and finally such outcomes as changes in values.

Finally and more broadly, we should be sensitive to the possibilities and problems of building images in the coming years, in the decades of mass higher education. On the one hand, for a college to be seen as different will be increasingly difficult when there are so many colleges. The meaning of college will be diluted and visibility will be obscured. In addition, a short supply of potential faculty may cause a college to draw an undistinguished faculty, which will sharply limit distinction. But at the same time, some conditions will favor bootstrap operations. Most important is the fact that colleges will be free of student shortage, an enormous constraint on their character. More colleges will have the opportunity to be selective, which will give them the chance to be special; that many will be encouraged to seek distinction is assured by the competition among colleges for status and faculty. More than in the past colleges that want to reach and maintain a high academic status will need to construct and communicate a noteworthy identity. We may expect images to be vigorously and quite diversely cultivated as colleges attempt to distinguish themselves in the mass market that lies ahead.

Notes

1. Robert H. Knapp and Joseph J. Greenbaum, *The Younger American Scholar: His Collegiate Origins* (Chicago: University of Chicago Press, 1953), 97.

2. John L. Holland, "Undergraduate Origins of American Scientists," *Science* 126 (3271): 433–37.

3. There is little literature on organizational images. For a humorous statement of the college images that are portrayed in college catalogues, see William C. Fels, "Modern College Usage," *Columbia University Forum* 2 (Spring 1959): 39–41. For a case of opinion research on corporate image that attempts to relate images to attraction of personnel, see Philip Lesly, " 'Corporate Image' and the Future Leaders of Business," *The Public Opinion Quarterly* 23 (Winter 1959–60): 547–53.

4. Data collected by the Center for the Study of Higher Education as part of a five-year study of selected colleges. Data reported in the essay, unless otherwise indicated, are from this study.

5. Paul Heist, "Results and Summary of 'Do You Know About These Colleges' Questionnaire" (Center for the Study of Higher Education, 1959 [mimeographed]).

6. The early publications of Reed College followed spellings (distinguisht, welcomd) recommended by the Simplified Spelling Board.

7. Quoted in "First Report of the President, 1910–1919," *Reed College Record* no. 34 (December 1919): 12.

8. Ibid., 15.

9. *Parade,* November 23, 1958.

10. *Fortnight,* January 1956.

11. *The Seattle Times,* April 18, 1957.

12. *The Christian Science Monitor,* March 23, 1957.

13. *The Seattle Times,* April 18, 1957.

14. Philip E. Jacob, *Changing Values in College* (New York: Harper & Brothers, 1957), chap. 6.

15. *The Educational Future of Columbia University,* Report of the President's Committee (New York: Columbia University, 1957), 7.

16. Ibid.

17. Norman Miller, "Academic Climate and Student Values," paper read at the Fifty-fourth Annual Meeting of the American Sociological Society, Chicago, September 3–5, 1959.

18. See Martin Trow, "Cultural Sophistication and Higher Education," in *Selection and Educational Differentiation*, ed. T. R. McConnell (Berkeley: University of California Center for the Study of Higher Education, 1959), 107–23.

19. Images "have, like switchmen, determined the tracks along which action has been pushed by the dynamics of interest." From H. H. Gerth and C. Wright Mills, eds. and trans., *Max Weber: Essays in Sociology* (New York: Oxford University Press, 1946), 280.

20. See Burton R. Clark, *The Open Door College: A Case Study* (New York: McGraw-Hill Book Co., 1960), chap. 4.

21. Heist, "Results and Summary."

INTRODUCTION TO CHAPTER 7

This essay on student cultures, written with Martin A. Trow, comes from an earlier age, one where the No. 2 lead pencil was a cutting-edge tool of the academic trade. We devised this typology during a coffee break spent in the International House on the Berkeley campus after escaping our regular office to make midmorning and midafternoon dashes across the street. On one such occasion, Trow grabbed an extra white paper napkin, pulled out his most trustworthy lead pencil, chewed on it, licked the point, and drew up a four-cell table by posing dichotomized dimensions, one at a right angle to the other, and voilà! We had four attractive boxes showing student identifications with their colleges vis-à-vis their involvement with ideas. We then designated names for these groupings: the academic, the collegiate, the nonconformist, and the vocational. For such on-the-spot imagination, the lead pencil was superior to ink-filled pens, which produced smeared prose in the hands of a left-handed writer—me—and superior to those ubiquitous punch cards that preceded the modern computer.

Trow and I conceded that this lead pencil scheme was only a heuristic, an aid to orderly thinking. Yet we did expand on the causes and consequences of each type of culture in a sizable essay published in *College Peer Groups*. Once the typology was published, its use was no longer in our control. To our continuing surprise, various sociologists and psychologists sought to quantify it in questionnaires and personality inventories. We soon lost track of what was going on in this regard—I know I did—because individually, we went on to other research. But the typology endured, undergoing scrutiny by scholars, who made sustained efforts to improve it. About its validity and standing today I have no idea. The No. 2 lead pencil did its job and soon left the published typology on its own. I have long maintained that authors are only responsible for the birth of their individual writings. Once out on the table for all to see, they have to take care of themselves. All the better if they stand up on the shelves in jacketed books, demanding occasional attention of the wandering eye, than become lost sooner in the miscellany of journals.

CHAPTER 7

The Clark-Trow Typology of Student Cultures

IN RECENT YEARS social scientists have turned their attention to the colleges and universities in which most of them work. Among the speculative questions that they are transforming into research problems is the perennial one: "What effect, if any, does their college experience have on students?" One approach to that question directs our attention to the relationships of students with one another. This has long been a central theme in the reflections of men concerned with higher education in America. Woodrow Wilson (1925), writing a half-century ago, made the following observation.

> The real intellectual life of a body of undergraduates, if there be any, manifests itself, not in the classroom, but in what they do and talk of and set before themselves as their favorite objects between classes and lectures. You will see the true life of a college . . . where youths get together and let themselves go upon their favorite themes—in the effect their studies have upon them when no compulsion of any kind is on them, and they are not thinking to be called to a reckoning of what they know.

We know from many sources that relationships among peers affect attitudes and behavior in a variety of ways; the subject is a continuing thread in sociological discourse and has been studied in many different contexts.[1] Work on this topic in the colleges has dealt primarily with the structure and processes of student groups and secondarily with their effects on members and on the larger systems of which the groups are part.

"The Clark-Trow Typology of Student Cultures," drawn from "The Organizational Context," in *College Peer Groups,* edited by T. M. Newcomb and E. K. Wilson, 17–26, 63–67. Chicago: Aldine, 1966.

104

Less well studied are the social forces and conditions that shape such groups: the features of social organization that generate and sustain the subsystems of student life. Our interest in this essay lies precisely in these determinants. We want to know the bearing of larger social structures on student life and relationships. From this perspective we will view the college peer group as the locus for a set of processes that intervene between the larger social systems and the outcomes of college education.

Two broad sets of factors shape the nature of the orientations and relationships of students in college. The first set flows from the character of the larger society. Students come to college with certain resources—material, moral, intellectual, emotional, and cultural. These resources are largely determined by the life experiences the students have had, and these in turn are shaped by the statuses they and their parents have held in the larger society. The prior social locations and experiences also shape aspiration: the kinds of lives the students envision for themselves in a rapidly changing society.

The second set of determinants derives from the nature of the colleges themselves: their historical development, their value climates, their structural features, and the shaping environment thus provided for student life. A college is not simply an aggregation of students, teachers, and administrators. Although the character of a college is greatly influenced by the nature of its staff and students, it also has qualities and characteristics that are to some extent independent of the people who fill its halls and offices at any given moment.

Throughout our analysis the one particular outcome of college upon which we wish to focus is the intellectual and cultural development of the adolescent and young adult. This analytical touchstone relates to the purposes of colleges. Colleges profess to be, and often are, civilizing agencies; they work to develop and refine the powers of intellect, perception, and feeling. Some students in some colleges "discover a new range of sensibility" under the influence of forces that "raise to the status of virtues certain humane feelings and actions which had until then been regarded as unimportant and even unmanly" (Nicholson, 1955). But to what extent does the civilizing process occur—for what kinds of students, under what conditions, and with respect to what sentiments and perceptions? Students bring to college a variety of interests and sentiments; in college they find support among their fellows for some of these and indif-

The Clark-Trow Typology of Student Cultures 105

ference or hostility toward others. But which are supported and which discouraged—subtle or crude ways of thinking, original or conventional conceptions, fresh or routine feelings and perceptions? And what forces in society and college affect the balance of influences that students have on one another?

Types of Student Culture

Instead of working with the formal properties of informal associations among students, we will focus on their normative content. Let us consider some of the orientations toward a college education that are represented on American campuses and that may be in competition on any one campus. These orientations are defining elements of student subcultures, in which they appear as shared notions of what constitutes right attitude and action toward the range of issues and experiences confronted in college. We will first distinguish several leading types of subcultures, then discuss some of the forces, both internal and external to the college, that shape the strength and distribution of the subcultures on any particular campus.

In passing, we wish to caution that the following are types of subcultures and not types of students, despite the fact that we often describe these subcultures by characterizing their members. First, an individual student may well participate in several of the subcultures available on his campus, though in most cases one will embody his dominant orientation. Second, these types of subcultures are analytical categories; the actual subcultures that flourish on any given campus may well combine elements of more than one of these types. Third, as will be seen, the analytical types simply break dimensions in half and hence oversimplify. These dimensions could be divided into a greater number of more homogeneous categories and combined in blends not here discussed or anticipated. Finally, we would not like to encourage the game of naming subcultures and then pigeonholing individuals, groups of students, or colleges. Rather, we think of this typology as a heuristic device for getting at the processes by which social structures shape student styles of life in different kinds of colleges.

COLLEGIATE CULTURE

The most widely held stereotype of college life pictures the collegiate culture, a world of football, fraternities and sororities, dates, cars, drinking, and campus fun.[2] A good deal of student life on many campuses revolves around this culture; it both provides substance for the stereotypes of movies and cartoons and models itself on those stereotypes. Teachers and courses and grades are in this picture but somewhat dimly and in the background. The fraternities have to make their grade point average, students have to hit the books periodically if they are to get their diplomas, some gestures have to be made to the adult world of courses and grades that provides the justification for the collegiate round.[3]

In content, this system of values and activities is not hostile to the college, to which in fact it generates strong loyalties and attachments. It is, however, indifferent and resistant to serious demands emanating from the faculty for an involvement with ideas and issues over and above that required to gain the diploma. This culture is characteristically middle- and upper-middle-class, for it takes money and leisure to pursue the busy round of social activities,[4] and it flourishes on, though it is by no means confined to, the resident campuses of big state universities. At other institutions, part-time work, intense vocational interest, an urban location, commuter students, all work against the full flowering of a collegiate subculture, as do student aspirations for graduate or professional school or, more generally, serious intellectual or professional interests on the part of students and faculty.

VOCATIONAL CULTURE

The countervailing forces of student poverty and vocationalism, on the one hand, and serious intellectual or academic interests, on the other, are strong enough to make the collegiate culture relatively weak on many American campuses that otherwise differ greatly. In the urban colleges that recruit the ambitious, mobility-oriented sons and daughters of working- and lower-middle-class homes, there is simply not enough time or money to support the expensive play of the collegiate culture. To these students, many of them married, most of them working anywhere from twenty to forty hours a week, college is largely off-the-job training, an organization of courses and credits leading to a diploma and a better job than they could otherwise command. These students have little attachment to the college, where they buy their education somewhat as one buys groceries. But like participants in the collegiate culture, these students are also resistant to intellectual demands on them beyond what is required to pass the courses. To many of these hard-driven students, ideas and scholarship are as much a luxury and distraction as are sports and fraternities. If the symbol of the collegiate culture is the football and fraternity weekend, the symbol of this vocationally oriented culture is the student placement office.

ACADEMIC CULTURE

Present on every college campus, although dominant on some and marginal on others, is the subculture of serious academic effort. The essence of this system of values is its identification with the intellectual concerns of the serious faculty members. The students involved work hard, get the best grades, talk about their coursework outside of class, and let the world of ideas and knowledge reach them in ways that neither of the forgoing types does. While participants in the collegiate subculture pursue fun, and the job-oriented pursue skills and a diploma, these students pursue knowledge: their symbols are the library and laboratory and seminar. If the faculty members who embody these values also represent the college as a whole, then this academic subculture is identified with the college. For these students, the attachment to the college, often as strongly felt as that among the collegiate crowd, is to the institution that supports intellectual values and opportunities for learning; the emotional tie to the college is through the faculty and through campus friends of similar mind and temper. This is the climate encouraged at the colleges that are academically strongest, and when colleges aim to upgrade themselves, it is the students already oriented in this direction whom they seek to recruit.

The products of this culture are typically aiming at graduate and professional schools; it is not surprising that they identify so strongly with the faculty and internalize the scholarly and scientific habits of mind and work as part of their anticipatory adjustment to future professional roles. These students are often oriented toward vocations but not so directly or narrowly as the lower- and lower-middle-class commuters who hold the consumer-vocational values described above; they choose "a basic general education and appreciation of ideas" more often than "provide vocational training" as the goal of education most important to them (Goldsen et al., 1960). In any case, it is not necessary to decide whether they are concerned with their studies more for the sake of learning than because of their career ambitions. The distinctive qualities of this group are, first, that they are seriously involved in their coursework beyond the minimum required for passing and graduation and, second, that they identify themselves with their college and its faculty.

NONCONFORMIST CULTURE

It is in this latter respect, identification with the college that "nonconformist," "intellectual," "radical," "alienated," "bohemian" students differ from their serious academic classmates. Some kind of self-consciously nonconformist subculture exists in many of the best small liberal arts colleges and among the undergraduates in the leading universities. These students are often deeply involved with ideas, both the ideas they encounter in their classrooms and those that are current in the wider society of adult art, literature, and politics. To a much greater degree than their academically oriented classmates, these students use off-campus groups and currents of thought as points of reference, instead of the official college culture, in their strategy of independence and criticism.[5]

The distinctive quality of this student style is a rather aggressive nonconformism, a critical detachment from the college they attend and from its faculty (though this often conceals a strong ambivalence), and a generalized hostility to the college administration. The forms that this style takes vary from campus to campus, but where it exists it has a visibility and influence far beyond its usually tiny and fluid membership. Its chief significance is that it offers a genuine alternative, however temporary, to the rebellious student seeking a distinctive identity in keeping with his own temperament and experience. In a sense it provides some intellectual content and meaning to the idealism and rebelliousness generated in adolescence in some parts of American society. While the preceding three types of students pursue fun, a diploma, or knowledge, these students pursue an identity, not as a byproduct, but as the primary and often self-conscious aim of their education. And their symbol is often a distinctive style—of dress, speech, attitude—that itself represents the identity they seek.[6]

The nonconformist subculture eludes easy characterization. It may, in fact, constitute a residual category, concealing within it quite different kinds of attitudes and orientations, some of which are on the rise, some of which are declining in their importance. Here, next to the fashionable bohemians and the compulsive rebels are those who already exhibit in college the radical cosmopolitanism and skepticism, the commitment to abstract ideas, and the alienation from merely "institutional" attachments that are marks of the intellectual.

The types of subcultures we have been describing emerge from the combination of two variables: the degree to which students are involved with ideas and the extent to which students identify with their college. If we dichotomize these variables, the above four types of student orientations, which provide the content of the most important and distinguishable student subcultures, emerge in the pattern shown in Figure 7.1.

These subcultures are fluid systems of norms and values that overlap and flow into one another on any one campus in ways that challenge the effort to distinguish them analytically. Yet that effort, for all the violence it does to the complexity of social life, appears justified by the light it promises to shed on colleges and their effects on students.[7]

Having distinguished these elementary types of subcultures, we can now raise some questions about the ways in which these subcultures are linked to the larger social structure and to the essential characteristics of colleges.

1. In what strengths and combinations are these orientations found in different types of colleges? Among the seventeen-thousand undergraduates on the Berkeley campus of the University of California, all these systems of values are represented in some strength; among the large number at a nearby state college, the collegiate, academic, and nonconformist subcultures are weak compared with the predominantly vocational orientation of the great majority. At small, academically elite schools, the academic subculture is clearly dominant, with nonconformist values represented, while both the vocational and the collegiate are weak. And at a large number of colleges, large and small, of average rank, the older collegiate values still reign supreme, tempered perhaps by an academically

Involved with ideas

		Much	Little
Identify with their college	Much	Academic	Collegiate
	Little	Nonconformist	Vocational

FIGURE 7.1. Types of Orientations of Four Most Distinguishable Student Subcultures

oriented minority but with the leaven of nonconformists almost wholly absent.

2. What are the social characteristics of the typical members of these different subcultures? Where do they come from in the social structure, and what are the links between their prior experience and their college orientation? There are distinctive patterns of experience that heavily condition the qualities and characteristics that students bring with them to college. Behind patterns of life experience lie social class, racial and ethnic ties, and religious identifications; it is the subcultures in the general population and their values, orientations, and aspirations that shape the orientations that most students initially assume toward college.

3. How do these biographical linkages differ in different kinds of colleges? We have already suggested the connections between lower- and lower-middle-class origins, strong mobility aspirations, and vocational orientations toward college work. But some students thus oriented will find themselves in a minority in, e.g., an Ivy League college, while others will find themselves among the majority in, say, a municipal college. How do these "similar" students deal with their college experience in these quite different situations?

4. What are the historical and structural characteristics of colleges that affect the character of their cultural mix? The purposes of an institution, its size and rate of growth, its historical traditions, its sources of funds and faculty, its physical location, the images of it held in different parts of the population—these and other factors shape the character of the student life within a college. The task is to specify how these forces operate.

Vocationalism and Liberal Education

THE TRIUMPH OF VOCATIONALISM

In discussing the determinants of student subcultures, we have dealt with a number of forces that work in one direction. We suggested earlier that vocationalism, as an orientation toward college and learning, is growing relatively stronger at the expense of both the collegiate and the academic. It is worth recapitulating some of the forces behind this tendency to see their mutually reinforcing effects.

1. *Expansion of higher occupations.* In considerable part, the expansion of higher education is a response to the growth of professional, managerial, and technical occupations that require advanced training. As a result of this change in the occupational structure, and also contributing to the change, the growth in the population in recent years has been very largely in fields of study that are directly vocational, such as business administration, engineering, and education.

The big three vocational curricula—business administration, engineering, and education—which account for nearly one-half of all undergraduate degrees, grew nearly twice as fast as the total number of college graduates in the four years between 1954–55 and 1957–58; the number of degrees earned in these fields increased by 49 percent as compared with an increase of 27 percent in all bachelor's and first professional degrees. Between 1957–58 and 1961–62, however, business and engineering stood relatively still in numbers, and only education, of these three fields, continued to grow rapidly. Training for the higher occupations is, of course, involved in the work of all the disciplines, in mathematics as well as in engineering (American Council of Education, n.d., 92).

2. *Education as the means of mobility.* Formal education has been the chief ladder of mobility for aspiring lower- and lower-middle-class people in America for many decades. Their movement toward college continues the secular trend toward more and more education that saw the growth of nearly universal secondary education in the thirty years between 1910 and 1940. People of lower social origins now increasingly see college as the prerequisite for the economic and social advancement of their children, and these perceptions are reflected in the rapidly growing college enrollments. When education is primarily an instrument for the achievement of higher status, rather than a way to maintain and legitimate it, it

is defined in primarily vocational terms—as a way of getting the training and diplomas that are needed for the better-paying jobs.

3. *Responsive character of public colleges.* This rapid expansion of college attendance among job-oriented children of lower social origins has been very largely in the public colleges. These colleges are generally free, conveniently located, and generous in admission. They are responsive to state and local demands and willingly train for the expanding array of occupations that require advanced skills. Comprehensively organized, they take on many characteristics of a large service enterprise. Their commitment to liberal education is partial rather than total.

4. *Bureaucratization of academic organization.* These comprehensive colleges are typically people-processing institutions, whose administrative staffs must deal with and organize the scattered activities of great numbers of students enrolled in a variety of programs. Relations between teachers and students under these conditions are typically in the mass, usually fleeting, and largely impersonal. Additionally, teachers' involvement with students is lessened by commitment to research, profession, and off-campus service. This tendency toward impersonal relationships among students and between students and faculty members fits vocational education, which aims to transmit technical information efficiently.

5. *Withdrawal of student involvement.* An increasing proportion of college students are enrolled in colleges that are largely nonresidential. Living at home and holding part-time or full-time jobs, students visit the college campus to attend class or use the library; they drop in and out of college, some finishing in six to eight years while many do not finish at all. In brief, the student role is narrowed to formal coursework and is squeezed in among other roles that are oriented off campus.

All these forces that are on the rise in American higher education tend to reduce the impact of college on the student in the older academic sense. Increasingly, students with narrow vocational interests enroll in colleges whose faculties and administrators are neither able nor strongly motivated to modify those interests and orientations.

The small distinctive colleges of high academic achievement, filled with talented upper-middle-class students headed for graduate school, are in another world. The academic subcultures that flourish in those colleges require a high average level of cultural sophistication, the inclination and leisure to cultivate intellectual interests, the help of personal attention from a devoted and able faculty, and the luxury of having merely to maintain rather than newly achieve high social and economic status. These schools will continue to play a role, especially in the country's intellectual life, out of proportion to the numbers of their graduates. But despite the worries of their presidents and professors about their effectiveness, these schools do not now pose the most difficult questions regarding the bearing of student life on higher education. It is in the large public colleges and universities, where vocationalism looms large, that the contribution of student life and its relationships to education becomes most problematic.

These problems do not arise solely in the United States. In every industrial society, recent immense advances of science, organization, and industry exert great pressures on higher education to become "the training institutions for the skilled manpower required by a complex technology" (Halsey, 1960). The USSR has gone farthest in making education an arm of the state and the economy. The Russians want no part of liberal or general humanistic education. They want no generalists—only specialists. Their main objective is to offer functional education so as to train, to mold, to develop the skills, the professions, and the specialists required by their long-run development programs—specialists who are capable of performing the tasks of running the industrial and bureaucratic machinery of the communist state. And in order to accomplish this, the Russians were, are, and will be training an army of scientists and technologists. "Although professing the aims of general and well-rounded education, the Soviet educational system in reality is uniquely geared to the training of specialized manpower" (DeWitt, 1960).

Even in England, where the university (and aristocratic) tradition of the cultivated man is strongest, the decades since the war have seen a greater emphasis on vocational and professional studies, especially in science and technology, although this movement has been slowed and contained by the elite conceptions of the university in that country (Halsey, 1960).

The great conflict on American campuses over the past fifty years has been between the academic and the collegiate subcultures, with the faculty upholding the intellectual values and the majority of students successfully opposing those with their own nonintellectual or anti-intellectual interests. Increasingly, however, the struggle will be between the vocational and academic subcultures, with the cleavage more nearly vertical—i.e., with proponents of each set of values found in the faculty as well as in the student body. Both the vocational and the academic orientations are "adult" in a way that the collegiate culture is not. While collegiate values and practices were widely condoned by college authorities, few adults in college were prepared to defend them as an adequate definition of the college experience. By contrast, the vocational orientation as the *primary* orientation to college is upheld in respectable quarters, finds expression in books on educational philosophy, and has many spokesmen among both college teachers and administrators. Thus, the expanding conflict between vocational and academic values is not likely to be as dramatic as the old, because the symbols are less clear.

The collegiate symbols were sufficiently outside the workaday adult world to be instantly recognizable in a cartoon or film, and their romanticization of adolescent vitality and irresponsibility made that world seem exciting, full of freedom and fun and unearned money. The academic subculture has its prestigious symbols: the academic procession and cap and gown, books, the library, the laboratory, and the classroom. But the vocational subculture is almost an adjunct of the adult world of jobs and work; it has as yet no defining symbols that distinguish it as a special college subculture, unless it be the engineer's slide rule in its orange case swinging from the belt. But it is inherently too humdrum and work-oriented ever to be very glamorous, a fact that affects both recruitment to it now and its fate as an alternative image and definition of higher education in the future.

The fact that the vocational orientation has no symbols of its own, but nevertheless is serious and is oriented to the adult world of work, allows it to borrow the traditional symbols of academia: so a picture of a college lecture hall or of students hard at work in a library can as easily be signs of vocational training as of liberal education. But the common use of the same set of symbols for vocational and academic subcultures makes it more difficult for issues between them to be joined, though the conflict is at the heart of fights over admissions policy, curriculum, and standards on many campuses. Although the cleavage between these cultures within colleges is not so sharply drawn along the traditional lines of academic status and rank, the outcomes of the conflict promise to be equally consequential, both for the experiences of students in college and, more broadly, for the nature and functions of higher education in America.

Notes

1. From reviews of the literature, see Katz and Lazarsfeld (1955) and Bales (1959). The classic work in education is that of Newcomb (1943). See also the articles in *The School Review* (*School Review* staff, 1963).

2. For a description and analysis of campus subcultures, see Angell (1928), Johnson (1946), and McConn (1928). For an early (1909) classic indictment, see Wilson (1925). For a recent sociological analysis of this student world, see Goldsen et al. (1960).

3. Goldsen et al. (1960, 73). The following are quotations from interviews with fraternity men in their sample.

> Lots of pledges come in with the idea that fraternity life means all fun and no studying. We quickly educate them. Not that we want grinds—no—we try to get them to maintain a respectable average. Nothing very glittering, of course, just respectable.

> We try to keep our house's grades up to standard. There's plenty of help for the brothers who fall behind. We have files of old examinations in almost every course that they can use in studying. We even assign certain men to tutor any brothers who need help. They don't have to get super grades. After all, when you get out of college nobody asks what your grades were. Just maintain a decent average.

4. In eleven universities across the country, fraternity members were found on the average to come from considerably wealthier homes than do independent students. In 1952 only 24 percent of the fraternity men as compared with 46 percent of the independents reported their fathers earning under $5,000. Computed from data of Goldsen et al. (1960, 71, Table 3.3).

5. Jencks and Riseman (1962). The academic, in their usage, refers to the pursuit of knowledge within some scholarly or professional discipline by experts and specialists (or their apprentices), whereas intellectual inquiry is the pursuit of wisdom—answers to perennial problems of living—through the play of intelligence rather than through specialized learning. As they observe, the official view holds that "the intellectual and the academic are largely synonymous," and they are concerned with those student organizations at Harvard that "have emerged to defend intellectual concerns against overt or covert pressures from the curriculum." Our typology to some extent cuts across this distinction: the academic cultures we speak of include students with genuine intellectual interests as well as "grinds" submissive to the demands of the faculty. In our typology, the members

of the academic subcultures tend to link their interests to the curriculum; the nonconformists pursue theirs outside it.

6. Nonconformist subcultures may provide opportunity and support for some of the processes of identity play discussed by Erikson (1956, 56–121). The relatively little attention given to nonconformist cultures in this essay reflects our ignorance about them and not their relative importance for American life and education.

7. This simple typology does not take into account other dimensions of student orientations that may be important for understanding the specific forms that student subcultures take. Research aimed at applying, extending, and refining this typology is currently under way at the Educational Testing Service, Princeton, and in Berkeley at the American College Testing Program as well. For a report of a study employing this typology, see Gottlieb and Hodgkins (1963).

References

Angell, R. C. *The Campus.* New York: Macmillan, 1928.

Bales, R. "Small Group Therapy and Research. In *Sociology Today,* edited by R. Merton. New York: Basic Books, 1959.

Erikson, E. H. "The Problem of Ego Identity." *Journal of the American Psychoanalytical Association* 4 (1956).

Goldsen, R. K., M. Rosenberg, R. M. Williams, Jr., and E. A. Suchman. *What College Students Think.* Princeton, N.J.: Van Nostrand, 1960.

Gottlieb, D., and B. Hodgkins. "College Student Subcultures." *School Review* 71 (Autumn 1963): 266–90.

Jencks, C., and D. Riesman. "Patterns of Residential Education: A Case Study of Harvard." In *The American College,* edited by N. Sanford. New York: Wiley, 1962.

Johnson, B. *Campus Versus Classroom.* New York: I. Washburn, 1946.

Katz, E., and P. F. Lazarsfeld. *Personal Influence.* Glencoe, Ill.: Free Press, 1955.

McConn, M. *College or Kindergarten?* New York: New Republic, 1928.

Newcomb, T. M. *Personality and Social Change: Attitude Formation in a Student Community.* New York: Dryden, 1943.

School Review staff. "Social Climates in School and College." *School Review* 71 (Autumn 1963).

Wilson, W. "The Spirit of Learning" (1909). In *Selected Literary and Political Papers and Addresses of Woodrow R. Wilson,* vol. 1. New York: Grosset and Dunlap, 1925.

INTRODUCTION TO CHAPTER 8

During the eight years I spent in the new Berkeley Center and in the old Berkeley Department of Education, I primarily pursued the fieldwork that lay behind *The Distinctive College,* worked on organizing an effective manuscript, and did some light teaching. But there was time to do other things. I participated in at least three summer conferences in the early 1960s; they were jointly sponsored by the Berkeley Center and the Western Interstate Commission for Higher Education. Of the two papers on academic organization and one on faculty culture I gave, one of them is included here as representative of all three. It illustrates the usefulness, indeed, even necessity, of maintaining a historical developmental perspective. It suggests that analytical frameworks and concepts employed five decades ago can still be useful today.

One view, dating from the 1960s, is the growing awareness that academic work has become highly professionalized. It is a profession that trains experts for all (or almost all) the other ones. The academic profession is many professions within a profession, and life turns out to be very different in the various subfields it encompasses. But how many commentators on university organization today even bother to recognize the clear differences between faculty (and student) life in the medical school, on the one hand, and the classics department, on the other, between astrophysics and economics, between philosophy and biology departments? To simply talk the talk around simplified journalistic images increasingly ignores the most obvious examples of fundamental differences in college and university realities. Since at least the 1950s, we have had extensive knowledge about the criss-crossing of disciplinary and institutional settings that mold faculty and student life into fundamentally different shapes. The academic world is characterized by a dizzying array of "small worlds, different worlds," a theme to which I return later.

CHAPTER 8

Organizational Adaptation to Professionals

A S WE PARTICIPATE in or study various faculties in American higher education, we observe decisions being made through informal interaction among a group of peers and through collective action of the faculty as a whole. Formal hierarchy plays little part, and we have reason to characterize the faculty as a collegium.[1] At the same time we sense that what we now observe is not a counterpart of the collegiality of the days of old. The modern faculty in the United States is not a body to be likened to the guilds of the medieval European university,[2] or to the self-government of a dozen dons in a residential college at Oxford or Cambridge,[3] or to the meager self-rule that was allowed the faculty in the small liberal arts college that dominated American higher education until the end of the past century.[4] The old-time collegium has modern reflections, as in the Fellowships of the colleges at Yale, but for the most part it is no longer winningly with us, and the kind of collegiality we now find needs different conceptualization. We also observe on the modern campus that information is communicated through formal channels, responsibility is fixed in formally designated positions, interaction is arranged in relations between superiors and subordinates, and decisions are based on written rules. Thus, we have reason to characterize the campus as a bureaucracy. But, at the same time, we sense that this characterization overlooks so much that it becomes misleading. Though the elements of bureaucracy are strong, they do not dominate the campus; and though they grow, their growth does not mean future dominance if other forms of organization and authority are expanding more rapidly.

"Organizational Adaptation to Professionals," in *Professionalization*, edited by H. M. Vollmer and D. L. Mills, 282–91. Englewood Cliffs, N.J.: Prentice-Hall, 1966. Used by permission.

The major form of organization and authority found in the faculties of the larger American colleges and universities, and toward which many small campuses are now moving, is now neither predominantly collegial nor bureaucratic. Difficult to characterize, it may be seen as largely "professional," but professional in a way that is critically different from the authority of professional men in other organizations, such as the business corporation, the government agency, and the hospital. To approach this unusual pattern, we first discuss trends in the organization and culture of the campus as a whole and then turn to the related trends in the organization and authority of the faculty.

We begin with broad changes in the nature of the campus because they condition the structure of authority. Authority is conditioned, e.g., by the nature of work, the technology of an organization. The mass assembly of automobiles does not allow much personal discretion on the part of the worker; surgery in the hospital operating room requires on-the-spot judgment and autonomous decision by the surgeon and one or two colleagues. To understand faculty authority, we need some comprehension of what academic work has in common with work in other settings and how it differs from work elsewhere. Authority is also conditioned by patterns of status. Status comes in part from formal assignment, hence men called deans usually have much of it, but status is also derived in academia from one's standing in a discipline, and this important source of status is independent of the official scheme.[5] Authority is also conditioned by traditional sentiments. Legends and ideologies have a force of their own. Conceptions of what should be are formed by what has been or by ideals handed down through the generations. The stirring ideologies of community of scholars and academic freedom are forces to be reckoned with when one is dealing with faculties and in understanding their organization. Thus, the work itself, the status system, the traditional sentiments, all affect authority.

Trends in the Social Organization of the Campus

Four trends in the campus, closely related, are as follows: unitary to composite or federal structure; single- to multiple-value systems; nonprofessional to professional work; consensus to bureaucratic coordination.

The history of American higher education is a history of movement from unitary liberal arts colleges to multistructured colleges and universities. The American college of 1840 contained 6 professors and 50 to 100 students;[6] in 1870, average size was still less than 10 faculty and 100 students. All students in a college took the same curriculum, a "program of classical-mathematical studies inherited from Renaissance education."[7] There was no need for subunits such as division and department; this truly was a unitary structure. In comparison, the modern university and college is multistructured. The University of California at Berkeley in 1962–63, with over 23,000 students and 1,600 "officers of instruction," was divided into some 15 colleges or schools (e.g., College of Engineering, School of Public Health); over 50 institutes, centers, and laboratories; and some 75 departments (including poultry husbandry, romance philology, food technology, and naval architecture). In 3 departments and 3 schools, the subunit itself contained over 50 faculty members. Such complexity is not only characteristic of the university: a large California state college contains 40 or so disciplines, grouped in a number of divisions; and even a small liberal arts college today may have 20 departments and 3 or 4 divisions.

The multiplication of subunits stems in part from increasing size. The large college cannot remain as unitary as the small one, since authority must be extensively delegated and subsidiary units formed around the many centers of authority. The subunits also stem from plurality of purpose; we have moved from single- to multipurpose colleges. Goals are not only more numerous but also broadly defined and ambiguous. Those who would define the goals of the modern university speak in such terms as "preserving truth, creating new knowledge, and serving the needs of man through truth and knowledge."[8] The service goal has a serviceable ambiguity that covers anything from home economics for marriage to research and development for space. A tightly integrated structure could not be established around these goals. Organizational structure accommodates to the multiplicity of goals by dividing into segments with different primary functions, such as liberal arts and professional training, scientific research and humanistic education. The structure accommodates to ambiguity of goals with its own ambiguity, overlap, and discontinuity.

We find some liberal arts disciplines scattered all over the campus (e.g., statistics, psychology), residing as components of professional schools and of "other" departments as well as in the appropriately named department. No neat consistent structure is possible; the multiple units form and re-form around functions in a catch-as-catch-can fashion. Needless to say, with a multiplicity of ambiguous goals and a variety of subunits, authority is extensively decentralized. The structure is federal rather than unitary, and even takes on some likeness to a loosely joined federation.

SINGLE- TO MULTIPLE-VALUE SYSTEMS

Most colleges before the turn of the century and perhaps as late as the 1920s possessed a unified culture that extended across the campus,[9] and this condition still obtains in some small colleges today. But the number of colleges so characterized continues to decline and the long-run trend is clear: the campus-wide culture splits into subcultures located in a variety of social groups and organizational units. As we opened the doors of American higher education, we admitted more orientations to college— college as fun, college as marriage, college as preparation for graduate school, college as certificate to go to work tomorrow, college as place to rebel against the Establishment, and even college as place to think. These orientations have diverse social locations on campus, from fraternity house to cafe espresso shop to Mrs. Murphy's desegregated rooming house. The value systems of the students are numerous.

The faculty is equally if not more prone to diversity in orientation, as men cleave to their specialized lines of work and their different perspectives and vocabularies. Faculty orientations differ between those who commit themselves primarily to the local campus and those who commit themselves primarily to their farflung discipline or profession; between those who are scientists and those who are humanists; between those who think of themselves as pure researchers or pure scholars and those who engage in a professional practice and train recruits. The value systems of the faculty particularly cluster around the individual disciplines and hence at one level of analysis there are as many value systems as there are departments.

Intense specialization characterizes the modern campus; academic man has moved from general to specific knowledge. The old-time teacher— Mr. Chips—was a generalist. He covered a wide range of subject matter, with less intensity in any one area than would be true today, and he was engaged in pure transmission of knowledge. In the American college of a century ago, the college teacher had only a bachelor's degree (in the fixed classical curriculum), plus "a modest amount of more advanced training, perhaps in theology."[10] There was no system of graduate education, there was no reward for distinction in scholarship, and the professor settled down into the groove of classroom recitation and the monitoring of student conduct. We have moved from this kind of professor, the teacher generalist, to the teacher of physics, of engineering, of microbiology, of abnormal psychology, and to the professor as researcher, as consultant, as professional-school demonstrator. We have moved from transmission of knowledge to innovation in knowledge, which has meant specialization in research. Taking the long view, perhaps *the* great change in the role of academic man is the ascendance of research and scholarship—the rise of the commitment to create knowledge. This change in the academic role interacts with rapid social change: research causes change, as in the case of change in technology and industrial processes; and such changes, in turn, encourage the research attitude, as in the case of competition between industrial firms, competition between nations, competition between universities. In short, the research component of the academic role is intimately related to major modern social trends.

In his specialism, modern academic man is a case of professional man. We define "profession" to mean a specialized competence with a high degree of intellectual content, a specialty heavily based on or involved with knowledge. Specialized competence based on involvement in knowledge is the hallmark of the modern professor. He is preeminently an expert. Having special knowledge at his command, the professional worker needs and seeks a large degree of autonomy from lay control and normal organizational control. Who is the best judge of surgical procedure— laymen, hospital administrators, or surgeons? Who is the best judge of theories in chemistry—laymen, university administrators, or professors of chemistry? As work becomes professionalized—specialized around esoteric knowledge and technique—the organization of work must create room for expert judgment, and autonomy of decision-making and practice becomes a hallmark of the advanced profession.

Not all professional groups need the same degree of autonomy, however. Professionals who largely give advice or follow the guidelines of a received body of knowledge require extensive but not great autonomy for the individual and the group. They need sufficient leeway to give an honest expert opinion or to apply the canons of judgment of their field. Those requiring great autonomy are those who wish to crawl along the frontiers of knowledge, with flashlight or floodlight in hand, searching for the new—the new scientific finding, the new reinterpretation of history, the new criticism in literature or art. Academic man is a special kind of professional man, a type characterized by a particularly high need for autonomy. To be innovative, to be critical of established ways, these are the commitments of the academy and the impulses of scientific and scholarly roles that press for unusual autonomy.

CONSENSUAL TO BUREAUCRATIC COORDINATION

As the campus has moved from unitary to composite structure, from single to multiple systems of values, from general to specialized work, it has moved away from the characteristics of community, away from a "community of scholars." A faculty member does not interact with most other members of the faculty. In the largest places, he may know less than a fifth, less than a tenth. Paths do not cross. The faculty lounge is no more, but is replaced by coffee pots in dozens of locations. The professor retains a few interests in common with all others, such as higher salaries, but he has an increasing number of interests that diverge. Even salary is a matter on which interests may diverge, as men bargain for themselves, as departments compete for funds, as scientists are paid more, through various devices, than the men of the humanities.

In short, looking at the total faculty, interaction is down, commonality of interest is down, commonality of sentiments is down. With this, coordination of work and policy within the faculty is not so much now as in the past achieved by easy interaction of community members, by the informal give-and-take that characterizes the true community—the community of the small town where everyone knows nearly everyone else, or the community of the old small college where the professors saw much of everyone else in the group. The modern campus can no longer be coordinated across its length and breadth by informal interaction and by the coming together of the whole. Informal consulting back and forth is still important; the administration and the faculty still use the lunch table for important business. But campus-wide coordination increasingly moves toward the means normal to the large-scale organization, to bureaucratic means. We appoint specialists to various areas of administration, we give them authority, and they write rules to apply across the system. They communicate by correspondence, they attempt to make decisions fairly and impartially by judging the case before them against the criteria of the rulebook. Thus we move toward bureaucratic coordination, as the admissions officer decides on admissions, the registrar decides on the recording of grades, the business officer decides proper purchasing procedures, and various faculty committees decide on a wide range of matters, from tenure to travel funds to the rules of order for meetings of an academic senate.

In sum: the campus tends toward composite structure, toward a multiplicity of subcultures, toward intense professionalism, and toward some bureaucratic coordination.

Change in Faculty Organization and Authority

The organization and the authority of the faculty accommodate to these trends in at least three ways: by segmentation, by a federated professionalism, and by the growth of individual power centers.

SEGMENTATION

As campuses increase in size, complexity, and internal specialization, there is less chance that the faculty will be able to operate effectively as a total faculty in college affairs, less as the governmental body we have in mind when we speak of a community of scholars. The decision-making power and influence of the faculty is now more segmented—segmented by subcollege, by division, and particularly by department. Since the interests of the faculty cluster around the departments, faculty participation in government tends to move out to these centers of commitment. Who selects personnel, decides on courses, and judges students? The faculty as a whole cannot, any more than the administration. Indeed, as departments and professional schools grow in size and complexity, even they often do not; it is a wing of the department or a part of the professional school that has the most influence. A liberal arts department that numbers forty to eighty faculty members may contain six or eight or a dozen specialties. The day has arrived when a department chairman may not even know the name, let alone the face and the person, of the new instructors in "his" department.

What happens to the governmental organs designed for the faculty as a whole? They move in form from Town Hall to representative government, with men elected from the various "states" coming together in a federal center to legislate general rules, which are then executed by the administration or the faculty committees that constitute an administrative component of the faculty. With the move to representative government, there is greater differentiation in participation: a few "actives" participate a great deal; a considerably larger group constitutes an alert and informed public and participates a modest amount; the largest group consists of those who are not very interested or informed and who participate very little. The structure of participation parallels that found in the larger democratic society, and apparently is normal to a representative mass democracy. The situation is, of course, vexing to those who care about faculty government.

PROFESSIONALIZATION

The authority of the faculty that flows out toward the departments and other units of the campus becomes located in the hands of highly specialized experts, and, as suggested earlier, takes on some characteristics of professional authority. Almost everywhere in modern large-scale organizations, we find a tug-of-war going on between administrative and professional orientations. In the hospital, the basic conflict in authority lies between the control of the nonmedical hospital administrator and the authority of the doctors. In industry, a fascinating clash is occurring between management and the scientist in the research and development laboratory.[11] The fantastic expansion of research and development has brought over four hundred thousand scientists and engineers into industry, there to be committed to innovation and to the development of new inventions to the point of practical utility. Many of these technologists have a high degree of expertise, a strong interest in research—often "pure" research—and they press for a large degree of freedom. Their fondest wish is to be left alone; they make the point that in scientific work it seems rational to do just that, that basic discoveries stem not from managerial direction but from the scientist following up his own initial hunches and the leads he develops as he proceeds. Management has found such men difficult to deal with; their morale suffers easily from traditional forms of management, and they present unusual demands on management to change and accommodate. In this situation, professional authority and bureaucratic authority are both necessary, for each performs an essential function: professional authority protects the exercise of the special expertise of the technologist, allowing his judgment to be preeminent in many matters. Bureaucratic authority functions to provide coordination of the work of the technologists with the other major elements of the firm. Bureaucratic direction is not capable of providing certain expert judgments; professional direction is not capable of providing the overall coordination. The problem presented by the scientist in industry is how to serve simultaneously the requirements of autonomy and the requirements of coordination, and how to accommodate the authority of the professional man and his group of peers to the authority of management and vice versa.[12]

The professional-in-the-organization presents everywhere this special kind of problem. He gains authority, compared to most employees, by virtue of his special knowledge and skills; he loses authority, compared to a man working on his own, by virtue of the fact that organizations locate much authority in administrative positions. The problem of allocation of authority between professionals and bureaucrats does, however, vary in intensity and form in different kinds of organizations. As mentioned earlier, advisors and practitioners need a modest degree of authority, while scientists and academics have perhaps the highest requirements for autonomy to engage in research, in unfettered teaching, and in scholarship that follows the rules of consistency and proof that develop within a discipline.

The segmentation of the faculty into clusters of experts gives professional authority a special form in academic organizations. In other situations, there usually are one or two major professional groups within the organizational who, if they are influential, substitute professional control for administrative control. This occurs in the case of medical personnel in the hospital who often dominate decision-making. The internal controls of the medical profession are strong and are substituted for those of the organization. But in the college or university this situation does not obtain; there are twelve, twenty-five, or fifty clusters of experts. The experts are prone to identify with their own disciplines, and the "academic profession" overall comes off a poor second. We have wheels within wheels, many professions within a profession. No one of the disciplines on a campus is likely to dominate the others; at a minimum, it usually takes an alliance of disciplines, such as "the natural sciences" or "the humanities" to put together a bloc that might dominate others. The point is that with a variety of experts—chemists, educationists, linguists, professors of marketing—the collective control of the professionals over one another will not be strong. The campus is not a closely knit group of professionals who see the world from one perspective. As a collection of professionals, it is decentralized, loose, and flabby.

The principle is this: where professional influence is high and there is one dominant professional group, the organization will be integrated by the imposition of professional standards. Where professional influence is high and there are a number of professional groups, the organization will be split by professionalism. The university and the large college are fractured by expertness, not unified by it. The sheer variety of the experts supports the tendency for authority to diffuse toward quasi-autonomous clusters. Thus, faculty authority has in common with professional authority in other places the protection of individual and group autonomy. It is different from professional authority in other places in the extremity of the need for autonomy and in the fragmentation of authority around the interests of a large variety of groups of roughly equal status and power. The campus is a holding company for professional groups rather than a single association of professionals.

INDIVIDUALIZATION

When we speak of professional authority we often lump together the authority that resides with the individual expert and the authority that resides with a collegial group of experts. Both the individual and the group gain influence at the expense of laymen and the general administrator. But what is the division of authority between the individual and the group? Sometimes group controls can be very tight and quite hierarchical, informally if not formally, as young doctors learn in many hospitals, and as assistant professors learn in many departments. The personal authority of the expert varies widely with the kind of establishment, and often with the rank and seniority. The campus is a place where strong forces cause the growth of some individuals into centers of power. We will review several of these sources of personal authority.

First, we have noted the expertise of the modern academy. The intense specialization alone makes many a man into king of a sector in which few others are able to exercise much judgment. Thus, *within* a department, men increasingly feel unable to judge the merits of men in specialties they know nothing about. The technical nature of the specialized lines of work of most academic men, then, is a source of personal authority. If we want to provide a course on Thomas Hardy, we are likely to defer on its content to the judgment of the man in the English department who has been knee-deep in Hardy for a decade. The idea of such a course would really have been his in the first place; Hardy falls within his domain within the English department, and his judgment on the need for the course will weigh more than the judgment of others.

Second, some professional experts now have their personal authority greatly enhanced by money. Despite his location within an organization, the professor in our time is becoming an entrepreneur. It used to be that the college president was the only one on campus, other than an enterprising and dedicated member of the board of trustees, who was capable of being an entrepreneur. Many of the great presidents were great because they were great at coming home with the loot—adventurers who conquered the hearts and pocketbooks of captains of industry and then with money in hand raided wholesale the faculties of other institutions. Presidents who can raise money and steal faculty are still with us, but they have been joined by professors. Kerr has suggested that the power of the individual faculty member is going up while the power of the collective faculty is going down because the individual as researcher, as scholar, and as consultant relates increasingly to the grant-giving agencies of the federal government and to the foundations.[13] He has direct ties to these major sources of funds and influence; indeed, he participates in their awarding of grants and even has problems of conflict of interest. A professor-entrepreneur, by correspondence and telephone and airplane trips, lines up money for projects. He sometimes arranges for the financing of an entire laboratory; occasionally he even brings back a new building. Even when the professor does little of the arranging, it is *his* presence that attracts these resources. He represents competence, and the grant-givers pursue competence.

The entrepreneurial activity and resources-gaining influence of professors, which extends down to assistant professors in the social as well as the natural sciences, has had remarkable growth since World War II, and the personal autonomy and power thus achieved in relation to others in the university is considerable. A professor does not have to beg postage stamps from a departmental secretary nor a two hundred dollar raise from the department chairman nor travel money to go to a meeting from a dean or a committee if he has monies assigned to him to the tune of $37,000, or $175,000, or $400,000. His funds from outside sources may be called "soft" funds, in the jargon of finance, but they are hard enough to hire additional faculty members and assistants, to cover summer salaries, and to provide for travel to distant, delightful places.

The following principle obtains: a *direct* relation of faculty members to external sources of support affects the distribution of influence within the campus, redistributing influence from those who do not have such contacts to those who do, and moving power from the faculty as a whole and as smaller collectivities to individual professors. In the university of old, members of the faculty achieved a high degree of influence by occupying the few professorial positions available in a structure that narrowed at the top. Their source of influence was structural and internal. The source of great influence in the modern American university is less internal and less tied to particular positions; it is more external and more tied to national and international prestige in a discipline, and to contact with the sources of support for research and scholarship that are multiplying and growing so rapidly.

The individualization in faculty organization and authority excites impulses in the faculty and the administration to establish some collective control, for much is at stake in the balance of the curriculum, the equality of rewards in the faculty, and even the character of the institution. But the efforts at control do not have easy going. Collective bodies of the faculty and the administration are hardly in a position, or inclined, to tell the faculty member he can have this contract but not that one, since the faculty member will define the projects as part of his pursuit of his own scholarly interests. When the faculty member feels that this sensitive right is infringed, he will run up the banners of academic freedom and inquiry, or he will fret and become a festering sore in the body politic of the campus, or he will retreat to apathy and his country house, or he will make it known in other and greener pastures that he will listen to the siren call of a good offer.

Third, personal authority of the professorial expert is increased in our time by the competitiveness of the job market. The expansion of higher education means a high demand for professors, and the job market runs very much in the professor's favor in bargaining with the administration. His favorable position *in* the market enhances his position *on* campus. He can demand more and get it; he can even become courageous. In the world of work, having another job to go to is perhaps the most important source of courage.

To recapitulate: faculty organization and authority tend in modern times to become more segmented, more professional in character, and somewhat more individualized. We are witnessing a strong trend toward a federated structure in colleges and especially in universities—with the campuses more like a United Nations and less like a small town—and this trend affects faculty authority by weakening the faculty as a whole and strengthening the faculty in its many parts. Faculty authority becomes less of a case of self-government by a total collegium, and more of a case of authority exercised department by department, subcollege by subcollege. The *role* of faculty authority is shifting from protecting the rights of the entire guild, the rights of the collective faculty, to protecting the autonomy of the separate disciplines and the autonomy of the individual faculty member.

Faculty authority in our time tends to become professional authority in a federated form. We have a loose alliance of professional men. The combination of professional authority and loosely joined structure has the imposing function of protecting the autonomy of the work of experts amid extensive divergence of interests and commitments. The qualities of federation are important here. The federation is a structure that gives rein to the quasi-autonomous, simultaneous development of the interests of a variety of groups. Within an academic federation, a number of departments, divisions, colleges, professional schools, institutes, and the like can coexist, each pushing its own interests and going its own way to a rather considerable extent. Professional authority structured as a federation is a form of authority particularly adaptive to a need for a high degree of autonomous judgment by individuals and subgroups.

This trend toward a federation of professionals is only part of the story. To hold the separate components of the campus together, we have a superimposed coordination by the administration, and, as Kerr has suggested, this coordination increasingly takes on the attributes of mediation.[14] The administration attempts to keep the peace and to inch the entire enterprise another foot ahead. The faculty, too, in its own organization, also counters this divisive trend with a machinery of coordination. The very fact of a diffusion of authority makes the faculty politician more necessary than ever, for the skills of politics and diplomacy are needed. There must be faculty mediators; men who serve on central committees, men with cast iron stomachs for lunch table discussions and cocktail parties, men who know how to get things done that must be done for the faculty as a whole or for part of the faculty. There must be machinery for setting rules and carrying them out impartially across the faculty. The modern campus is, or is becoming, too large and complicated for collegial or professional arrangements to provide the overall coordination, and coordination is performed largely by bureaucratic arrangements—e.g., the rulebook and definite administrative domains.

Federated professionalism within an organization, like many other trends, thus promotes countertrends. Specialization and individualization seriously weaken the integration of the whole. The weakness of collegiality or professionalism in the large organization, as suggested earlier in the case of industry, is that it cannot handle the problem of order, it cannot provide sufficient integration. Thus, the above trends in faculty organization and authority open the door to bureaucracy—more bureaucracy in the administration, more within the faculty itself. The modern large faculty, therefore, combines professionalism, federated structure, and bureaucracy—perhaps in a mixture never before evidenced in human history.

This combination of what seem contradictory forms of organization perplexes observers of academia. Is the faculty collegial? Yes, somewhat.

Is it split into fragments? Yes, somewhat. Is it professional? Yes, somewhat. Is it unitary? Yes, somewhat. Is it bureaucratic? Yes, somewhat. Different features of the faculty strike us according to the occurrences of the week or the events we chance to observe. The ever-mounting paperwork firmly convinces us that the campus is doomed to bureaucratic stagnation. The fact that the president often gets what the president wants convinces us that he really has all the authority. The inability of a campus to change a department that is twenty years behind in its field convinces us that departmental autonomy has run amok and the campus is lacking in leadership and in capacity to keep up with the times. One observer will see the campus as a tight ship, the next will speak of the same campus as a lawless place where power lies around loose. No wonder we are confused and no wonder that outsiders are so often even more confused or more irrelevant in giving advice.

But in the combination of forms of organization and the forms of authority that we find today within the campus and within the faculty itself, there are certain trends that are stronger than others and certain features that tend toward dominance. The society at large is tending to become a society of experts, and the campus has already arrived at this state. Expertise is a dominant characteristic of the campus, and organization and authority cluster around it. Because of its expertness, together with its ever-growing size, the faculty moves away from community, moves away from collegiality of the whole. The faculty moves toward decentralized or federated structure, and authority moves toward clusters of experts and the individual expert. Thus professional authority tends to become the dominant form of authority, and collegial and bureaucratic features fall into a subsidiary place. In short, when we say college, we say expert. When we say expert, we say professional authority.

Notes

1. A major type of collegiality is that involving collegial decision: "In such cases an administrative act is only legitimate when it has been produced by the cooperation of a plurality of people according to the principle of unanimity or of majority." Max Weber, *The Theory of Social and Economic Organization,* trans. A. M. Henderson and Talcott Parsons (New York: Oxford University Press, 1947), 400.

2. Hastings Rashdall, *The Universities in Europe in the Middle Ages,* ed. T. M. Powicke and A. B. Emden (Oxford: Clarendon Press, 1936), 3 vols.

3. C. P. Snow, *The Masters* (New York: Macmillan Company, 1951).

4. Richard Hofstadter and Walter P. Metzger, *The Development of Academic Freedom in the United States* (New York: Columbia University Press, 1955); George P. Schmidt, *The Liberal Arts College* (New Brunswick, N.J.: Rutgers University Press, 1957).

5. Logan Wilson, *The Academic Man* (New York: Oxford University Press, 1942); Theodore Caplow and Reece J. McGee, *The Academic Marketplace* (New York: Basic Books, 1958).

6. Hofstadter and Metzger, *Development of Academic Freedom,* 222–23.

7. Ibid., 226.

8. Clark Kerr, *The Uses of the University,* The Godkin Lectures, Harvard University, 1963.

9. Hofstadter and Metzger, *Development of Academic Freedom*; Schmidt, *Liberal Arts College.*

10. Hofstadter and Metzger, *Development of Academic Freedom,* 230.

11. See William Kornhauser, *Scientists in Industry: Conflict and Accommodation* (Berkeley: University of California Press, 1962); and Simon Marcson, *The Scientist in American Industry* (New York: Harper & Row, 1960).

12. Kornhauser, *Scientists in Industry.*

13. Kerr, *Uses of the University.*

14. Ibid.

INTRODUCTION TO CHAPTER 9

Why did I write this off-the-line article in the mid-1960s? Is it relevant to post-2000 concerns? Interorganizational analysis appeared often in the literature on organizations in the early 1960s. The work on curricular reform done by the Physical Science Study Committee (PSSC) in the post-*Sputnik* era intrigued me, especially when they tackled how reform could be made in the highly decentralized American "non-system" of schools, colleges, and universities. The National Science Foundation allocated funds to a voluntary committee of eight to ten leading scientists headquartered at MIT, not to state bureaucrats. During a two-year period (1956–58), this private committee developed new course materials for teaching science in secondary schools, trained teachers in their use, and persuaded many local educational authorities to adopt them. By 1963, these source materials were evidently very influential. The committee had blazed a way for collaborative action without bureaucratic dictate or placing trust in weak educational markets, i.e., in transactions without a coordinator. Its public-private alliance amounted to a third way—confederative organization heavily dependent on voluntary participation.

Unfortunately, this post-*Sputnik* reform effort ran out of steam in the face of the deeply rooted school structures of cities and states, which ultimately reasserted their control. Sound familiar? We do a poor job in America of learning from our successes as well as from our failures. Groups similar to PSSC are still active as I write these words in 2006, but local adoption of their recommendations by cities and particularly by the bureaucracies of the fifty state governments is repeatedly checkmated. Some states even deliberately use faulty data to hide ingrained defects in the K–12 system. Most outrageously of all, they even greatly lower their own benchmarks of achievement in order to report that high percentages of their students received a good secondary education. Some state politicians and bureaucrats are without shame when it comes to how they treat young people.

When students "graduate" from the twelfth grade while performing at sixth- and eighth-grade levels, something is broken in the system. And that gross anomaly, apparent for all to see—especially when we look at schools in other countries—goes on and on and on. What is broken in American education is the upper six years in the middle and senior high schools of the K–12 system. This defect deeply affects universities and colleges by thrusting upon them the huge burden of remedial education. More on this central, vexing matter appears in later essays, particularly in the one analyzing "what went wrong in America."

CHAPTER 9

Interorganizational Patterns in Education

AMONG THE MANY social trends that swirl around the school and college, three broad sets of forces stand out: the first is economic, the second demographic, and the third political. These forces create problems to which educational authorities must respond and, in responding, initiate effects that reverberate through the system and alter its structure. The direction and style of this change is only partly predicted by the traditional theory of bureaucracy and associated conceptions of administrative behavior. This essay explores some of the changes taking place that, if followed, lead to a research perspective at a tangent from the study of bureaucracy.

First the primary trends and outside forces that confront education are reviewed, then the way these external social changes affect the school and college. Next, a relatively new pattern of influences on educational decision-making and practice in the United States is specified in detail as illustration of the adaptation of organizations to social trends. Finally, a research perspective is presented that will help in understanding education in the modern world and at the same time contribute to theories of influence and organization. Both interorganizational analysis[1] and intraorganizational analysis are needed to comprehend the concert of action in American education. In any attempt to compare centralized and decentralized systems of action, it is necessary to understand the similarities and differences between influence within a bureaucracy and influence among bureaucracies, communication within the organization and communication between organizations, and initiative and innovation

Reprinted from "Interorganizational Patterns in Education," *Administrative Science Quarterly* 10 (September 1965): 225–37, by permission of vol. 10. © Johnson Graduate School of Management, Cornell University.

within an organization and parallel effort in a loosely joined federation or alliance or ad hoc confluence of interests.

Social Trends

The primary force of the economy on education lies in the increasing need for educational preparation and re-preparation for work.[2] One qualifies for work through education, and the threshold of qualification constantly rises as the bottom of the occupational structure sinks (decrease in unskilled jobs), the middle is upgraded in skills, and the top (professional and technical) expands rapidly. The organizations for formal instruction are charged with qualifying people for work and allocating them to an ever wider spectrum of job specialties. They thus come under heavy pressure to be continually oriented to the provision of expert labor. This pressure, already greatly expanded since 1945, is intensified by the emerging task of keeping men qualified to work through re-preparation, as a rapidly changing technology makes obsolescent old skills and jobs and new demands on competence. With this, education becomes more a part of the economic order than ever before. Seen as investment in human resources,[3] education is thereby increasingly viewed as part of both the local economy and the state economy, but particularly the national economy.

The pressures generated on education by the growing economic utility of the years spent in formal instruction are intensified by the growth in the general population and by the growing participation in education. A much enlarged school population results from a combination of high birth rate, which widens the population base, and high aspiration and high enrollment rate, which result in the school population more fully representing the base. Mass education is extending farther up the ladder of the school grades.[4]

The growing economic and demographic relevance of education contributes to a third major trend: the growth of political concern with education. If education is investment rather than consumption, if it is a major form of economic capital, then it must become a concern of those responsible for public policy. If there is growing involvement of the population in the schooling process, then, especially in democratic societies, education becomes a political issue on which parties and candidates can appeal to the electorate. The educational system is now probably the single most important issue in community government in the United States, and its importance as an issue in state government is growing rapidly. Most important, education has emerged as a national concern in the past fifteen years. Spokesmen for the national interest have come forth from many quarters. These include nationally visible individuals (e.g., James T. Conant, Admiral Rickover), major private foundations (Carnegie, Ford), established national associations (National Education Association, American Council on Education), and newly formed groups (Physical Science Study Committee, Council for Basic Education).

The national concern has its most potent form in the interest of the federal government in the outputs of education. The federal interest is, of course, actually an array of interests.[5] They have to do with manpower and unemployment, leadership and creativity, and urban and rural renewal, thus involving the Office of Education, which has a general mandate to serve education, the Department of Labor, and even the Bureau of the Budget. The critical interest is in the role of education in training men for work, with a particular focus on scientists and engineers for research and development. Here the National Science Foundation has a general mandate to strengthen science. The interest in scientists and engineers is sharply defined by diplomatic posture, military strength, and the missions, maintenance needs, and organizational character of the Department of Defense, together with the Atomic Energy Commission and the National Aeronautics and Space Agency. These interests that have emerged at the national level in the past twenty years are strong, central, permanent, and genuine. They are compelling enough to call forth attempts at national programs. Such programs must either be effected through the existing educational structure, by changing that structure, or bypassing it.

Economic, demographic, and political trends of the past two decades have, therefore, eliminated the economic and political irrelevance of education. No longer is education seen to have only long-run, indirect, and undifferentiated consequences, the effects subsumed under the global terms of cultural transmission and socialization of the young. Education is implicated in the training of experts for the labor force of a few years hence and is involved in present innovation efforts in research and development. It is a large and rapidly growing public expenditure in which the needs of allocation, coordination, and responsibility demand the attention of politicians and planners. It thereby becomes part of a larger order, that of political economy.

The Organizational Response

As modern social forces recast education as part of the economic and political institutions of society, numerous adjustments and adaptations are bound to occur within the single school system, in major segments of the educational system, and in the educational system as a whole. Examples of adjustments within the single educational organization are the adaptations of new technologies and the elaboration and professionalization of public relations, fundraising, and other boundary roles and activities. An adjustment among different units is the alliance of private colleges (Great Lakes Association, Associated Colleges of the Midwest, College Center of the Finger Lakes). The impulse here comes from the search for competitive advantage, particularly the need of small colleges to share expensive facilities and faculties and engage in joint fundraising as they compete with the large university, as well as with others of their size. This tendency to band together has in a few years proceeded sufficiently far that officials involved refer to it self-consciously as a movement.[6] The colleges that move toward confederation are attempting to solve organizational problems: how to grow and yet remain small; how to coordinate across a larger pool of activity while protecting unit autonomy.

No attempt is made here to catalogue the many adjustments. Instead, one major line of adjustment in the overall educational system is considered: the structure of influence and control. This has implications for educational administration and for research on organizations. The decentralized educational control in the United States has, through a long history, become tuned to the concerns of the individual school or college, the local community, and the separate state. What major changes can we discern in this decentralized control as it comes under increasingly heavy pressure to accommodate to modern social forces, particularly to the concerns that are national in scope and are defined by federal agencies and private national bodies?

There is some shift upward in the formal locus of educational decision-making, from the local to state level in public education, and from local and state to the national level in such programs as the National Defense Education Act of 1958. But much of the change taking place is in arrangements that lie in part outside the hierarchy of public offices. Indirect and subtle means of influence are being developed by many groups. The emerging patterns depend on voluntary relations among public agencies and private groups. In some degree, these arrangements serve as substitutes for or as alternatives to formal internal administration, i.e., to the national-state-local line of ministerial authority found in many countries. The patterns represent ways of influencing the grassroots level of operation in a field where no formal authority can impose cooperation.

One pattern is that of the private committee serving as connector between public authorities, notably between federal agencies and local authorities, as in the curriculum reform movement. The prototype was the work of the Physical Science Study Committee, the group of professors and secondary school science teachers under Professor Zacharias of MIT, who worked on changes in the instruction of high school physics.[7] The committee was financed by a federal agency, the National Science Foundation, and committees of the agency reviewed its work. The purpose of the committee was to improve the teaching of physical sciences in the secondary schools of the nation, which was considered inadequate at the time and was viewed as a national weakness.[8] The granting of funds for this purpose was well within the broad missions of the National Science Foundation, established by Congress in 1950, to strengthen basic research and education in the sciences. The first major component in the pattern of influence, then, was an agency in the executive branch of the federal government, whose breadth of mandate allowed initiation of influence without seeking legislative approval of specific formal programs. Private foundations also soon entered into the financial support of the curriculum reform group.

The committee to which the problem was delegated and the funds allotted was private and voluntary, having some of the attributes of an independent and impartial group of civic leaders. The committee set out to write a course for national school use, something that no federal agency could do directly because of probable congressional and popular opposition. Working at MIT away from the political arena, the committee in two years' time (1956–58), provided a "complex of schoolbooks, home-work assignments, laboratory guides, films, teacher's guides, laboratory apparatus, and classroom and college-entrance tests."[9]

The committee then saw to it that these materials would be actively promoted and made widely available throughout the nation by putting them into normal commercial channels. During the winter of 1959–60, the committee gave its printed materials to a schoolbook publisher, its new scientific equipment to a manufacturer of scientific apparatus, and its films to an education film distributor.[10] By these simple moves, the committee became an important mechanism of national influence. It had, in effect, made itself a research and innovation arm of the textbook in-dustry—more broadly, the course-materials industry—doing the research and development that the industry itself was not doing. No publisher has four and a half million dollars of venture capital (the cost of the physical science program) to develop the instructional materials for a course. The course-materials industry had been relatively passive, gearing innovation largely to market research and very little to research and development.[11] Thus, the commercial market itself provided little money and little im-pulse for improving courses. In the absence of national standards, where there are no nationwide governmental prescriptions about instructional materials, it is the national market for course materials that determines the quality of these materials.[12] The committee affected American educa-tion by changing what was available on the market, and, more important in the long run, by changing the passive relation of the course-materials industry to the market. The committee, incorporated as Educational Services, Inc. and broadened to include other disciplines in the sciences and social sciences (an important organizational phenomenon in itself), promises to revise its materials periodically and thus to remain an active, innovative arm of the industry. It is a national center of textbook revi-sion.

Teachers had to be taught how to use the new materials. The Na-tional Science Foundation initiated and supported a program of summer institutes that were voluntary throughout—for the colleges that offered them, the professors who directed and staffed them, and the teachers who came as students. The curriculum and the students of the institutes were made the responsibility of the individual colleges. The committee had to convince the directors of these institutes to use its materials. The directors were looking for the latest and best materials; they adopted the new materials and the institutes became part of the implementation of the new physics course. Finally, local educational authorities entered the pattern. They retained the formal choice as to whether to adopt the new materials, and their decision to enter was voluntary.

In summary, this pattern of influence was set in motion from the top, by a federal agency and a national private committee. The object was to affect general education practice, which was seen as a national weakness. The flow of influence was downward, through a chain of independent groups and organizations who found it in their interest to enter the alliance or compact. A federal agency provided the funds; a private nonprofit group received the money and developed a new course; commercial organizations made the new materials available to all units of the decentralized educational system; dispersed universities and colleges used the new materials to train teachers in all regions of the country; existing local authorities adopted the materials and allowed their teachers to reshape the local courses. In this pattern, decision-making was strongly influenced by the prestige of expertise. The National Science Foundation was expert and prestigeful; so also were the committee, the institutes, the teachers trained in the new materials. The very materials themselves traveled under the same aura.

Considering the voluntary character of the participation of each party, especially that of adoption by the local school district, the outcome of this pattern of influence is impressive. The new materials did not become available until after 1958; yet 40 to 50 percent of the students taking high school physics in 1963–64 and 1964–65 were studying the new materials.[13] Given the educational backwardness of some of the states, some of the rural areas, and some of the slums, it is doubtful if a national ministry with full authority over a national curriculum could have changed the study of physics more in the same period. The voluntaristic pattern has a major dysfunction in its present form, however, in that it undoubtedly increases the inequalities of education between the rich and the poor, and between the progressive and the backward school districts. The forward-looking districts will seek to adopt improved curricula, the backward will be less interested. The weakness suggests the remedy, a compensatory distribution of incentives to encourage and help the backward district to catch up.

Interorganizational Patterns

This pattern of influence, in which private groups serve as connectors between large public organizations and levels of government, is one that, with minor variations, is now widespread in the curriculum reform movement that is rapidly altering educational practice in the United States. (The secretariats of national academic organizations, such as the American Association for the Advancement of Science, are increasingly important agents in these relations.) The pattern is a way of concerting action without bureaucracy. It is one of a class of patterns whose growing importance points up the fact that unitary bureaucratic structure is just one way of consciously concerting action to achieve a goal.[14] These patterns, interorganizational in character, lie somewhat between the ways of concerting action that are commonly found within organizations, hence to be understood by a theory of formal organization; and the ways of concerting action that are commonly found in political arenas characterized by a formal decentralization of authority, and therefore to be understood by a theory of political influence, such as that which Edward Banfield has so brilliantly attempted to construct.[15] We need a theory of confederative organization or organizational alliance. Generalizations developed toward such a theory would reveal many points of contact and overlap in ideas about influence derived from the study of politics as well as from the study of internal administration. These interorganizational patterns converge with and become somewhat a part of political influence, in that they are the result of efforts to coordinate autonomous agencies, to unite effort *without* the authority of formal hierarchy and employee status. They are somewhat different in that they develop away from formal political arenas and often escape the constraints of political accountability. They move public policy away from the overt politician; in return, of course, some of their own members become covert public politicians.

One way to approach these new patterns is to think of them as in lieu of bureaucracy. This is a useful approach for comparative analysis of educational influence, since in some countries the study of influence in education must begin with the fact that there is a national organization of education with important elements of hierarchical and formal control from national ministries to the region, the community, and the individual school or college. In such countries, educational organization or educational administration or educational policy is related to this formal national system. This relationship is lacking in the United States, but an attempt is now being made to exert influence from the national center, and much of this influence flows outside bureaucratic channels.[16] It is fruitful to compare the patterns of influence among agencies with well-known features of bureaucratic organization, in each case suggesting the kind of relation between organizations in alliance that approximates the internal device.

AUTHORITY AND SUPERVISION

In a bureaucracy, authority and responsibility are delegated internally from position to position, from office to office, to handle problems effectively. In interorganizational patterns, where leverage of position is reduced, the handling of problems is less through formal structure, and more shared by specific agreement or presented by those who have responsibilities and problems but no rights of command to those who possess competence and such means of accomplishment as access to a necessary population. The shared or farmed-out responsibilities and problems are received by cooperating organizations that discover advantage in the relationship. Delegation is largely lateral rather than vertical and voluntary rather than mandatory. It is heavily adaptive to the technical authority of experts, even more than the new forms of lateral coordination developing within modern organizations to accommodate professionalism.

A corollary of the internal delegation of authority in bureaucracy is accountability up the line and supervision by those who occupy positions higher up the line. In the patterns that function in lieu of bureaucracy, a looser accountability and supervision is provided by a general agreement. Two or more independent organizations bind themselves together for a limited time and limited activities, often by the terms of a contract.[17] Then, in lieu of a superior official who commands and reviews, there are the legally enforceable stipulations of the contract.

In short, the sharing of problems, and hence of domains of work, under limited agreement is a counterpart to authority. It is an organizational invention, or rather an interorganizational invention, of no slight consequence for webs of organizations where authority is very decentralized.

STANDARDS OF WORK

In a bureaucracy, there is explication, formalization, and universal application of standards of work, from the administrators' code to the standards of the inspectors at the end of the production line. In interorganizational patterns, the setting of standards is less formal and more indirect. Standards-setting often takes the form of manipulating resources and incentives in a large market or economy of organizations. One device is to improve the quality of materials available on the market, through subsidized innovation, and then accord prestige for the use of the improved materials. Where the source of prestige behind the improved materials is very strong, as from leading scientists, foundations, or public officials, the prestige may be semi-commanding. A second device is to construct models of performance and encourage imitation, with prestige again a significant element of leverage.

PERSONNEL ASSIGNMENT

Within a bureaucratic organization, administrative performance is periodically reviewed and officials are replaced and reassigned to correct weaknesses in the organization. In interorganizational patterns, weak sectors are strengthened in other ways. The authority to reshuffle and replace men directly is lacking, but certain units of the alliance support weak sectors with resources they do possess—money and prestige. When officials in federal or private agencies thought they saw a national weakness in the curriculum of the secondary school, they were in no position to make changes in state and local personnel. They *were* in a position to use the leverage of money as well as the prestige of science to influence local authorities toward certain kinds of teachers and certain kinds of teaching materials.

RESEARCH AND DEVELOPMENT

In the modern organization, a research and development wing is often created to guarantee a flow of new ideas and innovations. In the patterns that are in lieu of bureaucracy, major agencies subsidize private innovative groups, contract for innovation, and then facilitate dissemination of the innovations to the field. Since this combination of subsidized research and dissemination of results is characteristic of many private foundations, this can be called "the foundation mechanism."

DECISION-MAKING

In a bureaucracy, solutions to problems take the form of deliberate decision. The organization assembles the elements of the problem, weighs the alternatives, and makes a purposeful or deliberate decision. In the patterns of influence that connect autonomous organizations, on the other hand, solutions to problems are less formally and consciously determined. The solutions approach is found in decentralized political systems, where the solution is a social choice, i.e., a resultant of the interaction of interested, autonomous organizations.[18] Influence exerted in a web of autonomous organizations often involves a decision that occurs in increments over time. In the pattern of curriculum reform, all the interested parties did not come together at one time. Their self-interest was not relevant at every stage. Different organizations were involved in the stages of creating new materials, retraining teachers, and adopting the new physics curriculum in the local school district. There was a rolling federation or alliance; the proposal for action was never a unified proposal but one composed of increments determined at different times; the decision resulted from the interaction of different parties at different stages.

These few sketchy parallels between bureaucratic and interorganizational patterns are sufficient to suggest one way of exploring the extensive area of social action, which lies outside of the formal organization and formal political arenas, but in which human effort is organized in quasi-formal or quasi-conscious ways by organizational agents. At least in education, social forces are greatly increasing the importance of this area that is not bounded by the kind of structures that have usually been designated as organizations. Leadership is moving into the interagency compact, the limited alliance, the consortium, the grants committee, the federation. Those who believe that the study of organizations is a valuable part of social inquiry need to extend their research perspectives so as to understand influence in interorganizational activity and comprehend the determinants of policy and practice among loosely joined organizations. To comprehend the shift to interorganizational administration and leadership would be to understand better the changing nature of administration inside the giant organization where large size and deepening expertise have fragmented command. Since many complex single organizations resemble the more structured interorganizations, there is no sharp line between the conceptions appropriate to such formal organizations and those necessary to the interorganizational scene.

Notes

1. On interorganizational analysis, see Sol Levine and Paul E. White, "Exchange and Interorganizational Relationships," *Administrative Science Quarterly* 5 (1961): 583–601; Eugene Litwak and Lydia F. Hylton, "Interorganizational Analysis," *Administrative Science Quarterly* 6 (1962): 395–420; James D. Thompson and William J. McEwen, "Organizational Goals and Environment," *American Sociological Review* 23 (1958): 23–31.

2. A. H. Halsey, Jean Floud, and C. Arnold Anderson, eds., *Education, Economy, and Society* (New York: Free Press, 1961): pts. I and II; Burton R. Clark, *Educating the Expert Society* (San Francisco: Chandler, 1962), chap. 2.

3. See special issue on "Investment in Human Beings," *Journal of Political Economy* 70 (October 1962).

4. Martin Trow, "The Democratization of Higher Education in the United States," *European Journal of Sociology* 3 (1962): 231–62.

5. Homer D. Babbidge Jr. and Robert M. Rozenzwieg, *The Federal Interest in Higher Education* (New York: McGraw-Hill, 1962); Charles V. Kidd, *American Universities and Federal Research* (Cambridge, Mass.: Harvard University Press, 1959).

6. John J. Wittich, ed., *College and University Interinstitutional Co-operation* (Corning, N.Y.: College Center of the Finger Lakes, 1962).

7. Paul E. Marsh and Ross A. Gortner, *Federal Aid to Science Education: Two Programs* (Syracuse: Syracuse University Press, 1962); Roald F. Campbell and Robert A. Bunnell, eds., *Nationalizing Influence on Secondary Education* (Chicago: Midwest Administration Center, University of Chicago, 1963); *Innovation and Experiment in Education* (Washington, D.C.: U.S. Government Printing Office, 1964); John I. Goodlad, *School Curriculum Reform in the United States* (New York: Fund for the Advancement of Education, 1964); Matthew B. Miles, ed., *Innovation in Education* (New York: Teachers College, Columbia University, 1964), especially chap. 10; Paul E. Marsh, "Wellsprings of Strategy: Considerations Affecting Innovations by the PSSC."

8. March and Gortner, *Federal Aid to Science Education,* chap. 10.

9. Ibid., 30.

10. Ibid., 63.

11. Ibid., 9–14.

12. Ibid., 14.

13. Goodlad, *School Curriculum Reform,* 24; *Educational Services Incorporated: A Review of Current Progress, 1965* (Watertown, Mass., 1965), 5.

14. Edward C. Banfield, *Political Influence* (New York: Free Press, 1961), *passim,* particularly chap. 11.

15. Ibid.

16. It has been argued that the United States already has a national educational system because of the extensive linkage provided by "ancillary structures." See Sloan R. Wayland, "Structural Features of American Education as Basic Factors in Innovation," in Miles, *Innovation in Education,* chap. 13.

17. On "federalism by contract," see Don K. Price, *Government and Science* (New York: Oxford University Press, 1962), chap. 3.

18. Banfield, *Political Influence,* 326–27.

INTRODUCTION TO CHAPTER 10

It is hard to convey to those who did not directly experience the militant actions of some students in the last half of the 1960s and early 1970s the intensity of emotional engagement, pro and con, that deeply affected colleges and universities in the United States. What would cause students to set fires in university libraries or place a bomb in a science building? What would cause administrators and outside politicians to turn National Guard troops loose on campuses to sweep students with bayonets drawn and to toss tear gas into academic buildings?

Arguably, the best scholarly attempt to capture the turbulent scene was *Academic Transformation: Seventeen Institutions Under Pressure,* (1973), edited by David Riesman and Verne A. Stadtman. Supported by the Carnegie Commission at the time, individual, knowledgeable participant-observers were commissioned to write articles. Funds were also allocated for further research and writing, and the resulting essays were sensitively put together and edited.

I was on the Yale faculty at the time and was asked to analyze the upheaval at Wesleyan University, a small traditional New England college about thirty-five miles away. I could easily commute between New Haven and Middletown for interviews, observation, and document analysis. Wesleyan was reeling from considerable turmoil over the actions of black militants on campus. What events had occurred? What had been the reactions of administrators, faculty, and students? Was the same thing happening elsewhere?

I included in my comparative framework the University of Wisconsin, where a bomb killed a graduate student, the University of California, Berkeley, and San Francisco State College, each of which experienced conflict among students and campus administrators sustained over many years; this dissension, among other outcomes, left faculty in some departments so bitterly split they would not speak to one another for years. I personally witnessed at Berkeley the intrusive role not only of student militants with a fondness for destruction, but also the reaction of National Guard troops armed with bayonets and tear gas.

The Wesleyan community, however, was able to bring about a more integrative outcome. They solved many problems by focusing on commitment to the university's traditions by the faculty and students in this old liberal arts college. In other words, their "moral capital" saw them through an ugly predicament.

This essay, highlighted by the concept of "moral capital," was the story I composed.

CHAPTER 10

The Wesleyan Story:
The Importance of Moral Capital

THE WESLEYAN UNIVERSITY of 1972 is a small place of complex character. A settled institution of ivy heritage and New England tradition, it changed sufficiently in the years after World War II that it is now widely considered progressive as well as stable, of first-rank academic quality as well as of solid virtue. Quiet self-alteration has made the college seem unproblematic throughout nearly all the recent years, not exciting but noteworthy as a model of how to adapt gently in an evermore turbulent environment.

In 1969, the college became front-page news as a small campus in serious trouble, with a stream of articles and accounts telling of militant black students clashing with whites, and how the campus was thrown into turmoil by demands, sit-ins, fights, and fires. Whispers could be heard in college administrators' circles "the Wesleyan problem." Had the college gone too far too fast in admitting blacks? Had it been too permissive in facing strident student demands? Had Wesleyan stumbled into crisis? Were there any lessons to be learned from its experience?

In order to interpret specific events and changes, we must, even in a brief essay, attend seriously to the historical development and the resulting identity of the college. Recent happenings can then be seen in context, assigned meaning—as they are by the knowledgeable actors in the situation—in relation to the flow and style of the institution. The context of events at Wesleyan is one where the advantages of substantial conventional capital, in the form of high income and competent staff, have

"The Wesleyan Story: The Importance of Moral Capital," in *Academic Transformation: Seventeen Institutions Under Pressure,* edited by David Riesman and Verne A. Stadtman, 367–81. New York: McGraw-Hill, 1973. Used by permission of the Carnegie Commission on Higher Education.

been joined by the advantages of moral capital, an accumulated strong self-belief formed around a legacy of moral understanding. To trace the development of these dominant features, we begin with a glance at Wesleyan's earlier history and then portray the critical change in the character of the institution in the last quarter-century.

The Historical Roots

In the distant retrospect of a later century, there was little that was unusual about Wesleyan University in its early years, for foremost were the practices and rhetoric of the search for survival so common among the private small colleges of the United States. Begun in 1831 by a group of Methodist clergymen full of determination but lacking in money, the college survived repeated financial and administrative crises while struggling to find an identity that would offer some security. Forced to muddle through for decades, the college stubbornly refused to die. Time and again at Wesleyan as during the depression of the 1870s (Peterson, 1964, 58–59), a small number of committed faculty, trustees, and churchmen rooted themselves in a logic of sentiments, keeping open an organization that any economic calculus would have sent to the grave. Their style involved a rhetoric of sacrifice: "the work of the college has been confined by the narrowness of its means"; we have been "neglected and forgotten by the church"; "[the] heroic professors [have] been submitted to personal sacrifices"; and "among the faithful and self-sacrificing friends of this institution, when it was poor and hungry and weak, must be recorded the honorable names of . . ." (*Semi-Centennial* . . . , 1881, 14, 17, 19). The early Wesleyan style also involved the common religious college dilemma of autonomy and dependence, in relation to the formal church of the parent denomination. At times the college drifted away from the church, as administrators sought self-determination, the faculty greater freedom in teaching, or the students more fun and games. At other times the college moved toward the church, to reassert religious values, obtain more money, or strengthen the traditional constituency.

In the early Wesleyan, the elders were also fond of preaching to the young, from the set lectures of the fixed curriculum to the discourse to the graduating class on *Early Piety: The Basis of Elevated Character* (Olin, 1851). The intent to elevate character within a closely guarded community generated a counterforce that Wesleyan shared with other colleges: the students revolted from time to time. Under a severely paternalistic president known for his "correct views," who was bound "to do my duty" (Peterson, 1964, 115), Wesleyan in the 1880s was a center of smoldering resentment that erupted finally, in 1887, when a day set aside for student hell-raising got out of hand and events escalated into a mass egging of the president (117).

Wesleyan also underwent the general evolution of the time. By the turn of the century, one could speak of Wesleyan and the other surviving New England colleges—after the changes of the 1870s, 1880s, and 1890s—as having modified greatly their control and atmosphere. Wesleyan's faculty had moved toward the concept of academic freedom made popular in the new universities of the American scene. The students had moved toward freedom in the classroom under the elective system and toward more control of their lives outside the classroom in the subculture of sports and fraternities. All the basic features of the New England college were there, with an occasional idiosyncracy such as the move into coeducation in 1872, a deviation corrected when the college returned in 1912 to the maleness of Amherst, Williams, and Bowdoin.

And so it went in the early decades of the twentieth century. The college was a solid WASP institution that occupied a respectable place in the little-Ivy triad along with Amherst and Williams. Moderation and tradition were the names of the place. The religious commitment eased toward a respectable nonsectarianism. Standards were stiffened gradually but never too severely. Although a university in name, the institution remained a liberal arts college that concentrated on undergraduate education. The student body grew from about three-hundred in 1910 to seven-hundred in 1940. Student life centered in residential fraternities. Either boy met girl at the weekend mixer for which the girls were imported from women's colleges, or the men traveled to where the girls were. There were no deep financial crises, no faculty upheavals, no abrupt transformations, no major unique efforts.

Clearly, just before World War II Wesleyan was a college with a defined social role that had evolved slowly over decades, with no distinctive thrust. Its evolved role, however, was no mean asset. Interpreted in the light of later development, the college had established a base camp solid in the aura of tradition and the loyalty of established alumni. The tradition included moral uplift in the character of the young, a generalized theme upon which a man with a mission, one incorporating old-fashioned virtues, could resonate a special effort to climb higher in both quality and morality. After the war came the shift to mission, with purpose first sharpened and more strongly defined from within, then embodied in new practices and structures, and finally felt as a spirit on the campus.

The Aims and Means of Change

Major change in the college was engineered during a presidency that spanned nearly a quarter of a century, from 1943 to 1966—that of Victor Butterfield. Butterfield had vision and the capacity to persist in the hard work of implementing it. He also happened upon several conditions that greatly facilitated the work of institutional change.

Butterfield based himself in tradition by stressing that the college would remain small, independent, and nonsectarian. On that foundation, he mounted an effort to seek "distinction for quality" and suggested that there be no compromise with this principle (Butterfield, 1955, 1). At the same time, however, Butterfield wanted an institution of great moral concern, one rooted deeply in a Christian humanism. A liberal college should have "faith," he persistently maintained, faith based on intellectual understanding and expressed, not through exhortation, evangelical appeal, or compulsion, but rather through the personal example of men of "full and coherent conviction . . . willing to share their insights and opinions" or men who, feeling that their most cherished values are highly personal and private, will simply "let their light so shine" (11). A sufficient number of such people would mean a "working spirit" of the whole that would be "by all odds the most important method of keeping the Christian tradition alive and vital and of giving it concrete and perpetually renewed meaning" (12). Butterfield's aims, then, were a combination of high academic quality and modernized Christian tradition.

Among the means of achieving these aims, the most important in Butterfield's view was the recruitment and retention of appropriate faculty. The faculty should be a heady mixture of academic talent and moral concern, characteristics that seemed increasingly antithetical within academic circles. The ideal faculty member would be both a ranking scholar and a saint among men. Fully aware that faculty selection was the main tool of institutional change, Butterfield kept himself deeply involved in recruitment. Right up to near the end of his term, long past the time when a man of lesser commitment would have retired to quieter activity in his office, Butterfield was still on the road looking for faculty or interviewing candidates on their visits to the departments and divisions of the college. His efforts became legendary, told in stories of how he wined and dined and talked the evening through with a scholar, encountered by design or chance anywhere in his travels, whose character and intellect seemed to him appropriate for the mission of the college.

Butterfield was fortunate, particularly in his early years in office, that many faculty openings occurred through retirement, wartime turnover, and institutional expansion. The men he recruited were often so impressive that they could not all be retained against the lure of an important university professorship or an inviting career in academic administration. A young Nathan Pusey was already on the scene in classics and was put to work shaping a freshman humanities program. David C. McClelland was brought into the psychology department in 1945, and the following year saw the arrival of Norman O. Brown in classics, Carl E. Schorske in history, and Steven K. Bailey in government—the latter to join two nationally known political scientists, Sigmund Neumann and E. E. Schattschneider, already on the faculty. Such appointments were evidence enough that Butterfield had a sharp eye for academic talent, men of high intellect and moral concern who could share in some degree his vision of what Wesleyan could become. The degree to which the faculty quickly became a Butterfield-selected group, quantitatively, was also impressive. One observer has calculated that "by the postwar period [about 1950] he had brought in fifty-four [72 percent] of the seventy-five members of the faculty" (Hefferlin, 1969, 48). In the later years of his term, the faculty was almost entirely composed of men added during his presidency.

The considerable enlargement of the faculty was made possible by a vast increase in financial resources. Here the story approaches by the unbelievable, as several trustees responsible for investment policy struck gold several times over. The purchase of an educational publishing firm that produced the *Weekly Reader*, read by millions of schoolchildren, proved so enormously profitable that good taste, invading competition, and the concern of the Internal Revenue Service over the nonprofit status of the college dictated a move to other investments. So the trustees sold the firm at great profit to Xerox Corporation, accepting in exchange Xerox stock that promptly took off on a success story of its own. The result of this and a few other bonanzas was that Wesleyan became, on a per capita basis, the richest college in the land. In 1962, its endowment was about $60 million, compared with about $30 million at Swarthmore—a well-financed college—and $5.5 million at poverty-stricken Reed. By 1966, its endowment had climbed to over $150 million, a truly fantastic sum for a small college. The institution had little difficulty in paying competitive salaries and financing expensive experiments as well as general expansion. It can even be said that for a few years the college had too much money.

The money and the faculty gave Butterfield and his senior colleagues the means of supporting and staffing a number of new programs and special units, among them a broad humanities course required of all freshmen, a Public Affairs Center (1955) incorporating within it the social science departments, and a Center for Advanced Studies (1959) that appointed visiting scholars and men of affairs (Herbert Read, C. P. Show, Daniel Patrick Moynihan, Richard Goodwin) and later became a Center for the Humanities. Departments grew in size and competence; some could even effectively staff graduate programs through the PhD. The campus experimented with subcolleges; in 1960 it had one in letters, one in social studies, and one in quantitative studies.

As at other colleges, the traditions of student life were stubborn and difficult to overcome. As late as 1955, the faculty felt that the fraternity system was "the most important single non-curricular force on the campus in the formation and development of student values" and were concerned that the fraternities remained anti-intellectual (*Report of the Educational Policy Committee . . .*, 1955, 61–62). But slowly student life swung toward the academic and the intellectual, even in the late 1960s toward the radical and the nonconforming. Membership in fraternities declined from about 85 percent of the student body in 1955 to about 35 percent in 1970. With students perceiving the fraternities as "an archaic, dying, and confining institution" and the college offering attractive alternative housing, the number of surviving frats declined from eleven to seven between 1968 and 1970 (Surgeon, 1970, 74). The students were coming predominantly (70 percent) from public high schools, and as the college became known as a liberal institution, even the students drawn from prep schools were more likely to be liberal or radical than conservative. In a survey of the class of 1972, only one in five would define himself politically as a conservative, while three in five held the campus middle ground as liberal, and one in five saw himself as radical (4–6, 43–45).

If the beginning of the Butterfield era was a move from passive role to active mission, the middle years were a time of embodiment of mission in structure, practice, and belief. There had been a particular leader, a special effort, a set of new practices, and, finally, what seemed to be a unified institutional character in which men believed deeply. There was a modest organizational saga, a story of special accomplishment that was rooted in historical fact but also romanticized into a sentimental belief.[1] There was a rhetoric of normative concern that mixed with a rhetoric of innovation. There was special meaning given to such terms as *liberal arts university* and *the little university* and a belief that Wesleyan, a small college, would experimentally and innovatively grow toward the commitments of a first-rate university but always with small scale, the liberal arts, and moral concern as primary values. Already in the early 1960s, one of the best historians of American higher education was describing Wesleyan as "moving toward a new integration of collegiate and university purpose" (Rudolph, 1962, 492).

The distinctive air of deep normative concern coupled with an attitude of innovation resonated well with the perspective of the Danforth Foundation, where the same sentiment of needed reform in American education, based on a Christian humanism, had taken philanthropic roots. Butterfield became a key figure in Danforth affairs; Kenneth Underwood, who Butterfield brought in as professor of social ethics and public affairs and later made head of the Center for Public Affairs, was for years closely connected with the Danforth group; and others on campus have been participants in Danforth seminars or have received Danforth awards for excellence in teaching. The convergence of values here between a college and a value-focused foundation was as natural as it was considerable. In the language of academic clichés, Danforthites set the moral tone of Wesleyan and were "swinging religionists" committed to reform and willing to work in reform efforts with completely secular men. Perhaps the most visible agent of this spirit in the late 1960s was John Maguire in religion, a man of charismatic tendency who left in 1970, taking a small cadre of faculty and recent graduates with him, to head up the troubled, experimental Old Westbury.

In the 1960s, Wesleyan contained a definite strain between well-round amateurism and professional competence, a tension that can be observed everywhere among the liberal arts colleges that have continued to take seriously the traditional view of liberal education as general and interdisciplinary in nature while at the same time attempting to meet the interest of faculty and students in competence in the specialized disciplines. Wesleyan's strong embodiment of a generalized moral concern, on the traditional side, and its upgrading to university-level scholarship, on the side of modern specialization, has ensured that the tension would be real. The high-caliber scholars whom Butterfield and his associates brought to the campus were not all perfectly balanced on the twin commitments of scholarship and morality. Predictably, prestigious faculty members would more often tilt toward the values of scholarship than toward those of general education and service to one's fellow man, and these sharp, high-priced people pressed to bring in men of their own type in making junior appointments from top graduate schools. Such men rejected the strand of Butterfield's thought that equated liberal arts with non-specialization and became impatient with both the latter-day Christian humanists and the traditional "Mr. Chips types" in the faculty who, full of warm sentiment about "little Wesleyan," held to undergraduate liberal education to the detriment of scholarly competence. The specialist-scholars, pushing beyond Butterfield's dream, generated a move in the 1960s to evolve from "the Academy to the University" ("The New University," 1961).

All was not sweetness and light, of course, since institutional tension, in practice, spells prolonged argument and even steady anger over the other man's foolish views. The spending of all that money in new centers and various experimental structures caused some friction and had some fracturing effect on unity. Then, too, the president had almost inevitably worn himself out, and in his final years in office others had to steady the college. Some toll was there, paid in the energies of men and in the coherence and dynamism of the institution.

But even within the ranks of the specialists, who at many universities are the non-loyal cosmopolitans ready to exit for the better offer, there were men devoted to the welfare of others and, convinced that Wesleyan had great if not unmatched virtues, were completely committed to the institution; e.g., Robert A. Rosenbaum, who had served for years in top administrative positions, Earl D. Hanson in biology, and William J. Barber in economics. Compared with other colleges and universities, many men were paid well in the coin of belief and morality as well as in that of salary and academic status. It was in this relatively healthy condition that the college moved into the special days of the late 1960s.

The Crisis of 1968–1970

In 1965, Wesleyan committed itself to admitting black students. In 1965–66, the admissions procedure brought in a small number of blacks, a group that suffered high attrition in the freshman year. An exceedingly vigorous effort under Jack Hoy, the director of admissions, brought a large jump during the next several years, to the point where, in 1969–70, blacks and Puerto Ricans numbered about 20 percent of the freshman class and 12 percent of the total student body of 1,400. This effort, in a small private college, was considerably in excess of what was occurring at the time in even many urban public colleges and universities, let alone in private institutions. For example, the Wesleyan enrollment of blacks alone in 1969–70 was about 10 percent, compared to 5 percent or less at Berkeley and Buffalo as well as at Columbia, Harvard, and Yale. Clearly, some internal adjustments would be necessary, perhaps some special tutoring for those blacks who were underschooled, but in the beginning there was little to draw upon by way of relevant experience at other colleges and hence adjustments had to be worked out as emerging problems revealed the failures of anticipation. At the same time, black students throughout the country were moving to militancy, with black separatism much on their minds.

In 1968–69, Wesleyan broke out with a rash of trouble. Black students were hearing racist slurs that they were no longer willing to dismiss as the highjinks of upper-class party boys in a few fraternities or as the hopeless stupidities of ultraconservatives in the town. Some were frustrated and angered by the problems set by inadequate scholastic preparation and by the misunderstanding generated by the linguistic and other cultural differences that separate lower-class blacks from upper-middle-class whites. The black students began, with an outspoken statement in the fall term to react collectively to personal and institutional "insensitivities," the latter including the absence of adult blacks on campus. A few months later, they moved to a specific demand that classes be cancelled for a day of education on Malcolm X and Martin Luther King; and, when the faculty voted a refusal, the black students orderly occupied for one day the main classroom building. The students proceeded during the spring term with more specific demands in which the central issue was the establishment of an Afro-American Institute that would help to bring black visitors to campus and to infuse black faculty into the normal departments. In the fall of the following year (1969–70), the troubles escalated in the form of specific and dramatic acts of violence and illegal activity: after a fight, the room of a white student was set on fire; shots were fired at a black administrator; many burglaries were occurring in the dormitories, and several blacks were arrested for armed robbery in the town. At one point, on the occasion of a homecoming weekend, the administration obtained an injunction against disruption by the blacks, a move that helped the college get peacefully through the weekend but, by stirring further resentment, helped cause continuing problems. The college now had significantly gotten the attention of the mass media and had gained national reputation as a college in trouble, signified notably by a long article in the Sunday magazine section of the *New York Times,* entitled "The Two Nations at Wesleyan University" (Margolis, 1970). The *Times* article, sure to excite alumni, donors, and parents of current and prospective students, spoke of white anger and fears, of increasing suspicion on both sides, and concluded on the note that "white students and black students do not even talk to each other" (64). When white and black students together wrote a letter objecting to the article, the *Times* reporter replied that they were wrong and that "the racial polarization at Wesleyan is genuine and runs very deep" (*New York Times Magazine,* 1970).

During the same period, white radicalism had also heated up, centered in 1968–69 on student demands that military recruiters be barred from campus. Out of the growing concern about the Vietnam War, some white students developed a confrontation with a navy recruiter. A joint faculty-student committee was set to work on the issue and came up with a quick report, complete with majority and minority recommendations. The faculty thereupon voted that Wesleyan should not bar any recruiters from campus; the students muddied the waters with a vote, on three alternatives, that was subject to varying interpretation. The faculty position prevailed, but the issue lingered.

Then in the spring of 1969–70, the concerns of white students and black students came together in the three issues of Cambodia, Kent State, and the New Haven trial of Bobby Seale and other Black Panthers, and the campus took part in the strike action of students that stretched from coast to coast. In the fall of 1970–71, the campus returned to a peaceful state, punctured once by an isolated bombing of a campus building, and it remained that way throughout the academic year.

Before and during the months of trouble, the campus had been working on various adjustments. Under sponsorship of the blacks, the college instituted a back repertory theater and a black arts festival as well as two courses in black history and culture. In the course of several years, more than twenty blacks were appointed to the faculty and a black associate provost was added to the administration. In response to the demands of early 1969, an Afro-American Institute was established and a historic John Wesley House was converted into a Malcolm X House. The college for several summers sent some blacks to compensatory education programs at other colleges, and when this effort seemed not to work, the campus turned to voluntary tutorials staffed by upperclassmen and teachers for anyone requesting help. Coursework could be spread out over five years. Perhaps most important was that in such a small college black students came to know with whom they could and could not work, person by person in the faculty, administration, and student body. As initial institutional naiveté was replaced by the hard realities of implementing a change, specific programs and specific individuals broke through what the blacks had seen as a solid structure of institutional racism. One could even make a case, as it has been made at the college, that the basic changes in structure and relationship were well under way by 1969–70, when, in several months of bad luck, a number of isolated incidents involving a few individuals snowballed into heightened group tension.

The trouble and strain were certainly enough to make the most dedicated supporters of the heavy admission of minorities doubt at times that the college had moved wisely in this effort. The resisters had much to point to in complaining that academic standards were eroding at a pace commensurate with the decline in law and order and sanctioned their general complaint with specific labeling of some departments as "gut departments for blacks." But the supporters would not retreat. Here interpersonal ties and regard for the institution had a part. Men of quite different persuasion on the specific issue were not only equally committed to the general institution welfare but also equally committed to be fair to one another and to the individual student. There were outstanding examples of personal caring, as when a faculty member quietly took out a mortgage on his house to bail out of jail a student whose values were completely antithetical to his own. The college held its basic unity and continued the effort to work out the necessary new adjustment.

Meeting the demands of blacks and coping with the wishes of white radicals were not the only items on the institutional agenda in the late 1960s. There was also a major self-study centered on other issues and some administrative reorganization. Upon Butterfield's retirement, Edwin D. Etherington was lured from the presidency of the New York Stock Exchange to become head of the college, and he immediately initiated a policy study. The study committee took up women's education and recommended the addition of undergraduate women. It also took up graduate education and the roles of the Public Affairs Center and the Center for Advanced Studies and recommended that the college proceed carefully into additional graduate programs, that the Center for Public Affairs be rejuvenated as a center for multidisciplinary work in the social sciences, and that the Center for Advanced Studies be replaced by a Center for the Humanities. The advanced learning programs, even when leading to the PhD, were to be interdisciplinary as much as possible, and the two interdisciplinary centers were to revolve around faculty and students rather than visiting fellows. The study group also examined the college's efforts in teacher education and recommended changes oriented to urban schools and community colleges.

Efforts to implement these recommendations began in 1968–69. On undergraduate education for women, the college accepted transfer students in 1968–69 and in 1969–70 and began admitting women as freshmen in 1970–71, toward the goal of having, by 1974, 700 women in a student body of 1,700. A woman was appointed as an associate provost. In advanced training, history and psychology became defined as the departments headed next for PhD programs, beyond the five (biology, chemistry, mathematics, physics, and world music) already there, and the new Humanities Center came into being. Teacher education was reconstituted as proposed.

Under Etherington, the college made several changes in structure and procedure designed to improve communication and make administration more effective at three levels. A student-faculty senate was created with legislative and advisory powers. The central administration was reshaped to give the president more time for long-run planning, changing the direct involvement of his office in many campus affairs that had been a hallmark of Butterfield's personal style. At the level of the board of trustees, the college added faculty members and students to trustee committees, and blacks, women, and younger alumni to the board itself. "Participatory governance" was clearly making some headway at Wesleyan.

In February 1970, Etherington resigned to run for political office. The chancellor, Robert Rosenbaum, filled in as acting president for a few months, and then Colin Campbell, who had come to the college with Etherington as executive vice president, was selected as the next president. Young and vigorous, tested on the firing line during the days and nights of tension, Campbell has won widespread respect and support on the campus.

As Campbell began his presidency in 1970–71, the view was growing that Wesleyan was overextended. The effort to implement the commitment to the education of blacks, with its attendant strains, together with the various other efforts reviewed above finally seemed too much at one time, especially as the financial problems of colleges hit even Wesleyan. The strains of 1968–70 thus led the college toward a hard look at priorities. Out of that examination, by the spring of 1971, there was forthcoming an unambiguous reassertion of the primacy of undergraduate liberal education. In the language of the new president: "we have faced the obligation to make hard choices in order to preserve our future"; "in reexamining the purposes for which Wesleyan stands, we have seen with renewed clarity the centrality of our commitment to excellence in undergraduate education"; "we must hone and harden our innovations to survive in a world of realities, a world of limited resources which we, no less than others, ourselves inhabit"; "survival at Wesleyan must continue to mean survival to innovate and excel" (*Remarks* . . . , 1971). The president went on to openly rank programs according to their importance to the undergraduate curriculum, giving first priority to core undergraduate programs and financial aid for undergraduates, the latter notably to support substantial numbers of minority-group students. He assigned second rank to the existing advanced work in some departments and the interdisciplinary Humanities Center; and he offered lowest priority to certain activities that "we do not view as central or significantly in support of undergraduate education here," e.g., the Wesleyan Press and the master of arts in teaching program (5–6). The press was put under review, the MAT program began a phasing out. A number of major decisions was yet on the agenda, the president added, but he concluded that "in the end the University will be leaner, stronger, healthier and better focused on its primary objectives as the result of today's challenges" (6).

The Importance of Moral Capital

Wesleyan is witness to the value of moral capital in a college. It underwent considerable stress in its days of trouble, paying a fair price for its rapid affirmative action in admitting blacks and the pulling and hauling that followed as one unforeseen change after another in internal structure and procedure was debated and then effected. The price paid would have been much higher, however, if the context had been one, observable elsewhere, in which interpersonal trust and institutional belief were in short supply. Under those conditions, campus conflict can all too readily exhaust the meager fund of trust and overwhelm frail belief in the goodness of the place. The result is a plunge below the threshold of goodwill and affirmative belief, setting in motion the vicious circle of suspiciousness and recrimination that polarizes a campus. In contrast, Wesleyan's character offered reserves that could be spent in a crisis to recover from deep stress before the dynamics of the vicious circle set in. As is evident elsewhere, a college that strongly believes in itself can withstand stresses, shocks, and even shortages of resources and carry on so effectively that it is widely heralded as a success.[2] Wesleyan is a notable instance of self-belief within which the personal morality of many on campus interlocks with an institutional morality. In the 1968–70 crisis the college had to draw critically on its moral accounts rather than its budgetary ones. Since those funds were considerable, the odds on recovery from the injuries of stress were high. Hence many at the college could not only believe in

1971 that the action on minorities was morally right and the troubles worth it but also feel that the institution was in good health and not vulnerable to repeated strain.

The effects of institutional crisis, then, are determined considerably by the institution's character as it enters into a period of stress. Perhaps what is true for individuals is true for institutions: a crisis, even severe illness, is not always a bad thing. The outcome depends upon the reserves of character and the predispositions that determine the capacity to cope. In the character and the coping of the institution we will find structure and procedure playing a part. But organizations of higher education are much dependant on normative rather than utilitarian or coercive bonds and we must also look to the role of ideas and values. The Wesleyan experience suggests the fascinating possibility that belief and concern remain the core of the healthy institution of higher learning.

Notes

1. On the buildup of sagas in college, see Clark (1970).
2. See the sections on Antioch and Reed in Clark (1970).

References

Butterfield, Victor L. *The Faith of a Liberal College*. President's annual report to the board of trustees, Wesleyan University, Middletown, Conn., 1955.

Clark, Burton R. *The Distinctive College: Antioch, Reed and Swarthmore*. Chicago: Aldine Publishing Company, 1970.

Hefferlin, J. B. Lon. *Dynamics of Academic Reform*. San Francisco: Jossey-Bass, 1969.

Margolis, Richard J. "The Two Nations at Wesleyan University." *New York Times*, January 18, 1970.

"The New University." Statement prepared by a group of Wesleyan faculty members, February 18, 1961.

New York Times, March 8, 1970.

Olin, Stephen. *Early Piety: The Basis of Elevated Character*, a discourse to the graduating class of Wesleyan University, August 1850. New York: Lane & Scott, 1851.

Peterson, George E. *The New England College in the Age of the University*. Amherst, Mass.: Amherst College Press, 1964.

Remarks by Colin C. Campbell, President, Wesleyan University, alumni luncheon, June 5, 1971. (Mimeographed.)

Report of the Educational Policy Committee to the Faculty of Wesleyan University, Wesleyan University, Middletown, Conn., 1955.

Rudolph, Frederick. *The American College and University*. New York: Alfred A. Knopf, 1962.

Semi-Centennial of Wesleyan University, 1881. (No publisher indicated.)

Surgeon, George P. *Political Attitudes at Wesleyan*. Unpublished student paper, December 1970. (Mimeographed.)

INTRODUCTION TO CHAPTER 11

I became interested in 1973 in the early evolution of a small new specialty that could be called the sociology of higher education, and I decided to write an article about it. I diligently reviewed the classics, from Max Weber through Thorstein Veblen to Logan Wilson's dissertation on academic man in 1942. I codified four energizing lines of research; I even estimated the future of research in this emerging field and passed down some lofty comments on massive trivialization and journalistic playfulness. I sought the high ground in praise of Durkheim. Looking back, I thought I had made some good points, even if it now seems somewhat pompous.

Well, it turns out that my early statement has achieved the standing of "foundational article" in a large 2007 collection. The volume contains a dozen reviews of many expanded subfields in the sociology of higher education. It is edited by Patricia J. Gumport, professor of higher education and vice provost for graduate education at Stanford University, and longtime contributor to volumes appearing on the Johns Hopkins University Press higher education list. The publication does me honor. When Gumport asked me if I wanted to add a comment in a concluding section, I responded with a brief note in chapter 11 to insist once more that researchers usefully converge on practitioner knowledge by searching for context-based patterns of action. Only time will show the lasting explanatory power of this point of view. But, without doubt, the Gumport collection is a major step forward in advancing a sociology of higher education.

CHAPTER 11

Development of the Sociology of Higher Education

A SOCIOLOGY OF higher education has emerged in the quarter-century since World War II. It is now a field with several important streams of interest: the two major foci of educational inequality beyond the secondary level and the social-psychological effects of college on students, and smaller literatures on the academic profession and governance and organization. In the 1970s, some parts of the field face the danger of expensive trivialization, others of substituting playful journalism for scholarly discipline. Encouraging prospects for the near future include more extensive development of comparative studies and analyses with historical depth. A useful additional step would be to counter the dominant instrumental definitions of education with approaches that center on the values, traditions, and identities—the expressive components—of educational social systems.

My purposes here are to review the development to date of the sociological study of higher education and, upon that base, to assess the strengths and weaknesses of current research and to point to the prospects for the future. The review is selective and the assessment biased by personal perception and preference. I would like to err in being open and catholic, since there are so many ways that sociological study of colleges and universities can render us more sensitive in coping with immediate problems as well as contribute to theory and method in sociology. But, in a limited essay, it is necessary to categorize roughly the work of the past and to highlight the more salient work. It is also realistic to face the fact

"Development of the Sociology of Higher Education," *Sociology of Education* 46 (Winter 1973): 2–14. Reprinted in Patricia J. Gumport, ed., *Sociology of Higher Education: Contributions and Their Contexts*. Baltimore: Johns Hopkins University Press, 2007.

169

of limited talent and resources as we turn to the future and to emphasize one or two perspectives that might best correct the defects of our current efforts.

The Past and the Present

The emergence and the substantial growth of a sociology of higher education have followed from the extensive educational expansion of the period since the end of World War II, especially that of the past decade, in semi-developed and developed nations around the world. The higher learning became problematic to social analysts as it became more important to the general population as well as to economic and governmental elites. The move toward mass participation in higher education has strained the traditional internal ordering of educational affairs. New demands have caused great problems of adapting externally to fast-changing sectors of society. The various demands, new and old, often pull in opposite directions: a dynamic, advanced economy, fueled by governmental concern about national strength, presses for a rationalization of training while a highly volatile culture of youth, fueled by the needs of the mass media and a youth industry, argues against such technical rationality, preferring a logic of sentiment and identity. Such strains, seemingly basic and reflected in various conflicts and disturbances, have led scholars to turn with wonderment, and often with some anguish, to the serious study of their own world. The 1960s saw a revitalization of the study of education in economics, political science, history, organizational analysis—and sociology.

We need only to look back a few years to see how recent is our concern. In the United States, we have had colleges since colonial days and universities since the last quarter of the nineteenth century. General sociology developed about the turn of the century and was a viable enterprise with a number of subfields by the 1920s. But among the subfields the sociology of education was a fragile enterprise until at least the 1950s; and within it, thought and analysis centered on the elementary and secondary levels. In its early state, the field was called "educational sociology," and its main journal was the *Journal of Educational Sociology*. It was based in teachers' colleges and the social foundations divisions of schools of education at the universities, where its task was to aid in the preparation of teachers and administrators for the public schools. One historical review of sociological inquiry in education in the period 1917–40 speaks of three subgroups: a general sociology group, concerned with the development of sociology; a policy group, interested in setting educational values and effecting social reform through the training of teachers and administrators; and a social technology group, seeking to develop a practitioner role around technical prescription on educational methods (Richards, 1969). Not one of these groups was successful in developing a prominent position either within education or sociology; and, of note for our purposes, none paid serious attention to higher education. The proper subject matter was the school, not the college and university.

We may connect two types of pre–World War II literature to the modern sociology of higher education. For one, broad statements in sociology and anthropology offered an undifferentiated view of education of all levels and types as a means of cultural transmission, socialization, social control, or social progress (Durkheim, 1922; Cooley, 1956; Ross, 1928; Ward, 1906). Of the broad approaches, Durkheim's seemingly conservative view of education as a dependent element in a slowly evolving web of institutions has been the most noted: education is "a collection of practices and institutions that have been organized slowly in the course of time, which are comparable with all the other social institutions and which express them, and which, therefore, can no more be changed at will than the structure of the society itself" (Durkheim, 1922, 65). Such statements, elaborating the basic sociological truth of the interdependence of social institutions, now seem both more appropriate, in the round, for 1900 than 1970 and for the elementary school than the university. Their import lay in establishing the terms of discussion for a long period, and even today they remain useful in recalling the specialist to the broadest conceptions of the social functions of education. Second, certain specific statements about higher education became established as classics but stood for decades in lonely isolation. The foremost instance in the basic theoretical literature is composed of Max Weber's statements on "Science as a Vocation" and "The 'Rationalization' of Education and Training," in which, following from his general insight on the rise of bureaucracy and specialization, he portrayed the tension between the generalist and the specialist—"the struggle of the 'specialist type of man' against the older type of 'cultivated man'"—as basic to many modern educational problems (Weber, 1946, 243). In retrospect, a highly useful line of inquiry could have developed three or four decades ago from the Weberian perspective on education, bureaucracy, and culture; but instead we have a notable instance of discontinuity in social research. The second instance of the striking specific classical statement was Thorstein Veblen's angry blast at the influence of businessmen and their mentality in the control and administration of colleges and universities, in his *The Higher Learning in America,* originally published in 1918 (Veblen, 1954). Veblen apparently was not followed for thirty years, until Hubert P. Beck's work *Men Who Control Our Universities* appeared in 1947 (Beck, 1947). Noting this discontinuity, we can well wish that Veblen had taken apprentices or had attracted followers whose work in turn would have established momentum in the analysis of power and control in higher education. A third instance of work that stood by itself for a long time was Logan Wilson's dissertation on university professors, published in 1942 as *The Academic Man: A Study in the Sociology of a Profession* (Wilson, 1942). There was no follow-up on this promising topic for a decade and a half, until Caplow and McGee's *The Academic Marketplace* (1958), and still today we do not have a book-length treatment of the university professor that is as serious and systematic as Wilson's effort of almost thirty years ago.

It is not until the 1960s that we discern a serious sociology of higher education in the sense of a subfield with a steady flow of writing and a specialty in which students take training, pursue it for a number of years, and accept a professional label. Two main directions of effort have become firmly institutionalized in these few short years, each representing a convergence of a sociological concern and a practical problem. The first stream is the study of inequality in education beyond the high school, particularly the search for the sources of inequality in social class, race, ethnicity, and sex. Inequality remains the root concern in the sociology of education around the world.

In American sociology, the basic field of stratification, concerned with class and race, was the base from which there developed a disciplined, empirically minded thrust into the study of education. In the 1930s and 1940s, a series of now-classic community studies (Lynd and Lynd, 1929, 1937; Warner and Lunt, 1941; Hollingshead, 1949) dramatized the impact of social class on the mobility of the young in the elementary and secondary school, including who finished high school and thus qualified for college. This sociological concern developed in the 1950s and 1960s into a serious tradition of statistical analysis (e.g., see the work of William Sewell and his students—Sewell and Armer, 1966; Sewell and Shah, 1967), and this concern followed mass education up into the college level. We now have an extensive journal literature of the social determinants of aspiration and achievement that includes the collegiate as well as the secondary and elementary levels of education, with increasing refinement around the issues germane to open admission and differentiation of institutions and tracks within a mass system, e.g., who goes to what kind of college and who completes the various degree levels. Here ideas on various overt and covert forms of channeling students and hence affecting seriously their social mobility have enlivened the literature and anticipated some current criticisms of schooling, e.g., the cooling-out function of certain practices in colleges (Clark, 1960), the difference between sponsored and contest forms of formal selection in educational systems (Turner, 1960), and the effects of counselors' categories of thought as labels placed on the young (Cicourel and Kitsuse, 1963).

The second stream is the study of the effects of the college years on the character, belief, and thought of students. An early study here was T. M. Newcomb's analysis of the effect of Bennington College on its girls (Newcomb, 1943), a classic work in social psychology. The topic was picked up again in the 1950s when Nevitt Sanford and his associates attempted a longitudinal examination of personality development in Vassar girls, a study that was only weakly sociological (Sanford, 1962), and when a group of Cornell sociologists compared the attitudes and values of students at eleven colleges and universities, noting some differences between public and private institutions in inputs and apparent effects (Goldsen et al., 1960). Since 1960, there has been a rapidly growing body of sociological writing, beginning with the study of Howard Becker and colleagues on the subculture of medical students (Becker et al., 1961) and the essay by Clark and Trow on types of undergraduate subcultures (see Newcomb and Wilson, 1966). Among the best studies reported later in the decade were the analysis of Becker, Geer, and Hughes of students' orientations to making the academic grade (1968) and the remarkable reanalysis of Bennington College by Newcomb et al. a quarter-century after his first study (1967). The study of life inside the campus and of its effects on the values, attitudes, and achievements of the student has become established rapidly, fueled by practical concerns of professors and administrators as well as the professional influence of senior investigators on colleagues and students. Research in this area also converges with that of psychologists who have been developing an even more extensive and intensive literature of the effect—or non-effect—of college on students (see Feldman and Newcomb, 1970).

Bordering on, and often converging with, this interest in student life is the late great concern with the causes of student disturbances. Stemming from the growing sense of academic crisis in the years since 1964, the writings on student unrest have come in waves from successively embattled campuses as all factions leaped to their pens and have been therefore long on ideology and short on research. This interest may yet find steady and creative academic bases in political sociology, e.g., in the comparative study of student movements (Lipset, 1966; Martinelli and Cavalli, 1970), and in the study of student life as related to the organization and governance of the college and university (Yamamoto, 1968; Kruytbosch and Messinger, 1970). But militant student action is a highly volatile phenomenon—witness the relative quiet riot of 1970–71—and its academic pursuit remains unsteady. A concern that escalated rapidly with the front-page headlines also may subside rapidly if student news becomes relegated again to the page behind the want ads or is assigned low priority as a campus problem when such matters as finance and faculty rights come to the fore.

Beyond these two main lines of inquiry, each of which centers on students, we may note two additional efforts that are otherwise focused. One is the study of "academic man," or higher education as a profession. Here we have the early study of Logan Wilson, noted above; some thoughts by Riesman on academic disciplines as power groups (1956); the efforts of Lazarsfeld and Thielens in *The Academic Mind* to study social scientists in a time of crisis (1958); the reflections of Caplow and McGee on the vagaries of the academic marketplace (1958); the delineation by John D. Donovan of *The Academic Man in the Catholic College* (1964); and the current, largely unpublished work of Talcott Parsons and Gerald M. Platt on "The American Academic Profession." Work is going forward in this line in other countries; e.g., the extensive investigation undertaken in the mid-1950s in West Germany, reported in Plessner

(1956), and the study by Halsey and Trow (1971) of the academic man in Britain. Most past work in this line has been conceptually ad hoc; but since there is now a thriving sociology of occupations and professions, the study of academic man can play effectively against this literature, e.g., on the strain between professional and bureaucratic orientations and the tensions common to the roles of professional men in complex organizations (cf. Clark, 1966).

The second subsidiary path takes the organizations of higher education as the units for study. Here conceptual leads have come from the literature on organization theory to which all the social sciences have contributed and the sociological field of complex organizations. The work includes the study of the dilemmas of the open-door college (Clark, 1960); the analysis of university goals (Gross and Grambsch, 1968); the creation of new perspectives on academic authority and power, including that of a subculture of administrators (Lunsford, 1970; Baldridge, 1971); the tensions of public experimental colleges (Riesman, Gusfield, and Gamson, 1970); and developmental analysis of organizational character and institutional self-belief (Clark, 1970). The organizational studies commonly are case studies oriented to exploration and discovery rather than to validation. Varying in rigidity, they shade off into journalistic vignettes and the writings of administrators and students of higher education that are not particularly sociological in intent or style.

This line of inquiry also extends at a more macrocosmic level into the organizations of sets of colleges and universities, including national systems of higher education. Here our appetites were whetted early by the skillful and provocative essays of Joseph Ben-David, the Israeli sociologist, on the effects of major structural differences among the systems of the most advanced industrial societies on flexibility, innovation, and change (Ben-David and Sloczower, 1962). Riesman has portrayed the rank-ordering and imitating propensities of the American system as a snakelike procession (Riesman, 1956); and Jencks and Riesman, within a wide-ranging description of the variety of colleges and universities in the American system, have interpreted the rise to power of professional scholars and scientists as the fundamental academic revolution of recent times (Jencks and Riesman, 1968). We have had an occasional illuminating country case study of a country outside of the advanced nations, as in Philip Foster's analysis of education and social status in Ghana (Foster,

1965). An educational literature on national systems has grown rapidly in the 1960s, but much of it remains in the general terms of manpower need, quantitative educational expansion, and national planning. The surveys of national systems have at least provided basic descriptive information comparatively assembled, on an ever larger number of systems of higher education (e.g., OECD, 1970), providing a base for more conceptually focused comparative inquiry.

The Future

Relatively young and unformed fields of study often are torn between intensive effort in one or two main lines of research and a desire to wander around testing the ground to find new and more sensitive approaches. The intensive effort allows us to refine empirically a few concepts and improve a few methods, with the possibility that we may finally pin something down. The wandering effort allows us to leapfrog from one idea to another, accelerating the conceptual game, with the possibility that we will come up with an exciting idea. These contradictory approaches are evident in the sociology of higher education, and each, with its evident virtues, carries its own dangers for the decade or two ahead.

The first approach has the danger of an inbred tradition of work, with increasing tunnel vision riveted on the trivial. The two most established lines of research mentioned earlier, those of educational inequality and college impact, will face this danger in the 1970s. The study of educational inequality is fast becoming a detailed and technical business in which only a few analysts, equipped with the latest statistical techniques, are competent. A tricky and complex problem does indeed call for the greatest possible methodological sophistication. But down that road also comes the career devoted to improving the reliability and validity of instruments of highly specific application. Our colleagues in educational psychology can attest to the stultifying and dead-end pitfalls of that particular academic procession.

In the study of college impact, we already have a relatively massive but trivial literature (cf. Feldman and Newcomb's review of 1,500 studies). If at last we have stopped attempting to measure the effects of specific courses on students, we seemingly still are stuck with a commitment to measure ever more carefully the year-by-year effect of one college after another—or perhaps several hundred of them simultaneously—on a host of specific attitudes. But the effort to sort out the determinants and the outcomes, particularly to comprehend the interactions between student inputs and campus structures, is increasingly costly in time and money. Is it worth it? Is it worth it for social science? It is helpful to stand back and recall that a fundamental if not the basic effect of college is to make college graduates out of high school graduates. Here the change is 100 percent in the surviving cohort: none of those entering college but all those receiving the degree are socially defined as college graduates. As John Meyer has put it, this is what colleges socially are chartered to do, to alter social statuses with this particular self- and public definition (Meyer, 1972). The consequences of the definition are enormous. In Meyer's terms: "Whether or not the student has learned anything—(and, we might add, become a little less religious or a little more liberal)—his job prospects, income potential, access to political and civil service positions, marital prospects, and other opportunities, are greatly altered" (Meyer, 1972, 110). Here the fundamental sociological thesis is that college effects occur primarily not at the level of attitudes and values but in the allocation of statuses and roles. This plausible argument should give some pause to those who would spend research fortunes on highly sophisticated, five-year, input-throughput-output analyses of small changes in specific values. In any event, the more sustained lines of work in the sociology of higher education already need this kind of direct challenging of their relative importance and possible contribution.

The second approach, that of the wandering analytical gypsy, will carry in the 1970s the danger of a game of vignettes. For many of us, it is more fun to go find another interesting case about which to write an interpretive story than to plug along in one vein seeking replication or the hard data of comparison. The result of drifting too far in this direction is a maximum of zig and zag, a minimum of accumulation, and even a reduction of scholarly discipline to journalistic play. The temptation is to be clever, even sardonic: the provocative phrase, rather than the truth, will set us free. Thus we are right on one page and wrong on the next, and only a few informed people are able to distinguish the one from the other. We will see much of this form of quasi-sociological writing in the 1970s, and what at one time is a fresh and useful ethnography can become a tiresome description of an endless number of tribes and a tangle of uncorrected interpretations. The ethnography will need conceptual focus and the hard criticism of those who insist on some systematic data.

The research of the 1970s clearly will include much comparative analysis, in line with the general drift of sociology toward comparative study, a development that should help correct the myopia that comes from too many days spent on scale reliability or on vignettes of the American college. The comparative work will entail a variety of analytical interests, e.g., inequalities in access, student life, institutional resilience and change, and governance and management of national systems. We also will gain from more historical investigation. The written history of higher education has been improving rapidly (cf. Hofstadter and Metzger, 1955; Rudolph, 1962; Veysey, 1965); there are young scholars who seem equally at home in sociology and history; and general sociology is clearly no longer uncomfortable with historical perspectives and materials. Historical studies instruct us about educational systems of the past, connections between educational trends and change in other sectors of society, and, most important for sociologists, the past-to-present development of existing systems. Developmental analysis carried out over decades of time can highlight fundamental institutional trajectories and hence suggest the potentialities and limitations of current institutional forms as they face new demands.

As one attempts to estimate the future for the lines of inquiry identified above, a latent common problem in approach and perspective becomes more manifest: how can the sociology of higher education take cues from, and make returns to, the concerns of educational practitioners without becoming a managerial sociology? It is not that we are so easily bought but that we are so much involved. Since education prepares the young for later life and professor-researchers are part of the training corps, we tend to perceive and define education in instrumental terms. Like administrators and reformers, we want to know who gets in and who gets out, what the students have learned and whether their personal character has been affected. Educational questions not only too easily set the sociological questions, but they also become voiced around immediate needs of administration and public policy, e.g., what specific issues are disturbing the students and hence what manipulations of structure and procedure will be advantageous? Even when our attitude is critical of present practice, we are still in the stance of defining the ends of educational work and arranging practices to be effective means to those ends.

One way to contain this tendency in part is to see higher education through the definitions presented by students and other subordinate actors, an approach practiced by Howard Becker and others in the symbolic interaction school of thought. A second way is to play against instrumental terms by seeking the expressive aspects of the system. Though colleges and universities begin as purposive formal organizations, they become, in varying degree, social institutions heavy with affect and nonrational involvement. For faculty and administrators, there are loyalties and lifestyles of the employing institution and the national discipline. For students, there are the feelings of group attachment or detachment that are constructed in the meeting of personal and institutional character. Research on attitudes and values of students and professors catches some of the personal side of expressive phenomena. What lags is research on institutional and system capacities to embody certain values in the thought and lifestyles of an evolving group. Macro-system analysis need not be limited to inputs and outputs and managerial manipulation of administrative structure. Compared to most other classes of complex organizations, colleges and universities apparently have a high propensity to order themselves through normative bonds and emotional commitment. We move toward a fuller understanding of their nature as we bring into view their variations as systems that at a given time are ends in themselves. We seek then for the evolution of value systems that give meaning to the lives of participants. We seek how the organized social system unconsciously absorbs the individual into a collectivity, promoting personal satisfaction in return. We seek group and institutional identities.

In historical connection, the present natural interest in effective delivery of educational services links well with the Weberian interest in bureaucratic rationality and the role of education in the certification of training. The corrective perspective emphasized here, in contrast, is rooted more in the Durkheimian concern with the role of morality and sentiment in social order. Durkheim saw schools as miniature societies that have their own particular moralities, ones developed over time as institutional character emerges as a reaction to institutional function. If colleges and universities as well as schools are places where society re-creates (and develops) itself in the young, then their values, traditions, and collective identities appropriately can be placed at the center of sociological attention.

References

Astin, A. "The Methodology of Research on College Impact," pts. 1–2. *Sociology of Education*, 43, nos. 3–4 (1970): 223–54, 437–48.

Baldridge, J. V. *Power and Conflict in the University.* New York: John Wiley, 1971.

Beck, H. P. *Men Who Control Our Universities.* New York: King's Crown Press, 1947.

Becker, H. S., B. Geer, and E. C. Hughes. *Making the Grade: The Academic Side of College Life.* New York: Wiley, 1968.

Becker, H. S., B. Geer, E. C. Hughes, and A. L. Strauss. *Boys in White: Student Culture in Medical School.* Chicago: University of Chicago Press, 1961.

Ben-David, J., and A. Sloczower. "Universities and Academic Systems in Modern Societies." *European Journal of Sociology* 3 (1962): 45–84.

Caplow, T., and R. J. McGee. *The Academic Marketplace.* New York: Basic Books, 1958.

Cicourel, A. V., and J. I. Kitsuse. *The Educational Decision-Makers.* Indianapolis: Bobbs-Merrill, 1963.

Clark, B. R. *The Open Door College.* New York: McGraw-Hill, 1960.

———. "Organizational Adaptation to Professionals." In *Profressionalization,* edited by H. M. Vollmer and D. L. Mills, 282–91. Englewood Cliffs, N.J.: Prentice-Hall, 1966.

———. *The Distinctive College: Antioch, Reed, and Swarthmore.* Chicago: Aldine, 1970.

Cooley, C. H. *Two Major Works: Social Organization and Human Nature and the Social Order.* Glencoe, Ill.: Free Press, 1956. (Originally published in 1909 and 1902)

Donovan, J. D. *The Academic Man in the Catholic College.* New York: Sheed and Ward, 1964.

Durkheim, E. *Education and Society.* Translated by Sherwood D. Fox. Glencoe, Ill.: Free Press, 1956. (Originally published in 1922)

Feldman, K. A., and T. M. Newcomb. *The Impact of College on Students.* 2 vols. San Francisco: Jossey-Bass, 1970.

Foster, P. *Education and Social Change in Ghana.* Chicago: University of Chicago Press, 1965.

Goldsen, K., M. Rosenberg, R. M. Williams, and E. A. Suchman. *What College Students Think*. New York: D. Van Nostrand, 1960.

Gross, E. G., and P. V. Grambsch. *University Goals and Academic Power*. Washington, D.C.: American Council on Education, 1968.

Halsey, A. H., and M. Trow. *The British Academics*. Cambridge, Mass.: Harvard University Press, 1971.

Hofstadter, R., and W. P. Metzger. *The Development of Academic Freedom in the United States*. New York: Columbia University Press, 1955.

Hollingshead, A. B. *Elmtown's Youth*. New York: John Wiley, 1959.

Jencks, C., and D. Riesman. *The Academic Revolution*. Garden City, N.Y.: Doubleday, 1968.

Kruytbosch, C. E., and S. L. Messinger, eds. *The State of the University: Authority and Change*. Beverly Hills, Calif.: Sage, 1970.

Lazarsfeld, P. F., and W. Thielens Jr. *The Academic Mind*. New York: Free Press of Glencoe, 1958.

Lipset, S. M., ed. *Student Politics*. Special issue of *Comparative Education Review* 10 (June 1966).

Lunsford, F. "Authority and Ideology in the Administered University." In *The State of the University: Authority and Change*, edited by C. E. Kruytbosch and S. L. Messinger. Beverly Hills, Calif.: Sage, 1970.

Lynd, S., and H. M. Lynd. *Middletown*. New York: Harcourt, Brace, 1929.

———. *Middletown in Transition*. New York: Harcourt, Brace, 1937.

Martinelli, A., and A. Cavalli. "Toward a Conceptual Framework for the Comparative Analysis of Student Movements." Paper presented at seventh World Congress of Sociology, Varna, Bulgaria, 1970.

Meyer, J. W. "The Effects of the Institutionalization of Colleges in Society." In *College and Student: Selected Readings in the Social Psychology of Higher Education*, edited by K. A. Feldman, 109–26. New York: Pergamon, 1972.

Newcomb, T. M. *Personality and Social Change*. New York: Dryden, 1973.

Newcomb, T. M., and E. K. Wilson, eds. *College Peer Groups*. Chicago: Aldine, 1966.

OECD (Organisation for Economic Co-operation and Development). *Development of Higher Education, 1950–1967: Statistical Survey*. Paris: OECD, 1970.

Parsons, T., and G. M. Platt. "The American Academic Profession: A Pilot Study." Typescript, 1969.

Plessner, H., ed. *Untersuchungen zur Lage der Deutschen Hochschullehrer*. Gottingen: Vandenhoeck und Ruprescht, 1956.

Richards, R. R. "Perspectives on Sociological Inquiry in Education, 1917–1940." PhD dissertation, University of Wisconsin, 1969.

Riesman, D. *Constraint and Variety in American Education*. Lincoln: University of Nebraska Press, 1956.

Riesman, D., J. Gusfield, and Z. Gamson. *Academic Values and Mass Education: The Early Years of Oakland and Monteith*. Garden City, N.Y.: Doubleday, 1970.

Ross, E. *Social Control*. New York: Macmillan, 1928. (Originally published 1901)

Rudolph, F. *The American College and University*. New York: Alfred A. Knopf, 1962.

Sanford, N., ed. *The American College*. New York: John Wiley, 1962.

Sewell, W. H., and J. M. Armer. "Neighborhood Context and College Plans." *American Sociological Review* 31 (1966): 159–68.

Sewell, W. H., and V. P. Shah. "Socioeconomic Status, Intelligence, and the Attainment of Higher Education." *Sociology of Education* 40 (1967): 1–23.

Turner, Ralph H. "Sponsored and Contest Mobility and the School System." *American Sociological Review* 25 (1960): 55–67.

Veblen, T. *The Higher Learning in America*. Stanford, Calif.: Academic Reprints, 1954. (Originally published 1918)

Veysey, L. R. *The Emergence of the American University*. Chicago: University of Chicago Press, 1965.

Ward, L. F. *Applied Sociology*. Boston: Ginn, 1906.

Warner, W. L., and P. S. Lunt. *The Social Life of a Modern Community*. New Haven, Conn.: Yale University Press, 1941.

Weber, M. *From Max Weber: Essays in Sociology*. Translated and edited by H. H. Gerth and C. Wright Mills. New York: Oxford University Press, 1946.

Wilson, L. *The Academic Man: A Study in the Sociology of a Profession*. New York: Oxford University Press, 1942.

Yamamoto, K., ed. *The College Student and His Culture: An Analysis*. Boston: Houghton Mifflin, 1968.

PART THREE

Cultivating Cross-National Insight

The essays in part III reflect a decision to learn more—much more—about the workings of institutions of higher education by engaging in cross-national research. The selections span almost three decades, from the 1970s through the late 1990s. That decision to commit to an international approach, a key one for my career, was weighed against other possibilities: I could simply have continued to study American higher education; I could have shifted my focus to the sociology of science or of professions. Possibly I could have scrutinized K–12 more closely. But the higher education terrain, the one in which I had accumulated expertise, was still challenging. Both its micro- and macro-organizational dimensions were largely unexplored. Building and broadening my expertise by tackling national systems seemed the right way to go; just thinking about doing organizational analyses of entire national systems was exciting. That ground was virtually virgin territory.

My wish to "go international" was enabled by a major workplace shift from a school of education at Berkeley to a department of sociology at Yale. A very attractive offer from Yale allowed me to concentrate on forging a cross-national perspective. I expected to engage in rebuilding a substandard department. But after two years serving as director of graduate studies in the reconstituted department and focusing on departmental matters, Yale was willing to fund a full-salary and year-long fellowship for research in Italy. Fieldwork done in 1969 became the basis for writing a case study of a large, fully nationalized, European system—the Italian one—which was very different from (and indeed the very opposite of) the decentralized American scheme. The resulting analysis, informed by several additional summer trips, became *Academic Power in Italy: Bureaucracy and Oligarchy in a National University System,* which was published by the University of Chicago Press in 1977. In it I described how the combination of state bureaucracy and faculty oligarchy has given Italy a deeply dysfunctional national university system.

After returning from Italy, I settled down to serve as department chair for three years and did a second stint as director of graduate studies. At the same time I helped to establish, and then headed up, a new comparative higher education research group. With financial support from Yale and grants from private foundations, the group comprised post-docs, recruited internationally from social science and history departments, who had acquired country-specific expertise in the course of their dissertation research. I clearly could not do the necessary intensive research by myself. And graduate students would not suffice: they would need years of front-end training, language study, and time in the field before producing results. John Perry Miller, then Yale graduate dean and first director of Yale's Institution for Social and Policy Studies, in which my research group was embedded, solved my problem. He suggested that working with post-docs was the answer.

Thus three contextual features facilitated my shift to an international perspective: a particularly supportive university; a well-funded opportunity to do my own field research abroad; and, most important, the opportunity to build a post-doc research group as *the* means of assembling diverse expertise.

I learned a great deal from the post-docs, graduate students, and visitors from abroad in the Yale group. One example of how well the group interacted was the production, analysis, and coordination of a seven-country study published after the group had been together for only a few years, *Academic Power: Patterns of Authority in Seven National Systems of Higher Education,* edited by John H. Van de Graaff, Burton R. Clark, Dorotea Furth, Dietrich Goldschmidt, and Donald F. Wheeler (Praeger, 1978). The group, in just six years, also issued over forty-five working papers, of which a good share later became published articles or chapters in books.

I continued to take on more involvements abroad and particularly enjoyed participating annually in summer conferences newly organized in England and Sweden. At home, a new group committed to comparative education had sprung up in New York City. James A. Perkins, formerly president of Cornell University, established the International Council for Educational Development. Perkins knew how to raise money from nearby foundations. Some he spent on long summer conferences in Aspen, Colorado, to which participants from abroad as well as within the United States had been invited. There I met Klaus von Dohnanyi from Germany, Alain Bienaymé from France, Ladislav Cerych from OECD, and Jan Szczepanski from Poland, who advocated strongly the advantages of daily napping for clarity of thought—a transnational bromide that agreed with me. Participants from the United States included Ernest Boyer and Barbara Burn. At the conferences led by Jim Perkins experts described education practices across national boundaries at long, informal exchanges held daily within view of the craggy Rocky Mountains and the music tent.

Perkins also spent his money on issuing some lasting publications. He published a set of brief monographs on the design, management, and effectiveness of systems of higher education in twelve countries, including Australia, Mexico, and Poland. A summary volume, *12 Systems of Higher Education: 6 Decisive Issues* (International Council for Educational Development, 1978), was based on these reports. The decisive issues (and contributors) included goals (Clark Kerr); planning and management (John Millett); coordination (my topic); flexibility and innovation (Brian MacArthur from the United Kingdom); measurements of efficiency (Howard Bowen); and comparative effectiveness (Clark Kerr). Many insightful ideas emerged in print in these essays; Kerr, for example, showed that statements about goals of higher education in one country after another had little to do with operational realities. Rather, they served primarily as a means of expressing the agendas of various interest groups. For good reasons, stated goals become similar to a laundry list. If you set down "trained manpower," make sure you list "transmission of a common culture." If you insist on "individual development," make sure you include "egalitarian access" and "public service." And so on. Soon the goals become hollow.

My chapter in this "decisive issues" volume forced me to struggle with patterns of national coordination from a comparative perspective. I started out with a straight line between extremes of state administration and market-type linkage, with France at one extreme and the United

States at the other. Kerr immediately pointed out that everything I had learned in my study of Italian higher education pointed to heavy coordination by means of an "academic oligarchy": university professors linked together in guild-like clusters. It became clear I needed a triangle, with systems exhibiting various combinations of three types. The struggle to make some sense of a "triangle of forms of coordination" took place here, a half-dozen years before it appeared as an important scheme in my 1983 *System* book. Endless chewing of No. 2 lead pencils saw me through.

By the end of the 1970s, I felt ready to attempt a basic book that would offer a new, well-structured way to compare higher education within and across national systems. That book became *The Higher Education System: Academic Organization in Cross-National Perspective* (1983). I devised a structure around the concepts of work, belief, authority, coordination, and change, and illustrated the scheme throughout with ample country-specific detail. The chapter on coordination spelled out the triangle comprising state, market, and university.

System became my magnum opus as well as the symbolic turning point of my career. From its cumulative findings, I set out in two concluding chapters to analyze conflicting basic values practiced in higher education and to create a model of what the most appropriate and productive national system would look like in the future. That model had many American characteristics, generally overlooked. I argued strongly for a clearer awareness of the bottom-heavy uniqueness of higher education and the resulting need to decentralize power, differentiate institutions and practice, and appreciate variety and disorder rather than uniformity and formal clarity. Such general findings induced from cross-national research seem to be even more relevant today than they were two decades ago.

From *System* onward, my primary effort was to cultivate grounded insights from cross-national observations. I became increasingly confident that I knew what I was talking about despite the staggering historical differences and unique characteristics of the various national systems. I thus moved to a more normative tone about comparative success and failure.

After retirement, upon my return to focused field research described in part IV, my insistence took another leap forward. It was now or never. Looking back, I can see that the writings in part III can be taken as milestones on the long road to understanding comparative systems, insights that culminated during the ten years between 1994 and 2004.

INTRODUCTION TO CHAPTER 12

To get started on my new comparative interest in the late 1960s, I decided to take on a fieldwork-based case study of an entire foreign national system of higher education. I wanted to focus on a large, fully nationalized European system that would be the very opposite of the American decentralized one. My choices soon narrowed down to France and Italy. France was atypical of other nationalized systems: it has a separate, elite, *grandes écoles* sector and a separate research sector (the National Center for Scientific Research—CNRS), which leaves the universities a weakened third party. Italy seemed to have a more typically general system, and it seemed more amenable to hosting an English-speaking foreigner who needed to engage in interviews and to use translators when necessary. Young Italian scholars available to me at the time had a good command of English and had studied in the United States at Columbia, Yale, and Berkeley. Students in sociology at the University of Rome could be hired as translating research assistants. So Italy it was.

But I had been warned by colleagues in international agencies in Paris that "no one could untangle the ways of the Italian system." Too much was subject to hidden hands, personal webs, incompetent ministerial and university personnel. Such warnings, embellished with detailed accounts, simply increased my desire to try my hand. Other outsiders from Britain and the United States had probed Italian economic and political systems. Why not grapple with the Byzantine elaborations of the educational sphere? So I set out in 1968 to find out who had power in the Italian national system and how they went about exercising it.

As I got bounced around between senior administrative personnel in the Kafkaesque huge educational ministry in Rome and senior and junior academics in the far-flung universities, especially Milan, Turin, and Florence, I finally figured out who the prime movers in the major areas of finance, personnel, and curriculum were. I learned a great deal about the

187

internal workings of a specific nationalized major system, and along the way, about higher education in other European countries. I also came to understand in some detail how exceptional the American system is.

I assembled my findings in *Academic Power in Italy: Bureaucracy and Oligarchy in a National University System* (1977), and wrote it with emphasis on the implications of the two concepts in the subtitle. I also contributed a chapter on Italy to the seven-country study, *Academic Power: Patterns of Authority in Seven National Systems of Higher Education*, edited by John H. Van de Graaff and other members of the Yale group at the time. Dorotea Furth from the OECD staff and Professor Dietrich Goldschmidt from the Max-Planck Institute of Education in Berlin participated in the volume as well.

The first part of this selection comes from the Italy chapter in the Van de Graaff volume. It offers a historical review of the development of the Italian system since the days when student and faculty guilds were the key organizing groups at the original University of Bologna. This surprising durable guild organization has persisted right down to the system I observed in the 1960s and 1970s. Its structure has stubbornly resisted major reform: "big bills" advocating change have failed time and time again when introduced in the national legislature. Implementation of small, incremental changes within the system has had little overall impact. Interlocked traditional controls have proven extremely difficult to overcome as late as the early twenty-first century. What we find in Italy, in confusing operation, is a deeply politicized guild system in which senior professors exercise strong oligarchical controls. A concluding page on "The Triumphs of Particularism" in an academic oligarchy has been taken from *Academic Power in Italy*. Here I locate the fatal weakness of combining ministerial control with faculty guilds.

Nationalization of higher education has become a huge failure in Italy. One top-down, across-the-system attempted reform after another has simply made matters worse. According to *The Economist*, as late as April 2007, the Italian unified national system is rife with patronage and cronyism. This leads to "gray power"—an inflated number of old professors who cling to their lofty jobs and power. Thirty percent of senior academics are over sixty-five. Perhaps those who understand the potential of regionalization (control by regional and city governments) and see the value of encouraging the invigorating growth of private institutions will yet prevail in carrying out root-and-branch reform.

Italians frequently refer to senior professors as *i baroni*. They are the linchpins of dysfunctionality throughout the system. The national formal structure needs to be broken up.

CHAPTER 12

Italy:

A Case Study of System Failure

THE GREAT AGE of university development in Italy took place between the twelfth and fifteenth centuries. Bologna was begun in 1158; Padua, Naples, Rome, and other universities of the present system had developed into substantial, recognized institutions before 1400; and more than two-thirds of the universities extant in the mid-twentieth century had been established by 1600. Only a few new universities, now mainly peripheral seats of learning, were started between the seventeenth and twentieth centuries.[1] The university is among the very oldest major social institutions of Italy, its antiquity surpassed only by that of the church and the communes. It existed long before a modern national state was created in the mid-nineteenth century.

Formed when guilds were the primary form for organizing urban work, the early universities were themselves guilds and guild federations, collective efforts by students and faculty to sustain self-regulating clusters of people with shared interests to control a small domain of activity and defend themselves against the other groups.[2] Italy was notable between the twelfth and the fifteenth centuries for the power of student guilds. As alien residents of city-states, students from other parts of Italy as well as other countries needed to band together in self-defense. At the same time, like the professors, they felt free to move the university from one city to another: "Townsmen and professors alike stood in awe of a body [the

Drawn from "Italy," in *Academic Power: Patterns of Authority in Seven National Systems of Higher Education*, edited by John H. Van de Graaff et al., 37–48. New York: Praeger, 1978. Copyright © 1978 by Praeger Publishers. Reproduced by permission of Greenwood Publishing Group Inc., Westport, CT; and excerpts from "Italy: A Case Study of System Failure," in *Academic Power in Italy: Bureaucracy and Oligarchy in a National University System*, 112–13. Chicago: University of Chicago Press, 1977. © 1977 by the University of Chicago. Used by permission.

university of students] which by the simple expedient of migration could destroy the trade of the former and the incomes of the latter."[3]

But townsmen and professors no longer had to stand in awe once they learned to make the university stand in place. By the fifteenth century, through the erection of permanent buildings, the entry of professors onto city payrolls, and the recruitment of hometown boys as students, city fathers and professors had established dominance over the students, and the most important chapter in the history of student power was at an end.[4] Henceforth, the important power struggles pitted faculty guilds against the encompassing chartering and administrative frameworks of church and state, particularly the latter, which funded and often attempted to regulate the academic guilds as they did the many craft and merchant guilds on whom, in turn, they were dependent. In their significant ties to city-states and provincial rulers, Italian universities may be considered "state universities" from the fifteenth century onward.

The ancient Italian universities were originally centers for professional studies, and like their counterparts in France and Spain, continued through the centuries to focus primarily on preparation for law, medicine, and public administration, the latter field generally drawing on law graduates. Between 1500 and 1850—centuries of decline for the universities and for the Italian peninsula as a whole—university activity was for long periods reduced virtually to the study of law alone.[5] Its fields of study already diminished, the Italian university became even less open than its counterparts in northern Europe to admitting and developing new fields as a way of adjusting to changing social demands. Science fared especially badly. Internal resistance meshed with a weak interest in scientific advances among Italian ruling circles and with the censorious resistance of the Catholic church mounted in the Counter-Reformation.[6] Conditions at the universities deteriorated further during the eighteenth and early nineteenth centuries, when a venerable institution such as Bologna, which in its earliest centuries attracted students by the thousands from near and far, was reduced to a few hundred students.[7] During this period of university decline, the entire peninsula suffered as it was turned into the battleground and playground of Austrian princes, French kings, and Spanish dukes. Too, the elite of the Italian city-states, unable to form a nation, not only feuded among themselves for three and a half centuries (1500–1850), but remained at the mercy of their more powerful neighbors who had managed to consolidate political control across the large entities that became the nations and empires of modern Europe.[8]

When the Italians finally were able to achieve national unification in the period 1850–70, they began a gradual nationalization of university support and control. The liberal leaders of the new nation, mainly Piedmontese of the Turin area who had been heavily influenced by French forms of governance and administration, began a trend toward both political and administrative centralization, drawing power from the cities and the regions and concentrating it administratively in the central offices of a set of national ministries and bureaus that would grow increasingly unwieldy and Balkanized.[9] They wanted, among other interests, an educational system that would help to make a nation, supporting national identification and unity over the divisive local loyalties of the old cities and provinces, over the disaffection of southern peasants and northern workers, and over the declared opposition of the church to a secular state that had conquered papal territory. An interest in trying to achieve equity and equality through unitary, uniform administration, much like France's, would also develop over time. All education was placed under a national ministry of education. The universities were given a direct, vertical relationship to the ministry, not even formally answering to an area prefect of the national government, much less to local or regional government.

As a result of this trend, which accelerated during the fascist period (1922–45), the century of development between the 1860s and the 1960s saw the national system achieve a virtual monopoly. In 1960, Italian higher education was conducted at 30 places: 24 universities supported primarily by the state and firmly within the states system, and 6 "free" universities, so called because they were supported mainly by cities, provinces, or private groups. The free universities needed recognition by the national system in order to grant a legitimate degree. Falling under general state supervision, they organized their affairs on the model of the state universities.[10] The 30 universities accounted for 98 percent of enrollment. Thus there were really no higher education institutions other than the universities, and there were no private-sector institutions truly independent of state authority.

The universities have varied widely in size. In 1960, the University of Rome had 45,000 students, Naples 28,000, while historic Pavia, Perugia, and Parma each had fewer than 5,000, and others such as Camerino and Macerata had only 1,000 or fewer. In the great student expansion of the 1960s, the disparities in size grew larger. By 1970, Rome had doubled to 90,000 students, Naples to more than 60,000, while small and moderately large universities were adding students in much smaller numbers. Disparities among the universities' fields of study were equally striking. A university in Italy can contain up to 12 faculties (*facoltà*). Nine of the faculties cover primarily professional areas: medicine, law, engineering, economics and commerce (mainly the latter), agriculture, teaching, architecture, veterinary medicine, and pharmacy. Three comprise what in the United States would be segments of the liberal arts: letters, science, and political science. The types of faculties are distributed unevenly among the universities. Some universities specialize in only one or two fields, whereas others are comprehensive, covering virtually everything that is recognized within the whole system. In 1960, e.g., the University of Rome had all 12 faculties, while Parma had 6, Sienna 3, and Macerata 1. A university with a faculty in letters might not have a science faculty. Some have neither.

The types of faculties vary enormously in power, as measured by such simple indicators as the number of chair-holders found throughout the national system: e.g., in 1960, medicine had about 440 and law 325, compared to about 65 in teaching and 40 in architecture. Each faculty is entered directly from the secondary level and leads to the single degree of *laurea* after 4, 5, or 6 years of study, with all graduates assuming the title of *dottore.*

Finally, the Italian universities have been part of a wider structure of elite selection. Universal elementary education did not take hold in Italy until the 1950s; its achievement was a government priority in post–World War II reconstruction and modernization. As elsewhere on the Continent, the secondary level was divided into elite schools (classical and scientific *licei*) that led to automatic admission to the university, and non-elite schools that ended in technical and teacher training. With the secondary schools serving as a screening mechanism, Italian universities as late as 1960 were admitting 5 percent or less of the age group. Mass education at the secondary level in the late 1950s and early 1960s meant that many more students would enter the open doors of the universities after 1965.

Levels of Organization

The operating levels of the traditional Italian system are somewhat similar to the German and French, following the Continental style of university organization. At the lowest level, the chair and institute are the organizational units, with the chair-holding professor doubling as director of a research institute or as the head of a main section within it. The structure places one man in full charge of both a teaching sector and a research sector, thereby making him a boss and encouraging the personalizing of power. Within his teaching and research domains, the professor personally selects junior personnel and acts as a sponsor in arranging their future careers as well as in deciding their current assignments. The power of the professor is also enhanced by his personal accumulation and filling of a wide network of roles: teaching on several faculties, even in cities far distant from one another, editing and managing a journal, engaging in outside professional practice, advising private organizations and local governments, and serving in posts in the national government, including the legislature and the cabinet. With so many other roles, professors have served only part-time as professors. How to make them full-time professors became an issue in the reform efforts of the 1960s and early 1970s. The professor's capacity to accumulate privileges and powers increases his stature in the local cluster, raising him even farther above the *assistenti* and others of lesser rank. Therefore, at the base of the national system, organization tends to be unitary, hierarchical, and particularistic. It may even be said that it is guild-like in vertical authority, with a master having extensive direct control over what are, in effect, journeymen and apprentices.[11]

The second level of academic organization in the Italian system has long been the faculty (*facoltà*). Numbering about two hundred in the system as a whole, the faculties are the inclusive units to which professors and students belong and hence are organizationally more important than the universities. In internal operation, the faculty is an assembly of chairs, a horizontal grouping of powerful persons who regulate the less powerful at level 1. The chaired professors, each representing certain subdomains and having one vote, come together in a faculty council (*consiglio di facoltà*) to decide on issues that fall within the collective domain of the faculty. As in Germany, the chairs elect their nominal superior, the dean (*preside*), who has little or no independent administrative power. Thus, the *facoltà* is not neatly unitary in authority structure, at least not by bureaucratic standards, but is more like a federation. Because it is a collegial body, with strong elements of collegiate monopoly, it is more horizontal than hierarchical. And because the colleagues who come together in the faculty council are fairly autonomous rulers of parts of the organizational countryside, decisions are influenced considerably by academic politics. The professors are much like senators representing different territorial interests, operating in a legislative body that dominates the executive. They must form majorities based on mutual regard for one another's established rights and territorial jurisdiction; senatorial courtesy mixes with bargaining, coalition formation, and occasional power plays. Here, as at the lower level, organization is guild-like, but now in the horizontal relation of a group of masters coming together to vote on common policy. The chair and faculty levels in Italy together place autocracy within collegiality, or, conversely, offer collegial relations among autocrats, having retained the vertical and horizontal relations that together characterize guild authority.[12]

At the next highest structural level, the university as a whole, organization is quite loose. The ruling body, the *senato accademico*, is an assembly of elected deans and certain other elected professors. Before the reforms of the 1970s, there was little or no representation of junior faculty or students. The nominal superior official, the *rettore*, is not bureaucratically appointed but is elected from the ranks of the chair-holders to a short term of three years. Without any power base beyond the professors, the rectors have remained amateur administrators, on rotating terms of office and subject to recall.

The bureaucratic side of university organization centers chiefly on the post of the administrative director, who is indeed appointed from on high. This civil servant often has a long stay in office and is expected to serve as an arm of the national government. Traditionally, administrative directors were relatively weak, serving as bookkeepers for faculties and universities run by academic notables. They have grown stronger in recent years as the university system has grown and the need for order and coordination has increased. But local professors have exercised general jurisdiction even over the business affairs of the university through an administrative council, on which they and the rector sit with the administrative director. Thus there are important similarities between the organization of the university and the faculty, most notably the considerable monopoly of collegial power by constituent professors. The main difference between them is the greater looseness of the university structure and the high degree of autonomy of the constituent faculties. As inclusive membership units, the faculties need not be physically grouped but may be scattered around a city. Little horizontal linkage has been needed among them in order to accomplish the necessary work. Thus, the structure of the university is loosely federative, virtually coalitional, with a minimal hierarchy. Constructed around the autocratic powers of its voting members, the university, like the faculty, allows for and even encourages the patronage and favoritism usually found among elected governors.

Above the university level in Italy, in the superstructure of academic control, there has been no major multicampus administration (level 4 in the comparative scheme), nothing that would parallel the German structure of state control (level 5), nor even any clustering of universities within regional administration of the national government. The structure connects the university to Rome, the national capital (level 6), specifically to a division of higher education within the mammoth ministry of public instruction, topped by a minister of education and his staff. Formal lines of authority, as in many other countries, flow upward from the minister to a chief executive and the national legislature. The national system has impressive powers. It decides admission policy. Graduation from one of its approved secondary schools ensures admission to the university system as a whole and the choice of faculty at a particular university. All degrees are awarded by the national system rather than by the individual university. All chair-holding professors and "stabilized" assistants are regular civil service personnel, placed in categories of status and salary that cut across the system. The system finances the universities and has paid up to 80 percent of their costs in recent years, the balance largely made up by student fees and income from a declining base of university-owned property and endowment.

As mentioned earlier, the fascist period increased educational centralization, thickening the common rulebooks applying to all university personnel. During this period even the curriculum became nationalized, with national codes specifying not only which fields of study would be available in the faculties of the various universities, but also naming the courses that were to be uniformly required throughout the country in each specialty, and listing what additional options were approved for each university. In short, admissions, finance, personnel policy, and curriculum were made uniform and centralized. Especially fascinating is the fact that after the fascists fell from power, the fat rulebooks were not thrown away or even seriously amended or reduced. The nationally codified rules and laws had become important sources of power for various bureaus of the fragmented national government and thus provided protection and advantage to whichever officials or groups had come to have their interest vested most effectively.

In the higher education sector, the chair-holding professors form a key group. The Italian system is noteworthy for the skill with which the professors have managed to parlay local power into national power. They hold considerable control over what goes on at the center; control is not lodged primarily with bureaucrats or nonacademic politicians. Power flows along lines of professional networks, nationally as well as locally. These networks connect decision-makers within the system. A generalist professor provides more coordination than a specialist professor, and the Italian professor-general in his elaborated and accumulated roles alone can help link parts of the center to one another, the top to the bottom, as well as parts of operating units to each other.

A second structural key is peer election, the wide national use of the elected committee. The center of the national system is interlaced with committees composed of professors, whether in the ministry of public instruction or the National Research Council. One such committee (Consiglio Superiore dell'Istruzione), at the apex of the structure alongside the minister, has had, for example, important powers of approval and veto over any changes in the nationalized curriculum. Research monies are given away by committees of professors meeting as segments of the National Research Council. The appointment of another chair-holder in the system involves an ad hoc committee of professors working at the center on behalf of the entire system. They must administer a national competition and select three victors, one of whom will get the chair— through often complicated processes of maneuver and exchange among individuals and faculties. In all such national committees, members are not appointed. They are elected by fellow professors, with the voting population usually decided along lines of related disciplines. This democratic procedure operates within a limited electorate, one totaling about three thousand professors nationally as late as the early 1970s. Coupled with peer election, of course, are peer review and decision.

It has been by means of unusual role accumulation on the part of individual professors and their uncommon peer control that a considerable collegial monopoly at the local level in the Italian structure has been transferred to the highest reaches of the national system. There is some role for bureaucrats in the central ministry, and many rules set forth bureaucratic lines in finance, curriculum, personnel, and other matters. Like states everywhere, the government is particularly concerned about the handling of state-allocated funds. Administrative officials, in the university as well as in the central office, are most likely to assert their bureaucratic position in accounting for the allocation of specifically budgeted monies. But bureaucratic coordination plays only a secondary role, to the point of functioning often as a façade for the professorial oligarchy that rules and coordinates the system. The influence of the professors even extends to important political offices, with chair-holders serving in the cabinet and legislature, where they occupy strategic positions on the education committees. Compared to the professors' stature and status, the permanent state officials, including planners, are embedded in a public agency known for the mediocrity of its personnel, within a public administration that in quality and effectiveness is generally ranked lower than that of Germany, France, and Britain.[13] The dullness of the bureaucracy has increased the need for academics to help provide the order mandated by the national system approach and, while so doing, to write their own privilege into the administrative rules and turn central control to their own advantage. Italians have had reason to speak of the professors as barons (*i baroni*) and, at times, of their country as professor-ridden.

Italian public administration is known for its weak horizontal coordination and its strong verticality, with segmental bureau controls extending downward from the center like stakes driven into the ground.[14] The higher education sector has some of this quality but it has two additional features. First, the top of the stake rests in the hands of those who are supposedly located far down the line, an imposing case of an internally located interest group controlling a segment of government and doing so through guild-like means of autocratic and collegial control; and second, the lowest operating units retain such impressive arbitrary power that the overall bureau, itself a Balkanized sector of the general government, is in turn Balkanized into several hundred faculties and several thousand chairs and institutes.

In the comparative perspective of the six levels of academic organization, the Italian structure is one that has concentrated power primarily at the bottom, secondarily at the top, and only weakly in the middle. The chair-holders, rooted in the lowest operating units, occupy not only the first level or organization but also the second and third: the substructure is in their hands, controlled from the bottom up by the guild combination of collegial authority superimposed onto a base of autocratic authority. Little effective supervision by bureaucratic arms of the central state or surveillance by external groups penetrates to these levels. In the secondary concentration of power at the top level, guild and bureaucracy are interwoven. Yet here too the structure is biased toward professorial control. The overall combination of faculty guild and state bureaucracy has finally and most notably meant weakness among a class of administrators whose interests would be vested in effective internal university and faculty coordination and in the linking of the universities to one another in multicampus and regional systems.

Reform and Change

As in other nations, recent demands for reform have hit the traditional Italian system hard. By 1960, it was clear that, because of the expansion and widening of access occurring in the 1950s at the lower educational levels, the university system would soon face much larger numbers of students whose social background and educational preparation would vary more widely than before. Such perceptions were articulated in reports in the early 1960s, and proposed university-reform legislation throughout the decade pressed for a number of changes.[15] There seemed so much to be done, on pragmatic as well as ideological grounds, that proponents of reform generally drafted "big bills," some with as many as a hundred clauses. All the political parties entered into prolonged debate; the junior academics, increasing rapidly in number and assuming more responsibilities, lobbied with increasing vigor; and some important scientists joined in, angrily arguing that the traditional structure worked against the development of science and reporting invidious international comparisons and critical external opinion.[16] But the professors as a bloc, together with some of the more conservative politicians, resisted change throughout the 1960s, and none of the big bills, some debated for three to four years, was passed. Exemplifying this lack of movement, throughout the entire postwar period the national government started no new universities until the founding of the University of Calabria in 1972. The old group of thirty universities had to absorb nearly the full impact of an expansion in which unchecked student traffic swelled the large urban universities to gigantic size. Universities that predated 1500, rooted in guild-like organization, now faced ever larger masses of students.

One result of resistance to change was, therefore, a severe overloading of the system. Also overextended was the effectiveness of the full professors themselves at some of the central universities, and particularly at the University of Rome. Having kept their ranks narrow, they were overwhelmed by the number of students and junior staff they had to supervise and somehow manage. A full professor working only part-time might face twenty assistants and a thousand students. The old guild ties, heavily dependent on personal intervention, were no longer adequate in such circumstances. By 1970, the system had moved into so deep a stage of institutional insufficiency that it was becoming apparent to groups outside as well as within the structure. Student discontent escalated rapidly after 1967 and helped to dramatize the tribulations of the greatly expanded student body. Their explosive outbursts shattered glass; their dogged occupation of buildings tied up some faculties for months at a time. But factionalism, fatigue, and its own organizational insufficiency soon weakened the Italian *movimento studentesco*, as they had in other countries.[17]

Beginning in 1969, when something had to be done to pacify some of the students some of the time, small changes were made. Access to all faculties was granted to the graduates of all the different kinds of secondary schools, replacing the streaming that had limited admission to graduates of the elite classical and scientific *licei*. The fixed national curriculum was made considerably more flexible when students were granted the right to devise individual programs of study. In practice, this entailed greater local determination of curriculum as students and faculties worked out requirements. The examination system was revised to allow students a better chance of passing within a given period, although faculty schedules now were even further crammed by time given to examinations. Too, "small laws" (*leggine*) gradually increased legal support and job security for teaching personnel below the chair-holder, with stabilization (essentially tenure) given to about 15,000 *professori incaricati* who already had assumed many duties of the full professors.

Most important, the academic ancien régime's unresponsiveness during the increasingly turbulent 1960s led to a diminished respect for the professors by groups other than the students. Such an erosion of their fundamental legitimacy made possible a shift in the distribution of power. The political parties, trade unions, and other outside groups grew more willing to intervene and to form temporary, active coalitions. In the fall of 1973, by means of an executive decree that bypassed normal legislative channels, the government rammed through what may prove to be substantial changes.[18] The major provision was a projected increase in the number of full professors from 3,500 to 10,000 in a few years' time. A second measure sought to weaken the politics of choosing professors for national personnel committees by substituting selection by lot for election by constituency. Other measures attempted to further stabilize the status of lower teaching personnel and to grant them more participation and representation in faculty bodies.

Meanwhile, beyond the purview of the established faculties, an interesting trend was accelerating. The Italian system has long provided an unpublicized option for local initiative: begin a university, university branch, or a faculty with local sponsorship and municipal financing, but without recognition by the national system; and then, before the first students have completed the work for a degree, have the new unit legally ratified, supported by national funds, and accredited to award the degree by lobbying the unit into the national system. This option recently has been exercised more and more, especially in the north, as local opinion, in the service of local need and ambition, has raced ahead of the system's willingness and capacity to respond. For example, embryonic subsystems seem to be forming around Milan and Turin, as small emerging units seek to collaborate for mutual advantage. Central Italy, long monopolized by the University of Rome, produced the new University of Chieti, which operates three campuses under a common budget. Such efforts are in the spirit of regionalization, a shift away from centralized government whose time may have come. It was promised in the Constitution of 1948 and even received some legislative action in 1970.[19] In short, increased activity at the local and regional levels may result first in a de facto and later in a de jure regionalization of the universities. The system has apparently grown too large to continue without some strengthened coordination at levels 4 and 5 in the comparative scheme.

The nature of change in Italian higher education is heavily conditioned by the nature of the traditional structure that was reviewed in the first two sections of this essay. The state monopoly has weakened greatly the leverage of market forces—e.g., the competition among institutions for faculty and students. The guild controls of the professors within that monopoly have blunted bureaucratic intervention and isolated planners from the most powerful constituency, the professors themselves. Even the power of professionalism has been vitiated, as many of the scholarly and scientific disciplines have been fragmented and impeded by the conservative local academic clusters.

By default, the real leverage rests with uncontrolled numerical expansion and politics. The events following recently instituted reforms, the post-1968 small laws, suggest that when political considerations are so basic, reform becomes a matter of adjustment through political incrementalism, studied indirection, and planned bargaining.[20] The government cannot pay steady attention because of its overloaded agenda. When it does pay attention, it deals from the weak position of coalition government and mediocre bureaucracy. The overcrowded higher education sector strains with internal conflicts. The junior faculty and exasperated external groups are able to exercise growing influence in favor of reform, against the entrenched capacity of the traditional chair-holders to dilute reforms forced upon them and to effect counter-reforms; the need for increased coordination among the Balkanized domains of the chairs and the faculties conflicts with the idea that the way to open things up is to increase the number of operating units and risk an even more fragmented structure. Small victories are won now and again: easier rites of passage for students; greater job security and higher rank for lower personnel; an increase in professorships that may spread power at the senior level and in time produce de facto departments.

An effort is under way in Italy to change the political dimensions of a heavily politicized academic system. The general structural drift is toward establishing, where an entrenched power monopoly once stood, a political arena in which exchanges will be made, bargains struck, and tacit agreements reached by a larger number of groups that have an interest and stake in the structure of the system. The political alterations may then in turn provide an opening for such administrative changes as strengthened campus coordination that will help faculty federations become modern universities.

To summarize our interpretation of the nature of academic control and coordination in Italy: national bureaucracy, as structured in Italy, could not coordinate effectively, particularly in matters of personnel and curriculum. Coordination has been provided chiefly by negotiation and exchange within the ranks of the lords who by tradition *and* formal position have been authorized to rule individually over bits of the countryside. An old elite system, locally rooted, worked out some national coordination by elaborating mechanisms of oligarchical connection between local and national levels and constructing devices for oligarchical interplay at the national center. Principles of oligarchical *authority* determine the structure of control; principles of oligarchical *politics* determine the processes of allocating position, resources, and power. Bureaucratic principles do intrude, but at a second level of importance, and bureaucratic rules amount to petty harassment of those who obtain and exercise power on other grounds. It is indeed then the case that the doctrines and practices of bureaucracy serve to mask oligarchical control. In so doing, they help to maintain the legitimacy of a purportedly public system in which much has been given to the private use of a few.

Notes

1. Hastings Rashdall, *The Universities of Europe in the Middle Ages,* new ed. in 3 vols., ed. F. M. Powicke and A. B. Emden (Oxford: Oxford University Press, 1936) (1st ed., 1895), vols. 1 and 2; and *International Handbook of Universities: And Other Institutions of Higher Education,* 5th ed., ed. H. M. R. Keyes and S. J. Aitken (Paris: The International Association of Universities, 1971), 550–73.

2. Rashdall, *Universities of Europe, passim,* especially vol. 1, 149–51; Charles Homer Haskins, *The Rise of Universities* (Ithaca, N.Y.: Cornell University Press, Great Seal Books, 1957); Alan B. Cobban, "Medieval Student Power," *Past and*

Present, no. 53 (1971): 28–66; J. K. Hyde, "Commune, University, and Society in Early Medieval Bologna," in *Universities in Politics: Case Studies from the Late Middle Ages and Early Modern Period,* ed. John W. Baldwin and Richard A. Goldthwaite (Baltimore: Johns Hopkins Press, 1972), 17–46.

3. Rashdall, *Universities of Europe,* vol. 1, 165.

4. Ibid., 218, and vol. 2, 61–62; Cobban, "Medieval Student Power," 36–37, 42–48.

5. Richard L. Kagan, personal communication. On the weakness of historical research on universities in the centuries after 1500 (the end point of Rashdall's coverage), and on developments in Spanish universities in the early modern period, see his *Students and Society in Early Modern Spain* (Baltimore: Johns Hopkins University Press, 1974).

6. Joseph Ben-David, *The Scientist's Role in Society: A Comparative Study* (Englewood Cliffs, N.J.: Prentice-Hall, 1971), chap. 4, "The Emergence of the Scientific Role."

7. Matthew Arnold, *Schools and Universities on the Continent* (London: Macmillan, 1868), 109–11; Edith E. Coulson James, *Bologna: Its History, Antiquities and Art* (London: Oxford University Press, 1909), 159–60.

8. Denys Hay, "Introduction," in *The New Cambridge Modern History,* vol. 1, *The Renaissance, 1493–1520,* 1st paperback ed., planned by G. R. Potter, ed. with a preface by Denys Hay (Cambridge: Cambridge University Press, 1975), 7.

9. On the evolution and structure of Italian government, see Robert C. Fried, *The Italian Prefects: A Study in Administrative Politics* (New Haven: Yale University Press, 1963); Dante Germino and Stefano Passigli, *The Government and Politics of Contemporary Italy* (New York: Harper and Row, 1968); Joseph LaPalombara, *Interest Groups in Italian Politics* (Princeton: Princeton University Press, 1964).

10. Burton R. Clark, *Academic Power in Italy: A Study of Bureaucracy and Oligarchy in a National University System* (forthcoming), chap. 1, "University."

11. Ibid., chap. 3, "Oligarchy," and chap. 5, "Guild."

12. Ibid., chap. 5, "Guild."

13. Luciano Cappelletti, "The Italian Bureaucracy: A Study of the *Carriera Dirrettiva* of the Italian Administration" (PhD diss., University of California, Berkeley, 1966). Published in Italian, in revised form as *Burocrazia e Società* (Milan: Dott. A. Giuffrè Editore, 1968); Ezra N. Suleiman, *Politics, Power, and Bureaucracy in France: The Administrative Elite* (Princeton: Princeton University Press, 1974), 75–79.

14. John Clarke Adams and Paolo Barile, *The Government of Republican Italy,* 2nd ed. (Boston: Houghton-Mifflin, 1966), 221; Germino and Passagli, *Contemporary Italy,* 163.

15. Clark, *Academic Power in Italy*, chap. 4, "Reform."

16. For example, the so-called Brooks Report on OECD on Italian science. Organisation for Economic Co-operation and Development, *Reviews of National Science Policies: Italy* (Paris: OECD, 1968).

17. Federico Mancini, "The Italian Student Movement," *American Association of University Professors Bulletin* 54, no. 4 (Winter 1968): 427–32; Guido Martinotti, "Italy," in *Students, University and Society*, ed. Margaret Scotford Archer (London: Heinemann Educational Books, 1972), 189–93; Gianni Statera, *Death of a Utopia: The Development and Decline of Student Movements in Europe* (New York: Oxford University Press, 1975).

18. Clark, *Academic Power in Italy*, chap. 4, "Reform." This urgent measure was announced by the government on October 1 and became law sixty days later (Law 766, November 30, 1973).

19. On the limitations and possibilities of regionalization in Italy and France, see Sidney Tarrow, "Local Constraints on Regional Reform: A Comparison of Italy and France," *Comparative Politics* 7, no. 1 (October 1974): 1–36.

20. The political and administrative constraints on planning in Italy as well as in France and Britain are discussed in Jack Hayward and Michael Watson, eds., *Planning, Politics and Public Policy* (Cambridge: Cambridge University Press, 1975).

INTRODUCTION TO CHAPTER 13

"Order and Disorder" appeared in an unusual place. *Dialogue* was a "quarterly journal of opinion and analysis on subjects of current intellectual and culture interest in the United States." Published by the U.S. Information Agency, it was intended for foreign readers. This issue featured a special section of five articles on "the world of dance," including a piece by James Watson, of *The Double Helix* fame, about competition in science; a lead article by Seymour Martin Lipset on socialism in America (or the lack thereof); one by Joan Didion on being part of the "derisive barefoot population" of California; and a mélange of other ad hoc pieces, one of which was my article on higher education. I found myself in good company indeed.

I had just finished writing *Academic Power in Italy* and was ready to get back to the American system. I wanted to focus on how the U.S. framework differed from all other national systems of higher education. This short piece (no footnotes allowed) was written as clearly as I could write it for a wide audience here and abroad. Putting my thoughts down on paper helped me to realize, more than ever, that taking an internationally comparative view of higher education would become the modus operandi of the next phase of my work.

Lipset, near the end of his career, was famous for initiating lectures with the statement that he who knows only one national system knows none. A true comparativist! Using a cross-national perspective analytically, he was able to account for the absence of socialism in American politics—one of his basic components of American exceptionalism. Powerful thinking. And so it is for the higher education sector of society. Through comparison of nations, key differences and similarities can be empirically identified. After having observed the Italian system intensively, I came to appreciate the energizing variety displayed by institutions at home more than ever.

CHAPTER 13

Order and Disorder in Higher Education

THE AMERICAN SYSTEM of higher education contrasts radically with the modes of organization prevalent in most developed as well as developing countries. Seen from the vantage point of European and English modes of academic organization alone, the American system stands as a special case not only by virtue of its huge size, but also its dispersion of control, variety of institutional forms, and a host of characteristics such as extensive student choice and high faculty mobility.

These special features that constitute the American deviation may even be seen as a bit of basic good luck. For they help make a national structure capable of handling mass higher education in the face of contradictory cultural and technological demands. This favorable condition has not been produced by planning and grand design; hence, no one can take credit for it. Rather, it has evolved out of a specific sequence of struggles to create postsecondary institutions under the special conditions of nation-building in America.

The first organizational form to emerge in American higher education was not the university composed of multiple colleges, as at Oxford and Cambridge in England, but the small unitary college now known as *the private liberal arts college*. Unlike medieval universities abroad, which originated as guilds of master professors (or occasionally students), colleges in America were organized from the top down, as founding groups in the colonial period set up boards of managers (called trustees) to hire and fire teachers, appoint and dismiss presidents, and otherwise be responsible for the enterprise. Trustee authority thus became entrenched, before either administrative or faculty authority. By the time these small

"Order and Disorder in Higher Education," *Dialogue* 10, no. 4 (1977): 74–81. Abridged from "The Benefits of Disorder," *Change* 8, no. 9 (October 1976): 31–37. Used by permission of *Change: The Magazine of Higher Learning* and Heldref Publications.

colleges began to multiply rapidly in the westward expansion of the nineteenth century, the place of trustees was firmly legitimated and institutionalized, accepted as an inherent part of the way one went about the higher learning.

Trustees as Managers

When the *private university* emerged as a second sector in the last half of the nineteenth century, placing graduate and professional schools in a tier atop the undergraduate college, it too adopted the trustee mechanism. The crucial test came with the development of a third sector, *the state university*. Nearly everywhere else in the world, publicly supported schools and universities were placed within a bureau of government, with "the public interest" expressed through political and administrative officials. In contrast, the American state university was placed in the hands of appointed or elected laymen, following the trustee example that had been developed in the private sector. The same pattern was followed when publicly supported *teachers' colleges* appeared and when the two-year *junior colleges and community colleges* emerged in the twentieth century, as the American short-cycle unit for which European systems are still searching. The trustee board simply became the American mechanism for combining public accountability with the professional autonomy of academicians.

With trustees in charge, administrative services did not develop at some higher level but became grouped under them in the form of campus administration. Administrative authority began to emerge as a force of its own with the use of strong college and university presidents during the late nineteenth and early twentieth centuries. Power flowed increasingly from the hands of trustees, first into the presidency and then gradually into the hands of a larger group of campus administrators. This development, natural to the American scene, also stands in sharp contrast to developments and practices elsewhere.

In most systems, such as those in France, Italy, Germany, and Sweden, where authority has been divided between clusters of professors and a state ministry, such intermediate administration has had little or no place. The professors continued to rule locally through collective decision-making, while the national ministry of education (as in France), or a subnational ministry (as in Germany), took care of general administration, from budget making to civil service procedure for most personnel, and often appointed its own representatives to serve as administrative directors at the universities. It has been chiefly in the United States that strong administration developed at the campus level as a child of trustee control and with a power base independent of both state officials and faculty members.

Faculty Power

The concept of faculty authority was a late development in the United States. In the first half of the nineteenth century, when the unitary college began to be divided in order to handle specialization, the department emerged as an operating unit. Within it, limited personal rule could develop in specialties, and the faculty members together could decide on certain matters, somewhat in the style of the chair-holding professors in Europe, who combined personal control within the domain of the chair with collective control within the domain of the faculty.

But in contradistinction to the experiences of other major countries, the U.S. academic department from the beginning was encapsulated in an established unitary administrative structure. The chairman, responsible to administrative superiors as well as to colleagues, became a classic case of the managerial man-in-the-middle caught, like the foreman, between "management" and the "workers." Professors have had to win responsibility in certain areas of decision-making, preeminently curriculum and selection of personnel, within the context of powers already possessed by other groups. This has been true for collective bodies (such as academic senates) at organizational levels above the department, as well as within the department itself.

A Multiplicity of Structures

The persistence of these organizational forms has produced for the twentieth century an uncommon multiplicity of forms of control within institutions. The fact that the public sector was never nationalized into one inclusive system, but developed as fifty independent state structures added greatly to the dispersal of control. And each of the five major types of colleges and universities mentioned above has great diversity within it. The private university sector, for example, contains leading research universities, more modest secular universities, and Catholic universities that have retained an important religious commitment. In the past quarter-century, we have seen also the considerable development of superstructures of control, at the levels of the multicampus system, and at the state level as a whole. In addition, there exists a complicated arrangement of federal bureaus and quasi-coordinating associations at the national level.

Awareness of the differences in the structure of national systems can help to explain why reform in one country may need to move in a direction contrary to change in another. Recent reform in the highly differential American system has been directed largely at improving integration at state and national levels, with a pronounced upward drift of authority to help pull things together. In contrast, the French and the Italians are faced with the need to move authority downward, since they have become impressed of late with the vices rather than the virtues of the nationalized structures they have constructed during the last 100 to 150 years. These European reformers are struggling to break up nationally standardized forms, flirting with decentralization and even genuine regionalization. Some of them want to allow more institutions to develop outside of public authority, a move that would go down hard with conservative national ministers wedded to a unified approach as well as with leftist reformers opposed in principle to private initiatives.

The Difficulties with Mass Education

To watch other nations struggle with their derived structures as they edge toward higher education and anticipate future needs of state and society is to be struck with the great difficulty that most face in three areas. The first is how to adapt a singular structure to plural needs. Mass systems must be more differentiated than elite ones, as they absorb a more heterogeneous clientele, respond to new demands from the labor market, and attempt to cover a wider range of knowledge. But the unitary nationalized system resists mightily that needed differentiation. Any important proposal for change in one part or another becomes a national issue requiring debate and enactment at the center and implementation across the system.

The second difficulty is how to develop greater national flexibility.

Modern systems of higher education have to respond faster to changing demands than did systems in the past. But the unified frameworks are notoriously rigid, with modern planning and administrative implementation of reforms likely to increase the rigidity as new offices and levels of coordination are piled on top of the old.

Third, what can be done about the fact that, as organized systems become larger, unified control from the top loses effectiveness? It is not possible even with modern computers and communication networks to stay on top of the requisite knowledge or to direct sensibly the myriad adaptations that others must make to local conditions and their own special contests. The need increases everywhere for heterogeneity, flexibility, and dispersed control.

Main Features of U.S. Higher Education

It is precisely in these three areas that the disorderly American structure shows to best advantage. This structure may not lend itself to exact imitation, but its main (and interconnected) features may suggest possible directions for more rigid and centralized university systems.

DECENTRALIZATION OF ACADEMIC POWER. More than in any other major national system of higher education, the exercise of power is fragmented. The private academic sector holds genuine nongovernmental power in autonomous enterprises that number over a thousand. The public sector has fifty state divisions, which are fractured into subsystems within the states and fractured again at the institutional level where individual major campuses have accumulated considerable power.

CORPORATE PRIDE AND INITIATIVE. Hundreds of individual colleges and universities are responsible for their own welfare. Trustee authority and administrative authority are vested directly in promoting the local institution, encouraging faculty members to consider the welfare of the whole campus as well as the strength of their own specialized sectors. The result has been unusual corporate pride and initiative, a feature of American universities noted at the turn of the century by Max Weber, the great German sociologist, as he bemoaned the loss of local responsibility in universities in his own country that had come under strong interference from a Prussian ministry of education.

Rough Competition

COMPETITIVENESS OF THE SYSTEM. No other major system of higher education engages its constituent colleges and universities in so much competition. This is a natural outcome of the long struggle for institutional survival and advantage under conditions of radical decentralization. Competition has been self-generating, as competing colleges raised their claims, took faculty and students from one another, and altered the affections and loyalties of various publics. As in a competitive sector of industry, the game can be rough and life hard. In a time of a depressed economy, as during the past five years, hundreds of institutions literally have to fight to remain alive, several dozen actually die each year.

Some institutions move to diversity (as in industry), to reduce the vulnerability of relying on one or two competencies that may become unwanted; others choose to strengthen their claim of distinctiveness and thereby try to carve out a protected position. Surprising feats of survival are accomplished, as institutional loyalists keep alive colleges that by rational accounts should have died. Still other institutions move closer together, the better to fix prices, share resources, and otherwise escape the insecurities of sharp competition. And some give up considerable autonomy in return for more state funding, since a niche in a governmental budget is the best guarantee of survival.

Foreign observers are often astonished to see "the higher learning" subjected to a wild interplay of uncontrolled forces, when "obviously" a ministry of education, aided by planners, could establish an intelligent order. Indeed, many Americans are equally dismayed. Politicians in Washington, as well as in the state capitals, press for a more unified higher education establishment that will speak with a single voice rather than make claims at cross purposes; superboards and governors in the states seek a formal division of functions that will cut into redundancies and check future institutional aggrandizement. Yet the competitiveness remains sharp, not easily eliminated in a system where it has become deeply embedded in the states, in types of institutions, and in individual schools.

Expanding Student Choices

ENHANCEMENT OF CHOICE. The extent of personal choice depends on institutional alternatives and the chance to select and move among them, including the opportunity of making one or more mistakes and having second and third choices of institutions and programs. Many systems abroad are not well geared for this. Transfer from a faculty of law to a faculty of the humanities within the same European university, let alone from one institution to another, can be difficult or costly in lost time. In addition, a national system may either be composed of a single type of organization, the university, or may place the university, with its limited options, in such a dominant position that all other institutions of higher education are a poor second-best. Choice is narrowed and constrained accordingly.

In comparison, the range of student choice in the American system is staggering. Hundreds of thousands of students each year migrate from one college to another. No other country has such vast numbers pouring in through the relatively open doors of academically unselective colleges, with the chance later, if desired, of moving onto more selective campuses.

CHECKS AND BALANCES. The American system at all its levels is full of countervailing forces. In the superstructures of control, no single national bureau or political party dominates; no one state towers over the rest. Accrediting associations insist on minimum standards but do not hold everyone to a higher level. They thus function quite differently from governmental bureaucracies in other nations that attempt to equalize all institutions, or subsets of them, in unified systems. Within institutions, the fragmentation of power among trustees, administrators, and faculty clusters provides an informal as well as formal check-and-balance system.

AN ADAPTIVE, FLEXIBLE NATIONAL SYSTEM. Even the checks and balances operate largely within limited sectors of the system, leaving the major parts somewhat free to move in different directions in response to consumer and labor force demands and internal ambitions. The elite undergraduate college at Princeton may never include paraprofessional medical programs, but several noted liberal arts colleges in the Midwest have already done so, as they find students both in short supply and interested in job-entry skills. Liberal arts colleges have long individually devised back-door adaptations, such as taking in a nursing program for a local hospital to help pay the bills while managing not to list it in the catalogue. Many private urban universities, religious and secular, have long been service institutions, adapting themselves to the purely occupational needs of students. A thousand community colleges have adapted to whatever needs were felt in local communities and urban neighborhoods.

The cumulative result is that the American system overall can be made to expand or contract rapidly, as well as to face at once in a number of different directions. The expansion may be sloppy and uncontrolled, as it was during the 1950s and 1960s; the contraction may be brutish and opportunistic, as it has been during the past five years. But change in either direction is easier in the decentralized U.S. structure than in countries where designed change means national debate and additional national legislation, where the universities are entrenched in the national budget and their personnel in the national civil service.

The Costs of Dispersion

Lest this appear a completely rosy picture, I should mention briefly the costs of such a system, some of which cannot be afforded elsewhere. Disorder breeds intellectual confusion. Purpose gets shaded, even lost; it is hard to say what education is doing overall. The system contains much overlap: institution-builders will continue to drive rational beings mad with their plans to construct two expensive duplicate facilities within fifteen miles of one another when everyone knows that one could handle all reasonable needs.

The comparative perspective highlights two great dangers in the future drift of reform, and both are named monopoly. One is the monopoly of a single type of organization. The experience of national systems caught with only the university form but needing to find their way into mass higher education teaches that no single form is sufficient. Stretching and overloading the traditional university is the best way to weaken its traditional functions. One needs only to imagine the already comprehensive American state university, taking on all the additional tasks and roles of the state colleges, community colleges, religious private colleges, etc. In all likelihood, research would be the loser, as teaching time drove out research time and as politicians found that the consumers of teaching had more votes than the consumers of research.

Avoiding Monopoly of Power

The other danger is the monopolization of power by any single interest group, be it an external interest group, a political party, state officials, superboard staff, trustees, campus officials, faculty, or students. A monopoly of power may initially serve as a great instrument of change. But if that monopoly is allowed to continue, it can become the source of rigidity in itself if it reflects the interests and perspectives of just one group. In the increasingly turbulent organizational environments of the past quarter of this century, no small group is going to be smart enough to know the way. Even if one were, there would be a number of other groups still making legitimate claims. The touchstones of viability will be differentiation among organizational types and balance of power among organized groups that have a stake in the system.

In common with other nations, America faces the need to balance unilinear and multilinear trends. The unilinear trend, as in other sectors of society, is toward the embracing larger system, at state, provincial, and national levels, and even, as in Western Europe, toward a larger academic common market. The multilinear trend is toward differentiation and diversification that reflects a host of group interests and allows for spontaneous adjustment in the thousand and one segments that compose the organized complexity of modern higher education.

The multilinear structure deposited on America's doorstep by history gives the forces of dispersion a fair chance to resist the forces of integration. With a little attention, a little wisdom, and a little luck, we should be able to maintain the balance.

INTRODUCTION TO CHAPTER 14

It took me three decades—the 1970s through the 1990s—to fully develop a new, useful framework for comparing universities and academic systems across nations. Midstream, the *System* book set forth my thinking along these lines; it has become my most notable and important effort.

When I put some thought into how to structure the book, I shifted away from the usual common schemes of historically sequential chapters and the traditional four separate categories of student, faculty, trustee, and administration to a structure suggested by a set of distinct sociological groupings. Three basic "elements of organization"—work, belief, and authority—were what I wanted to start with. Two more chapters on national integration and change completed the scheme. The book thus confronts five generic questions about academic systems. How is work arranged? How are beliefs maintained? How is authority distributed? How are systems integrated? How does change take place?

Responses to these questions are interesting in their own right. But they also lead toward systematic answers to "issue" questions, which are commonly treated in an ad hoc manner, without too much thought about the organizational structure. What determines access? How can general education be supported? Can higher education be further democratized? Is graduate unemployment inevitable? All such matters are heavily conditioned by the structural bases pursued in *System*. To excavate the basic system structure is not to avoid the issues that confront administrators, faculty, and students in their daily rounds. Rather, it is to find the underlying "carrying vehicles" of these issues.

The conceptual and empirical grounding of these chapters encouraged me to end on a normative posture in two concluding chapters. In one of them I center attention on conflict among four disparate basic values, social justice, competence, liberty, and loyalty. I emphasize how conflict is accommodated by a variety of structural arrangements within universities and among institutional sectors within systems. Taking an international view helps greatly in uncovering possible answers.

At the least, we see participants working over long periods of time in various national systems to propose evolving structural compromises that forward a wide array of values. Resolving conflict is never an either-or choice. Universities are quite capable of keeping in mind a half-dozen or more ambitions and goals, let alone a basic three or four. They are multipurpose organizations to a fault. As such, they are compromised systems that require modest expectations; "failure" is often a shortfall against high expectations, about how much will get done, how fast it will happen, and how superior will be the result. Uncertainty comes from facing simultaneously the challenges of equality *and* excellence *and* liberty *and* loyalty. Heavily insistent values assert their own pressure, one by one, for accommodation in ambivalent situations.

CHAPTER 14

Coping with Conflicting Values:

An International View

IN AND AROUND higher education, various groups press broad values upon the system. The claims come from all sides: business executives, union leaders, church officials, minority representatives, journalists and other stray observers, spokesmen for the family. The groups increasingly articulate the primary values through government, since government is *the* modern sponsor and hence the crucial part of the environment within which higher education resides. Vague societal values are brought down out of the clouds of free-floating rhetoric as they are defined in the chambers of the legislature, the meeting rooms of the political parties, the hallways of the executive branch, especially the department or ministry of education, and the offices of such bodies as the superior council of public instruction, the grants committee, and the national academy of science. We no longer need to guess about which values really count from among those presented in polls and in textbooks; nor do we need to turn to philosopher-kings for new statements on essence and eternal truth, for we observe the values expressed by powerful groups as they act out their interests in and around the system.

Cross-national comparisons help immensely in identifying basic values and their transformations into pressing interests, since we can thereby note underlying issues that key actors seem to face in common across many countries, even as they do so in different degrees and in situations that dictate dissimilar responses. Any given country may also understate a particular value, at least for a time, thereby submerging what others more

Based on *The Higher Education System: Academic Organization in Cross-National Perspective*, chap. 7, 240–62, 290–91. Berkeley: University of California Press, 1983. Used by permission.

clearly project. Nations make major blunders in higher education as they ignore certain primary values and concentrate on others. They may swing in their efforts from one pole to another. An international view then supports normative postures that have some warrant in observed national experiences. We can advise the modern state, especially when its current commitments overlook what is obvious elsewhere.

The Basic Values

Three basic sets of values are inescapable in the expectations of attentive publics in the modern period, the interests of government officials themselves, and the attitudes of academic workers. One set may be denoted as justice, a second as competence, and a third as liberty. A fourth orientation, powerfully developed by government itself, we may call loyalty. Actions carried out on behalf of these values often clash, even contradict one another, necessitating accommodations that soften conflict and allow simultaneous expression.

SOCIAL JUSTICE

A national valuation of social justice—fair treatments for all—is pressed upon modern academic systems as a set of issues of equality and equity, first *for* students and second *by* faculty, other staff, enterprises, and sectors *for themselves*. With respect to students, equality is taken to consist, in ascending order of stringency, of equality of opportunity in the sense of access, equality of opportunity in the sense of treatment once admitted, and equality of outcome or reward. These broad conceptions of equality are variously defined, with significant effects. It is one thing to hold to a strict definition of equality of access whereby entry is determined by the academic qualification of the individual without regard to such "extraneous" characteristics as race, class, creed, or political affiliation, and quite another to define equality of access in a looser, more populist fashion as an open door for all, subordinating criteria of merit as defined by academic achievement.

Systems that profess open access but find only a third or less of their youth "qualified for higher education" clearly are using the first interpretation. The systems of Great Britain and nearly all of the European

Continent, and indeed most of the world, remain in this category, even as they expand manyfold from the time when only several percent of the population entered and even as an open-door concept becomes rhetoric and policy. "Open door" is taken to mean entry for all those who meet certain qualifications exacted by secondary schools, or the institutions of higher education, or both. In contrast, systems that let in anyone who wants to enter are clearly using the second interpretation.

Entry without particular academic merit is apparent in the U.S. system, where some students entering four-year colleges and universities are still reading at the eighth-grade level—products of automatic or social promotion in the lower grades—and some students entering the most modern and open of the community colleges, as in California, are illiterate in one language and sometimes in two. In lesser degree, this more open interpretation is found in the systems of countries as diverse as Japan, Canada, and Sweden—the latter, among the countries of Europe and Scandinavia, offering those who want to go to college the best chance to do so, regardless of academic background. This can be done by going to work for a few years, awaiting the twenty-fifth birthday, and then entering college under the 25-5 plan (later 25-4) established in 1977. Everywhere in democratic societies, equality of access is a strong and seemingly now-permanent value, and the trend in definition has been toward the looser form, under which virtually anyone can get in, in one way or another, at one time or another.[1] Even modern authoritarian and totalitarian regimes are hardly able permanently to ignore claims for equality of access: indeed, to the extent that these regimes promise greater fairness in society, as do the more socialist ones, they emphasize this value.

Beyond access, the interest in justice for students appears as a demand for uniform standards across a system so that students in given fields will be treated equally and will be given certificates of equal value. This point of view was institutionalized a long time ago in the university systems of such countries as France and Italy, in which the degree is issued by the national system as a whole and not by the individual institution, backed by the claim that training has been similar in programs throughout the nation. Ironically, although equal treatment is seen in modern reform as a more stringent definition of equality than is equal access, it developed in many systems at a time when access was sharply limited and decidedly unequal. For the few who were admitted, treatments—programs—were to be standardized, and rewards—professional degrees—were to be similar across institutions. The nationalization of systems of higher education typically entails some movement in these directions. The demand for these forms of equality also typically strengthens as access widens, with various groups seeing them as the full flowering of a true democratization. After equal access, the refrain goes, the next steps are equal treatment while in the system and equal rewards upon leaving.

Personnel and whole enterprises also steadily pursue equitable treatment, since "have-nots" have a driving and permanent interest in parity with the "haves." Uniformity is the seemingly obvious cure, in the eyes of many professors, institutional administrators, union leaders, and central officials alike. This form of equity is expressed in official insistence on fair shares for institutions and programs as well as for individuals. Bureaucracy and democracy here converge, as stressed by Susanne Hoeber Rudolph and Lloyd I. Rudolph in their study of Indian higher education:

> If bureaucratic uniformity is an important aspect of the genetic imprint that was impressed on the Indian education system, democracy has served to reinforce the propensity to uniformity. Andhra officials, like officials in other states, are likely to think uniformity a self-evident virtue. The union ministry of education, in establishing a national committee to formulate a "model act" for all universities, reflected India's educational heritage. The committee's charge contained bureaucratic notions that uniform rules might "neaten up" the confusion and conflict and perhaps "cure" the diseases that seemed to afflict academia. . . . Differences suggest the possibility of privilege and invite uniformity as a possible cure.[2]

The concept of fair share is so ubiquitous in public administration that evenhandedness, or balance, comes to mean that budget increases and decreases are to be shared as evenly as possible. As put by an observer of Japanese budget-making: "Balancing represents avoidance of comparisons among programs and their merits by implying that simply because they are similar they should receive the same or equivalent budgets."[3] Equity is a natural concern of the bureaucrat. Thus, the claims of administrators and faculty in the polytechnic colleges of the British system for salary levels and research support on a par with those of the universities found support in the British government. In the United States, state colleges find some support in the logic of state politics and administration in their efforts not to be treated as second best; and the lesser campuses of multicampus state universities can find support for parity with the flagship campus. It is difficult for officials, elected or those under civil service, to argue for differences in personnel treatment and rewards across and within categories of institutions. They can find legitimate reasons to support differences, but those reasons must then come from such other values as competence.

Bureaucratic efforts to be orderly bring together the principle of fair shares for everyone with a process of coercive comparison, whereby unequal treatments are revealed, made invidious, and leveraged by ideology and power. Norms of impartiality and objective treatment are brought into play, whether in Japan, the United States, France, or Poland. And, what is critical, the placing of universities and colleges in larger systems highlights dissimilarities and magnifies differences. If we are part of one system, how come *they* are getting so much more than we? Such comparisons become coercive as they become operationalized in the representation of interest within the system and in the normal efforts of the various parts to obtain more resources for their work. Lower administrators and professors have a vested interest in knowing what other departments, faculties, and universities are getting, and then arguing for parity whenever others get more. The have-nots have a more coercive claim in the integrated systems that they be brought up to parity than they would if they were in a separate system or systems. And, under bureaucratic norms, the higher levels of the system are vulnerable to such internal demands, since fair administration means all hands should be treated equally without regard to heritage, distinctive character, accumulated pride, and personal opinion.

That administered systems are often explicitly dedicated to a general equalizing of their many parts is made particularly clear when a national system offers national degrees. Such degrees become ludicrous if the programs of study and the standards of passage are markedly dissimilar. "The state" is vouching for the preparation, certifying that the many graduates of the many institutions have met common standards. The nationalized mode is one in which central administration works over decades to honor such commitments by spreading thousands of administrative categories across institutions.

COMPETENCE

A second powerful set of values emphasize competence. So many social groups need a capable system of higher education, one effectively organized to produce, criticize, and distribute knowledge, one that can send forth, in a reliable stream, people well prepared for occupational performance and civil life. The state needs qualified people, preferably outstanding ones, as do the professions and private firms. Everywhere there is talk about improving or maintaining the quality of education overall, or at least in certain fields that appear deficient or are connected to a deepening national need (e.g., economic analysis or military preparation).

The true believers in "excellence" have no trouble in presenting dramatic arguments. When you are wheeled into the operating room, do you want an incompetent surgeon behind the knife? It is widely deemed inadvisable to become seriously ill in countries that have low-quality medical education. Or, if our planners must be tutored in the dismal science of economics, why should we allow them to receive admittedly mediocre instruction? If they got the best, the argument goes, we could at least reduce the probability of grand mistakes in national policy. Or, why is it necessary for our otherwise advanced nation to remain on the periphery in one scientific field after another—an argument heard even in technologically advanced Japan as critics castigate the country for a tradition of imitating rather than inventing and blame the academic system for not producing more Nobel Prize winners.[4] The preference for competence comes in so many sizes and shapes: the work of academic individuals and groups; the quality of students at entry and exit; the effectiveness of institutions and systems; general education; professional preparation; research; criticism—even competence in achieving social justice. As within any other broad set of values, internal contradictions will abound: to be very good at one thing means a concentration in it that courts weak capacity to do well in other endeavors.

Academics themselves often root their own individual and group self-interest in quality of performance, since so many of them belong to fields within which judgments on capability are made across the borders of institutions and even, as we have seen, across national systems. The more scientific the discipline the more those within it judge virtue on the basis of international standards. The status-award systems of most individual disciplines and professions use quality as an important criterion to the point where perceived competence dominates positional power: e.g., a brilliant assistant professor is "better" than a mediocre full professor. A unified academic profession may also perform this way across much, if not all, of a national system. Great Britain is the foremost case of quality control by peer surveillance: the practice of external examiners means that professors of different institutions test one another's students and thereby indirectly but immediately evaluate the quality of one another's performance. This procedure encourages critical comment, much of it informal and oblique, about the teaching and the research of others. The contrast is most noticeable with the U.S. system, which, lacking similar peer surveillance of curricula and student performance, has never been able to judge teaching across institutions the way it does research. Perhaps the most important way to improve teaching competence in large systems is to concentrate on practices that entail peer intrusion, lifting the veils that normally shroud the teaching behavior of individual professors and departments. Peer witnessing can enter where political and bureaucratic surveillance dare not, and ought not, tread, because it is self-defeating.

Basic to competence is the robust fact that fields of study are structures of knowledge that have to be mastered by those who teach and those who learn. The general framework of education cannot take any shape at all that will fit other values but must be constrained by the relatively fixed forms constructed in the many fields as ways of organizing knowledge.[5] There is science, mathematics, and languages; grammar, logic, induction, and deduction. So-called soft subjects such as history are still complex, sufficiently pyramidal and sequential that those who would be called competent must work their way from lower to higher levels of understanding, from a superficial to a genuine grasp. Mastery of subject matter and related analytical skills is an inescapable aspect of formal learning, one not likely to be overlooked by all observers all the time, even if some groups or states for a while pretend otherwise. Nations that dump their interest in competence, through neglect or through attending to their values, are forced in time to turn around and face it. For example, China attempted to give low priority to academic competence during the period known as the Cultural Revolution, as reflected in the practice of forcing professors and students to spend large blocks of time in the rice fields or in some other way of participating in the work of the poorly educated masses.[6] But, at the end of the 1970s, with much fanfare, the public policies and some of the relevant practices of the central regime swung back toward a posture that would allow professors and students to concentrate on what they know most intimately and are able to do best.

It is possible to make the pursuit of excellence into a lethal habit, whether in research on human subjects, in the discovery of more ways of mass destruction, or in the emphasis on grades and credentials that leads to mental breakdown and suicide in young people. High concentration on competence in any one field, institution, or system has its costs. Perhaps most common now among the costs observed and heartily disliked by many is a certain lack of democracy. Whenever there are centers of excellence, a few are chosen and the many left out. The exclusion stimulates a counterargument that there should be a democratization of knowledge: if knowledge is power and it is concentrated, more effort should be made to scatter it. Then, too, the pursuit of self-interest on the part of competent specialist groups may or may not serve the general welfare. "Elite functions" are necessary, but they will always be in tension with mass participation and certain democratic ideals.

LIBERTY

A third set of values that plays upon systems of higher education links together choice, initiative, innovation, criticism, and variety. The central idea in this complex is liberty, connecting to traditional values expressed in Western political thought and emphasizing freedom of action as the basic condition for exercising choice, encouraging initiative, engaging in innovative behavior, sustaining criticism, and inducing variety. Liberties are sought by groups and institutions in higher education as well as by individuals. Departmental groups seek self-determination within the university; the university presses for autonomy from the state and from outside groups. The desired states of freedom are argued as a basis for wider choice in lines of action, more leeway in criticizing past and present policy, and so on, actions that in the aggregate extend variety. The subvalues of this complex interact: a variety of institutions extend the range of choice for students, teachers, and administrators alike; extension of choice on the demand side tends to lead to more innovation and variety on the supply side, as institutions respond differently to a wider set of demands and carve out different niches.

This set of values includes the powerful academic ideologies of freedom of research, freedom of teaching, and freedom of learning. Those who do research claim maximum freedom is necessary at work if they are to do their job properly and help science and scholarship to advance. Those who teach have long elaborated the notion that they must be free to say what they please without retribution if society is to benefit from self-criticism and wrongs are to be righted. Those who learn, in a variety of nations, assert individual choice in what they will study and even in what way and at what pace they will pursue learning. Freedom of the learner was given great dignity in the nineteenth-century German university, as the doctrine of *Lernfreiheit*—essentially, freedom to learn—was linked to and placed on a philosophical plane with the freedom to teach. The freedom of students to engage in social criticism and political action has had strong doctrinal support in Latin America since the 1920s, including the idea of the campus as a sanctuary for student expression. In general, freedom for one's own group is near the core of most group self-interest. Students have been no less influenced by this value than professors, even if they are less powerfully positioned in most systems to sustain a doctrine, press their claims, and effect their hopes.

Basic to this set of values is the desire for individual self-expression, not only among academics and intellectuals but among larger proportions of the general populace. Democratic values raise expectations of individuality—freedom, taken to mean more people allowed to do as they please. Economic progress lifts more people to a standard of living where time and resources are available for something beyond dawn-to-dusk labor. Rising educational levels encourage expectations about the enriched life that was formerly the province of the few. Consumers, then, come to education, especially higher education, with a variety of marginally differentiated hopes and desires that combine various aspects of self-development, such as increased autonomy, with occupational preparation and enhanced life chances; e.g., to be free and expert, therefore a computer consultant; to be altruistic but rich, therefore a lawyer who saves some time for helping the poor.

The demands of students upon nearly all advanced higher education systems clearly have multiplied tremendously, in part because of the more heterogeneous labor market into which they will later plunge, but also because the spreading valuation of individual self-expression argues against the "lockstep" of uniform programs and standard progression. Each individual literally can see higher education differently, come to it differently in preparation and personality, and ask for an individual arrangement. Linked to the desire for self-expression is a desire for variety and even for eccentricity. More people think that higher education can help them to be creative—and creative people, in myth and fact, have long modeled to the world how richly rewarding it is to be inconsistent and eccentric.

LOYALTY

There is always a body of interests brought to bear in higher education that is centered in the operation of the state, a group of interests bound up in the survival of regimes and the identity of nations. "Loyalty" is perhaps the best name to apply to this complex that stretches from the limiting of criticism to the linking of the system to national integration. To overlook this set of values would be to avoid issues that are at the heart of the higher education question in one country or another.

Particularly poignant is the depth of the clash in values in many new underdeveloped nations that causes politicians and academics to collide head-on. The academics typically wish to pursue their work in line with their own adjustments of metropole models and international standards. But the national political and bureaucratic leaders seek to build a nation by promoting a singular symbolic identity, integrating diverse tribes and factions, constructing the infrastructure essential to nationhood (such as transportation and communication networks), and delivering on promises of a better life. In addition, they often are impatient with democratic forms—seeing them as dangerous to unity and slow in producing results— and prefer authoritative rule for a variety of reasons. Hence, they not only expect higher education to march shoulder-to-shoulder with other branches of government in the cause of nation-building but also expect the university administrators and professors to follow the definition of nationhood, its ends and means, decided upon by the leader and his immediate staff. The relation between higher education and government, then, often tilts toward domination by government. Fealty to the state looms large. It is more difficult than in advanced nations to dissociate the tasks of the university from the tasks of the state.

This set of values, like the others, has its own contradictions. What the state wants from the higher education system may be at least three different types of relevance: socioeconomic relevance, defined in terms of practicality and professionalization; cultural relevance, referring to cultural revival and national identity; and political relevance, defined as good citizenship and commitment to political goals. The first means an emphasis on technology, natural science, and specific professional training. The second hinges on competence in the humanities and the social sciences, with a particular focus on one's own country, but allowing for freedom of inquiry and exposition in those fields. The imperative of political relevance places primacy upon conformity, uniformity, and discipline. As James A. Coleman notes in the case of African universities: "The ideology of relevance applied to frail new universities imposes upon them a heavy overload which is patently compounded when the demands upon them are so inherently contradictory."[7]

Basic to the state-university relationship everywhere are the boundaries established for outspoken criticism of state actions and societal conditions. The boundaries can indeed be very wide: fools have to be suffered gladly in British academic life by state officials because there is virtually no way to get rid of them. No direct orders can be given to block employment or disbar promotion or restrict salary. No leverage against the employing institution is available for its "mistaken" toleration. The boundaries can also vary markedly within a single system, in line with its diversity. In the United States, toleration varies by state—greater in New York than in Mississippi; by level—greater in universities than in community colleges; by degree of public support—greater in excellent liberal arts colleges than in mediocre ones.

The limits on criticism can be especially wide also where sharp criticism of government and society has become a way of life in higher education institutions—the many countries, advanced and developing, where university and government exist virtually as two different cultures, and students expect both to be critical and to play out their personality development in politics. Criticizing and struggling against the government is a way of life in faculty and student subcultures in Italy and France, as it has been in such Latin American countries as Mexico, Chile, and Argentina whenever the government is something less than harshly authoritarian. In the many Latin countries, the posture of criticism, of course, is a dangerous game—often more persistent, more strident, more violent than that found elsewhere, but then subject to a crackdown by the state and a severe tightening of the limits of expression when a hostile regime comes to power, often by coup, or when under a benign regime state officials feel pushed too far.

Finally, the wide boundaries for criticism can contract sharply when authoritarian regimes come to power and act vigorously to stay the flow of critical comment. And narrow boundaries are institutionalized as one-party regimes remain in power and have the will and the means to define opposition as illegitimate and even illegal. Hence, in the worldwide picture, loyalty and subservience to the will of the state are primary values, even if they do not appear on the front of the stage in Sweden or Britain, Japan or the United States. They are prominent in most new nations in Asia and Africa and in authoritarian states everywhere.

Conflict and Accommodation

Any sensible administrator asked to confront directly and to reconcile these four orientations would undoubtedly seek other employment. Fortunately for officials, the system, not particular individuals, does most of the work of reconciliation. System accommodation proceeds largely by indirection and delayed interaction—by analogy, more in line with the urgings of Niccolò Machiavelli to temporize, temporize than with the injunctions of those management theorists who would have us clarify goals, order priorities, and implement objectives, all by five o'clock.[8] In higher education, any major enterprise is a compromise of conflicting values, and system organization is compromise written large. But some organizers are poor compromisers, more often for reasons of ideology than intelligence. System compromising can be badly done, as certain values become set in the concrete of position and power and then deny an adequate realization of other ends.

The conflicting values press behavior in contradictory directions and encourage antithetical forms and procedures. The value of social justice presses toward open-door admission, mass passage, and uniform graduation. But the interest in competence everywhere argues for selection at the outset, a willingness to fail and weed out, and for graded certification that will label some persons as more capable than others. The clash between equity and excellence on the issue of entry and certification has been widely noted in educational debate during the decades since World War II, especially in the 1960s and 1970s. The problem is found in communist as well as democratic nations. Educational policy in the USSR has vacillated between emphasizing admission based on performance and admission based on social status, i.e., preference given to working-class and peasant youth. The result has been that "the quality of graduates has declined whenever social status has been the major criterion, but has increased whenever performance has been stressed." One value or the other had to give; or, a compromise might evolve.[9]

> The current situation may be seen as representing a compromise between ideological commitment to equality of opportunity and the necessity of meeting the skill needs of an increasingly complex economy. It is clear that in spite of recent reforms aimed at increasing the enrollment of working class and peasant youth in institutes and universities, the regime is very reluctant to give much weight to nonperformance criteria, and hence the overall impact of the reforms has been small. The manner in which the reforms have been implemented also indicates that educators are themselves reluctant to forgo universalistic criteria.

Similarly in the German Democratic Republic (East Germany): the attempt to proletarianize DDR education has competed with the desire

> to recruit the most gifted students wherever they are found and train them so that they are able to serve DDR industry in the most productive way possible. . . . A victory of dogma over pragmatism . . . is apt to be brief and ineffectual.[10]

Less noted in both policy deliberations and research is how liberty enters the fray, playing at times against both equity and competence. For equity, fair shares is the name of the game and therefore procedures must be set that apply across the board. The competence camp also presses for uniform arrangements, generally called standards—well-constructed barriers to entry, required sequences of courses and examinations for passage, and quality controls on certification. But liberty is contrary to both, pressing away from both fair shares and standardized forms and toward a maximizing of choice and a celebration of variety.

Under full sail, liberty means autonomous faculty individuals acting with little regard for group norms and individual students seeking individualized programs of study with little worry for common standards. Institutional liberty carries with it the likelihood that institutions will vary all over the map in what they do, including the marketing of shoddy goods to uninformed customers in the soft underbelly of a diverse system. Those who want to ensure competence by measuring individuals against norms and standards obstruct such free choice and institutional self-determination. In turn, liberties can clearly be diminished by equity-induced uniformities despite the general hope that greater justice will bring more opportunity and choice. For example, a research assessment of widened admission to higher education in Sweden by means of the much-acclaimed 25-5 scheme pointed out that

> the strivings after fairness have resulted in its opposite: owing to excessively complicated rules and a gigantic central admission procedure the individual's possibility of asserting himself has suffered. Moreover, the system may disfavor applicants with unusual qualifications, social handicaps or the like.[11]

A generalized demand for fairness and equality in the Swedish case has led to increased bureaucratization and centralization, which in turn diminished individual choice. It also lessened the fairness that comes from taking unusual qualifications or disadvantages into account. Judging individuals by criteria plugged into a central computer, as was begun in the Federal Republic of Germany in the 1970s, cannot help but have mixed effects in areas of individual choice and freedom to act.

Loyalty often conflicts straightaway with all three of the other values, subordinating justice, competence, and liberty in the name of a single higher good. When regimes are preoccupied with loyalty of faculty and students, little heed is given to equal treatment or competent training or freedom of choice.

Without doubt, the structure of a higher education system must be full of contradictions, inconsistencies, and compromises if it is to express effectively these four disparate primary values. As systems modernize, as they move from less to more accessible education, they widen and deepen their elemental strains and dilemmas by having to attempt significantly to embody these values. Each system must do so with forms and practices, institutionalized in earlier decades, that are interlocked with one another as well as with various structures in the larger society. Thus, post-1980s, we need not wonder why modern systems of higher education should exhibit a bewildering mixture of the open and the closed, the elitist and the democratic, the flexible and the rigid, the traditional and the modern.

But all is not hopeless chaos. There are broad system arrangements that seem to reconcile these values better than others do. We can assess how conflict among such fundamental interests is structurally abated. Although systematic inquiry into such matters has hardly begun, six ideas deserve the light of day.

IDEA ONE. Conflict among such basic values in higher education is accommodated better by diverse than by simple structures. The more diverse national systems are more capable of reconciliation than the simple ones. Systems are pushed toward diversity by multiple values. A composite of *un*like segments and procedures (1) permits better immediate response to different known demands; (2) allows varied later adjustments to the unknown and unanticipated; and (3) provides a more ambiguous total space within which conflicting actions taken in the name of justice, competence, liberty, and loyalty can be played out. The sunk costs of each of the values are not so directly challenged since the true believers of each value get at least some territory of their own, are able to work their way around others, and find it difficult to determine who is doing what to whom. Those who are capable of holding several values in mind at the same time find some structural supports for each and maneuver by shifting priorities over time.

We have mapped the basic horizontal and vertical dimensions on which the needed differentiation occurs. Within their institutions, systems can and do generate more fields and programs side by side at any level of training and more levels arranged in a progression of increasingly advanced tiers. Among their institutions, systems can and do proliferate institutional types, arrange the types in functional and status hierarchies, and make permeable the boundaries between the sectors so that students can move from one to another in search of different types and levels of training. Diversification is the key to how higher education systems effect compromises among a plurality of insistent values. Simplicity demands confrontation among contradictory points of view.

IDEA TWO. In the service of competence, the most crucial form of diversification in modern advanced systems is vertical status differentiation among institutions. A moderate degree of hierarchy allows status to be awarded to institutions and sectors on grounds of perceived quality and encourages them to compete on this basis. One might immediately object and say that competence can be achieved better by administrative controls that seek to establish minimal standards and to reward outstanding performance. But we have seen the complexity of tasks in higher education systems and the impelling need for the many parts to be at least semiautonomous. It becomes virtually impossible, even self-defeating, to attempt to ensure competent effort in most of the system by top-down oversight, planning, and administration. Formal coordinators are in a steady state of frustration as critics demand that they move to improve the system and rulers send down commands from on high, but the levers of basic change remain remote if not hidden completely. The problem becomes sociological: namely, to find the ways to hook group and institutional self-interests to chariots of ambition. There must be something to be won by all those who man the understructure, working harder to be better. That something is higher status and its associated rewards.

Ralf Dahrendorf has argued effectively that both options and linkages ("ligatures") are necessary to enhance the life chances of individuals.[12] Options are possibilities of choice, the alternatives of action given in social structure. Linkages, no less important, are bonds that anchor persons and their actions and give meaning to choices. Those who are socially stitched together have some basis for judging where their choices will take them and what is worth doing. Without social links, choice becomes pointless; with ligatures, choice has coordinates. Further, undergirding both choice and linkage is hope, hope prodded not by utopian images but by realistic awareness that some individuals, groups, organizations, or countries possess what others aspire to. Thus status inequality makes for hope, for both individuals and institutions. Institutional hope springs from institutional differences rather than from similarities.

The question of balance in hierarchical arrangements immediately occurs. The sharply peaked hierarchy in France, Britain, and Japan can isolate several institutions in elite positions and block out all others. The flat hierarchy characteristic of the Italian system can block the incentives for enterprises to strive hard to better themselves. A middle ground provides the openness and the incentives, the grounds for hope. Institutions can compete for better personnel, and hence young scholars can flow from one institution to another in search of better conditions of work. Institutions can shift their clienteles toward the higher-quality inputs of their betters. There are many reasons to worry about academic drift, but competence as it is understood in the system and society at large is not one of them. Drift is toward "better"; it is a standards-serving process because it pursues status, and status is linked to perceived standards. This is a prime reason why status hierarchies are not as bad as they are normally viewed, through the modern perspectives of democracy. Where status hierarchies do not exist, there will be strong pressure to create them in order to guarantee a bottom-up search for competence.

The importance of institutional status hierarchies in promoting competence has been stressed by "best-science" advocates. Modern science at its best requires concentration of talent and resources. It can hardly be promoted by equalizing and thereby scattering talent and funds across institutions and programs. France in the West and the communist nations in general have tried to assist "best-science" by investing in a separate research structure—the national academy approach. The Federal Republic of Germany has used the many institutes of the Max-Planck shelter. But if best science, best scholarship more broadly, is to have protective and supportive locations within the higher education system itself, then there must be concentrations, some favorable treatment within and especially among institutions.[13]

The problem is to couple some hierarchy with some openness, pluralism, and peer review—a problem noted in classic form by Henry A. Rowland, an American scientist and exponent of best-science elitism who attempted to specify in the 1880s what needed to be done to improve the science of physics in the United States.[14] The existing system of four hundred institutions he likened to a cloud of mosquitoes: hardly any could be compared with the "Great academies" found in Europe, which provided "models of all that is considered excellent" and thereby stimulated physicists to their "highest effort." There had to be some concentration of talent in physics in a few first-class universities. Best science required an institutional pyramid, commanded at the heights by a best-science elite and open to talent at the bottom. All levels of the hierarchy would need to be pluralistic, with groups of physicists divided along lines of specialty, training, and geography and having access to many journals and granting agencies. The U.S. system, especially after World War II, did indeed evolve in the direction that Rowland had advocated.

In sum, institutional hierarchy can be and often is a form of quality control. It portions out status, respect, and rewards on grounds of perceived competence, utilizing both public opinion and peer assessment. It can and often does concentrate resources efficiently for the carrying out of expensive tasks, from the forming of bureaucratic elites to the manning of research laboratories. The problem is how thereby to preserve high standards and, at the same time, allow for institutional and individual mobility.

IDEA THREE. In the service of liberty, the most essential form of diversification is the creation and maintenance of different sectors and subsectors, down to the point of allowing institutions to be individually distinctive. Within the general system, enterprises need the freedom to initiate on their own and thereby choose a line of development. Much choice, we may note, can be made available within universities and colleges that are highly diverse in themselves, such as the "educational city" that we call the American state university. But there are limits to size and complexity of the individual enterprise that, when exceeded, cause severe problems of overload in work and management and confusion in organizational character. Institutions that try to do it all, replicating within their structures all that is found within the system at large—superinstitutions, we might call them—suffer some of the same problems of overload and characterological confusion as persons who try to be superwomen or supermen. What is critical is that certain bona fide group interests will be resisted or suppressed. No matter how extensive its internal diversity, an institution will still have some dominating points of view that will cause it to handle some activities badly, if not to prohibit them entirely.

The classic case in one country after another in recent years has been the resistance of university professors and administrators to short-cycle education and recurrent education. The resistance is motivated by a host of reasons that need not be explored here, but it has clearly weakened these forms of education. The groups that wish to carry the new values and work them up in operations need the freedom to choose for themselves. Increasingly it is necessary to divide up the work among institutions so that different units can wholeheartedly devote themselves to different tasks. Professional training at many levels, general education of different types and for different kinds of students, research of quite different complexities and ranging from the most basic to the heavily applied—all can be assumed by different structures of support and sorted out by planning or unplanned evolution or a combination of the two.[15] Separate institutions are typically less coupled than the parts of a single organization and hence can reap the benefits of flexibility that inhere in loose coupling.[16]

Thus, a prime reason why undifferentiated national systems cannot manage modern higher education very well is that they do not provide enough liberty for a range of ideas, activities, and supporting groups. Preeminently in academic systems, ideas have a right to be born, even at some inconvenience to system coordinators and their search for integration. Despite the confusion, duplication, and overlap thereby produced, a vast complex of institutional types and marginally differentiated institutions is the name of the game for liberty and innovation in modern higher education. But the problem is how to maintain a high level of institutional liberty and individual choice without limiting equality too severely and weakening standards too much. In this, permeable boundaries are crucial. Diversity becomes more acceptable to those with their eyes on equality if the diverse channels of participation are void of dead ends. Having second and third chances and the possibility of transferring from one sector to another, from one institution to another, diminishes the disagreeable effects. Similarly, diversity and a high degree of individual choice become more acceptable to those with their eyes on competence and consumer protection if some academic surveillance, such as accreditation, operates across sectoral and institutional lines, maintaining some minimal standards and reining in the roguish behavior on the part of institutions and their staffs that sometimes amounts to consumer fraud.

IDEA FOUR. Justice in higher education is most effectively implemented if it is institutionally disaggregated instead of applied in a blanket fashion across a system. As we have seen, competence and liberty require sectors and hierarchies; merit and choice entail differences and rankings, unlike segments seen as relatively high and low, noble and less noble, even as systems strain to blur the perceptions of the differences. Hence, if these two values are to be served even modestly well, systemwide equal access, treatment and outcome are not possible.

The idea of disaggregating justice is not a popular one, since equity issues loom large on the national agenda in many countries, attracting parents, students, politicians, and administrators alike to promise that inequities can be wiped out by sweeping measures. But systemwide attacks on equity issues in higher education have great potential for boomerang effects as they try to flatten institutional differences and command a system to be unitary, thereby undercutting the grounds for competence and liberty. Since the system cannot be made operationally unitary and differences are maintained and enlarged, high expectations of equality are inevitably frustrated. Sooner or later, the vision of equity must center on fairness in segments of the whole and even, if possible, at the level of the individual institution.

Systems may thereby help contain the self-defeating tendency of the pursuit of equality. As Ralf Dahrendorf has noted, equality has a built-in frustration effect.[17] Behind the demand for equality is the wish to extend opportunity: how can more people come to enjoy more life chances? But many life chances defy continuous extension, since to increase them past a certain point is to destroy them. The acquisition of a degree increases one's chances in life as long as the degree has some special value in the eyes of others. To be valuable, it cannot be possessed by all. As soon as most persons can have it, it adds little or nothing to life chances. The declining value of the high school degree, the associate in arts degree, and the bachelor's degree in the American system illustrates this point. It is a bitter irony for those who vigorously pursue the equalization of access, treatment, and outcome in higher education that the end results, if achieved, would be relatively worthless. Everyone would have the same thing but be worse off. A more sophisticated concept of extension of opportunity is required, one rooted in the differentiation rather than integration, pluralities rather than unities. Justice in academic systems must be varied and specific, attached to contexts that promote different competencies and, in their aggregate, widen the play of liberty.

IDEA FIVE. State control of higher education works better by long-run rewards than by short-run sanctions. States can have intervention strategies that respect the peculiarities of institutions organized around multiple fields of knowledge, places where the values of justice, competence, and liberty must be exercised. But governments are inclined to reach for direct controls, rules that reduce day-to-day discretion. The model is: do this job in the following manner; do not deviate from this procedure; make sure every professor teaches twelve hours a week and reports periodically on how he spends his time. Negative sanctions are emphasized, eliciting defensive strategies from those to whom the sanctions are applied.[18] Then, too, when goals are not easily measured and compliance can at best be only partially evaluated, such sanctions soon lose effectiveness, frustrating those who try to apply them.

In contrast, governmental guidance can be effective over the long run where governments concentrate on setting broad directions of development, maintaining the quality of the professional personnel, and supervising the system in the mediated form, previously identified, in which the balance of control shifts from government to academics at successively lower levels. The key is the attractiveness of higher education as an area of employment—is talent attracted or repelled?—and the quality of professional socialization—are controls internalized in the individual academic and the operating group that make for responsible behavior? The state can have its "accountability" in the form of general oversight alone, if professional controls within the system hold academics accountable to one another and to general norms of objectivity and fairness. Enlightened oversight is the way to go, since no matter how precisely governmental officials attempt to define objectives, the outcome will largely depend upon the cooperation of those in the system.

IDEA SIX. Value ambivalence in higher education is mirrored in structural ambivalence. Modern complex higher education systems are mixed in character, rather than tending to one pole or the other, e.g., public or private, equity or excellence, liberty or loyalty. Like individuals, collectivities can be fanatical for a time, but the costs of pursuing only one set of values soon becomes too high and counter-reforms set in to restore the place of other values. The inherent contradictions of these systems in effecting basic social values lead to mixed structures.

We may learn from a similar situation in health care. After noting the virtues and vices of private, public, and mixed systems of health, Aaron Wildavsky concludes that "what life has joined together no abstraction may be able to put asunder. . . . By the next century, we may have learned that a mixed system is bad in every respect except one—it mirrors our ambivalence"[19]—ambivalence over extension of treatment, equal access, high quality, more choice, professional independence, responsiveness of doctors to patients' needs, personal control over personal costs, cost containment at the collective level, etc. No one likes mixed systems except the majority of those who participate. An all-private system makes sense on paper, especially on the note pads of economists; a fully public one is similarly an impressive theoretical model, particularly in the minds of governmental planners. But what we get in reality are ambivalent systems comprised of some of each, produced by the push and pull of contradictory values and interests. Likewise for the primary values considered here: only ambivalent structures can express the ambivalence contained in value opposition and contradiction.

Compromised systems also require modest expectations. We have seen that "failure" is often a shortfall against high expectations about how much will get done, how fast it will happen, and how superior will be the results. Many persons and groups, beginning with politicians, have a vested interest in promising large and quick results as they struggle competitively for favor in political and bureaucratic arenas. But systems that must interpret, embody, and implement a wide range of contradictory values need modest expectations on the possible realization of any single goal. Such realistic hope goes hand in hand with the growing uncertainty that attaches to policy and action. Organizational theory has come to emphasize the uncertainties produced within modern organizations by environments that change more rapidly than in the past. But it is not merely rapid change that is at work. It is also pressures, within and without, of heavily bearing values that have grown more numerous. Uncertainty comes from facing the challenges of equality *and* excellence *and* liberty *and* loyalty more fully than before. Modest expectations are an accommodation to this ambivalence of situation and response.

Notes

1. See Dorothea Furst, "Selection and Equity: An International Viewpoint," *Comparative Education Review* 22 (1978): 259–77.
2. Susanne Hoeber Rudolph and Lloyd I. Rudolph, eds., *Education and Politics in India: Studies in Organization Science and Policy* (Cambridge, Mass.: Harvard University Press, 1972), 171.

3. John Creighton Campbell, "Japanese Budget Barnsu," in *Modern Japanese Organizations and Decision-Making,* ed. Ezra F. Vogel (Berkeley, Los Angeles, and London: University of California Press, 1975), 71–100.

4. See Michio Nagai, *Higher Education in Japan: Its Take-Off and Crash* (Tokyo: University of Tokyo Press, 1971), chap. 3, "The Tasks of the University."

5. Noel Annan, "Equality in the Schools," in *Whatever Happened to Equality,* ed. John Vaisey (British Broadcasting Corporation, 1974), 89–102, especially 101–2.

6. John Shea, "Background Paper: Education in China," in *Observations on the Relations between Education and Work in the People's Republic of China,* Report of a Study Group (1978) (Berkeley, Calif.: Carnegie Council on Policy Studies in Higher Education, 1978), 33–47.

7. James S. Coleman, "The State and the University in the Republic of Zaire," paper presented at a conference on Politics and Education, Western Regional Comparative and Education Society, University of California, Santa Barbara, November 1981. Quotation from p. 29.

8. Machiavelli on reform: "I say, then, that inasmuch as it is difficult to know these evils at their first origin, owing to an illusion which all new things are apt to produce, the wiser course is to temporize with such evils when they are recognized, instead of violently attacking them; for by temporizing with them they will either die out of themselves, or at least their worst results will be long deferred." Niccolò Machiavelli, *The Prince and the Discourses* (New York: Modern Library, 1940), chap. 33, *Discourses,* p. 200. Machiavelli's point of view comes closer to the attitudes appropriate for reform in modern public administration than those that propose sweeping reform as a way of reconstructing a system from the top to the bottom.

9. T. Anthony Jones, "Modernization and Education in the U.S.S.R.," *Social Forces* (1978): 522–46. Quotations from pp. 536, 544.

10. Thomas A. Baylis, *The Technical Intelligentsia and the East German Elite* (Berkeley, Los Angeles, and London: University of California Press, 1961), 51.

11. Lillemor Kim, "Widened Admission to Higher Education in Sweden (The 25/4 Scheme): A Study of the Implementation Process," in *Implementation of Higher Education Reforms,* ed. Ladislav Cherych and Paul Sabatier (Paris: Institute of Education, European Cultural Foundation, unpublished), 60. Later published in *Great Expectations and Mixed Performance: The Implementation of Higher Education Reforms in Europe* (Stoke on Trent, U.K.: Trentham Books, 1986).

12. Ralf Dahrendorf, *Life Chances* (Chicago: University of Chicago Press, 1979), chap. 6, "Inequality, Hope, and Progress."

13. On the need for "elite" components within "mass" universities and colleges, and modern systems generally, see Martin Trow, "'Elite Higher Education': An Endangered Species?" *Minerva* 14 (1976): 355–76; and Clark Kerr, "Higher Education: Paradise Lost?" *Higher Education* 7 (1978): 261–78.

14. Daniel Kevles, *The Physicists: The History of a Scientific Community in Modern America* (New York: Vintage Books, 1979), 43–44, 375.

15. See Joseph Ben-David, *Centers of Learning: Britain, France, Germany, United States,* an essay prepared for Carnegie Commission on Higher Education (New York: McGraw-Hill, 1977), especially 165–69, 180–82. Ben-David concludes that "the feeling of crisis and anomie that prevails in many academic circles . . . derives mainly from internal causes, namely, the difficulties of systems of higher education to accommodate within their existing structures their new and extended functions" (180–81).

16. For outstanding discussions of loose coupling, see Karl Weick, "Educational Organizations as Loosely Coupled Systems," *Administrative Science Quarterly* 21 (March 1976): 76–86.

17. Dahrendorf, *Life Chances,* 94, 118.

18. Guy Benveniste, *Bureaucracy and National Planning—A Sociological Case Study in Mexico* (New York: Praeger, 1970).

19. Aaron Wildavsky, "Doing Better and Feeling Worse: The Political Pathways of Health Policy," *Daedalus* 106 (1977): 105–21. Quotation from p. 122.

INTRODUCTION TO CHAPTER 15

When I wrote the concluding chapter for *System* (1983), I wanted to portray what an effective higher education system would look like in the post-1980s future.

I argued vigorously against centralizing decision-making power in the hands of state officials or any other single group. We know by now that arbitrary power imposed to break the stale cake of custom and move things along in the short run leads, in a few years' time, to the greatest danger of all—monopolistic power exercised top-down. Start with the minister of education and take it from there. Seek order by means of formal order. Even insist that one size can fit all.

The opposing set of views I asserted in *System* emerged from observations and comparisons of higher education in many different countries. What makes modern higher education viable, productive, and capable of progress? A forthright, upfront answer is that power should be divided, variety supported, and ambiguity legitimated. Because universities and national systems are steadily evolving into unique, more complex units, a vast array of institutions and programs are needed. And openness to innovation is prized.

Most of all, reform efforts should avoid reducing complex realities to a single issue. When the matter of how to overcome the "average" poor performance of American students in their first two undergraduate years arose in 2006, e.g., rarely was it specified that this average was derived from statistics offered by several thousand different universities and colleges. That pathetic average has nothing to do with student average performance at Harvard—or at North Carolina State University or at Carleton College in Minnesota or at the University of Utah or at California State University, San Diego. It is simply a fabricated figure that squeezes out all the varieties of American higher education. It is an average that reflects the low student academic achievement associated with the large number of open-door two-year *and* four-year colleges that welcome students each fall with no questions asked about merit. This soft underbelly of student low achievement is a standard part of the variety of institutions in the United States—the part that is most directly reflected in remedial programs following on from poor secondary school education. Consider also student admissions based on religious faith, or for their tuition payments directly needed to pay faculty salaries, or for any number of reasons associated with local availability and continuity.

How many times since World War II have reform groups used simplified national "averages" to claim that the education system has put "the nation at risk"? Refusing to learn from history, one national reform group after another in the United States has chosen to repeat that chestnut. They make no serious effort to locate the problem: bottom-feeding institutions that very democratically open their doors to poorly prepared students who missed having a decent secondary school education—and to those newly arrived immigrants eager to get a college education even if they start out illiterate in two languages. To look at it another way—these places go a long way in offering a second, third, or fourth chance in a non-formal, madcap, and nebulous system of higher education. They are part of the American accommodation of conflicting values.

CHAPTER 15

The Case for Bottom-Heavy Federalism

THE COMPROMISE AMONG conflicting values that allows their parallel realization may logically be effected by a single authority. It is not difficult to find theories that portray the individual political leader or senior administrator rationally choosing among a set of values, establishing priorities for all time, or rearranging them from year to year. It can then be but a short step to the possibility that the powerful state can provide a workable resolution to the problems of multiple demands and conflicting values in each institutional sector that falls within its reach: simply put wise people in charge, an authoritative chief informed by expert staff. But we cannot depend on the wisdom of Leviathan, especially after witnessing so many lessons to the contrary in the twentieth century. And our analysis of the higher education system has shown one functional reason after another why all-powerful bodies prove particularly ineffectual in this sector. The task structure alone gives the modern system a low threshold in tolerating concentrating authority. More quickly than in other activities, the system becomes "overcentralized." Nations that run elementary and secondary education on a thoroughly nationalized basis, for example, right down to inspector generals visiting the classroom, are not able to operate higher education in a similar fashion.

But the large lessons of history almost seem beside the point as statesmen and politicians, administrators, and professors and students, seeking solutions to pressing problems, generate responses that in the aggregate move to concentrate control. There are always ample reasons to centralize, since it is the central government that is best poised to make massive attacks on common problems. Issue by issue, various groups seek a

Based on *The Higher Education System: Academic Organization in Cross-National Perspective*, chap. 8, 263–76, 291–92. Berkeley: University of California Press, 1983. Used by permission.

central response to their will, and immediate effects are visible within the short-term perspective of governmental officials, elected or appointed, who need to show results. But the second-order effects, those that change the underlying structures, are difficult to identify and, once identified, difficult to analyze. They are also beyond the horizon for those who are politically and administratively nearsighted, and thus are systematically avoided. Furthermore, their constituency is small and confused.[1]

This phenomenon of unanticipated and undesired long-run effects of concentrated purposive action is clearly exacerbated in the higher education sector. The underlying characteristics of postsecondary activity are difficult to perceive and appreciate. They make any system peculiarly troublesome, recalcitrant to the central touch. But it is upon these characteristics that realistic preferences for the organization of higher education need to be constructed. The preferences are most directly applicable to advance systems in industrialized democracies, but they also bear on the evolution of other systems if they wish to do the work of modern higher education effectively. In its broadest dimensions, the case is three-sided: it is essential to divide power, support variety, and legitimate disorder. To link these preferences to the uniqueness of higher education is to end where we began the search.

The Division of Power

There is value in perceiving higher education as a power struggle. This approach builds on the Weberian legacy in classical sociological thought: modern societies are replete with irreconcilable values; organized social life is then a power struggle, since it is power that ultimately determines whose values gain priority and who pays the costs. That necessary struggle has increasingly moved inside the webs of organization that constitute societal subsectors.[2] Thus, if a number of values and interests are each to have some emphasis in a higher education system, and respective supporters are to pay some of the costs, then organizational power must be divided in one way or another. Divided power permits partial expression of particular values in the sector overall, or full expression of each in some part of the system, or both.

Undivided power thereby becomes the greatest single danger in the operation of a system of higher education. Anything approaching a monopoly of power will express the concerns and perspectives of just a few groups, shutting out other interests. The history of higher education exhibits such effects. Students in some medieval Italian universities, through student guilds, could hire and fire professors and hence obtain favors from them. Senior faculty in some European and English universities during the past two centuries were answerable to no one and hence could sleep for decades. Dominating trustees in some early American colleges could and did fire presidents and professors for not knowing the number of angels dancing on the head of the ecclesiastical pin, or, in the twentieth century, for simply smoking cigarettes and drinking martinis. Autocratic presidents in some American institutions, especially teachers' colleges, have run campuses as personal possessions. State bureaucratic staffs and political persons in Europe and America, past and present, democratic, and nondemocratic, have often been heavily dominant in ways that retarded progress and limited the effectiveness of the system. Such concentrations of power have sometimes served well, protecting scholarship or helping to build distinctive enterprises, or even breaking open an immobilized system. But they do not work well for long, soon freezing organization around the points of view of just a few.

In the complex and turbulent settings of the last part of the twentieth century, no limited group can be wise enough to know the way, including the central staffs now most likely to evolve into near-monopolies of control. State and party officials in East European countries have been forced to back off from total dominance, limiting the constraints of their manpower planning to allow, among other things, more room for the judgments of professors and the choices of students. Various countries in Western Europe are attempting to reverse a long trend toward centralization in order to shift decision-making out to the many segments of the periphery, closer to participants and to the realities of local operating conditions.

The underlying reason for all this is that organized systems of any complexity are increasingly replete with reciprocal ignorance. The expert in one activity will not know the time of day in another. Given the breadth of subjects they cover, such ignorance must be uncommonly high in developed systems of higher education. The chief state higher education officer may not even be able to do long division, let alone understand high-energy physics, whereas the professor of physics, able to understand

Einstein, is incompetent in the everyday matters of system coordination. And business firms and government agencies have been driven to greater dependence on the judgment of authorities in different parts of the organization as their work becomes more rooted in expertise. The loosely woven texture of the effective university is a relevant model of how to function as those at the nominal top become more ignorant.

A central concentration of power also promotes a vicious circle of politicization, an excess of effort to influence action through political pressure. When the corridors of power are like a sharply tapered funnel, they become exceedingly crowded. All interested parties must push themselves forward in the limited space, encouraging a politico-administrative version of the war of all against all.

The classic political doctrine for advocating a division of power is federalism. James Madison and some of the other founding fathers who wrote the U.S. Constitution set out to devise a divided, balanced, and limited government that could steer between the mischief of fragmenting fractions and the mischief of excessive control. The government overall should be pluralistic, promoting justice within a framework of diversity. Without monopoly, but with linkage, each branch or part could check the likely usurpations of the others.[3] The primary way to guarantee any major degree of democratic control through state regulation would be to use a federated structure that puts the regulation on a divided and piecemeal basis and forces parts of the system to check and balance one another. Madison spoke of a double security for the rights of individuals: two or more levels of government would control one another and, at the same time, the division of government into several interacting branches would cause each level to control itself.

This classic conception of divided and self-checking control can be applied to the internal composition of organizations and major sectors of society. The complex university in itself tends to become a federal system: semiautonomous departments and professional schools, chairs and faculties, act like small sovereign states as they pursue distinctive self-interests and stand over against the authority of the whole. After noting the growing importance of the department in the English university, produced partly as an unintended consequence of expansion, A. H. Halsey and M. A. Trow comment that it is not fanciful to see the modern university as a federation of departments each facing outwards toward the research councils for research funds and toward schools and other universities for students and staff while at the same time living together on a campus with faculty boards and the Senate as mechanisms for negotiation and arbitration of their divergent interests.[4]

Graeme C. Moodie and Rowland Eustace also take note that in the English university "there is an important sense in which the 'higher' bodies seek validation from the 'lower.' Whatever the precise boundaries of departmental autonomy, its existence makes of every university a 'federal' structure rather than a strongly centralized system."[5] Federalism in higher education begins in the antithesis between discipline and enterprise.

But the problem is how to extend that principle to whole systems, particularly those that are formally unified. We need to apply the principle to the higher layers, emphasizing that control should look more like patchwork than cloth consistent in color and shape. We hardly need to worry about excessive patchwork, since the basic processes of the superstructure work to systematize, to tidy up. How then are checks and balances maintained? A middle ground has two essential features: the top levels of the system should themselves be pluralistic; and intermediate bodies should mediate between the central authorities and the many levels of the understructure, buffering one from the ungainly ways of the other.

Agency pluralism at the top of higher education systems is an important line of defense against the error of a monopoly of power. Pluralism generally evolves from the natural pursuit of agency self-interest. Rare is the national system in which all matters of research and higher teaching are handled in a single ministry or department: even in relatively simple systems, ministries of agriculture, departments of defense, bureaus of mining, and institutes of health support universities, colleges, and research centers in whole or in part and have their own academic constituencies. Each headquarters office is then in part the representative of a particular set of operational interests, struggling for their welfare. Considering their typically intense need for highly trained experts, for the upgrading and retraining of professional personnel, *and* for the pleasing of constituencies, governmental agencies across the board can hardly stay away from higher education. Thus, agency conflict at the top is natural. It should be expected and encouraged. But there are strong inclinations to discourage it, even to seek to eliminate it. In the name of economy and efficiency, reform seeks to eliminate overlap and duplication. Conventional wisdom continues to view monopolies in the public sector as good, overlooking the need for pluralism within the governmental structure itself, in the governance of such a complicated and basic function as higher education.

Equally important is the buffering of control provided by intermediary bodies and forms. Levels of organization can and do check one another: when the Swedes inserted a regional level of governmental supervision during the 1970s, they created a possible counterforce to central direction as well as to university self-control. Different forms of authority also can and do balance one another: in the U.S. system, trusteeship, institutional bureaucracy, and faculty collegial control, individually and collectively, balance against state bureaucracy and legitimate political control. The central idea is to have forms that will offer different compositions of interest and expertise at successively higher or lower levels. In its golden age (1920–65), the British University Grants Committee (UGC) came close to the ideal. The processes of resource allocation at the top and the bottom were influenced by different mixtures of interests and expertise. Holding intermediate powers between the university people and the governmental officials, the UGC clearly protected one from the other. There were many informal features of trust and friendship, and common background among political, administrative, and academic elites, that helped make the committee work as well as it once did. But it is the form, the primary structure itself, that has been the most important invention in twentieth-century higher education in buffering central control by intermediate bodies.

The necessary division of power in academic systems should perhaps go by some other name than federalism, since the federal principle is so much attached to the U.S. experience and little valued and discussed in many countries. But one can take the long view and make the case, as has S. Rufus Davis, that the constitutional framework established in Philadelphia in 1787 was

> an evolutionary accident, as it were, brought into being out of the historical experience of all those who, from whatever motives, from whatever beliefs, for whatever purpose, or in whatever form, had ever

sought the benefits of association without surrendering their identity as individuals.[6]

Thus, leaving aside the specifics of the American experience and form, the federalist principle is one appropriate for the internal constitution of major organized sectors of society. In higher education systems, individuals and groups, while strongly tempted to go their own way, must perforce seek "the benefits of association." But the need to preserve and strengthen individual and group identities is uncommonly high, for the good of the whole as well as in the service of self-interests. When freedom of research, freedom of teaching, and freedom of study are seriously curtailed, the system as a whole suffers. And such freedoms are protected to the extent that near-monopolies of power are restrained and a diffusion of power promoted.

Short-run thinking, affected so much by immediate problems, will cause systems to err in one direction or the other in seeking to rearrange the structure of power. If choice can be made, it is safer to err toward the mischief of multiple factions entailed in excessive fragmentation and minimal overall control; for to move in the other direction is to ease toward the mischief of monopoly entailed in excessive order and strong formal integration. The latter is much the greater error, the one that reduces sharply the structural flexibility required for later progress.

The Support of Variety

The case for a division of power is also a case for the support of variety. While monopoly tends toward narrowness, a multiplicity of authorities is likely to produce greater variety, even when subject to the effects of academic drift. Further, a direct case needs to be made for deliberate support of variation in institutional types and academic forms. As the values we wish to implement become numerous, more varied tools are needed to serve them. Then, too, growing complexity increases our uncertainty, leaving us more than ever unsure about facts and their interpretation as well as the policies and strategies to be derived from them. We are then best served by several approaches to major problems—different attacks on general education, different forms turned loose to promote short-cycle education, multiple types of research centers devoted to the cure of cancer or the reduction of air pollution. It also makes sense to have several universities or colleges doing virtually the same thing in the same locality, since conflict and struggle can promote their achievement. When such comparison is possible, errors in programs and institutional types may be caught and brought to light before they become entrenched. Error is also compensated for when one or more sets of institutions provide an alternative that serves as a bypass around the breakdown of another. Higher education may be the worst sector for putting all of one's eggs in one basket.

The observable need to support variety in the higher education system draws theoretical sustenance from the concept of rational redundancy. Martin Landau has convincingly argued the virtues of redundancy in administrative and social systems as well as in biological and physical ones.[7] An airplane is badly designed when it has only one way of putting down the wheels. Transportation in and out of cities works best when people have different ways of getting to work. The human body can recover from a heart attack when secondary muscles around the heart take over from damaged primary ones. In language, spoken or written, we repeat ourselves to increase reliability and to reduce errors of communication. Political systems are well designed when the whole is more reliable than any of its parts, because of a redundancy of structure, particularly power centers. Auxiliary precautions are built in and compensating responses made possible that overcome weaknesses and failure in any number of different parts. Likewise for major organizations and their larger webs. They also need ways to allow rules to be broken and units to operate defectively without doing critical injury to the whole.

In the face of such an obvious need for redundancy, orthodox theory in public administration has long been wrong:

> For the public administration rationalist, the optimal organization consists of units that are wholly compatible, precisely connected, fully determined, and, therefore, perfectly reliable. The model which represents this dream is that of a linear organization in which everything is arrayed in tandem. It is as if the entire house is to be wired in series. . . . Organizational systems of this sort are a form of administrative *brinkmanship*. They are extraordinary gambles. When one bulb blows, everything goes. Ordering parts in series makes them so depen-

dent upon each other that any single failure can break the system. It is the old story of "For want of a nail . . . the battle was lost [emphasis in original]."[8]

Thus, while conventional wisdom assigns to redundancy such meanings as needless, costly, excessive, and bad, it is preferable to emphasize its usefulness, its necessity, in considerable degree in modern organized systems.

The importance of variety in academic forms reverses the commonsense assumption that coordination means to pull together. Instead, the most important coordination issue is differentiation. With the dominant pressures in the higher levels taking the form of standardization, integration can literally take care of itself. There is so much momentum behind it as to carry it too far. But the relative success of modern systems increasingly depends on a command structure that allows for myriad adaptations to specific contexts and local conditions. A unified system coordinated by a state bureaucracy, or by an interlocking network of bureaucratic and oligarchical controls, is not set up to work in this way. It resists differentiated and flexible approaches. Thus, the crisis of stalemated structure, as in France of the late 1960s that shakes the nation. Thus, near-permanent crisis of a system, as in Italy of the 1960s and 1970s, possessed by a rigidity difficult to break. Coordination in these instances had so much settled down in particular narrow channels that it became out of phase with the organic understructure and the changes it would normally promote.

Hence, the central problem for coordinators becomes that of how best to anchor different roles for different institutions and groups in the system. *The* enemy of top coordinators should not be the messy, chaotic ways of students, faculties, and institutions, but the planned and unplanned convergence of the basic operating forms upon one another—the natural production of sameness that comes from status-seeking in the field as well as from administration in headquarters. One can find insightful officials throughout the world who have grasped this point. A first level of awareness is shown in discussion of the need for "planned differentiation." A more penetrating awareness seeks diversity by creating conditions of autonomous action—planning for unplanned change, as it were—and giving legitimating help, by means of pronouncements and rewards, to those who accept and create limited niches. Thus, in the United States, some state chancellors have advocated that "statewide system leaders have a responsibility to *articulate* the virtues of institutional diversity, and to seek to distribute resources to reward institutions for doing well the more limited tasks associated with such diversity."[9] The basic work of legitimating an institutional role, or an ecological niche for a subsector, naturally falls to those on the spot. But those higher up the line can help or hinder. They can then bless those flowers that come up beautiful and hearty, and curse the weeds that foul the garden.

All those who advocate pluralism must admit to the vices of autonomous action, among which is the simple fact that the drift of the market can steadily undercut the crucial differentiation of institutions and sectors. Anchorage for the parts must develop—in budgets, rewards, and doctrines; coordinators need explicitly to encourage, against converging flows, distinct bases of support and authority that help to stabilize different roles. This requires a willingness to ride with a bothersome division of authority within the upper levels, since multiple sources of sponsorship and supervision will be the best guarantee of diversity. Multiple agencies protect multiple types, and a power market of competing agencies supplements the economic-and-status market of competing institutions and corrects for some of its failures.

Thus in supporting variety, the central procedural concern is the relative and interacting contribution of planned and autonomous actions. Both are needed and both are operative everywhere, but in varying combinations that include radical imbalance. At this time in history, with current combinations tilting toward controlled action, support on the organic side is needed. The appropriate role for statesmen in higher education systems is to create and maintain broad frameworks that encourage constituents to generate changes that are creatively adaptive to a myriad of local contexts and, in the aggregate, thereby diversifying.

The Legitimation of Disorder

If educational powers are to be extensively divided and if coordinators are to take the support of diversity as central, then we need appropriate rationalizations—administrative doctrines and broader ideologies that tell officials they are doing all right when the system as a whole looks like a mess, nearly everyone in the system feels powerless, and no one can clearly identify who is doing what to whom. The doctrine of federalism, of pluralism, is a crucial part of the answer. But there is more that is needed: direct praise for ambiguity, two cheers for disorder.

An appropriate normative sense of the situation has been emerging at a rapid rate in efforts of the past several decades to understand the complexity of modern organizations and the decision-making that ostensibly takes place within them. Norton E. Long argued cleverly a quarter of a century ago that government could be and is coordinated by the play of political action in and around it rather than by top-down command in neat hierarchies. By the end of the 1950s, Charles E. Lindblom had presented his classic, persuasive case that muddling-through was a normal, rational, and effective means of decision-making in complex organizations operating in complex settings. Astute government watchers among organizational theorists have portrayed in recent years the increasing ambiguity of governmental structure and action, within large agencies as well as in the government as a whole, as bureaus develop individual personalities and are taken over by professional groups. The highlighting of the functions of redundancy has obvious normative use. Aaron Wildavsky and his associates have shown the complexities of governmental action that defeat or greatly attenuate the implementation of policy. Other recent work has emphasized the point that so-called decisions, again in complex settings, are more the result of accretion than of clear, decisive judgment. The school of thought developed by James March and his colleagues during the 1970s, epitomized in the organized-anarchy metaphor, extended the growing awareness of complexity and related ambiguity to university organization.

The additional doctrine now needed for direct application to higher education systems as a whole is one that emphasizes and praises the benefits of disorder. Above all others, higher education systems need a disorder within which individuals and groups autonomously overexert themselves and consult informally and quasi-formally with one another, thereby achieving the effectiveness that formal controls are unable to produce. Given the tasks, beliefs, and authorities of the system, this is the only way over the long run. Systems are effective when they maximize their own possibilities, and maximizing what dozens of varied groups of professionals can do along the bottom side of the higher education system means the encouragement of their initiatives and choices.

At the top, the doctrine of disorder emphasizes redundancies among policy systems—never let one set of policy-makers decide; and contingencies among policies—act tentatively, expressing policy through a series of experiments. In place of "adaptive specializations," such as more powerful planning units, high officials can seek "adaptive generalizations," such as multiple and overlapping policy systems and the flexible capacity to zig and zag, go forward and pull back on mistakes, that comes with a tentative approach.[10] If these arguments are too general, specific ones can be offered: e.g., do not write changes down in national laws, for then you will rigidify them, magnify their errors, and diminish future flexibility; do not put academic personnel into a general civil service if you can help it, for you will push rewards toward the serving of time and minimize the incentives for creativity.

Under the doctrines of disorder and mixed systems, central officials can restrain themselves in seeking consensus and contentment in the system as a whole.[11] Colleges and universities themselves do not need a great deal of consensus, since their structures and activities are only mildly interdependent. The larger systems are even less so. Higher education requires a fair amount of discontent so that people will speak up about what they think is going wrong, in a system where arcane knowledge can hide error from generalists. Top officials can also seek to restrain consistency. Otherwise they may be opting for revolution over evolution. If a system avoids the zigs and zags of change in order to be consistent, its need for change builds up and its capacity to accept change weakens. The drift is then toward the revolutionary situation, the day when changes can no longer be held off but the old regime has lost the capacity to adapt. Fortunately, the low interdependence of some units in any complex higher education system facilitates some experimentation with an inconsistent variety of innovations and strategies. But central officials and planners seldom believe this to be desirable and try to move in the opposite direction. It is ironic that they should be so involved in brinkmanship and the construction of revolutionary situations as they seek to be rational and consistent and to offer stability and happiness.

The Uniqueness of Higher Education

It does not make much sense to evaluate business firms according to how much they act like universities, nor economic systems according to their resemblance to higher education systems. Neither does it make any sense to do the reverse; yet it is built into current commonsense and management theory that we do so. We persist in peering at higher education through glasses that distort, producing images that render more confusing a terrain that is naturally difficult. The first source of trouble is in the borrowed assumptions that steer our vision, assumptions that are no longer appropriate even in the first instance. For good reasons, large business firms stray far from idealized conceptions of economy and efficiency, and we have learned to expect the economic system as a whole to be divided, varied, and ambiguous. We now know that government departments, having a character of their own, will not behave according to business models, and that "the political system" is a vast and opaque web of conflicting tendencies. So, too, and more so, for the higher education system. It may be smaller in scale than the economic or political system, but it contains extended and unique complexities. The imagery of "organization" and "system," the very terms themselves, lead us to expect simplicity—simplicity that must be there and will be found if we are only intelligent enough. But if the higher education system was ever simple, it will not be again. We are looking at inordinate and uncommon complexity.

To understand that complexity much better than we currently do requires that we retreat somewhat from general theorizing across the major organized sectors of society and concentrate on analysis of particular realms. A sector is taken seriously when we seek its own ways of dividing work, promoting belief, and distributing authority, its own ways of changing and its own conflict of values. Once those ways are known, then features held in common with other societal subsystems appear readily enough. But to begin from the assumptions of other sectors is to misperceive and underestimate the unusual parts in the mixture of the common and the unique. In each case, the unique ways, we have cause to believe, center around the tasks of the system. For higher education, we have seen, the tasks are knowledge-centered. It is around the formidable array of specific subjects and their self-generating and autonomous tendencies that higher education becomes something unique, to be first understood in its own terms. Just one general effort alone, the creation of knowledge, remains poorly comprehended until we grasp the fact that "difference and plurality are part and parcel of the moral world of discovery and invention."[12] Field by field, the academic search for progress leads to alternative interpretations of the world. Uncertainty rather than the grail of truth characterizes the frontiers of knowledge, and mortals can offer only different and changing approximations of the truth. Knowledge will remain a divided and imperfect substance. In its fissions and faults we come closest to a root cause of the many odd ways of the higher education system.

Notes

1. See James Douglas and Aaron Wildavsky, "Introduction: The Knowledge Foundation in the Era of Big Government," in *Russell Sage Foundation: The Future and the Past* (New York: Russell Sage Foundation, 1979), 50–51.

2. See Kenneth McNeil, "Understanding Organizational Power: Building on the Weberian Legacy," *Administrative Science Quarterly* 23 (1978): 65–90.

3. James Madison, in *Federalist Papers* numbers 10, 47, 48, and 51, argues that (1) factions are the price as well as the product of liberty; (2) the many necessary factions should be able to represent and express themselves, rather than be suppressed by a dominant faction or centralized state; (3) toward that end, formal powers should be divided between several levels of government; and (4) central government should be composed of separate and distinct branches that are able to check and balance one another. Madison concluded that security for the rights of the people is not found in charters or in appeals to humanity but in "the multiplicity of interests" that characterize a free society. See *The Federalist Papers: Alexander Hamilton, James Madison, John Jay* (New York: New American Library, Mentor Books, 1961).

4. A. H. Halsey and M. A. Trow, *The British Academics* (Cambridge, Mass.: Harvard University Press, 1971), 111–12.

5. Graeme C. Moodie and Rowland Eustace, *Power and Authority in British Universities* (Montreal: McGill-Queens University Press, 1974), 61.

6. Rufus S. Davis, *The Federal Principle* (Berkeley, Los Angeles, and London: University of California Press, 1978), chap. 4, "The United States Model, 1787." Quotation from pp. 119–20.

7. Martin Landau, "Redundancy, Rationality and the Problem of Duplication and Overlap," *Public Administration Review* 29 (1969): 346–58.

8. Ibid., 354.

9. R. E. Lieuallen, "The Ecological Frame of Mind," in *The Monday Morning Imagination: Report from the Boyer Workshop on State University Systems*, ed. Martin Kaplan (New York: Praeger, 1977), 152.

10. Hugh Heclo, "Policy Dynamics," in *The Dynamics of Public Policy: A Comparative Analysis*, ed. Richard Rose (Beverly Hills, Calif.: Sage Publications, 1976), 237–66.

11. See Bo L. T. Hedberg, Paul C. Nystrom, and William H. Starbuck, "Camping on Seesaws: Prescription for a Self-Designing Organization," *Administrative Science Quarterly* 21 (1976): 41–65; and George Ecker, "Administration in Higher Education: Making the Most of Ambiguity," *Review of Higher Education* 3 (1979): 23–31.

12. Ralf Dahrendorf, *Life Chances* (Chicago: University of Chicago Press, 1979), 157.

INTRODUCTION TO CHAPTER 16

By the time *The Higher Education System* was published in 1983 (it became my basic book), Adele and I had turned our attention to launching three successive four-day summer seminars. The first, in 1982, focused on eight different disciplinary perspectives—including the historical, the political, and the economic—and their varied approaches to systems of higher education. This mini-conference resulted in *Perspectives on Higher Education*. I wrote one of the basic chapters, "The Organizational Conception," and also the concluding one. For this collection, we chose part of the latter.

I do not remember how the perspectives topic came to mind. I do remember being increasingly impressed, as I attended conferences in Europe and Latin America, with how the work of historians and political scientists and scholars other than sociologists shed some light upon the fast-growing complexities of higher education. Bringing together eight disciplinary perspectives voiced by international experts then seemed a good idea. At the same time, I wanted to garner some funds from one or more private foundations to support a new comparative higher education group I established at UCLA after I moved there in 1980. The foundation that proved most responsive was the Exxon Education Foundation, then under the thoughtful leadership of Robert Payton, president, and Arnold Shore, program officer. They agreed to fund a first summer seminar—and after its success—a second, "The School and the University," and then a third, "The Academic Profession," making the early to mid-1980s a busy time for Adele and me and for the small group of post-docs and graduate students who gradually became involved.

Each summer conference had a clear focus. Papers were prepared by eight to ten experts; at least two others were commissioned to offer a critique on each subtopic; and then the assembly of about twenty-five specialists engaged in discussion for half a day. After the conference the papers underwent needed redrafting and strenuous editing. Clarity of language becomes a major problem in international conferences, particularly when papers reflecting different disciplinary terminology are to be integrated and published.

At the conferences we were able to draw upon the insights of accomplished scholars. At the first one, e.g., Harold Perkin, the English social historian, and Simon Schwartzman, the Brazilian specialist in the development of science, participated. The twenty-five experts assembled during the three years included Sheldon Rothblatt, the Berkeley historian, and Gareth Williams, the English economist—both senior figures—and also such rising younger scholars as Gary Rhades, the sociologist in my research group, Rune Premfors, the Swedish political scientist, and Klaus Huefner, the German economist. The strangers in our midst provided lively mutual exchanges and a marvelous camaraderie, from which we all surely profited.

The essay presented here highlights eight large "truths" drawn from the disciplinary perspectives for thinking about policy and administration. An example is the central role prestige plays as a special coin of exchange. Over the years, the book has proven to be useful for teaching graduate students how the various disciplines can offer insights in the study of higher education.

CHAPTER 16

Useful Disciplinary Perspectives in Probing Higher Education

IF THESE eight ways of thinking about higher education are beamed toward "policy" and "administration," is there any discernible relevance and enlightenment? One can recommend an unmediated immersion by individual policy-makers and administrators in broad subjects, a personal search for ideas and frameworks useful in grappling with practical problems. But life is short, and time this month much shorter, and compelling duties usually preclude such reading. We might also hope to have scholars closely associated with policy-makers, connecting "truth" to "power" as they whisper advice in the ear of the prince. But this type of involvement also infrequently obtains. The movement of perspectives, ideas, and insights normally contains many steps, with much slippage and reinterpretation along the way. . . .

Our final effort in integrating these eight approaches is to give a clear picture of their potential relevance to those who have practical concerns. Out of each perspective a central idea is extracted and presented as a guide to thought. Necessarily broad in formulation, and a far cry from the direct engineering of solutions, each of these ideas conveys a view of the higher education system that surely is not new to many practitioners but, just as surely, is new to others. And even for the most thoughtful policy-makers and administrators, some of the expressed ideas may clarify what has been intuitively known. Together, the eight ideas become a battery of explicit thoughts that may help firm judgment amid the swirling disarray of everyday problems and pressures. If they serve only to point to crucial long-run features of the higher education system, for those

Based on *Perspectives on Higher Education: Eight Disciplinary and Comparative Views*, edited by Burton R. Clark, chap. 9, 268–73. Berkeley: University of California Press, 1984. Used by permission.

whose obligations steadily pull attention to short-run decisions, they will be touchstones for informed judgment.

The eight large "truths" mined from the eight perspectives may be simply summarized:

1. The higher education system is rife with political action and hence may be fruitfully viewed as a political system. But the political processes of highest importance differ qualitatively at different levels. "Politics" at the bottom is different from "politics" at the top. Hence it is no longer useful to argue about whether the system as a whole is primarily a collegium or a bureaucracy, an open system or a closed system, and so on. At any one time, it may be professional politics at the operating level, bureaucratic politics at higher administrative levels, and corporatist politics, e.g., at the level of state action. In any event, bona fide "interests," inside and outside the formal boundaries of the system, are always multiple, and they increase as the system becomes more complex. Hence, political processes are endemic and steadily multiply in number and type. The quality of politics in the system, conditioned by tasks and beliefs, is then a necessary object of observation and thoughtful evaluation by scholars and administrators alike.

2. Mechanisms of finance are central stabilizers of the higher education system and crucial levers of reform and change. They steer decentralized and loosely coupled parts that are otherwise difficult to touch. They make real the expression of state power, defining it broadly as guiding frameworks, when lump sums are disbursed, or narrowly as direct special controls, when categorical budgeting dominates. They become institutionalized particularly around enrollment, funding from higher to lower levels largely on the basis of number of students enrolled or anticipated. Hence, they can be manipulated by all parties concerned, not just by top formal coordinators, by attracting or repelling students or altering the ways in which they are counted. Thus, all chairs, departments, faculties, colleges, and universities, as entities, engage in "economic behavior," seeking to increase their share of resources. The more economic ones come closest to the day-to-day problems of administrators and offer opportunities for some manipulation. There are good reasons why administrators see economists as the most relevant social scientists, even in settings when their predictions are more wrong than right. At least they offer predictions, and in concrete numerical terms.

3. The individual disciplines and professional fields of study are authoritative segments in the social organization of any modern system of higher education. These "thought groups" fragment individual enterprises. They also fragment the academic profession, making it a conglomerate unlike other professions. Hence, no simple model of professional organization, any more than a bureaucratic model, points to the nature of the thought groups. Turning the understructure of the university and the system into a unique operating level, one characterized by fragmented professionalism and even guild-like arrangements, the disciplinary imperative demands that administrators be sensitive to the nuances of differences among subjects and their supporting groups. It also requires rejection of most of what a student learns about "management" while formally studying this art. More discriminating models of university organization, descriptive and normative, will develop as scholars and practitioners take seriously the imposing place of disciplinary organization among the unique features of the higher education system.

4. Prestige is a special coin of exchange in higher education, for individuals, groups, enterprises, and even whole national systems. The ambition and the work that go into winning a Nobel Prize, or a less-known award in a scholarly field, are simply the extreme example of a more general phenomenon in which effort is tied to recognition more than to profit. Particularly in the more competitive sectors and systems, personnel exert and overexert themselves to increase their own status. Institutions do likewise, again especially in the more competitive settings, with higher status seen as the bridge to larger resources as well as a better life. Hence, institutional hierarchies become major mechanisms of allocation and coordination. Where they are somewhat open to status-climbing by upwardly mobile institutions, or to central manipulation, they may be powerful mechanisms for change. If they are closed and fixed, they are grounds for resentment and despair. Key to the positive efforts of open-status hierarchies is their encouragement of hope, a panoply of motivations in individuals, departments, and universities that things will be better if more strenuous efforts are deployed. Hence, sophisticated policy-makers and administrators are as sensitive to the meaning and use of prestige and hope as they are to the incentives of money and other material rewards. Prestige and hope are instrumental tools, means to important ends.

5. Beyond prestige, the symbolic side of organization has special

power in a sector of society that is organized around bundles of knowledge, staffed by "men of ideas," and intensely professionalized. Only the church among the major sectors of society is seemingly so laced with cultural imperatives. Each discipline or professional area of study becomes a subculture with self-elaborating and autonomy-seeking tendencies. The academic profession overall is permeated with such stirring ideologies as "freedom of research" and "freedom of teaching." Each institution develops symbolic representations of itself, in self-image and public image, which affect resources. Especially in competitive settings, these collective representatives are steadily cultivated, turned into powerful legends or sagas. Even in noncompetitive contexts, universities and colleges are readily transformed into romanticized objects of love and affection, more quickly converted into "communities" than are organizations in business and public administration. Thus, a sophisticated executive in this sector of society is one who understands the symbolic imperatives, especially the separate culture-building tendencies of disciplines and enterprises.

6. Science is increasingly a special world, a dynamic republic of special interests seeking favorable conditions outside as well as within higher education. The strain toward autonomy is pressing; the scientific sector develops hegemony that is not coterminous, or identical in interest, with that of higher education. The latter system has more to do, spreading its attention to activities that are nonscientific or only weakly scientific in nature. But science either has to be well accommodated within, spread throughout, or centered in well-supported segments, or it will flow toward outside locales. If badly accommodated, research becomes divorced from teaching and the scientific norms of universalism are weakened within the academic profession and individual universities and colleges. Notably, higher education then loses the prestige and legitimacy conferred by modern science. Hence the care and feeding of science are enduring responsibilities for statesmen in all sectors of higher education as they concern themselves with the long-run status and effectiveness of the system.

7. Policy implementation is considerably more difficult than policy formation. Almost anyone can quickly formulate a policy—uninformed voters and preoccupied legislators do it all the time—but it takes sustained efforts and special competencies to implement effectively most policies that are enacted. The difficulties increase in systems where authority is diffused, purposes are ambiguous and contradictory, and the

operating structure steadily grows more complicated. Higher education scores high on all such characteristics. The veto points are notably numerous; a host of interest groups can stand in the way. Hence, attenuation of policy is normal, and slowness in implementation is natural. And much incremental adjustment is the order of the day, pulling expectations of global change down to a more modest level. To do otherwise is to multiply the unintended and undesired consequences of policy and to excite major boomerang effects. Intelligent policy formation and implementation become step-by-step experimentation, zigging and zagging through unclear alternatives, pulling back from wrong starts, and finally blessing the small beginnings that prove they are worth larger application.

8. There is always history. All important phenomena within the higher education system are shaped by their developmental flow. Structures and processes laid down at any time tend to perpetuate themselves. In a sector with much diffusion of authority and a rich symbolic life, forms become deeply institutionalized in various parts of the systems. They rarely need to prove comparative efficiency and effectiveness, for effective measures cannot be devised when significant outcomes are multiple, long-run, ambiguous, and intangible. The basic forms develop protected niches, even more under state authority than under market interaction, and become ends in themselves. Hence they project themselves powerfully into the future. They also shape what comes after them, since they occupy the domain of work and embody the common understanding of what higher education is and how it should proceed. A finely honed sense of historical development is extremely useful for those who practice, in politics and administration, the art of the possible.

At the same time an existing set of structures and processes will develop deficiencies that help generate an interest in reform. The odds of disappointment particularly increase as we ask a system to do much more than previously in effecting contrary values and interests. The true believers in any one value are particularly prone to such disappointment and will seek changes that promise more of what they want. Forces for change are always operative in modern systems, in tension with the forces of stability and perpetuation.

Our eight examinations of higher education offer no solutions to contemporary problems, but in providing perspectives they help make simple solutions and deep despair both seem less compelling. In common, they also make us realize that a national system of higher education is increasingly not a mere epiphenomenon, dependent for its direction upon the political order, or the economic forces of production, or "the world system." There are decisive processes within as well as without, mechanisms for growth and qualitative change that are an integral aspect of the functioning of the system. There are abundant conflicts and contradictions, forces and counterforces, to upset the status quo from within. There are beliefs that select and reinterpret environmental pressures and condition the responses of the system. There is room for autonomous initiatives, even for the adoption of ideas and forms taken from counterparts in other societies. The transferring of ideational materials from one society to another, long a major path of change, will loom ever larger as communication and learning across national borders increase. The agents of the higher education systems will do much of the exporting and importing, obeying their own logics and generally acting without asking anyone's permission.

The habit of thinking cross-nationally will soon be as important for those who administer higher education as for those who study it. Historians tell us appropriately that if you want to know where you are going, it helps to know where you have been. We may add: it also helps to know where you are. That sense of place depends on coordinates that locate one's own responsibilities and efforts in larger frames. Scholars can now help practitioners sense their latitude and longitude on an international grid, identifying on a broad and basic scale the universals and the particulars in their own systems and their own work. The comparative grasp can thereby help to clarify the destination of each system in the years to come. It also significantly adds meaning to a multitude of personal efforts, granting importance and even additional dignity to what must be faced in the office next Monday morning. A comparative capacity has become a rich resource in practical thinking as well as in scholarly analysis, and nowhere more so than in the practice and study of higher education.

INTRODUCTION TO CHAPTER 17

The second four-day summer conference supported by the Exxon Education Foundation was held at UCLA in 1983. Over twenty-five participants were seated at the table with ten experts, whose papers were discussed intensively by two reviewers and then by the entire group. The topic we focused on this time was the all-important matter of the relationship between secondary and higher education. This connection has long been a troubling one in the United States; it was now a matter of national concern. A report, *A Nation at Risk: The Imperative for Educational Reform* (1983), prepared by a National Commission on Excellence in Education and published by the U.S. Department of Education, described the situation. It portrayed a breakdown in education so deep as to threaten the welfare of the nation. The problem and its solution virtually asked for a comparative approach. We assembled experts from France, Germany, Great Britain, Sweden, Japan, China, Latin America, and Africa, as well as from the United States. The results were published in *The School and the University: An International Perspective* (1985).

When we compared the educational structure found in the United States with those in Europe and Japan, we saw that our public, comprehensive, secondary schools had a major weakness. They operated as local monopolies under local control, with far-flung mandates to do everything. After writing up "the distinctive American problem" in the concluding chapter of the book, we took our critical assessment to a broader audience by publishing two papers in *Phi Delta Kappan* (1985) under the provocative subtitle of "What Went Wrong in America." Our indictment was severe, even cold-blooded. Others could sing the praise of the American common school. We sought to report on the dark side of a school-university relationship that had gone very wrong. We here draw upon the second of these two papers.

How do matters stand two decades later in the early twenty-first century? The effort to promote academic excellence in U.S. secondary schools has degenerated into state-by-state testing of all students for levels of "proficiency." But national prescriptions under "No Child Left Behind" have deliberately left the definition of proficiency to the individual states. As of 2006, a number of states took this leeway to dumb down their tests, slashing their own standards in order to report a high number of students as proficient. They are willing to thereby label undereducated students as educated.

CHAPTER 17

The High School and the University:

What Went Wrong in America, Part 2

TAKEN TOGETHER, the commission and task force reports and research studies that appeared during 1983 and 1984 constitute a staggering indictment of U.S. secondary education.[1] They portray U.S. high schools as confused about their mission and irresolute about their program and standards—as flattening the hopes of the best teachers, sapping the energies of nearly everyone involved, and stifling public good will. According to the reports, U.S. high schools neither inspire students nor educate them well.

The reports follow with a variety of recommendations: require all students to take a foreign language, establish a universal core curriculum, rebuild the secondary curriculum around the "new basics," return to the "three essentials" (English, mathematics, and history), group courses into larger units, establish rigorous and measurable standards for graduation, lengthen the school day or school year, and somehow find a way to pay teachers higher salaries and improve their working conditions. On the whole, however, the reports and studies evade organizational issues.[2]

Yet, as long as the institutional arrangements that preclude effective action remain in place, recommendations from on high—enunciated by national commissions and by directors of broad national studies—will make little difference. Such recommendations do not change the structures that establish the incentives that shape motivations and steer behaviors.

We should have learned this lesson from our efforts to reform U.S. education after the Russians put *Sputnik I* into space in 1957. Those earlier

"The High School and the University: What Went Wrong in America, Part 2," *Phi Delta Kappan* 66, no. 7 (March 1985): 472–75. Used by permission.

attempts at reform did not change the basic structures of schooling, and the school agenda had a momentum of its own. Therefore, appeals to school boards and administrators, to teachers, and to university administrators and faculties to move in the direction of "excellence" affected their motivation and behavior only briefly. Then the ongoing situational imperatives took over again.

Five features work together to bias the upper level of U.S. secondary education against excellence in preparing students for higher education. These features are universal education, comprehensive schools, downward coupling, local control, and local monopoly. In turn, U.S. higher education is biased against serving effectively in the selection and training of teachers for the high school. What ought we to be doing, during the current wave of reform, to root out these institutional biases against excellence?

A Strategy of Focused Variety

Cross-national comparison can be a tool for self-analysis, with other countries serving as mirrors that offer different reflections on our own system of education. And reflections from the European mirror reinforce an idea that has already come to many observers of and participants in U.S. education: our system of secondary education would benefit from more institutional variety.

Several efforts in this general direction are already under way. For example, New York City offers students a number of specialized alternatives to the comprehensive high school—ranging from the outstanding Bronx High School of Science to secondary schools that focus on the performing arts, the humanities, commerce, and the health professions. Cincinnati is now a laboratory for experiments on the use (and abuse) of specialized high schools. San Francisco has Lowell High School, which accepts only students who have earned high grades and who have performed well on a special test. Led by North Carolina, several states are now experimenting with public boarding schools for outstanding students in science and mathematics. Meanwhile, parents and students are more open to private school options today—sometimes because they wish to escape the travails of racial integration, sometimes because they are disappointed with the academic performance of comprehensive public high schools.

The specialized high school becomes biased toward the development of talent. Whatever its area of specialization, each such school can seek to attract faculty members with special skills and interests in that area, to assemble a critical mass of students who can support one another's endeavors, and to develop a focused sense of joint enterprise between teachers and students.

With a sufficiently large enrollment, a generous budget, and strong leadership, a comprehensive high school can sometimes build such clusters of talent internally. However, as the number of fields of study and the number of subspecialties increase, the variety often becomes too great to assemble clusters of talent effectively. Nor can the overall size of a comprehensive high school be steadily increased, because problems of order soon become too great.

Diversity is enhanced when comprehensive schools differ from one another not just by neighborhood, but academically as well. Japan is a case in point. Japanese secondary education is universal; entry and graduation rates in that nation exceed even those of U.S. secondary schools. Japan has also moved energetically toward mass higher education. Its more than one thousand universities and colleges—including five hundred community colleges—vary greatly in type and degree of selectivity. Moreover, the American occupation that followed World War II caused Japan to adopt the comprehensive secondary school. How, then, does secondary education in Japan differ from secondary education in the United States?

The important differences stem from a willingness in Japan to make sharp distinctions among students when they enter secondary schools and again when they enter institutions of higher education. Schooling is uniform in Japan only through grade 8. In the first eight grades, Japanese students—like their American counterparts—are assigned to schools strictly on the basis of their areas of residence. Thus, the early years of schooling in Japan provide "a solid base of relatively equal opportunity."[3]

But the Japanese feared that comprehensive schools at higher grade levels would cause all students to sink toward the lowest common denominator. The system of education that had dominated in Japan from the Meiji Restoration to the time of the American occupation was built on the premise of selectivity at the secondary level, with some schools modeled on the strongly academic German *Gymnasium* and other schools offering several vocational tracks. Thus differentiation at the secondary level was deeply ingrained in Japanese thought and practice—so much so that, when the Americans pushed the Japanese to adopt comprehensive secondary schools during the occupation, the Japanese transformed these comprehensive schools into something quite different from what the Americans had in mind.

The Americans expected the Japanese to establish secondary schools that were similar to one another in program and in quality of instruction, with each school functioning as a monopoly within its designated attendance area. Instead, the Japanese deliberately differentiated their comprehensive schools and placed them in large districts that typically include "five or more schools" that are "explicitly recognized as varying in quality."[4]

Thus, in Japanese secondary education, comprehensiveness has been married to selectivity. Students have to compete for admission, and the better students are given first option on the specific schools they wish to attend. Because the top schools attract only superior students, they need offer only a college-preparatory curriculum. This has turned the top comprehensive high schools in Japan into specialized schools that focus strictly on academics.

Examinations play an important role at this first stage in the selection process. High school entrance examinations in Japan "sort each age cohort into what amounts to an eight- to 10-tier high school ranking system."[5] Strict selection takes place again when students transfer from secondary to higher education, and students from the better secondary schools are in a superior position to do well in this second sorting. Thus the downward influence—from higher education to secondary education to elementary education—is extremely strong in the Japanese system of schooling. Indeed, the university dominates the secondary school in Japan, and the secondary school dominates schooling at the elementary level.

Meanwhile, competition among Japanese schools raises academic standards and student achievement. In order to attract the better students, each public school scrambles to be perceived as better than the others, and the most successful ones guard their images as elite institutions. In addition, private secondary schools in Japan educate a greater proportion of college-bound students (more than 40 percent) than do private secondary schools in the United States, and many private schools in Japan develop strong ties with particular universities. These private schools compete with—and push—Japanese public schools.

Japanese secondary education can serve neither as a direct model nor as a blueprint for secondary education in the United States. The culture and the social structure of Japan differ too much from those of the United States. However, from his study of the Japanese high school, Thomas Rohlen has arrived at two telling observations that can help inform our thinking about the broad directions that U.S. school reform should take:

1. "The merit principle and hierarchical differentiation are inseparable in public education."[6] Efforts to make all public schools identical work against efforts to achieve higher levels of academic excellence.

2. "Progress towards social equality that cannot be integrated with the pursuit of general excellence has no long-term viability."[7] (I might add that the definitions of both *excellence* and *viability* will increasingly be established cross-nationally, as the school systems of all nations compete against the international pacesetters in achievement, both in schooling and in the workplace.)

As reflected in the Japanese mirror, then, the shortcomings of U.S. secondary schools have their roots in a lack of differentiation, a low degree of hierarchy, and an intolerance of competition. Of all the international mirrors, the Japanese mirror most clearly shows that the U.S. comprehensive high school is *not* selective; rather, it is concerned first with equity and second with social integration, while excellence as a concern places only a distant third.[8] However, if competence is the long-range goal of education, Americans may have to be willing to differentiate among students— and even to allow schools to drift into hierarchies—at the same time as they pursue the goals of educational equity and social integration.

Clearly, we Americans need a strategy for injecting some variety into our system of secondary education. Virtually every recent national study and report has called for a clearer definition of the mission of the U.S. high school; this appears to be an operational impossibility, however, unless we divide the purposes of education among different types of upper-secondary schools. There is little chance that the profusion of purposes—stated and unstated—of the comprehensive urban high school can be narrowed and reshaped into goals specific enough to drive behavior and to provide teachers and students with a clear sense of joint enterprise. Specialized secondary schools have the inherent advantage of greater coherence. Because of their distinctive character, it is much easier for such schools to establish a sense of collective enterprise—and the same thing is true of distinctive U.S. colleges.[9]

Institutional variety at the secondary level also makes possible centers of excellence that will restore some prestige to teaching. These centers of excellence will provide jobs for teachers whose exceptional command of their disciplines aligns them closely with colleagues in higher education. The colleagues in higher education, as well as top government officials and the general public, will respect the work of these uncommon secondary teachers. Moreover, those secondary schools and teachers with enhanced prestige will motivate less-blessed schools and teachers to raise their standards and improve their performance. Finally, high prestige will once again bring talented recruits to teaching. Declining prestige in recent years has been a major blow to the entire system of secondary education.

A strategy for injecting some variety into U.S. education during the remainder of this century must satisfy two conditions. First, it must allow us to retain those comprehensive schools that have somehow managed to create a strong sense of purpose and to uphold respectable intellectual standards. There must be thousands of such high schools in the United States, survivors from the era of the common school. Second, the strategy must allow for differentiation among students but not create more racial segregation and social inequality than already exist under the practice of school monopoly by neighborhood.

This second condition should not be difficult to meet, since the neighborhoods from which the comprehensive schools now draw their students are characterized by relatively fixed socioeconomic and racial differences (especially in the major metropolitan areas, where the problems of racial segregation and social inequality are most severe). Specialized secondary schools can mix students from different racial and socioeconomic backgrounds more easily, since they do not have to restrict their admissions to certain geographic areas.

An imaginative approach to variety would also permit larger numbers of students to attend comprehensive and specialized secondary schools simultaneously. An artistically talented student, for example, might attend a comprehensive school in the morning and a school for the performing arts in the afternoon—or attend the two schools on different days of the week or month. Such schooling arrangements are more democratic than the ones currently in force because they give students and their parents greater freedom of choice.

Both the Japanese system of secondary education and the American system of higher education demonstrate that schools do not *have* to be structured as monopolies. Clearly, U.S. high schools can compete with one another in ways that enhance the viability of the entire education enterprise. Taken together, Japanese secondary education and U.S. higher education also suggest one important benefit of institutional hierarchies: by recognizing perceived excellence, such hierarchies motivate thousands of educators to higher levels of effort and achievement than central administrators can ever hope to induce through controls and demands.

While reformers in the United States tinker with such changes as requiring four years of English instead of three, requiring students to take one or more courses in computer science, and requiring high school graduates to pass a test of functional literacy, some of the rest of us should be studying the wisdom of pushing our comprehensive high schools toward competition and specialization. We need experimental action and solid research to determine the extent to which competition and specialization can and should invade upper-secondary education in the United States. One thing is already clear, however: we must begin to challenge the existing institutional structure of U.S. secondary education. The comprehensive high school can no longer carry the burden alone.

No single organizational structure is necessarily the best one for schooling at all times, in all places. A change *from* specialized schools *to* comprehensive schools sometimes makes sense; indeed, European school systems are trying to make this transition right now—an effort aimed particularly at reducing the privileges traditionally associated with graduation from one of the classical or scientific schools. But the introduction of a greater number of specialized schools into a secondary system that is dominated by comprehensive schools is equally appropriate at another time or in another place. Greater variety and more experimentation are especially necessary today in the one national system of education that has most completely adopted comprehensive schools as the norm—the U.S. system.[10]

Introducing variety into the U.S. system of secondary education will be difficult enough. But significantly reducing the bias of U.S. colleges and universities against serving effectively in the selection and training of high school teachers seems likely to prove an even more difficult task.

Top-flight research universities in the United States need to find ways to institutionalize a campus-wide commitment to move teacher education to the center of academic life. But how to go about this task is not at all clear, since teaching school will continue to be a poorly paid occupation with relatively low status and will thus continue to attract less-able individuals, with whom professors at research universities do not wish to deal. To enhance the status of teacher education and to cause research universities to see the training of teachers as part of their mission will require new programs, restructured ideals, and strong leadership.[11] We will need to move toward greater variety in methods of teacher training and retraining.

Leading private universities, e.g., may find it more feasible to develop programs aimed at upgrading teachers who are already at work in nearby school systems than to initiate extensive pre-service training programs. Professors in particular disciplines are likely to find specialized secondary schools in their own or related fields more interesting than comprehensive high schools; hence, they will probably be more willing to recruit and train teachers for specialized schools. In other words, we should expect different segments of higher education to take on different types of teacher training for different types of schools.

At the core of the problem of upper-secondary schooling in the United States is the simple fact that the comprehensive high school is badly overloaded with responsibilities and goals. Running in every direction at once, the comprehensive high school is losing its sense of purpose. Athletics, extracurricular activities, and the norms of autonomous adolescent culture are quickly becoming the only sources of meaning from which to build unity.

Teachers feel the diffusion and deflection of purpose in upper-secondary education, as well as their own loss of moral authority and control. So they reduce their commitment; sometimes they even leave the classroom and the school system; often they tell others to look elsewhere for rewarding work. Meanwhile, students drift; they lack purpose and, frequently, challenge; boredom ranks high on their list of complaints. When students finally graduate, most observers agree that their achievement level is relatively low.

For the urban comprehensive high school, even social integration goes by the wayside. The shining ideals of the common school fall before the harsh realities of neighborhoods segregated by race, ethnicity, or social class. Millions of students end up more trapped than liberated by forced assignment to neighborhood schools. Clearly, operating as a near-monopoly, the comprehensive secondary school tallies up educational and social costs that weight heavily against the many virtues we have historically attributed to this tool of democratic education.

The institutional biases against excellence can be gradually reduced by a long-term strategy of fundamental structural change. Central to that strategy is greater choice for upper-secondary students, teachers, and school administrators. Methods of increasing choice include schools-within-schools, specialized schools, private schools, networks of school that share special programs, and competitive comprehensive schools. Greater variety in the types of school units operating within and outside of the comprehensive public high school would end the sameness, rigidity, boredom, and alienation that are the end products of structural uniformity.

For many social institutions, just as for individuals, variety is the spice of life. This is especially true at the level of education where compulsory common schooling gives way to voluntary participation and alternative ways of moving from youth to adulthood.

Notes

1. See, in particular, National Commission on Excellence in Education, *A Nation at Risk: The Imperative for Educational Reform* (Washington, D.C.: U.S. Government Printing Office, 1983); Task Force on Education for Economic Growth, *Action for Excellence: A Comprehensive Plan to Improve Our Nation's Schools* (Denver: Education Commission of the States, 1983); College Entrance Examination Board, *Academic Preparation for College: What Students Need to Know and Be Able to Do* (New York: CEEB, 1983); Twentieth Century Fund Task Force on Federal Elementary and Secondary Education Policy, *Making the Grade* (New York: Twentieth Century Fund, 1983); Ernest L. Boyer, *High School: A Report on Secondary Education in America* (New York: Harper & Row, 1983); John I. Goodlad, *A Place Called School* (New York: McGraw-Hill, 1983); and Theodore R. Sizer, *Horace's Compromise: The Dilemma of the American High School* (Boston: Houghton Mifflin, 1984).

2. For an excellent analysis of this aspect of the reports, see Paul E. Peterson, "Did the Education Commissions Say Anything?" *Brookings Review* (Winter 1983): 3–11.

3. Thomas P. Rohlen, *Japan's High Schools* (Berkeley: University of California Press, 1983), 307. See also William K. Cummings, *Education and Equality in Japan* (Princeton, N.J.: Princeton University Press, 1980).

4. William K. Cummings, "Japan," in *The School and the University: An International Perspective*, ed. Burton R. Clark (Berkeley: University of California Press, forthcoming).

5. Rohlen, *Japan's High Schools*, 308.

6. Ibid., 313.

7. Ibid., 326.

8. In *The Egalitarian Ideal and the American High School* (New York: Longman, 1983), Philip A. Cusick concludes that "the dominating element" in the U.S. high school is its "obligation to the egalitarian ideal" (106). Some teachers may have preferred a different system, stronger on merit, Cusick says, but they have "accepted the social burden of 'having to take everybody and keep them all happy'" (116). More than twenty years ago, Martin Trow noted that "the American value of equality is most deeply rooted" in the schools—that the schools try hard to avoid the invidious distinctions that inhere in matching the more academically able students with the more able teachers ("The Second Transformation of American Secondary Education," *International Journal of Comparative Sociology* [September 1961]: 161).

9. Burton R. Clark, "The Organizational Saga in Higher Education," *Administrative Science Quarterly* (June 1972): 178–84.

10. Among the major recent reports on what has gone wrong in U.S. secondary schooling, *Horace's Compromise*, by Theodore Sizer, comes the closest to proposing a strategy of focused variety and extensive experimentation. Sizer sees mediocre sameness and chronic boredom as institutionalized in the comprehensive school. Meaningful reform necessitates "a variety of school settings," he says (216). The individual school should "retreat from the objective of 'comprehensiveness'" (137). After advocating a particular set of core requirements, Ernest Boyer also suggests "elective clusters" and "specialty schools" (*High School*, 128–30). In *A Place Called School*, John Goodlad argues for the strengthening of common schooling from kindergarten through grade 12. However, he goes on to praise "key schools," "magnet schools," and "demonstration schools"—all of which involve choice—for providing "exemplary models" (299–301). Of course, such schools are competitive and hierarchical.

11. Gary Sykes, "Teacher Education in the United States," in Clark, *The School and the University*.

INTRODUCTION TO CHAPTER 18

The third four-day seminar in the series supported by the Exxon Education Foundation was planned for the summer of 1984, but because the Summer Olympics had captured all campus housing at UCLA for its athletes that year, we had to find accommodations elsewhere. After submitting a request to the Rockefeller Foundation, we were granted the use of its awesome Villa Serbelloni conference center in Bellagio, Italy, for the week that spanned July and August. Rockefeller covered all on-site costs, as I recall; additional funds from the Carnegie Foundation for the Advancement of Teaching as well as from the Exxon Education Foundation covered travel expenses of all participants. So off we went to Lake Como, all thirty of us—arriving from different directions—to discuss the academic profession across nations, disciplines, and universities. We were not at all unhappy that we had been bumped out of Los Angeles.

The first part of the conference focused on national settings: Britain, Germany, France, the United States. Walter Metzger, the Columbia University historian, offered a particularly detailed coverage of the complicated momentum of the American setting, topped off with the concept of "substantive growth"—the growth of knowledge—including its causes and its lasting fundamental effects. Here was history brilliantly put to use to advance contemporary understanding.

The topic of disciplinary and institutional context comprised the second half of the conference. Together, Guy Neave and Gary Rhoades compared the European "academic estate"—a corps in the governmental civil service—with the American academic profession. Tony Becher added his work on "the cultural view" offered in the earlier Perspectives conference. If we are to grasp what steers modern universities, he forcefully asserted, we must absolutely, indisputably, focus on the cultures of the many disciplines. UCLA post-docs Sydney Ann Halpern and Kenneth P. Ruscio reported on their early findings of the UCLA research project on the American professorate. They portrayed and carefully explained the complex interiors of medical schools and the layering of academics in major institutional sectors that become very different professions, as between teaching oriented and research oriented.

In short, we think *The Academic Profession* sheds considerable light on how academics—their work and beliefs—are conditioned and affected both by their national setting and by the increasingly powerful thrust of the disciplines. The forms of academic organization that most strongly steer academic behavior are best pursued by searching for similarities and differences across national, disciplinary, and institutional contexts. The final chapter of *The Academic Profession*, on which we draw here, speaks to the many contradictions embedded in this strange key profession.

CHAPTER 18

Differentiation and Integration of the Academic Profession

The Layering of the Profession

As systems of higher education become more complex, the academic profession inescapably becomes more differentiated. What was a university profession becomes a postsecondary profession. In one country after another, academics locate in institutions quite different from the traditional university, even in ones designed to counter university practices. There may even be special sectors, as in the classic case of the *grandes écoles* in France, that evolve into a position superior to that of the universities. In every country where they develop, the differentiated sectors position themselves in a prestige hierarchy.[1] The academic profession is thereby systematically layered.

Such layering has three primary dimensions, the first of which is the sheer extent of differentiation, the number of recognized major divisions. Italy has had one sector—a unified national system of public universities.[2] Britain in recent decades has been strongly binary—university and nonuniversity, the "independent sector" and "the public sector." France has a tripartite division: the *grandes écoles*, the universities, and a powerful separately funded set of research units. The United States has a sixfold breakdown at minimum—public and private universities, public and private four- and five-year colleges, public and private two-year colleges—

Based on *The Academic Profession: National, Disciplinary, and Institutional Settings,* edited by Burton R. Clark, chap. 9, 377–99. Berkeley: University of California Press, 1987. Used by permission.

and a ten- to twentyfold one when analysts more closely approximate the realities of differences among three thousand institutions.[3] In all cases the sectors differentiate the work and careers of academics. They also differentiate academic authority in different proportions of collegial and bureaucratic, oligarchic and managerial. They may or may not strongly differentiate academic beliefs, a matter to which I will return.

A second dimension of the layering of the profession by sectors is the firmness and clarity of the division. The dividing lines may be hard and clear with categorical divisions, or soft and ambiguous with fuzzy separations. State action tends to produce the first, market interaction the second. The formal bracketing of institutions in a national system works to produce categorical divisions, since the central government must decide on an overall framework, apportion institutional titles, and define budget allocations. It needs clear categories, large and small, to help it decide which institutions ought to do what. It seeks to control institutional aggrandizement. France is one clear case of such categorical division, with the separation of academic workers in three virtually watertight compartments ratified by explicit and detailed separate civil service definitions for *grandes écoles* instructors, university personnel, and full-time researchers in the third stream. Britain has moved rapidly toward the categorical approach. The binary policy set down in the mid-1960s clearly divides English academic life into distinct parts, each topped (in the early 1980s) by a specific coordinating body that constantly struggles to clarify its mission and jurisdiction.

In contrast, a non-unified, more market-like system produces ambiguous divisions as well as multiple ones. There is not sufficient formal control to lay down an embracing scheme and to keep institutions from wandering somewhat as they pursue individual ambitions. Again, the United States is the classic case: public and private sectors blend into one another; teachers' colleges shade into comprehensive colleges that offer graduate work. These colleges in turn overlap with "service universities" that do little research and produce only a few PhDs. Ambiguity surrounds the boundaries of the many layers. Only the two-year colleges establish a clearly separate category, because the collegiate work of their faculties is limited to the first two years. Even here radical decentralization of control has allowed community colleges to roam around in the higher education domain, where they absorb much of the country's adult education clientele in a catch-as-catch-can fashion, including persons who already have a BA, MA, or PhD.

A third dimension of layering is the degree of homogeneity within declared or observed strata. Governments may lay down clear categories, but they have enormous difficulty in making institutions into carbon copies of one another within those boxes. Thus in France it turns out that the *grandes écoles* sector, normally described as monolithic, is actually composed of quite different places, individualistic in nature and under private as well as public sponsorship. In Britain the university and non-university sectors are each internally complex, with differences that cause observers to remark that certain polytechnics ought to be classified as universities and certain universities as polytechnics. In each case some of the internal diversity had developed in the past and had existed before the government ascribed major demarcations. But institutional diversity in higher education is a restless thing: it is steadily produced in the normal course of affairs as institutions work out individual niches in the ecology of the whole, each ultimately having a unique configuration of ambition, organizational capability, and environmental constraint.

In the United States, nearly all the major layers of academic life are internally heterogeneous as well as blurred at the boundaries. Among private universities, for example, some are secular and others are religious, some are privileged bastions of research and high scholarship—veritable think tanks—and others offer academics the chance to labor at low pay while teaching many courses in the salt mines of undergraduate vocational curricula in a downtown center serving students who read at a pre-college level. In turn, the hundreds of private liberal arts colleges range all over the map in quality of staff, student selectivity, purity of program, and secular commitment. Even among public institutions often formally treated as if they were alike, much college-by-college differentiation individualizes the conditions under which academics work; the overall beliefs from which they take meaning; and the patterns of control that apportion authority within their ranks and between them, the administrators, and trustees. Among the nineteen campuses of the California State University System (the state college part of the California planned tripartite structure), the large, urban, relatively prestigious campuses in San Diego and San Francisco are very different locales for academic life than the small, more isolated, less prestigious centers in Bakersfield and Humboldt.

Over the long run the increasing complexity of knowledge drives institutional differentiation, which in turn powerfully divides the academic profession. The profession is inescapably layered, turned into a hierarchy of subprofessions organized by institutional sectors that vary in status. The odds on achieving a parity of esteem between noted professors in leading universities and part-time teachers in two-year programs seem no higher than the odds on developing a classless society. Differentiation overwhelms; and prestige is a valuable commodity in the higher education system and its mainline profession.

This is not to say that this trend is unopposed. There are always important social, administrative, and academic interests that want it otherwise. Social groups strongly committed to egalitarian ideals are deeply offended by the invidious distinctions found in a layered profession: they seek to effect, generally through left-of-center governments (as in Sweden), singular frameworks that embrace all academic units under the umbrella of "university." Administrations committed to bureaucratic ideals of fairness find layering troublesome to administer and defend: they move toward an institutional form of comparable worth. The "have-not" academics located in the lower reaches of the prestige hierarchy have a self-interest in parity: they press government for official redress. Thus various groups within and without seek a planned de-differentiation.

Furthermore, unplanned delayering takes place through academic drift. "Lower" institutions attempt to converge on "higher" ones as they are driven by the ambitions of professors and administrators to make a better world for themselves. They want a converging profession, with more institutional look-alikes and greater similarity in work and rewards. Especially in countries where central governments are little inclined or poorly positioned to plan convergence, drift is the main counterforce to layering. But all such forces, planned and unplanned swim upstream against the strong flow of differentiation. One may use common labels and all-embracing formal frameworks, but the differentiation of subjects, services, and clienteles does not thereby cease. And differentiation means that dissimilar components possessing different social and personal value will, in the nature of things, be ranked.

Among the features of institutional layering that affect the unity of the profession none loom larger than the permeability of sector boundaries; it is not the number of sectors that is decisive, but whether the sectors are sharply separated or blur into one another. A two-sector system that operates as two distinct compartments divides the profession into halves that cannot trade with each other. A ten-sector system in which sectors overlap, boundaries are blurred, and intersector mobility of staff is possible places the internal differentiation of the profession on a gradient. Some trade flourishes: students acquire credit in one type of institution which is good currency in another; faculty members may move from a college to a university or vice versa, or, barring such personal mobility, they may at least have a sense that they are somewhat interchangeable in training, talent, and value with colleagues in other places. Permeability is a foundation on which a number of integrating mechanisms, discussed later, may be strengthened. It is formal categorical layering that most splits the profession or estate into separate worlds.

The Disciplinary Bases of the Profession

Everywhere higher education is organized primarily by discipline. This specialized form of organization knits together historians and historians, psychologists and psychologists, chemists and chemists, thereby cutting across institutions and institutional sectors, fragmenting them internally.[4] The discipline (and the professional area of study) is a domain of knowledge with a life and dynamic of its own. Norton Long, in a classic essay published over thirty years ago, cogently pointed out that such scientific disciplines as physics and chemistry are "going concerns with problems and procedures that have taken form through generations of effort and have emerged into highly conscious goal-oriented activities."[5] These going concerns are not organized to carry out the will of nominal superiors in organized hierarchies; instead they develop their own incentives and their own forms of cooperation around a subject matter and its problems. Disciplines have conscious goals. In fact it is their intentions and strivings and not those stated as the broad aims of higher education which determine the real goals of the many departments, schools, and sub-colleges that make up the operating levels of universities and colleges. The operating units are as much if not more the arms of the disciplines as they are the arms of the institutions, especially when research is emphasized over teaching and specialized training is more important than liberal education.

It is no wonder, then, that universities and colleges are a bottom-heavy form of organization. Each internal disciplinary unit has self-evident primacy in a front-line task, each possesses the authority of its own field, and each takes its behavioral cues from peers, departmental and individual, located elsewhere in the country and the world. It is not astonishing that the academic profession as a whole is primarily fragmented rather than integrated by professionalism, because professional attachment forms first around the discipline. The academic profession is qualitatively different from all other professions in the extent of this fragmentation. It is inherently a secondary organization of persons located in numerous diverse fields that operate as primary centers of membership, identity, and loyalty.

Tony Becher has emphasized and clarified how the very knowledge base of a discipline shapes thought and behavior within it: physics leads to a culture different from that of political science, with Einstein, Heisenberg, and Oppenheimer as heroic figures in the one and Machiavelli, de Tocqueville, and Dahl as defining (if not heroic) figures in the other.[6] The disciplines develop different ways of training and initiating new members, and they influence how members specialize, interact with one another, and move among positions within the field.

The main disciplinary fault line perhaps lies between members in professional schools and those in letters and science departments. Medicine and its branches in dentistry and nursing is the extreme case of the professional school setting that is infused more with the orientations and practices of an outside profession than with those of the faculty in the "basic disciplines." Faculty roles differ by categories of full-time and part-time, clinical and academic, tenured and non-tenured, in a way qualitatively different from the relatively singular track of status and rank that letters and science departments seek to uphold.

But our conception of disciplines-within-the-profession cannot stop with a one-way account of the disciplinary imperative shaping the profession, because the disciplines are shaped in turn by the manner in which the profession develops in national contexts. A crucial instance is found in the differences between chair and department organization. The traditional clustering of junior and support personnel around the single senior chair-holder in traditional Continental systems balkanized many disciplines. "Invisible-college" linkages, which extend across the universities of a nation as like-minded researchers and scholars write, phone, meet, and otherwise communicate with one another, are broken and are restricted to local clusters when the institute directed by a senior professor publishes a non-refereed journal, sponsors the work of its own members to the virtual exclusion of others, and renders the careers of young scholars dependent on the goodwill and patronage of the padrone and his circle. Such blockages within disciplines break cardinal rules of the scientific ethos when they restrict the wide distribution of ideas and the results of research, weaken the corrective capacity of critical review, and make a career placement more dependent on sycophancy than scholarly achievement.

In contrast, department organization tends to break up such individual-centered fiefdoms, distributing power locally among a number of full professors all equal in formal power, and in lesser amounts to associate and assistant professors on a gradient of rank and responsibility. Local members are then free to participate in the larger circles of the discipline: the rawest of recruits are found at the front of the room at national and international meetings of associations and societies, presenting the results of their own research and learning how to communicate and compete in the larger arenas. Sponsorship still counts, and institutional location measurably adds or detracts. But compared to chair sponsorship and its tendency toward inbreeding, under organization by department individuals are more on their own. And in the competitive race for status in which American university departments engage, the recruitment and retention of talent becomes pressing. Inbreeding is suspect, a weakness to be guarded against, since the odds are normally high that the best person is not one's own.

In short, fragmentation of the academic profession by discipline is as fundamental and consequential as fragmentation by type of institution. The disciplines are powerful points of commitment and identity in those systems where organizational forms encourage individual scholars to be cosmopolitans. However, the disciplines are themselves fractured where the institutional foundations encourage academics to be locals. The disciplinary imperative may well be *the* driving force in modern higher education. But it is powerfully shaped in turn by the imperatives of the institutional sectors and the large structures of incentive and reward that characterize the national settings.

The Question of Authority

In higher education professional authority is distributed in disciplinary, institutional, and governmental frameworks.[7] Within each modern national system, the academic profession develops its own grassroots organization in the disciplinary foundations and then uses those forms as the principal base for extending influence in the institutional and national arrangements. For the profession, the road to power is essentially from the bottom up. And that road is paved with blocks of knowledge. If knowledge is power anywhere, it is so in the academic world.

The characteristic forms of professorial influence are personal rulership and collegial control. Systems of higher education are saturated with the personalized rule of superiors over subordinates. Individual professors supervise and otherwise command the work of students and often the labors of junior teachers, researchers, and support staff, with the judgments of superiors circumscribed neither by bureaucratic rules nor by collegial norms that would foreclose individual discretion. The personal rule of professors has historical roots in the dominance of the master in early academic guilds; it is functionally founded on sheer expertise: "She's the only one around here who knows anything about that subject." It allows the personal leeway that seemingly promotes creative thought and critical detachment; it receives strong ideological backing in the central academic doctrines of freedom of teaching and research. Highly personalized control is even promoted by national bureaucratic structures in which professors acquire niches in the civil service and accumulate projected rights and privileges. In many daily interactions and ongoing relationships, individually they may do as they please, whether choosing research topics or grading the work of students or providing institutional and community services. There may be a myriad of rules in nationalized systems that multiply each year, but enactment is one thing and enforcement another. Whenever bureaucracies encapsulate the academic profession, investigative procedures are notably weak.

Collegial rulership is also pervasive. Collective control by a body of peers is a classic form of traditional authority, one that has worn well in academic systems. Widespread in the academic world from the twelfth century to the present, it is congenial to the expression of expert judgment and has exceedingly strong ideological support in the blended doctrines of academic and scientific freedom. Collegiality is the form of authority about which the profession expresses the greatest pride. It has democratic, anti-bureaucratic overtones, as decisions are to be made not by a boss but by a group of peers; equality is operationalized in one-person-one-vote procedures.

The characteristic academic compound of the personal and the collegial amounts to guild authority. The individual master has a personal domain within which he or she controls or heavily influences subordinates—in the classroom, the laboratory, the tutorial session, the supervision of the dissertation. The masters then come together periodically as a body of nominal equals to exercise joint control over a larger territory of work—a specialization within a department, a department, a school, a faculty, or the entire university. The controlling stratum in a guild is composed of persons who are simultaneously autocrats and colleagues; they are bosses with individual rights of command as well as good democrats who submit to the rule of a limited populace. The combination has worn well. It may tilt toward the personal, and edge into the dangers of particularistic judgments patronage. Or it may tilt toward the collegial, then to face the weaknesses of logrolling and suppression of individuality. But whatever the balance, this guild-like compound commonly dominates the authority substructure of institutions and national systems, even those that are heavily weighted with top-down bureaucratic and political constraints.

From their operative bases in departments, chairs, and institutes, academics stretch their authority in two directions. The first thrust is upward in the structure of institutional, regional, and national administration. At the institutional level, the academics' favorite collective bodies—senates, faculties, and the like—contend with campus bureaucrats, trustees, and other laypersons who have been granted some voice. Faculties then work out shared authority with these groups, or they slip into an adversarial posture based on interest groups. At the system levels, they gain privileged access to central councils and offices, even becoming the most important members of bodies that allocate financial resources and decide on personnel appointments. They institutionalize peer review within one central body after another, most notably in science councils. They advise officials throughout government. In the transactions of higher education, they often become the most important constituency for bureaucratic and political officials. By means of election, appointment, and informal exchange, academics transfer their discipline-rooted local power into some significant degree of system-wide academic oligarchy. National systems may be, and have been, legitimately ruled by professors.

The second direction in which academics extend their forms of governance is in regional, national, and international disciplinary organizations, which mostly take the forms of associations and societies. Stepping out of their local shops, the masters, journeymen, and apprentices form large interrelated guilds, usually now called professional associations—e.g., Western Sociological Association, American Sociological Association, International Sociological Association—to help extend control over membership and practices. Within these associations they develop special sections that recapitulate the practicing specialties of the disciplines. Further, they link their associations in larger clusters—a national academy of science, a social science research council, a council of learned societies. Such associational structures may be and often are powerful centers of authority and influence, reflecting sharply the disciplinary thrusts of academic effort.

In the extreme case of the United States, where great disciplinary specialization has built on the strong American tradition of voluntary association, the forming and strengthening of one's own national association is a key part of the legitimation of a field of study. Hence one finds hundreds of such specialized associations that supplement the all-encompassing associations in such mainline disciplines as physics, economics, and English: the Society for Italian Historical Studies, the American Folklore Society, the Psychometric Society, and the American Association of Teacher Education in Agriculture. These American associations are a powerful class of organizations that are entirely separate from such institutional ones as the Association of American Universities and the Association of American Colleges. The latter, also numerous, are clubs for presidents and other administrators. The papers presented at meetings of these two major classes of academic organizations could hardly be more dissimilar, with the one focused on the separate subjects of the many disciplines and specialties—"Toward a Reconsideration of Marx, Weber, and Durkheim"—and the other on institutional concerns and administrative problems—"Some Thoughts on a New Program of Student Personnel Services."

Professorial authority thus comes well equipped, with a supporting base in local personal and collegial forms and with two main branches upward from that base, one to influence and possibly control the coordinating machinery of institutions and systems, the other to organize academics in national and international disciplinary frames that operate separately from the institutional structures.

But much has happened in the twentieth century, particularly since World War II, to oppose professorial authority and to change its nature. Higher education may or may not be the pivotal institution of modern society, but it is now too valuable and too expensive for governments to ignore. Harold Perkin, in an extended historical perspective, characterizes the modern period as one in which the university's traditional autonomy is increasing at the mercy of the bureaucratic corporate state and its employer associations, its trade unions, and its professions. Higher education itself tends to become a corporate bureaucracy; it is encased in a series of nested administrative units and is often structured internally around numerous strata of personnel that organize around their own particular interests and that lobby the government accordingly. Bureaucratic coordination has its own means of increased influence: it expands jurisdictions, adds layers, enlarges the administrative workforce, makes administration more specialized, expands the rulebook. Political coordination has also gained almost universally in recent decades. As higher education assumed a higher priority in government budgets, politicians found there were votes and responsibilities to be reaped, and outside interest groups sought greater influence. The counterforces to academic self-rule have clearly become more conspicuous, working mainly through the offices of the modern administrative state.

In certain settings academic self-rule has, critically, divided along a new dimension. "The academic estate" in the systems of Continental Europe has developed a basic fissure along lines of rank: junior faculty divides from senior faculty to an extent qualitatively different from the academic structure found in Britain and America. The schism in Europe is linked to the chair-faculty structure typical until the 1960s. Senior figures were sharply set off and especially as patrons had extensive power over junior staffs. Expansion overloaded this relationship: junior faculty numbers became much larger, absolutely, and relatively to the number of professors. Patronage became less dependable, advancement more doubtful, and feelings of exploitation and powerlessness were exacerbated. Finding courage as well as power in their swollen numbers, the younger faculty then organized themselves as a stratum, turning to trade union activity or to associations of their own that pressured and worked through governmental bodies to redistribute power in universities. "Participation" and "democratization" became the watchwords, and from operating units to central councils, the junior faculty acquired new rights. Their efforts were initiatives from within that helped to replace the chair-faculty structure with new units of organization. In the process a fragmentation of the academic estate by rank became formalized in laws that spelled out respective rights, and in union and associational bodies that represented academic interests.

Looking more broadly across national systems, sheer size clearly strains traditional informal give-and-take, the collegiality idealized in bygone days. Academic senates move toward representative government in place of direct democracy: a few are elected to go to meetings, representing disciplines and professional fields of study. Academic unions spread and take on more adversarial postures. The ways in which the profession organizes itself move from the informal toward the formal, from the soft to the hard. Though authority is always political, we can say that authority in the modern academic profession has become more political. It is more sharply so, with the profession and its many parts more intensely involved in conflict over who does what to whom.

But beneath all the strengthening of the hands of bureaucrats, politicians, and corporate groups, and beneath the segmenting and hardening of academic interests, the sense of professional expertise grows ever more important as a cornerstone of autonomous academic authority, for individuals and for groups large and small. When asked who is qualified to judge him, the academic will surely answer that not administrators, not trustees, not members of the general public, not even all the members of his discipline or professional area of study can do so. He will accept only those few who are schooled and proven in his specialty. The more academic people specialize, the greater is their sense of separateness. Their bundles of knowledge are the basis for their power. And that foundation of authority, grounded in disciplines and in institutional locations, continues to expand. The silent drift of authority to expertise helps explain why, in the face of so many bureaucratic and political interventions, academics go on running faculties, departments, and institutes, maintaining a primacy of influence in those matters about which they care most.

The Integration of the Profession

Professions, like organizations, are integrated along the two dimensions of social structure and normative order.[8] Either dimension may be weak or strong and the two lines may or may not correlate closely. The academic profession is a fascinating case of structural and normative integration, one that requires some stretching of a sociological imagination. Fragmentation is the play of institutional and disciplinary differences that set academic people apart from one another. The forces of fragmentation run strong: specialization will not cease, institutional differentiation goes on. We know that with each passing decade the academic division of labor will become finer and more extensive. What then still binds, if anything, in this profession of professions? Where do we look if we wish to search for the forces of integration?

THE STRUCTURE OF INTEGRATION

Within disciplines roles emerge that serve to link specialists. A study of the specialties found in high-energy physics in Britain offered the principle, "When roles became segmented one role will emerge whose function it is to bind the separate components into a cohesive group."[9] Some specialists specialize as generalists. In a host of fields, methodologists and theorists serve as such specialists, working with methods or ideas that reach across subfields. Among disciplines, in turn, interpersonal linkages form around problems not special to a particular discipline, as in Latin American studies, education, health, or environmental pollution. Here the interdisciplinary groups serve to lure specialists out of their tunnels, at least some of the time, to mix with others on general topics. Professional schools increasingly are hotbeds of such crosshatching of specialty and broad subject.

At the level of institutions, senior professors take up all-campus tasks. Professorial oligarchy may be strongly integrative: leaders of an academic senate move toward integrating frames of reference as they struggle with such campus-wide issues as the criteria for promotion to tenure. Central administrators often become key sources of integration. The campus head—president, vice chancellor, rector—may symbolize the whole. The administrators who specialize, such as a vice president for finance or a dean of student affairs, generally bridge across the many divisions of academic specialization. In short, the bureaucracy integrates. And so on, up the line, through the system-building arrangements in multicampus universities, the administrative and professional linkages that form in major institutional sectors, the regional networks, and the national system. Formal linkages are apparent almost everywhere. And relatively invisible informal and quasi-formal ties that form webs of relationship around the formal lines are, in most settings, likely to play an even greater role.

Central to our understanding of the possible integration of the academic profession in its increasingly varied settings in different countries is a recognition of how membership in small units may be a link to membership in large ones. Here our story of disciplinary and institutional fragmentation may be turned on its head. If individuals can be simultaneously citizens of California and the United States, or of Berlin and the Federal Republic of Germany, or identified with Tuscany and also Italy as a whole, academics can be simultaneously members of a discipline and members of the academic profession as a whole, members of both a particular institution and a national system. Using a pluralist explanation of integration, the discipline and the institution may be seen as units that mediate between the individual and the profession at large. The refrain would be: "I am an academic biologist, therefore I am a member of the academic profession," as biology so obviously belongs to the academic world. We can adopt an essentially federalist perspective on a profession composed of autonomous segments: in belonging to the smaller state, one is made part of the larger nation. Thus a professor of biology at Stanford is linked to the American professoriat at some minimal but still significant level, so long as his discipline and his institution fall within the socially defined boundaries of the higher education sector of society. And each affiliation separates academics from nonacademics to some degree. In short, there is a natural federalism in the composition of the profession in which dualities of membership, power, and status may link as well as divide.

Unlike institutional differences, disciplinary differences are confronted by compensatory integrating mechanisms that are normative. The norms of science have spread as a professional ethos, penetrating one discipline after another. This spread is the hidden agenda of the infusion of science into higher education. Academics in the various disciplines understand that they are committed to the advancement of knowledge. They all respect research. They develop shared procedural expectations: that information should be shared, that evidence should be reviewed impartially, that academics are responsible for some self-regulation. Academics think of plagiarism and the falsification of research results as the worst occupation crimes, compared to which running away with a colleague's spouse or money pales into insignificance. Stealing ideas and falsifying research are severely judged because they violate basic academic codes of intellectual honesty and the pursuit of truth. There seem to be some norms widely held within national systems, and even across them, which may serve to link institutional sectors as well as to embrace disciplines in a single normative order.

There may be large elements of professional consensus, broader still than scientific values, which are best sensed in a general anthropological perspective. Ronald Dore has argued persuasively that in Japan, the United States, and in most other countries academics commonly believe that brighter is better and that higher social placement based on quality is legitimate.[10] There is a primary belief in the intrinsic value of academic quality and the related awarding of prestige to individuals and institutions. With all its inequalities, a prestige hierarchy is thereby valued. In Dore's terms, there is a "consensual hierarchy." And inside this consensus, such disparate items as school marks, salary levels, and campus prestige march together. And once these hierarchies are institutionalized in national systems, such values are held particularly strongly by elites who are in a position to dominate. This type of value consensus is also a primary source of academic drift: academics push their own institutions toward the posture of those that are in a more favored position. Call it hope or color it envy, the ambition that causes institutions to converge indicates a consensus about quality and what is most worth doing.

Perhaps even more basic are the academic interpretations of the concepts of community, freedom, and individualism. The guild has long spoken of itself—locally, nationally, and even internationally—as a "community of scholars." And still today in universities with tens of thousands of anonymous students, several thousands of professors who are strangers to one another, and many thousands of support staff, we find professors and administrators voicing the same doctrine at lunch in the faculty club, at meetings of the academic senate, at all the occasions when wounds need to be bound, and for all time at inaugurations and commencements. Consciously manipulated or honestly stated, the idea of communality clearly serves to integrate. It goes with the flowing robes, the colorful banners flapping in the breeze, the spires of academic architecture, and the flagstones of college landscaping. The academic profession remains uncommonly able to turn "corporate bureaucracies" into "communities," able to extract rich meaning and emotion from the shining ideals of educating the young, advancing the frontiers of knowledge, and otherwise serving society—all requiring, according to academics, the loving hands of a community of craftsmen rather than the ministrations of a body of corporation employees. Doctrines of community, blessed with loving overtones of togetherness, still serve.

Even more salient is the academic interpretation of freedom, one that at first glance seems to lead to radical individualism. Academics enshrine the idea of freedom in one or more of three forms: freedom of research, freedom of teaching, and freedom of learning. They thereby strongly value a reasoned individualism. As put by Émile Durkheim, the ideal of individualism "has as its primary dogma the autonomy of reason and as its primary rite the doctrine of free inquiry."[11] Individualism may become a shared value, one that academics sense they share and one that inculcates respect for the choices and actions of others. For instance, academics readily understand that individual divergence may be good for collectives:

> Where most other social institutions require their members to adopt convergent values and practices, universities—and, to a growing extent, polytechnics and colleges—put a premium on creative divergence. Individual distinction, competitively assessed, in research or consultancy or scholarship, is held to strengthen the reputation of the basic unit which has housed and sponsored the work, and more remotely that of the institution which has provided resources for it.[12]

Serving as a flexible normative frame, individualism has an elective affinity for the always varied nature of academic work.

The Integration of Profession and Society

In the relationship of the academic profession to the general society, one dimension ranges from elite bonds to mass linkages. Close to the first pole is the pattern in Europe in which the profession links directly to the senior civil service, to advance levels of schoolteaching, and to a few leading outside professions, preeminently law and medicine. In that classic European relationship, the profession taught a few students a few subjects to certify them for a few occupations. Research, if carried out, was to be pure, detached from the immediate preoccupations of the world. Elite occupations, high-status students, and respected subjects interacted in a virtuous circle of status enhancement. The profession became part of a larger exclusive network. It profited from social exclusion and earned credit for isolating itself from business and commerce, as well as from the overwhelming majority of the population. It sharply limited its student clientele and its coverage of subjects and services and was able to avoid activities considered vulgar. The tasks of stocking government with top-grade officials and preparing able individuals to staff the best secondary schools were central. Tack on preparation for the learned professions and of course for the academic world itself, and not many "relations to society" were left to worry about.

Close to the other pole of mass linkages is the pattern prevailing in the United States, where the profession early became absorbed into trying to do everything for everybody. Employment in government was never the first resort for graduates: it was far more prestigious to become a captain of industry or commerce. And the outside professions could be less learned: e.g., forestry, social work, librarianship, and nursing, as well as law and medicine. Great masses of young people—15 percent of the age group by 1940—were admitted to undergraduate programs to improve their minds and characters by means of the ever-elusive "liberal education," as well as to acquire job skills by means of a host of vocational-technical-technological programs. They were then sent forth with a bachelor's degree in hand to find whatever jobs they could, even to tend homes and raise children. Compared to European counterparts, the American academic profession has been unparticular about what it does. Its internal diffusion has been part of a broad, ambiguous connection to society and its needs. In a classic pattern toward which many other countries are now moving, a broad coverage of clientele and fields of study has gone hand in hand with a broad array of services and linkages to many parts of society. In the European pattern, everyday life and academic life were separated by a wide breach. In the American pattern that breach became minimal.

In a democratic age it is written in stone that the elite pattern brings with it the great danger of limited popular support. This is the outcome that has now become such a threat to the British academic profession, where the barriers to mass access remain so rugged and the outputs to industry relatively meager. In contrast, the mass pattern, at once diffuse and disorderly, "buys" popular support.

Running parallel to the dimension of elite-to-mass linkage is one of closeness to government. The European academic pattern of distance from society correlates with closeness to government; the American pattern in contrast incorporates closeness to the general economy and to a plethora of societal institutions and groups but displays relatively considerable distance from government. One of the most revealing points for Americans working cross-nationally is the European academy-government proximity, where, simply, the academic estate is so intimately a part of the state as to be embedded in its civil service. Not only does government monopolize the financing of the estate, but it does so in the most intimate way possible: through direct salary subsidy allocated according to civil service rank and privilege, with all the bureaucratic classifying and rule-making that is a normal part of modern governmental procedure. Academics are then a national profession, an estate situated within the state. This fundamental structure underpinning means that, willy-nilly, the internal affairs of the estate are then automatically translated into relations with the state.

The now classic case is the uprising of the academic subclass, the junior faculty, in Europe in the 1960s and 1970s. To effect their interests, as pointed out earlier, they hardened their interest group representation and took their case directly to government, using trade unions and other outside groups to pressure government officials. Confirmation or rejection of academic interests then became an intensely political matter. Left-of-center governments tended to support the junior faculty, students, and others who were the party of change in the distribution of power within the estate; right-of-center governments favored the senior professors, even to the point of mounting counterreformations. The point is clear: when the academic estate is intimately a part of government, it is vulnerable to changes in the dominant political ideologies of government.

In the United States, in contrast, the profession is housed in private as well as in public institutions. Membership in the private places is the antithesis of civil service: each institution behaves like a private corporation or a voluntary association—"a tub on its own bottom"—hiring, promoting, and firing on its own. In public institutions there is an awareness of being on the public payroll but little sense that one has joined the organized ranks of state public employees, and of course no sense of embeddedness in any national corps. Overhead administrative services are located primarily in campus administrative offices or in academic system-wide administrative locations in the states, rather than in state offices. Many state university systems have considerable constitutional autonomy (e.g., the University of California), which helps to push the profession away from the embrace of government. Trustees often became a buffer, representing the institution to the state rather than the other way around.

The private housing of the profession that is significant in Japan as well as in the United States is more widespread elsewhere in the world than is usually seen.[13] And what we may expect to increasingly see in more countries and in more sectors within them is a pattern of mixed public and private support in the financing of the profession, with a greater number of lines of support in each: basic institutional funding from two or more levels of government; multiple public channels for support of research; governmental student aid, arranged in various packages; private contributions to endowment; private annual support; parental payments for tuition. The public-private distinction in the financial base is being replaced in many countries by a distinction between single and multiple sources. The effects of the latter are crucial to the autonomy of the modern profession. A single source is able to make broad moves, leaving the academy and the professoriat vulnerable to massive intervention. Multiple sources spread dependency, building a certain redundancy into the capacity of the system and its main profession to survive and prosper. Multiple dependencies are a source of institutional and professional autonomy.

Autonomy within the modern pattern of mass integration may be a more than adequate substitute for the autonomy of the old arrangement in which, in various countries, the academic profession was isolated from mass pressures. The autonomy offered by multiple dependencies is untidy. But this disarray seems to be near the core of any explanation of how, e.g., the American professoriat can be so dependent on the goodwill of so many different groups in society and at the same time be so highly autonomous in its most prestigious institutional sectors and disciplines. Complex financing makes for ruggedness in comprehensive academic institutions and a comprehensive academic profession.

THE DIVERSIFICATION OF CLIENTELE SERVICES

As sectors and disciplines proliferate, so do academic services. Different sectors admit different arrays of students and send graduates to different job markets. Disciplines and professional studies are notoriously different in their services to applicants and graduates. Some admit only a few on highly selective grounds and later certify them for well-paying prestigious occupations, while others admit virtually all applicants with little regard to achievement or aptitude and then graduate survivors who must maneuver in an open job market. Any intelligent account of how the academic profession serves society by means of its service to individual clients has to recognize the differentiation and diversity intrinsic to the profession. The transition from higher education to work becomes more segmented, as internal diversity comes to an ever-finer division of labor in the general society.

And so for the services bound up in relationships with major donors, public and private. Government receives various types of professional cadres from the academy to serve its many diverse bureaus—from the road-building engineers to policy analysts, from foresters to doctors— in an endlessly widening array. The corporate executive depends on a lawyer on one side, an economist on the other, and an accountant in front, as obligatory fountainheads of professional advice, all to be gotten from different parts of the academy and all to be trained in diverse divisions of the firm. Rich firms can pay for the very best and hence recruit from top sectors of universities and colleges. Enterprises with modest resources work farther down the line, taking graduates of less prestigious institutions, right down to the night-school lawyer and the graduate of a barely accredited business administration program. Segmentation is the basic trend in the service relationship between those who do the academic training and the major institutional donors who finance their work.

But the academic profession does much more than merely service individual, governmental, and corporate clients directly. Its more ultimate commitments are rooted in its role as a central location for the handling of knowledge. There is the cultural heritage to be preserved, ample reason in itself in well-organized institutions to place the university library at the center of the campus and to be proud of having millions of books, most of which are seldom if ever used. There is the commitment to the creation of new knowledge, embedded in the research imperative. There is the task of shaping the minds of future generations, sometimes even their characters, which is institutionalized in the most common duty of the profession, that of teaching. A broad involvement in the care and feeding of knowledge means a fiduciary relation to society's culture in general. These broad societal services are the bases for the loftiest ideals and pretenses of the profession, the one on which claims of professional altruism can best be founded. Always ambiguous and always edging into myth and cant, the services to knowledge, culture, and future generations are part and parcel of what the profession is about. They are also the outcomes of academic effort that are most remote to the touch of efficiency criteria and accountability demands. Hence they are the strongest bases for claims of trust: if you cannot direct their work, you have to trust them to get it right.

The One and the Many

What was always so is now much more so: the academic profession is many professions, a loosely coupled array of varied interests. The nineteenth- and twentieth-century expansion of higher education has multiplied the settings that are the foundations of academic work, belief, and authority. Student clientele has shifted from elite to mass; subjects have proliferated in a broadening stream of knowledge; outputs of graduates and services are unremittingly numerous and varied. Moving further into complexity, the profession comes to resemble a caucus of subprofessions, and that array, we have seen, will be arranged differently in different countries by the interaction of national, institutional and disciplinary settings on which we have concentrated. National contexts shape the institutional and disciplinary ones, as in the nineteenth-century Bonapartist definition of a single national university for all of France. Disciplinary thrusts condition all national and institutional settings, as in the sweep to power first of physics and then of biology in all advanced systems in the twentieth century. And institutional arrangements shape national and disciplinary ones, as when competitive sectors of universities, colleges, and short-cycle units diverge and converge in a market dynamic. What we see is a proliferation that can no longer, if it ever properly could, be characterized in a global type. The profession is the many and not the one.

Still, we sense strands that help to hold this profession of professions together, within a country and even internationally. There are the memberships we have identified that link academics in segments by discipline and by institution, with those segments in turn tied into the academic system. There are the shared understandings we have fleetingly highlighted: the commitment to subject, the awareness that specialization pays, the mandate of the pursuit of truth, and the converging understanding that academics ought to differ in thought and behavior. What remains particularly problematic is the strength of such bonds, often intangible and remote, against the forces of fragmentation. Since the reach of this profession is so great, we have mainly emphasized its division into autonomous segments. We have been taken with "the many." But in the many there remain some signs of the one. The profession remains a puzzle, a subject clearly in need of a variety of perspectives that may stimulate the imagination and point further analysis in quite different directions.

This modern "key profession" is a product of eight centuries of higher education in the Western world. Inescapably, it will continue to have a central role in society, even as it becomes more difficult to grasp. If social analysis pursues worthy problems, then it will invest more fully in the effort to grasp the constancy and the change in the lives of academics and to base views of their work and their services on fact rather than fiction. To date, such inquiry has occurred only in fits and starts, with long pauses in between. Perhaps reflection and research will lead to the day when we systematically will know much more about the one and the many, and the interaction between the two, in a profession that is an art as much as a science, a place where dreamers dream alongside tinkerers who tinker, all in the name of the highest values of society.

Notes

1. On institutional sectors and hierarchies in higher education, see Clark, *Higher Education System,* 53–69, 254–62; and Trow, "Analysis of Status," chap. 5.

2. See Clark, *Academic Power in Italy.*

3. See the Carnegie classifications of the 1970s, as reported in Carnegie Council on Policy Studies in Higher Education, *Classification of Institutions of Higher Education.*

4. On the cross-cutting of disciplines and enterprises in a grand matrix of academic organization, see Clark, *Higher Education System,* 28–34; and Clark, "Organizational Conception," chap. 4.

5. Long, *Polity,* 83.

6. See particularly Becher, "Cultural View," chap. 6.

7. The following section draws heavily upon Clark, *Higher Education System,* 110–23.

8. The following section draws heavily upon Clark, *Higher Education System,* 102–6.

9. Gaston, *Originality and Competition in Science,* 172.

10. Prepared comments at the Bellagio Conference, July 30–August 3, 1984, for which the papers of this volume were originally prepared.

11. Durkheim, "Individualism and the Intellectuals," chap. 4, quotation from p. 49.

12. Becher and Kogan, *Process and Structure in Higher Education,* 110.

13. See Geiger, *Private Sectors in Higher Education*; and Levy, *Higher Education and the State in Latin America.*

References

Becher, Tony. "The Cultural View." In *Perspectives on Higher Education: Eight Disciplinary and Comparative Views,* edited by Burton R. Clark, 165–98. Berkeley, Los Angeles, and London: University of California Press, 1984.

Becher, Tony, and Maurice Kogan. *Process and Structure in Higher Education.* London: Heinemann, 1980.

Carnegie Council on Policy Studies in Higher Education. *A Classification of Institutions of Higher Education.* Berkeley, Calif., 1973. Rev. ed., 1976.

Clark, Burton R. *Academic Power in Italy: Bureaucracy and Oligarchy in a National University System.* Chicago: University of Chicago Press, 1977.

————. *The Higher Education System.* Berkeley, Los Angeles, and London: University of California Press, 1983.

————. "The Organizational Conception." In *Perspectives on Higher Education: Eight Disciplinary and Comparative Views,* edited by Burton R. Clark, 107–31. Berkeley, Los Angeles, and London: University of California Press, 1984.

Durkheim, Emile. "Individualism and the Intellectuals." In *Emile Durkheim on Morality and Society,* edited by Robert N. Bellah. Chicago: University of Chicago Press, 1973.

Gaston, Jerry. *Originality and Competition in Science: A Study of the British High Energy Physics Community.* Chicago: University of Chicago Press, 1973.

Geiger, Roger L. *Private Sectors in Higher Education: Structure, Function, and Change in Eight Countries.* Ann Arbor: University of Michigan Press, 1986.

Levy, Daniel C. *Higher Education and the State in Latin America: Private Challenges to Public Dominance.* Chicago: University of Chicago Press, 1986.

Long, Norton. *The Polity.* Chicago: Rand McNally, 1962.

Perkin, Harold. "The Historical Perspective." In *Perspectives on Higher Education: Eight Disciplinary and Comparative Views,* edited by Burton R. Clark. Berkeley, Los Angeles, and London: University of California Press, 1984.

Trow, Martin A. "The Analysis of Status." In *Perspectives on Higher Education: Eight Disciplinary and Comparative Views,* edited by Burton R. Clark, 132–64. Berkeley, Los Angeles, and London: University of California Press, 1984.

INTRODUCTION TO CHAPTER 19

Sometime in 1983 Ernest Boyer, then president of the Carnegie Foundation for the Advancement of Teaching, and I discovered that, coincidentally, we wanted to know more about the American professoriate. I also felt that by concentrating so much on other countries I had lost touch with what was going on at home. Boyer wanted to study the professoriate primarily by national survey, using Princeton and his shop as a base. I wanted to do intensive, largely qualitative fieldwork. It turned out that we completed two studies (and two books) with two different methodologies. He gave me a generous three-year grant, including some additional financial help for the third Exxon-supported conference in Bellagio, Italy. The Carnegie grant principally allowed me to assemble a staff of two post-docs and up to a half-dozen graduate students. Kenneth Ruscio, the political scientist post-doc from Syracuse University, turned out to be an outstanding fieldworker, who stayed with the project for the scheduled two years in the field. Graduate students, particularly Ron Opp, helped out substantially by finishing up the fieldwork as well as by categorizing transcribed interview materials. Throughout the study, Gary Rhoades, who was with me as a post-doc for four or five years beginning in 1982, helped us to choose what avenues to pursue and constructively criticized emerging interpretations.

My study was a major exploration of how the American professoriate was differentiated into many subprofessions organized around subject matter and institutional locations. The staff conducted interviews in six disciplines and in sixteen institutions in a matrix of joint locations in the eastern, midwestern, southern and western regions. In writing *The Academic Life: Small Worlds, Different Worlds* (1987), I wanted to show the vast differences between academic life in the universities, the small liberal arts colleges, and the community colleges. The book also pointed to the fundamental differences *within* universities, e.g., between life in the medical school and in the humanities departments.

Doing the research was fascinating. We greatly benefited from intensive face-to-face prolonged interviews, especially when respondents elaborated on their contradictory feelings that could not be explained in checkmark questionnaires. I became convinced more than ever that researchers who do not delve into job-based differences within academia fall into misleading, simple-minded stereotypes. What good is it to state that "on the average" American academics teach 9 hours a week, when the reality is 2 to 20? In fact, major clusters in different institutions vary teaching hours at 2 to 6, 9 to 12, and 15 to 20. Lazy journalistic simplicities are enemies of the truth. A caveat: be wary of the mean and other measures of central tendency that squeeze out the truth of diverse stories.

The book is large and complicated; I traced the "logic" of the American academic profession through three historical stages. I saw that the inner logic of the third, modern stage agrees with the argument made throughout the classic study, *The Academic Revolution* (1968) by Christopher Jencks and David Riesman. They argue that the interests of a large plurality of academic professions determine the evolution of American higher education. What goes on in departments and professional schools—and is carried forward by them—is basic. With so much at stake in how the many academic professions comport themselves, the central problem becomes maintaining the strength of the academic calling—the absorbing errand.

Meaningful research into the ways of academia must delve into a multitude of small worlds that are very different. How is the academic calling shaped and strengthened in these disparate places? Political scientist Jane Mansfield offers a useful, tripartite typology of interests in her writings about forms of democracy: *self-regarding,* a preference for purely personal gain; *other-regarding,* in which we make the good of another individual or group our own; and *ideal-regarding* in which one's own good is identified with the realization of broader social outcomes.[1]

I think young academics can keep in mind—and fulfill—these three forms at the same time. Listen up! Here is a trifecta worthy of your attention! The odds are good; the results can be a beautiful payout as you seek to take on an absorbing errand. You do for yourself *and* for your department *and* for the advancement of science or the education of the young. We know from in-depth interviews that this convergence of interests occurs in academia even in many unlikely locations.

Note

1. Jane J. Mansfield, *Beyond Adversary Democracy* (Chicago: University of Chicago Press, 1983), 26.

Reference

Jencks, Christopher, and David Riesman. *The Academic Revolution*. Garden City, N.Y.: Doubleday & Company, 1968.

CHAPTER 19

The Logic of the Profession

Culture and the institutions that sustain it have always depended on enlightened patronage. That is as true for the modern, sophisticated research university as it was for Michelangelo and Mozart. It is a somewhat more recent truth, however, one born out of the rise of modern organizations, that their fate lies largely in the hands of those who work in them.

—ROBERT M. ROSENZWING, *The Research Universities and Their Patrons* (1982)

Our thesis is that the human coefficient of intellectual activity is of the utmost importance . . . the producers are an essential part of the product.

—LOGAN WILSON, *The Academic Man* (1942)

The shape of American higher education is largely a response to the assumptions and demands of the academic professions.

—CHRISTOPHER JENCKS AND DAVID RIESMAN, *The Academic Revolution* (1968)

THE MARCH OF KNOWLEDGE across the world of work has created tribes of professionals whose manners and mores intensely affect human affairs. Behind every set of desks there lurks a would-be profession, knowledge specialists who devise ideologies, certificates, and associations to back their claims. As they cultivate their own social systems and cultures, these carriers of intellectual activity perpetuate distinctive

The Academic Life: Small Worlds, Different Worlds. A Carnegie Foundation Special Report, chap IX, 257–75, 336–37. From Princeton, N.J.: The Carnagie Foundation for the Advancement of Teaching, 1987.

human coefficients, special styles that spring readily to mind when we think about each profession or encounter doctors, lawyers, psychotherapists, and interior designers. Each group develops strange patterns as it goes about isolating and commanding a domain of work. Mystification is routine: "we" cannot know what "they" know unless we are willing to undergo their training and join their circle. Given the difficulties they cause and the powers they acquire, "we" would undoubtedly, if we could, do without them, or at least supervise them closely. But we cannot do either. Across the endless array of traditional professions, latter-day professions, semiprofessions, and would-be professions, those who seek particular products and services have to take the producers, and largely on faith.

Among these mystifying occupations that elaborate powerful identities for individuals and groups, the academic profession is at once the easiest to approach and the most difficult to understand. Many individuals, as students, were once within its walls; many serious observers, as faculty, are part of it. Penetration is no problem, participant-observers are abundant. But the two-way differentiation on which we have concentrated erects major screens. Exacting internal specialization spells mutual ignorance, striking everyone somewhat dumb on the spot. Any specific way of knowing is also a way of not knowing. The individualization of many types of institutions further removes academics from one another and presents a confusing and contradictory organizational maze to outside observers. The pattern of mystification we find in professions generally is repeated within the omnibus profession, making it strange to insiders and outsiders alike.

The Third Moment

It was not always so, since the profession was simple before it became complex. Along the road of elaboration in America, we can distinguish three stages. The professional origins of academia were much weaker in the United States than in Europe. Though faculty on the Continent and in Britain from the beginning clung to their own guilds, hunkering down within them when under assault from church or state, American academics began as little groups of hired hands. Throughout the long colonial period and well into the nineteenth century, they were clearly pre-disciplinary and pre-professional, not yet given to specialization. Attempting to impart a common culture of the more educated classes, their relatively fixed body of common knowledge robbed them of the authority of expertise. Looking back, we see them as amateurs. Many stayed in academic work only for a few years before moving on. Substantively and organizationally, their defenses were weak. The academic occupation had little chance to mystify.

Distinctive academic ways developed gradually over the course of the two centuries that stretched from the establishment of Harvard in 1636 to the Civil War years. In the first half of the nineteenth century, specialists were already hard at work elaborating particular subjects. Scientific knowledge was beginning to move beyond the ken of amateurs and generalists. The academic specialist then fully triumphed over the generalist when major disciplines became separate professions in themselves. From the 1870s onward, in a second state of occupational development, the departments of universities and colleges increasingly took charge. They positioned the influence of academics on a firm base of expertise.[1] Joined by many outside fields that set up shop in new professional schools, the disciplinary specialists gave muscle it did not have before to the embracing profession. At the same time, the scale of academia, although many times larger than in the first stage, allowed a lingering sense of oneness. Commonalities could be found in the myths of "the professor," the sense of calling that we now associate with "the old days" of the small campuses of the decades before World War II, and the unifying leadership of the leading scholars who graced the halls of the American Association of University Professors (AAUP). Modern professionalism had arrived, but it was still enveloped in strong pretenses of community.

For those desiring a strong, unified profession, moment two was the golden age, reflected locally in the growing privileges of the department and the senate and nationally in the unities of the disciplinary associations and the AAUP. Faculty appeared to have crawled out from under the dominance of trustees and administrators, seizing control of the basic operating units and manning an all-campus professional structure that had primary influence in many local matters. In institutions of any substantial standing, the president increasingly had to spend his or her capital of residual power prudently, for, if squandered, stern votes of "no confidence" issuing from the senate would speed departure. A much-used rhetoric of "shared authority" recognized that the faculty knew best in such central matters as selecting staff and deciding curriculum. Their doctrines of freedom of research and freedom of teaching were now undergirded with the privileges of personal autonomy.

The quarter-century since 1960 has seen the full flowering of a third professionalization moment. A "postmodern" complexity has evolved, a startling cross hatching in which segmentation of sectors has interacted with the fragmentation of subjects to give differentiation a quantum leap. Professional school faculties have grown and solidified in universities, establishing large and powerful domains that are out of control as well as out of sight of the letters and science departments; English has little sway over engineering and none over medicine. Within the letters and science core of the universities, general education and liberal education—long on the defensive—have become causes for the saving remnant, so distant are the realities of departmental separation from the pieties of curricular integration. Up and down the hierarchy of institutions, as well as across each type, innumerable nonprofessions, semiprofessions, and newly legitimated professions present their subjects and have them dignified, right down to the trades of hair styling and auto mechanics. It has become virtually impossible to name a subject that someone, somewhere, will not teach; "the profession" is in no position to take responsibility for it, especially to prohibit it. In a radically fractured profession, the less respectable operations are marginalized rather than outlawed. Degree mills come and go, chased by a few state investigators who in no way come from the ranks or represent professional self-control. In a national system composed to do all things for all people, even to repeat the work of the elementary school, the profession is far from a controlled sector of employment. In the third moment the academic profession has no boundaries. It steadily diffuses; the stretch goes on.

We only understand the contemporary American academic profession if we grasp the magnitude of its dispersion into parts that whirl off in different directions. There still are small components, religious and secular, which are gloriously old-fashioned. Some operate as presidential autocracies, while others approximate a community of scholars. A few faculties still exist in the form of fellowships where sherry precedes dinner on Thursday night, a collective habit that favors rumination on the eternal verities. But other parts take radically different shapes: the cancer ward is a place where clinical faculty interact intensively with many levels of auxiliary personnel and practice an applied art of great immediacy. The expansion of nominal universities, state colleges, and especially community colleges during the past quarter-century has notably put the majority of academics in locales far from the fellowships of the old-time colleges and the special worlds of the top private universities. Organizationally, those academics may have a champagne taste, but what they get is bottled beer.

In this latter period, though disciplinarians remain much in charge at the top of the hierarchy of institutions, consuming students and responding managers take charge in the non- and slightly selective institutions.[2] The triumph of clientele has been institutionalized in the administrative (and faculty) responses that have put one-third of the professoriate on part-time assignment. A large share of the profession has crawled back under the control of trustees and administrators, with the unionization response adopted as the new road to an adversarial unity of academic workers. Largely created in the 1960s and 1970s, the deprofessionalized bottom of the professoriate leads off into the camps of the gypsy scholars, the new nomads who personally pay the price for consumer-driven flexibility. In the organized tools of mass higher education that assign faculty to the lower one-third to one-half of the clientele in ability and resources, the third moment is a major regression. For the professoriate as a whole, the costs of mass higher education have been high.

Thus, over the long course of three centuries, the character of the intellectual moment in American academic life has changed remarkably. What academics could seize at the beginning was only short-term work as generalists. They then developed posts that turned jobs into lifelong careers that could be taken on their own terms but that still centered on undergraduate residential life. A qualitative shift occurred only when research and specialized scholarship measurably enhanced prestige and power. Academics then had a world of their own: what they thought and what they did became peer oriented and discipline-driven. But this condition was not to be a permanent answer for everyone: in a twentieth-century evolution, centrifugal forces have qualitatively diversified academic conditions. If research settings became always more esoteric, operating as configurations of rare expertise that the laity cannot fathom, other settings have adapted to the imperatives of general teaching for an open-access clientele.

Powering the shift from the first to the second to the third intellectual moment have been the substantive and reactive forms of growth, which operated under the special conditions of intense competition and emerging institutional hierarchy. Substantive growth drove the evolution into the second stage. It was not demands of clientele, but, rather, demands of expanding knowledge that most caused generalists to be replaced by specialists. The clients, especially in the undergraduate classroom, would have preferred to keep teachers who were centered on students' interests and who spoke a general language. But self-amplifying science and scholarship had other designs for higher education. Since expanding knowledge could only be handled by greater specialization, graduate students soon became more important than undergraduates, the PhD more weighty than the bachelor's degree.

In the third stage the full weight of reactive growth has come into play. There could well be sizable assemblies of academics who served "elite" functions, but there had to be even larger congregations who served "mass" functions, academics who would carry the burdens, while facing the challenges of the open door. There could be institutions that competed nationally for the highest prestige, the best faculty, and the best students, but there had to be many more institutions that would adjust to the demands of unselected students within the limits of local and regional catchments. Faculty growth that followed student growth, in a system characterized by competition and hierarchy, shifted faculty toward an other-directed posture in which clients replaced peers.

The Profession and the Organization

In the evolution of intellectual moments, professors changed their interests and caused universities and colleges to adapt accordingly. Persuasive is the observation offered by Christopher Jencks and David Riesman that American higher education has been mainly shaped by its resident professional groups. But this conditioning of system by profession has occurred primarily in the uppermost levels of the institutional hierarchy, where a central institutional interest forms around the faculty interest in substantive growth. The organization as a whole then becomes tremendously supportive of the disciplinary commitments of academics. Presidents as well as peers prod professors to become more productive in research and scholarship, thereby competitively enhancing the organization while ostensibly serving the nation and the world.

But other organizational settings of the profession march to quite different drummers. They have not been fashioned to express substantive growth. Major institutional sectors provide different tasks and conditions of work, different institutional identities and histories, different covering authorities, different career paths, and different associational networks. Crucial in the shaping of the profession is the organizational determination of the mix of the two primary tasks, research and teaching. That mix comes close to determining everything else about academic life. Where the combination tilts heavily toward research, it follows that disciplines will be powerful and departments strong; freedom of research will be the reigning ideology; research-centered professors will speak lovingly of the faculty as the core of the university and will walk carefully around the plenitude of faculty prerogatives. But when the mix is all teaching and no research, then disciplines will fade in importance and departmental nationhood will be weaker. Freedom of research will no longer be a relevant ideology. Professors will form associational links relevant to their type and level of teaching and will pull away from research circles. Careers will be defined locally, sharply limited in mobility, and rooted in seniority rights. Administrators will be more managerial and, law permitting, will precipitate a unionization response that moves faculty-administration relations into contractual formalities.

Academics know what wins the day in their disciplines. Hence, the vast majority want to do some research, and publish a little, even if teaching is their first love. The ideal of combining research and teaching is deeply fixed in American academic consciousness. Field by field, it burns bright. But for a half or more of the professoriate, organizational restraints on research are heavy to the point of near-prohibition, particularly when we count the swollen ranks of the part-timers. As we move down the status hierarchy, organizational imperatives increasingly dominate faculty preferences. The faculty role is specified as only undergraduate teaching, then becomes teaching only in the first two undergraduate years. Academics then maneuver in a sharply limited occupational space that is organizationally defined.

What is so attractive about the university setting for so many faculty members is the reduction of those kinds of organizational constraints. As "teaching load" is lightened, the organization liberates academic time. But it does so only to turn it over to the full might of research expectations that are set and monitored more by the faculty than by the administration. The research university reeks of professional dominance, with professors constantly sliding from the role of employee into that of salaried entrepreneur, going largely their own way in managing their time, their research, and their teaching. They develop a strong sense of nationhood in their own department, ruling it by collective decision-making and holding administrators at arm's length from the core tasks. Since trustees have ultimate authority and make occasional large decisions, and since the administrative staff steadily elaborates bureaucratic controls, the setting is far from innocent of contrary forces. But the greater power lies in subjects, the stuff of academic work itself. Those most directly involved in the evolution of the subjects are the beneficiaries of the constant widening and deepening of the knowledge base of academic life.

The interaction between profession and organization produces a fundamental divide among professors that appears in the many dimensions of professionalism. As we ascend the institutional hierarchy, we find professors facing peers for recognition and reward. As we descend, we encounter professors facing students for direct satisfaction and long-term viability and legitimacy. Major segments of the foremost universities function much like think tanks. The more a university moves in this direction, the better its competitive advantage in recruiting faculty. Only the financial need for tuition income, or state allocation based on number of students, acts as a major brake on this tendency. Students are not the point: what counts is recognition afforded by peers. In sharp contrast, the two-year college teacher finds that students are nearly everything, *the* source of daily satisfaction, *the* basis for a successful career. A community college has no chance to become a think tank. Instead, the nature of its work moves it toward the character of a comprehensive secondary school.

Opposing forces thus tend to split the academic profession in two.

The upper part in a hierarchy of prestige becomes more professionalized: it is more fully based on arcane knowledge, more involved in peer judgment, more independent of clientele demands and related market forces. The bottom half, especially the bottom one-quarter, becomes less professionalized: it is committed to introductory materials that many can teach, more dependent on student reaction than peer approval, and heavily driven by market demands. Not far from the "shopping mall high school" we find the shopping mall community college.[3] Up the hierarchy we find inner-directed organizations in the hands of professionals; down the line we observe other-directed organizations that are client-driven. Perhaps it cannot be otherwise in a system of higher education that simultaneously seeks to function under a populist definition of equality, where all are admitted, and also tries to serve the gods of excellence in the creation and transmission of all rarefied bodies of knowledge.

In this odd occupation, professionals who primarily answer to peers are certain to be fundamentally different from professionals who are heavily dependent on consumer clientele.[4] The first group have to prove they are producing knowledge, the second that they are making enrollment.

Benefits have costs, strengths have weaknesses. Operating as a professors' medium, the university has difficulty in being responsive to undergraduate students. As professors turn to their research and their graduate students, freshman and sophomore students get the short end. Since the turn of the century, and especially in the post-1945 decades, the task of teaching beginning students has drifted toward the margin of reward and interest. Year in and year out, major universities, including private ones, send away brilliant young teachers, rather than give them tenure when their scholarship does not measure up. Such action often precipitates howls of protest from undergraduates and a march across campus to the president's or chancellor's office, where the loss is duly noted but allowed to stand. Such repetitive professional behavior on the part of the evaluating academics results not from personal willfulness but from the underlying structure of commitments and related rewards. Noting that "administrators give lip service to teaching excellence, whereas major universities promote staff members primarily on the basis of distinction in research and conspicuousness of publications," Logan Wilson remarked four decades ago that "the most critical problem confronted in the social organization of any university is the proper evaluation of faculty services, and giving due recognition through the impartial assignment of status."[5] This underlying problem has not and will not go away. In the inability to reward undergraduate teaching, we find the Achilles heel of the American research university.

In contrast, operating as a students' medium, the community college has difficulty in being responsive to the faculty's need for engagement in scholarship. Disciplinary involvement drifts toward the margin, attenuating scholarly competence and all the intrinsic satisfactions and extrinsic rewards that come with it. In the academic profession it is more blessed to produce than to distribute. When academics are denied all possibilities of engaging in research or scholarly practices, they are removed from the profession's central system of rewards. Then the Achilles heel is found in a winding-down of the scholarly model and a loss of academic respect. The central problems of one sector are virtually opposite the central problems of the other.

Serious reform that seeks to reduce weaknesses while retaining strengths has to address different conditions and effects. Reforms at the university level have to seek a substructuring of the undergraduate function that, in addition to the departmental structure, breaks up the large campus into more personal and more tangible parts: honors programs, subcolleges formed around residences or broad fields of study, special sets of seminars for freshmen and sophomores. The "college" has to be given strong symbolic definition within the university, challenging administrators and faculty to creatively alter rewards for the professoriate, even at the risk of creating a division between a teaching faculty and a research faculty. Some small gains are made in stiffening the teaching criterion in promotion decisions. But with competition for scholarly status powerfully concentrating the institutional mind, the tides run strong in the opposite direction.

Reforms in the all-teaching settings have an even more difficult time. They have to strengthen the incentives for scholarship, to maintain faculty competence in one field after another in which knowledge and technique change at a rapid rate. Many four-year college faculties sense the danger of residing in the backwaters of academia. Community college staffs are worse off. They are pushed toward a marginality that virtually cuts them out of the academic profession. Heavy teaching loads are at the heart of the problem. Here, small gains can be observed as faculty manipulate their twelve- and fifteen-hour loads to gain more time for keeping up with their fields. The lesser liberal arts colleges are able to look to the leading colleges as models of how to combine some research and scholarship with a primary commitment to undergraduate teaching. But the tides run strong in the other direction. The institutional need for students and the costs of lighter teaching loads powerfully set the institutional bias.

The Logic of the Profession

What is finally most useful to grasp are the inherent propensities of this profession, the drives that task and context set for the long term. Primary in the profession's logic is the hegemony of subjects, a characteristic of professions that is magnified in the academy. From the tyranny of subjects there follows the duality of commitment to discipline and institution that is the organizational heart of higher education. And from the liberating force of subjects there follows the intrinsic motivations that turn academic work into a calling.

THE HEGEMONY OF KNOWLEDGE

Lord Eric Ashby once postulated three main environmental forces acting on systems of higher education: consumer demand, manpower needs, and the patron's influence.[6] All external to the system itself, they enter mainly by means of reactions and translations that take place in the channels of system organization and institutional administration. Consumer demands for access, e.g., operate through admission requirements and procedures that are defined by government or are set by the competition of institutions in a market in which applicants and institutions freely interact; labor market demands penetrate the system through the employment anticipations of students, the lures offered graduates by employers and occupational sectors, and placement linkages that have been established between higher education and employment. Professors and administrators are involved in the transactions that bring these external forces to bear internally. Academics may shape decisively the one or the other: when their own committees guard the doors of admission or their internal interests perpetuate certain occupational programs at the expense of others. In both cases they interact with the outside world. They essentially operate much like administrators, even observe an administrative rationality. Frequently they leave such matters to administrators—those in admissions and placement offices—or hand the work to committees on which a few serve in the name of the many. The forces are external; the reactions are "organizational."

A fourth force of knowledge internal to the system and around which reactions are "professional" stands in sharp contrast. As Ashby noted, any higher education system has "its own articles of faith by which its practitioners live," or prefer to live, producing an "inner logic." That inner logic "does for higher education systems what genes do for biological systems: it preserves identity; it is a built-in gyroscope." The articles of faith are closely rooted in the very materials on which academic subunits center their work. As knowledge is newly created by research, and is reformulated and repeatedly transmitted in teaching and service, its force continuously bubbles up from within daily operations, right in the palm of the professional hand. The logic, the identity, the very rationality of the academic profession is thereby rooted in the evolving organization of those categories of knowledge that disciplines and professional fields of study have established historically and carried into the present, producing an inertia that powerfully prefigures the future. This rationality changes everything. If consumer demands, job placements, and the interests of patrons were the only imperatives, academic organization would more nearly resemble standard bureaucratic organization. It is the primacy of cognitive materials and their internal shaping influence that make the difference, turning so many universities and colleges into knowledge-driving organizations possessed by a bottom-up bias. Viability does not depend on the capacity of top-down commands to integrate parts into an organization whole. Instead, it depends on the quality of the performance of the basic units as nearly self-sufficient entities that do the work of disciplines and reflect their concerns.

In knowledge-driven organizations, where knowledge is the end as well as the means, a fragmented but intense professionalism is the only effective guarantor of standards. Covering authorities cannot offer a guarantee: they are too remote from the laboratory and classroom, too lacking in control of subject to effect useful control over persons. The better universities and colleges are the ones that have adapted their organization to the logic of subject dominion. They then become organizations that are inherently more centrifugal than centripetal.[7]

In the rationality of academic professionalism, peer surveillance serves as the main corrective for error, poor performance, and deviance. Such surveillance is most powerful in the task of research, for then it can be done on relatively visible products and by national and international observers as well as by local colleagues. Virtually cut loose from administrative chiefs, research professors answer to disciplinary sets of judges who effect controls in their judgmental reactions to preprints, articles, conference presentations, books, and a five- or ten-year body of work. However, the surveillance is much less powerful in the task of teaching, for then it must be done almost entirely by local observers and over classroom performances not typically in the public domain. As teaching takes over from research, the thrust of disciplinary controls is lessened, opening the way to the power of external demands, especially consumer satisfaction. The inner logic is muted.

In contradistinction to the more nationalized systems of higher education in Europe, and generally elsewhere in the world, the American system also operates, as I have stressed, at the more macro-level by the rationality of competition within a status hierarchy. Institutions that are in or anywhere near the upper quarter of the institutional hierarchy compete sharply for those academics considered to be the primary producers in creating knowledge. The effective institution is one most effective in this competition, working by the simple rule that faculty are the central resource. The effective institutions trumpet their success: the ambitious ones renew their bids. State governments even enter the competitive picture by awarding chairs and other special resources to their flagship public institutions to help them increase their bidding power and their chance of garnering faculty whose aggregate prowess and prestige will lift the institution another notch in research capability and national renown. Deeply entrenched in the commanding heights of the American professoriate, this competitive ethic drives the academic profession, segment by segment, as much as it does the institutions. The competition goads individual academics, their departments, and their invisible colleges.

But, as with subject domination, the rationality of competition shifts significantly from settings controlled by research to ones possessed by teaching. In the lower-status sectors of the hierarchy, the absence of research means that institutions are no longer competing for the status that follows from the reputation of scholars. If they compete to any degree, all-teaching institutions contend for control of student catchments or directly for individual students, making students rather than faculty the central resource. Financing is more strictly student-driven, and prestige of faculty as scholars adds little to the equations of viability and success. Rational behavior then dictates a shift from the disciplinary game to the institutional one. The rationality of the commanding heights of the many subject fields gives way to one, centered on the character of the student body, which is more subject to administration and hierarchy. Professionally, the situation is problematic: the centrality of faculty is sharply questioned, even strongly denied with the shift to temporary and part-time employment. The unionization response, as in elementary and secondary education, then entangles professionalism with unionism.

THE DUALITIES OF COMMITMENT

Given its disciplinary base and its grand diffusion of primary loyalties, this particular profession is more federative than any other. Subjects become states; disciplinary involvements are set off from institutional affiliations, and the two commitments frequently operate at cross purposes. The old distinction between "cosmopolitans" and "locals" pointed to the extremes in which either the discipline or the enterprise emerges as the commitment that subordinates the other. Always belonging to both specialty and locational groups, the academic professional has to work out a balance between the ways of each.

This primary duality becomes ambiguously elaborated in the American system. The radical decentralization of public authority in fifty states and the separation of a private sphere of authority composed of 1,500 autonomous institutions further fragments disciplines and types of institutions as it blocks all the formal integration provided by common civil service status in nationalized systems. It is then not a case of simple polarities between discipline and institution, but of types of disciplinary ties differing from one another as memberships in types of institutions differentiate academics.

We also have taken note of the growing unboundedness of this maverick profession, particularly in the form of temporary and part-time personnel whose certification is only weakly controlled if at all, and who perforce wander in and out of the system at the will of institutional administrators and sometimes personal desire. As boundaries are erased, the simple matter of counting the number of academics becomes a tortured exercise in arbitrary, ambiguous definitions. Now adding to the lowered boundaries between inside and outside is the growth of academic-like work external to the academy, occurring somewhat in the military establishment but most strongly in the world of business. "Scholars in corporations" is not a make-believe term.[8] For over a quarter of a century, Bell Laboratories have served as the prototype of the research facility in the business world whose collection of PhD talent in the sciences is equal to that of the leading universities. Other firms have joined in; they also teach and provide for the creation of new knowledge. They produce PhD-level scholars along with recruiting the university's products. The research and development division of many firms takes on a structure and develops a culture resembling that of the research university. Inside business, formal "schools" and "colleges" have now arrived; their privilege of granting degrees is a clear indication the academic profession has found yet another home.

Sociologists who paint on large canvases have had good reason to depict professions as major standardizing and unifying forces in modern society, on a par with, and even replacing, bureaucracies in producing "isomorphism"—similarities in structure and process.[9] Such observers see both patriots and mercenaries in particular occupations capturing territories of work as they grant membership only to those who enter through controlled gates, subscribe to sanctioned procedures, obey a common code—however loose its definition—and establish a common dominance over clients and auxiliary personnel. But the idea of isomorphism ill-fits the academic profession. A profession of professions is inherently centrifugal, especially when each of its subprofessions is driven by a research imperative that constantly enlarges and otherwise unsettles its own knowledge foundations. Polymorphism is the dominant trend; differentiation is more prized than commonality. The academic profession is qualitatively different in its extreme pluralism of contents and commitments.

Any dependable integration that comes about across the multitudinous commitments of the American profession is a product of overlapping connections among differences. From the hardest of the sciences to the softest of the humanities, from the purest fields to the most applied, adjacent fields overlap and even interpenetrate. In the institutional chain the many types of universities and colleges do not operate as watertight compartments but rather border upon and overlap one another, often to the point of heavily confusing the efforts of classifiers to draw lines between them. The fish-scale model of integration is an appropriate one. Hence disciplines and institutions are not only isolating tunnels. They are also mediating institutions that tie individual and small groups into larger holes of system and profession.

In its extreme heterogeneity the American academic profession is virtually a miniature of the extended diversity of groups that make up American society. Integration is largely unity in diversity, with slight family ties among the resilient and often unmeltable separate groups. Such plurality is dependent on broad respect for differences and on trust in the choices of others.

THE ABSORBING ERRAND

Henry James once wrote that true happiness "consists of getting out of oneself, but the point is not only to get out, you must stay out, and to stay out, you must have some absorbing errand."[10] Professions provide such errands, offering serious long-term assignments that captivate and motivate. They take on the coloration of secular religions that inculcate hope, promote a sense of service, and hold out the promise of earthly rewards. Professionals get out and stay out of themselves most fully when they make their tasks a part of themselves. In its many embodiments, the American academic profession exhibits the capacity to engage individuals on such absorbing errands, providing long careers that have a moral life of their own. Professors in a wide range of institutions and disciplines in America find motivation and satisfaction in the very thing itself—in research, or in teaching, or in both.

But the errands are always heavily conditioned by organization, sometimes to the point of descending spiral. Schoolteaching is the clear case in American education. It has endured a critical loss of spirit; its "professionalization project" became stalled, even reversed.[11] Under adverse organizational conditions, elementary and secondary school teachers have had their autonomy and authority subordinated to administrative controls, trustee supervision, and preferences of laymen. In a long downward slide propelled in part by defensive reactions of teachers themselves, careerism has considerably replaced calling. The bargain between teachers and students frequently becomes: I will not bother you if you do not bother me. In the "shopping mall high school," the resident profession has great difficulty in maintaining an absorbing errand.

American higher education is not immune to the conditions that lead to a loss of errand. Conditions in colleges and universities slowly but surely deprofessionalize the professoriate. Most perilous are the sectors where open access and the search for clientele has turned purpose into all things for all people. Then the administrative need to adjust flexibly to floating clienteles becomes more important than the need to have faculty define dominant duties and develop in-house cultures rich in professional meaning. Only true missionaries—always in short supply—can maintain an absorbing errand when the promise of career is reduced to a lifetime of teaching largely remedial composition or remedial mathematics for a revolving-door clientele that is easy in and quickly out.

A generalization of academic work that empties it of advanced contents has become a greater threat to the vitality and standing of the academic profession than all the intense specialization about which American reformers have routinely complained. From an extensive study of faculty in community colleges based on in-depth interviewing, Earl Seidman cogently concluded that "the community college as an institution has eroded the essential intellectual core of faculty work."[12] The perils of student-centeredness are greater than the dangers of professional dominance. In the shopping mall college, intellectual stagnation is a clear and present danger. For sure, the intellectual core runs down.

At the end of his classic essay on science as a vocation, published in 1919, Max Weber offered a set of striking observations that highlighted the richness, actual and potential, of the academic life.[13] Concentrating on "the inward calling" for science, "the personal experience" of science, he pointed to the passion that often lies behind the apparent coldness of strict specialization. Noting that enthusiasm is a prerequisite of inspiration, he spoke of the "strange intoxication" of the scientist when he feels that "the fate of his soul depends upon whether or not he makes the correct conjecture at this point of this manuscript." Dramatizing that rational thought can and should be pursued with passionate devotion, he ended his observations with a ringing affirmation of the fulfillment that the scientific-cum-academic calling can bring. Against those who "tarry for new prophets and saviors," he held up the duty of intellectual honesty, insisting that "in the lecture-rooms of the university no other virtue holds but plain intellectual integrity." Hence: "We shall act differently. We shall set to work and meet the 'demands of the day', in human relations as well as in our vocation. This, however, is plain and simple, if each finds and obeys the demon who holds the very fibers of his very life."[14]

Under all the strengths and weaknesses, the autonomies and vulnerabilities, of American academic life, we can sense the problem of calling. When academic work is just a job and a routine career, then such material rewards as salary are front and center. Academics stay at their work or leave for other pursuits according to how much they are paid. They come to work "on time" because they must; they leave on time because satisfactions are to be found after work is concluded. But when academic work is a calling, it "constitutes a practical ideal of activity and character that makes a person's work morally inseparable from his or her life. It subsumes the self into a community of disciplined practice and sound judgment whose activity has meaning and value in itself, not just in the output or profit that results from it."[15] A calling transmutes narrow self-interest into other-regarding and ideal-regarding interests: one is linked to fellow workers and to a version of a larger common good. It has moral content, contributing to civic virtue.

Professionalization projects aim to provide chariots by which multitudes of workers wend their way to a calling, there to find motivating demons as well as the glories of high status and the trappings of power. The academic profession has demons in abundance in the fascinations of research and the enchantments of teaching. Many academic contexts offer a workaday existence rich in content and consequence: as a confederate gathering, the academic profession's continuing promise lies in the provision of a variety of such contexts. In that promise lies the best hope in the long term for the recruitment and retention of talent. But when organization and profession fail one another, the errands run down, the demons disappear, and talented persons search for other fascinations and enchantments.

Near the end of the twentieth century, American higher education is a varied story of success and failure that has only begun to be disentangled by those willing not just to yearn for lost virtues but to take seriously its contradictory complexities. One cannot understand America's three thousand institutions of higher education without grasping how they are variously conditioned by the divergent ranks of the academic profession. And one cannot understand the profession without grasping the enormous differences exacted by different institutional frameworks. The American academic profession has become different worlds. The miracle is that organization and profession between them still often provide the errands that offer the rewards of personal fulfillment and a sense of societal service.

Bureaucracy is needed in academia, since formal organization is compellingly necessary if researchers are to do research, teachers are to teach, and students are to learn. But if the tools of professionalism are to be put to good use in the promotion of academic activity, the supporting organizations must be essentially profession-driven, offering conditions that heighten the intrinsic rewards of teaching and research and the intrinsic satisfactions of the academic life. Only professional norms and practices are positioned, person by person, in everyday activity to constructively shape motivation and steer behavior. Grasping this point, academic statesmen seek to create the conditions of professional inspiration and self-regulation. Failing to grasp the logic of the profession, indeed the very requirements of an effective modern system of higher education, narrow management attempts to substitute the nuts and bolts of bureaucratic regulation. Then the calling is reduced, the errand loses its fascination.

The third moment of professionalization has fragmented American academia into a thousand parts. But inside the many ranks and beneath the weariness of hurried toil, something extraordinary often resides. In our cultural world the academy is still the place where the devotion to knowledge remains most central, where it not merely survives but has great power. Many academic men and women know that power and still believe in it. They glow with that belief. In devotion to intellectual integrity, they find a demon who holds the fibers of their very lives.

Notes

1. Walter P. Metzger, "The Academic Profession in the United States," *The Academic Profession: National, Disciplinary, and Institutional Settings,* ed. Burton R. Clark (Berkeley, Los Angeles, and London: University of California Press, 1987); Christopher Jencks and David Riesman, *The Academic Revolution* (Garden City, N.Y.: Doubleday, 1968); and Laurence R. Veysey, *The Emergence of the American University* (Chicago: University of Chicago Press, 1965).

2. David Riesman, *On Higher Education: The Academic Enterprise in an Era of Rising Student Consumerism* (San Francisco: Jossey-Bass, 1980).

3. On the similarity of American schools to shopping malls, see Arthur G. Powell, Eleanor Farrar, and David K. Cohen, *Shopping Mall High School* (Boston: Houghton-Mifflin, 1985).

4. John P. Heinz and Edward O. Laumann have portrayed the American legal profession as divided primarily by the character of the clients served: the distinction between corporate and individual clients divides the bar into two separate "hemispheres." See John P. Heinz and Edward O. Laumann, *Chicago Lawyers: The Social Structure of the Bar* (New York: Russell Sage, 1982). The distinction between peer and consumer clienteles that we have observed in the academic profession may be applicable to a number of other professions, where the orientation to research and innovation is stronger than it is in law: e.g., medicine—now a part of "the health sciences"—architecture, and engineering.

5. Logan Wilson, *The Academic Man* (London: Oxford University Press, 1942), 219, 112.

6. Eric Ashby, "The Structure of Higher Education: A World View," occasional paper no. 6 (New York: International Council for Educational Development, 1973).

7. Jan-Eric Lane, "Academic Profession in Academic Organization," *Higher Education* 14, no. 3 (June 1985), 241–68.

8. Nell P. Eurich, *Corporate Classrooms: The Learning Business* (Princeton: The Carnegie Foundation for the Advancement of Teaching, 1985).

9. Paul J. DiMaggio and Walter W. Powell, "The Iron Cage Revisited: Institutional Isomorphism and Collective Rationality in Organizational Fields," *American Sociological Review* (April 1985), 147–60.

10. Comment attributed to Henry James: exact reference unknown.

11. Gary Sykes, "Teacher Education in the United States," in *The School and the University: An International Perspective,* ed. Burton R. Clark (Berkeley, Los Angeles, and London: University of California Press, 1953).

12. Earl Seidman, *In the Words of the Faculty: Perspectives on Improv-*

ing Teaching and Educational Quality in Community Colleges (San Francisco: Jossey-Bass, 1985), 275.

13. Max Weber, "Science as a Vocation," in *From Max Weber: Essays in Sociology*, ed. H. H. Gerth and C. Wright Mills (New York: Oxford University Press, 1946), 129–56.

14. Ibid., 156.

15. Robert N. Bellah, Richard Madsen, William M. Sullivan, Ann Swidler, and Steven M. Tipton, *Habits of the Heart: Individualism and Commitment in American Life* (Berkeley, Los Angeles, and London: University of California Press, 1985), 66. In exploring individualism and commitment in American life, Bellah and his associates, in four research projects, mainly pursued love and marriage, therapy, and several forms of civic or political participation among upper-middle-class people. Unfortunately, they concentrate for only a few pages on the world of work, where, especially for upper-middle-class professionals, much commitment is centered. See pp. 65–71 and pp. 287–90, where the call for reform centers on "a reappropriation of the idea of vocation or calling."

INTRODUCTION TO CHAPTER 20

This essay, drawn from the concluding pages of *The Academic Life*, highlights a central point: academic life in many institutions in the United States is capable of becoming an "absorbing errand"—one sufficiently strong to cause intrinsic rewards to triumph over extrinsic ones. As put by one interviewee, "psychic gratification" prevails to the point that "if I had to do it over, I sure would be a professor again." This person clearly has an emotional commitment to academia, despite its impediments.

But what about the widespread work conditions that adversely affect this sense of calling? We know, as reported frequently in interviews, that part-time work, low pay, and poorly prepared students negatively affect intrinsic rewards. Part-time work lowers self-esteem in a major way; low wages are thoroughly demoralizing; and, worst of all, teaching poorly prepared students robs the job of its serious subject matter. Here in the United States the would-be scholar is first required to do the teaching that should have been done in high school to raise student comprehension and capacity sufficiently to enable the assumption of college-level efforts—a difficult task for both student and teacher. Here again we note how defective secondary schooling deals a wasteful, dispiriting blow to higher education.

I beg the reader's indulgence for my propensity to take liberties with repetitive exhortation of what I believe are key ideas. In this case, I stress the importance of absorbing errands. Max Weber in the nineteenth century referred to this emotional commitment as the academic calling. However it is labeled, we need to be aware of its central importance in academic work.

CHAPTER 20

The Absorbing Errand

IN A MATERIALISTIC AGE that measures occupational success in dollars, academic work in the United States marches to a different drummer.

Whether located in research universities, four-year colleges, or two-year colleges, professors often refer to their work as a noble activity. Professors find personal reward and social value in their daily rounds as they invest themselves in undergraduate instruction, train graduate students as the next academic generation, create new knowledge through research and critical scholarship, and help preserve the parts of the cultural heritage for which they are centrally responsible.

Contrary to the bleak picture of disarray and despair, even greed and sloth, that sometimes has been painted by commentators during the 1970s and 1980s, an intensive study associates and I carried out between 1983 and 1985 found no crisis throughout the profession, no thundering loss of faith and commitment. What we found instead, in one locale after another, was a stubborn, even confident, affirmation of the value of the academic life.

How come? What comprises this affirmation? What lies behind it? If a professor teaching introductory accounting to remedial students in a community college can passionately report exhilarating experiences in the classroom, something unusual must be going on, something intangible that may be readily overlooked, especially when observers come armed with cynical perspectives.

What we encountered time and again was the capacity of the two primary tasks of teaching and research to commit individuals to the academic cause, thereby infusing life with meaning. No matter where we turned among diverse fields of study and quite different types of institutions, we found professors whose eyes lit up and whose voices moved

"The Absorbing Errand," *AAHE Bulletin* (March 1988): 8–11.

beyond cold objectivity when they spoke about what teaching meant to them, or about why research possessed their souls, or about why the combination of teaching and research, if not the best of all possible worlds, was the nearest thing that earthly employment was going to offer.

A two-year college instructor was not speaking for herself alone, it turned out, when she said, "To me it is not boring. To me it is challenging, to me it is fun, it is exciting. . . . I like to be up front, I like talking in front of people, I like putting an affect on someone. I like the ability to light a spark in someone and see that they like that, and to say that I helped that person make a decision. . . . because [of] what I gave to them and how I dealt with them. . . . I like the immediate reward that you get from dealing with students—good, quick recognition."

Another community college instructor, who had worked previously in a major corporation, added: "Obviously, we don't get paid very much, and you have to get psychic gratification to make up for that lack of financial rewards. . . . I can't imagine wanting to go back into a corporation full-time. I didn't find it terribly satisfying. . . . The fundamental mission of [that] organization is unimportant to me. And *this* mission is important to me."

At the other end of the institutional continuum, in the leading research universities, the rewards of critical thought and inquiry lend considerable zest to the lives of many professors. An early infatuation that became lifelong was expressed by a physicist: "There is no substitute for dealing with the things that we [physicists] deal with. I mean I'm just as crazy about that as I was when I was fourteen or fifteen years old. . . . I knew I had this inclination, I just never thought I would do it. And it's the only way."

And, in a second case: "Oh, I couldn't do anything else. . . . If you want to solve problems or do anything original or creative, then it's one of the few places [where] it can be done. . . . So I'd say if I had it to do over again, there are a few things I would do differently, but I sure would be a professor again."

The interest in coupling teaching and research stretches strongly into the second- and third-level universities and into the four-year colleges, public and private. A professor of English in a lesser university explained: "My primary goal when I came here was to be an outstanding teacher. I didn't want to be just competent; I wanted to be an outstanding teacher.

The other goal that I set for myself was my goal as a scholar, and that was to write well. I wanted people to read what I had to say about Joyce and say 'he writes well on Joyce.' To read someone who writes well on someone who writes well is, I think, a goal that I set for myself."

In a public comprehensive college not long out of its days as a teachers' college, another professor came on strong: "I am thoroughly immersed in my discipline, which is English literature. I am of the view that a person teaching in higher education is by definition an active, functioning, publishing scholar. This feeds the teaching, this maintains the enthusiasm, this keeps the juices flowing. . . . I really don't understand how one can function in the academic setting without being engaged in some research."

In short, to have the research demon by the tail can be a lifelong pleasure, combining a sense of craftsmanship, originality, and success, and a feeling that the juices are flowing, in teaching as well as in scholarship.

In a very substantial number of our field interviews, we found we were witnessing the triumph of the intrinsic over the extrinsic. Small wonder then that a Carnegie survey of five thousand academics in 1984 found that an overwhelming proportion of regular faculty were satisfied with their profession, despite a fall in salaries during the preceding decade and much concern about poorly prepared students. Nine out of ten reported that their present institution was either "a very good place" or "a fairly good place" for them. When asked to respond to the statement "If I had it to do over again, I'd not become a college teacher," only one in five agreed even mildly. Less than one in ten strongly agreed, and they were outnumbered 6 to 1 by those who emphatically took the opposite view that they would again become a professor.

Academic jobs, then, retain in considerable measure the capacity to become infused with a sense of calling. As recently defined by Robert Bellah and his associates in their critical assessment of American individualism, (*Habits of the Heart*, 1985, 66), a calling "makes a person's work morally inseparable from his or her life. It subsumes the self into a community of disciplined practice and sound judgment whose activity has meaning and value in itself, not just in the output or profit that results from it." When we are socialized into a calling, and then possessed by it, we commit ourselves to others in the service of a cause.

How does this come about? Academic work frequently hooks self-interest of the narrow sort to interests that encompass others and that connect to ideals. In a prize-winning book in political science, entitled *Beyond Adversary Democracy* (1980), Jane J. Mansbridge has argued persuasively that many of us as citizens are capable of simultaneously pursuing three forms of interest: an interest that is *self-regarding*, where our objective is some form of personal gain; an interest that is *other-regarding*, where our object is to advance the welfare of a group to which we belong; and an interest that is *ideal-regarding*, where we labor to serve one or more broad social purposes or principles.

In my view, modern professionalism aims to fuse these three forms of interest. Academic work is particularly equipped to do so. Certainly we all pursue self-interest of the narrow sort, whether for sheer material gain or for the delights of prestige and higher status; and on every campus we can point to those whose interests stop here. But we can in most locales point to a much larger number who have sincere regard for the advancement of their department and for the learning of their students and for the good name of their institution. They care about peers or students, and generally both.

And higher education remains alive with captivating ideals. How else do we interpret the finding of the Carnegie survey that nine out of ten American professors believe that education is the best hope for improving the human condition? What arrogant nonsense, one is tempted to say. But they—we—believe it, in overwhelming numbers.

Our in-depth interviews found professors also attached to the belief that they serve society while serving knowledge, by creating, refining, conserving, and disseminating it. They also reported the pursuit of truth as a touchstone, to the point where the worst crime is plagiarism. Plagiarism is a high crime because it entails a theft of knowledge, a stealing of intellectual property that poisons the reward systems. Professors, in various ways, also remain strongly attached to the ideal of academic freedom, and they portray the personal freedom thereby gained as an extremely attractive aspect of academic life.

Many years ago, Henry James wrote that true happiness "consists of getting out of oneself, but the point is not only to get out, you must stay out, and to stay out you must have some absorbing errand."

James's literary metaphor is surely akin to the idea of a calling; to the concept of the intrinsic; to the notion that we can be simultaneously self-regarding, other-regarding, and ideal-regarding—*and* to the warranted assertion that academic professionalism, in the America of the late twentieth century, reflects more of the bright side than the dark side of the coin of professionalization. Because, when we talk with people in the academic world, listen to them in the fullness of their own terms—in locations away from the public settings where they put on the masks of cold objectivity and critical detachment—their absorption in academic errands shines through.

That's the good news. Now for the bad news.

The bad news is that there are powerful conditions that undermine all that I have highlighted. There are conditions that have evolved in our system of higher education that weaken the intrinsic rewards, that push self-interest away from the embrace of other-regarding and ideal-regarding interests, that run down the absorbing errands that motivate and satisfy.

What are these conditions? The most important one by far is part-time work. For good short-run reasons, academic managers, often joined by rank-structure faculty, have moved something like one-third of all academics onto part-time status. Many community colleges, and a goodly number of four-year colleges, have a half or more of their faculty on part-time assignment.

This shift has been a disaster for the professoriate. The many terms used by part-timers and others denote the deeply troubling position they are in: gypsy scholars, displaced academics, migrant laborers of academe, the academic proletariate, marginal academics, disposable dons, freeway scholars. All serve in a market for piecework.

Nothing *de*professionalizes an occupation faster and more thoroughly than the transformation of full-time posts into part-time labor. And the part-timers are the first ones to say so, as they report the dismal conditions of work and status under which they labor, the straight-out exploitation to which they are subjected, the intense brutalizing of the ideals of the profession that they experience.

The second condition that reduces our absorbing errands is more difficult to specify and more subject to misunderstanding. It entails a weakening of the intellectual core of academic work. It is most prevalent where instructors teach only introductory materials of the most general sort, and then often to poorly prepared students. Hence it is a particularly threatening condition in the open-door community colleges that are overloaded with remedial work, and in four-year colleges that admit applicants without regard to preparation and ability. The energies of college teachers then become concentrated on introductory subject-matter, and some members of the staff have to work with students who are initially functioning at a ninth-grade, or a sixth-grade, or even a third-grade level. In crude terms, the subject-matter has to be "dumbed down," often twice over. The effect on teachers is to erode the vitality that comes from commitment to subject and the related identity as scholar. When the subject base is only elementary, intellectual juices may well stop flowing.

Open access and an eager search for clientele in postsecondary education have major costs with which we have yet to reckon. Only true missionaries—always in short supply—can maintain a calling, an absorbing errand, when the promise of career is reduced to a lifetime of teaching largely remedial composition, or remedial mathematics, for a revolving-door clientele that is easy in and quickly out. The simplification of academic work that empties it of advanced content is a substantial threat to the vitality of the academic profession, a condition that appears to bring more harm than all the intense specialization about which American reformers have routinely complained.

The third adverse condition is one that has been widely discussed: the lessening of material rewards. There are limits to how much "psychic satisfaction" can substitute for the pay check. The old car needs a new motor; the house needs its leaky roof repaired; and braces for the children's teeth become a necessity—even for those who read books, attend art films, and identify themselves as intellectuals. Lack of money is one of the two chief complaints of academics in our discussions with them— "the biggest problems is [that] the pay is not good enough"—the other being, as mentioned earlier, the poor preparation of students. The material rewards do count for something, often a lot, and in the 1970s and early 1980s, in some fields and in many institutions, they had not kept pace.

Basic reform in higher education—reform that takes seriously the fundamental structure of the system and the systematic constraints and rewards under which academics operate—needs to address these conditions.

Responsible institutional action can chip away at the overload of part-time work to bring it down to a level where the faculty core of institutions is measurably strengthened. As Ernest Boyer has recommended in the foreword to my book, *The Academic Life* (1987), institutions need to justify educationally as well as financially why, e.g., more than 20 percent of faculty teaching undergraduates should be part-time. Salary deprivation can be altered also, with apparently some improvement in many institutions in the past several years. Academics are better paid, of course, when they are in short supply, and the academic labor market should evolve in this direction in the 1990s.

The toughest condition to change is the one involving the simplifying of academic work to the point of a virtual loss of subject matter. This one cuts deep into the identity of teachers as scholars, especially when the global reference group includes faculty in the research universities and the selective four-year colleges. But if this condition were raised to a higher level of consciousness in those community colleges where it is pervasive, and there defined as a major problem, a number of incremental steps could be taken.

Those teaching only introductory materials need professional associations, or parts thereof, that are appropriate to their interests; and this process is under way (e.g., a Community College Humanities Association, a Community College Social Science Association). These first-tier instructors need regular contact with subject matter counterparts in four-year colleges and universities. And they need a sabbatical clock that works, and that can be sped up. Nothing makes the intellectual juices flow again like a year back in the university library, advanced seminars, and laboratories. For the great majority of academics, disciplinary involvement is a key anchoring point. Then, too, staff can be differentiated so that some members, lodged in learning resource centers, identify themselves and support one another as learning specialists—another small evolution that is well under way.

In conclusion, I want to stress that what we see in the academic world depends very much upon where we look. American academic life is very uneven.

In the world's most diverse system of higher education, the professoriate is enormously differentiated by type of institution as well as by disciplinary specialization. Hence we cannot speak clearly and act effectively when we think in a simplistic fashion about "*the* professor in *the* college," or "*the* university professor."

Simple statements to the effect that professors do not teach enough, or professors spend too much time doing research, become nonsense. Many professors in sectors we can clearly identify teach too much rather than too little. And in those sectors one can readily make the case, as our respondents did, that academics have too little time for scholarly renewal, let alone for research, rather than too much. Context is everything.

Those who wish to shape public policy on higher education become sophisticated and relevant only as they learn to speak in the language of differentiation, specifying what settings they have in mind when they try to make one point or another. And it clearly does not hurt if researchers get out of their offices, away from their computers, and enter into sustained discussions with colleagues in far-flung locales.

As we root around in the different worlds, the many small worlds, of academe, what should occupy our attention the most is the strength of academic errands. Supporting conditions for these errands vary from one field to another, and from one institution to another, but the basic tasks of teaching and research are inherently attractive forms of work, and it takes massive adverse conditions to reduce seriously the strength of the academic calling in the system as a whole. The faculty remains the central resource, the key asset, for institution-building, and sturdy institutional character depends on their deep commitment.

Thus, as observers or administrators or policy-makers, we need to attend to the conditions that help, and the conditions that hinder, the forging of a commitment by faculty in which narrow self-interest is hooked to the twin chariots of service to others and service to ideals.

At the heart of the matter are the ways by which teaching and research (*and* college administration) exert their fascinations. Why do we so often invest our sum of living in our academic assignments? Why do we so often attempt to ignore the need to sleep, and to treat the flesh as a piece of torn luggage that the spirit must drag after it? Whatever the fuller explanations, those of us who work in higher education are more advantaged than abused by the simple fact that our work so readily becomes a haunting and haunted business. At the least, we come to know that there is more, much more, to life than getting and spending.

References

Bellah, Robert N., Richard Madsen, William M. Sullivan, Ann Swidler, and Steven M. Tipton. *Habits of the Heart: Individualism and Commitment in American Life*. Berkeley, Los Angeles, and London: University of California Press, 1985.

Clark, Burton R. *The Academic Life: Small Worlds, Different Worlds*. Princeton, N.J.: Carnegie Foundation for the Advancement of Teaching, 1987.

Mansbridge, Jane J. *Beyond Adversary Democracy*. Chicago: University of Chicago Press, 1980.

INTRODUCTION TO CHAPTER 21

I include a second essay that briefly highlights a basic argument from *The Academic Life* (1987). After describing some details of disciplinary and institutional differences in the academic life in American higher education, I turn to the gritty question of what, if anything, integrates the country's professoriate. Michael Polanyi's meritorious idea of "chains of overlapping neighborhoods" and Donald T. Campbell's notion of "a continuous texture of narrow specialties," both dating from the 1960s, answer that question. And so does sociologist of science Diana Crane when she writes about ideas of "overlapping memberships among cultural communities" (1982).

The central energizing idea is integration through overlapping parts—rather than through membership in a grand corps, identical socialization, or commonly held values. *E pluribus unum* can come in many shapes.

CHAPTER 21

The Academic Life:

Small Worlds, Different Worlds

> The American professoriate is enormously differentiated by discipline and type of institution on such primary dimensions of professionalism as patterns of work, identification, authority, career, and association. Integration across the professoriate no longer comes primarily from similarity of function and common socialization, but from the overlap of subcommunities and the mediating linkages provided by the ties of discipline and institution.
>
> —*Educational Researcher* 18, no. 5 (1989)

TODAY, NEAR THE END of the twentieth century, the American system of higher education is highly diversified, steadily dividing along the two basic lines of discipline and type of institution. As the system goes, so does the academic profession reap, evolving into a multisided occupation composed of many different professions, semiprofessions, and nonprofessional fields. I want to explore the nature of this extreme differentiation, particularly its self-amplifying tendency, and then suggest some largely hidden links that may yet connect academics one to another even as common values and experiences recede.

The Growing Division of Labor

The modern differentiation of the American professoriate means straightaway that we deceive ourselves, and others, every time we speak in simplistic terms of *the* professor in *the* university, or *the* college professor. Disciplinary differences alone demand a more exacting approach in

"The Academic Life: Small Worlds, Different Worlds," *Educational Researcher* (June–July 1989): 4–8. Used by permission.

which the field of competence and study is front and center. In the leading universities, e.g., the clinical professor of medicine is as much a part of the basic workforce as is the professor of English. The medical academic can be found in a cancer ward, interacting intensively with other doctors, nurses, orderlies, laboratory assistants, a few students perhaps, and many patients in a round of tightly scheduled activities that may begin at seven in the morning and extend into various evenings and weekends. Such academics are often under considerable pressure to generate income from patient-care revenues: they frequently negotiate with third-party medical plans and need a sizable administrative staff to handle patient billing. Salary may well depend on group income that fluctuates from year to year and that is directly affected by changes in the health care industry and by the competitive position of a particular medical school–hospital complex. Hence salary may not be guaranteed, even in a tenured post. Sizable research grants must also be actively and repetitively pursued, and those who do not raise funds from research grants will find themselves loaded up with more clinical duties.[1]

The humanities professor operates in a totally different environment. Teaching "loads" are in the range of four to six hours a week. Office hours are at one's discretion; administrative assignments vary considerably with one's willingness to cooperate. The humanities academic typically interacts with large numbers of beginning students in lecture halls, in an occasional turn in introductory classes; with smaller numbers of juniors and seniors, in specialized upper-division courses; and then with a few graduate students in seminars and dissertation consultation, around such highly specialized topics as Elizabethan lyric and Icelandic legend. Much valuable work time can be spent at home, away from the "distractions" of the university office.

About what is one thinking and writing? Attention may center on a biography of Eugene O'Neill, an interpretation of what Jane Austen really meant, an effort to trace Lillian Hellman's political passions, or a critique of Jacques Derrida and deconstructionism. Professors seek to master a highly specialized segment of literature and to maximize individual interpretation. The interests of humanities professors are reflected not only in the many sections and byways of such omnibus associations as the Modern Language Association, but also in the specificities of the Shakespeare Association of America, the Dickens Society, the D. H. Lawrence Society of North America, the Speech Association of America, the Thomas Hardy Society of America, and the Vladimir Nabokov Society. Tocqueville's famous comment on the propensity of Americans to form voluntary associations is nowhere more true than in the academic world.

Disciplinary differences are of course not limited to the sharp contrast between life in a medical school and in a department of English. The work of Tony Becher and others on the cultures of individual disciplines has shown that bodies of knowledge variously determine the behavior of individuals and departments (see especially Becher, 1987). Disciplines exhibit discernible differences in individual behavior and group action, notably between "hard" and "soft" subjects and "pure" and "applied" fields; in a simple fourfold classification, between hard-pure (physics), hard-applied (engineering), soft-pure (history), and soft-applied (social work). Across the many fields of the physical sciences, the biological sciences, the social sciences, the humanities, and the arts, fieldwork reveals varied work assignments, symbols of identity, modes of authority, career lines, and associational linkages.[2] More broadly, great differences in the academic life often appear between the letters and science departments and the many professional school domains in which a concern for the ways and needs of an outside profession must necessarily be combined with the pursuit of science and truth for its own sake. Far from the popular images of Mr. Chips chatting up undergraduates and of Einsteinian, white-haired, remote scholars dreaming up esoteric mathematical equations are the realities of academic work that helps prepare school teachers, librarians, social workers, engineers, computer experts, architects, nurses, pharmacists, business managers, lawyers, and doctors—and, in some academic locales, also morticians, military personnel, auto mechanics, airport technicians, secretaries, lathe operators, and cosmetologists. As Robert Wiebe (1967) and Walter Metzger (1987) have noted in historical detail, American higher education has been generous to a fault in admitting former outside fields into the academy, thereby administering a dose of legitimacy.

Because research is the first priority of the leading universities, the disciplinary differentiation of every modern system of higher education is self-amplifying. The American system is currently the extreme case of this self-amplification: its great size, decentralization, diversity, and competitiveness magnify the pursuit of new knowledge. The reward system for this self-amplification began to emerge a century ago, when Johns Hopkins and other new upstart universities competitively prompted Eliot at Harvard and others in the old colleges of the day to speed up the nascent evolution from the age of the college to the age of the university. This evolution turned professors loose to pursue specialized research and to teach specialized subjects at the newly created graduate level, even as students were turned loose to pick and choose in an array of undergraduate courses that was to become ever more bewildering. The reward system of promoting academics on the grounds of research and published scholarship has become more deeply rooted in the universities, and would-be universities and leading four-year colleges, with every passing decade. The many proliferating specialties of the disciplines are like tributaries flowing into this mammoth river of the research imperative.

The most serious operational obstacles to this research-drive amplification are the limitations of funding and the institutional need to teach undergraduates and beginning graduate students with packages of introductory materials that they can understand. Then, too, there remains in the American system the long-standing belief in the importance of undergraduate liberal or general education. The saving remnant of academics who uphold the banners of liberal and general education are able to sally forth in full cry periodically—the 1920s, the late 1940s, the 1980s—to group some specialties into more general course offerings, narrow the options in distribution requirements from, say, four hundred to one hundred courses, insist that teaching take priority over research, and in general raise a ruckus about the dangers of the specialized mind. Meanwhile, however, campus promotion committees continue their steady scrutiny of the record of research and scholarship. Central administrators work actively to build an institutional culture of academic first-rateness as that is defined competitively across the nation and even internationally on the basis of the reputation of noted scholars. Sophisticated general educators and liberal arts proponents in the universities recognize the primacy of the substantive impulse and learn how to work incrementally within its limits.

Institutional Differentiation

As powerful as are the self-amplifying disciplinary differences in dividing the professoriate, institutional differentiation now plays an even more important role. Useful classifications of the 3,400 accredited institutions in American higher education now run to twenty categories of major types—and still leave unidentified such important subtypes as historically black colleges, women's colleges, and Catholic colleges (Carnegie Foundation for the Advancement of Teaching, 1987). The creation of individual niches within the types has become a high art, especially among private universities and colleges but not limited to them—a self-amplifying tendency propelled by competition for resources, clientele and reputation. The extensive differentiation places most academics in settings other than that of the research university. We find a third of them in public and private four-year colleges and "comprehensive colleges," numbering together about 1,200, that offer degree work as far as the master's. Another fourth to a third are to be found in the nearly 1,400 community colleges.

These major locales exhibit vast differences in the very basis of the academic life, namely, the balance of effort between teaching and research. Teaching loads in the leading universities come in at around 4 to 6 hours a week, tailing down to 2 to 3 hours—a class a week, a seminar a week— more often than rising above 6. The reciprocal is that faculty commonly expect to spend at least half their time in research, alone or in the company of a few advanced graduate students. We need not stray very far, however, before we encounter teaching loads that are 50 percent, 100 percent, and 200 percent higher. What are called "doctorate-granting universities," rather than "research universities," exact teaching loads of 9 to 12 hours. So too for liberal arts colleges, especially outside the top 50. In comprehensive colleges, loads of 12 hours a week in the classroom are common. In turn, in the community colleges, the standard climbs to 15 hours, and loads of 18 and 21 hours are not unknown. And as we move from the top of the institution hierarchy to the bottom, faculty involvement shifts from advanced students to beginning students; from highly selective students to open-door clientele; from young students in the traditional college age group to a mix of students of all ages in short-term vocational programs as well as in coursework leading toward a bachelor's degree.

In the community colleges, students in the college-transfer track are now numerically overshadowed by students in terminal vocational programs, and both are frequently outnumbered by non-matriculated adults who turn "college" into "community center."

The burdens of remedial education are also much heavier as we descend the hierarchy. The open-door approach, standard in two-year colleges and also operational in four-year colleges that take virtually all comers, confronts college teachers with students in the classroom who are still operating at a secondary-school, and even an elementary-school, level. Then, to add insult to injury, as we descend the hierarchy, we encounter more part-time academic work. During the past two decades, the ranks of the part-timers have swollen to two hundred thousand or so, a third of the total academic workforce, with heavy concentrations in the less prestigious colleges and especially in community colleges, where a half or more of the faculty commonly operate on a part-time schedule.

At the extreme opposite end of the institutional hierarchy from those who serve primarily in the graduate schools and graduate-level professional school in the major universities are the full-time and part-time teachers in English or mathematics in downtown community colleges who teach introductory and subintroductory courses over and over again—the rudiments of English composition, the first course in mathematics—to high school graduates who need remediation and to adults struggling with basic literacy. As faculty pointed out in interviews, "scholars" are then transformed into "mere teachers," serving in a fashion more similar to high school teaching than to university work.

With the very nature of academic work varying enormously across the many types of institutions that make up American postsecondary education, other dimensions of the academic life run on a parallel course. If we examine the cultures of the institutions by discussing with faculty members their basic academic beliefs, we find different worlds. Among the leading research universities, the discipline is front and center, the institution is prized for its reputation of scholarship and research, and peers are the primary reference group. A professor of physics will say: "What I value the most is the presence of the large number and diverse collection of scientists who are constantly doing things that I find stimulating." A professor of biology tells us that his university "has a lot of extremely good departments . . . there are a lot of fascinating, interesting people here." A political scientist adds that what he values most "is the intellectual level of the faculty and the graduate students. . . . Good graduate students are very important to me personally and always have been, and having colleagues that are smart is important." And a professor of English told us that his institution "is a first-rate university . . . we have a fine library, and we have excellent teachers here, and we have first-rate scholars." Academics in this favored site have much with which to identify. They are proud of the quality they believe surrounds them, experiencing it directly in their own and neighboring departments and inferring it indirectly from institutional reputation. The strong symbolic thrust of the institution incorporates the combined strengths of the departments that in turn represent the disciplines. Thus, for faculty, disciplinary and institutional cultures converge, a happy state indeed.

The leading private liberal arts colleges provide a second favored site. Here, professors often waxed lyrical in interviews about the small college environment tailored to undergraduate teaching: "It is a very enjoyable setting. The students are—the students we get in physics—a delight to work with"; "I can't put it in a word, but I think that it is one of the least constraining environments I know of"; "it is a better form of life"; or, "My colleagues are fantastic. The people in this department are sane, which in an English department is not always the case." These institutions retain the capacity to appear as academic communities, not bureaucracies, in their overall integration and symbolic unity.

But soon we encounter sites where faculty members are troubled by inchoate institutional character and worry about the quality of their environment. In the lesser universities, and especially in the comprehensive colleges that have evolved out of a teachers' college background, at the second, third, and fourth levels of the institutional hierarchy, the setting was often summed as follows:

> I think the most difficult thing about being at an institution like [this one] is that it has a difficult time coming to terms with itself. I think the more established institutions with strong academic backgrounds don't have the problem that an institution that pretty much is in the middle range of higher educational institutions around the country does. I'm not saying that [this institution] is a bad institution, but it certainly doesn't have the quality students, the quality faculty, the

quality programs of the University of Chicago, Harvard, Yale. . . . When it talks about standards, what sort of standards? When it talks about practicality, how practical does it have to be? . . . It doesn't have a strong sense of tradition.

Compared to the research universities, the overall institutional culture is weaker and less satisfying for many faculty members, at the same time that disciplinary identifications are weakened as heavy teaching loads suppress research and its rewards.

In these middle-level institutions, professors often spoke of their relationship with students as the thing they value most. Students begin to replace peers as the audience of first resort. That shift is completed in the community colleges, with the identifications of faculty reaching a high point of student-centeredness. In a setting that is distinctly opposed to disciplinary definitions of quality and excellence, pleasures and rewards have to lie in the task of working with poorly prepared students who pour in through the open door, e.g.: "We are a practical teaching college. We serve our community and we serve . . . the students in our community, and give them a good, basic, strong education. . . . We are not sitting here on our high horses looking to publish"; and "I really do like to teach, and this place allows me to teach. It doesn't bog me down with having to turn out papers." In the community colleges, the equity values of open door and open access have some payoff as anchoring points in the faculty culture. But in the overall institutional hierarchy, where the dominant values emphasize quality, selection, and advanced work, the community college ideology can play only a subsidiary role. The limitations cannot be missed: "It would be nice to be able to teach upper-division classes."

As for work and culture, so go authority, careers, and associational life. To sum the story on authority, at the top of the institutional hierarchy faculty influence is well and strong. Many individuals have strong personal bargaining power; departments and professional schools are strong, semiautonomous units; and all-campus faculty bodies have dominant influence in personnel and curricular decisions. University presidents speak lovingly of the faculty as the core of the institution and walk gently around entrenched faculty prerogatives. But as we descend the hierarchy, faculty authority weakens and managerialism increases. Top-down command is noticeably stronger in the public comprehensive colleges, especially when their genetic imprint is that of a teachers' college. The two-year colleges, having evolved mainly out of secondary systems and operating, like schools, under local trustees, are quite managerial. Faculty then feel powerless, even severely put upon. Their answer has been unionization. The farther down the hierarchy of prestige we go, the more widespread do unions become, especially among the public-sector institutions.

To sum the associational life of faculty: in the leading universities, faculty interact with one another across institutional boundaries in a bewildering network of disciplinary linkages—formal and informal; large and small; visible and invisible; local, regional, national, and international. When university specialists find "monster meetings" not to their liking, they go to participate in a smaller division or section that best represents their specific interests, or, as of late, they find kindred souls in small, autonomous meetings of several dozen people. The jet set is everywhere, from physicists pursing high-energy physics to professors of English off to a conference in Paris on structuralism. As we move down the hierarchy, however, there is less reason to be involved, less to learn that is relevant to one's everyday life, and the travel money is gone from the institutional budget. Then, academics do not go to national meetings, or they go only if the national association comes to their part of the country and develops special sessions on teaching—or they break away to form associations appropriate to their sector. Community college teachers have been developing associations in such broad areas as the social sciences and the humanities and in such special areas of teaching as mathematics and biology, and doing so on a home-city or home-region as well as national basis.

Different worlds, small worlds. The institutional differentiation interacts with the disciplinary differentiation in a self-amplifying fashion that steadily widens and deepens the matrix of differences.

What Integrates?

If academic life in America is so divided, and the future promises even greater fragmentation, does any integration obtain? I mentioned at the outset that common values and experiences recede. When we searched in faculty interviews for common beliefs, we found some possible cultural linkages in widely used expressions. As faculty members attempted to formulate what professors have in common, they turned often to expressions about serving knowledge, searching for answers, and striving for new understanding. We frequently encountered norms of academic honesty in which plagiarism—the stealing of someone else's intellectual property—is the worst crime of all. The ideology of academic freedom was often raised, with personal freedom portrayed as an extremely attractive aspect of academic life that, like recognition, sometimes serves in lieu of material rewards.

But we had to scrape to find values that might still be widely shared, sensing that so often the same words had different meanings. Academic freedom means in one context primarily the right to pursue research and publish as you please; in another, the right to give failing grades and the right not to punch in and out on a time clock for so many hours on campus each day. The concern about plagiarism drops off sharply among those in all-teaching settings; the norms of academic honesty then more often refer to fair grading and fair treatment of students. In short, the ongoing differentiation not only erodes common values but also gives stated common values different meanings in different contexts.

Because this is the case, a search for common values is not now the best way to identify linkages among professors. The claim that academics must and should find their way back to agreement on core values becomes more unrealistic with each passing year. Instead, as commonness recedes, we have to determine how "unity in diversity" comes about. One path to such unity is normative systems that hook self-interest to larger institutional chariots. In the normal course of their work, biologists or political scientists or literature professors can serve simultaneously their own achievement, the progress of their department and discipline, and the education of the young, the advancement of scholarship, and other ideals that give meaning to the academic world. The bright side of modern professionalism, especially its academic version, is that self-regarding, other-regarding, and ideal-regarding interests can be blended and simultaneously served. (These three forms of interest have been brilliantly conceptualized in Mansbridge, 1983.) In an age of specialization, academic callings are constructed primarily in the many cultural homes of the individual disciplines. Tunnel by tunnel, the disciplines *qua* professions serve as critical centers of meaning and as primary devices for linkage into the larger world.

Further, the disciplines do not exist simply as isolated tunnels, linking individuals in parallel chains that never meet. Both in their coverage of empirical domains and as modes of reasoning, they overlap. Michael Polanyi (1967) has acutely observed that modern science consists of "chains of overlapping neighborhoods" (72). Donald T. Campbell (1969) has stressed that a comprehensive social science, or any large domain of academic knowledge, is "a continuous texture of narrow specialties" (328). Multiple specialties overlap much like the scales on the back of a fish. That overlap produces "a collective communication, a collective competence and breadth" (330). In attempting to figure out how cultural integration may coexist with diversity in a highly differentiated society, Diana Crane (1982) has observed that the social system of science is an appropriate model: "Contemporary science comprises hundreds of distinct specialties, but each specialty has connections, both intellectual and social, with other specialties. . . . Cultural integration occurs because of overlapping memberships among cultural communities that lead to the dissemination of ideas and values" (239). What we find, in science and in academia, are "interlocking cultural communities" (241).

In the subcultures of academe, it is a long way from physics and chemistry to political science and sociology, let alone history and literature. As cultural communities, however, physics and chemistry overlap with mathematics, which connects to statistics, both of which in turn link importantly to the "hard" social sciences of economics and psychology. They in turn shade into the softer disciplines of political science, sociology, and anthropology, fields that readily shade into the perspectives of history and then further on into the humanities. Also, more broadly, the letters and science disciplines serve as academic links to professional fields. They contribute substantive materials; and, as the "basic" disciplines, they continue to define what is scholarly.

Our imagery of cultural overlap is also heightened when we see the academic world stretching from center to periphery in the form of institutional as well as disciplinary chains. Institutionally, the hard core of academic values in the American professoriate is found in the leading research universities and top liberal arts colleges. The first exemplifies modern science and advanced scholarship; the second upholds the much-respected tradition of liberal education for undergraduates. These locales are centers whose cultural influence radiates first to adjacent types of institutions and then in weakening rays to institutional sectors more divorced in character. The top ten universities are a powerful cultural magnet to the second ten, the top twenty to the top fifty, the recognized universities to the many comprehensive colleges that so dearly want to be recognized as universities. The many different types of institutions do not operate as watertight compartments—witness the high transferability of course credit—but rather overlap to the point of heavily confusing the efforts of classifiers to draw lines between them.

The analytical handle is the idea of integration through overlap. Then we no longer need to think as observers or participants, that integration can come about only by means of some combination of identical social-ization, similarity of task, commonly held values, and united member-ship in a grand corps or a single association. Academics need not think that they must somehow pull themselves together around a top-down pronouncement of a fixed set of values and a universal core curriculum, swimming against the tides of history and seeking a return to a gold age that never was. As we probe the nature of the modern academic life, especially in America, it is much more fruitful to grasp that integration can come from the bit-by-bit overlap of narrow memberships and specific identities. Specialties and disciplines, and whole colleges and universities, may serve as mediating institutions that tie individuals and small groups into the whole of the system.

For a profession that is so naturally pluralistic, and for which the fu-ture promises an ever-widening complexity of task and structure, a large dollop of pluralist theory is not a bad idea. The many dualities of com-mitment to discipline and institution, and the many linkages among units on these primary lines of affiliation, provide an academic version of the great federal motto: *E pluribus unum.* Whatever the future unities of the academic life in America, they will have to be rooted in the developmental differences that inhere in the ways of modern academe.

Notes

1. Unless otherwise indicated, all empirical materials reported in this essay come from a 1973–75 study that centered on 180 intensive faculty interviews in the six fields of physics, biology, political science, English, business, and medicine, in sixteen universities and colleges, chosen nationally to represent six types of institutions, from leading research universities to community colleges. The interviews, taped and transcribed, led to lengthy protocols that could be variously grouped and analyzed by discipline and institutional type. Some quantitative data from the 1984 Carnegie faculty survey were also available and used. Fuller description of the research study can be found in *The Academic Life* (1987), Introduction and Appendix A.

2. These five categories of work, culture, authority, career, and association, defined as primary dimensions of academic professionalism, are developed as central chapters in *The Academic Life* (1987) to group and analyze the rich materials obtained in the 1983–85 field interviews.

References

Becher, T. "The Disciplinary Shaping of the Profession." In *The Academic Profession: National, Disciplinary, and Institutional Settings,* edited by B. R. Clark, 271–303. Berkeley and Los Angeles: University of California Press, 1987.

Campbell, D. T. "Ethnocentrism of Disciplines and the Fish-Scale Model of Omniscience." In *Interdisciplinary Relationships in the Social Sciences,* edited by M. Sherif and C. Sherif, 328–48. Chicago: Aldine, 1969.

Carnegie Foundation for the Advancement of Teaching. *A Classification of Institutes of Higher Education.* Princeton, N.J.: Carnegie Foundation for the Advancement of Teaching, 1987.

Clark, B. R. *The Academic Life: Small Worlds, Different Worlds.* Princeton, N.J.: Carnegie Foundation for the Advancement of Teaching and Princeton University Press, 1987.

Crane, D. "Cultural Differentiation, Cultural Integration, and Social Control." In *Social Control: Views from the Social Science,* edited by J. P. Gibbs, 229–44. Beverly Hills, Calif.: Sage, 1982.

Mansbridge, J. J. *Beyond Adversary Democracy.* Chicago: University of Chicago Press, 1980.

Metzger, W. P. "The Academic Profession in the United States." In *The Academic*

Profession: National, Disciplinary, and Institutional Settings, edited by B. R. Clark, 123–208. Berkeley and Los Angeles: University of California Press, 1987.

Polanyi, M. *The Tacit Dimension.* Garden City, N.J.: Doubleday, 1967.

Wiebe, R. H. *The Search for Order, 1877–1920.* New York: Hill and Wang, 1967.

INTRODUCTION TO CHAPTER 22

You can tell by its tone that this book review was fun to do. At the same time, the central issue on which I focused was painful twice over. I knew the Berkeley scene well—the two authors were former colleagues—and I was located at the UCLA school of education, one of the other "ed schools" reviewed in the book, when I wrote the review. More important, the strain between university norms and professional practices in such schools generally runs deep, much more so than in schools of medicine, law, engineering, and business. Thereby hangs the tale.

CHAPTER 22

Schools of Education:

The Academic-Professional Seesaw

*E*D *SCHOOL* BEGAN as a communiqué from the front in The Hundred Years' War of the Ed Schools. Serving successively as chairs of the department of education in Berkeley, Geraldine Clifford and James Guthrie were in the front lines, carrying the tattered flag of their small garrison of irregulars during the difficult days of the late 1970s and early 1980s, when—as seasoned veterans will recall—the heavy shelling directed at the exhausted education troops from elsewhere on campus threatened to drive the survivors into the bay.

When it comes to hand-to-hand fighting and the agony of a long retreat, the authors know whereof they speak. Only a last-minute reprieve by the campus CEO stayed the advance of the opposing forces. Some reconnoitering by committees, and a pinch or two of rational calculation, caused cooler heads of both sides to realize that a national scandal was in the making.

It was one thing for Yale, a private university, to close its department of education in the 1950s. It would have been quite another matter if the country's leading public university campus had done so—and in the early 1980s no less. To have closed the Berkeley department (and school) would have been the wrong move at the wrong time, a public statement of academic irresponsibility likely to be judged infamous across the country. After all, beyond research and teaching there is "public service," especially to train those who will teach the young. A truce was called: the ed school would survive. But it had been a close call.

"Schools of Education: The Academic-Professional Seesaw," *Change* (January–February 1989): 60–62. Used by permission of *Change: The Magazine of Higher Learning* and Heldref Publications.

Bloodied but still intact, Clifford and Guthrie sat down for six months to write an account of what went wrong in Berkeley. An early report was prepared but then shelved, they tell us, partly in deference to the delicate position of an incoming dean, and in part because scholarly instincts prevailed. The authors turned to more encompassing inquiry: first, to compare the development of five schools of education in leading universities (Chicago, Berkeley, Harvard, Stanford, Columbia) and then, in a second surge, to add another six institutions (Ohio State, Michigan, Minnesota, Illinois, Wisconsin, UCLA) to give a comparative frame of eleven cases. Ten of these schools and departments had histories dating back to the nineteenth or early twentieth century. UCLA was added as a late developer that had moved rapidly into the front ranks and also as a major campus within the University of California system that seemed a success story.

One a historian and the other a policy analyst, Clifford and Guthrie offer a statement that combines enormous historical detail, a set of fascinating case studies of recent developments, and vigorous judgment on what went wrong and how things can be set right. In three long chapters they trace the historical development of education schools during the 1900–1940 period, with those decades defined as "the formative years." A second set of three chapters, equally detailed and more fully given over to comparative case studies, analyzes the problems and purposes of leading schools during the three decades of 1955–85, defined as "the years of maturity." A concluding chapter offers advice, bringing together their "brief" for professional education.

In the first three chapters devoted to the years leading up to 1940, now over a half-century behind us, there is more told than most readers will want to know. Moving around in the developmental record of ten institutions, and often beyond, Clifford and Guthrie provide a full-bodied account of the generic problems and genetic defects of this particular type of professional school when it is situated within the confines of leading universities.

Horace Mann and others in the mid-nineteenth century might argue for independent professional schools for teachers—"normal schools"— but by the end of the century, education, like other would-be professions, was moving into the universities, even if the great bulk of teacher training remained in the normal schools. From the beginning, in order to distinguish themselves from the normal schools, the university departments of pedagogy sought to emphasize the theoretical or philosophical aspects of teaching. And virtually from the beginning "the siren call" of graduate education—and scholarship and research—was heard and heeded, leading to the awarding of the PhD as well as the EdD. The claims of scholarship—of theory—were staked out so early on that Clifford and Guthrie note with acuity that the field outran its knowledge base, that it had to manufacture a literature: a not uncommon problem in American minor professions, and one that was to bedevil education.

A fundamental tension between the academic and the vocational, between theory and practice, was soon set into the character of these schools, one that deepened as the host universities engaged in their twentieth-century take-off. By the end of the 1940s, America's leading universities had developed into world-class institutions in the context of a competitive national system of higher education in which research production and scholarly output increasingly became *the* basis for personal, departmental, and institutional status.

Throwing their net of analysis across many institutions, Clifford and Guthrie are able to move beyond the excellent account of "the uncertain profession" given by Arthur Powell in his history of the Harvard Graduate School of Education. So, too, are they able to flesh out in great detail in one case study after another the composite picture offered by Harry Judge in his widely quoted Ford Foundation account from the early 1980s of the deep and troubling strains of leading American schools of education. There is much here to admire and to be grateful for.

Particularly fascinating (because of the Berkeley experience's substantial role in the overall story) is a key chapter in the second part that contrasts the recent experiences of the Berkeley and UCLA schools of education, an analysis that "provides the grounds for the recommendation in the concluding chapter." UCLA's school "prospered . . . achieving the kind of balanced appearance that others also sought" while "Berkeley's fell on hard times, for reasons we dissect in excruciating detail."

And what were the grounds for the differences? UCLA developed considerably around professional schools. The administration was relatively supportive. A major University Elementary School (UES) functioned as a lab setting and, along the way, picked up sufficient public support to see it through more than one effort to suppress it. Most of all intelligent and sustained leadership in the deanship and the UES gave positive visibility, able defense, continuity of effort, and recruitment efforts and opportunities (in the case of the department) that attracted a research-minded faculty appropriate to the rapidly rising standing of UCLA as a research university. That faculty, most of the time, managed not to shoot itself in the foot. The school went academic, institutionalizing a deep commitment to research and scholarship, but at the same time it was able to maintain a professional-practice base of operations in the lab school and in other activities to which it could repair when the pendulum swung too far toward the strictly academic. Virtuous circles were generated in which campus respect for the school was well above the threshold of viability, let alone of survival.

Meanwhile in Berkeley, the bad news was virtually unrelieved. If we think of things that could go wrong, we find they all happened in Berkeley. The campus had developed considerably around the letters and science disciplines—especially the sciences—giving great power to those on campus most likely to place education well down past the salt and to wonder out loud at frequent intervals whether it even belonged at the university table. The attitude of the campus administration, as Clifford and Guthrie ably document, varied for many years between benign neglect and punitive starvation. School leadership was critically lacking. Between 1975 and 1983, there were a total of nine "acting deans," "dean designates," and "deans." One appointed dean, a campus physics professor, resigned within a few months even before his term in office officially began, charging broken promises on the part of the administration. Tired cynics refer to this disastrous state of affairs as "revolving door leadership," even a "dean-a-week" system.

Internally, the school was also divided between a hierarchical and research-minded faculty and a body of supervisors of teacher education. To make things worse, a group of educational psychologists within the school clamored incessantly for separate nationhood or an escape down the hallway to the psychology department. And then, as if to give complete validity to campus perception that the school was hopeless, some faculty members in the school insisted on shooting themselves and the school in the foot, engaging at one time or another in such practices as giving "A" grades to undergraduates who otherwise were on academic probation and letting students grade themselves.

In the authors' tough judgment, their own school "was characterized by a singular absence of enlightened followership." There was an "enemy within," as well as an "enemy without." Had the faculty acted otherwise, they note, "it is quite possible that subsequent investigations and administrative actions would have been prevented or moderated."

Resources eroded. The school's "agency" was increasingly displaced to other campus units; by 1976 only about 12 percent of the campus's education research was being done by the school. Four external studies of the school mounted during the crisis period of 1976 to 1982, with the last two offering a preferred opinion, or clear recommendation, that the school be closed. One report noted that the school was caught in a series of vicious circles. And so it was. The generic tension between research and practice was played out here in the worst possible way.

Clifford and Guthrie would be less than human if their perceptions of the state of schools of education in leading research universities were not heavily conditioned by the battering of a worst-case scenario. Nobody promised them a rose garden, but what happened was ridiculous. In answer, as their subtitle emphasizes, their book is a brief for professional education. Their judgments, subtly interwoven throughout the book, are brought together in a strong concluding chapter entitled "Places of Action and Places of Analysis." Their advice is: more action, less analysis.

They see the leading schools of education as vulnerable institutions that have engaged in "dysfunctional coping strategies." These strategies—"interdisciplinary appeasement," "academic intensification," and "the route of social science legitimacy"—are seen by them as part of a confused effort to ape the letters and science department. The schools hire social scientists, emphasize research and the PhD, and make joint appointments with academic departments. This is the wrong way to go, they maintain.

The right way is to turn to the profession rather than to the academy, putting relationships to the schoolhouse ahead of relations to the rest of the university: "schools of education must take the profession of education, not academia, as their main point of reference." This means in practice, among other things, that the majority of the faculty should be *qualified and engaged* in the training of beginning professionals; that substantial professional criteria should be included in faculty appointment and promotion decisions; and that the PhD should be rejected as a graduate degree in education. To intensify relationships with other units of the university is *not* the way to go.

But there is no gainsaying the simple fact that these schools of education reside in research universities. The host is the university, not the school. Schools of education in the universities may be adrift, but their anchorage—for resources, moral support, and legitimacy—has to be first in the university harbor (Rhoades, 1989). These schools will have to go on answering to academic norms: it cannot be otherwise. They do not have, and will not have, the prestige and power of engineering or, now, business administration, let alone law or medicine, to push back the central academic norms. They cannot become enclaves, funded and independent. They will have to balance themselves as best they can on the academic-professional seesaw, attempting to steady the oscillations and climbing back on every time they are thrown off.

And there is no gainsaying a second simple fact: the great bulk of teacher education is handled by other institutions. For example, the nine campuses of the University of California train only 5 percent of California teachers, while the nineteen campuses of the California State University ("state college") system train over 75 percent, and the numerous private colleges and universities contribute 20 percent. The center of gravity for teacher education in the country lies, and will continue to lie, in the state colleges and other locales outside the research universities. It is deeply structured in the American system that the leading universities are, quantitatively, only minor players in this activity. Thus the university ed schools are neither equipped by their campuses nor positioned in the larger system to be major providers.

What these schools can do is what they are attempting to do: to engage in basic and applied research that hopefully will aid practice; to sustain small-scale lab schools and teacher education laboratories where applied research and professional development can take place; and to offer advice and leadership backed by the prestige of their campuses in local, state, and national initiatives.

Several years ago, as a twenty-year sequel to his classic article "The Science of 'Muddling-Through,'" Charles E. Lindblom wrote an essay entitled "Still Muddling, Not Yet Through" (1979). This is not a bad slogan for schools of education in America's universities. They will continue to have ambiguous and conflicting missions; they will continue to have, with only incremental improvement, a weak, diffused knowledge base; they will continue to relate to a mass, low-status occupation of schoolteachers who, in turn, have children as clients; they will continue to be pushed and pulled between university norms and professional practice; they will continue to find campus status problematic. There will be little agreement on essential research, on how to teach, and, especially, on how to teach people to teach.

But the evidence offered by Clifford and Guthrie, and by others, shows that some schools of education in the research universities have learned how to muddle along better than others. While the Berkeley school became for a while so debilitated that it could not hold two thoughts in mind at the same time, other schools more fortunate in their institutional cultures—and especially in their leadership and internal followership—learned how to operate with multiple identities, even if they were to swing decade by decade from one emphasis to another. These schools are not yet through. In the 1980s a number of them, including Berkeley, are having a better time of it. And even as they involve themselves more in professional practice, the successful schools extend and deepen their research base. There is no future in turning away from the values of the university. The right brief for ed school is scholarship *and* professional education.

References

Judge, Harry. *American Graduate Schools of Education: A View from Abroad.* New York: Ford Foundation, 1982.

Lindblom, Charles E. "Still Muddling, Not Yet Through." *Public Administration Review* (November–December 1979).

Powell, Arthur. *The Uncertain Profession: Harvard and the Search for Educational Authority.* Cambridge, Mass.: Harvard University Press, 1980.

Rhoades, Gary. "Change in an Unanchored Enterprise: Colleges of Education." *Review of Higher Education* (1989).

INTRODUCTION TO CHAPTER 23

The opportunity to write this essay in 1992 as part of a transatlantic dialogue between European and California experts came about because the Paris-based Organisation for Economic Co-operation and Development (OECD) was engaged in preparing a "country report" on higher education in the United States.

Not least because of its ample sunshine, California was selected as a proxy for a huge, diversified country. Even so, the three-person visiting team, ably chaired by A. H. "Chelly" Halsey, the British sociologist, only had, as I recall, three weeks to visit at the many campuses of the University of California, the California State University system, private universities, and community colleges up and down the state. An exhausting, impossible task, but the committee still managed to write up a report that initiated considerable discussion at later meetings held at OECD headquarters in Paris and back in California. The publication to which I contributed the following essay included a half-dozen pieces edited by Sheldon Rothblatt. Included were an "ex ante" view of the 1960 California Master Plan for Higher Education by Clark Kerr and a concluding "dialogue in California" by Halsey. All in all, a well-focused, thoughtful, small book.

My answer to the queries raised in Europe about how useful "the California model" was for reform in other countries was first to insist that California was not a nation; it had to be understood as a state operating competitively in the larger national context. In my essay I quote remarks made by David Gardner, then president of the entire University of California system, who was extremely frank in explaining how this set of research universities responded to the national competition. His comments alone make this transatlantic dialogue valuable, as it brings to light basic university maneuvering in an internally competitive setting that even U.S. observers generally do not know about.

Second, I called attention to the tripartite structure of organizations institutionalized in the 1960 Master Plan: three sets of sector dynamics ("inner logics," in the terminology of subsystems), each facing in a somewhat different direction, were set up. Thus, California becomes a possible model only when we take into account both the national competition and the dynamics of a three-part structure.

At the end of the essay I criticize the OECD habit of always searching for broad national policies and formal plans capable of steering a system. But how systems are planned and how they actually work are two quite different things. A plan or stated policy can be just some prosaic talk that has little or no effect. Reality resides in what constituent universities and colleges actually do. The OECD country reports are long on the first and short on the second.

CHAPTER 23

Is California the Model for OECD Futures?

THE QUESTION POSED as my topic is whether California can serve as the model for OECD futures, or more broadly, whether California's postsecondary arrangements are exportable. This query was apparently the underlying theme of the spring 1989 "confrontation meeting" in Paris between California higher education representatives and OECD examiners and delegates. The first requirement of a good answer to this question is a thorough understanding of the dynamics of the California system. And to fashion an explanation of how this system works, and why it works the way it does, we need to add to the OECD Examiner Report by pushing off in two directions.

Two Angles of Vision: Up and Down

We should first bring the nation back in and put California in its proper place as a state. We need to highlight telling features of the U.S. system of higher education as a whole that are understated and even overlooked entirely when we tear California out of its natural habitat and pretend it is a nation. Here we ascend the scale of organization to a more inclusive level of context and motivation. Second, I want to reverse direction and move within the California system to examine critical features of its three major sectors of public higher education. Since these sectors are powerful actors, we need to grasp their self-amplifying tendencies. Each sector

"Is California the Model for OECD Futures?" in *The OECD, the Master Plan, and the California Dream: A Berkeley Conversation,* edited by Sheldon Rothblatt, 61–77. Berkeley, Calif.: Center for Studies in Higher Education, University of California, 1992. Used by permission.

has dynamics that are not well explicated when we fix on environmental forces such as demographic trends and the formal intentions of state planners. We need to bring faculty and institutional administrators back into the picture, especially in a state system, and a national system, in which the springs of action are much more at the bottom than at the top. My two angles of vision—the one up, the other down—come together in an effort to explain how a thoroughly bottom-up system of higher education works.

Bringing the Nation Back In

We can capture much of the special nature of American higher education, seen in cross-national comparison, in five primary characteristics: large size; radical decentralization; extreme diversity; intense competition; and a high degree of institutional initiative.[1]

LARGE SIZE

The U.S. system is so large that it deserves to be called colossal. Over 3,400 institutions, just on the accredited lists, is a mind-boggling number. Despite the geographic space that is provided in a continental nation for institutions to get out of each other's way, this exceedingly large number spells high organizational density overall, and high density within such major subsectors as doctoral-granting universities (200), comprehensive universities and colleges (600), liberal arts colleges (600), community colleges (now 1,400) and detached specialized institutions (600). Great size is also indexed by 13 million students and 800,000 faculty. The U.S. student body is considerably larger than the entire population of such small European countries as Sweden, Norway, Finland, and Austria. The American system has virtually as many faculty as the British system has students. In sheer size, the U.S. system, on various measures, is 10 times, 20 times, 50 times larger than national systems, large and small, found on the European Continent. We must not overlook the effects of such huge size; it interacts with the other primary characteristics to produce a special kind of system.

RADICAL DECENTRALIZATION OF CONTROL

Among all advanced industrial nations, the American system exhibits extreme decentralization of control. Some 1,800 private institutions proceed largely on their own in finding niches in the ecology of the system. One by one they find the money to support themselves, assemble their own staff, and build their own student body. Only a few other systems, notably in Japan and Brazil, have tasted privateness on any scale that approaches that of the United States. And in the U.S. picture, privateness has great historical depth, a richly embellished tradition, and much prestige in the form of leading institutions, among both the universities and the four-year colleges.

When we turn to public higher education, we find fifty systems, a bottom-heavy federalism in which state support and state authority dominate that of the national government. It is this breakup of public control that in the first instance makes sense of an OECD effort to study California alone. The private and public dispersion together constitute a unique national structure of control, one that in cross-national comparisons is positioned at the far end of a tight-to-loose continuum of control.

EXTREME INSTITUTIONAL DIVERSITY

The Carnegie classification reported in the OECD review, the best that we have, contains ten major categories of institutions that become twenty when the public-private distinction is run through each of them. And still the classification does not distinguish such important groupings as women's colleges, black colleges, and Roman Catholic colleges. A classification with a finer mesh soon runs to thirty or forty categories, many of which still exhibit much internal variation, e.g., lumping together as top research universities institutions that have 35 million federal research dollars with ones that have six and eight times that amount. If we try to make use of thirty or more categories we get lost among the trees and cannot see the forest. But when we work with fewer categories in order to see the forest—when, e.g., we speak of three public sectors and a private sector in California—we radically understate the vast differences among individual institutions and groups thereof that have developed in a largely unplanned fashion.

Decentralized public and private control set in motion a long time ago a restless proliferation of institutions. Back in the first half of the nineteenth century, long before the age of the college gave way to the age of the university, institutions were created under local initiative in numbers and at a rate unheard of in other countries. At a time when England had two places, Oxford and Cambridge, the United States developed hundreds of separate colleges. But as academic scientists in the late nineteenth century pointed out, what the United States had, by the standards of Europe, was a swarm of mosquitoes rather than a few soaring eagles. The eagles began to soar in the last three decades of the century, and in considerable number. Such leading private colleges as Harvard, Yale, and Princeton transformed themselves into full-bodied universities; such new private institutions as Johns Hopkins (1876), Clark University (1889), Stanford University (1891), and the University of Chicago (1892) were composed as universities; and each state soon sought to have at least one institution that could claim substantial university character. By 1900, decentralized control had led to a large number and wide range of universities. When the exclusive club—a voluntary association—known as the American Association of Universities (AAU) was formed in 1900, it had fourteen charter members (eleven private and three public), and many other campuses lined up at the door seeking admission. In 1990, the AAU has fifty-six members—and there is even a longer line at the door! At the same time, in a setting where institutional initiative was unbounded and stimulated, non-university institutions, public and private, continued to proliferate, giving the United States a census of institutions that already approached a thousand at the turn of the century.

The decentralization of control and the institutional diversity that were well in place by the turn of the century have ensured a twentieth-century system characterized by sharp competition for faculty, students, and institutional status. Compared to that found in other nations, the U.S. system is an open one in which competitive disorder and a market-like status hierarchy heavily condition the ways that institutions define themselves, seek resources, and arrange the conditions for research, teaching, and learning. Foreign observers, unaccustomed to the competitive mode, often see these ways as decidedly unacademic, even brutish. Notably, the habit of competition extended to the development of big-time sports, a benefit and an affliction that universities in other countries have managed to do without. Using a full measure of counterfactual thinking—what if the Ivy League had not given birth to the sports monster in the last decades of the nineteenth century?—it is now safe to say that if the Ivies had not done so someone else would have. Competitive big-time sports comes with the territory. Indeed, as is well known, athletic prowess often comes first, with an institution then straining for several decades to build a faculty that the football team can be proud of.

HIGH INSTITUTIONAL INITIATIVE

A system that is at once decentralized, diversified, and competitive encourages initiative, an entrepreneurial spirit, in individual universities and colleges. To stand still is to fall behind, since others will be moving ahead by amassing financial resources, fashioning attractive packages for recruiting and retaining faculty, increasing the stipends for graduate students, trying to improve the quality of undergraduate life, and painting an evermore glorious public image. Within this localization of initiative, trustees, administrators, faculty, students, alumni, and assorted well-wishers can join hands. The leading private universities are especially well-situated for this exercise of competitive initiative. But public universities increasingly have done well in the twentieth century in the game of status. They have learned how to compose comparison groups of private and public universities, and otherwise exercise comparison, that help them to increase salaries, lower teaching loads, support sabbatical leaves, increase the ratio of graduate to undergraduate students, and, in general, to remind the officials of their own state that decline is just around the corner unless they increase allocations and allow for university autonomy.

The competitive university, public or private, is thus an active autonomy seeker. Universities everywhere push for autonomy from the controls of state, church, and other patrons. But the search for autonomy is measurably strengthened when responsibility is localized. Sophisticated trustees mark their time in office as successful or not according to how much their efforts contribute to a comparative strengthening of their institution. Campus presidents, chancellors, and a whole range of local administrators have careers on the line that depend on how well they do while in local office. Professors build effective research domains in "their" institutions according to their initiatives in competitively raising support from research-funding sources. Hence, responsibility and initiative interact in the construction of institutional capability to resist the control of patrons. Decentralized systems tend to remain decentralized because the structure of incentives encourages key institutional actors to initiate autonomous actions.

The drive for autonomous institution-building has had a striking budgetary outcome: sources of financial support have multiplied. The best guarantee of institutional autonomy in modern universities is to have not one major source of financing, as in the case of the national treasury in unified systems, but many sources. This strategic lesson has not been lost on either private or public universities. Both types steadily extend and diversify their portfolio of revenue sources. The private universities diversify their lines of support from private supports and users; they eagerly tap the many federal pipelines of research funding and student support. The state universities have shown a remarkable capacity in recent years to raise very large sums of money from private sources in major development drives, leaving in place, as at UCLA, a capability to go on raising, e.g., one hundred million dollars each year in the form of additional endowment or gifts for immediate use. As funding diversifies, the power of any one patron to call the shots across the full range of institutional actions is reduced and institutional flexibility is increased. Versatility is added to variation.

The competitive university is also uncommonly subject to self-elaboration. American universities received a strong push toward elaborate structuring in their formative years in the late nineteenth century when, out of competitive interaction, a distinct graduate level of courses and credits in the basic disciplines was laid down over the older undergraduate college, providing a "vertical university" hybrid that has turned out to be highly useful throughout the twentieth century. A professional school structure also developed within the universities that has increasingly become lodged at the post-bachelor's level, separating intense professional preparation from the undergraduate years and thereby divorcing it structurally from the general education and liberal education practices that remain deeply rooted in the expectations of "the college years." The tripartite arrangement of undergraduate college, graduate school, and professional school has kept disparate functions somewhat out of each other's way.

While highlighting the central role played by competition and initiative, I have spoken mainly of research universities. But I do not mean to suggest that competition and initiative are characteristic of only our two hundred doctoral-granting institutions, out of the total institutional population of about 3,500. Far from it. The hundreds of private four-year colleges are in a very competitive situation in which finance, student body, and faculty are largely determined by local institutional effort. The huge sector of comprehensive universities and colleges—formally non-doctoral-granting, but heavily invested in graduate and professional education—is no stranger to the competitive mode of interaction, as colleagues from the California state university system can testify. In my second section I want to make a special point about the competitive dynamics of the CSU system. And the community colleges, about which more later, are part of a general free-for-all for undergraduate student clientele.

In short, competition is the central process of the American system of higher education. We cannot go far in understanding higher education in California unless we first seize upon this process and attempt to grasp its complicated interplays. It is central to the great international success of Californian and American higher education in the last half of the twentieth century, to the making of universities as intellectual magnets that attract talent from around the world, thereby allowing the system as a whole to take up the role of the international center of learning that Germany held in the nineteenth and early twentieth centuries. The competitive process is also central to our systemic weaknesses, from our great variability in standards to our sins of pride in the presentation of institutional images.

The central role played by competition is not easy for American or foreign observers to grasp: it cannot be seen in the same ready way as state master plans. It does not appear quantitatively in charts and graphs, as in the case of demographic trends and state finance. It is not often referred to in *The Chronicle of Higher Education*, while every other week there is another account of lawmaking in national and state capitals and another account of what William Bennett has said.[2] But competition is never far from the minds of faculty and institutional administrators, and even of system-level administrators. Thus it was at the OECD confrontation meeting in Paris last spring that President David Gardner of the University of California kept bringing up the force of competition, especially when the discussion turned to research policy and to the relationship of postsecondary education to the economy. A typical OECD question was posed at one point to the Californians: "Is the absence of a well-defined State research policy seen as a major obstacle in maintaining the competitive position of California in the country as a whole and in the world?" Gardner replied:

> We receive [at the University of California] $200 million a year from the state of California for research. . . . We use that money to provide the basic infrastructure, i.e., provision for those personnel and facilities that enable us, as a university, successfully to compete at the national level for basic research funding from the agencies of the federal government that provide $800 million to the University of California through a peer research review process. . . . There is not in that process [of state support] any clear formulation of research policy as such, but there is a policy to equip the University of California with the capacity to compete for research. The state's policy is to make us a competitor for the federal dollar for research.[3]

Note how the state and a constituent university system join hands to compete with other states and other state systems, and with private institutions; note that the state puts up one dollar to help the university get four more dollars from the "feds" (a game that is systemic in American federalism); and note that the state, the main provider of support, is not in the business of defining research areas and targets, but rather attempts to aid the university in building the basic infrastructure, the enhanced capacity, to compete effectively in the national system.

President Gardner noted further that when the national government pulled back significantly in recent years in its funding of research facilities and equipment, the state of California, again compared to most states in the country, funded equipment and space generously, putting "California at an advantage compared with those states that are not funding the infrastructure."[4] Note how the university can seek to move between two primary funding sources, always with an eye on competition with other institutions and systems. And it can strike a convincing posture that what is good for the university is good for the state of California. We may also note in passing that even just using the more explicit categories, federal funds for research amount to only about 60 percent of the university's research expenditures. Beyond the 40 percent provided by nonfederal sources lies the simple but imposing fact that faculty time for research is the most important subsidy of all in the support of research, and it is largely built into the state allocations for faculty salaries.

So it went at the meeting in Paris. Gardner also took some pains to point out in reply to another question that the university seeks to ratchet up its salary schedule by using a comparison group of "eight other distinguished American universities," public and private. He stressed that competition with private universities is a primary problem—and well he might, given the pace-setting role of Stanford, MIT, Princeton, Harvard, Caltech, Chicago, and so on.[5] At still another point the California delegation pointed to the increasingly "serious competition from other states which have begun to argue successfully that California already has too large a share of the nation's research and development resources," this in regard to such failures in national competitions as the Supercollider and the National Earthquake Center, major federally funded facilities that somehow ended up in other states.[6] The game is a rough high-stakes game; it is evermore an intensely competitive game. Notably, it is not grasped by focusing on the internal features of the state Master Plan. Indeed, when the Paris meeting turned to "Planning and Links" in its fourth and final session, there were the Californians, state commission and all, still insisting that "the underlying concern [is] to keep California fully competitive with the other 49 states."[7]

If the national picture insists that we put institutional and state competition first in our analysis of American higher education, it also brings in the role of the national government, a large topic that I will put aside as both obvious and deserving of much more space than available here. Suffice it to say that most of the resources that come out of Washington do so in a competitive mode. Funds for students go to students to use where they please, hence they enhance choice in the consumer market of higher education. Funds for research still largely issue from the competitive process of peer review, although the congressional-earmarking political procedure that bypasses peer review has recently become a significant phenomenon.

Instead of pursuing the role of national government, which becomes virtually the most important topic in understanding steerage and coordination in centralized systems, it is more helpful to point to the coordination that takes place in the American system as a whole in nongovernmental channels. One means of coordination is found in voluntary association. A second pathway is market-like interaction.

Tocqueville was right: Americans are prone to form voluntary associations. As soon as three people find they have something in common they set up an association to further the cause. And nowhere more than in higher education, where every disciplinary specialty demands and develops an association (or a major division of one); where every distinguishable set of institutions insists upon a representative association; where a complex of buildings in Washington centered around One Dupont Circle is chock-full of associations of presidents, graduate deans, business officers, registrars, and other administrative specialists who staff the campus bureaucracies. The decentralization of the American system virtually demands voluntary linkages as a countervailing force, as a way of linking individuals across institutions along functional lines. Given their central values and their taste for autonomy, academics also much prefer to be "association persons" than to be "organization men." Association is their answer to bureaucracy. For institutions and their administrators, it is an answer to the pitfalls of unbridled competition.

Thus, the American system may have no national ministry and no national form system of control; in comparative perspective, it is only loosely structured by normal bureaucratic and political tools of state authority. But voluntary association offers a substitute system, one that is bewildering and hard to capture. This form of linkage is both visible and invisible, simultaneously formal, semiformal, and informal. No peak association, or single set of ties, commands all the rest. Lines of affiliation loop through and around one another, with no regard for unifying principles of order, logic, and accountability. The gaps and the redundancies are too numerous to count. But voluntary coordination goes with the flow of academic life and institutional self-development. As reasons to associate develop, linkages are formed. When the reasons pass, the related associational linkages die on the vine. More than in other countries, the voluntary ties make for a changeable, even a disposable, structure of national coordination, thereby promoting system flexibility. Voluntary associating is a good way to have structure follow changes in knowledge, and follow changes in institutional capability, rather than have knowledge and capability heavily constrained by national bureaucratic order. Association follows particularly well the many contours of academe. Turned loose by decentralization, and stimulated by the dark side of competition, it is, in the American setting, a primary component of the logic of the higher education system.

The other major pathway of national coordination that remains hidden in the American system, but that is so central to its functioning, is the order that emerges out of market-type interaction. The U.S. system has an extremely complicated consumer market within which institutions find students and students find institutions. State master plans seek to guide significant chunks of this market, as in the admissions standard set for the University of California (UC) and California State University (CSU) campuses. But student choice remains very high, with private and out-of-state alternatives and multiple in-state choices for those with decent achievement records. The private institutions, in turn, one by one, seek to build secure niches in this otherwise wild-and-woolly market.

The national system also has an extremely large and active labor market in which institutions recruit faculty and new recruits find jobs, and in which job mobility is high compared to other countries. This market is a crucial one for institutions, since faculty are the essential personnel and the basis for institutional aggrandizement. It is a finely honed market, one tailored by the detailed specifications of departments in search of faculty and by the specialisms that newly trained academics bring with them to the job search.

Finally, there is the overall institutional market in which the bottom line is not profit but prestige. Reputation is here the main commodity of exchange; relative prestige not only guides the choices of consumers and workers but also a vast array of institutional attitudes and actions. High-prestige institutions markedly affect the behavior of other institutions, generating the tides of academic drift wherein institutions imitate and converge. In the general institutional market we observe the interplay between public and private sectors, with the one over time seizing upon the weaknesses of the other, including the gaps that go unfilled. The private universities and colleges significantly shape the public sectors in this country. In some cases they provide "the more," in other cases, "the better," and in still other cases, "the different." While there has been much "state creep" in the past quarter-century, with state and national governments exercising more supervision, there has been also much "market creep" as institutions wiggle their way to more autonomy and alter their character. The individual campuses of the University of California have more self-determination now than they did a quarter-century, a half-century, ago. A good prediction is that the campuses of the CSU system will move toward more self-determination in the 1990s. Under the steady pounding of size and complexity, the center of large formal systems cannot hold. As operative authority (in contrast to ultimate authority) slips off to operating organizations, market-like interaction is strengthened, in the form of interaction among enterprises that are at least semiautonomous in competing for personnel, clientele, financial resources, and prestige.

When an activity comes under state control, there is a bias for aggregation. Things are to be added up. OECD reviews themselves are exercises in adding things up. OECD delegates at the Paris review of the California report asked time and again, how do you plan this, and how do you plan that, how do you integrate everything into a meaningful whole, how do you make things up? But when an activity such as higher education is in a market-like context, it comes under a bias for disaggregation. Things are not added up in one heap, in one place. They are to be left in their piecemeal state. "System" is then an altogether different matter.

The Dynamics of Sectors

Now that we have brought the nation back in, particularly to highlight competition and institutional initiative in an American-type system, we can turn back to California universities and colleges and understand better the constraints and the facilitations under which they operate, the incentives that prod them, the logics that become embedded in their character. Lord Ashby has noted that any higher education system has "its own articles of faith by which its practitioners live," producing an "inner logic." That inner logic "does for higher education systems what genes do for biological systems: it preserves identity; it is a built-in gyroscope."[8] Applying this perspective to the different sectors of California public higher education we can ask: what are the inner logics, the built-in gyroscopes, of the UC system, the CSU system, and the community college system?

The University of California, in all its vastness, is the easiest to grasp.

It is a foremost case of the American research university about which much of my previous comment has centered. From within, the university is strongly steered by the research imperative. The domination of this imperative is reflected in the criteria by which faculty are hired and promoted, in the strength of graduate programs in the basic disciplines, in the importance given to PhD production over bachelor's degree production in the minds of the faculty, and in the related flow of attention from the undergraduate level to the labs, the seminars, and the students of the graduate level. On this later point, David Gardner, at the Paris meeting, was frank in the extreme. Acknowledging the weaknesses that are systemic in the university in its balance of undergraduate teaching and graduate level research and teaching he said:

> We don't know any other way of doing it. The state of California would not pay for a research university if we only offered instruction to graduate students. Indeed they would not pay, in my opinion, for a university that only offered the last two years in undergraduate instruction. The only way we manage is to admit students at the freshman level in large numbers and redirect the money that is appropriated for them to the graduate programme. . . . The quality of the faculty that we can attract to the University of California arises from the quality of the graduate programme, not from the quality of our freshman students, and the presence in the University of California of a very distinguished faculty, whether they teach freshmen or not, sets the intellectual tone for the university and permeates and infuses every aspect of its work.[9]

The inner logic is clear: the University of California is first of all committed to research. Second, I might add, it is committed to professional education, most of which takes place at the graduate level. Third, it is committed to the general education of undergraduates.

When we turn to the CSU system, the story becomes more clouded. The OECD report on California paid relatively little attention to this mammoth system of universities; American observers generally do the same thing. The research university is seen as interesting because of its research prowess and its dominating prestige; the community colleges readily capture attention because of their open access and their apparently central role in issues of equity. But what of this in-between sector of "state colleges" turned into non-doctoral-granting universities? What can we make of them? What is their inner logic, if indeed one exists? We should make a very great deal of them, for they matter greatly. After all, among other things, they train 75 percent of the schoolteachers of the state, while the University of California trains 5 percent.

What is very clear about this sector of institutions across the nation is the long evolution of many of its members from humble "normal school," to somewhat stronger "teachers' college," to a more diversified "state college," to a much weightier, comprehensive university structure with extensive work at the master's level and finally to full-throated university standing as a place of research and PhD output. Nationally, this sector is the strongest instance of academic drift, and so it is in California. There is steady, unrelenting pressure at the campus level to evolve into full university stature. The sources of this strong tendency are many. As we search across the nineteen (now twenty) campuses of the CSU system, across disciplines within them, and across successive cohorts of new faculty, we find that institutional leadership plays a part, that geographic location has influence, that size and the historical buildup of organizational resources must be weighed in the scales. Most of all, we see that the desire to do research and the capacity to do research grows in successive generations of faculty. The faculty have PhDs, they are well-trained, they come from the research universities. They have the desire and they have the skill, and, Master Plan or not, the campuses, at different rates and to different degrees develop a research capability.[10]

Once again in the 1987 Master Plan review CSU was denied the privilege of giving the doctorate. But there is nothing in state master planning, U.S. style, that can keep campuses from raising research funds. Thus it is that the CSU campus in San Diego, at the cutting edge of this evolution, now receives more than $50 million a year of federal research funds, surpassing at least two of the University of California campuses and thereby adding considerably to the overlap of the CSU and UC systems. Other CSU campuses are following the lead, in a game they all can play. And why not? If the competence is there, why not invest in it? If the state wants more science and technology out of its system of higher education, it can increasingly find it in the CSU system, with perhaps greater attentiveness there to applied research, near-market technology transfer, and the local and regional needs of industry.

CSU will remain heavily invested in undergraduate work. But its inner logic is that it will also continually stretch up from its base in bachelor's and master's programs to the research capability of existing research universities. The stretch will be quite different on different campuses and in different disciplines. It will accelerate in some periods, slow down in others. But the easiest prediction of all is that in the year 2000, CSU will be more invested in research and research-related graduate training than it is now. More awarding of the doctorate will come to this system, even as now found in joint-doctorate arrangements with the University of California and private universities.

Can we even speak of an inner logic in the community college system? California community colleges, in some number, go back as far as the 1920s. Born out of the secondary system, they have been comprehensive rather than specialized, open access rather than selective. Over time they have become increasingly comprehensive in program and clientele.[11] Their extensive work in adult and continuing education, in remedial education (where they do the unfinished work of our weak K–12 system), in short-term occupational training, as well as in the programs that parallel the first two years of traditional colleges, stretches their character to the point where the problem of organizational identity is critical. California community colleges have become much more than colleges. They are also community centers in which the easy in-and-out traffic can make observers think of participants in a shopping mall. A sentiment even grew among some community college leaders during the 1970s to not worry about the college label and to accept fully a community-center identity.

This drift turned out to be a loser's game: the state prefers to pay for colleges and not for community centers. The 1980s have seen an effort to call the community colleges back to an academic core centered on two-year programs for matriculated students and to better articulation of coursework with CSU and UC campuses for transfer students. But diffuse character is now systemic; transfer students are a minority of participants; and with state funding based on enrollment, the colleges are very enrollment-driven and clientele-sensitive. Thus, the community colleges march to a different drummer. They do not do research; disciplinary peers are not the audience of first resort for faculty; and competition is not based on scholarly reputation. Instead, their open door and their program comprehensiveness render them dependent on local clientele demand. Their central ongoing problem of identity is how to construct and maintain an inner logic that sets boundaries and convinces outsiders that they are indeed colleges.

California as the Model for OECD Futures

Now that we have higher education in California back in its proper place as part of the national system of higher education, and now that we have out on the table some of the basic dynamics of California's three massive sectors of public postsecondary education, we can return to the original question: "Is California the model for OECD Futures?" The answer is clearly "no." Even the relevance of California as a mirror for reflection, as a setting from which we can draw some lessons, depends on a tough-minded willingness to look at the pros and cons of the American system overall. Let us recapitulate in order of importance.

To take any lesson from California-cum-America means to recognize first the primacy of competition and the institutional initiative that it promotes. Any system abroad that is not prepared to undergo the risks of competition cannot learn much from California. To go the route of enhanced competition and institutional self-aggrandizement means that much steerage must move from state authority to the uncontrolled outcomes of interactions in a higher education consumer market, even more in an academic labor market, and most of all in the interplay of institutions in a reputational market.

Second in primacy is coordination by means of voluntary (nonstate) linkages. To give a simple example: we find hundreds of institutions using the same day of the year to mail out offers of acceptance to students and the same date by which students must respond, without either state or national government entering the picture. We find numerous agreed-upon ways of behaving in which state authority does not enter. The various markets are not left completely unguided to leave everyone in an Hobbesian state. Much guidance is worked out along functional lines by administrators and faculty with the system. A so-called market system of higher education promotes professional authority over bureaucratic authority; it generates linkages across the national system that are devised by faculty and administrators at lower levels as they go about their business. There is much devised coordination. It is simply more hidden than in the state-command system. It is also more flexible.

Only thirdly do we come to the determination of California higher education by state planning. The California Master Plan only sets a few broad parameters. The bite of that plan lies largely in the definition of boundaries between the CSU and UC systems in undergraduate admissions, research investment, the awarding of the PhD, and the possession of several expensive professional fields. The Master Plan is reviewed about once a decade. Meanwhile the institutions make their own way, individually building as best they can and thereby, in the aggregate, causing long-term evolutions that the state can only partially guide. As I have indicated, the state is not fully in control of the evolution of the CSU system, of its growing inner logic of research orientation. Within the UC system the individual campuses are clearly universities in themselves. As they diversify their financial bases, they are "state assisted": they are also federal government assisted, private donation assisted, student fee assisted, and hospital income assisted. The budget of the University of California, Los Angeles, is about one-third from the state of California. Its federal research funds in 1988 totaled over $200 million a year, placing UCLA, by itself, fifth in the nation. In addition UC San Francisco is seventh, UC San Diego, eighth, and UC Berkeley (which, unlike the other three, does not have a medical school), sixteenth. In 1990, California has twenty-nine public universities, nine in the UC system, twenty in the CSU system. They vary greatly in character, and nearly all are entrepreneurial to a degree that would be uncommon in other countries. A good share are determined to develop their own character, and they are positioned to go a long way in doing so. State guidance is a force to be understood only after we understand competition, institutional initiative, and voluntary coordination in the national system as a whole.

If there is one specific lesson that comes out of the California-cum-U.S. model it is one that other countries generally learn the hard way. This is the lesson of multiple patronage. The first injunction becomes: do not allow higher education institutions to come under the sway of a single patron, which in our day and age is nearly always the national government, specifically in the form of an education ministry. At the end of the twentieth century, a diversified funding base is a necessary condition for dependable, sustained institutional autonomy. It is also a necessary condition for rapid adaptability on the part of universities and colleges in fast-changing environments. Diversify, diversify, we might say, do not let any source of money escape your eye, for only then can you reduce dependency on a patron capable of excessive, even punitive, control. The capacity of national governments to turn hostile in their relation with higher education is better documented with each passing decade. The Australian and British systems in the 1980s are only the latest dramatic examples.

So let us take from the California scene what the California institutions of higher education most exemplify. In his 1972 book on American higher education, done for Clark Kerr's Carnegie Commission, Joseph Ben-David had a chapter entitled, "How the System Works: Enterprise, Competition, and Cooperation." He began the chapter by saying: "The most important condition of the system has been that, composed of independent units, the institutions have had to compete with each other for community support, students, and faculty." He added "This also applies to state universities."[12] Exactly. To understand the U.S. model, or the model provided by any one of the fifty states, one must look first for enterprise, competition, and cooperation, the latter considerably of a voluntary nature. If there is a California model, it is an enterprise model, a model of nongovernmental coordination, a model of loose confederation of diverse institutions, public and private and, above all, a competitive model. As Clark Kerr pointed out in his explanation at the Paris conference of how the California Master Plan was devised in 1960, this type of system depends on agreements among internal groups that are more like treaties than plans.

Policy versus Reality

Finally, "the California model" reveals a distorting bias in the nature of the country reports on higher education that OECD periodically commission. OECD sends out Examiners to look for policies and for planned arrangements. The report at hand is entitled, *Higher Education in California*. It discusses early on why California was chosen as the focus for "another of the OECD's reviews of national policy." But for any country, OECD ought to be most interested in how higher education actually works. *How a national system of higher education is planned and how it works are two quite different things.* Modern vibrant systems of higher education are notoriously bottom-heavy; they are steered more from below than from on high, more by the thrust of the disciplines and by the yearnings of institutions than by the directives of central bodies. If policy and planning are made the center of attention, primary dynamics of the system will be missed or only weakly captured—anywhere, and most so in the American system.

The California case teaches that OECD could serve better the practical understanding of the processes of systems of higher education—their springs of action—if its studies were directed more to how each system works. Policy and planning could then be understood in their limited roles. They could be more realistically grounded in the ongoing realities and capabilities of these quite uncommon systems of effort and achievement.

Notes

1. For extended analysis of these five features, see Burton R. Clark, *The Higher Education System: Academic Organization in Cross-National Perspective* (Berkeley and Los Angeles: University of California Press, 1983), and *The Academic Life: Small Worlds, Different Worlds* (Princeton: The Carnegie Foundation for the Advancement of Teaching, 1987), especially chap. 3, "The Open System," 45–66.

2. Former director of the National Endowment for the Humanities and subsequently secretary of education.

3. OECD, *Higher Education in California* (Review of National Policies for Education) (Paris: OECD, 1990), 102. Hereafter *Review.*

4. Ibid.

5. Ibid., 103.

6. Ibid., 106.

7. Ibid., 117.

8. Lord Ashby, *The Structure of Higher Education: A World View,* International Council for Educational Development, occasional paper no. 6, 1973.

9. *Review,* 104–5.

10. Françoise Alice Queval, "The Evolution Toward Research Orientation and Capability in Comprehensive Universities: A Case Study of the California

State University System" (unpublished doctoral dissertation, University of California at Los Angeles, 1990).

11. Arthur M. Cohen and Florence B. Brawer, *The American Community College*, 2nd ed. (San Francisco: Jossey-Bass, 1989), *passim.*

12. Joseph Ben-David, *American Higher Education: Directions Old and New* (New York: McGraw-Hill, 1972), 25.

INTRODUCTION TO CHAPTER 24

This essay was challenging to write and ended up being somewhat murky to read. It is perhaps an example of how an effort to theorize produces turgid prose. I wanted to highlight the sources and consequences of ever-increasing complexity in the tasks and operations of modern higher education. I tried first to describe sources of complexity: higher education is expected to do more for other sectors of society; we press it to develop new knowledge and conserve an expanding cultural heritage; we move from elite to mass to universal access for students; graduates need preparation for an expanded job market; academic subjects, one by one, imperialistically expand their scope—witness history and economics!

Next, I turned to describing how coping with complexity occurs through structural differentiation and fragmented professionalism. And, last, I addressed the question of "what integrates"? Here I move to such ideas as interlocking cultural communities and spontaneous orders discussed in an earlier essay drawn from *The Academic Life*.

Conceivably, there is a very concrete way to look at how complexity is finally handled. It lands daily on the desks of provosts as departments, one by one, press warranted claims for greater resources. Complexity is then steered by decisions to fund more here, continue sunk costs over there, and cut allocations—abruptly or gradually—to some unlucky third parties. What finally forces solutions *on the ground in particular universities*, is the lack of money to fund everything. Theoretical possibilities give way to the brute realities of local choices; practice exerts its primacy. At the institutional level it steers and limits.

At least this is one cogent, rational way to escape turgid theorizing about the problem of complexity. Follow the money!

CHAPTER 24

The Problem of Complexity in Modern Higher Education

THE BASE SIMILARITY of modern systems of higher education is that they become more complex. To cope with the unrelenting pressures of complexity, national systems adjust their historic configuration of beliefs, interests, and structures. Hence, to pursue the very nature of this fundamental academic trend, to suggest its more important causes, and especially to seek its compelling effects, is to explore basic modes of evolution. Among the modes of adaptation, we undoubtedly will find some impressive cross-national similarities. But close analysis will surely also reveal large differences that follow from unique national traditions. Guided by the response sets of established orders, nations must necessarily cope with complexity in somewhat different ways. Any theory of convergence that highlights a common drift into complexity, and similar forms of accommodation, will need in time to shade into a theory of divergence that observes individualized national evolutions. In this early analysis, particularly to establish some opening categories, I will concentrate on what seems everywhere operative.

The Forces of Complexity

With each passing decade a modern or modernizing system of higher education is expected and inspired to do more for other portions of society, organized and unorganized, from strengthening the economy and invigo-

"The Problem of Complexity in Modern Higher Education," in *The European and American University since 1800: Historical and Sociological Essays,* edited by Sheldon Rothblatt and Bjørn Wittröck, 263–79. Cambridge: Cambridge University Press, 1993. © Cambridge University Press. Reprinted with the permission of Cambridge University Press.

rating government to developing individual talents and personalities and aiding the pursuit of happiness. We also ask that this sector of society do more in its own behalf in fulfilling such grand and expanding missions as conserving the cultural heritage and producing knowledge. This steady accretion of realistic expectations cannot be stopped, let alone reversed.

Where among modern nations can we expect a return to the education of a relatively homogeneous 3 to 5 percent of the age group? Instead, systems slide over the long run along the track of elite to mass participation (even if some do not slide very well and stall at minor inclines), relating to more heterogeneous clienteles as they include more students drawn from more segments of the populations. Input demands multiply, extending the tasks of teaching and increasing the congruences that must be fashioned if individual desires and institutional capabilities are to mesh.

Second, where among modern systems can we expect a return to educating for only governmental elites and several leading professions, the dominant pattern historically in Europe? Instead, as graduates move on to both private and public employment and to a widening range of occupations generally, systems steadily extend their connections to occupational life. On its output side, higher education without doubt is tied to an expanding societal division of labor. Again, the pressure to enlarge the system's bundle of tasks is great, even irresistible.

Third, where among modern systems of higher education can we expect the resident profession to turn away from a widening involvement in the production of knowledge as well as in its refinement and distribution? As a force for enlarging the complexity of higher education, this substantive impulse, embedded in modernity, becomes the steadiest pressure of all. It is driven by the pace set in the international communities of many disciplines, with the biological sciences now the most vivid instance. It is propelled by the disciplinary rewards of specialization that lead to a Virginia Woolf Society and a Conference Group on Italian Politics. It is promoted by the interests of national governments in the fruits of basic science, and by regional and local economic interests in such useful R&D as the improvement of fisheries in Alaska, oil plant management in southern Norway, and computer services in the cities of northern Italy. The fascinations of specialized research, pure and applied, steadily deepen. Even where a major research sector has evolved separate from universities, as in France and in the Soviet model, university professors seize opportunities to engage in knowledge production and revision within their own shops as well as across the street in the laboratories and offices of the academy. There is no way to keep them away: indeed, they are generally the ruling research oligarchs.

With disciplinary linkages operating across institutional and national boundaries, subjects are in the driver's seat. There is quite literally no way to stop the field of history from expanding its boundaries of coverage in time and space and from proliferating its arcane specialties—nor political science nor economics nor sociology nor anthropology. The basic disciplines are inherently imperialistic.[1] Then, too, new specialties, interdisciplinary as well as disciplinary, are steadily added. By a process of parturition, they have been and are born out of mother fields: broad approaches to science gave way to such specific scientific disciplines as chemistry, geology, biology, and physics in the early and mid-nineteenth century; all-encompassing social subjects gave rise to economics, political science, sociology, and anthropology in the latter part of the century. By processes of importation and dignification, outside endeavors are brought in and lowly fields, new and old, are raised to respectability: modern languages and technology in the past; management and computer science during the recent decades. Such interdisciplinary fields as environmental studies, peace studies, women's studies, and ethnic studies now struggle with varying success to plant a foot squarely in the door of legitimation.

As research both intensifies and diversifies, the academic division of labor accelerates even faster than the rapidly shifting societal division of labor.

Thus, in whatever direction we turn, we confront complexity. If we take research, teaching, and public services as broadly stated missions of higher education, each becomes over time an elaborate, steadily differentiating set of expectations and tasks. If we pick up on the three categories of general higher education, advanced professional education, and research and training for research that were creatively established in a cross-national perspective by Joseph Ben-David, the outcome is the same.[2] Each is a confused maze. General education can never be whole again, despite periodic efforts to declare its rebirth around this or that person's list of core values and essential subjects. Professional education shades off in endless permutations: from early-childhood learning specialists to international economic planners just within the single field

The Problem of Complexity in Modern Higher Education   387

of education; from airport mechanics to secretaries to cosmetologists in short-cycle vocational higher education. As academia trains for both high and low vocationalism, the culture of one outside occupation after another, in an endless stream, intrudes into the higher education systems itself. A relevant staff takes up residence within it, directly representing yet another part of the occupational world. Finally, research and training for research, as already emphasized, is the wildest card of all. Virtually without limit, it is a cultivation of the new.

Then, too, when developing societies seek to modernize their systems of higher education, those systems evolve toward an open-ended, ambiguous complexity. Further, when systems in the modern period work out new relations with industry, their tasks multiply. When they seek to accommodate a wide range of local interests by means of regionalization, utilizing different local adaptations, they move farther down the road of task diversity.

Therefore, how to handle the complexity of tasks and responsibilities necessarily becomes the root problem of system adaptation. Modern systems must do more and more, invest in the new on top of the new, go from uncertainties to still more uncertainties. How, then, do they face up to the multiplication of tasks? What accommodations produce an organized social complexity that works?[3]

Coping with Complexity

The growing diversity of tasks pushes modern systems of higher education toward a number of systemic accommodations. Most important is structural differentiation, an adaptive trend that in its various forms deconcentrates the overall system. Closely related is the elaboration of academic professionalism, within which academics specialize their interests and commitments in a widening array of subjects and institutions.

SELF-AMPLIFYING STRUCTURAL DIFFERENTIATION

National systems of higher education have operated in the twentieth century with one type of institution, two or three types, or ten, twenty, or more types.[4] It is now no secret that the more simply structured systems (e.g., Italian higher education today, the Swedish system up to the expansion of the past two decades) have had the greater difficulty in coping with the growing complexity of tasks. Without an arsenal of organizations that are differently competent, they simply expand their one or two main forms—in particular, the national public university—and turn them into conglomerates within which an expanding welter of interest groups fight out all the battles that are involved in doing everything for everyone. Compromises among such competing competencies as undergraduate and graduate studies, practical training and pure scholarship, the humanities and the sciences, are made all the more difficult as the "have-nots" seek equality with the "haves." Vicious circles of interaction are readily generated in which various major and minor interests block one another's development. The need grows for a separation of tasks whereby groups can get out of each other's way and find organized supportive niches. Sooner or later a working agreement emerges, at least tacitly, that the old-line university really cannot do—does not want to do—short-cycle higher education, and hence there is created or allowed to evolve institutes of technology and two-year colleges and other units that pass out first degrees of their own. Sooner or later it becomes reasonably clear that in trying to do well the expanding bundle of tasks involved in the traditional lines of university performance and status, the dominant sector really cannot do—does not want to do—extensive adult or continuing education, especially at less than the most advanced levels, and then we see the creation of an open university or a set of user-friendly regional colleges. Hence, sectorization, in many country-specific forms, can be seen as a general answer to the overloading of simple structures. If additional types of institutions are not created or permitted to emerge, the all-in-one conglomerates increasingly become nominal forms, political pretenses to academic unity, while cramping the organized space within which new units undertaking new tasks must find their way. Bypasses and add-ons are then hard to come by.

Notably, despite the convergencies induced by emulative academic drift, the main university sector itself begins to break up into different types of universities. The rising costs of big social science, big humanities, and big arts, as well as big science, increasingly ensure that money will not be passed around equally. Within the different major subject clusters, and often discipline by discipline, there will be centers of excellence and centers of non-excellence. If not, high costs spread across the system will drive down access to the system at large; *and,* highly talented people who want to sit with other highly talented scholars and scientists, but are not allowed to so concentrate, will flow into the emerging pipelines of brain drain. As different university combinations develop, statesmanship then includes the elaboration of subsector ideologies that blunt invidious comparisons and justify second-best and third-best statuses. Have-not institutions may desire and actively seek a single non-invidious central niche; but complexity reverses the tide and moves them in the other direction. In an evolution that is natural for adaptive species, systems move toward more niches rather than fewer.[5]

National systems of higher education have also operated in the twentieth century with control systems that vary from heavily centralized to radically decentralized. It is now no secret among the more centralized cases that the center cannot hold, that one or more national offices, or academic oligarchies, cannot manage in a top-down fashion the sector of society that is most naturally bottom-heavy in its location of disparate expert judgment and that is most naturally resistant to all-system command. We find curious cross-mixtures of centralizing and decentralizing imperatives. Centralization readily captures our attention. After all, the evolution of the British system during 1965–85 is already a classic example ready for the textbooks. Central ministerial control in France, when loosened for a few years by crisis-level resistance of faculty and students, seems to snap back into place like a rubber band that has been stretched too far. Then, too, after the events of the past two decades, Swedish academics are no strangers to *dirigisme.*

But the flow of control is not all one way, and systems strain to accommodate the conflicting imperatives of centralization and decentralization. Behind the impulse to decentralize lies the simple fact that the evermore swollen professional underbelly of higher education gives the central cadres a "knowledge problem" they cannot handle.[6] It is well known that scientists and scholars grope toward truth by an unending, elaborate process of mutual criticism and discovery. Even with the best academics on top, secure in central offices, they cannot effectively substitute their judgment to short-circuit that process. They will not know what is going on at the bottom, in the many departments, laboratories, and programs, in sufficient detail to be able to plan science and scholarship effectively. They are not able to miniaturize the social structure of scholarly interaction and change. Since they are unable to recapitulate the understandings of thousands of professional operatives, many thousands of bits of tacit knowledge will escape them, no matter how much they amass information. Then, the adaptive structural response is to engage in a layering of authority. In the nationalized systems, decentralization introduces a regional or provincial level of institutional grouping and public accountability.[7] The center is encouraged to devote itself to the setting of a broad "outline of policy" or a broad "framework." In the federal systems, two levels of government continue to vie for influence; with, e.g., Australia now relatively top-heavy, the Federal Republic of Germany a case of balanced federalism, and Canada and the United States still radically decentralized.

Particularly in the large nations, growing complexity tends to call out and/or strengthen regional structures. But even these structures find supervision of other than a most general kind extremely difficult to effect in the face of the individualized professionalism that increasingly characterizes the specialties tucked away in hundreds of corners inside the institutions. The institutional levels then become the best hope of the formal integrators: that at the all-campus level, and at a divisional level within the institution, supra-disciplinary gatherings of faculty and administrators can establish boundaries, allocate budgets, maintain some common internal rewards and sanctions, conduct foreign affairs, and otherwise offer some semblance of a civic order—all within the bounds of the broad frameworks established by those higher up in the national ranks whose job descriptions call for the construction of guidelines.

Now looming large internationally in the differentiation of structures of control is the havoc wreaked upon unitary ideals and approaches by privatization. The two largest systems of higher education in the Western world, the American and the Japanese, have been heavily shaped by their critically important private sectors. In the American case, the private institutions have been historically dominant; they presently number 1,500 or about one-half of all institutions, they contain 20 to 25 percent of the enrollment, and, in both the four-year sector and the university sector, the leading private institutions set the pace for the public brethren. The top fifty four-year colleges are all private; among the top ten universities, six or seven are private. In the Japanese case, the private sector became *the* vehicle for mass entry, handling 75 to 80 percent of students. It has a variety that stretches from degree mills to institutions now positioning themselves quite high in the institutional hierarchy. In these two leading cases, in particular the American one, the construction of individual institutional niches is a high art.

Especially outside Europe, the encouragement of private higher education is very much on national agendas. Even in Europe, the matter is more than a passing rumor. The recent major studies by Roger Geiger and Daniel Levy have shown that as analysts bring into view the Philippines as well as France, Brazil as well as Sweden, we find that the pros and cons of privatization are situationally rooted.[8] There are many forms of privateness—mass and elite, secular and religious, central and peripheral, parallel and divergent in relation to state-supported institutions. In such large cases as the United States, the private sectors may exhibit three or four major types of privateness. Private development has many modern appeals. It can reduce state costs. It often absorbs discontents that otherwise continue to agitate government. It offers alternatives to perceived failures of the state sectors. As part of a broad zig-and-zag adaptation to complexity, private types of universities and colleges may emerge not only in a largely unplanned fashion but also receive support from central officials seeking new paths of development or simply ways to make their own jobs easier.

The tendency to have both public and private sectors in the overall system can have extremely powerful effects at the institutional level. Competition is likely to be enhanced. *And* individual institutions enhance their viability by diversifying their financial base. Private institutions find their way to public treasuries; public institutions learn that money exacted from private sources is as spendable as funds allocated by governments. As institutions mix multiple public sources with numerous private ones, they create individualized institutional packages. They also strengthen their defenses against sources that turn ugly. For institutional autonomy in the late twentieth century there is no more urgent dictum than that of avoiding the situation of all financial eggs in one basket. Multiplying the channels of resource allocation becomes a key form of adaptation.

At the level of institutional structure, one hardly needs to argue the case that institutions, whether nominally specialized or comprehensive, elaborate themselves year-by-year horizontally and vertically: horizontally in more departments, more organized research units (ORUs), and more interdisciplinary programs (IDPs); and vertically in degree levels and levels of oversight. As example: a strategic planning committee at my own institution is examining its entire academic and business organization with an eye toward reorganization that can better position the campus for competitively enhanced strength by the year 2000. There is much agreement that central bodies operated by the faculty as well as the administration are overloaded, yet at the same time many units on campus are relatively unsupervised. ORUs and IDPs are scattered all over the place, greatly extending the network of basic units that traditionally consisted mainly of departments. The ORUs and IDPs are clearly adaptive units, set up to accommodate research interests, and, separately, teaching interests, that are not well supported by the departments. They may report hardly to anyone; or if they have a reporting line, a central official may find that the number of significant units for which he or she is responsible is twenty not ten, thirty-five not fifteen. Then, too, Berkeley and UCLA have had much experience with centralized faculty personnel structures that increasingly become *the* Achilles heels of faculty retention, promotion, and long range development. Central bodies become bottlenecks that turn three-month actions into ones that stretch over nine, twelve, and fifteen months. Institutions that are awake take these phenomena seriously and try to do something about them: notably, by enlarging the central apparatus so that it can subdivide itself; by more clearly separating critical decisions from routine ones; and, most important, by deconcentrating operational responsibility to the divisional level. Who among us cannot report similar problems of coping with complexity inside the university?

At the disciplinary level, it is clear enough that we all confront an irresistible emergence of new subjects that we ignore at our peril and to which we respond by underpinning them with new and varied organizational units. The disciplinary dimension of the system-wide matrix of disciplines and institutions is restless and self-generating, with an expansionist dynamic, as suggested previously, that has cross-national affiliations behind it. International conferences illustrate this dynamic. They encourage the professionalization within many countries of emergent, multidisciplinary fields such as "comparative higher education." The fields are structurally propped up by a center here and a center there, a cluster of semiorganized interested scholars within a university in one country, and a cluster scattered across a half-dozen universities in another. The true believers among us ache for more solid foundations in and among the basic disciplines and the professional schools. In comparative higher education, we measure progress by the firming of small bases in an Hiroshima ORU, an Amsterdam center, a coupling of a half-dozen researchers in a study of the Italian professoriate that seeks to utilize a comparative perspective. We note the intellectual progress, or lack of it, over the years in successive conferences in Lancaster and Stockholm in the books and articles produced by second- and third-generation scholars. Who radically differentiates the academic world? We do. As we pursue scholarship, we differentiate structures as well as ideas and literatures.

Self-Elaborating Academic Professionalism

In a current book on the American professoriate, I portray American academics as having evolved from a first to a second and then to a third "intellectual moment."[9] In a first stage that spanned the colonial period and even stretched into the nineteenth century, academics in my country were temporary hired hands, tutors taken on for a few years before they went off to other work. Academic positions then gradually solidified into a lifelong occupation, one that developed into a fullblown profession (in the modern sense of the word) on the back of specialization. The age of the university that supplanted the age of the college, starting roughly in the 1870s, gave the occupation a second intellectual moment in which a semi-integrated professionalism obtained. At its initiation (1915) and during the quarter of a century leading up to World War II, the American Association of University Professors was able to draw upon the leadership of such distinguished scholars at leading research universities as John Dewy, E. R. A. Seligman, and Franklin Giddings at Columbia, Roscoe Pound at Harvard, Richard T. Ely at Wisconsin, and Arthur O. Lovejoy at Johns Hopkins. It could reasonably pretend that it represented the interests of *the* professoriate, even if more academics stayed out than enlisted in its cause.[10]

The third intellectual moment that has developed during the four decades since 1945 is of an increasingly different character. Academic work is not only set apart in the hands of numerous clusters of trained experts who can claim special knowledge, but it is also greatly differentiated by institutional type. This fragmented professionalism puts involvement and commitment at a different level, that of the disciplines and the institutional types, and turns the American Association of University Professors and its several major rival union organizations increasingly into units of secondary and often nonacademic affiliation.

Particularly instructive is the night-and-day contrast between the extremes of life in the leading research universities and the community colleges. The two-year units have grown so much that they now embrace one-third of all students (four million by head-count!), and one-fourth to one-third of faculty. Their faculties teach fifteen hours a week, almost entirely in introductory courses, to students many of whom are still performing at the secondary level and who need remedial attention. More students are "terminal vocational" than "academic transfer," and even more are non-matriculated adults. Facing a student body that comes and goes on a short time schedule, the institution needs a disposable faculty. As a result, they have turned to part-timers, enlarging their ranks to the point where they outnumber full-time staff. (One-third of the American professoriate is now part-time.)

Hence we can observe two broad avenues of de-professionalization, or at least a casting of academic work in forms far removed from those of the leading universities: work moves from full-time to part-time, with the part-timers ("gypsy scholars," "academic nomads," "freeway scholars") piecing together a livelihood as best they can; and work loses its advanced intellectual content, with "scholars" becoming "teachers" who have positions markedly similar to those of American secondary schoolteachers. Discipline matters much less, since few are doing the advanced things in their fields that differentiate disciplines.

Across the many fields located in the large universities, we find significant differences in workloads and orientations of faculty in the sciences as contrasted to the humanities; and, more broadly, between life in the professional schools and in the letters and science departments. The latter divide is an important schism. One-half of the faculty in the universities is in the professional schools, where work is clinical as well as scholarly, and where it is increasingly set off in the graduate tier, away from the problems of undergraduate teaching. The demands of the professional-practice dimension, and the tension between it and the academic side, have already produced a plethora of additional faculty roles—clinical, part-time, non-tenured, tenured without a salary guarantee—as an internal differentiation that makes the professional schools decidedly differ from the letters and science departments, even as it helps those schools to cope.

In such professional features, as well as in system characteristics, the American case is an extreme one. But in its extremity it is revealing, often exhibiting in relatively stark form what is more muted in other systems. What it helps to reveal in this case is that the academic profession steadily decomposes itself as it responds to the complexities of input and output demands and especially to the substantive imperative of research and scholarship. The profession separates into constituent parts that multiply within its ranks. As it does so, we may intuit, existing controls—professional and bureaucratic—are thrown out of whack. If knowledge is power, then new knowledge is new power, expanded knowledge is expanded power, and fragmented knowledge is fragmented power. Then not only do central administrative cadres have a knowledge problem they cannot handle, they have a control problem that grows steadily larger before their eyes. Power steadily accumulates at the operating levels of the system, shielded from easy penetration by arcaneness and ambiguity in its knowledge foundation. Those who would gather all academics in a unified profession also find that the ground slips from under them. Academic professionalism produces power, but it produces it in a highly fragmented form. The natural self-elaboration of our profession turns it into a mosaic of small worlds, different worlds.

Coping with Structural Differentiation and Fragmented Professionalism: What Integrates?

So much has been made of the defects of academic professionalism that we overlook its compelling contributions. Academic reform in the United States, centered on a strengthening of undergraduate general education that is purportedly necessary to save the nation, castigates the disciplines for their narrowness. Reform in Sweden has attempted to realign undergraduate education around interdisciplinary clusters that are labor market defined. In both cases, the drift of recent reform underestimates what focused professionalism accomplishes for faculty, students, and the system at large.

Academic specialization is one response to the inherent limitations of the human mind. Individuals increasingly cannot expect to cover such major areas as "the social sciences" or "the humanities." It is increasingly odd that we think undergraduate students can and should master such broad domains. As it delineates restricted areas of inquiry and of facts, specialization—compared to non-specialization—leads toward mastery and a sense of competence. Most important, specialization develops a particular kind of structured thinking that we call a discipline.[11] In contrast, theme courses and purportedly interdisciplinary studies typically focus on topics, not intellectual structure. The discipline is treated as a subject matter rather than as a structured method of analysis. Overlooked then is the reality that particular kinds of questions have their own specific systems of analysis. When a question pertains to gross national product, the ways of thinking of physicists and classicists cannot help very much; those of economists can. When a question pertains to Dante's fourth level of Hell, the perspectives of economists become totally irrelevant while the accumulated insights of classicists become relevant. Specialization has the rational bases that are the foundation of the modern academic enterprise.

It is around the modern structures of reasoning that we call disciplines that academics develop their professionalism. Since that professionalism is closely tied to disparate fields, each a self-aggrandizing concern, we appropriately portray it as enormously fragmented. But we can also see that professionalism is a crucial way in the modern occupational world by which self-interests are hooked to larger institutional chariots. In the normal course of his or her work, a biologist or a political scientist or a professor of literature can simultaneously serve and blend self-, other-, and ideal-regarding interests:[12] one's own achievement; the progress of one's department and one's disciplinary group; and the furtherance of scholarship, the education of the young, and a host of other ideals that give meaning to the academic life. Who in our own invisible college is serving only narrow self-interest? Our colleagues in other specialties are surely doing no less to serve others and to serve ideals, even when they "selfishly" seek greater monetary rewards, higher status, greater individual and group autonomy, and more power. In an age of specialization, academic callings will reside basically not in broad theme courses or in labor market–defined subjects but in the cultural homes the disciplines construct around their individual structures of knowledge and reasoning. Tunnel by tunnel, the disciplines are simultaneously *the* centers of meaning and *the* devices for cosmopolitan linkage.[13]

Further, the disciplines do not simply exist as isolated tunnels, linking individuals in parallel chains that never meet. In coverage of empirical domains, and as modes of reasoning, they overlap. Harold Perkin has described the historian as "a kind of licensed rustler who wanders at will across his scholarly neighbors' fields, poaching their stock and purloining their crops and breaking down their hedges."[14] As poachers, the historians have good company: modern disciplines are inherently imperialistic. Anthropologists who use to hanker after lost tribes now turn back on their own advanced societies to pursue domains as they please—the ethnography of the classroom, or the hospital, or the business firm. Sociologists are prepared to offer a sociology of whatever human activity you can think of. You cannot keep economists out of anything, since they are sure they have the keys to the analytical heavens of the social sciences. The boundaries between political science and sociology are so blurred that top scholars in the one can actually be elected to high office in the mainline associations of the other.

We now have at hand a useful vocabulary for conceptualizing and elaborating on this phenomenon. Michael Polanyi has spoken of modern science as consisting of "chains of overlapping neighborhoods."[15] Donald T. Campbell has stressed that a comprehensive social science, or any other large domain of knowledge, is "a continuous texture of narrow specialties." Multiple narrow specialties overlap much like the overlap of scales on the back of a fish. That overlap produces "a collective communication, a collective competence and breadth."[16] When we take this perspective seriously, the implications for reform are breathtaking. Efforts to fill gaps between fields, and to bridge fields, by training scholars who have mastered two or more disciplines are doomed to fail. Such efforts are like trying to make the Mississippi River run north instead of south: better to go with the natural flow, and use it. The way to proceed is to make those organizational inventions that will encourage narrow specialization in interdisciplinary areas. The interdisciplinarian must "remain as narrow as any other scholar." The slogan for reform (overdressed in academic rhetoric) becomes "collective comprehensiveness through overlapping patterns of unique narrowness."[17]

In a creative essay on how cultural integration may coexist with cultural diversity in a highly differentiated society, Diana Crane has acutely observed that the social system of science is an appropriate model:

> Contemporary science comprises hundreds of distinct specialties, but each specialty has connections, both intellectual and social, with other specialties. . . . Cultural integration occurs because of overlapping memberships among cultural communities that lead to the dissemination of ideas and values.

What we find are "interlocking cultural communities."[18] As we extend this formulation to academic fields more generally, we can say that while modern academia is a system powered by specialization and hence by diverging interests, it may also be a system that allows for a collective comprehensiveness that is integrative.[19] The analytical handle is the idea of integration through overlap. We no longer need to think that integration can come only from similarity of function, or common values, or united membership in a grand corps. We do not need to ask that we all become Mr. Chips, nor that we pull ourselves together around four values and a core curriculum, nor that we enter a national civil service and join one union. We can understand that integration can come from the bit-by-bit overlap of narrow memberships and specific identities, with specialties and disciplines—and whole colleges and universities—serving as mediating institutions that tie individuals and small groups into the enclosure of the whole. For a realm that is so naturally pluralistic, and for which the future promises an ever-widening complexity of task and structure, a large dollop of pluralist theory is not a bad idea.

This line of thinking pushes us toward the relatively unexplored phenomenon of the associational linkages that academics themselves fashion. My recent study of the American academic profession found that, in the United States at least, the associational structure of the academic profession mirrors the ongoing contest between centrifugal and centripetal academic forces.[20] "Splinteritis" is everywhere. The country has something in the order of 350 associations that are largely or importantly academic, from the omnibus American Association for the Advancement of Science (AAAS) to the John Dewey Society and the Society for Nursing History.

The Problem of Complexity in Modern Higher Education 399

Each major association, be it the American Physical Society, the American Psychological Association, or the Modern Languages Association, finds itself steadily subdividing into numerous major divisions along subject matter lines, which then divide still further into subsections. As the associations grow substantively, tracking and furthering their respective fields, they incorporate more specialties and sow the seeds of their own fragmentation. If they are not accommodative, even quick on their feet, specialists break away to form their own associations. The American associations are also now subdividing internally and externally by type of institution: e.g., the community college sector has interests so far removed from those of the research universities that instructors in this realm have and are constituting the likes of the Community College Humanities Association, the Community College Social Sciences Association, and more discipline-centered ones in mathematics and biology.

Academics associate voluntarily from the bottom up. They fashion informal individualized sets of ties on their own campuses. They participate in quasi-formal local, regional, and national groups of a dozen or several dozen people who meet separately or within the program of the "monster meetings." The informal ties link to the quasi-formal, and the quasi-formal to the formal. The small groups connect to large ones that link up in gigantic conglomerates, as when a regional disciplinary association connects to a national one that in turn participates in one or more national and international "umbrella" associations. Professional associating follows well the many natural contours of academe.

Conclusion

As national systems of higher education seek the means of enhancing flexibility and responding adaptively, in the face of ever-expanding complexity, they undoubtedly can assist themselves through some state targeting. While large countries may permit diffuse coverage of all subjects, small countries undoubtedly have to be selective, opting to invest only in certain fields. State-guided limitations—coercive simplicity—is one way of trying to control complexity. But beyond such planned responses lie more adaptive profession-led and market-led forms of differentiation and integration. These latter forms depend on more spontaneous, unplanned developments.

The profession-led responses on which I have concentrated depend in higher education upon competitive discovery processes. The give-and-take of scientific fields, and other fields of scholarship, are, at the level of the individual, an "anarchy of production." But out of a furious turmoil of lower-level disorder a higher-level order can and does evolve. This more spontaneous road to order depends on the interacting competencies, tacit and explicit, of thousands of individuals. They try to help things along by establishing such bottom-up forms of their own devising as informal, quasi-formal, and formal associations. "Spontaneous orders" are likely to be central to a fruitful, changing integration, offering a "mutual coordination in which the actions of each participant both contribute a kind of pressure to the actions of other participants, while simultaneously being guided in its own actions by similar pressures contributed by others."[21]

Associating professionally with one another in webs of relationship that form and evaporate as substantive interests change, academics evolve structures that follow the development of knowledge, rather than the other way around. Flexibility is gained by escaping both from the iron cage of bureaucracy and from the professional iron cage that is wrought whenever close unity among academics is achieved.[22] Specialization that creates so much freedom, and allows order to follow function, deserves at least two cheers.

The problem of complexity is not without its surpassing ironies. Try as we might to theorize it and to order it in boxes, the idea of complexity implies the primacy of practice over theory.[23] There is an old joke in science that research is what I am doing when I do not know what I am doing. As a minor paraphrase, complexity is perhaps what we have to think about when we do not know what to think. Émile Durkheim drew a powerful bead on the problem when he argued that generalization was a sort of pride, a refusal to accept the personal restraints and social obligations imposed by complexity, while specialization was an implicit means of adaptation to complexity.[24] This precept for occupational practice can and has been translated into a precept for thinking about politics, the economy, and other social orders: do one's narrow duty and let the complex whole take care of itself. Theory then must not only maintain a modest sense of limits but also deeply appreciate ambiguity.

At the same time, it still seems to remain the case that only general theoretical reflection, together with a sense of history, will enable us to think through the operation and meaning of our complex social institutions in a systematic way. At the least, when we think about complexity in higher education we are driven to return to fundamental exploration of the ways that spontaneous orders develop within and outside of officially enacted structures. Such an approach is particularly appropriate in the analysis of a major sector of society—higher education—in which a diffuse profession-led specialization and integration are so clearly the main alternative to bureaucratic allocation and linkage.

Notes

1. On the basic processes of substantive growth in the academic profession and academia at large, see Walter Metzger, "The Academic Profession in the United States," in *The Academic Profession: National, Disciplinary, and Institutional Settings*, ed. Burton R. Clark (Berkeley and Los Angeles: University of California Press, 1987), 126–47.

2. Joseph Ben-David, *Centers of Learning: Britain, France, Germany, the United States* (New York: McGraw-Hill, 1977).

3. For a much-overlooked intensive and extensive modern exploration of the problem of societal complexity, see *Organized Social Complexity: Challenge to Politics and Policy*, ed. Todd R. LaPorte (Princeton, N.J.: Princeton University Press, 1975).

4. See Burton R. Clark, *The Higher Education System: Academic Organization in Cross-National Perspective* (Berkeley and Los Angeles: University of California Press, 1983), 53–62.

5. On the application of a biological evolutionary perspective to system diversity, see Robert Birnbaum, "System Arguments for Diversity," in *Association for the Study of Higher Education Reader in Organization and Governance in Higher Education*, ed. Robert Birnbaum (Lexington, Mass.: Association for the Study of Higher Education, rev. ed., 1984), 411–23. This article is taken from his larger study, *Maintaining Diversity in Higher Education* (San Francisco: Jossey-Boss, 1983).

6. For a modern treatment of the "knowledge problem" as viewed by an economist advocating a radical agenda for turning away from planning, see Don Lavoie, *National Economic Planning: What is Left?* (Cambridge, Mass.: Ballinger, 1985), chap. 3.

7. Symptomatic is the reaction now (1987) developing in Britain to the centralized powers of the University Grants Committee and the Department of Edu-

cation and Science: eleven northern universities are contemplating a go-it-alone plan that would loosen the planning controls from London. They are discussing whether to agitate for the creation of a northern regional university council, which would take over the job of detailed nationalization from the University Grants Committee and foster cooperation among the eleven.

See "Northerners Bid to Plan Their Own Universities," *The Times Higher Education Supplement*, no. 753 (April 10, 1987): 1.

8. Roger L. Geiger, *Private Sectors in Higher Education: Structure, Function, and Change in Eight Countries* (Ann Arbor: University of Michigan Press, 1986), and Daniel C. Levy, *Higher Education and the State in Latin America: Private Challenges to Public Dominance* (Chicago: University of Chicago Press, 1986).

9. Burton R. Clark, *The Academic Life: Small Worlds, Different Worlds* (Princeton, N.J.: The Carnegie Foundation for the Advancement of Teaching, 1987).

10. Metzger, "The Academic Profession," 167–68.

11. My formulations in this paragraph have drawn upon Thomas Sowell, "Recipe for Change on Campus," a review of Ernest L. Boyer, *College: The Undergraduate Experience*, in *The Wall Street Journal*, April 9, 1987.

12. The concepts of self-regarding, other-regarding, and ideal-regarding interests are drawn from Jane J. Mansbridge, *Beyond Adversary Democracy* (Chicago: University of Chicago Press, 1983), 24–26.

13. On the basic role of the disciplines as separate cultures and as communities of knowledge, see the work of Tony Becher as represented by his book, *Academic Tribes and Territories: Intellectual Enquiry and the Culture of Disciplines* (Milton Keynes: Open University Press, 1989).

14. Harold Perkin, "The Historical Perspective," in *Perspectives in Higher Education, Eight Disciplinary and Comparative Views*, ed. Burton R. Clark (Berkeley and Los Angeles: University of California Press, 1984), 17.

15. Michael Polanyi, *The Tacit Dimension* (Garden City, N.J.: Doubleday, 1967), 72.

16. Donald T. Campbell, "Ethnocentrism of Disciplines and the Fish-Scale Model of Omniscience," in *Interdisciplinary Relationships in the Social Sciences*, ed. Muzafer and Carolyn Sherif (Chicago: Aldine, 1969), 328, 330.

17. Ibid., 328, 331.

18. Diana Crane, "Cultural Differentiation, Culture Integration, and Social Control," in *Social Control: Views from the Social Sciences*, ed. Jack P. Gibbs (Beverly Hills, Calif.: Sage, 1982), 239.

19. Clark, *The Academic Life*, chap. 5.

20. Ibid., chap. 8.

21. Lavoie, *National Economic Planning*, 67.

22. On bureaucracy and profession as twentieth-century iron cages, see Paul J. DiMaggio and Walter W. Powell, "The Iron Cage Revisited: Institutional Isomorphism and Collective Rationality in Organizational Fields," *American Sociological Review* 48 (April 1985): 147–60.

23. Harlan Wilson, "Complexity as a Theoretical Problem: Wider Perspectives in Political Theory," in *Organized Social Complexity,* ed. LaPorte, 281–331, 307.

24. Ibid., 315, 331.

INTRODUCTION TO CHAPTER 25

At the time I wrote this piece the existing American literature on higher education was fixated on the undergraduate years. The Feldman-Newcomb review (1970) and the follow-on review (1991) by Pascarella-Terenzini showed that over four-thousand studies had been done on undergraduates. The attention of legislators and the general public was also focused on who goes to "college" and what happens to them by the time they take the bachelor's degree—if they do.

Meanwhile, large numbers of students were going on for master's degrees; faculties spent considerable time with them, often more than they did with undergraduates. Advanced students doing theses and dissertations often had a one-on-one relationship with a mentor. University presidents spoke fondly of the PhD and other top professional degrees, particularly in medicine and law, as "the crown jewels" of the research university. But the literature, then as now, did not at all reflect the importance of "the graduate school." What was this domain like in America? What structures that supported advanced work did other nations have? Here was a subject virtually begging for cross-national analysis.

The work of Joseph Ben-David, the Israeli sociologist, stimulated my interest in pursuing the most advanced level. During the 1960s and 1970s, he had usefully combined a comparative sociology of science with a comparative sociology of higher education. His classic book, *The Scientist's Role in Society* (1971), was followed six years later by *Centers of Learning: Britain, France, Germany, United States* (1977). In the latter volume he compared how those four nations had organized the support of academic research and research training while also engaged in professional and general education. I was struck by his acute observations on national differences, especially by his explanations of how the organization of the research university sector in the United States led to American dominance in academic research during the last half of the twentieth century. I wanted to dig further into the organizational details of this phenomenon. Thus, I decided to take on the "big four" systems and add Japan to the mix.

When approached, Lawrence Cremin, the outstanding historian of education and then the dynamic president of the Spencer Education Foundation, warmed on the spot to what I wanted to do. He arranged a major grant that would fund this five-country study. I determined I could not do the needed intensive work alone nor could I proceed effectively by assembling a group of post-docs who would work out of a UCLA office: the study would require an international team of researchers. The key members became Guy Neave on France; Claudius Gellert on Germany; Tony Becher, Mary Henkel, and Maurice Kogan of Britain; Morikazu Ushiogi on Japan; and a new post-doc, Patricia J. Gumport, recruited to do the American field research.

We did a first-year analysis of how each of these countries developed the graduate level. The five national teams took different analytical perspectives. Their talents varied across historical, anthropological, and policy interests. I also encouraged them to write their national reports in a holistic fashion that would follow the special contours of tradition and structure each country offered.

In the second year we focused on interviewing in disciplines: physics, economics, and history in all cases, plus in such strong fields as engineering in Japan and biological sciences in the United States. Here, in Tony Becher's words, we reached for a "view from the ground." Two papers on each country led to an edited volume, *The Research Foundations of Graduate Education: Germany, Britain, France, United States, Japan* (Clark, 1993). I emphasized the distinctive capability of American graduate education in the concluding chapter.

Here I could be an organizational analyst on a grand scale: "Cross-national comparison reveals how much specific organization matters. It matters a great deal to have formally recognized graduate schools. It matters considerably to have departments rather than chairs as the primary operational units. It matters to have research clusters subsumed within teaching settings but also capable of raising much of their own funding. It matters that universities, departments, and research groups compete for prestige and resources" (378). I also came to a contrarian understanding of the modern integration of research activities with teaching and learning. That is what the 1997 article reprinted here is all about.

A second volume, written by me, emerged from this five-country study: *Places of Inquiry* (1995). I concentrated on the organizational devices by which German universities had institutionalized research in the nineteenth century and compared that arrangement to the mechanics that structured the graduate school part of American universities in the twentieth century. Here I specified the late twentieth-century conditions that pulled research apart from teaching and learning and the modern conditions that fostered their close integration. The "research-teaching-study nexus" is the core of a compatibility thesis—one that in recent years has been seen by others as well as by me—as appropriate for undergraduate and K–12 education, as well as for advanced scientific and professional education. Research-based study is an effective way to prepare students for life in an inquiring society.

Reference

Clark, Burton R., ed. *The Research Foundations of Graduate Education: Germany, Britain, France, United States, Japan*. Berkeley, Los Angeles, and Oxford: University of California Press, 1993.

CHAPTER 25

The Modern Integration of Research Activities with Teaching and Learning

NO ISSUE IS MORE basic in modern higher education than the relationship between research and teaching. And no issue occasions more superficial thought and retrogressive criticism both outside and inside the academy. In the United States, but not there alone, an incompatibility thesis had increasingly been voiced during the 1980s and early 1990s. We repeatedly hear assertations that when university professors do research they avoid teaching, that the time they spend on one is time taken from the other, that deep interest in research entails low interest in teaching, and, notably, that when academics do research they abandon students. Though popularized mainly by outside critics, we find this oppositional view even reflected in standard survey questions posed by academics in studies of academics. Professors are asked: Are you interested in research or in teaching? Do you spend your time in research or in teaching? Which does your institution emphasize? Universities seemingly accept the thrust of the incompatibility thesis when they defensively answer criticisms with lame rebuttals that professors really do not run off to do research as much as is claimed, that critics can find professors in "the classroom" if they only look hard enough and sympathetically comprehend all the many things that academics have to do.

A contrary perspective, here developed from cross-national research, offers a better purchase on the role of research in education [8, 9]. A broad compatibility thesis, one that applies to national systems of higher education generally, asserts that research activity can and does serve as an

"The Modern Integration of Research Activities with Teaching and Learning," *Journal of Higher Education* 68, no. 3 (May–June 1997): 241–55. Used by permission.

important mode of teaching and a valuable means of learning. The thesis can be extended by the warranted observation that research-based teaching and learning become more important in higher education with every passing decade. In its strongest and most normative form the thesis becomes a claim that student involvement in research is an efficacious way to educate throughout the educational system the great mass of students as well as the elite performers, for the inquiring society into which we are rapidly moving.

The following analysis first anchors the compatibility thesis in an ideal-type concept of a research-teaching-study nexus. I then offer a brief historical overview of how close approximations to the nexus became organizationally embedded in universities, first by means of the German nineteenth-century construction of what in retrospect we can call "the academic research group," and then, under twentieth-century conditions, by the American addition of "the advanced teaching group" within a graduate school framework. This latter organizational enactment, revealed by cross-national comparison of the basic units of modern universities, is a critical component of the comparative advantage that American universities achieved in the last half of the twentieth century. A third section points to the possibility of much greater use of research-based teaching and learning in U.S. undergraduate programs and refers to reform efforts in American elementary and secondary education that stress student involvement in research. Overall, the compatibility thesis highlights an inquiry model of education.

A full-fledged inquiry model redraws the main fault line in higher education. Instead of the dichotomous distinction between research and teaching that is now so common, it distinguishes types of institutions and educational levels in which research, teaching, and learning are closely linked from those settings where they are separated. The incompatibility thesis is then seen as simplistic, overlooking critical linkages. As a guide for reform, it points in the wrong direction, not serving well either the general society or the academy. Instead of fewer, more educational sites should be constructed as places of inquiry.

No effort is made here to refer to the existing American literature on the research-teaching connection. That literature is centered on undergraduate "teaching," a faculty activity located primarily in the undergraduate lecture hall and undergraduate instructional classroom. "Research" is then viewed as a separate faculty activity, one that may be quite removed from teaching and opposed to it in the use of academic time. I deliberately do not use this usual way of framing the research-teaching connection. Rather, I want to construct an imagery that is rooted first of all in the teaching and learning that takes place in the advanced laboratory (or seminar) and especially that which takes place in the course of dissertation research. Let us examine a "research-teaching-study nexus" in which three activities are closely fused, a nexus in which engagement in research—or inquiry, more broadly—is the means of teaching and the pathway offered for student learning.

The Research-Teaching-Study Nexus

In every major modern national system of higher education, some academics routinely use research activities as a powerful mode of instruction and a means of student involvement. In departments, in research centers, and even in such interdisciplinary programs as environmental studies and African studies, professors assemble students in laboratories and seminars to pursue research agendas. Prototypically, a professor and a group of students engage in a joint research project or agree on what different but allied topics the individual students will pursue and what methods they will use. Members of the seminar or the laboratory report back to each other in periodic meetings and informal conversations and explain the tentative results of their inquiries, including blind alleys and trivial outcomes. Much discussion and criticism ensues, led by the professor or another member of the academic staff.

In such settings, common in advanced higher education, teachers clearly teach by means of research activities, and students are engaged in the educational process via those activities and learn through that engagement. Dissertation research, generally pursued after seminar or laboratory participation, even more powerfully provides teaching and learning organized around research activity. The student pursues research for one or more years as the primary means of learning; from initial prospectus to finished dissertation, members of the academic staff guide and supervise the various stages of the student's effort.

Academics who have taken research-based degrees, especially the PhD, and whose normal work includes much research-based teaching will find the above description a commonplace observation. Its familiar patterns are part of their conventional wisdom, the backbone of their assertion that research and teaching must be kept together. But in many settings now found in universities and colleges the connection is greatly loosened, and students may be only marginally involved or not involved at all. Professors may spend part of their time in esoteric research and then spend another part lecturing from codified materials, textbook and all, to beginning and intermediate students whose elementary grasp of subjects places them far from research frontiers. Traditional utterances by academics about their need to engage in research and teaching, voiced by academics in every modern society, can then unwittingly support the claim that students are left out, especially when universities supply one large lecture hall after another where students in the thirty-fifth row can just about make out the face of the teacher, peering at her as if through the wrong end of a telescope.

A construct that points to research-based learning as well as research-based teaching is called for, a three-way conception that includes students and their learning as a primary element. As an ideal type, the concept of a "research-teaching-study nexus" highlights a complete blending of research activities, teaching activities, and study activities, an intermingling so thorough that it is hard to tell where one ends and the other begins. In this form of education, research activity is the glue that holds together teaching and learning. Through research the professor teaches, and simultaneously, the student studies and learns. Research integrates teaching and learning.

The concept of a research-teaching-study nexus has historical echoes in the 1810 formulations of Wilhelm von Humboldt. In the words of Margarita Bertilsson, Humboldtian thought was an "extravagant ideology" [3]. Humboldt sought to connect everything to everything else in four "unities": not only should the reformed German university of the nineteenth century unite research and teaching, but it should also unite through philosophy the various empirical sciences and unite science and general upbringing and unite science with universal enlightenment. Underlying all these desired unities, however—especially the unity of research and teaching—would be the commitment to discovery. Humboldt saw higher education as something quite different from elementary and secondary education. The lower levels, he maintained, "present closed and settled bodies of knowledge," while higher intellectual institutions "conceive of science and scholarship as dealing with ultimately inexhaustible tasks: this means that they are engaged in an unceasing process of inquiry." The relation between teacher and student then becomes different: "At the higher level, the teacher does not exist for the sake of the student: both teacher and student have their justification in the common pursuit of knowledge" [33, p. 249]. Seekers one and all, teachers and students were to be viewed as co-researchers. Amid much ambiguous idealism that clouded Humboldtian doctrine, here was the sustaining formulation that put the creation of new knowledge and the revision of old ideas first among the tasks of higher education.

Construction of the Nexus in University Organization

Humboldtian ideology served to open up conceptual space and especially to rationalize the intentions and actions of new disciplinarians who, especially in the decades between 1820 and 1870 in the German system, took up the cause of one new scientific field after another, preeminently chemistry and physics. The disciplinarians' pursuit of self-interest and related experimentation with basic unit organization led to the birth of a new generic form: the academic research group. The main tools of this new formation were neither the lecture nor the didactic classroom, nor the reading of canonical texts, but discovery-oriented activity in new teaching-research laboratories and teaching-research seminars.

A classic case and influential model of what Humboldtian thought came to mean in actual practice, as worked out by the new specialists as they sought to establish themselves and to engage in research, was the laboratory organized and directed by the chemist Justus Liebig in the small provincial university of Giessen beginning in 1826 and lasting for three decades [15, 12]. The laboratory started out as a training school for pharmacists similar to others of its type. But Liebig was determined to do research, to contribute new knowledge in successive waves, while teaching existing knowledge and expanding research technique. He did so in a way that gave his laboratory a competitive advantage over old and new rivals at other universities. He learned to concentrate lectures in a summer semester, leaving the entire winter for practice work in the laboratory. He set research problems for students; he invented simpler and more reliable instruments for chemical analysis, making it possible for students of varying levels of insight and skill routinely to produce elementary analyses at a much accelerated rate. Student investigations became standard, first centering on problems the director set around his own interests and capabilities and then going beyond them. Matriculants shifted from would-be pharmacists to chemists. By the 1840s, competitive advantage was fully at hand. Frederic L. Holmes commented: "Liebig's command of so large a group of advanced students to whom he could give experimental projects useful both to their training and to his interests enabled him to exploit new research openings with only a few students, to compete with him" [15, pp. 162–63].

Other chemists who were to leave their mark—Bunsen at Heidelberg, Kolbe at Leipzig, Baeyer at Munich—and such influential new physicists as Franz Neumann at Königsberg found the research-teaching laboratory or seminar to be their primary tool [24, 27]. Instruction was no longer based primarily on lecture courses and traditional written materials or left to self-instruction. Teaching now revolved around practical exercises in techniques of quantification, innovative design of instruments, and group review of problems and results. Such professors could pontificate about Wissenschaft and Bildung all they wanted, but in practice they were promoting the mental and material tools involved in the *labor* of science—a distinctive set of investigative techniques newly characteristic of a discipline. Students learned to follow certain rules of investigative protocol and rigorous techniques of investigation. As students were pulled into the new laboratories and seminars both as research trainees and research performers, they notably gained an intimate involvement that did not, and still does not today, obtain in the lecture hall, or in any classroom no matter how small, where the professor presents codified knowledge and students are expected to absorb the best of the past. Now, as teaching was blended with research activity, study was folded into "the unceasing process of inquiry" that Humboldt had sought to place first in the orientation of universities.

Working outward from this Germanic base, the idea and the practices of education by means of discovery processes have spread during the past one-and-a-half centuries across academic systems in developed societies and in all less developed societies that seek entry to the international gold standard of science and critical scholarship. (In 1995 these latter societies stretched from Hong Kong to Brazil to South Africa.) The idea of research-based teaching and learning has become deeply entrenched in academic thought, even to the point of unconscious assumption; such operational tools as the research-teaching laboratory and the inquiry-oriented seminar have become fixed in many academic structures as standard operating procedure.

But two basic trends in the twentieth century, especially during the past half-century, have changed markedly the conditions that enable the historic nexus and organizational arrangements that best enact it. For one, the trend from elite to mass to universal higher education [31] brings enormous growth in the teaching of beginning and intermediate students who ostensibly must master codified elementary material before they can go forward to advanced work. The problems of "undergraduate" education then weigh heavily, demanding attention and resources: "teaching-first" settings acquire a strong rationale. Second, the trend from simple to complex knowledge, captured in the concept of substantive growth [23], enormously complicates every discipline, placing research frontiers and advanced levels of training farther away from rudimentary knowledge. In an often self-amplifying fashion, the research dynamic extends and intensifies knowledge. If the biological sciences (more broadly, the biomedical fields) offer the most dramatic example of rapid change in knowledge in the past two decades, all the scientific fields, including the social sciences, and most of the humanities notably history, exhibit unending specialization and differentiation. The facts are shattering: in mathematics, journals number more than 1,000 and review journals use a classification that includes over 4,500 subtopics arranged under 62 major areas [21]; in psychology, the American Psychological Association is structured around 45 major specialties [20], and one of these large fields (social psychology) reports that it is comprised of 17 subfields [14]; in history, the output of materials from 1960 to 1980 apparently equaled in magnitude all that was published from the time of the Greek historian Thucydides in the fourth century BC to the year 1960 [32].

The two primary trends of enlarged access and knowledge growth greatly increase the costs of higher education. Governments increasingly indicate that they are not prepared to pay the unit costs of mass higher education at the level of elite education. They also make clear that they are not willing to pay throughout a national system for the increasingly high costs of research and research-based teaching and learning. By state planning or unplanned adaptation, institutions overwhelmingly centered on undergraduate instruction, with lower unit costs, are differentiated from ones that are heavily research-centered. Even among the institutions designated as universities, some are fully research-invested, some partially so. Still others operate largely without a research base and give themselves over to preadvanced teaching and routine preparation for one or more professions.

Such differentiation among institutions is also increasingly supplemented by differentiation within them. Degree levels and types of degrees multiply; the teaching of first-year students and of doctoral and postdoctoral students becomes two contrasting ends of a lengthening sequence. As noted with great reluctance by German academics in the mid- and late-1980s, the opportunity to blend research activity with teaching and learning in that historic system has shifted from the preadvanced to the graduate level [16]. Inside universities a non-research faculty, primarily in the status of "university lecturers," has also grown up in many national systems alongside the old-line faculty of professors privileged to do research and granted appropriate conditions of time and resources [25, pp. 44–46]. In short, during the past half-century, the idea and practices of research-based teaching and learning have become more segregated. They are not in command at the present time across modern systems of higher education. They are well supported only in particular locales, in certain university sectors, and there primarily at advanced levels of training.

The American university, in providing such concentration, has stood out with increasing prominence during the twentieth century. Other national systems have been largely "one tier" [6, pp. 49–53]. With general education completed at the secondary level, as in European systems, students enter higher education to specialize. A long first-degree program of study historically has led to professional qualification and ostensibly to mastery of disciplinary knowledge in the letters and science fields to a level similar to the American master's degree. The few students who stayed on beyond that point could then take a post as a research worker at the university or plunge directly into the research work of the doctoral dissertation. Little or no formal structure was needed for this second stage; a connection to a mentor would do. The American university, in contrast, has had two tiers throughout the twentieth century. Because the general education of students had not been completed at the secondary level, the first tier has been preoccupied with its provision. Students generally are not admitted as freshmen to a discipline but to an undergraduate college as a whole, there to face first the requirements specified for a liberal or general education. Some specialization begins with selection of a major, generally for the last two years of the four-year program, but intense specialization in most fields does not begin until after the first degree when students move to the graduate level. This second major tier of study notably involves another round of selection and national redistribution of students in which disciplinary department and professional schools finally assume the primary role in selecting students.

The graduate school emerged in the last quarter of the nineteenth century, in what reformers then called "the vertical university," after a half-century of struggle and experimentation, in which various efforts were made to accommodate the research imperative and substantive growth within the limits of the classical four-year first degree [30, pp. 23–35; 13, pp. 1–20]. The established "college" proved to be an immovable object; disciplinary specialization became the irresistible force. The college framework was kept, but disciplinary specialization was given "the graduate school." Advanced training thereby acquired a distinctive organizational home, one that increasingly had its own full set of admission criteria, course requirements, periodic testing, and sequences of research activities.

In cross-national comparison, the American graduate level of disciplinary departments and the professional schools that are fully located at the graduate level stand out as a frame for teaching across a broader swath of knowledge than what specialized research groups can provide. The many courses and requirements of graduate programs are staffed by what we can call the advanced teaching group, an assembly of faculty in the department or professional school as a whole responsible for the training and certification of advanced students who seek higher degrees. These basic units also usually contain multiple research groups organized by specialists. Faculty and students move back and forth between the two types of groupings. The research groups offer the mentor-apprentice relationship that continues to serve as the primary vehicle for the transmission of tacit knowledge [35, pp. 122–32; 18, pp. 232–37].

But by themselves the research groups offer little knowledge about other specialties in the broader field of study. The growing amount of tangible knowledge in each field is then provided in the mandatory and optional courses the department faculty as a whole defines as necessary for competence. The coursework may be placed first, occupying two to three years, before full entry into intense research as the basis for the dissertation. Or the coursework and the research work may run somewhat more parallel, as when students in chemistry enter a research group at the same time they enter the parent department. In either case, the department becomes a collective mentor, a guide to preparation for research. Generally, the shift from preparation *for* research to learning from involvement *in* research occurs over several stages in which students are increasingly plunged into research activity.

Thus, under modern conditions, the research-teaching-study nexus is provided *organizationally* in a systematic and massive fashion by the type of university basic unit that combines a teaching group with research groups, a hybrid framework that can provide relatively broad disciplinary knowledge (and even some work in cognate fields) with highly specific specialty knowledge. National systems other than the American are now groping toward this framework, notably in Europe [26]. The first formal British graduate school was established in 1991 at the University of Warwick. By 1994 more than twenty universities in the United Kingdom had established graduate schools, and about a hundred joined a new national Graduate Council.

On the global scene during the 1990s, the organization of a systematic framework for research linked to advanced research training is a key item of basic change in universities. Officials and academics in such fast-moving societies as Hong Kong and Korea make clear that they have no intention of being left behind. They wish to do world-class research in their universities, draw on an international talent pool, and train promising students at the cutting edge of research. What they need then are organizational patterns that uphold the research-teaching-study nexus.

Those patterns fall mainly into four combinations. In descending order of tight integration, they are: a Type I nexus, the inclusion research department that contains a broad-based teaching group and one or more specialized research groups; a Type II nexus, the combination of department and one or more related campus research centers, a dual structure now common on the campuses of American and British universities in which academics and chosen advanced students move back and forth across a department-research center divide to be members of teaching and research groups; a Type III nexus, a combination of university department and non-university research group, a more complicated arrangement common in Germany, with its plethora of outside major research institutes (Max-Planck, Fraunhofer, etc.) and even more common in France, with its broad dual structure of universities and CNRS laboratories, in which professors, full-time researchers, and students have to move across major sector boundaries (with different career structures) in order to link teaching frameworks and specialist research groups; and a Type IV nexus, a spreading pattern characteristic of teaching-first universities, the weakest case, in which research activity, only lightly present, can only weakly serve as a primary foundation for advanced teaching and study.

In their monumental work on the development of physics in Germany, Christa Jungnickel and Russell McCormmach noted that three things are needed for effective local presentation and advancement of a discipline: research activity by established scholars, advanced training of students by means of research, and a comprehensive course of study [17, p. xvii]. The Type I setting offers all these elements in one place and with the same people collectively involved. The Type II setting offers all elements but places them in different intra-university locales and with somewhat different persons engaged. The Type III setting concentrates research activity by placing it in a separately supported locale, but leaves more problematic whether students gain access to that locale and whether any course of study is included. The Type IV setting is weak on all three components, particularly in support of research activities.

Specified organizationally in the context of late twentieth-century mass higher education and high knowledge sophistication, these four types of the research-teaching-study nexus provide terms appropriate for both examination of university organization in any one country and cross-national comparison of university sectors.

Research-Based Teaching and Learning in the General Educational Structure

As noted above, modern conditions of higher education tend to move the research foundations of teaching and learning within higher education from the undergraduate to the graduate level, especially to doctoral programs. For staff and students alike, the doctoral level is where the commandment to do research most fully takes over. And it is by concentrating on doctoral training that we learn how nineteenth-century German modes of research-based teaching and learning became supplemented by twentieth-century American arrangements to provide in great profusion strong versions of the three-way connection. But a strong case can also be made that student participation in a research environment is a highly appropriate form of teaching and learning in preadvanced programs, from the entry year onward. Regardless of its specific nature, a research project involves a process of framing questions, using reliable methods to find answers, and then weighing the relevance of the answers and the significance of the questions. Student research activity is then, at root, a scholarly process for learning how to define problems and map a line of investigation. It is also a way to induce critical thinking and to develop inquiring minds, an active mode of learning in which the instructor provides an analytical framework and some particular ways of solving problems but does not offer answers to be written down, memorized, and given back. Even when resources and setting do not permit an actual plunging of preadvanced students into projects, small or large, instructors who bring a research attitude into their teaching are likely to exhibit some features of the processes of inquiry. Good educational reasons abound why academics, when told they must only teach, resist a flight from research.

Thus it should come as no surprise that faculty in the best undergraduate-centered liberal arts colleges in the United States report they are involved in research. They view research as necessary for effective undergraduate teaching in both the short run and the long term and as essential for their personal development, standing, and identity as productive academics [7, pp. 73–85; 22]. Treating some undergraduates as research assistants, they offer a mentor-apprentice relationship. Many American university faculty members bring some undergraduates as well as graduate students directly into research activity. In the 1990s a small national movement is under way that encourages the "research collaboration" of undergraduate students and faculty [19, 34]. Professors are more than ever aware that involvement in research activity can increase the general motivation of undergraduates to learn as well as stimulate their interest in specific subjects.

The educational uses of research have also not escaped the partisans of reform in K–12 education. J. Bruner argued cogently three decades ago that schools should promote active learning through discovery and problem-solving [4, 5]. R. J. Schaefer even advocated at the time that some schools should be centers of inquiry, operating in part as "centers for the production of knowledge about how to carry out the job" [28, pp. 1–2]. He rightly stressed that teaching cannot be an intellectual calling when it mainly consists of a routine distribution of knowledge in packaged form. If teachers operated as scholar-teachers, with action research giving them a work life more like that of university professors, they could then also serve as role models for students preparing for lifelong learning. Teachers and students alike should have the opportunity to engage in inquiry and thereby become better inquirers.

During the 1980s and early 1990s, numerous reform efforts in K–12 education have moved toward the idea of teaching by means of staff and student involvement in research. Reform in mathematics and science education has sought to move schoolteachers and their students toward a broad problem-solving approach, as opposed to computation [1, 11]. T. Sizer's Coalition of Essential Schools, with its emphasis on student as worker, teacher as coach, and "learning how to learn," seems substantially inquiry oriented [29]. Professional Development Schools seek to strengthen school-university collaboration and to have teachers involved in inquiry [10, p. 289]. Particularly striking have been the special programs developed for high-flying students in science that have been long in place in such elite settings as the Bronx High School of Science and Stuyvesant High School in New York, settings backed by the prestigious and spirited annual national Westinghouse Science Talent Search. Here secondary schoolteachers clearly engage students in research. And the specialized academic schools of New York City are not alone in heavily emphasizing inquiry. Many other schools throughout the United States in states varied as Virginia, Illinois, and California have picked up on the general idea that young people need to be taught to do research and at some point to be actually involved in research [2]. Once the merits of a research program are appreciated, numerous secondary schools have or can develop the capacity to be substantially more research oriented.

Educational Sites as Places of Inquiry

We need to move conceptually beyond the dichotomy of research *and* teaching. Drawing a fault line between these two principal faculty activities, the incompatibility thesis portrays teaching and research as distinctively different operations that are basically opposed to each other. But if a line must be drawn, it should be drawn between research-based teaching and learning (where much blending of these three activities occurs) and teaching and learning centered on codified material and lacking an inquiring attitude. The extremes of these two forms are found within higher education in doctoral education and routine instruction of first-year students. An informed grasp of the relationship of research to teaching and learning depends on an understanding of graduate schools and advanced programs as well as undergraduate instruction and the needs of beginning students.

A culture of inquiry has important advantages in educational sites. Elementary and secondary schools increasingly find close encounters with research to be powerful ways to stimulate student motivation and enhance learning. Forward-looking universities and colleges promote such encounters in undergraduate work, as an essential part of a liberal or general education, even as the universities embed them all the more deeply in master's and especially doctoral programs that serve as natural locales for a tight research-teaching-study nexus. From high-school diploma to the doctorate, graduates will increasingly need habits of mind necessary for informed and disciplined problem-solving. For life in an inquiring society, one where information becomes knowledge and knowledge occasionally becomes wisdom, a sense of inquiry and a related research enlightenment may be the best common tools that higher education can offer its graduates.

References

1. Alper, J. "Scientist Return to the Elementary-School Classroom." *Science* 264 (1994): 768–69.
2. Berger, J. *The Young Scientists: America's Future and the Winning of the Westinghouse.* Reading, Mass.: Addison-Wesley, 1994.

3. Bertilsson, M. "From University to Comprehensive Higher Education: On the Widening Gap between '*Lehre und Leben.*'" Stockholm: Council for Studies of Higher Education, 1991.

4. Bruner, J. *The Process of Education.* New York: Vintage Books, 1963.

5. Bruner J. *Toward a Theory of Instruction.* Cambridge, Mass.: Harvard University Press, 1966.

6. Clark, B. R. *The Higher Education System: Academic Organization in Cross-National Perspective.* Berkeley and Los Angeles: University of California Press, 1983.

7. Clark, B. R. *The Academic Life: Small Worlds, Different Worlds.* Princeton, N.J.: Carnegie Foundation for the Advancement of Teaching, 1987.

8. Clark, B. R. (ed.) *The Research Foundations of Graduate Education: Germany, Britain, France, United States, Japan.* Berkeley and Los Angeles: University of California Press, 1993.

9. Clark, B. R. *Places of Inquiry: Research and Advanced Education in Modern Universities.* Berkeley and Los Angeles: University of California Press, 1995.

10. Cohn, M. M., and R. B. Kottkamp, *Teachers: The Missing Voice in Education.* Albany: State University of New York Press, 1993.

11. Cullotta, E. "Science Standard Near Finish Line." *Science* 265 (1984): 1648–50.

12. Fruton, J. S. *Contrasts in Scientific Style: Research Groups in the Chemical and Biochemical Sciences.* Philadelphia: American Philosophical Society, 1990.

13. Geiger, R. L. *To Advance Knowledge: The Growth of American Research Universities, 1900–1940.* New York: Oxford University Press, 1986.

14. Hewstone, M. "Social Psychology." In *The Encyclopedia of Higher Education,* vol. 4: *Academic Disciplines and Indexes,* edited by B. R. Clark and Guy Neave, 2150–63. Oxford: Pergamon Press, 1992.

15. Holmes, F. L. "The Complementarity of Teaching and Research in Liebig's Laboratory." In *Science in Germany: The Intersection of Institutional and Intellectual Issues,* edited by K. M. Olesko, 121–64. Philadelphia: History of Science Society, 1989.

16. Huber, L. "A Field of Uncertainty: Postgraduate Studies in the Federal Republic of Germany." *European Journal of Education* 21 (1986): 287–305.

17. Jungnicke, C., and R. McCormmach. *Intellectual Mastery of Nature: Theoretical Physics from Ohm to Einstein,* vol. 1: *The Torch of Mathematics 1800–1870.* Chicago: University of Chicago Press, 1986.

18. Kanigel, R. *Apprentice to Genius: The Making of a Scientific Dynasty.* New York: Macmillan, 1986.

19. Kolson, K. and D. Yuen. "On Reconciling Teaching and Research." *AAHE Bulletin* 45 (1993): 7–10.
20. Leary, D. E. "Psychology." In *The Encyclopedia of Higher Education,* vol. 4: *Academic Disciplines and Indexes,* edited by B. R. Clark and Guy Neave, 2372–50. Oxford: Pergamon Press, 1992.
21. Madison, B. L. "Mathematics and Statistic." In *The Encyclopedia of Higher Education,* vol. 4: *Academic Disciplines and Indexes,* edited by B. R. Clark and Guy Neave, 2372–88. Oxford: Pergamon Press, 1992.
22. McCaughey, R. A. "But Can They Teach? In Praise of College Professors Who Publish." *Teachers College Record* 95 (1993): 242–56.
23. Metzger, W. P. "The Academic Profession in the United States." In *The Academic Profession: National, Disciplinary, & Institutional Settings,* edited by B. R. Clark, 123–208. Berkeley and Los Angeles: University of California Press, 1987.
24. Morrel, J. B. "Science in the Universities: Some Reconsiderations." In *Solomon's House Revisited: The Organization and Institutionalization of Science,* edited by T. Frangmyr, 51–64. Canton, Mass.: Watson Publishing International, 1990.
25. OECD. *The Future of University Research.* Paris: OECD, 1981.
26. OECD. *Post-Graduate Education in the 1980s.* Paris: OECD, 1987.
27. Olesko, K. M. *Physics as a Calling: Discipline and Practice in the Königsberg Seminar for Physics.* Ithaca, N.Y.: Cornell University Press, 1991.
28. Schaefer, R. J. *The School as a Center of Inquiry.* New York: Harper & Row, 1967.
29. Sizer, T. R. *Horace's Compromise: The Dilemma of the American High School.* Boston: Houghton-Mifflin, 1984.
30. Storr, R. J. *The Beginning of the Future: A Historical Approach to Graduate Education in the Arts and Sciences.* New York: McGraw Hill, 1973.
31. Trow, M. A. "Problems in the Transition from Elite to Mass Higher Education." In *Policies for Higher Education,* 51–101. Paris: OECD, 1974.
32. Van Dijk, H. "History." In *The Encyclopedia of Higher Education,* vol. 4: *Academic Disciplines and Indexes,* edited by B. R. Clark and Guy Neave, 2009–19. Oxford: Pergamon Press, 1992.
33. Von Humboldt, W. "On the Spirit and the Organizational Framework of Intellectual Institutions in Berlin." Translated by Edward Shils. *Minerva* 8 (1970): 242–50.
34. Weaver, F. S. (ed.) *Promoting Inquiry in Undergraduate Learning.* San Francisco: Jossey-Bass, 1989.
35. Zuckerman, H. *Scientific Elite: Nobel Laureates in the United States.* New York: Free Press, 1977.

INTRODUCTION TO CHAPTER 26

Sometime in the mid-1990s I was asked to specify new categories for higher education research. I believe I responded to this charge at a meeting of the Consortium of Higher Education Researchers in Rome (CHER) along with four other senior members of the organization—Ulrich Teichler (Germany), Frans van Vught (Netherlands), Guy Neave (France), and Maurice Kogan (England). Hardly a decade old, this self-selecting, self-conscious group of fifty or so members could be highly contentious at times. This meeting was no exception. The Europeans argued vigorously over the best way to do research: historical approaches, quantitative surveys, and hypothesis-testing were among the methods proposed.

Because I came to the conference with a couple of ideas I wished to promote, I did not get involved in the intra-European squabbles. I was still quite taken with the concept of "substantive growth" brilliantly set forth by Walter Metzger at the Bellagio conference in 1984. Metzger's paper later appeared in *The Academic Profession* (1987), the collection of papers Adele and I edited. Then, too, I also continued to be amazed by fast-moving differentiation of knowledge in one discipline after another, from the physical and biological sciences to the social sciences and humanities. This story emerged as Guy Neave and I were working on volume 4 of *The Encyclopedia of Higher Education* (1992), a volume devoted to the development of disciplines.

Here was ample evidence of an inescapable phenomenon—substantive growth—that shook universities at their very core. Here was a phenomenon begging for attention. The essay offered here was my effort to get other scholars to pay attention to it.

An enormous, worldwide growth in knowledge, in and around universities, I soon reasoned, would make some universities quicker on their feet. Innovative organization would surely result. What we needed to do

424

was to study this second phenomenon. And I was already doing just that. Beginning in 1994, I was actively engaged in field research that led to the books and papers that are featured in part IV. I aimed to search for—and encourage others to search for—the armature, the organizational tools of change.

CHAPTER 26

Substantive Growth and Innovative Organization:

New Categories for Higher Education Research

DURING THE PAST THREE decades, the growing international literature in the study of higher education has largely centered on three
large areas of concern: the transition from elite to mass higher education;
the changing relationship between governments and universities, with attendant concerns of university governance and authority; and the integration and differentiation of higher education systems. We now know
a great deal about these broad issues. The development of mass higher
education has been widely tracked. Its role in expanding the size of institutions and systems, swelling budgets, increasing popular involvement,
and stimulating governmental interest has been duly noted. The place of
government in university affairs has been extensively pursued, virtually
on an annual basis, with governments portrayed as moving closer during
one period and stepping back in another as they vary their approaches to
resource allocation, audit, accountability, and assessment. We now know
that governments and universities are not "partners." They are two parties with different interests and priorities that sometimes converge and
sometimes sharply conflict. In turn, system differentiation and integration
have become the concern of much research. As they grow larger and more
complex, national systems generally create new types of institutions and
additional degree levels, thereby differentiating personnel, resources, and
clienteles. But many systems at the same time also seek to maintain or
create unified administrative frameworks in order to subordinate status

"Substantive Growth and Innovative Organization: New Categories for Higher
Education Research," *Higher Education* 32 (1996): 417–30. Used with kind permission of Springer Science and Business Media.

differences and simplify system organization. Together, the above three concerns have fixated attention on student inputs and graduate outputs, governmental agendas, and the nature of the institutional fabric of entire national systems.

Now institutionalized in the interests of sponsors and researchers in a large number of countries, these issues will remain for the foreseeable future a standard part of the international research agenda. Thus composed, however, the agenda has a strong downside. For one, it is set too much by the interests of sponsoring government. Relatedly, it attends too much to the surface of current events, particularly to passing debates about formal policies and the enactment of laws. Largely pursuing macro trends and structures, it has undervalued micro dynamics and determinants. Notably, without a serious weighing of alternative explanations, the developed research agenda assumes that the shift from elite to mass participation—student expansion—has been the primary twentieth-century trend in changing the nature of universities and academic work. That assumption in particular leads research away from a host of critical features. Much of the essential story about the development of higher education is left out. Overall, the current main lines of research amount to an unbalanced agenda that may increasingly mislead researchers and research-informed practitioners.

Let us look at what else must not be left out. What is so basic that when overlooked it will cause all understanding to be distorted? One answer is the disciplinary dimension of universities and systems, a line of influence that has its own determinants and wide-ranging effects that shape higher education institutions from bottom to top. Knowledge organization in the form of self-augmenting subjects is an independent force, one that increasingly operates internationally. Its development often runs counter to student demands. It presents governments with ongoing problems of oversight and steerage that are only partially solvable. It increasingly complicates university organization and presents hard choices in institutional policy. We need to know much more about knowledge expansion, especially as it interacts with student expansion.

A second answer is the growing importance of internal university organization. As they grow more complex, national systems generally find they must decentralize authority to individual institutions and then somehow create conditions that encourage the institutions to become proactive, self-determining enterprises. Here we enter the realm of institutional flexibility and innovation, new organizational forms and environmental relations, reconciliation of newly strengthened administrative values with traditional academic values, and niche-building in competitive supranational orbits of universities. We need to know much more about universities as organizational actors and how they go about changing their ways.

Thus the agenda for this essay: to stake out the two topics of substantive academic growth and innovative university organization.

Substantive Academic Growth

To better identify the disciplinary dimension as a commanding category for future research, I first explore the proliferating base of academic knowledge, highlighting the concept of substantive growth. Subsidiary sections then argue that substantive growth and mass higher education are frequently in conflict, and that an understanding of universities as primarily places of inquiry points to the widespread existence of, and growing value of, inquiry-based teaching and learning. The knowledge base of higher education offers interesting possibilities in a fast-changing world of reconciling research specialization with the growing need for a population of problem-solvers.

THE PROLIFERATING BASE OF ACADEMIC KNOWLEDGE

We have known for some time that a national system of higher education is a grand matrix of dual locations in which an academic belongs to a subject and to an institution, with professional identity based increasingly throughout the nineteenth and twentieth centuries on a discipline, or a disciplinary subspecialty, or occasionally on an interdisciplinary subject that in time becomes a new specialty (Clark, 1983, 28–34). The two basic commitments of the academic worker mean that disciplinary and institutional modes of linkage converge in the basic units of universities, the primary working groups of the academic world. The core membership unit is discipline-centered, even as it operates as an arm of a particular university. The historical story of disciplines is one of unrelenting generation of new fields and specialties, with a growing rate of change, while the contemporary picture is one of intense specialization that on a worldwide scale is uncontrollable. Disciplinary differentiation is many times greater than institutional differentiation.

In an overview of how new disciplines emerged in American higher education during the course of the nineteenth and early twentieth centuries, Walter Metzger has provided a rich account conceptualized as "substantive growth" (Metzger, 1987, 126–47). Metzger identified four processes that lead to this form of growth: *subject parturition*, in which new fields are born out of older ones, such as chemistry, geology, astronomy, physics, and biology out of such mother fields as natural philosophy and natural history; *program affiliation* and *subject dignification*, in which formerly excluded fields are admitted to the family of legitimate subjects, as, e.g., such professional fields as medicine and law and such previously low-rated fields as modern languages and technology in the United States; and *subject dispersion*, in which a field extends its coverage, such as the field of history constantly spreading its wings to cover more eras, locales, and activities. Metzger has shown that these processes sped up dramatically after 1880. The gestation period for new subjects became shorter and shorter; subject dignification ran amok; and subject dispersion, as we can now observe in anthropology, economics, psychology, and sociology in the social sciences, has become a virtually genetic form of subject imperialism and aggrandizement.

By the beginning of the twentieth century, American academic commentators were pointing to "the explosion of human knowledge" as a master key in explaining massive changes taking place in higher education. One college president turned historian put it quite simply: "As knowledge has grown, the course itself has grown. Every enlargement of the domain of knowledge has ultimately resulted in the enlargement of the academic field" (Metzger, 1987, 133). But the relationship has not been simply one-way, with quantum-of-knowledge driving the academy. Rather, the academy has been an increasingly active agent in expanding knowledge. A more secularized faculty was more receptive to new and varied forms of knowledge. More important across nations, two other trends worked in close concert: the institutionalization of academic research and the organization of academic specialties (Metzger, 1987, 134–37). As research became a primary academic activity, academics produced knowledge systematically and in increasingly large quantities. As academic specialties became organized within universities as the building blocks of organization, in the form of departments and research institutes, and organized externally as learned or disciplinary associations— national in membership and specialized in scope—they became interest groups that systematically promoted the expansion of research and the growth of knowledge. Increasingly well-muscled in organizational forms, the research imperative became in the twentieth century the primary source of substantive growth.

The nineteenth century takeoff in the substantive growth of universities occurred earlier and on a much larger scale in German higher education than in the American system or elsewhere. From 1820 onward, new disciplinarians in the German academic world were hard at work developing teaching-research laboratories and teaching-research seminars to maximize the research productivity of their own clusters and research training within them. The perceived capability of individual basic units and whole universities became increasingly based on research prowess (McClelland, 1980, 187–255). In a radically decentralized political system of nearly forty sovereign states (in the pre-unified German territories), higher education ministers promoted this change as they competitively sought to build their own universities by seeking out and rewarding first-class research talent (Ben-David, 1977, 97–103). A growing governmental interest in notable scholarship helped to propel a major expansion based on growth in knowledge before enlarged consumer demand appeared on the scene. While student numbers increased very little during the half-century between 1820 and 1870, the funding of research dramatically increased. Ministers fed the funds directly to the research-centered institutes and seminars that were controlled by the new disciplinarians, bypassing the traditional professors who could exercise a conservative hand.

Thus, substantive growth set the basic shape of the first national set of research universities. When enlarged consumer demand came along after 1870 in Germany, it was the research-structured university that became organizationally enlarged.

For the late twentieth-century picture, recent research has offered highly useful perspectives and data on the proliferating base of academic knowledge. Pursuing departments as tribes attached to territories—cognitive territories—Tony Becher, Mary Henkel, and Maurice Kogan have reported a bewildering variety of academic cultures that attach to major specialties within disciplines as well as to entire fields of study (Becher, 1989; Becher, Henkel, and Kogan, 1994). Researchers in Japan, the United States, Germany, Britain, and France found in a five-coutnry study of graduate education and academic research that the number and variety of disciplines, specialties, and inter- or multidisciplinary subjects everywhere steadily increases (Clark, 1993; Clark, 1995a, b). The *Encyclopedia of Higher Education* (Clark and Neave, 1992), in a volume devoted to disciplines, reported the development of academic fields that ranged from classics and linguistics to neurobiology and computer science. The disciplinary essays offered shattering facts about the arcane worlds of the disciplines. For example: in mathematics, 200,000 new theorems are published each year, periodicals exceed 1,000, and review journals have developed a classification scheme that includes over 4,500 subtopics arranged under 62 major topic areas (Madison, 1992). In history, the output of literature in the two decades of 1960–80 was apparently equal in magnitude to all that was published from the time of the Greek historian Thucydides in the fourth century BC to the year 1960 (van Dijk, 1992). In psychology, 45 major specialties appear in the structure of the American Psychological Association, and one of these specialties, social psychology, reports that it is now comprised of 17 subfields (Leary, 1992; Hewstone, 1992). And the beat goes on. In the mid-1990s, those who track the field of chemistry were reporting that "more articles on chemistry have been published in the past 2 years than throughout history before 1900." *Chemical Abstracts* took 31 years to publish its first 1 million abstracts, 18 years for its second million, and less than 2 years for its most recent million. An exponential growth of about 4 to 8 percent annually, with a doubling period of 10 to 15 years, is now seen as characteristic of most branches of science (Noam, 1995).

When disciplines are grouped in major sets, "the medical sciences" are increasingly seen as a separate group alongside of, rather than subsumed under, "the biological sciences." Those who specialize in molecular biology or neurobiology are cognitively a long way from those now working in such specialties as immunology and pharmacology. A fast-growing set of "engineering sciences" has taken up residence alongside the "physical sciences." An expert in astronomy might know what time it is in space but she will not know the time of day in materials engineering. With so many important academic specialties available for coverage, the disciplinary volume of the *Encyclopedia* could have appropriately grown from forty to sixty or eighty essays. But even as it stands the volume offers an education in how fields emerge, grow, subdivide, and recombine.

Processes of subject parturition and subject dispersion are everywhere at work. The ongoing differentiation of subjects runs ahead of our imagination, let alone our empirical grasp, about what is going on within the knowledge foundations of higher education and indeed of intellectual life generally. Disciplinary fragmentation is arguably *the* source of ever-growing system complexity, a source more powerful in its effects than the expanded inputs of students and the more varied outputs to the labor force on which we generally concentrate when observing the scale and scope of modern universities and national systems of higher education. Notably, decisions about the inclusion and exclusion of various disciplines, and of various specialties within them, and of how to group disciplines in multidisciplinary and interdisciplinary arrays, loom large in institutional differentiation. In short: academic territories are first of all subject territories, even while they are clientele territories and labor market territories.

How do we go about studying substantive growth? We can track it over long periods of time by pursuing developments along discernible lines of university and disciplinary organization:

1. growth of basic units (departments and non-departmental academic units), in particular, universities by subject, and then by university and national system of subject
2. growth of types of courses, majors, and degrees, by university and national system
3. growth and substructuring of disciplinary associations within national systems, noting in particular their role in spanning the boundaries of universities and national systems
4. growth of disciplinary journals and article production
5. growth of recognized research topics and related research clusters

Simple mapping along such lines can lead straight on into more subtle inquiries, field by field, that allow close assessment of Metzger's processes (and other processes) of substantive growth. In so doing we will learn much, e.g., about how systems of higher education relate to their environment. Are they largely isolated from the general society? Do they have major parts that are interfused with outside groups? When we bring regional, national, and international disciplinary associations into view we find that they increasingly span both the formal boundaries of universities and the entire higher education system (Clark, 1987, 233–54). Members come from different universities and from inside and outside the academy. Academics and nonacademics freely and regularly associate with one another. In such subjects as chemistry and the engineering sciences, the vast majority of participants in the discipline, including its researchers, are located outside in non-university settings. Thus, boundary spanning in academic systems seems more a matter of the nature of different disciplines, and of the bottom-up changing interests of disciplinarians, than it is a matter of student numbers or governmental edicts or overall administrative control.

When we concentrate on subject-centered forms of organization in higher education, we find "splinteritis" everywhere, not only in the biological and medical sciences where the rate of change is currently the highest but throughout the other sciences, the social sciences, and the humanities. Self-amplifying substantive growth continues to divide higher education into small worlds, different worlds. The problems thereby presented for university management and change are increasingly severe, in many cases surpassing the magnitude of the problems introduced by increased access and the need to educate a much larger number and greater variety of students.

In sum: alongside the study of student expansion we need to place the study of knowledge expansion. Alongside the trend from elite to mass higher education we need to place the trend from simple to complex knowledge. The basic problems for the future are seemingly more set by the growing complexity of knowledge than they are by the growing complexity of student aggregations. The differentiation of knowledge also plays a primary role in the growing complexity of academic and outside labor markets.

SUBSTANTIVE GROWTH VERSUS MASS HIGHER EDUCATION

Substantive growth can be distinguished in a useful dichotomy from *reactive growth*—growth in faculty, facilities, and system size that principally follows from increases in student numbers we associate with the concept of mass higher education. Interaction between these two forms of growth clearly takes place: they often coexist and feed upon one another. But one may proceed while the other stalls. The pressure of substantive growth seemingly never ceases, while student enrollments sometimes level off and even decline. Most interesting is the possibility that substantive and reactive growth are often so much in conflict that they set painful systemic dilemmas for higher education.

Simply stated, substantive growth is knowledge-led and generated largely by research, while reactive growth is student demand–led and generated by student enrollment. Faculty are intensely tuned to substantive growth, while system officials and university administrators are obliged to give high priority to coping with student expansion and to governmental and popular interest in increased access. Substantive growth leads to more esoteric academic specialties that organizationally become elite enclaves; reactive growth demands mass structures and a great expansion of remedial, introductory, and intermediate teaching. Substantive growth encourages the development of advanced degrees and graduate programs; reactive growth greatly expands lower degrees and undergraduate education. Substantive growth becomes the principal "demand" on one set of institutions in a differentiated national system, while reacting to consumer demand becomes the primary influence in another set: e.g., in the American system, a hundred research universities, particularly private ones, at the one extreme, and 1,400 community colleges at the other.

Notably, research-centered universities that can limit their size do not have to worry about reactive growth. They leave that form of reaction to other institutions. They are positioned to take a more selective slice of faculty and student talent. What they do worry about, year by year, department by department, is whether they are making the right choices in their recruitment and research support within various fields and whether they are moving ahead, standing still, or falling behind in substantive capability relative to other universities and non-university enterprises.

RESEARCH-BASED TEACHING AND LEARNING

Mindful of substantive growth and its primary role in shaping universities, we can learn much in future research by drawing the main faultline in faculty activities not between research and teaching but between research-based teaching and learning and teaching and learning based on already codified materials (Clark, 1995a, b). In many national systems of higher education, particularly at the most advanced levels, much teaching and learning is essentially accomplished by direct engagement in research and by preparatory training closely related to ongoing research, e.g., in laboratory and seminar groups, student dissertations, and courses in research methods. At the same time, much teaching and learning must be based on an ever-expanding base of accumulated knowledge, e.g., in introductory lectures and didactic classroom settings in which teachers expound on the wisdom of the ages or pass on standardized disciplinary knowledge. Both forms are essential in modern higher education. But many observers grasp only the latter form of teaching and learning, particularly as it appears in introductory or undergraduate education. Research and teaching are then often viewed as incompatible. Time spent on one is time withdrawn from the other.

However, when the first form is grasped and kept in view, research and teaching are seen as highly compatible. From Australia to Finland, academic opinion research finds that university professors overwhelmingly assert this compatibility. And when we note that students are directly involved, we can speak of a research-teaching-study nexus that is an invaluable component of modern research universities. While the heartland of research-based teaching and learning has tended everywhere to shift from the undergraduate to the graduate level, immersion in research activity remains a highly appropriate form of undergraduate instruction and even, increasingly it seems, in elementary and secondary education. Modern nations increasingly need a wide network of inquiring minds. What better way to prepare problem-solvers than to have them learn by means of inquiry? We should expect a growing tide of educational reform to be based on student involvement in research-based activity.

Substantive growth in academic systems can be highlighted in two broad propositions:

1. The more advanced the knowledge base of a *national system* of higher education, the more it is driven by knowledge expansion. Propelled by the research imperative, the knowledge base is considerably self-accelerating. The larger and deeper this resource, the greater is the self-propulsion. The dynamic of "the

more, the more" is heavily at work, leading to an expanding knowledge gap between highly developed nations and most developing societies. The growing gap comes from the competitive advantage of strong knowledge production.

2. The more advanced the knowledge base of a *university*, the more it is driven by knowledge expansion. The dynamic of the more, the more leads to a growing knowledge gap between leading research universities and non-research-based segments of the higher education system. The competitive advantage of strong knowledge production also obtains.

National systems of higher education and individual universities within them need to be increasingly self-conscious about how to best cope with knowledge expansion, the disadvantages of the knowledge gap, and the advantages of strong knowledge production. The question of how to best cope with substantive growth leads straight on to the next category for future higher education research.

Innovative University Organization

The second topic that should become a major category for higher education research in the near future is organizational change. Change that involves an overall adaptation of universities is much on the agenda of practitioners, and there is ample reason to think that the problem is systemic. The rate of change in key parts of the societal environment of universities steadily increases, e.g., in the service sector of the economy. The higher education sector itself is subject to the steady pounding of knowledge growth and its induced rapid change in subjects that I have earlier emphasized, as well as to the need to accommodate new types of students and changing relations with job markets, the features of modern higher education that I have subsumed under the concept of reactive growth. Finally, there seems little doubt that the situation of individual universities within the higher education complex is becoming more competitive, within national systems and especially across national lines. Universities have to be more entrepreneurial, in a word, more capable of finding new ways to proceed that can be mixed with traditional procedures. The topic of institutional transformation may be seen to have both theoretical and practical import. How do universities, as organizations, go about changing their ways, even their overall character? What are the essential tools in various national contexts and across national systems by which universities become innovative organizations?

I initiated a small study during 1994–95 designed to explore this topic on the European scene. Case studies of five universities in five different national settings are under way, entailing repeated visits over a two-year period. The institutions selected are reputedly entrepreneurial/innovative in their national context and have developed that character over a period of five to ten years or more. They are the University of Twente in The Netherlands, the University of Warwick in England, Chalmers University in Sweden, Strathclyde University in Scotland, and the University of Joensuu in Finland (Clark, 1995b; Clark, 1996).

Amid the many peculiarities and uniquenesses of the individual institutions, I am attempting to identify common organizational features that may be conceptualized as "essential elements" in the formation of the entrepreneurial/innovative university. Five leading ideas used at the outside to give some tentative structure to interviews, observations, and document analysis have given way, midstream in the research, to four tentatively identified elements. A critical feature of these elements is that they are heavily interactive, growing in strength in a spiraling circle of definition and support over a decade or so.

In brief review, the first element is an innovative self-defining institutional idea—an ambitious vision, we might call it. The idea or vision, gradually worked out, becomes a significant feature, however, only when it is effected in specific organizational structures and processes. Thus a second element is a strengthened and better integrated administrative core, a central group or small set of central groups that acts on behalf of the institution as a whole while also reaching down into the organization to connect to basic units. A central problem here is to reconcile new managerial attitudes with traditional academic perspectives. The evidence from the case studies thus far indicates it can be done.

A third important element is a funding base that frees up discretionary funds. Such funds are sometimes fashioned within mainline institutional channels of support (where trusting governments are again ready "to leave the money on the stump"), but discretionary income is most dependably fashioned in second and third funding lines in which the institution goes out and gets money from research councils and from a plethora of "private" or nontraditional sources. As governments retrench in their mainline support of universities (as share of total support), "hard money" goes soft, while ostensibly soft sources together become a new form of hard money. The central managerial group uses the newly won discretionary money to fund new ventures and to strengthen selectively the things the university would like to carry forward from the past to the future.

The third piece of necessary infrastructure, constituting a fourth element, is a developmental periphery—a set of organizational programs and specific operational units, largely but not wholly outside the traditional departments, that fashion new environmental relationships as they flexibly reach outside old boundaries. Units in the developmental periphery reach out to city councils, professional associations, and, preeminently, business firms. They are often involved in continuing/recurrent education of professionals. They help graduates to start firms, and then help them to develop those firms. They may even enter directly into product development and get in the business of providing venture capital. In European settings, some units in the university developmental periphery have experts knowledgeable in the bureaucratic ways of the European Union, including a capacity to translate "Euro-speak" into a clear language that researchers at the home institution can understand. When a middle-size European university in the mid-1990s has a hundred European Community–funded projects, there is reason to think that uncommon entrepreneurship is being exercised.

Beyond the above four elements, set forth in a 1995 progress report on my research (Clark, 1996), a fifth possible essential element yet to be explored is a "stimulated heartland"—an activation of the traditional basic units of the university in which the new organizational vision and the new organizational ways become widely embodied in the university at large. Beyond strengthened administration, more discretionary funding, and a useful developmental periphery, the whole entrepreneurial effort must sink into and come to characterize the traditional departments and faculties. They too become more willing and capable to "get up and go," to seek new sources of support, to actively expand old ones, and to make hard decisions locally on what new and old features to invest in and what ones to diminish or avoid. Self-management that is entrepreneurial in nature in the basic units notably entails selective substantive growth:

selective support of "steeples" among departmental research specialties and instructional programs; selective support of substantive weaknesses that should be turned into strengths; and selective elimination of cognitive territories that ought not or cannot be turned into strengths. Whatever the final conceptualization of this fifth element, it will clearly need to encompass the fusion of traditional academic outlooks with the new administrative capability of the innovative university.

This brief review of some ideas gained midstream in a research project is offered as an example of how research on innovative university organization can go forward. Now more than ever we need to understand universities in many nations as potentially active agents. Why do some become quite active, to the point of self-renewal, while others do not? When authority is decentralized from government to university, as recently occurred in a number of European countries, some institutions seize the organizational moment while others do not. Institutional ambition matters. Implementing ambition by means of effective organizational tools matters a great deal. We can learn much about modern university life by studying why some universities become strongly change oriented and how they then explore new things that might come to be useful as well as more effectively exploit what they already know how to do.

Conclusion

A focus on universities as knowledge-based institutions driven by substantive growth leads finally to an ultimate issue: is it possible that the virtual explosion in information and knowledge that has occurred during the past half-century might produce an increase in wisdom in the twenty-first century? If we can move from information to knowledge, can we on occasion move from knowledge to wisdom—to an enhanced capacity to use knowledge in an informed and discerning fashion and thereby to select the best ends and means in a wide range of activities? An organizational perspective applied to an evermore complex world suggests that increases in wisdom will not stem primarily from solitary charismatic figures or a few great minds rising up from lonely contemplation to offer large insights. Instead, sustainable wisdom will more likely follow from the ways that some productive, collective enterprises go about organizing themselves to engage selectively in the proliferating base of knowledge.

In universities, the selective efforts include recombinations of old fields as well as risk-taking investment in new fields. Such only partially conscious reworkings of the knowledge base, operating in a context of ever greater scale and scope, may offer more opportunities to make small breakthroughs in the centering of knowledge, both generalized breakthroughs that integrate whole bodies of arcane materials and a continuous stream of specialized breakthroughs that enlarge the circle of knowledge with small salients into the unknown.

Future wisdom, it seems, achieved in small steps, will be both more multitudinous and collective. It is less likely to come in the form of large shifts in paradigms and more likely to consist of incremental gains in understanding the present and estimating the future. An ever-widening band of inquiry, supplemented by inquiry-based teaching and learning in a wide range of topics, may not produce another Aristotle, but it offers the possibility of an extended democracy of inquirers out of which wiser understandings and choices can more abundantly flow.

At the least, those who study higher education across the nations of the world should seek to better understand the relationship between knowledge and wisdom under conditions of ever greater complexity. Required is much research that produces knowledge about the conditions and effects of knowledge as it is variously produced, integrated, and distributed. As part of that effort, we need to know more about universities as learning organizations in which self-assessment and self-regulation lead to cycles of self-enhancement. Organizational imagination based on self-knowledge is surely superior to imagination based on organizational ignorance. More than at present, effectively organized universities can be places of instructed imagination in which knowledge about how better to reorganize knowledge leads to better uses of knowledge. Perhaps we will find that certain ways of organizing knowledge offer the possibility of sustained insight, even to the point of a systematic claim on wisdom.

References

Becher, T. *Academic Tribes and Territories: Intellectual Enquiry and the Cultures of Disciplines*. Milton Keynes: Society for Research into Higher Education and Open University Press, 1989.

Becher, T., M. Henkel, and M. Kogan. *Graduate Education in Britain*. London: Jessica Kingsley, 1994.

Ben-David, J. *Centers of Learning: Britain, France, Germany, United States*. New York: McGraw-Hill, 1977.

Clark, B. R. *The Higher Education System: Academic Organization in Cross-National Perspective*. Berkeley and Los Angeles: University of California Press, 1983.

———. *The Academic Life: Small Worlds, Different Worlds*. Princeton: The Carnegie Foundation for the Advancement of Teaching and Princeton University Press, 1987.

———, ed. *The Research Foundations of Graduate Education: Germany, Britain, France, United States, Japan*. Berkeley and Los Angeles: University of California Press, 1993.

———. *Places of Inquiry: Research and Advanced Education in Modern Universities*. Berkeley and Los Angeles: University of California Press, 1995a.

———. "Leadership and Innovation in Universities: From Theory to Practice." *Tertiary Education and Management* 1, no. 1 (1995b): 7–11.

———. "Case Studies of Innovative Universities: A Progress Report." *Tertiary Education and Management* 2, no. 1 (1996): 53–62.

Clark, B. R. and G. Neave, eds. *The Encyclopedia of Higher Education*. Vol. 4. Oxford: Pergamon Press. 1992.

Hewstome, M. "Social Psychology." In *The Encyclopedia of Higher Education*, edited by B. R. Clark and G. Neave, 4:2150–63. Oxford: Pergamon Press, 1992.

Leary, D. E. "Psychology." In *The Encyclopedia of Higher Education*, edited by B. R. Clark and G. Neave, 4:2136–50. Oxford: Pergamon Press, 1992.

Madison, B. L. "Mathematics and Statistics." In *The Encyclopedia of Higher Education*, edited by B. R. Clark and G. Neave, 4:2372–88. Oxford: Pergamon Press, 1992.

McClelland, C. E. *State, Society, and University in Germany, 1700–1914*. Cambridge: Cambridge University Press, 1980.

Metzger, W. P. "The Academic Profession in the United States." In *The Academic Profession: National, Disciplinary, and Institutional Settings*, edited by B. R. Clark, 123–208. Berkeley and Los Angeles: University of California Press, 1987.

Noam, E. M. "Electronics and the Dim Future of the University." *Science* 270 (1995): 247–49.

van Dijk, H. "History." In *The Encyclopedia of Higher Education*, edited by B. R. Clark and G. Neave, 4:2009–19. Oxford: Pergamon Press, 1992.

INTRODUCTION TO CHAPTER 27

The invitation to contribute to a *Daedalus* volume in the mid-1990s was attractive. After having written papers, I and other participants would take part in a small, focused meeting in Cambridge to critique each other's rough drafts—all expenses paid. It meant a chance to reach a large audience of intelligent readers. And it gave me one more shot to write about differentiation in the American academic profession—this strange one-of-a-kind profession of professions, one broken up by disciplinary and institutional locations into thousands of different, small worlds. My paper pressed three arguments: that across the dispersed professoriate more academics teach too much rather than too little; that more of them are increasingly marginalized in part-time assignments; and that increasing political and bureaucratic controls denigrate the intrinsic rewards of this kind of work.

This essential but peculiar profession of professions can be improved neither by top-down state controls nor by the vagaries of drifting markets. My focus on "uniqueness and troubles" ends with a call for more attention to "the conditions of professional inspiration and self-regulation."

Intelligent planners, state officials, and university administrators put their money on intrinsic academic rewards.

CHAPTER 27

Small Worlds, Different Worlds:

The Uniquenesses and Troubles of American Academic Professions

THE ACADEMIC PROFESSION is a multitude of academic tribes and territories.[1] As in days of old, it is law, medicine, and theology. It is now also higher-energy physics, molecular biology, Renaissance literature, childhood learning, and computer science. Built upon a widening array of disciplines and specialties, it hosts subcultures that speak in the strange tongues of econometrics, biochemistry, ethnomethodology, and deconstructionism. Driven by a research imperative that rewards specialization, its fragmentation is slowed, though not fully arrested, by limited resources to fund all the new and old lines of effort in which academics would like to engage. Already very great, knowledge growth builds in a self-amplifying fashion. Subject differentiation follows not in train, not least in a national system of universities and colleges, such as the American, that is both hugely based on research and generously inclusive in adding subjects to the now-endless list of what legitimately can be taught. As subjects fragment, so does the academic profession, turning it evermore into a profession of professions.

No less important in the differentiation of the academic profession in America is the dispersion of faculty among institutions in a system that, when viewed internationally, must be seen as inordinately large, radically decentralized, extremely diversified, uniquely competitive and uncommonly entrepreneurial. A high degree of institutional dispersion positions American faculty in many varied sectors of a national "sys-

"Small Worlds, Different Worlds: The Uniquenesses and Troubles of American Academic Professions," *Daedalus* (Fall 1997): 21–42. © 1997 by the American Academy of Arts and Sciences. Used by permission.

tem" that totaled 3,600 institutions in the mid-1990s: 100-plus "research universities" of high research intensity; another 100 "doctoral-granting" universities that grant only a few doctorates and operate off a small research base; 500 and more "master's colleges and universities," a catch-all category of private and public institutions that have graduate as well as undergraduate programs, offering master's degrees but not doctorates; still another 600 "baccalaureate colleges," heavily private and varying greatly in quality and in degree of concentration on the liberal arts; a huge array of over 1,400 2-year colleges, 95 percent public in enrollment, whose individual comprehensiveness includes college-transfer programs, short-term vocational offering, and adult education; and finally a leftover miscellany of some 700 "specialized institutions" that do not fit into the above basic categories.[2]

These major categories in turn contain much institutional diversity. Buried within them are historically black colleges, Catholic universities, women's colleges, fundamentalist religious universities and colleges, and such distinctive institutions as the Julliard School (of Music), the Bank Street College of Education, and Rockefeller University. The American faculty is distributed institutionally all over the map, located in the educational equivalents of the farm and the big city, the ghetto and the suburbs, the darkened ravine located next to a coal mine and the sunny hill overlooking a lovely valley.

Disciplinary and institutional locations together compose the primary matrix of induced and enforced differences among American academics. These two internal features of the system itself are more important than such background characteristics of academics as class, race, religion, and gender in determining work-centered thought and behavior. These primary dimensions convert simple statements about "the professor" in "the college" or "the university" into stereotypes. We deceive ourselves every time we speak of *the* college professor, a common habit among popular critics of the professoriate who fail to talk to academics in their varied locations and to listen to what they say. Simple summary figures and averages extracted from survey, e.g., "68 percent of American professors like their mothers" or "On the average, American professors teach eight and a half hours a week," also should be avoided. Understanding begins with a willingness to pursue diversity.

Different Worlds, Small Worlds

The disciplinary creation of different academic worlds becomes more striking with each passing year. In the leading universities, the clinical professor of medicine is as much a part of the basic workforce as the professor of English. The medical academic might be found in a cancer ward, interacting intensively with other doctors, nurses, orderlies, laboratory assistants, a few students perhaps, and many patients in a round of tightly scheduled activities that can begin at six in the morning and extend into the evenings and weekends. Such academics are often under considerable pressure to generate income from patient-care revenues; their faculty groups negotiate with third-party medical plans and need a sizable administrative staff to handle patient billing. Salaries may well depend on group income, which fluctuates from year to year and is directly affected by changes in the health care industry and the competitive position of a particular medical school–hospital complex. Even in a tenured post, salary may not be guaranteed. Sizable research grants must be actively and repetitively pursued; those who do not raise funds from research grants will find themselves encumbered with more clinical duties.

The humanities professor in the leading universities operates in a totally different environment. To begin with, teaching "loads" are in the range of four to six hours a week, office hours are at one's discretion, and administrative assignments vary considerably with one's willingness to cooperate. The humanities academic typically interacts with large numbers of beginning students in introductory classes in lecture halls; with small numbers of juniors and seniors in specialized upper-division courses; and with a few graduate students in seminars and dissertation supervision around such highly specialized topics as Elizabethan lyric and Icelandic legend. Much valuable work time can be spent at home, away from the "distractions" of the university office.

About what is the humanities academic thinking and writing? Attention may center on a biography of Eugene O'Neill, an interpretation of what Jane Austen really meant, an effort to trace Lillian Hellman's political passions, or a critique of Jacques Derrida and deconstructionism. Professors seek to master a highly specialized segment of literature and maximize individual interpretation. The interests of humanities professors are reflected not only in the many sections and byways of such omnibus associations as the Modern Language Association but also in the specificities of the Shakespeare Association of America, the Dickens Society, the D. H. Lawrence Society of North America, the Speech Association of America, the Thomas Hardy Society of America, and the Vladimir Nabokov Society. Tocqueville's famous comment on the propensity of Americans to form voluntary associations is nowhere more true than in the academic world.

Disciplinary differences are of course not limited to the sharp contrast between life in a medical school and in a department of English. The work of Tony Becher and others on the cultures of individual disciplines has shown that bodies of knowledge variously determine the behavior of individuals and deparments.[3] Disciplines exhibit discernible differences in individual behavior and group action, notably between "hard" and "soft" subjects and "pure" and "applied" fields: in a simple fourfold classification, between hard-pure (physics), hard-applied (engineering), soft-pure (history), and soft-applied (social work). Across the many fields of the physical sciences, the biological sciences, the social sciences, the humanities, and the arts, face-to-face research reveals varied work assignments, symbols of identity, modes of authority, career lines, and associational linkages. Great differences in the academic life often appear between letters and science departments and the many professional school domains in which a concern for the ways and needs of an outside profession must necessarily be combined with the pursuit of science and truth for its own sake. The popular images of Mr. Chips chatting up undergraduates and Einsteinian, white-haired, remote scholars dreaming up esoteric mathematical equations are a far cry from the realities of academic work that helps prepare schoolteachers, librarians, social workers, engineers, computer experts, architects, nurses, pharmacists, business managers, lawyers, and doctors—and, in some academic locales, also morticians, military personnel, auto mechanics, airport technicians, secretaries, lathe operators, and cosmetologists. For over a century, American higher education has been generous to a fault in admitting former outside fields, and new occupations, into the academy—a point made by historians of higher education and of the professions.[4]

Because research is the first priority of leading universities, the disciplinary differentiation of every modern system of higher education is self-amplifying. The American system is currently the extreme case of this phenomenon. Historic decentralization and competitiveness prompted Charles William Eliot at Harvard and others at the old colleges of the last half of the nineteenth century to speed up the nascent evolution from the age of the college to the age of the university. This evolution turned professors loose to pursue specialized research and to teach specialized subjects at the newly created graduate level, even as students were turned loose to pick and choose from an array of undergraduate courses that was to become ever more bewildering. Throughout the twentieth century and especially in the past fifty years, the reward system of promoting academics on the grounds of research and published scholarship has become more deeply rooted in the universities (and would-be universities and leading four-year colleges) with almost every passing decade. The many proliferating specialties of the knowledge-producing disciplines are like tributaries flowing into a mammoth river of the research imperative.

The most serious operational obstacles to this research-driven amplification are the limitations of funding and the institutional need to teach undergraduates and beginning graduate students the codified introductory knowledge of the various fields. There also remains in American higher education the long-standing belief in the importance of liberal or general education—a task, we may note, that Europeans largely assign to secondary schools. The saving remnant of academics who uphold the banner of liberal and general education are able to sally forth in full cry periodically—the 1920s, the late 1940s, the 1990s—to group some specialties into more general courses, narrow the options in distribution requirements from, say, four hundred to a hundred courses, insist that teaching take priority over research, and in general raise a ruckus about the dangers of the specialized mind. Meanwhile, promotion committees on campus continue their steady scrutiny of individual records of research-based scholarship. Central administrators work to build an institutional culture of first-rateness, as it is defined competitively across the nation and the world according to the reputations of noted scholars and departments. Sophisticated general educators and liberal-arts proponents in the universities recognize the primacy of the substantive impulse and learn how to work incrementally within its limits.

INSTITUTIONAL DIFFERENTIATION

As powerful as self-amplifying disciplinary differences have become in dividing the American professoriate, institutional diversity now plays an even more important role. This axis of differentiation places approximately two-thirds of American academics in settings other than that of doctoral-granting universities. We find about a fourth of the total faculty in the colleges and universities that offer degree work as far as the master's; a small share, about 7 percent, in the liberal arts colleges; and a major bloc of a third or so (over 250,000) in the nearly 1,500 community colleges.[5] In student numbers in 1994, the universities had just 26 percent of the total enrollment; the master's level institutions, 21 percent; the baccalaureate colleges, 7 percent; the specialized institutions, 4 percent; and the community colleges, 43 percent—by far the largest share.[6] The two-year colleges admit over 50 percent of entering students. It is no secret that academics in this latter section do an enormous amount of this work of the system at large.

These major locales exhibit vast differences in the very basis of academic life, namely, the balance of effort between undergraduate teaching and advanced research and research training. Teaching loads in the leading universities come in at around 4 to 6 hours a week, occasionally tapering down to 2 to 3 hours—a class a week, a seminar a week—while sometimes, especially in the humanities, rising above 6. The flip side is that faculty commonly expect to spend at least half their time in research, alone or in the company of graduate students, other faculty, and research staff. We need not stray very far among the institutional types, however, before we encounter teaching loads that are 50, 100, and 200 percent higher. The "doctoral-granting universities" that are not well supported to do research often exact teaching loads of 9 to 12 hours, as do the liberal-arts colleges, especially those outside the top 50. In master's colleges, loads of 12 hours a week in the classroom are common. In the community colleges, the standard climbs to 15 hours and loads of 18 and 21 hours are not unknown. Notably, as we move from the research universities through the middle types to the 2-year institutions, faculty involvement shifts from advanced students to beginning students; from highly selected students to an open-door clientele; from young students in the traditional college age group to a mix of students of all ages in short-term vocational programs as well as in coursework leading toward a bachelor's degree. In the community colleges, students in the college-transfer track are numerically overshadowed by students in terminal vocational programs, and both are frequently outnumbered by non-matriculated adults who turn the "college" into a "community center."

The burdens of remedial education are also much heavier as we move from the most to the least prestigious institutions. The open-door approach, standard in two-year colleges and also operational in tuition-dependent four-year colleges that take virtually all comers, means that college teachers are confronted with many underprepared students. Those who work in the less-selective settings also more frequently work part-time. During the past two decades, the ranks of the part-timers have swollen to over 40 percent of the total academic workforce,[7] with heavy concentrations in the less prestigious colleges and especially in the community colleges, where over half the faculty operate on a part-time schedule. At the extreme opposite end of the institutional prestige hierarchy from those who serve primarily in graduate schools and graduate-level professional schools in the major universities we find the full-time and, especially, part-time teachers of English and mathematics in downtown community colleges, who teach introductory and subintroductory courses over and over again—the rudiments of English composition, the basic courses in mathematics—to high school graduate who need remediation and to adults struggling with basic literacy.

With the nature of work varying enormously across the many types of institutions that make up American postsecondary education, other aspects of the academic life run on a parallel course. If we examine the cultures of institutions by discussing with faculty members their basic academic beliefs, we find different worlds. Among the leading research universities, the discipline is front and center, the institution is prized for its reputation of scholarship and research, and peers are the primary reference group. A professor of physics says, "What I value the most is the presence of the large number and diverse collection of scientists who are constantly doing things that I find stimulating." A professor of biology tells us that his university "has a lot of extremely good departments . . . there are a lot of fascinating, interesting people here." A political scientist adds that what he values most "is the intellectual level of the faculty and the graduate students. . . . Good graduate students are very important to me personally and always have been, and having colleagues that are smart is important." And a professor of English states that his institution "is a first-rate university . . . we have a fine library, and we have excellent teachers here, and we have first-rate scholars." Academics in this favored site have much with which to identify. They are proud of the quality they believe surrounds them, experiencing it directly in their own and neighboring departments and inferring it indirectly from institutional reputation. The strong symbolic thrust of the institution incorporates the combined strengths of the departments that in turn represent the disciplines. Thus, for faculty, disciplinary and institutional cultures converge, creating a happy state indeed.

The leading private liberal-arts colleges provide a second favored site. Here, professors often waxed lyrical in interviews about the small-college environment tailored to undergraduate teaching: "It is a very enjoyable setting. The students—the students we get in physics—are a delight to work with," "I can't put it in a word, but I think that it is one of the least constraining environments I know of," "It is a better form of life," or "My colleagues are fantastic. The people in this department are sane, which in an English department is not always the case." These institutions retain the capacity to appear as academic communities, not bureaucracies, in their overall integration and symbolic unity.

But soon we encounter sites where faculty members are troubled by inchoate institutional character and worried about the quality of their environment. In the lesser universities, and especially in the comprehensive colleges that have evolved out of a teachers' college background, at the second, third, and fourth level of the institutional prestige hierarchy, the setting may be summed up in the words of one professor:

> I think the most difficult thing about being at an institution like [this one] is that it has a difficult time coming to terms with itself. I think the more established institutions with strong academic backgrounds don't have the problem that an institution that pretty much is in the middle range of higher educational institutions around the country does. I'm not saying that [this place] is a bad institution, but it certainly doesn't have the quality students, the quality faculty, the quality programs of the University of Chicago, Harvard, Yale. . . . When it talks about standards, what sort of standards? When it talks about

practicality, how practical does it have to be? . . . It doesn't have a strong sense of tradition.

Compared to the research universities, the overall institutional culture is weaker and less satisfying for many faculty members at the same time that disciplinary identifications are weakened as heavy teaching loads suppress research and its rewards.

In these middle-level institutions, professors often spoke of their relationship with students as the thing they value most. Students begin to replace peers as the audience of first resort. That shift is completed in the community colleges, with the identifications of faculty reaching a high point of student-centeredness. In a setting that is distinctly opposed to disciplinary definitions of quality and excellence, pleasure and rewards have to lie in the task of working with poorly prepared students who pour in through the open door. For example: "We are a practical teaching college. We serve our community and we serve . . . the students in our community and give them a good, basic, strong education. . . . We are not sitting here on our high horses looking to publish" and "I really do like to teach, and this place allows me to teach. It doesn't bog me down with having to turn out papers." In the community colleges, the equity values of open door and open access have some payoff as anchoring points in the faculty culture. But in the overall institutional hierarchy, where the dominant values emphasize quality, selection, and advanced work, the community-college ideology can play only a subsidiary role. The limitations cannot be missed: "It would be nice to be able to teach upper-division classes."

As go work and culture, so do authority, careers, and associational life. To sum up the story on authority: in the leading universities faculty influence is relatively strong. Many individuals have personal bargaining power; departments and professional schools are semiautonomous units; and all-campus faculty bodies such as senates have primacy in personnel and curricular decisions. University presidents speak lovingly of the faculty as the core of the institution and walk gently around entrenched faculty prerogatives. But as we move to other types of institutions, faculty authority weakens and managerialism increases. Top-down command is noticeably stronger in public master's colleges, especially when they have evolved out of a teachers' college background. The two-year colleges, operating under local trustees much like K–12 schools, are quite managerial. Faculty in these places often feel powerless, even severely put upon. Their answer (where possible under state law) has been to band together by means of unionization. The farther down the general hierarchy of institutional prestige, the more widespread the unions become, especially among public-sector institutions.

To sum up the associational life of faculty: in the leading universities, faculty interact with one another across institutional boundaries in an extensive network of disciplinary linkages—formal and informal; large and small; visible and invisible; local, regional, national, and international. When university specialists find national "monster meetings" not to their liking, they go anyway to participate in a smaller division or section that best represents their specific interests, or they find kindred souls in small, autonomous meetings of several dozen people. In the other sectors, however, involvement in the mainline disciplinary associations declines; there is less to learn that is relevant to one's everyday life, and travel money is scarce in the institutional budget. Academics then go to national meetings when they are held in their part of the country. They look for special sessions on teaching; they break away to form associations (and journals) appropriate to their sector. Community-college teachers have developed associations in such broad areas as the social sciences and the humanities, e.g., the Community College Humanities Association, and in such special fields as mathematics and biology, e.g., the American Mathematics Association for Two-Year Colleges.[8]

Different worlds, small worlds. Institutional differentiation interacts with disciplinary differentiation in a bewildering fashion that steadily widens and deepens the matrix of differences that separate American academics from each other.

Systemic Problems

When we pursue the different worlds of American professors by emphasizing disciplinary and institutional conditions, deep-rooted problems that are otherwise relegated to the background or only dimly perceived come to the fore. Five systemic concerns may be briefly stated as problems of secondarization, excessive teaching, attenuated professional control, fragmented academic culture, and diminished intrinsic reward and motivation.

SECONDARIZATION AND REMEDIATION

The long evolution from elite to mass to universal access in American postsecondary education has not been without its costs. One major undesirable effect is a change in the conditions of the academic life that occurs when academics confront poorly educated students who come out of a defective secondary school system and flow into higher education by means of open access. Academic work then revolves considerably around remedial education. Faced with entering students whose academic achievement is at the level of ninth-grade English, faculty first have to help the student progress to the twelfth-grade or traditional college-entry level, thereby engaging in the work of the high school. Mathematics instructors may find themselves facing students whose achievements measure at the sixth-grade level and hence need to complete some elementary schoolwork as well as their secondary education. Well known by those who teach in nonselective four-year colleges and especially in community colleges, this situation may seem surprising, even shocking, to others. But like the night and the day, it follows from the structure and orientation of American secondary and postsecondary education. If secondary schools graduate students whose achievement is below the twelfth-grade level, as they commonly do, and if some colleges admit all or virtually all who approach their doors, then college faculties will engage in K–12 work. Remedial education is spread throughout American higher education, from leading universities to community colleges, but is relatively light when selectivity is high and quite heavy when selection is low or even nonexistent.

The problem of teaching poorly prepared students is compounded in the two-year college by its concentration on the first two years of the four-year undergraduate curriculum and on short-term vocational and semiprofessional programs. This curricular context calls for repetitive teaching of introductory courses. Since community colleges experience much student attrition during and after the first year of study, due to a variety of personal, occupational, and academic reasons, teaching is concentrated in first-year courses. In each department it is usually the general introductory course or two that must be taught over and over again, with little or no surcease. Upper-division courses, let alone graduate courses, are rarely available. While some course diversity can be found at the second-year level, the departmental task is to cover the introductory materials semester by semester, year in and year out. The teaching task is then closer to secondary school teaching than what is found in selective universities. The task of remedial education adds to the downward thrust, requiring subcollege work on a plane below the regular first-year instruction.

Inherent and widespread in current American education, this teaching context receives relatively little attention in academic and public discussions. It is virtually an institutional secret that academic life is so often reduced to the teaching of secondary school subjects. With due respect to the difficulties of the work, and the often deep devotion of involved staff to the welfare of underprepared students and immigrant populations, this widely found situation amounts to a dumbing down of the intellectual life of academic staff. Subject content is limited to codified introductory material. Education euphemisms allow us to blink at this undesired effect of American-style comprehensive secondary schooling and universal higher education, but they do not allow us to escape it. The situation marginalizes faculty. Eroding "the essential intellectual core of faculty work," it deprofessionalizes them.[9]

EXCESSIVE TEACHING

The complaint that professors do too much research and too little teaching has been prevalent for almost a hundred years. When William James wrote about "the PhD octopus" shortly after the turn of the century, he pointed to the increasing preoccupation of professors in the emerging universities with specialized research, graduate students, and doctoral programs. Since then the protest of too much research has been a perennial battle cry of the American reformer seeking more emphasis on undergraduate programs and on their general or liberal education components in particular. The 1980s and early 1990s have seen a strong resurgence of this point of view inside and outside the academy. Careful critics beamed their messages at research universities, would-be universities, and even four-year private and public colleges that have opened their faculty reward systems to the research imperative. They understand that professors teach when they supervise students in the preparation of master's and doctoral theses. They are sometimes aware that in the best private liberal arts colleges professors involve their undergraduate students in research as an effective way to teach and to learn.[10] But the critical comment overall has turned into a generalized charge that "professors" should do less research and more teaching, meaning undergraduate teaching. In the popular press, and even in the academic press, careful targeting is forgone. In the extreme, a minimization of teaching by professors is portrayed as part of a "scam."

But across the dispersed American professoriate, the reality is the reverse: more academics teach too much than teach too little. Fifteen hours of classroom teaching each week is far too much for the maintenance of a scholarly life; even twelve hours is excessive. But as noted earlier, most institutional sectors present such loads, specifying assignments that are two to three times greater than that of professors in research-based institutions. Twelve and fifteen hours a week in the classroom at the college level tend to push professors out of their disciplines. A sense of being a scholar is reduced as the "physicist" becomes entirely a "teacher of physics," the "political scientist" a "teacher of political science"—and then mainly as teachers of introductory courses only. Interest flags in what is going on in the revision of advanced topics; command of the literature weakens. Excessive teaching loads apparently are now becoming a source of academic burnout, importing into higher education the teacher burnout long noted as a problem in the K–12 system. A 1989 Carnegie Foundation faculty survey found that the share of the full-time faculty "intending to retire early" was 25 percent in research universities, 26 percent in liberal arts colleges, and a huge 49 percent in two-year colleges.[11] A setting characterized by heavy introductory teaching propels academics toward early retirement twice as much—one-half of the total staff!—as settings where professors have light teaching loads, involvement in research, and a more scholarly life as traditionally defined.

WEAKENED PROFESSIONAL CONTROL

As indicated earlier, command structures are not unheard of in American colleges and universities. Professors in research universities and leading private four-year colleges certainly encounter trustee and administrator influence. Their professional position is also increasingly challenged by the professionalization of administrative occupations clustered around central management; in the words of Gary Rhoades, "faculty are increasingly 'managed' professionals in organizations increasingly run by 'managerial professionals.'"[12] But academics in these favored sites generally have strong countervailing power of a professional kind that is rooted in their personal and collective expertise. Department by department, professional school by professional school, they exercise much internal control. They expect to dominate in choosing who to add to the faculty and what courses should be taught. They expect to be consulted in many matters rather than to receive orders from those in nominally superior positions. But in public and private comprehensive colleges and especially in community colleges, the foundations of authority change. Subject expertise becomes more diffuse, occasionally amounting only to sufficient knowledge in the discipline to teach the introductory course to poorly prepared students, while at the same time the role of trustees and administrators is strengthened, sometimes approaching the top-down supervision found in local school districts. Such managerialism is particularly evident in public-sector institutions, especially when they are exposed to state assertations of accountability.

Adding greatly to the vulnerability of academic professionals to political and administrative dictate is the marginal position of part-time faculty. In all institutional sectors, part-timers have long been with us: witness the traditional use and abuse of faculty spouses in part-time work in foreign-language departments of research universities. But the use of part-timers grew greatly during the past two decades as a form of mobile and inexpensive labor. It unfortunately turns out that floating student "clienteles" require dispensable academic staff, hence the deteriorating situation for staff in community colleges where a majority of faculty now serve part-time. The part-timers themselves have only marginal influence, and their large numbers weaken the influence of full-time faculty vis-à-vis trustees and administrative staff. A relatively powerless proletariat exists in American academic life, centered in employment that is part-time and poorly paid.

Experiments are under way in the two-year colleges, we should note, to create new forms of academic professionalism that are centered on "the disciplines of instruction" rather than on disciplinary affiliation.[13]

This approach emphasizes the importance of translating knowledge into more understandable forms by such means as course revision and media preparation. Certain attitudes about teaching, as well as forms of teaching, become the possible basis for professional identity. But while community college instruction has become a career in its own right, it remains highly unlikely that a strong sense of professionalism can be constructed when disciplinary foundations are weak, part-time work is the main form of employment, and top-down bureaucratic control remains widespread.

FRAGMENTED ACADEMIC CULTURE

All-encompassing academic values are increasingly hard to find in American academic life. The claims frequently made by reformers that academics must somehow find their way back to agreement on core values and assume an overarching common framework become less realistic with each passing year. Different contexts, especially institutional ones, promote different values. Even common terms assume different meanings. "Academic freedom" in one context means mainly the right to do as one pleases in pursuing new ideas; in another, the right to teach evolution in a college where the local board of trustees is dominated by creationists; in yet another, the right to join an extremist political group. Promotion criteria vary from an all-out emphasis on research productivity to weight put solely on undergraduate instruction, from complicated mixtures of teaching and research and several forms of "service" to heavy weighting of years on the job and seniority rights. As mentioned earlier, professional schools must value their connection to outside professions as well as to other parts of their universities, thereby balancing themselves between two sets of values in a way not required in the letters and science departments. The grounds for advancement then become particularly contentious. All such differences in outlook among academics widen as differentiation of academic work continues.

DIMINISHED INTRINSIC REWARD AND MOTIVATION

Under all the strengths and weaknesses of American academic life, we find the persistent problem of the professional calling. When academic work becomes just a job and a routine career, then such material rewards as salary are placed front and center. Academics stay at their work or leave for other pursuits according to how much they are paid. They come to work "on time" because they must (it is nailed down in the union contract); they leave on time because satisfaction is found after work is concluded. But when academic work is still a calling, it "constitutes a practical ideal of activity and character that makes a person's work morally inseparable from his or her life. It subsumes the self into a community of disciplined practice and sound judgment whose activity has meaning and value in itself, not just in the output or profit that results from it."[14] A calling transmutes narrow self-interest into other-regarding and ideal-regarding interests: one is linked to peers and to a version of a larger common good. The calling has moral content; it contributes to civic virtue.

Professionalization projects seek to provide vehicles by which multitudes of workers are transported to a calling, where they find intrinsic motivation as well as the glories of high status and the trappings of power. The academic profession is lucky in that it has abundant sources of intrinsic motivation in the fascinations of research and the enchantments of teaching. Many academic contexts offer a workaday existence rich in content and consequence. As a confederative gathering, the academic profession's continuing promise lies considerably in the provision of a variety of contexts that generate "absorbing errands."[15] In that promise lies the best hope in the long term for the recruitment and retention of talent. But when such contexts fade away or become severely weakened, the errands run down and talented people search for other fascinations and enchantments. The systemic problems I have identified—secondarization, excessive teaching, weakened professional control, fragmented academic culture—point to structural and cultural conditions that run down the academic calling.

What, If Anything, Can Be Done?

In a large, decentralized, and competitive system of higher education apace with great differentiation of institutions and disciplines, student growth and knowledge growth have badly fractured the American academic profession. From a cross-national perspective, the resulting system has had major advantages. More than elsewhere the system at large has been able to combine academic excellence and scientific preeminence with universal access and weak standards. It has been flexible, even to a fault, with various sectors adjusting to different demands and numerous colleges and universities fashioning individual niches. But a heavy price has been paid, not least in the systemic problems I have identified that seriously weaken the American academic workforce. The ever-extending differentiation that is integral to the success of the system produces a host of academic subworlds that downgrade the academic profession overall. They establish conditions hostile to the best features of professionalism.

Can these conditions be reduced, reversing the drift toward secondarization, the weight of excessive teaching, the weakening of professional control, the fragmentation of academic culture, and the diminishing of intrinsic motivation and reward? These weaknesses do not just hurt the professoriate; they also injure universities and colleges. They undermine the hopes of the nation that a well-trained and highly motivated professoriate will continue to staff an academic system second to none.

Four broad ideas can frame future directions of reform. First, *the intellectual core of academic work throughout the system should be protected and strengthened*. It may be helpful to students in the short run to offer them remedial instruction; it may be helpful to high-turnover clienteles and tight institutional budgets to invest heavily in part-time academics. But such major developments are injurious to the state of the academic profession and hence in the long term to the institutions that depend upon its capability. Higher education has enough to do without including the work of the secondary school. Success in secondary school reform that instilled serious standards for the high school diploma would be a major step for those who teach in postsecondary education. Part-timeness needs to be taken seriously, since nothing runs down a profession faster than to shift its work from full-time labor requiring credentialed experts to an operation that can be staffed by casual laborers who must live by their wits as they flit among jobs. Limits on the use of part-timers can be set in institutions: 20 or 25 percent of the total staff is enough; 50 percent is highly excessive and should be seen as institutionally injurious.

Second, *constant attention must be paid to the integration of academic personnel with managerial personnel*. As the gap grows between "faculty" and "administration" inside universities and colleges, faculty seek to promote their special interests more and administrators increasingly see themselves as the only ones who uphold overall institutional concerns. "Shared governance" only works when it is shared to the point where some academics sit in central councils and the rest of the academic staff feel they are appropriately represented, or where decision-making is extensively decentralized to deans and department heads and faculty sit close to these newly strengthened "line managers," or in various other complicated combinations of centralized and decentralized decision-making.

Personal leadership has its place in academe, but the window of opportunity for arbitrary top-down policy generally does not last very long. Anything worth doing in a university or college requires a number of people who want it to happen and will work at it for a number of years. Academic values, as defined by the academic staff, need to be constantly mixed throughout the organizational structure with the influence of the new managerial values that will be even more necessary in academic institutions in the future than they are now. The linking of academics with overall, long-term institutional interests is central in academic management; with it comes extended professional authority.

Third, *indirect forms of linkage among divergent academic cultures need to be better understood and promoted.* The search for clarified common goals comes up empty-handed. Rhetoric that embraces complex universities and colleges falls back on eternal clichés about research, teaching, and service. Meanwhile, the separate departments and professional schools go on generating their separate cultures. How do these cultures then connect, if at all? Both as modes of reasoning and as knowledge domains, they often have some overlap with neighboring fields. With interdisciplinary fields also helping to bridge the gaps, the many specialties of academics may be seen (in the words of three acute observers) as connected in "chains of overlapping neighborhoods." The connections produce "a continuous texture of narrow specialties," a "collective communication," and "a collective competence and breadth." Academics are partially integrated through "interlocking cultural communities."[16] Then, too, the socialization of graduate students into academic ways still counts for something—an integrating force among university graduates spread out among different types of institutions. Models of behavior also radiate from one type of institution to another. For example, the image of liberal education most strongly embodied in small private liberal arts colleges clearly serves as a model of what undergraduate education in large public four-year colleges could be if appropriately funded and properly carried out. The many different types of institutions comprising the American system do not operate as value-tight compartments.

Fourth, *the intrinsic rewards of the academic life need to be highlighted and respected.* As earlier reported, academics in diverse settings point to the special joys of teaching, or of doing research, or of combining the two. They speak of the pleasure of shaping the minds of the young, of making discoveries, of carrying forward the intellectual heritage of the nation and the world. They sense that at the end of the day they may have done something worthwhile. They point to such psychic rewards as reasons to be in academic work and as reasons to resist the lure of greater material rewards elsewhere. There is still some devotion to a calling.

Academic fanatics who are fully caught up in this now oddly shaped calling can even feel, as Max Weber put it in a famous essay, that they are in the grip of "a demon who holds the fibers of their very lives."[17] We find the academic demon everywhere: in the professor so intensely interested in her writing that she never checks the clock; in the college teacher who acts way beyond the call of duty as personal mentor and substitute parent for marginal students; in the academic scientist who is in the laboratory instead of home at two o'clock in the morning; in the lecturer who will not stop talking long after the bell has rung and has to be forced out of the lecture hall or classroom; in the dying academic who works up to the last week, even the last day. George Steiner wrote of the world of "the absolute scholar" as "a haunting and haunted business," a place where "sleep is a puzzle of wasted time, and flesh a piece of torn luggage that the spirit must drag after it."[18]

Even in modest dosages, academic professionalism centered on intrinsic features of the work at hand leads to committed productivity that political and bureaucratic controls cannot generate—nor can "market forces" guarantee. Those who seek to replace professional commitment with the nuts and bolts of bureaucratic regulation run down the calling; they take intellectual absorption out of the absorbing errand. Wise academic leaders and sophisticated critics sense that only professional norms and practices are ingrained, person by person, in everyday activity to constructively shape motivation and steer behavior. They then attend to the conditions of professional inspirations and self-regulation. Positioned between state and market, academic professionalism, however fragmented, remains a necessary foundation for performance and progress in higher education.

Notes

1. This essay is based largely on two books and two prior articles that report the results of research on academic life in Europe and America: Burton R. Clark, ed., *The Academic Profession: National, Disciplinary, and Institutional Settings* (Berkeley and Los Angeles: University of California Press, 1987); Burton R. Clark, *The Academic Life: Small Worlds, Different Worlds* (Princeton, N.J.: Carnegie Foundation for the Advancement of Teaching and Princeton University Press, 1987); Burton R. Clark, "The Academic Life: Small Worlds, Different Worlds," *Educational Researcher* 18, no. 5 (1989): 4–8; and Burton R. Clark, "Faculty: Differentiation and Dispersion," in *Higher Learning in America: 1980–2000*, ed. Arthur Levine (Baltimore: Johns Hopkins University Press, 1993), 163–78. For other research-based studies of American academics reported in the 1980s and 1990s, see Martin J. Finkelstein, *The American Academic Profession: A Synthesis of Social Scientific Inquiry Since World War II* (Columbus: Ohio State University Press, 1984); Howard R. Bowen and Jack H. Schuster, *American Professors: A National Resource Imperiled* (New York: Oxford University Press, 1986); and Robert T. Blackburn and Janet H. Lawrence, *Faculty at Work: Motivation, Expectation, Satisfaction* (Baltimore: Johns Hopkins University Press, 1995).

2. Carnegie Foundation for the Advancement of Teaching, *A Classification of Institutions of Higher Education* (Princeton, N.J.: Carnegie Foundation for the Advancement of Teaching, 1994), xiv.

3. Tony Becher, *Academic Tribes and Territories: Intellectual Enquiry and the Cultures of Disciplines* (Milton Keynes: The Open University Press, 1989).

4. See Walter Metzger, "The Academic Profession in the United States," in *The Academic Profession: National, Disciplinary, and Institutional Settings*, ed. Clark, 123–208; and R. H. Wiebe, *The Search for Order, 1877–1920* (New York: Hill and Wang, 1967).

5. Arthur M. Cohen and Florence B. Brawer, *The American Community College*, 3rd ed. (San Francisco, Calif.: Jossey-Bass, 1996), 86.

6. Carnegie Foundation for the Advancement of Teaching, *A Classification of Institutions of Higher Education*, xiv.

7. For tracking the growth of part-time faculty, see David W. Leslie, Samuel E. Kellams, and G. M. Gunne, *Part-Time Faculty In American Higher Education*

(New York: Praeger, 1982); Judith M. Gappa, *Part-Time Faculty: Higher Education at a Crossroads*, ASHE-ERIC Higher Education Research Report no. 3 (Washington, D.C.: Association for the Study of Higher Education, 1984); and Judith M. Gappa and David W. Leslie, *The Invisible Faculty: Improving Status of Part-Timers in Higher Education* (San Francisco, Calif.: Jossey-Bass, 1993).

8. Cohen and Brawer, *The American Community College*, 98.

9. Earl Seidman, *In the Words of the Faculty: Perspectives on Improving Teaching and Educational Quality in Community Colleges* (San Francisco, Calif.: Jossey-Bass, 1985), 275.

10. See Robert A. McCaughey, *Scholars and Teachers: The Faculties of Select Liberal Arts Colleges and Their Place in American Higher Learning* (New York: Barnard College, Columbia University, 1994).

11. Carnegie Foundation for the Advancement of Teaching, "Early Faculty Retirees: Who, Why, and with What Impact?" *Change* (July–August 1990): 31–34. On burnout in community colleges, see Cohen and Brawer, *The American Community College*, 90–93.

12. Gary Rhoades, "Reorganizing the Faculty Work Force for Flexibility," *Journal of Higher Education* 67, no. 6 (November–December 1996): 656.

13. Cohen and Brawer, *The American Community College*, 96–100.

14. Robert N. Bellah, Richard Madsen, William M. Sullivan, Ann Swidler, and Steven M. Tipton, *Habits of the Heart: Individualism and Commitment in American Life* (Berkeley and Los Angeles: University of California Press, 1985), 66.

15. A metaphor attributed to Henry James. Exact reference unknown.

16. For a fuller account of these metaphors and perspectives offered respectively by Michael Polanyi, Donald T. Campbell, and Diana Crane, see Clark, *The Academic Life*, 140–42.

17. Max Weber, "Science as a Vocation," in *From Max Weber: Essays in Sociology*, ed. H. H. Gerth and C. Wright Mills (New York: Oxford University Press, 1946), 156.

18. George Steiner, "The Cleric of Treason," in *George Steiner: A Reader* (New York: Penguin Books, 1984), 197–98.

INTRODUCTION TO CHAPTER 28

As is its wont, UNESCO, the sprawling United Nations agency, invited huge numbers of university planners and administrators from around the world—and scholars as well—to attend a five-day congress in Paris in the fall of 1998 on the development of higher education.

No doubt participants came to enjoy the delights of the city and each other's company but perhaps also to learn something substantial about universities, useful advice that could be transported to home locales to solve practical problems. The Czech Embassy in Paris took the occasion to award Comenius Medals to a half-dozen or so scholars and administrators from various countries. I, as a medallist, was asked to give "The Comenius Lecture" in a large auditorium infused with anxiety-producing klieg lights. As speaker, I could see only the first two rows of the audience. Rather intimidating.

The cavernous setting called for brevity—hence only twelve pages—and maximum clarity—hence all the simplicity I could muster—for a huge audience with diverse linguistic backgrounds and a wide range of sophistication about higher education reform. I sought to enliven the address with catchy mantras. When I discussed system organization, "diversify, diversify" and "learn by experimentation" became the bywords. In university reform: "top-slice and cross-subsidize"; engage in "collegial entrepreneurialism."

I took as a source for my talk my recently published *Creating Entrepreneurial Universities,* (1998). The book was part of a series assembled by Guy Neave, research director of the International Association of Universities (IAU) located in the UNESCO Paris framework. I drew upon Michael Shattock's insightful papers written about his University of Warwick experience and those of Peter West about his University of Strathclyde know-how; I also had recourse to Jussi Välimaa's knowledge about experimentation in Finnish higher education.

464

This lecture appeared to be well received. Was there any long-term effect? I have no idea. At least some researchers seemed pleased I had staked a strong claim for the relevance of research to practice.

CHAPTER 28

University Transformation for the Twenty-First Century

JOHN AMOS COMENIUS WAS A forward looking man, a deeply dedicated reformer. In his own way, in his own time, he pressed hard for the improvement of "everything in life," emphasizing reform in the education of adults as well as in the education of children—in higher education as well as in primary and secondary education. [1] The relevance of Comenius to higher education has long been clear. James Bryant Conant, the most important president of Harvard University in the twentieth century, noted a half-century ago that Harvard had a "peculiar indebtedness to John Comenius," describing him as "the principal authority on education in Europe" at the time of Harvard's founding in the small colony of Massachusetts in the early 1600s. "The spirit of Comenius," Conant said, "should make possible in every generation that fresh envisaging of educational problems which he, against overwhelming odds, forced upon his contemporaries." [2]

In the spirit of Comenius, I will be forward looking in my brief remarks, and will do so in a way that is appropriate for our own age. I am a researcher, with a broad interest in reform and innovation. And I come from a research community, an interdisciplinary international community of researchers who concentrate on the study of higher education. That community has produced ideas in recent years that broaden and deepen the realistic comprehension of problems and possibilities that practitioners—government officials, university administrators, university faculty—must have as they cope day by day with the problem of adjust-

The Comenius Lecture: "University Transformation for the Twenty-First Century." Presented at the UNESCO World Congress on Higher Education. Paris, October 4–9, 1998. Used by permission of UNESCO Publishing.

ing evermore complex universities to an uncertain and rapidly changing world.

Waxing bold, as Comenius would have us do, I will attempt a fresh envisioning of educational problems we face in common. The basic question we need to confront is: what most needs to be done to strengthen universities for the fast-moving world of the twenty-first century? The question, research now tells us, should be broken into two parts: first, what can and should be done at the level of whole national systems of higher education, particularly in the relationship of universities to government? Here we face issues of governmental support and steerage. The second question becomes: what can and should be done at the level of university action, particularly to enable universities to engage in new activities while bringing forward traditional academic values and practices? Here we face issues of university autonomy and initiative.

What Can Be Done at the System Level?

We now know that national systems of higher education can help strengthen universities in two primary ways. For one thing, they can formally differentiate types of institutions, i.e., they can establish a broad division of labor in which universities have different responsibilities— different relationships to student demand, to labor force requirements for trained graduates, to societal expectations in solving social problems, and to different bodies of knowledge. We now know that no university can possibly cover the waterfront of all demands now made on higher education, and no university can cover the waterfront of expanding and fast-changing knowledge. Therefore, a division of labor among institutions is required: broad master plans that establish broad types of institutions doing different things have a useful place. The differentiation phenomenon is no longer the mystery it once was. The research community has pursued this phenomenon, producing significant insight about its various patterns and their pros and cons.[3]

The lesson is: diversify, diversify. Higher education systems need a variety of instruments in order to even begin to do all the many things that higher education ought to do for society in the twenty-first century.

The other primary way in which government officials and other patrons can help strengthen universities for the difficult days ahead is to sponsor institutional experimentation. In the university system of Finland, the process is known as "learning by experimentation."[4] One institution is asked, or allowed, to experiment with a radical form of budgetary decentralization; another is asked, or allowed, to experiment with a new flexible workload scheme, in which faculty can adjust their individual workload from year to year. Results from each experiment can be evaluated after two or three years, and then, if valuable, applied or encouraged in the system at large.

In the search for new ways to proceed and to make our way into the unknown future, experimentation has a very large advantage: it avoids the massive mistakes made when central legislative bodies and ministerial officials mandate reforms across the entire system without preliminary testing. Since there is no way by means of untested reasoning that central planners can know enough about all local contexts and constraints, the Big Plan, or Big Bang, approach maximizes the unanticipated and undesired consequences of broad policies. Unfortunately, central governments are biased toward this road to failure. It is better, much better, to take the time to experiment, especially as uncertainty clouds our vision about what paths to take.

The twin injunctions to diversify and to experiment imply a government posture of light steerage of universities. University activities become increasingly complicated. The activities are subject to change at a more rapid rate than in the past. Many university subjects are highly esoteric. The ongoing work of universities in research and teaching steadily moves beyond the effective reach of close central supervision. And universities do not respond well to top-down commandments from government. Ministerial plans enunciated from on high are often shot down even before the ink is dry. Governmental "management" of higher education now needs more than ever to be light rather than heavy, soft rather than hard, indirect rather than direct, and after-the-fact rather than before. Governments have to learn anew that they have to trust their universities.

And, at best, whole systems of higher education are blunt instruments for innovation and reform. They work best when they liberate the initiatives of institutions and the energies of departments and research groups. The future capabilities of higher education are most determined not by what goes on at the top of national systems but at the bottom. Which brings us to the individual universities that constitute the main operating units of each system.

What Can Be Done at the Institutional Level?

I had the opportunity to tackle this basic issue directly in a research study carried out between 1994 and 1997, a study that focused on five European universities that for a decade or more had been working hard to change their own character. The institutions were the University of Warwick in England, the University of Twente in The Netherlands, Strathclyde University in Scotland, Chalmers University of Technology in Sweden, and the University of Joensuu in Finland. I treated each university as a case study of institutional change, with its own uniquenesses and peculiarities. But as the research proceeded I was also able to tease out some elements of change that these five universities, variously located, had in common. I came to call these elements "pathways of transformation," and was able to use them to frame the case studies.

The study allowed me to interact closely with the institutions I was studying, in a rich and rewarding way that I had not experienced before. "Practitioners" were my teachers; "practice" rather than prior "theory" was the basis for my results. My conclusions have been reported in three papers that have appeared in the new journal, *Tertiary Education and Management,* the journal of the European Association for the Institutional Research (EAIR), and then most fully in a book entitled *Creating Entrepreneurial Universities,* published a few months ago by Pergamon/ Elsevier Science as part of a series of books assembled by the International Association of Universities located in the UNESCO framework in Paris.[5]

How have these universities gone about strengthening their capacity to respond and develop in a fast-changing world? For one, they have developed a *stronger steering capacity,* one that integrates faculty and administrators. They have generally strengthened the position of the rector, the dean, the department head, locating some authority and initiative in particular persons. We may say they have strengthened personal authority, the kind we usually associate with the concept of leadership. But, more important, they have strengthened the capacity of *groups* of faculty and administrators to make hard choices on behalf of the entire university—or at lower levels, on behalf of an entire faculty, or an entire department.

The capacity to make hard choices on behalf of an entire university means that one or more central groups are able, in a useful phrase, "to top-slice and cross-subsidize." From various university incomes, some money is taken off the top to constitute a strategic fund, or rector's fund. That fund is then used to not only to support new ventures but also to support valuable traditional programs that need additional subsidy. Michael Shattock, the registrar at the University of Warwick, has stressed that cross-subsidy within the university is quite necessary, that "it is to the university's advantage that those departments that can generate income should support those departments that are simply unable to do so." [6] The ability to top-slice and cross-subsidize is an operational definition of a modern strong capacity to steer a university.

Second, these institutions—and others, we may note, that were not in my study—have learned how to build new units that reach directly to the outside world. They have constructed a *developmental periphery,* largely of interdisciplinary research centers and programs, that supplements the traditional structure of discipline-based departments. Such new units bring outside points of view into the university and bring in funds from industry and from governmental departments other than the ministry of education. They build in new capabilities to work on societal problems, such as environmental degradation and pollution control. For example: the University of Joensuu, located in rural Finland not far from the Russian border, has developed an expertise in sustainable forestry that has worldwide utility. Chalmers University of Technology in Sweden has developed research centers focused on cleaning up exhaust emission that include researchers from industry. Such centers now often find that knowledge transfer can flow from industry to the university as much as the other way around.

Third, the study shows how universities build a culture of change, even a culture of entrepreneurship, that extends across the traditional departments that constitute the academic heartland, as well as across the invigorated central committees and the new outreach units. As that culture is extended, entrepreneurialism becomes understood as a phenomenon of groups as well as of individuals. We may then speak of *collegial entre-*

preneurialism. Peter West, the secretary of the University of Strathclyde, pointed out in a recent paper that this finding of mine echoes the teaching of the Chinese sage of many centuries ago, Lao Tzu, who said:[7]

And when the deed is done,
The missions accomplished
Of the best leaders
The people will say
"We have done it ourselves."

Entrepreneurialism works in universities when faculty as well as administrators can say "we have done it ourselves." Collegiality—that much treasured resource of traditional universities—is then no longer overwhelmingly biased toward defense of the status quo, even the status quo ante. Instead, it becomes biased toward change.

As individual universities learn how to become more proactive, even entrepreneurial, they extend themselves internationally. Leaving aside old passivities, they reach out, to colleagues and institutions in other countries, even to universities halfway around the globe, East-to-West, North-to-South. Universities that adopt an attitude of taking care of themselves—instead of sitting by the side of the road waiting for someone to help them—are universities that learn both how to compete better and how to cooperate better. They fully realize that they are part of an international arena that is increasingly competitive. They become sensitive to the need to find niches in the international ecology of higher education, niches in which they can survive and prosper around distinctive competencies that they fashion. At the same time, entrepreneurial universities also seek out international ties and learn how to cooperate with other universities. Testing their own capabilities and limits, they realize that they cannot even begin to cover the waterfront of expanding knowledge without the help of other institutions. They realize that there is strength in numbers, and in joint efforts, to work on such world-level problems as war, depression, poverty, sustainable environments, and the construction of civil society. Today, much more than a quarter-century ago, universities are learning from one another across national lines how best to go about the university business. Entrepreneurial universities are particularly active in this regard.

Conclusion

The universities of the world have entered a difficult era. They face an overload of demands made upon them; they find their governmental patrons retreating from full coverage of costs; they are plagued with rigidities in their traditional structure; they are unsure about what new structures and programs to create and how to go about creating them. The financial picture is particularly troubling. Good universities are expensive; great universities are very expensive. And one government after another has made clear that it can—or will—pay for only part of the bill. No wonder that so many speech-makers—those who "talk the talk"—issue dire predictions about all the growing weaknesses of universities and about dark days that lie ahead, even to predict that universities will not survive.

But universities, as organizations, have two large advantages. For one, they have shown over centuries of history that they have great staying power. Even when revolutionaries and emperors have abolished them, they have come bouncing back. For the second, universities *have* adapted to every passing age, and they are now showing anew that they can construct the means of renewing themselves, transforming themselves, to become adaptable organizations. As they become more conscious of the strengths and weaknesses of their own traditional character *and* of the means of transformation they have at their disposal, they are positioned to become learning organizations. No one really knows what universities will be like in 2025, and farther down the road in 2050, and a hundred years after the millennium. Universities will indeed have to experiment their way from the present to the future—from one decade to the next—by exercising more initiative and by risking new approaches. Adaptive universities construct a portfolio of small experimental steps, changing that portfolio from one decade to the next as they learn what works and what does not, and as they sense what new opportunities should be explored.

Thus, we can say that as national systems of higher education learn to experiment, they become *learning systems.* As universities develop an adaptive character, they become *learning organizations.* Higher education thereby becomes in large part a self-guiding society that can find its way from one decade to the next in the new century that lies before us.

In this emerging society, and in the spirit of Comenius, we can "in every generation" newly envision the basic educational problems. The problems become opportunities.

Notes

1. D. Capkovà, *Comenius and Education*, in *The International Encyclopedia of Education*, 2nd ed., ed. Torsten Husén and T. Neville Postlethwaite (Oxford: Pergamon/Elsevier Science, 1994), vol. 2, 880–84; UNESCO, *John Amos Comenius, 1592–1670: Selections*, introduction by Jean Piaget (Paris: UNESCO, 1957); John Edward Sadler, *J. A. Comenius and the Concept of Universal Education* (London: George Allen & Unwin, 1966); Daniel Murphy, *Comenius: A Critical Reassessment of His Life and Work* (Dublin: Irish Academic Press, 1995).

2. Quoted in Murphy, *Comenius*, 224.

3. Burton R. Clark, *The Higher Education System: Academic Organization in Cross-National Perspective* (Berkeley and Los Angeles: University of California Press, 1983); Ulrich Teichler, *Changing Patterns of the Higher Education System: The Experience of Three Decades* (London: Jessica Kingsley, 1988); Guy Neave, *Homogenization, Integration, and Convergence: The Cheshire Cat of Higher Education Analysis*, in *The Mockers and Mocked: Comparative Perspectives on Differentiation, Convergence and Diversity in Higher Education*, ed. V. L. Meek, L. Goedegebeure, O. Kivinen, and R. Rinne (Oxford: International Association of Universities Press and Pergamon-Elsevier Science, 1996); 26–41; Meek et al., *The Mockers and Mocked, passim.*

4. J. Välimaa, *A Trying Game: Experiments and Reforms in Finnish Higher Education, European Journal of Education*, no. 2 (1994): 149–63.

5. Burton R. Clark, *Creating Entrepreneurial Universities: Organizational Pathways of Transformation.* (Oxford: Pergamon/Elsevier Science, 1998).

6. Michael Shattock, "Optimizing University Resources," paper delivered to the Conference of European Rectors, April 1994, 4.

7. Peter West, "Address to University of Twente," paper delivered at the Twente Seminar on Entrepreneurial Universities, May 19–20, 1998, 6.

INTRODUCTION TO CHAPTER 29

Comparativists doggedly want to solve problems by looking at how one country compares to others. Such comparisons can suggest useful "lessons" about what to do and what not to do. I wrote this piece sometime in the mid-1970s and originally published a version of it in *Change* in 1978. It became the concluding chapter in a book of valuable articles about higher education in American society, compiled by Philip G. Altbach, Robert O. Berdahl, and Patricia J. Gumport. It cycled through three editions and continued to be used during the 1980s and 1990s. The editors chose to bookend the collection with my caveat that the efforts to improve U.S. higher education overall by greater top-down control are likely to lead to highly undesirable long-term consequences.

Europeans have been trying to decentralize, to move away from deeply entrenched rigidities embedded in governmental control. Americans, however, have been seeking to centralize higher education systems and substitute new inclusive levels of coordination, state and national, that promise administered order. My warning was, and is still: be careful what you wish for. Be wary of the isolation of American thought inside a nationalistic tunnel vision. The growth and influence of the new U.S. Department of Education, in particular, needs to be closely watched as it becomes the established bureaucratic arm of national government—a ministry in the making.

This warning is all the more relevant as I write this essay, in the early twenty-first century, than it was a decade or two earlier. The national Department of Education, given full-cabinet status, and backed by the president, does indeed vigorously seek ways to steer American higher education, private as well as public, from community colleges to liberal arts colleges to leading research universities. In 2005, e.g., the education secretary, Margaret Spellings, created a federal Commission on the Future of Higher Education, chaired by a Texas businessman, Charles

474

Miller, who had been associated with accountability testing in that state. This Spellings Commission was set the task of creating a *"comprehensive national strategy for higher education."* It was to identify what improvements were most needed in the system at large and how they could be effected. What went wrong with higher education, the chairman early complained, was that no one was really in charge.

When last heard from in 2007, the commission had bogged down considering a wide array of preferences brought to the table by different interest groups. These preferences were increasingly resisted by those, from diverse geographical regions, who advocated decentralized institutional and state controls. It was resisted culturally—in principle—by representatives of the private Ivy League universities (think MIT) *and* by those from the large, major flagship state universities (think Michigan) *and* by those from open-door community colleges—over one thousand of them—who together admit close to one-half of all entering students.

The chairman, much inclined to issue a stern message, turned to highly critical consultants, who prepared papers with a decidedly negative tone about the faults of the system and the complacency of institutions within it. The regular members of the commission fought back to develop a gentler document more acceptable to those in the system. The result, according to Robert Zemsky—a highly active commission member—was "a mild scolding" that "proposed little that was new and much that was neither possible nor likely."[1]

That the commission cared about what universities do beyond their efforts in general education in the first two undergraduate years was not evident. Nothing at all was said about advanced professional education in medicine, law, engineering, business, and an expanding array of semi-professions; about the performing arts; or about world-class scientific research that would allow the United States to compete effectively against systems like the ones in Finland and Singapore, which are committed to strengthening their best universities. Very important, this commission does not appear to understand the competitive dynamics of the higher education system and the resulting institutional initiatives it promotes.

Thus my warnings are still relevant. Those who would attempt to reform American higher education need to understand the downside of national planning and central bureaucracy, and especially the dangers of monopoly control. They need to understand that university autonomy should be strengthened, not weakened, that state-by-state competition keeps adaptive change in motion.

Anyone who studies other countries intensively will have seen futures that do not work. Comparative vision has become virtually necessary for long-run vision. It promotes an outlook sensitive to unanticipated and unwanted consequences of over-concentration on short-term solutions to immediate problems. Seymour Martin Lipset, a convincing comparativist, once said that he who knows only one system knows no system. The Spellings Commission is a case in point. It knows no system.

Note

1. Robert Zemsky, "Using Information Technology to Enhance Academic Productivity," *The Chronicle of Higher Education*, January 26, 2007, 139.

CHAPTER 29

The Insulated Americans:

Five Lessons from Abroad

IN THINKING ABOUT postsecondary education, Americans tend to remain isolated and insular. The reasons are numerous: ours is the largest national system; we know this massive complex is the system most widely acclaimed since the second quarter of this century; we are geographically separated from the other major national models; we have many unique features; and we are busy and have more pressing things to do in Montana as well as in New York than to ask how the Austrians and Swedes do it. But there is a great deal to learn about ourselves by learning about the experiences of others in this important sector of society, and it is wise that we learn in advance of the time when events force us to do so.

To use an analogy: American business could have studied the Japanese way of business organization, and the German way, and even the Swedish way a quarter of a century ago instead of waiting until virtually forced to do so in the 1970s by worsening competitive disadvantage and deepening worker discontent. Cross-national thinking encourages the long view in which, for once, we might get in front of our problems. We might even find out what not to do while there is still time not to do it. The perspectives that I draw from comparative research indicate that we are now making changes that not only deny the grounds on which we have been successful to date but will probably lead to arrangements that will seriously hamper us in the future.

To help develop a broad analytical framework within which legislators, chief executive officers, educational officials, faculty, and others can

"The Insulated Americans: Five Lessons from Abroad," in *Change* (November 1978): 24–30. Also in *Higher Education in American Society* (3rd ed.), edited by Philip G. Altbach, Robert O. Berdahl, and Patricia J. Gumport, chap. 16, 365–76. Amherst, N.Y.: Prometheus Books, 1994.

make wiser decision in postsecondary education, I will set forth some rudimentary ideas in the form of five lessons from abroad. The basic points are interconnected. The first three of these lessons are largely "do nots" or warnings, and they set the stage for the final two, which are affirmations of what should remain central in our minds as we think about leadership and statesmanship in postsecondary education.

1. *Central bureaucracy cannot effectively coordinate mass higher education.* Many nations have struggled for a long time to coordinate higher education by means of national administration, treating postsecondary education as a subgovernment of the national state. The effort has been to achieve order, effectiveness, and equity by having national rules applied across the system by one or more national bureaus. France has struggled with the possibilities and limitations of this approach for a century and a half, since Napoleon created a unitary and unified national system of universities. And Italy has moved in this direction for over a century, since the unification of the nation.

Many of the well-established systems of this kind, in Europe and elsewhere, have not only a nationalized system of finance, but also: (a) much nationalization of the curriculum, with common mandated courses in centrally approved fields of study; (b) a nationalized degree structure, in which degrees are awarded by the national system and not by the individual university or college; (c) a nationalized personnel system, in which all those who work for the university are members of the civil service and are hired and promoted accordingly; and (d) a nationalized system of admissions, in which federal rules determine student access as well as rights and privileges. Such features naturally obtain strongly in communist-controlled state administrations, such as East Germany and Poland, where the dominant political philosophy affirms strong state control, based on a hierarchy of command. In some countries, such as West Germany, heavy reliance on central bureaucracy takes place at the state or provincial level of government rather than at the federal level, but often the results are not less thorough.

Back in the days of "elite" higher education, when the number of students and teachers was small, this approach worked to some degree—and we now know why. A bargain was struck, splitting the power between the bureaucrats at the central level and the professors at each institution. There were few middlemen—no trustees, since private individuals were not to be trusted with the care of a public interest, and not enough campus administrators to constitute a separate force. Professors developed the personal and collegial forms of control that provided the underpinnings for personal and group freedom in teaching and research. They elected their own deans and rectors and kept them on a short-term basis. Hence the professors were the power on the local scene, with the state officials often remote, even entombed hundreds of miles away in a Kafkaesque administrative monument. State administration sometimes became a bureaucracy for its own sake, a set of pretenses behind which oligarchies of professors were the real rulers, nationally as well as locally. The public was always given to understand that there was single-system accountability, while inside the structure power was so fractured and scattered that feudal lords ruled sectors of the organizational countryside. In general, this was the traditional European mode of academic organization—power concentrated at the top (in a central bureaucratic staff) and at the bottom (in the hands of chaired professors), with a weak middle at the levels of the university and its major constituent parts.

But the unitary government pyramid has become increasingly deficient over the last twenty-five years as expansion has enlarged the composite of academic tasks as well as the scale of operations. As consumer demand grows, student clienteles are not only more numerous but more varied. As labor force demands proliferate, the connections to employment grow more intricate. As demands for knowledge multiply, inside and outside the academic occupations, the disciplines and fields of knowledge increase steadily in number and kind. The tasks that modern higher education is now expected to perform differ in kind from those demanded traditionally in other sectors of public administration, and the challenge is to find the structure best suited for these new roles. There is a need to cover knowledge in fields that stretch from archeology to zoology, with business, law, physics, psychology, you name it, thrown in. Across the gamut of fields, knowledge is supposed to be discovered—the research imperative—as well as transmitted and distributed—the teaching and service imperatives. On top of all this has come an accelerated rate of change that makes it all the more difficult for coordinators, who tend to be generalists, to catch up with and comprehend what the specialists are doing.

Clearly, a transition from elite to mass higher education requires dramatic changes in structured state and national systems. The success of mass higher education will increasingly depend on: (a) plural rather than singular reactions, or the capacity to face simultaneously in different directions with contradictory reactions to contradictory demands; (b) quicker reactions, at least by some parts of the system, to certain demands; and (c) a command structure that allows for myriad adaptations to special contexts and local conditions. A unified system coordinated by a state bureaucracy is not set up to work in these ways. The unitary system resists differentiated and flexible approaches.

In such countries as Sweden, France, and Italy, many reformers in and out of government are now beginning to realize this, so that the name of their game at this point in history is decentralization—efforts to disperse academic administration to regions, local authorities, and campuses. But this is extremely difficult to do through planned, deliberate effort. Federal officials with firmly fixed power do not normally give it away—abroad any more than in the United States—especially if the public, the legislature, and the chief executive still hold them responsible. But at least things are changing; responsible people in many countries have become convinced that the faults of unitary coordination far outweigh the virtues, and they are looking for ways to break up central control. They are almost ready to take seriously that great admirer of American federalism, Tocqueville, who maintained over a century ago that while countries can be successfully governed centrally, they cannot be successfully administered centrally. There is surely no realm other than higher education where this principle more aptly applies.

Meanwhile, the United States, historically blessed with decentralization and diversity, within states as well as among them, is hankering after the promised virtues: economy, efficiency, elimination of overlap, less redundancy, better articulation, transferability, accountability, equity, and equality. Our dominant line of reform since World War II has been to impose on the disorder of a market system of higher education new levels of coordination that promise administered order. We continue to do this at an accelerating rate. In fact, if our current momentum toward bureaucratic centralism is maintained, first at the state level and then at the national, we may see the day when we catch up with our friends abroad or even pass them as they travel in the direction of decentralization.

Unless strong counterforces are brought into play, higher education at the state level will increasingly resemble a ministry of education. Administrative staffs will grow, and the powers of central board and staff will shift increasingly from weakly proffered advice toward a primary role in the allocation of resources and in the approval of decisions for the system as a whole. Legislators, governors, and anyone else looking for a source to berate, blame, or whatever will increasingly saddle the central board and staff with the responsibility for economy, efficiency, equity, and all the other goals. And the oldest organizational principle in the world tells us that where there is responsibility, the authority should be commensurate. The trend toward central political and bureaucratic coordination is running strong. Just how strong can be easily seen if we compare state structures of coordination between 1945 and 1975. Robert Berdahl, Lyman Glenny, and other experts on state coordination have noted that in the 1960s alone a remarkably rapid centralization took place, with the states shifted from structures of little or no formal coordination to coordinating boards with regulatory powers.

To see just how fast such an evolutionary trend can change matters at the national level in a democratic nation, we have only to observe Great Britain. Like us, the British were long famous for institutional autonomy. As government money increasingly became the sole source of support, they devised the ingenious University Grants Committee (UGC), which, between 1920 and 1965, became the foremost world model for how to have governmental support without governmental control. But things have changed in the past decade. UGC, which initially received its moneys directly from the treasury and doled out lump sums with few questions asked, now must work with and under the national education department.

The national department has always supervised and sponsored the non-university sector, which operates without a buffer commission. But recently it has become a more aggressive instrument of national educational policy as determined by the party in power and senior administrators in the department. Along with the UGC, it has been swept along toward a stronger regulatory role. Now, in the mid-1970s, central offices in Britain ask all kinds of questions of the institutions, favor one sector at the expense of another, tell some colleges previously out of their purview to close their doors, and suggest to other universities and colleges that they ought not attempt A, B, and C if they hope to maintain the good will of those who must approve the next budget. Britain is still far from having a continental ministry of education, but evolution in that direction has recently been rapid. For the best of short-run reasons, the central administrative machinery is becoming the primary locus of power.

Our own centralization is first taking place at the state level. This allows for diversity and competition among the state systems, some outlet for personnel and students when any one system declines or otherwise becomes particularly unattractive, and the chance for some states to learn from the successes and failures of others. Apparently, it can pay sometimes to be an attentive laggard. But we are certainly heading in the direction of bureaucratic coordination. Most important, our central offices at the national level have adopted a different posture in the mid-1970s from one or two decades earlier. We have already bowed to the quaint notion of taking away federal moneys flowing to an institution when it fails to obey a particular federal rule. Such an approach characterizes the sternest type of relationship between government and higher education in democratic countries with national ministries of education.

Our national policy will ricochet around on such matters for some years to come, while federal officials learn to fit the punishment to the crime. But the new world of national coordination into which we are moving rapidly was made perfectly clear by Secretary of Health, Education, and Welfare Joseph Califano, in a speech at the 1977 meeting of the American Council on Education. In front of an audience of hundreds of university and college presidents, he pointed out that since a recent bit of legislation opposed by academics was now national law, they would have to "comply," and he would have to "enforce." From the market to the minister in a decade! Others in Washington, inside or outside of government, feel free these days to speak of "federal supervision of education."[1] Where one stands depends largely upon where one sits, and those who sit in Washington, consumed by national responsibilities and limited to a view from the top, will generally stand on formal coordination, by political and bureaucratic means, of national administration.

In short, we could learn from our friends on the European Continent who are now realizing that their national and often unified administrative structures can't cope with mass higher education. Particularly, we could take a lesson from the British, who evolved rapidly in the past decade toward dependence on central bodies as an answer to the immediate demands of economy and equity. But as matters now stand, it appears that we will not do so. Rather, we seem determined to learn the hard way, from brute experience.

2. *The greatest single danger in the control of higher education is a monopoly of power,* for two good reasons: a monopoly expresses the concerns and perspectives of just one group, shutting out the expression of other interests; and no one group is wise enough to solve all the problems. The history of higher education exhibits monopolies and near monopolies by various groups. Students in some medieval Italian universities, through student guilds, could hire and fire professors and hence obtain favors from them. Senior faculty in some European and English universities during the past two centuries were answerable to no one and hence could sleep for decades. Trustees in some early and not-so-early American colleges could and did fire presidents and professors for not knowing the number of angels dancing on the head of the ecclesiastical pin, or, within our lifetime, for simply smoking cigarettes and drinking martinis. Autocratic presidents in some American institutions, especially teachers' colleges, ran campuses as personal possessions; and state bureaucratic staffs and political persons in Europe and America, past and present, democratic and non-democratic, have often been heavily dominant.

A monopoly of power can be a useful instrument of change: some states in Western Europe, normally immobilized in higher education, have effected large changes only when a combination of crisis events and a strong ruler produced a temporary monopoly, e.g., France in 1968 under DeGaulle. But the monopoly does not work well for long. It soon becomes a great source of rigidity, resisting change and freezing organization around the rights of just a few.

In the increasingly complex and turbulent organizational environment of the remaining quarter of this century, no small group will be smart enough to know the way. This holds even for the central bureaucratic and planning staffs, who are most likely to evolve into near monopolies of control. State and party officials in East European countries have been finding out that they cannot, from on high and by themselves, effect even so simple an exercise as manpower planning—allotting educational places according to labor force targets. They have been forced by their errors to back off from total dominance and to allow more room for the academic judgments of professors and the choices of students. As mentioned earlier, various countries in Western Europe are attempting to halt and reverse a long trend of centralization in order to move decision-making out to the periphery, closer to participants and to the realities of local operating conditions.

All organized systems of any complexity are replete with reciprocal ignorance. The expert in one activity will not know the time of day in another. The extent of ignorance is uncommonly high in systems of higher education, given the breadth of subjects they cover. The chief state higher education officer may not be able to do long division, let alone high-energy physics, while the professor of physics, until retrained and reoriented, is ignorant in everyday matters of system coordination. Here is a fundamental feature of modern organized life: while higher education has been moving toward the formation of large hierarchies traditionally associated with business firms and government agencies, those organizations have been driven to greater dependence on the judgment of authorities in different parts of the organization as work becomes more rooted in expertise. That authority flows toward expert judgment is evident in such mechanisms as peer review and committee evaluation. The organized anarchy of the university remains a useful model of how to function as those at the nominal top become more ignorant.

3. *Another great danger in the control of higher education is domination by a single form of organization.* No single form will suffice in mass higher education. Here again some of our European counterparts have been fundamentally unlucky and we can learn from their misfortune. The European university has been around for eight centuries, predating in most locales the nation-states that now encompass it. Over the centuries, the assumption grew that genuine higher education meant university education, and that made it difficult to bring other forms into being or to give them prestige. Thus, some nations were swept into mass education with only the nationally supported public university legitimated as a good place to study. As a result, since 1960, this dominant form has been greatly overloaded, with large numbers of students and faculty making more and more heterogeneous demands. This has weakened the traditional function of the university—basic research. In many European countries it is now problematic whether most basic research will remain within the university as teaching time drives out research time and as gov-

ernments sponsor and protect the science they think they need by placing it in research institutes outside the university systems. Differentiation of form has to occur, but it will happen the hard way in those countries where one form has enjoyed a traditional monopoly.

In the United States, we are in fairly good shape on this score, despite recent worry about homogenization. We have at least five or six major sectors or types of institutions, and the best efforts to classify our three thousand institutions reveal no less than a dozen or more categories, taking into account extensive differences among the hundreds of places now called universities, the still greater number called colleges, and the one thousand community colleges. Here no single form dominates the system. But we may have cause to worry about voluntary and mandated convergence.

4. *Institutional differentiation is the name of the game in the coordination of mass higher education.* Lesson four is the flip side of lesson three, but the point is so fundamental that it can stand restatement. It answers the most important, substantive question in high-level system coordination and governmental policy: will and should our universities and colleges become more or less alike? The pressure of the times in nearly all countries is heavily toward institutional uniformity. Yet cross-national comparison tells us that differentiation is the prime requirement for system viability.

One of the great pressures for institutional uniformity derives from the search for equality and equity. For a long time in this country the notion of what constitutes educational equality has been broadening. At first, equality of access simply meant equal chances of getting into a limited number of openings—selection without regard to race, color, or creed. This changed to a position that there should be no selection, that the door should be open to all. But while this idea was developing, a differentiated arrangement of colleges and universities was also taking shape. Everyone could get into the system, but not into all its parts: we differentiated among the roles of the community college, the state college, and the state university, made differential selection an important part of the process, and allowed private colleges and universities to do business as they pleased. This saved us from some of the deleterious effects of letting everyone in. Now the idea of equality is being carried a step further as observers and practitioners take critical note of our institutional unevenness. The effort will grow to extend the concept of educational equality to mean equal treatment for all. To make this possible, all institutions in a system should be equated.

Europeans have already had considerable experience with this idea. It has been embedded in those systems comprising a set of national universities and not much else. The French, Italians, and others have made a sustained attempt to administer equality by formally proclaiming and often treating the constituent parts of the system as equal in program, staff, and value of degree. Still, back in the days when selection was sharp at the lower levels, only 5 percent or less graduated from the upper secondary level and were thereby guaranteed a university place of their choosing. But mass elementary and now mass secondary education have virtually eliminated the earlier selection in some countries and racially reduced it in others. As a result, much larger numbers have come washing into the old undifferentiated university structure, like a veritable tide, with all entrants expecting governmentally guaranteed equality of treatment. There has been no open way of steering the traffic, or of differentiating, which is surely the grandest irony for a national system founded on rational, deliberate administrative control.

This European version of open-door access has recently generated enormous conflict within almost all the European systems. Unless some way is found to distinguish and differentiate, everyone who wants to go to medical school has the right to attend; everyone who wants to go to the University of Rome will continue to go there—when they last stopped counting, it was well above 150,000; and the French apparently had over 200,000 at the University of Paris before a deep crisis forced them to break that totality into a dozen and one parts. Ideally, more degree levels, with appropriate underpinnings, will also have to develop, since the heterogeneous clientele, with its more uneven background and varied aptitude, needs programs of different length and different stopping places. But to attempt to effect selection, assignment, and barriers now, precisely at the time when the doors have finally swung open, is morally outrageous to the former have-nots and to the political parties, unions, and other groups that articulate their interests. The battle rages on the national stage, with virtually all education-related ideologies and interests brought into play. In America, we have been saved from this by a combination of decentralization and differentiation.

Other strong pressures for institutional uniformity come from within higher education systems themselves. One is a voluntary movement of sectors, now referred to as academic drift, toward the part that has highest prestige and offers highest rewards. The English have had trouble resisting such convergence, since the towering prestige of Oxford and Cambridge has induced various institutions to drift toward their style. In addition, administered systems tend toward mandated convergence. Within the European unitary systems, this is expressed in the thousand and one details of equating salaries, teaching loads, laboratory spaces, and sabbatical leaves. Have-nots within the system become pressure groups to catch up with the haves (e.g., in America, state college personnel seek equality with university personnel). Then, too, impartial and fair administration demands system-wide classifications of positions and rewards, with salaries for everyone going up or down by the same percentage. From Warsaw to Tokyo there is a strong tendency in public administration generally to expand and contract in this fashion, equalizing and linking the costs, with the result that future costs become more restrictive.

Since the historical development of our institutions has presented America with the necessary differentiation, a central task is to maintain it by legitimating different institutional roles. We have been relatively successful in initiating tripartite structures within our state systems, but cannot manage to fix this division. A classic case is the unstable role of the state college. In one state after another, the state colleges will not stay where they are supposed to, according to plan, but at a blinding rate—i.e., within a decade or two—take on some or all of the functions of universities, alerting their printers to the change in title that soon will be lobbied through the legislature. In contrast, the two-year colleges have accepted their distinctive role and—outside of Connecticut and a few other backward states—have prospered in it.

This has been in the face of predictions, a quarter-century ago, that two-year colleges would renounce their obviously undesirable role and evolve into four-year institutions. That convergence was cut off at the pass, more by the efforts of community college people themselves than by weakly manned state offices. There came into being a community college philosophy and a commitment to it, notably in the form of a "movement." Some leaders even became zealots, true believers, glassy eyes and all. Around the commitment, they developed strong interest groups with political muscle. Today, no one's patsy, they have a turf, the willingness and ability to defend it, and the drive and skill to explore such unoccupied territory as recurrent education and lifelong learning to see how much they can annex. When did we last hear about a state college movement? If the name of the game is institutional differentiation, the name of differentiation is legitimation of institutional roles.

5. *Planning and autonomous action are both needed as mechanisms of differentiation, coordination, and change.* The difference between the acceptance of roles and the trend toward convergence, both here and abroad, suggests that we cannot leave everything to the drift of the marketplace. Unless the anchorage is there for different roles, institutions will voluntarily converge. Clearly defined roles stand the best chance of surviving. A strong state college was never far from a weak university in the first place. It took only the addition of a few more PhDs to the faculty and a little more inching into graduate work in order to say: why not us? Teachers' colleges were once quite different from universities, but as the former evolved into comprehensive state colleges, their institutional role became fuzzier and harder to stabilize. In contrast, our two-year units were inherently different from universities. Perhaps the rule is: organizational species that are markedly different can live side by side in a symbiotic relation; species that are similar, with heavily overlapping functions, are likely to conflict, with accommodation then often taking the form of convergence on a single type.

Distinct bases of support and authority seem to contribute to the stability of differentiated roles. The French have a set of institutions, the *grandes écoles*, that continue to be clearly separated from the universities; many of them are supported by ministries other than the ministry of education. In Britain, teachers' colleges until recently were a distinctive class of institutions, operating under the control of local educational authorities. Now that the national department of education has been sitting on them, their separate and distinct character is undergoing erosion. In the United States, the community colleges worked out their separate identity primarily under local control. They came into higher education from a secondary school background and, straddling that line, have often been able to play both sides of the street. This local base has afforded some protection.

So if we must plan and coordinate at higher levels, as we must to some degree, then we should be deliberately attempting to separate and anchor institutional roles. And as formal coordination takes over, multiple sources of sponsorship and supervision will be the best guarantee of institutional diversity. Multiple agencies protect multiple types and check and balance each other. A power market of competing agencies will replace the market of competing institutions.

But not all developments must be planned. A higher order of statesmanship is to recognize the contribution—past, present, and future—of autonomous action and organic growth. There are numerous reasons for pointing our thinking in this direction. One is the basis for our relative success: the strength and preeminence of American higher education is rooted in an unplanned disorderliness that has permitted different parts to perform different tasks, adapt to different needs, and move in different directions of reform. "The benefits of disorder"[2] ought not be inadvertently thrown away as we assemble permanent machinery for state and national coordination.

There is another reason for putting great store in emergent developments. Whether we can effectively plan diversity remains highly problematic. The arguments for planned diversity are strong: state higher education officials surely can point to some successes in the past two decades, as in the case of new campuses in the New York state system that have distinguishing specialties. But we must not congratulate ourselves too soon, since our immature central staffs have not had time yet to settle down as enlarged central bureaucracies loaded with responsibilities, expectations, and interest group demands.

Our central coordinating machinery has not been in place long enough to become the gathering spot for trouble. But the news from abroad on such matters is not promising. The experience of other countries suggests that the balance of forces in and around a central office, especially in a democracy, may not permit planned differentiation to prevail over planned and unplanned uniformity. One of the finest administrators in Europe—Ralf Dahrendorf, now head of the London School of Economics—recently addressed himself to "the problems expansion left behind" in Continental and British higher education and saw as central the need to distinguish, to differentiate. He confessed that he had reluctantly come to the conclusion that deliberate differentiation is a contradiction in terms.[3] Why? Because in the modern world the pressures to have equal access to funds, equal status for all teachers, and so on, are too strong.

People who are held responsible for getting things done are, by the nature of their roles, inclined to value and trust deliberate effort over spontaneously generated developments. But it is the better part of reality to recognize what sociologists have long seen as the imposing weight of the unplanned. As put by Dahrendorf in taking the long view in Britain and Continental Europe: "The more one looks at government action, the more one understands that most things will not be done anyway, but will happen in one way or another."

Our central procedural concern ought to be the relative contribution of planned and autonomous actions, especially in regard to differentiation. Both are needed and both are operative, so we need to add support to the organic side. We shall need to be increasingly clever about planning for unplanned change, about devising the broad frameworks that encourage the system's constituents to generate, on their own, changes that are creative and adaptive to local contexts.

In the changing relation between higher education and government, higher education is becoming more governmental. It moves inside government, becomes a constituent part of government, a bureau within public administration. On this, perspectives from abroad are invaluable, since we are the laggards who can look down the road that others have already traveled. No small point from abroad is transferable, since context is everything, but the larger portraits of relations should catch our attention, principally to stimulate our thinking about options, potentialities, and limits.

Lessons from abroad help us construct longer timeframes through which to analyze the character of our institutions. For example, in considering the problem of a new U.S. Department of Education, we need to ask what it will look like a decade, a quarter-century, a half-century hence, when it is many times larger in personnel, greatly extended in scope, vertically elaborated in echelons, and well established as a bureaucratic arm of the state alongside Agriculture, Labor, and Commerce. Up to this point, the largest advanced democratic country to attempt to order higher education by means of a national department has been France, a country one-fourth the size of the United States, where the effort has been crowned with failure and the name of reform is decentralization. We will be the first nation to attempt to "supervise" three thousand institutions in a country of over 200 million people by means of double pyramids in which a national department is placed over the state structures, with both levels exercising surveillance over private as well as public institutions. Before taking that step, we need to gain more perspective on what we are doing.

Especially under the time constraints of governmental policy-making, our canons of judgment nearly always suffer from overconcentration on immediate problems and short-run solutions. Comparative vision helps to correct these defects, thus reducing the probability of unanticipated, unwanted consequences. Anyone who studies other countries intensively will have seen futures that do not work.

Notes

1. See Samuel Halperin, "The Federal Future in Education," *Change* (February 1978).
2. See *Change* (October 1976).
3. Ralf Dahrendorf, *Life Chances* (Chicago: University of Chicago Press, 1979).

Revealing the Armature of University Change

I continued to do research and write after I retired from UCLA in 1991 at the age of seventy. The University of California in the early 1990s offered—three years in a row—attractive retirement packages. Expensive senior professors on all its campuses were encouraged to shift from a cash-poor payroll to a cash-rich retirement account. I took advantage of the offer in the first round. I retained my office and was able to continue to use the faculty center and other facilities. Adele and I gradually organized an office at home, one she fully integrated with the technical facilities available on campus. And, delightfully, my emeritus status freed me of all expectations of attending faculty meetings.

But I wasn't really ready to step down entirely. I looked at some options and reviewed ventures still underway. A project I had recently directed—the five country comparison of graduate education—was essentially done, awaiting publication. Because "call-back" teaching was possible, I chose to teach my course in comparative higher education for two additional years. Student interest at the time was modest, however, and my own wish to continue teaching waned. I was also finishing up on an ambitious four-volume encyclopedia of higher education, coedited with Guy Neave, published by Pergamon Press in 1992. Neave and I were proud of this encyclopedia; the entries did not ramble across topics from A to Z. One large group consisted of 130 country reports; another major component uniquely presented discipline-based essays to emphasize that universities and colleges are built around subject matter.

Could or should I take on another study during my retirement years? Trying to balance the positives and negatives, it became clear by 1994 that what I most wanted to do was one more research study on my own, without post-docs, graduate students, or international colleagues—just myself out in the field as in the early days. I wanted to go back to my core competence, if it was still there, and do an old-style institutional analysis of specific universities. Since I was well seasoned in European higher education, I could do it abroad, I was sure, this time around. I would figure out the details as I went.

Word had it that a handful of European universities were on the cutting edge of change. They were reported to have taken major steps in reforming their own character to become more innovative and adaptive. They would be worth examining intensively. I gradually fixed on five of them, variously located in Europe (England, Scotland, The Netherlands, Sweden, and Finland). Harriet Zuckerman in the Mellon Foundation was willing to back the study with a three-year grant. I made ten visits to the five institutions during 1994, 1995, and 1996 to interview, observe, and analyze documents. Working close to practice, I interacted quite freely with practitioners; I spent considerable time with finance officers who could explain local income categories, which could then be aligned with those of other universities in the study. Annual meetings of the European Association for Institutional Research (EAIR), which included both researchers and practitioners, were good settings for presenting my ongoing research. At a first session, in a pre-research paper, I specified what I hoped to do, and then followed up with midstream findings at the next annual meeting. When the research had been concluded and reported upon at a third meeting, I went on to write *Creating Entrepreneurial Universities: Organizational Pathways of Transformation* (1998). Organized around the five-country case studies, I highlighted five internal elements that seemed to play a primary role in transforming a university from a traditional posture satisfied with the status quo to one with an innovative, entrepreneurial outlook eager to embrace change.

The book centered on the right topic at the right time. Based on it I gave addresses and wrote papers to encourage researchers and practitioners to consider its ideas. It acquired such vigorous backers as Michael Shattock, famous for his central role in the pathbreaking transformation of the University of Warwick; Peter West, lead administrator at the University of Strathclyde, who used the book in conferences and training exercises in such disparate places as Malaysia, Malawi, and Stockholm; and

Franz van Vught, director of the fast-growing Center for Higher Education Policy Studies (CHEPS) at the University of Twente in Holland. The original five universities banded together with five others to create a new European Consortium of Innovative Universities (ECIU). I was gratified that, for a brief moment in 2000, the ECIU crowned me "the Godfather of Entrepreneurial Universities"! In truth, I only put a large label on the overall phenomenon of what the universities themselves had done and were doing. I could have called them proactive or innovative universities; with mixed feelings, however, I chose the more pointed but controversial concept of entrepreneurial university.

What I had to say in the book prompted a spirited debate at a major international conference. Convened in Paris in 2000 by the Institutional Management in Higher Education Program of the OECD, the meeting was devoted to the topic "Beyond the Entrepreneurial University." I gave a plenary address; the presidents of the five universities I had studied (Warwick, Strathclyde, Twente, Joensuu, and Chalmers) made presentations on the five common elements I had identified. Other participants entered the discussion, pro and con. Even though I was very heartened by new papers presented on case studies from around the world, I was discouraged—mainly annoyed—when traditionalists expressed the sentimental view that entrepreneurial universities were destroying the very soul of the university. Ministers were prominent among such soul talkers.

The meeting motivated me to pursue a second round of research in 2000–2003. One reason for doing this was to see if my original set of five European universities had developed capacities to go on changing. Second, I introduced more cases internationally distributed—fourteen all together—including six in the United States. Since fieldwork trips were now beyond my physical capability, and I did not seek special funding, I had to rely mainly on documents. Source documents were easy to get; universities publish annual reports and additional information about themselves on the Web. Hence, thinking and writing was done out of our home office; Adele vigorously edited and processed the work. A fourteen-case analysis, including ones in Africa, Latin America, and Australia led to a second book in 2004, *Sustaining Change in Universities: Continuities in Case Studies and Concepts*. Major chapters in this volume were the basis for the first two essays in this part of the book.

The two, brief final essays are heavily normative. Chapter 32 points to a disconnect between researchers and practitioners in understanding how universities operate and suggests how that breach can best be bridged. The concluding essay, written in 2007 from unpublished reflections, highlights the importance of an ethnographic approach and case study narratives in understanding universities.

Part IV embraces research carried out during my retirement years. It increasingly focused on the means—the armature—of how universities change. On this task, I think we made some serious progress.

INTRODUCTION TO CHAPTER 30

This selection, published in a European journal, drew largely on the concluding chapter of *Sustaining Change,* my 2004 book. I wrote the book as a follow-up to the earlier one, *Creating Entrepreneurial Universities* (1998). This second book went far beyond the first. It included my analysis of some fascinating case studies originally produced by other scholars: David Court, on Makerere University in Uganda; Andres Bernasconi, on the Catholic University of Chile; and Simon Marginson, on Monash in Australia.

Most important, *Sustaining Change,* as revealed in this selection, moved my analytical framework forward in two significant ways. For one, it shifted my focus from transformation to changes that persist. It concurrently loosened the inflexibilities of the original set of concepts by setting forth the fluid idea of "amplifying variations," a concept borrowed from musical theory. Variations always stay in touch with an original theme but amplify it in new formulations. How useful it was for me to think along these lines when analyzing similarities and differences among forward-looking universities on an international scale! I hope others find the new adaptability fruitful.

By turning to variations, each of fourteen cases becomes instructive in itself. One by one the cases become exemplary instances of how universities can develop a continuous forward motion—a *steady state of change*—by blending specified building blocks and modes of operation with key uniquenesses of place and time. By adopting a change-oriented stance, they can keep up with—even get ahead of—a fast-moving world. I stress how an organizational, continuous steady state of change differs from the conventional steady equilibrium exhibited in traditional universities.

Other researchers will need to further explore how to simultaneously retain common elements while being mindful and appreciative of the unique. Careful analysis of entire universities has to bridge the gap between generalized themes and local contextual variability. However we conceptualize those themes, reality has to finally rule the world of generalization. The search goes on. I hope this condensed reading will serve as an example of what can be done.

CHAPTER 30

Delineating the Character of the Entrepreneurial University

Creating Entrepreneurial Universities: Organizational Pathways of Transformation reported in 1998 an effort to grasp how a few proactive universities in Europe, during the 1980s and early 1990s, had gone about changing the way they operated. It presented in parsimonious fashion five institutional narratives and five concepts induced from the case studies. The universities chosen were the University of Warwick in England, the University of Strathclyde in Scotland, the University of Twente in The Netherlands, the University of Joensuu in Finland, and Chalmers University of Technology in Sweden. The integrating concepts pointed to diversified university income, strengthened steering capacity, extended developmental periphery, stimulated academic heartland, and embracing entrepreneurial culture. The interaction of case studies and concepts leaned toward practical wisdom—to combine research for understanding with research for use. Findings were discussed and used internationally.

Sustaining Change in Universities—subtitled *Continuities in Case Studies and Concepts*—(2004) greatly enlarges the earlier analysis. It presents fourteen institutional narratives that span the globe. From that empirical pursuit, I offer concepts that combine transformation with sustainability and go on to depict a new rounded character that universities can develop to unhinge themselves from the status quo and collegially commit to change.

In search of exemplars—clear prototypes and strong examples of entrepreneurial action—the chosen universities include the original five Eu-

"Delineating the Character of the Entrepreneurial University," *Higher Education Policy* 17 (2004): 355–70. Used by permission.

499

ropean universities carried forward to 2000; three very innovative and widely distributed universities—the University of Makerere in Uganda as a proactive prototype in Africa, the Catholic University of Chile as a leading example of major change among Latin American universities, and Monash University as a cutting-edge instance of the entrepreneurial university in Austrialia; and, finally, six diverse research universities in the United States, which exemplify aggressive institution-building under the spur of intense competition—Stanford, MIT, Michigan, UCLA, North Carolina State University, and Georgia Institute of Technology. The emerging conceptual framework, developed as I rotated among cases, includes the five original pathways of transformation clarified further and five new ideas on how university transformation can be sustained, and altered practices turned into a steady state of change.

As each university is unique when it comes to combining common elements with particular features, the case studies also produce "amplifying variations" of the overall themes. Thus, we find Chalmers throwing light on how to go about continually generating centers of initiative, the Catholic University of Chile dramatizing the way to modernization of an old-fashioned faculty in a decade and a half, and the University of Michigan revealing how a massive public university actively multiplying resources can match up to the sharp competition of the richest private universities in the world. The exhibited variations are as much a source of transferable insight as the old and new concepts that bring order to wide-ranging empirical inquiry. Universities operating in complex environments develop complex differentiated answers.

Drawing principally upon the final chapter of the new book, this essay concisely presents key features of change-promoting organization in universities and highlights the growing centrality of university-led action. Both descriptively and normatively, my analysis emphasizes the value of a third way between state and market. I offer a brief for the growing advantages of entrepreneurial universities in the twenty-first century.

Key Features of Entrepreneurial Organization in Universities

With many reasons to stay in the traditional box, with steady-state inertia wedding institutions to the status quo, a large number of globally dispersed universities, perhaps a majority, will not venture very far down the road of self-induced major change. All the more impressive are the feats of those universities that not only overcome their fear of failure before setting out on a journey of transformation, but also accomplish to a significant degree the second miracle of maintaining the will to change for a full decade and beyond. Incrementally, and on many fronts, they evolve into a new steady state oriented toward future change. They sustain a transformation, and more.

The capacity of an institution to be highly proactive must be rooted in altered organizational foundations. For a university to be appropriately and productively entrepreneurial, it needs to acquire the right kind of organization, one that allows the institution to be in a state of continuous change and adapt effectively to a changing society, and also one that allows its groups and individuals to become more effective than previously. The traditional box needs to be replaced by an organizational framework that encourages fluid action and change-oriented attitudes. Structures are inescapable, but they can be made into ones that liberate, that tutor groups and individuals on how to be smart about change.

Key features of the new type of organization can be briefly summed up in two parts: transforming elements, newly clarified; and sustaining dynamics that construct a steady state of change.

TRANSFORMING ELEMENTS REVISITED

THE MANY POSSIBLE SOURCES OF SUPPORT. The first element for transformation, a diversified funding base, can be more fully understood when we break down funding sources into:

1. *other government sources* (other than the core-support department)
2. *private organized sources,* particularly business firms, philanthropic foundations, and professional associations
3. *university-generated income,* e.g., alumni fundraising, garnered research-contracts, profits from patents.

Each subcategory offers numerous possibilities, and the three major sources imply virtually no limit on possible streams of support. Some but not all universities that are transforming turn heavily to student tuition, and we learn from international cases that tuition is not the only substantial alternative to state support; in reality, it may be the fourth or fifth in terms of magnitude. Some proactive universities turn to business firms in a major way, but, on the other hand, many show industry sources only as a minor item in their piecuts of income sources.

ENTREPRENEURIALISM IN UNIVERSITIES NOT SYNONYMOUS WITH COMMERCIALIZATION. Income from industry is repeatedly outweighed by income from other government departments where research monies are won competitively from national departments of science, health, economic development, energy, and defense; it often contributes less than the monies gained annually from alumni and endowment; and it can readily be exceeded by income from "auxiliary services," especially when this category includes the presence of a large medical complex with substantial income from patient care and biomedical research.

Financially, self-reliance lies in a broad portfolio of income sources. The legitimacy of the portfolio depends on educational values guiding monetary decisions. There must be things the university will not do no matter how much money is offered, e.g., permitting donors to select faculty. Conversely, there must be "useless" things it insists upon doing, e.g., cross-subsidizing the teaching of classics and philosophy because it is an institution committed to cultivation and transmission of a cultural heritage as well as to economic progress.

For those who wish to explore possible new income sources, a simplified inventory of a baker's dozen may help:

- public core support: national and/or provincial ministries
- support from other public agencies at the same level of government: ten to twenty at the very least (and more may be found)
- support from public agencies at other government levels, e.g., provincial, state, county, city
- support from large business firms
- engagement with small- and medium-sized firms, particularly spin-offs
- philanthropic foundations, both large and small
- professional associations (for professional development education)
- university endowment income

- university fundraising from alumni and willing supporters
- student tuition and fees, applied to foreign students, graduate students, and continuing education students
- student tuition and fees from domestic undergraduate students
- earned income from campus operations, a varied array of academically driven activities plus spun-off, stand-alone, and self-financing activities
- royalty income from patented and licensed invention and intellectual property

Non-core sources often feed and encourage one another. National and provincial government departments may offer joint support for particular programs; business firms and professional associations may share costs of certain courses; wealthy private supporters may contribute funds to build endowment; tuition gained from foreign and graduate students may be used to reduce costs for domestic undergraduate students. The greatest gain in independence comes from tilting the resource base toward university-generated and directly controlled sources.

ALIGNING THE STRENGTHENED STEERING CORE. The second element is an administrative backbone stretching from central bodies to major faculties and on to baseline departments and institutes. Balancing influence across multiple levels is an almost constant problem in entrepreneurial universities. New ventures include new interest groups; aggressive departments seek more autonomy so they can race ahead; central bodies worry about integration of the whole and about how to support weak departments and functions. In the steady reinvention of a productive balance, faculty participation in central councils is a critical component—improved steering capacity depends considerably on collegial connections between academics and administrators in daily operations and both become responsible for the legitimacy of the funding portfolio. Absent the new class of change-oriented administrators, faculty can readily find comfort in old niches. Absent the faculty, and administrators bent on efficiency and effectiveness can become forgetful of educational values. Shared governance is essential, but in new or adapted forms. And it helps greatly in building a strong steering core if supporting state ministers, instead of specifying a standard governance structure, allow universities to develop different practices appropriate to their own settings.

Effective entrepreneurial universities are neither extremely centralized nor decentralized; they are administratively strong at the top, the middle, and the bottom. They introduce professionalized clusters of change-oriented administrators at all levels—development officers, technology-transfer experts, finance officials, sophisticated staff managers—to help raise income and establish better internal cost control. Maturing entrepreneurial universities develop a bureaucracy for change as a key new component of their character. Such agents clearly form part of the cost of production. They are as valuable a means of production as are faculty.

BASIC FORMS OF AN EXTENDED DEVELOPMENTAL PERIPHERY. The third category was devised as a way of accounting for the presence of an increasing number of operating units that were clearly not traditional, discipline-centered departments. These units particularly take the form of interdisciplinary and transdisciplinary research centers focused on a wide range of societal problems, from global warming to improvement of public administration, from third world development to urban renewal. The extended periphery is also dotted with units of teaching outreach, proliferating under such labels as continuing education, lifelong education, distance education, and professional development. As part of their daily efforts, these research and teaching instruments cross old university boundaries to bring in populations, general and specific, not previously in the picture.

Such base units have natural allies in the bureaucracy for change built up in the steering core. Just as each new source of funding requires a university office, so the new units of the developmental periphery, the office of continuing education, e.g., require specialized offices to develop and process their activities. Numerous administrative units paralleling the many research and teaching units of outreach are part of what makes the entrepreneurial university a proactive place. Awareness of their importance is one more step in eradicating old impressions that the university remains a place where only disciplinary departments provide research and teaching, and only young people are taught. New assemblies of subjects—cognitive territories varying in content, time, and place—require supporting tribes in both operating units and the administration, resulting in greater organizational density.

ENTREPRENEURIALISM IN HEARTLAND DEPARTMENTS. The fourth element recognizes that strong universities are built on strong departments. Entrepreneurial universities become based on entrepreneurial departments—dynamic places attractive to faculty, students, and resource providers. Heartland departments do not fade away; instead, as traditional knowledge territories expand and intensify, their supporting tribes become more important. What the old departments are willing to do gets done; what they oppose is slowed down or eliminated along the way. The most frequent mistake made in attempts to transform universities is for a management team to proceed on its own without involving faculty and their departments from the outset. Even more mistaken are efforts by ministers to attempt to effect within-university change by command and control from their remote perches.

Some departments can and will move faster than others in understanding the benefits of entrepreneurial actions—their own as well as those located elsewhere in the university. Generally, science and technology departments lead the charge, enabled by sources of support directly available to them and prepared by their experience in administrating costly projects, labs, and equipment. However, this is not always the case. At the University of Makerere in Uganda, the first stage of recovery from severely depressed academic conditions was led by social science and humanities departments and "soft" professional fields positioned to readily pick up on new ways of increasing "private" sources of support. As they did in teaching law, they could become "customer friendly" by adding new courses sought by potential students and outside organizations and scheduling them at convenient times. When external funding for science and technology becomes available, departments in these fields—at a later stage of institutional development—will readily become more entrepreneurial.

Altered heartland departments, then, are a necessary part of the bargain that is transformation. As they work harder to acquire the habits of change for themselves, they become part of the sustaining foundation of the entrepreneurial university. Minimally, departments positioned to raise income should be encouraged to do so by other departments, and thereby to contribute to the welfare of the entire university as well as their own. It is then a second-order problem to work out—fight over!—who decides what share of the enhanced resources each gets.

INSTITUTION-WIDE ENTREPRENEURIAL CULTURE

Organizational culture, seen as the realm of ideas, beliefs, and asserted values, is the symbolic side of the material components featured in the first four elements. Always ephemeral, often wispy to the touch, it escapes empirical identification. However, it is there: participants in universities today are even schooled to conceive of culture and point to its appearance in concrete practices and particular beliefs.

Central to the drama of the fifth element is its relative intensity. High intensity was frequently exhibited among the cases I studied. Warwick remains an entrepreneurial prototype in part because of its aggressive idealization of "the Warwick Way." Building upon the "foundation" character it acquired in the early 1990s, Chalmers intensely believes it is distinctly capable of enacting change in the Swedish setting. The Catholic University of Chile proudly asserts its character as a leading case of a new "exceptionalism" in Latin America. And Monash in Australia "knows" very well it is the leading entrepreneurial university in all of Southeast Asia, or at least one of the top two or three. All six U.S. universities analyzed—two private, four public—exhibited vigorous assertion of distinct identities containing a forward-looking orientation. Competitive striving for prestige intensifies entrepreneurial culture.

As the competition heats up, nationally and internationally, more universities are encouraged to move toward an entrepreneurial state of mind. If they reach high cultural intensity, they acquire confident self-images and strong public reputations that enable institutional advance. New true believers are affronted to even think of sliding back into a traditional box. Rather, their historical account, their saga, points to the volition they have assembled and used. They believe they have the willpower to continue to move forward.

SUSTAINING DYNAMICS AND THE STEADY STATE OF CHANGE

Beyond clarifying essential features of the initial pathways to transformation, the analysis presented in the new book put forward a set of ideas that saw those elements in supportive interaction that turned into a steady state of change. Expressed as dynamics, they were labeled the dynamic of mutually supporting interaction, the dynamic of perpetual momentum, and the dynamic of embedded collective volition. These concepts trace the processes by which transformation becomes *sustainable*. They help fill in what I claim as a new steady state in entrepreneurially transformed universities, a state that inclines them to go on changing. That new mode, defined in juxtaposition to the commonly known steadiness of traditional universities, is difficult to achieve. However, it is well worth the effort. It is less risky than the risk of inertia. It takes universities beyond survival, to achieve a consequential effectiveness in the twenty-first century.

Many U.S. universities, e.g., acquired a steady state of change in the last half—and especially the last quarter—of the twentieth century. The flywheel of forward motion was their willful effort to develop and maintain high prestige. They diversified income, strengthened their steering capacity, developed an elaborate complex of boundary-spanning research centers, encouraged traditional departments to become involved in new ventures, and spread an entrepreneurial culture. Interaction of such basic elements was deepened by the simple fact that competition ruled out any stopping point. Even universities with the highest status had to be on guard against accumulating comparative weaknesses and to move to make timely repairs. Administrators and faculty at the University of California, Berkeley, e.g., noted that their set of biology departments, somewhat in disarray in the mid-1980s, had slipped in national and international standing. Urgent repairs were soon undertaken—reconstituting departments, regrouping research teams, constructing an expensive new physical plant, investing in new promising faculty—and the desired level of observable effectiveness was restored.[1] In the face of increased competition, Harvard adjusted, in 2003, its long-standing prohibition against awarding tenure to young academics, no matter how outstanding their promise, by granting a tenured full professorship in the humanities to a thirty-two-year old woman who was on the verge of moving to the West Coast. Competition is very favorable to talented individuals.

When universities search for prestige they build upon the "natural" striving of academics to acquire a reputation and enjoy the company of productive teams and departments.[2] High-reputation departments and research groups act like magnets in attracting able faculty and students. Stanford and MIT, Michigan and UCLA, North Carolina State University, and the Georgia Institute of Technology have all exhibited in the American system an ingrained willingness to build high research intensity as a means of competing vigorously for prestige and resources. That intensity has become increasingly characteristic of the top fifty (and more) U.S. universities. It is a stunning, self-sustaining phenomenon. This particular steady state is a competitive advantage of the first order for the system at large as well as for individual universities.[3]

The Modern Pathway to University Self-Reliance

Two decades ago when I first compared national systems of higher education (*The Higher Education System*, 1983), I constructed a triangle of major forms of system coordination by placing "state" authority in one corner (with the USSR located nearby), "market" in a second (with the United States as nearest case), and "academic oligarch" in the third (with Italy in mind).[4] Despite its crudeness, this triangle of coordination became a useful heuristic. Others could place national systems in a three-dimensional space by estimating their comparative combinations of state control, market-type influence, and institutional self-control. They could then pursue subcategories of political-bureaucratic, professional, and market forms of system integration. Under market coordination, I pointed to basic types of markets appearing in higher education, consumer markets, academic job markets, and institutional markets, and concluded by stressing that (a) these markets were often shaped by state-sanctioned authority, and (b) privileged institutions, possessing the most desired parts of the markets, could exert even more influence than state authorities in determining continuities and changes in system capabilities.

The triangle can be usefully updated by insisting on a qualitative difference between market coordination and coordination effected by state officials and universities themselves. Lindblom, in his exacting analysis of "the market system," reminds us that markets are "mindless and purposeless." Although each kind of market in itself provides "coordination without a coordinator," abstract "market forces" do not decide anything. They may push and constrain but outcomes are "proximately decided by human beings often in tough negotiations with each other."[5] In short, people and organizations pursue purposes; markets do not. Those who pursue purposes attempt to carve out slices of markets—a specific consumer market, a specific labor market, a specific financial market, a specific reputational market—favorable to their cause. In higher education, state agencies and universities themselves are deliberate designers of mutual adjustment. Both seek to define and use mindless markets.

Reputational markets in which mutual adjustment takes place among universities play a key role. Markets in which reputation becomes the main commodity of exchange turn universities into prestige-maximizing institutions. Reputation is so crucial because it guides the attraction (and retention) of administrators, faculty, students, and resources. When a prestigious university, public or private, annually receives thirty-thousand applications for five-thousand openings in the next entering class, and can itself make the selection, it has extensive control of its "consumer market." It is not bothered by the vagaries of the large arenas of interaction—regional, national, and international—between universities and would-be students. While competing with other highly selective institutions, it can broadly select whom it wants.

Without doubt Lindblom is also correct when he stresses that "all real-world coordinating systems are hybrids in which centrality [central control] and mutual adjustment depend on each other."[6] Two hybrids now count most in the university world: one where centrality consists of state agencies and a second in which universities themselves assume primary command and make a wide range of mutual adjustments in related markets.

Thus, in sharp contrast to the widespread use of anthropomorphic depictions of markets as actors who are elated or disappointed, who run and jump and otherwise act up, let us understand markets not as steering forces but as conditioning arenas of interaction. Steering takes place in how purposive organizations and individuals make use of those arenas. For as long as they have existed, universities have had consumer markets in which they find students, labor markets in which they find faculty, and institutional markets in which they amass reputation. What has changed is that ever more complex universities have become enmeshed in many more market-type relationships than in the past, and have become greatly differentiated by the amount of self-control they are able to exercise. In this context, we comprehend collegial entrepreneurialism as a road to a keenly desired high degree of market control.

If we put markets in their proper place, we then come down to two main pathways of guided development. The first is not only state-led but also system-centered and top-down in viewpoint. The second is not only university-led but institution-centered and bottom-up in understanding and advocacy.

A modern example of the pursuit of the state-led pathway, a 2002 consulting report for the Scottish Higher Education Funding Council, titled "Higher Education in Scotland: Orchestrating an Adaptive Knowledge-Based System," is instructive. It recommends a search for a "unified Scottish vision," one to be enunciated in an "authoritative and long-term statement of Ministerial policy" and "endorsed by the sector and other key stakeholders." The document implies that all participants ought to agree on one blueprint; reform can then proceed by means of "strategic management at the system level."[7]

Going down this well-worn path, universities in the United Kingdom have had to accept identical measurement scales placed on all eighteen Scottish universities (and over one-hundred universities in the United Kingdom)—to assess their research performance (research assessment exercises, RAEs) and their teaching quality (in separate assessments). This system generated simplified quantitative ratings with direct effects on both the reputation and financing of individual universities. Such system-level assessments mean that national subject-based review committees bypass the central offices and overall integration of universities and slice right down to individual subject departments to rate them quantitatively against their peer departments in other universities. The ratings follow a would-be standardized format in which over sixty different subject panels of judges (in the U.K. and Scottish cases)—from chemistry to economics, law to social work—are assumed to grade with equal severity. Anyone familiar with the subject-matter composition of universities knows this is impossible and close follow-up research has shown that the panels necessarily have to think and act in different ways.[8] Consistency across subjects is not even remotely possible. However, the fact remains that people who believe in this approach live among us. The funding councils, working on behalf of government, want simple numbers to which they can attach financial rewards and punishments. The outcome has been a bitter adversarial relationship between government and universities in which universities (and some subject panels) seek to "game" the assessments to get high scores, and funding bodies reciprocate by announcing belatedly that they will not pay for all the grade inflation, and change the rules after the game is played.

Along this pathway, the *dirigiste* tendency in an officially integrated system comes strongly into play. That tendency produces a homogenizing effect in molding universities, even if differential sums magnifying differences between the "haves" and "have-nots" are parceled out. What the favored few possess and practice becomes the model. With all institutions rolled up into one system, extended comparisons up and down the line are inescapable with the less favored aspiring to equate themselves by way of benefits and pay.

Scottish academic critics of the 2002 consulting report highlighted the dangers of its government-centered approach:

- The focus becomes too much centered on universities as an economic good, losing the "social and cultural dimensions of our work."
- The report did not "face the funding realities": if "growth in public funding for higher education is going to dry up even further, we need an honest debate about alternative means of funding future development. . . . Universities are likely to spend even more time than they do now searching out new income streams."
- Scottish universities need to be enabled "to compete successfully with their counterparts in the rest of the UK and overseas." More needs "to be done to create the right environment for change at institutional level . . . a positive environment for change."
- "The trappings of central management control—stricter planning guidelines, performance targets and reporting systems—all in the name of public accountability . . . will drain energy and purpose from the sector and stifle initiative and enterprise— the very qualities that Ministers are trying to promote in other parts of the economy." Above all, one should "avoid a *dirigiste* approach."[9]

The state-led pathway is clearly not one appropriate for change in complex universities in the fast-moving environment of the twenty-first century. System-wide changes are notoriously slow in formation and blunt in application. And where is the positive environment for change, the promotion of initiative and enterprise, the rewards for universities finding their own configurations of new income streams, the stimulation of leadership in the operating units where all the activities of research, teaching, and learning are located? In an IT world, how can the many parts of universities experiment with, differentiate, and alter their use of information technology according to its constantly changing fit with diverse subjects and forms of teaching?

A *juxtaposing* example of the pursuit of the institution-led pathway of change is the Kerr-Carnegie model of reform that developed from a twelve-year effort (1967–80) by two successive study groups, supported by the Carnegie Foundation and led by Clark Kerr, to analyze the U.S. system of higher education.[10] In this sustained effort, over one-hundred books and technical reports examined such institutional sectors as private liberal arts colleges and community colleges; such curricular and disciplinary slices as the undergraduate curriculum and legal education; and such organization and governance components as state policy-making and the college presidency. Ever concerned about year-by-year crises, the Kerr groups issued recommendations along the way, e.g., on such matters as financing and equity in access. However, although the successive committees were loaded with intellectual firepower and public stature, they did not sit down to write, from their collective wisdom, an integrated document on the strengths and weaknesses of the country's system of higher education, the shaping trends of the time, and what needed to be done. No government money was involved, no political white papers were prepared to make the case for certain system-backed changes. The study group clearly obeyed the dictum to do no harm: no institution, no segment of the system, was held up for ridicule; no college or university was tarnished or punished financially by low or middling scores on crude measures.

The final report of the Kerr-Carnegie assessment looked to the future under the curious title of *Three Thousand Futures: The Next Twenty Years for Higher Education*. Why three-thousand? Why not "the future of the system?" Because

at least 95 percent of all campuses underwent some significant change in the 1970s: they gained or lost enrollment, or opened or closed, or merged, or shifted to public control, or changed from one institutional category to another. Alteration of condition or status was almost universal: continuation of the status quo, almost non-existent. Each campus has had its own individual recent history and is likely to have its own individual future. Institutions of higher education have been riding off in all directions and will probably continue to do so: 3,000 different institutions face 3,000 different futures.[11]

The Kerr groups did not pretend that all the institutions are of a kind, that a particular liberal arts college is like a particular research university, or that even two top research universities are carbon copies of each other or should be. The specific institutions are the ones that matter— the different heritages, their different geographic locations and regional environments, and the differences in firmly established configurations of academic subjects and programs. And this is the way it should be when the values of institutional diversity and initiative are placed front and center. Then the "advice to state governments," in 1980, was to "prepare financing formulas that will encourage diversity and new initiatives." States should stop pre-audit controls over expenditure, ease the possibility of transfer of funds within institutions, provide for portability of state financial aid to students, and allow institutions to keep the private funds they raise.[12]

The Kerr-Carnegie model offers a transferable logic in how to think about reform and change in higher education. Begin by shifting attention to the institutional level, focus on development from past to present to possible futures, and then take it from there. So, if Scotland has eighteen institutions in its designated higher education system, there are eighteen stories of past, present, and possible future development. Reformers can drop all pretense that St. Andrews, Edinburgh, Strathclyde, and the Royal Scottish Academy of Music and Drama are cut from the same cloth and should somehow undergo a common system evaluation. These institutions are diverse, and their valuable identities and competencies will only be harmed by homogenizing pressures.

The mantra for reform then becomes complex universities operating in complex environments require complex differential solutions. In other words, each university requires its own unique solution.

On the university-led pathway, reform avoids, at all costs, a one-size-fits-all mentality. It encourages institutions to freely carve out their own solutions, in combinations of the traditional and the new. These new measures reflect their particular possibilities as well as their particular constraints—and especially, their particular acts of will. Movers and shakers insist on system actions that enable differentiation and competition; they are aware that these broad conditions are necessary for future institutional competence at home and for the growing international competition generated by ambitious universities in Europe, Australia, Singapore, and China, e.g., and, in the United States, in North Carolina, and Georgia as well as in California, Michigan, and Massachusetts. The home system needs to turn universities loose so they can develop capacities to adapt rapidly to change, and thereby to compete. The state has to find a new platform for trust—"a light touch"—perhaps to verify in a general way, every five to ten years, just how well various universities are doing. As legislators, ministers, and state planners grow increasingly remote from the realities of universities, their best hope is to enable those in the institutions to do the job.

On the institution-led pathway, at the cutting edge the extremely proactive place will be hard at work early Monday morning to turn problems into solutions that comprise a stronger capacity for adaptive change. Pursuing such institutional cases around the world, I sought answers to the two simple questions of how they transformed their character and how they are able to sustain a capacity to go on changing. In their common answers, we find the necessity of collegial forms of entrepreneurialism is to work well in universities. Above all, we find institutional will that reflects assertive ambition. Facing the same external forces, some universities change extensively, some change moderately, and some hardly change at all. The demands of the day clearly do not produce change. What counts are the responses summoned from within by diverse universities.

This side of the calamities of war, fire, and earthquake—and repressive governmental tyranny—the future of universities rests in their self-reliance. The study of modern academic entrepreneurialism teaches, and teaches well, that, one by one, as the twenty-first century unfolds, universities will largely get what they deserve. The lucky ones will have built the institutional habits of change.

Notes

1. Trow (2003, *passim*).
2. Smelser and Content (1980, 7). The authors noted in a study of the U.S. academic labor market that competition for academic talent "is simultaneously a competition for individual services and a competition between universities trying to advance or solidify their own position in the prestige hierarchy." See also Becher (1989) and Ziman (1991).
3. Herbst (2004, 5–21). See also Herbst et al. (2002, *passim*) and CEST (2002), i–iv.
4. Clark (1983, chap. 5, *Integration*, 131–81).
5. Lindblom (2001, 41, 23, 83). See also Fligstein (2001) and Dobbin (2002, 64–65). A growing group of economists and sociologists argue persuasively that economic behavior is a subcategory of social behavior and must be explained socially, that states and societies are the "architects" of markets. They stress that as governments create the rules under which markets operate many different kinds of modern economy can be found, e.g., in Sweden, Japan, France, Germany, and the United States. The logic of their system-level analysis may readily be applied to an institutional sector, such as higher education, in which state and university shape the architecture of markets. The cultures and norms—and power—of the universities shape their relevant markets.
6. Lindblom (2001, 27).
7. PA Consulting Group (2002, *passim*).
8. McNay (2002, *passim*).
9. PA Consulting Group (2002, comments by Sir Alan Langlands, 3 pages unnumbered).
10. Clark (2003, *passim*).
11. The Carnegie Council of Policy Studies in Higher Education (1980, 199).
12. Carnegie Council of Policy Studies in Higher Education (1980, 203–04).

References

Becher, T. *Academic Tribes and Territories: Intellectual Enquiry and the Cultures of Disciplines.* Milton Keynes: SRHE and Open University Press, 1989.
Carnegie Council on Policy Studies in Higher Education. *Three Thousand Futures: The Next Twenty Years for Higher Education* (summarized in *A Summary of Reports and Recommendations* [1980]). San Francisco: Jossey-Bass, 1980.

CEST *La Suisse et la Champions League Internationale des Institutions de Recherche 1994–1999*. Bern, Switzerland, CEST 2002/6. Summary (in English): i–vi, 2002.

Clark B. R. *The Higher Education System: Academic Organization in Cross-National Perspective*. Berkeley: University of California Press, 1983.

———. *Reform That Matters: University-Led Change*, in *Creating and Sustaining Entrepreneurial, Innovative Universities*. Glasgow: University of Strathclyde, 2003. (Lectures given at the University of Strathclyde by Burton Clark and Michael Shattock, September 2002.)

Dobbin, F. "Markets Are Social Animals." *Contexts* (Summer 2002) 64–65.

Fligstein, N. *The Architecture of Markets: An Economic Sociology of Twenty-First Century Capitalist Societies*. Princeton, N.J.: Princeton University Press, 2001.

Herbst, M. *The Production-Morphology Nexus of Research Universities: The Atlantic Split, Higher Education Policy* 17 (2004): 5–21.

Herbst M., et al. *MIT and ETH Zurich: Structures and Cultures Juxtaposed*. Bern, Switzerland, CEST, 2002.

Lindblom, C. E. *The Market System: What It Is, How It Works, and What To Make of It*. New Haven: Yale University Press, 2001.

McNay, I. *Assessing the Assessment: An Analysis of the UK Research Assessment Exercise 2001, and Its Outcomes, with Special Reference to Research in Education*. Paper Presented at International Forum of the Association for the Study of Higher Education (ASHE), Sacramento, Calif., November.

PA Consulting Group. *Higher Education in Scotland: Orchestrating an Adaptive Knowledge-Based System. A Report for the Scottish Higher Education Funding Council*, Edinburgh, 2002.

Smelser, N. J., and R. Content, *The Changing Academic Market: General Trends and a Berkeley Case Study*. Berkeley: University of California Press, 1980.

Trow, M. *Leadership and Academic Reform: Biology at Berkeley*. Available at http://ishi.lib.berkeley.edu.cshe.mtrow/. 2003.

Ziman, J. *Academic Science as a System of Markets, Higher Education Quarterly* 45, no. 1 (1991): 41–61.

INTRODUCTION TO CHAPTER 31

This essay, drawing upon a major chapter in *Sustaining Change in Universities*, focuses on the unusual dynamics of the American system of higher education. The system is squarely non-ministerial; it does not locate universities and colleges under specific branches of national government, as is common elsewhere in the world. Instead, control is widely dispersed among hundreds of private institutions as well as many public universities and colleges that fall under one or another of the fifty state governments. A vast array of institutions is driven entrepreneurially in the fundamental sense that they, one by one, have to take care of themselves.

This is a long-standing state of affairs. Competitive diversification became solidified in the attitudes of small colleges in America as far back as the early nineteenth century. Competition then intensified immensely as public and private universities developed after 1870 and took over the commanding heights of the system. This competing stance became so ingrained during the twentieth century that by the year 2000 many state public universities were joined at the hip with their own state government in state-by-state rivalry.

"Genetic entrepreneurialism" points to the way a highly differentiated and intensely challenging non-formal "system" shifts initiative to the institutional level. Robustly aroused entrepreneurialism has causal antecedents in the way the system as a whole is put together. Its effects include high international standing for fifty or more U.S. universities, public and private. They are a restless, ambitious lot.

When I was asked to contribute to the second issue of a new annual journal published in English by the Research Institute for Higher Education at Hiroshima University, I was very pleased to submit this piece about competitive dynamics in the U.S. system. Reformers in Japan have recently been trying to change, root and branch, their ministry-dominated system. I hope this essay helps, both in Japan and in other societies.

CHAPTER 31

Genetic Entrepreneurialism among American Universities

M Y BOOK, *Sustaining Change in Universities* (Clark, 2004), offers fourteen case studies of proactive universities: five accounts pursue sustaining developments during the late 1990s in the European universities previously studied in *Creating Entrepreneurial Universities* (Clark, 1998); three narratives based on the work of other scholars portray transformed universities in Africa, Latin America, and Australia; and six brief cases of institutional development range across diverse universities in the sprawling U.S. system. Drawing on the new volume, this essay concentrates on striking outcomes of the American unplanned arrangement. I spell out broad interacting features of a non-formal national system that widely generate institutional initiative, encouraging entrepreneurialism. I then turn to the historical and contemporary development of the University of Michigan as an exemplar of public university initiative. In a concluding section, I highlight state-by-state competition on top of private-public competitiveness that amplifies institutional striving and achievement. The multisided competitive dynamic pushed development during the last half of the twentieth century of over fifty U.S. universities, viewed on an international scale, to a very high level of research-led capacity.

Competitive Generation of University

The American system of higher education is markedly different from all other national systems. It combines very large size, extreme decentralized

"Genetic Entrepreneurialism among American Universities," *Higher Education Forum* 2 (March 2005): 1–17.

control, great institutional diversity, sharp institutional competition, and substantial status hierarchy.[1] Its key structural feature is radical decentralization of authority. It is a system composed both of major private sectors, in which over two thousand private universities and colleges of all sizes operate under individual boards of control, devising their own viable niches, and of numerous public sectors in which another 1,600 institutions fall primarily under the fifty states rather than the national government (*Chronicle of Higher Education*, 2002).

This fundamental condition of decentralized public and private control in a large country set in motion, a long time ago, a restless proliferation of institutions. Long before the age of the college gave way to the age of the university, institutions were created in the first half of the nineteenth century in large numbers and at a rate unheard of elsewhere. At a time when England had four places of higher education—ancient Oxford and Cambridge, new Durham and London—the United States had developed hundreds of separate small colleges. But as academic scientists in the late nineteenth century were to point out, what the United States had, by the standards of Europe, was a swarm of mosquitoes rather than a few soaring eagles. Numerous eagles began to soar in the 1870s, 1880s, and 1890s. Some leading private colleges, preeminently Harvard, Yale, and Princeton, transformed themselves gradually into full-bodied universities, in competition with such new private institutions as Johns Hopkins (1876), Clark University (1889), Stanford University (1891), and the University of Chicago (1892), all constructed as universities from the outset.

At the same time, each of the proliferating number of states sought to have at least one public institution that could claim a substantial comprehensive character: University of Wisconsin and University of Georgia, e.g. Stirred by the commitments of the land-grant tradition, one or more public universities in many states also prized their service to the state's general population, beginning with the admission of sons and daughters of farmers and workers. But private universities set the model of a quality research university. When a self-selecting club—the American Association of Universities (AAU)—was formed in 1900 to jointly vouch for quality, it had eleven private and three public members. At the same time, in a setting where institutional initiative was unbounded and stimulated, both public and private non-university institutions continued to proliferate—small private colleges increased in number rather than died away, and teachers' colleges grew everywhere, giving the United States at the turn of the century a census of accredited institutions that approached the unbelievable number of one thousand.[2]

The structure and diversity, well in place by 1900, ensured a twentieth-century system characterized by sharp competition for faculty, students, resources, and status. Comparatively, the U.S. system became an open one—no inclusive official structure, no national ministry of education—in which competitive disorder and a competitive status hierarchy heavily conditioned the ways that institutions defined themselves, sought resources, and arranged internal conditions for research, teaching, and learning. Foreign observers, unaccustomed to the competitive mode, often saw these ways as decidedly unacademic, even brutish. Well they might. The habits of competition soon extended to the development of big-time sports—a benefit and an affliction that universities in other countries have managed to do without. Big-time competitive sports came with the territory; athletic prowess even sometimes arrived first, leaving some institutions for a time in the situation of building faculties their football and basketball teams could be proud of. Institutions similarly placed can still be found in 2000, giving university presidents a headache second only to that produced by having to contend with a major medical school.[3]

Throughout the twentieth century, diffusion of control localized initiative. Private institutions had to survive and prosper largely on their own; public ones, considerably influenced by the independence and achievements of the leading private universities and four-year colleges, also sought self-constructed autonomy, under, over, and around the mandates of state and federal government. The system's disorderly and competitive conditions encouraged a large number of institutions (but not all, of course) to build institutional willpower.

Since no one institution can represent the play of this widespread dynamic in many different sectors, I discuss briefly in my new book six cases that, each in its own way, exhibit a high level of local initiative and self-determination: two leading private universities, Stanford in northern California and MIT in Massachusetts; two flagship-level state universities, North Carolina State University and Georgia Institute of Technology, not as well known at home and abroad as the first four, in which we find a determination, under current competitive conditions, to work out new forms of university enhancement. These latter cases also highlight the state-by-state competition that flourishes in a fifty-state federal system of university sponsorship in which education officials do not get together across state lines to establish common rules and limit competition, as occurred in the German federal system, or surrender their control to national government, as happened in Australian federalism, but instead join together with universities and firms in their own state (or own region of the country) to compete more effectively against other states and regions.

The University of Michigan is a grand example of powerfully exerted local initiative, old and new, in a major U.S. public university. We can observe institution-building in action where local ambition is steadily enlarged, right down to important steps taken in the 1980s and 1990s.

University of Michigan: Public University Exemplar

The University of Michigan in Ann Arbor, a small city about forty miles from Detroit, has long stood as a flagship institution in its state's higher education system and as first—or second—among equals in a group of major public universities in the neighboring states of Wisconsin, Minnesota, Illinois, Indiana, and Ohio, the American mid-continental academic heartland. Dating from a small college established in the late 1830s, when Michigan formed its state government, by 1900 the university acquired both the loyalty of a good share of the population of its home state—a place for our sons and daughters, with an exciting football team—and a substantial academic competence and status that earned it an invitation— it was one of three public universities along with Wisconsin and California—to sit at the table of the new Association of American Universities whose majority members consisted of private self-anointed pace-setters stretching from Harvard to Chicago to Stanford.

When Slosson wrote a major research-based assessment of *Great American Universities* in 1910, he selected fourteen top universities defined by annual expenditure on instruction: nine private universities, Harvard, Yale, Princeton, Cornell, Columbia, Pennsylvania, Chicago, Johns Hopkins, and Stanford; and five state universities, Michigan, Minnesota, Wisconsin, Illinois, and Berkeley (California). Michigan was first among the public institutions, just behind three of the private universities, Harvard, Columbia, and Chicago, and above such notables as Yale, Cornell, and Princeton. By that early date, Michigan had already stood "for more than a half century as the typical and leading State university" (Slosson, 1910, ix–x, 182).

In transforming an existing college into a university, two strong presidents played a defining role during the last half of the nineteenth century. Henry P. Tappan and James B. Angell had each made the transatlantic pilgrimage to Germany before assuming office and had returned full of enthusiasm for a research-centered approach. They had seen the future. But enamored of "Prussian ideals," Tappan (1852–63) was so much ahead of the times that he was "summarily and ungratefully dismissed after 10 years." A decade later Angell (1871–1909) then proved to be the right man at the right time to transform an undergraduate-centered college into a comprehensive research university, American-style. He organized a graduate school in 1893, *and* built faculty strength in medicine, law, and engineering, *and* by 1908 had more undergraduate students (over 4,400) than any other university in the country (Slosson, 1910, 187–202). The college level served well in linking the university to the population of its state. The growing graduate realm reached to the nation and promoted specific streams of income: the law school, second largest in the country, drew nearly 70 percent of its students from outside the state and they paid higher fees than Michigan students; in medicine, more than half came from other states (199).

Here were early steps, taken a century ago, toward a leading model of how U.S. public universities could evolve into hybrid forms in which adaptive self-steerage would largely dictate the institution's path of development.

Two active decades highlight the trajectory of the Michigan phenomenon in the twentieth century. During the 1930s, under presidential leadership that was "decidedly sympathetic toward faculty research," the university engaged in a "general devolution of administrative authority away from presidents and regents toward the deans and departments," and appointed representative executive committees at those operating levels. With much influence exercised from the bottom up, academic values of the faculty entered strongly into the determination of university policies (Geiger, 1986, 209–10).

Equally important was a further major shift toward non-state revenue. The university actively sought private donors—but carefully. "Not wanting their donors to appear to lessen the state's responsibility, they sought restricted [earmarked] gifts for purposes that the legislators would be unlikely to support." By the end of the decade, the university had pulled in $44 million in gifts of various types. A good share of the new money went into lasting assets in the form of buildings and endowment. Increasingly, the voluntary support went to the improvement of research. A key donation by Horace Rackham went to the construction of a building for the graduate school and the endowment of research (210–11).

A financial division of labor—a very early one in the history of modern higher education if viewed internationally—emerged in which state core support covered general operating expenses, while voluntary contributions went to support research activities, graduate education, enhancement of the quality and standing of such specific units as the law school, and a slow but sure buildup of endowment. The search for such support encouraged the university to be a leader among public universities in organizing alumni: their assistance first centered on the undergraduate realm, dormitories and student unions, e.g., and then subsequently moved to research support and graduate program development. Diversification of income was well on its way; it positioned Michigan to compete against leading private universities across the nation, particularly for faculty, as well as against other flagship public universities from its Midwestern backyard to the West Coast.

Michigan became an extremely entrepreneurial university in the 1980s and 1990s, considering its age, size, and solidity. Starting in the 1970s, for a variety of economic, political, and cultural reasons, its core support from the state became increasingly undependable. Between 1980 and 1983, e.g., the state allocation rose at an average annual rate of 1 percent and largely continued at this stagnating level throughout the 1980s and 1990s. This was not enough for growth, and was nowhere near what was needed to finance an outstanding university. The university responded strongly: it would "privatize" heavily by greatly increasing income from non-state sources with which it was already familiar.

First, it had long developed a battery of tuition charges differentiated by level (graduate/undergraduate), discipline, and residence (out-of-state/ home state). It now raised these lines "prodigiously." Instate tuition was elevated to the top of the national range. The university became "the first university to charge higher tuition to upper-classmen and graduate students, and these premiums were increased as well." With a huge demand from outside the state—its prestige drew students from such student-exporting states as New Jersey and New York—"it became the only state university to set non-resident tuition at levels comparable to private universities." As a result, tuition revenues, which were one-half the size of the state appropriations in 1980, exceeded them by 40 percent in 2000 (Geiger, 2004, chap. 4).

Second, in the 1990s, drawing on its strong tradition of voluntary support, the university vigorously expanded gift income from alumni and other willing supporters to build the largest endowment among single state universities. "Only a handful of public universities derive significant revenue from endowments, but Michigan's potential annual contribution in 2000 approached $5000 per student" (Geiger, 2004, chap. 4).

Third, Michigan grew its research base by investing in major research initiatives and in the parallel development of large organized research units (ORUs). It became in the 1990s the largest performer of academic R&D of all U.S. universities, private or public—a stunning achievement, given the high level observed in such leading cases as Stanford and MIT. Toward expansion of its research infrastructure, a $5 million 1986 grant from a private foundation was used to establish a permanent Presidential Initiative Fund. Successful in attracting faculty initiatives in high-risk/ high-reward areas, it soon grew into a larger Strategic Research Initiatives program, under the vice president for research. It provided between $5 and $10 million *each year* to "seed and stimulate innovative research," out of which came new research units, defined as "hubs for collaborative work." By 2000, the university had over 160 such units, more than one-half of them established in the 1990s (Geiger, 2004, chap. 4). The university then topped up its research infrastructure with a $200 million Life Sciences Institute as a massive investment in future biological and medical research; dual faculty appointments linked the huge medical school and the large basic College of Literature, Science, and the Arts. Responsibility for new undergraduate courses was scrupulously written in. The Institute was thereby "structured to have an impact on the entire university" (Geiger, 2004, chap. 4).

Fourth, income from "auxiliary services" became the largest sum of all, due to revenue brought in by a huge medical school–teaching hospital complex from third-party payments for patient care—an operation so complicated and expensive that it was spun off as a separate incorporation in the early 2000s.

Income diversification had arrived on a grand scale. All these major streams and their tributaries greatly enlarged the means for steady, substantial budgetary growth. The vigorous developments of the 1980s and 1990s put in place an income-snowballing effect clearly evident at the beginning of the twenty-first century. A twenty-year trend report for 1984–2003 indicated that an initially large budgetary base became colossal in the space of a few years. In 1984 the "all funds budget" for the Ann Arbor campus was already four-fifths of a billion dollars ($824 million), certainly a solid base that reflected previous diversification of income. By 1991, a mere seven years later, the total budget had doubled to over a billion and a half ($1,690 million). At the end of the 1990s, in 2000, income had doubled again, making it annually over $3 billion ($3,200 million). Three years later—in the midst of a major national economic downturn—annual increases in income had pulled the university up to over $3,800 million—approaching the $4 billion mark.

How were such staggering increases possible in a comprehensive public university? While income from traditional core support ("state appropriations") went from $161 to just $364 million, income from tuition and fees shot up from $130 to about $600 million. Federal dollars for research increased from $108 to over $530 million. And to add to the pot, hospital income (and expenditure) had moved from $270 to over $1,700 million. Even "other external" sources generated in fundraising had become a significant item at over $200 million (University of Michigan, 2003).

In sum: the university's revenue in absolute dollars doubled during the 1980s, doubled again during the 1990s, and grew by another one-fifth between 2000 and 2003, even as state core support was falling to 10 percent and less of the total. When "hospital" revenues are put to one side, the state contribution to the rest of the university, other than the medical complex, still amounted to less than 20 percent. This particular U.S. "state university" had clearly moved to "state-assisted university" and then on to "privately-financed public university."[4] It had become, in my terms, a "self-reliant public university"—a much more self-directed non-profit organization than a state agency or a business firm.

The large size of Michigan—similar to that of other public universities, such as Wisconsin, Berkeley, and UCLA—along with its demonstrated capacity to raise major resources from a multiplicity of public and private donors, gives it competitive strength. Out of a total enrollment of 37,000 in 2000, one-third of the students, 13,000, were at graduate school level. This large assembly of advanced students was greater than the overall student population of Yale (11,000)—and three times the size of that institution's graduate student body; it was double the total size of Princeton (6,400). The result is a comparatively large number of doctorates awarded annually, 629 in 2000. This placed Michigan fourth among the public universities and fourth among all U.S. universities. The highly selective private universities do extremely well in attracting postdoctoral appointees, but here, with 728 in 2000, Michigan was sixth among public universities and a respectable tenth nationally (Lombardi et al., 2001).

Large size in U.S. public universities starts with huge undergraduate enrollment. Michigan at the end of the 1990s had 24,000 undergraduates. The university has long had the reputation of being student-friendly, part of its attractiveness for out-of-state as well as for in-state applicants who make it their first choice. In the reform efforts of the 1980s and 1990s, the university paid special attention to the undergraduate base. Beyond the resources of a huge library system, dispersed in myriad locations, the university created a Media Center to bring new technology directly to the students. It also created attractive special courses and programs that allowed some students to participate in "research/creative projects," "service learning," and even "writing in the discipline." National magazines and newspapers gave Michigan high marks for quality of undergraduate education—as high as third overall among public universities and fifth for "best value" for the money in the public sector (University of Michigan, 2002).

Attention was further focused on undergraduates when Michigan intensely committed itself to "affirmative action." A "diversity initiative," sustained over years of negotiation and adjustment, became known as *The Michigan Mandate: A Strategic Linking of Academic Excellence and*

Social Diversity. The mandate insisted that "diversity and excellence are complementary and compelling goals for the University." The implementation of a succession of "opportunity programs" let the university dramatically improve social diversity on campus. Over a decade, students, faculty and administrative staff from underrepresented groups more than doubled; the graduation rates of minority students rose to the highest among public universities; promotion and tenure success of minority faculty members became comparable to their majority colleagues; and a growing number of appointments of minorities were made to leadership positions (Duderstadt, 2000a, 204, 207).

Specific actions taken under the diversity mandate on minority access were challenged in two court cases that simultaneously reached the U.S. Supreme Court in 2003. The university interpreted new rulings to mean that race could indeed be considered in admission decisions, but could not be stated in quota-like numerical fashion. The case received enormous attention over many months preceding and following the decisions. Michigan, among all the universities of the country, was a standout for its forthright boldness. It became a heroic institution to many, but an institution that had gone a stage too far for others. It certainly had not been a passive, heads-down observer of the struggle over a major national issue, one that involved social diversity in business corporations and the military as well as in universities.

For the undergraduates also there was always the great excitement of the nationally ranked sports teams, particularly in football, where heritage stretched back over a century. Always a headache for university administrators and faculty to maintain some semblance of academic control over a domain that operates under deeply entrenched dynamics of its own, big-time sports led to embarrassing scandals. Heavily emphasized competitive sports attached to a university are a major drawing card for students, staff, and alumni alike, at Michigan as much as anywhere. A price had to be paid institutionally for deeply undesirable effects on academic integrity. James Duderstadt, a former president, wrote after retirement a major volume on specific actions that universities needed to take to "clean up" the sports realm while recognizing its continuing utility (Duderstadt, 2000b).

Behind diversification of income, constructing a huge developmental periphery, building change orientation in heartland departments, and spreading an embracing entrepreneurial culture was a highly proactive steering core topped by successive able presidents and provosts that stretched during the 1980s and 1990s from Harold Shapiro (1980–87), who went on to become president of Princeton, to James J. Duderstadt (1988–96), who stayed on at the university, to Lee Bollinger (1997–2002), who went on to become president of Columbia University, to Mary Sue Coleman (2002–) after the turn of the century. Duderstadt played a particularly vigorous role in restructuring the university to enable adaptive change. A visionary about the open-ended possibilities of a massive self-determining university, Duderstadt drew a distinction between the traditional view of strategy that "focuses on the fit between existing resources and current opportunities" and a "*strategic intent*" "that cannot be achieved with current capabilities and resources." The intent deliberately creates a misfit between resources and ambition: through this, "we are able to challenge the institution to close the gap by building new capabilities."

These new capabilities are not built, however, by grand leaps in design. Rather, they emerge out of *logical incrementalism*, "a small-wins strategy, relying on a series of steps to move toward ambitious goals." The planning process is evolutionary, and it "moves from broad goals and simple strategic actions to increasingly complex tactics." Experimentation should constantly be under way, and the organization ought to be prepared to take aggressive action on newly discovered fruitful pathways. Duderstadt was pleased he was known for a decision-making style of "fire, ready, aim," as he launched "yet another salvo of agendas and initiatives." Anything to move the elephant! Anything to stay away from "traditional planning approaches [that] were simply ineffective during times of great change" (Duderstadt, 2000a, 266).

"The University of Michigan had become a better, stronger, more diverse, and more exciting institution" as a result of the transforming efforts of the 1980s and 1990s, concluded Duderstadt. Organizationally, the university had institutionalized "an exploratory approach to the future," one that took seriously "our basic character as an inquiring institution" and depended on experimentation and discovery as "the most realistic near-term approach" (Duderstadt, 2000a, 275, 277).

Pride of achievement had clearly deepened pride of place: stubborn continuity linked past and present to any emergent future. But, most important, step-by-step this hugely complicated university had learned some secrets of perpetual change.

The Stimulus of Competitive Federalism in Amplifying Institutional Initiative and Achievement

The Michigan case highlights the stimulating role played by competition among the top ten to twenty private U.S. universities. Michigan always has Wisconsin, Berkeley, and UCLA in view as markers of comparative achievement, as well as such private high achievers as Columbia, Cornell, and Stanford. When we turn to other ambitious public universities we find in addition that the competitive instincts of the fifty states also enter importantly into institutional stimulation. We find universities frequently joined at the hip with their immediate state to jointly square off against other state based pairs, a systemic process across the country in which at least one-half of the fifty states are vigorously involved. Two recent U.S. studies offer case study data.

One study, focused on case-by-case analysis of "new university roles in a knowledge economy," pointed to developments in ten public universities, which involved close university–home state relationships: North Carolina State, Georgia Tech, Virginia Tech, and Texas A&M in the South; Ohio State, Pennsylvania State, Purdue (Indiana), and the University of Wisconsin in the Midwest; University of Utah in the Rocky Mountains region; and the University of California at San Diego on the West Coast (Tornatsky, Waugaman, and Gray, 2002). A second analysis focused on "science-based economic development" noted university-state collaborations that stretched from Maine to Louisiana to Kansas to Montana to Oregon (Raymond, 1996). And what do we find? Three cases typify.

In Ohio, a major industrial state, the large, well-settled flagship public university, Ohio State University, "has gone through something of a renaissance over the past four years," involving "an exciting rethinking of mission, goals, and investment—particularly as they pertain to contributing to the knowledge economy of the state." The university now "aspires to be Ohio's leading asset in growing a knowledge-based economy." This entails developing higher *national* stature in selected areas of research and scholarship, with such specific targets for 2010 as having "10 programs in the top 10, and 20 in the top 20." In short, to become Ohio's leading asset in the new age, Ohio State has to develop additional organized capabilities that will place it higher in national standing, in competition with other major universities, public and private, located in all the other states (Tornatsky et al., 2002, 55–56).

As other universities in other states are similarly engaged in national benchmarking—top 100, top 50, top 20, top 10—the aimed-for status is a moving target, forced upward by the achievements of others. The higher the aim, the tougher the competition, because such deeply entrenched institutions as Harvard and Stanford, Berkeley and Michigan, are already sitting on the commanding heights. And the problems of focus and niche development become acute, requiring sharp internal assessment of possible match-ups between organizational capabilities and changing external possibilities. Greater differentiation, rather than simple imitation, becomes a vital requirement. And standing still becomes a means of falling behind.

The University of California, San Diego (UCSD), is a powerhouse West Coast university that has risen rapidly in national and international stature to give the UC system a third flagship that rivals Berkeley and UCLA. Started late, in 1960, UCSD has used the high-quality base of the UC system as a launching pad for both investing heavily in a relatively few areas of science (instead of trying to be all things to all people), and opening itself to external partnerships with industry and the community. Among all the private and public universities of the country, after just four decades of existence by the end of the century, it ranked tenth in faculty quality and sixth in total research funds. Its research funds exceeded Berkeley's, in major part because it has a medical school and Berkeley does not.

At the same time the university has seen itself "as very much a corporate citizen of San Diego, with an associated responsibility to build the economy and well-being of the region." It has explored "new modes of university-industry cooperation and new approaches to economic development strategy": as early as 1985 it had underway a major "connect program" as an economic development organization focused on technology-based entrepreneurship. The university has played a critical role in the transformation of San Diego into "an entrepreneurial, technology-based economy" (Tornatsky et al., 2002, 129–36). With a thousand firms and more developing and locating in the region, the San Diego area has become California's second silicon valley, and UCSD serves as the anchor university.

My final example of successful state-university partnering is the University of Utah, the most prominent higher education institution in Utah, which has increasingly become recognized internationally as a distinguished American university. With enrollment exceeding 25,000 in 2001, its students came from "every Utah county, every state in the nation, and 102 foreign countries." The university stresses that it has "a long tradition of service and outreach to the state and the mountain region." Much of its research program is organized in more than forty centers and institutes, eleven of which are "state-supported centers of excellence . . . explicitly designed to maximize industry partnering and technology commercialization." Historically the state has not been a national center for industry or finance. But in recent years university and state have worked together to develop a "burgeoning Utah technology economy," where university spin-offs have turned into successful small and middle-size companies. Considerably aided by "a robust and customer-friendly set of policies and procedures coupled with an enabling organizational culture" at the university, Salt Lake City has been viewed increasingly as a technology-oriented metropolitan area, and has been ranked in one national magazine 1997 report as sixth in the world on an indicator of new technology development (Tornatsky et al., 2002, 137–38). In short, in a "Utah culture" of entrepreneurially led economic change, the university and the state, especially the major city, have been mutually supportive and closely linked.

In sum: intense institutional competition within cities and states and across the country is virtually a genetic characteristic of the U.S. system of higher education. Universities seek their own betterment not only as measured against their own past performance but also against the contemporary achievements of other universities. As they seek higher status, they avoid the standing still that would put them on a downward escalator. They seek position on sets of upward escalators of reputation that enhance their claims on faculty, students, and financial resources. On an upward competitive spiral, some of the U.S. universities—fifty and more—have by the early years of the twenty-first century become awesome performers. They have become international benchmarks of high academic achievement.

Some up-to-date quantitative evidence of international standing comes from the Center for Science and Technology Studies (CEST) in Bern, Switzerland, which in 2002 constructed a census, "The Worldwide Champions League of Research Institutions." It was based on bibliometric analysis of nearly one thousand institutions that had significant quantities of research papers published in indexed international journals, as reported by the Institute for Scientific Information (ISI). The researchers wanted to assess the performance of Swiss research on an international scale and then additionally to benchmark the famed Swiss Federal Institute of Technology Zurich (ETHZ) against the American MIT. The results were startling. At the system level, "there appears to exist a performance gradient which separates U.S. research universities from those of the rest of the world. . . . Only 6 out of the top 50 most influential universities are non-U.S. universities. . . . ETHZ is the only university in these top 50 not based in an Anglo-Saxon country and the only one located in continental Europe (the other 5 non-U.S. universities being located in the United Kingdom and in Canada)" (Herbst, Hagentobler, and Snover, 2002, i–iv).

Bibliometric analysis has well-known defects. It crudely replaces institutional and system complexities with simple numbers that obscure more than they reveal. It places a premium on the use of English and downgrades work done in other languages. It does not capture applied research as completely as basic research. Still, the crude measures of publication and citation offered by this form of analysis are readily understood and widely used. And if we take them as approximations, they can be justified as useful analytically. Thus, the world share of any country in research literature output can be studied field by field and aggregated for such major groupings as life and physical sciences. Output can be broken down by university, department, research group, and individual researcher.

The great buildup of the American research base, primarily located in over two hundred "Doctoral/Research Universities," was captured in ISI data that showed the U.S. share of world scientific literature in the 1980s was between one-third and two-fifths (about 37 percent), a share greater than that of Britain (9 percent), Germany (6 percent), France (5 percent), and Japan (7 percent) combined. The U.S. share in life sciences was about 40 percent in sheer volume and over 50 percent in frequency of citations; in physical sciences, about 35 and 50 percent, respectively (Clark, 1995, 137).

The American framework of academic research has clearly helped to position a large number of universities (and departments) to become world leaders. By the mid-1980s, international citation analysis in 4 subfields of chemistry found 18 to 20 of the top 25 universities and 8 to 9 of the top 10 to be American; in electrical engineering, 20 of the top 25 were American, with 4 in Britain and 1 in Japan (Clark, 1995, 139). A special inquiry mounted by a British economist for his own discipline, using a set of indicators of research productivity, showed that among the top 25 departments in the world, 21 were American, 3 were British, and 2 were Israeli (Portes, 1987). A knowledgeable American observer, Henry Rosovsky, former dean of arts and sciences at Harvard University, was considerably justified in stating in the late 1980s "between two-thirds and three-fourths" of the leading universities in the world were in the American system (Rosovsky, 1990, 29–36). The 2002 Swiss data on research output indicated that this long-standing story still exists a decade later. It is deeply systemic.

When ETHZ was benchmarked directly to MIT, the results were again startling. Although this Swiss university was the best of the best on the European Continent—Nobel Prize winners and all—when compared to MIT, an institution of similar size, "the total number of publications in the fields qualifying for the Champions League differs in favor of MIT by a factor of almost 3" (Herbst et al., 2002, iv). Of the twenty-five major fields assessed, MIT outperformed ETHZ in nineteen. "In those fields where MIT has higher publication counts than ETHZ, MIT normally dominates ETHZ by factors of 2 to 10." At a given output level, "MIT sustains roughly 35% to 140% more fields." If "we look at citations, MIT's position vis-à-vis ETHZ is even stronger than in the case of publications" (72).

The Swiss study stressed that any comparisons of the much smaller European university systems and the huge U.S. system should not be made between gross system averages—share of publications per inhabitant, e.g.—but should first grasp the vast differences that exist among over 250 universities in the U.S. system, where universities in the top quarter doctoral programs greatly outperform those in the bottom quarter, on publication and citation counts, on number of doctorates produced. The top fifty U.S. universities are much higher on a wide range of benchmarks than those in the bottom half and especially in the bottom quarter. Comparing four universities that ranged from "the very prominent to the nearly invisible," Gumport found in the late 1980s such huge differences as $200 million in federal research contracts at the high extreme and $3 million at the low end; in fact, the low ranked university has less research funding than many departments in universities in the first and second quartiles (Clark, 1993, 261–93). And MIT is very high in the top cohort. Clearly it is not the average U.S. performance that "should be a benchmark for a small European nation of ambition, but the performance of 'peer regions' within the United States, e.g., California, Massachusetts, the Research Triangle in North Carolina, regions in Georgia and Texas. . . . Better yet, we should concentrate on comparing individual institutions, a path pursued now by CEST. . . . if the average U.S. program is the benchmark for Swiss universities, the wrong targets have been chosen" (Herbst et al., 2002, 74). The university label has been widely distributed among—even freely assumed by—institutions in the United States that do little or no research. Their hope to change that condition may be a motivator, but it is not synonymous with reality.

Bearing on the ETHZ-MIT comparison, the Swiss researchers raised the question of the "morphology" of universities and went on to speculate about a morphology of leading U.S. universities that could account for their greater strength, and specifically about a morphology of MIT compared to that of ETHZ. The researchers judged that the critical differences were neither simply a matter of size and mass, nor of greater publish-or-perish pressures in the United States. One quantitative item they picked up was a lower student-teacher ratio at MIT than in the European counterpart. But leading public universities in the United States normally have higher ratios than their private counterparts, closer to 20 to 1 than 10 to 1, and they still manage to come out very high on national and international scales. More revealing in the Swiss data was the number of senior faculty: 910 at MIT compared to 340 at ETHZ, a difference approximating 3 to 1 (Herbst et al., 2002, 27).

No simple morphological differences will go very far in explaining the American outcomes. Institutional differences are complex, built up in the character of individual universities over long periods of time. As seen in my study, complexity necessitates case studies that can describe the play of idiosyncratic features perched on top of the role of common elements found in classes of institutions. In total morphology, there is only one MIT and one ETHZ.

But there are indeed some widely-shared features among the better universities in the American system. From among the universities reviewed in my book we can extract some of these.

DELIBERATE CONSTRUCTION OF UNIVERSITY SELF-RELIANCE. Whether at Stanford or MIT, Michigan or UCLA, North Carolina State or Georgia Tech, we find diversification of income, with a wide range of private and public contributors; strengthened steering capacity, from top to basic units; extended outreach capability, a collaboration with a wide range of business firms and public agencies; strong willingness in heartland departments to develop adaptive outlooks, including teaching and service for older populations (especially professional development); and a widespread broadening of interests in the academic culture to include the interdisciplinary and transdisciplinary alongside the disciplinary. In short, we find a strong version of the elements of transformation and sustainable change that I developed originally from studying proactive universities in Europe and now seen to be at work at different levels of academic achievement in change-minded universities in Africa, Latin America, and Asia.

DELIBERATE BUILDUP OF RESEARCH INTENSITY. The universities exhibit an almost exuberant push to develop a wide range of research groups and clusters. Large numbers of senior faculty, rather than just one or two, direct research areas. Junior faculty are relatively free to initiate and carry out projects and explore new lines of inquiry. Young non-tenured faculty participate as voting members of departments, rather than serve only as assistants to a head professor. Department organization mixes junior and senior faculty with graduate students, post-docs, and some undergraduates in a modernized version of a research-teaching-study nexus.[5] The research capacity of a university is greatly enhanced—intensified—when more faculty, varying in rank, are added and left free to innovate. A rapid buildup of research intensity stood out in the Michigan story, indexed by high numbers of academic researchers, funded research grants, and total research income. This feature stands out in U.S.–Continental Europe comparisons.

INGRAINED WILLINGNESS TO COMPETE ACTIVELY FOR INSTITUTIONAL PRESTIGE. Constantly at work to protect and increase their standing in a competitive system, where to stand still is to fall behind, highly proactive U.S. universities seek to attract better faculty, better graduate students, better undergraduates, better administrators—and even better trustees. As stressed at the outset, a competitive status hierarchy has been operative as the key system characteristic throughout the twentieth century. It has steadily included more institutions, enlarging the pool within which rugged competition has stimulated greater self-reliance and increased research intensity. More public universities have slipped away from the traditional posture of being fully state-led and have moved closer to private universities in a large, growing nonprofit sector. MIT and ETHZ differ first of all, we can add, in that MIT, past and present, is fully a private university, free to select its own students and is thoroughly embedded in the national system as an exemplar of successful non-state institution, while ETHZ has been and remains a major public university operating within a state-defined "open admission policy" (Herbst et al., 2002, 27) and embedded as an exemplar in Europe of a particularly successful state institution.

It is hard to exaggerate the importance of competitively striving for prestige in the American system of higher education. Players include borderline community colleges, small private liberal arts colleges known nationally and locally, Catholic universities, Lutheran colleges, women's colleges, historically black institutions, masters' level universities, and doctoral-granting research universities. The universities in particular are indeed what economists would call "prestige maximizers": their bottom line is prestige rather than monetary profit.

Accumulated prestige is central in that it allows a university to exert some control over a variety of markets it encounters. Prestige critically shapes interactions between universities and would-be students in consumer markets. It enters, often decisively, into mutual adjustment between universities and prospective faculty in academic labor markets. It weighs upon the minds of possible employers of graduates entering the general labor markets. It conditions agreements between universities and such external institutions as banks in financial markets. Most of all, accumulated prestige is the coinage by which universities and colleges place one another in higher education's reputation markets.

In "the third way" of university development pursued in the concluding chapter of my book—third between state and market—a determined bid for performance-based high prestige is an essential part of the character of the proactive, self-reliant university.

My explanation of the centrality of institutional competitive initiative in the creation of robust world-class universities in the American system of higher education may possibly serve as a corrective to widely held beliefs in European and Japanese governments that top-down governmental initiatives can readily and powerfully move universities along this all-important road. The central lesson from the American experience is that universities have to be given a great deal of autonomy—backed by trust—upon which they can strengthen their self-steering capacity. The American experience is one of universities individually traveling down an entrepreneurial road to self-reliance. They are handcrafted, not mass-produced. Adaptive change in capacity for research, teaching, and student learning is fashioned incrementally over decades of sustained effort. Above all, rather than state-led, it is institution-led. There is no state substitute for university autonomous self-development.

Notes

1. For greater elaboration of these characteristics, see Clark (1987), chap. 3, "The Open System"; also Clark (1990); and Clark (1995), chap. 4, "The United States: Competitive Graduate Schools."

2. For extensive coverage of the development of American higher education, especially the university sector, see Geiger (1986) and (1993).

3. On these twin headaches for university administration in the United States, see Duderstadt (2000a) and (2000b).

4. Duderstadt (2000a, 304, 310, 312–31). Convinced that we are witnessing the emergence of new "learning structures," even "new civic life forms," Duderstadt has strongly argued for a nomenclature of "private-financed public university" and similar terms. His vision, based on the Michigan development, leads to two radical conclusions: that "America's great experiment of building world-class public universities supported primarily by tax dollars has come to an end"; that "the autonomy of the public university will become one of its most crucial assets, perhaps even more critical than state support for some institutions."

5. On nineteenth- and twentieth-century versions of the research-teaching-study nexus, see Clark (1995), particularly chap. 1 on Germany, chap. 4 on the United States, and chap. 7 on conditions of integration of the nexus.

References

Chronicle of Higher Education. Almanac 2002–3. August 30, 2002.

Clark, B. R. *The Academic Life: Small Worlds, Different Worlds.* Princeton: Carnegie Foundation for the Advancement of Teaching and Princeton University Press, 1987.

———. "The Organizational Dynamics of the American Research University." *Higher Education Policy* 3, no. 2 (1990): 31–35.

———. *Places of Inquiry: Research and Advanced Education in Modern Universities.* Berkeley: University of California Press, 1995.

———. *Creating Entrepreneurial Universities: Organizational Pathways of Transformation.* Oxford: Pergamon/Elsevier, 1998.

———. *Sustaining Change in Universities: Continuities in Case Studies and Concepts.* Maidenhead, England: Society for Research into Higher Education and Open University Press, 2004.

Duderstadt, J. J. *A University for the 21st Century.* Ann Arbor: University of Michigan Press, 2000a.

———. *Intercollegiate Athletics and the American University: A University President's Perspective.* Ann Arbor: University of Michigan Press, 2000b.

Geiger, R. L. *To Advance Knowledge: The Growth of the American Research Universities, 1900–1940.* New York: Oxford University Press, 1986.

———. *Research and Relevant Knowledge: American Research Universities Since World War II.* New York: Oxford University Press, 1993.

———. *Knowledge and Money: Research Universities and the Paradox of the Marketplace.* Palo Alto: Stanford University Press, 2004.

Gumport, P. "Graduate Education and Research Imperatives: Views from American Campuses." In *The Research Foundations of Graduate Education: Germany, Britain, France, United States, Japan,* edited by B. R. Clark, 261–93. Berkeley: University of California Press, 1993.

Herbst, M., Urs Hagentobler, and L. Snover. *MIT and ETH Zurich: Structures and Cultures Juxtaposed.* Bern, Switzerland: Center for Science and Technology Studies (CEST 2002/9), 2002.

Lombardi, J. V., D. D. Craig, E. D. Capaldi, D. S. Gater, and S. L. Mendonca. *The Top American Research Universities: An Annual Report from The Lombardi Program on Measuring University Performance.* Gainesville: The Center at the University of Florida, 2001.

Portes, R. "Economics in Europe." *European Economic Review* 31 (1987): 1329–40.

Raymond, S. U. (ed.). *Science-Based Economic Development: Case Studies Around the World.* New York: The New York Academy of Science, 1996.

Rosovsky, H. *The University: An Owner's Manual.* New York: W. W. Norton, 1990.

Slosson, E. E. *Great American Universities.* New York: Macmillan, 1910. (Reprint Edition, 1977. New York: Arno Press.)

Tornatsky, L. G., P. G. Waugaman, and D. O. Gray. *Innovation U.: New University Roles in a Knowledge Economy.* Research Triangle Park, N.C.: Southern Growth Policies Board, 2002.

University of Michigan. Recent Rankings for Academic Programs at the University of Michigan—Ann Arbor, 2002.

———. All Funds Budget Table, University of Michigan—Ann Arbor, 1984–2003.

INTRODUCTION TO CHAPTER 32

We approach the end of this volume with two brief source documents that reflect my zeal for context-based research. The first short statement, taken up at this point, comes from a collection of papers devoted to an up-to-date assessment of the sociology of higher education assembled and edited by Patricia J. Gumport. She began her 2007 collection with an article I wrote in 1973, in which I had attempted a comprehensive assessment of this field in its early state—one that developed largely between the end of World War II and the early 1970s. That paper appears as the eleventh item in this collection of essays.

When Gumport was preparing her volume, she asked me if I would like to add a final comment. I should have sensibly said no. But at the time I had been increasingly concerned about a large chasm between researchers and practitioners in how they go about understanding universities. So I wrote a short, grumpy piece pointing to a need to overcome the research-practice disconnect if we wanted to make serious progress in this field.

That cleavage can be effectively bridged if more higher education researchers would do as I have done: to reason from "best practices," a trope used in other fields, and to do so at the level of whole universities. We find tested practices in exemplary cases linked together in a defined context. Those noteworthy universities can be captured best by writing case study narratives that report on combinations of common elements and key singularities each university possesses.

Research that seeks to explain the organized workings of higher education should avoid ungrounded theorizing ("I think that . . ." "I believe that . . ." "Critical theory indicates that . . .") that spins off into vacuous space. Instead, research gains credibility as it positions itself close to the gravitational pull of tested reality.

CHAPTER 32

Overcoming the Disconnect between Researchers and Practitioners

THERE IS NO LONGER any doubt about it. The disconnect between researchers and practitioners in understanding universities remains acute. Researchers write mainly for one another, armed with disciplinary and interdisciplinary perspectives. Early in their careers, they test hypotheses generated from a review of the literature. As they grow older, they aim to generate "theory," ensuring turgid prose. Ruminating among broadly stated schemes, as presently practiced in the sociology of higher education, they publish articles in journals that practitioners do not read. For their part, practitioners turn to one another to gain insight into how to handle ongoing specific concerns. For them, academic theorizing is imprecise and remote—a case of talking the talk far removed from local operating complexities. Researchers aim too high and attempt to explain too much. Practitioners—the staffs of U.S. foundations included—aim too low and fall into ad hoc discussions. When questions of how change comes about in universities take the stage, the gap widens.

This disconnect in how the university is analyzed is similar to how business firms were studied up to the 1960s. But in the ensuing four decades, faculty in business schools closed the gap between research and practice by means of case study analysis, concentrating on exemplary institutions and best practices. The resulting literature on General Electric alone is a subspecies, filling bookshelves and classroom assignments. Case studies of firms, good and bad, today constitute the basic tools of instruction.

Recently, researchers studying American education levels K–12 have seriously tackled the research-practice disconnect. Ellen Condliffe Lage-

Based on "A Note on Pursuing Things That Work," in *Sociology of Higher Education*, edited by Patricia J. Gumport, chap. 11, 319–24. Baltimore: Johns Hopkins University Press, 2007.

mann observed in a 2001 Spencer Foundation annual report that by operating close to practice, "use-driven" or "practice-based" research on elementary and secondary education has sought to link fundamental understanding with immediate application (Lagemann, 2001). Beyond education studies, in the wider scientific scene, Donald E. Stokes challenged the old dichotomy between basic and applied research. In the late 1990s, he stressed combining research for understanding with research for use, using as "a model case the fundamental yet use-inspired studies by which Louis Pasteur laid the foundations of microbiology a century ago" (Stokes, 1997). Stokes asserted a modern "dynamic paradigm" that would help renew the compact between science and government and, even more broadly, the connection between basic science and American democracy.

A new approach, then, has spread throughout many societal sectors and realms of analysis. It centers on use-inspired, practice-driven research that can serve also as research for basic understanding.

We who study university change can reduce the research-practice disconnect by two means immediately at hand. First, we can reason inductively from the experience of on-the-ground practitioners. We can convene seminars on what works. We can give primacy to the hard reality of observed practices in defined settings: from departments and research centers to broader schools and faculties, to all-encompassing central administrators, academic senates, and coalitions of faculty and managers. Only secondarily do we glance at broad frameworks developed in the study of business and public administration—resource dependency, path dependence, isomorphism, management by objectives, total quality management. These borrowed approaches never get to the point of how decisions are collectively fashioned in complex universities, each loaded with unique features in an extended portfolio of missions and programs, general and specific, that need rebalancing from year to year.

In the complex realities of practice, we can pursue what works. We find out what significant organizational changes Stanford made in the last half of the twentieth century to become an outstanding university (undergraduate education included) noted for talent-attracting magnetism. We find out how Michigan and Wisconsin continue to prosper in research *and* in teaching *and* in service as public U.S. universities, even as they extend themselves to include new populations and outside business and professional groups. We watch North Carolina State University experimentally fashion a separate niche alongside Duke University and the University of North Carolina, to give the state of North Carolina increasing strength in its research triangle. We take seriously the question of how U.S. universities raised themselves up to a collective posture whereby they dominate in international assessments—recently carried out in Switzerland (Herbst, Hagentobler, and Snover, 2002), Britain (*Times Higher Education Supplement*, 2004), and China (Institute of Higher Education, Shanghai Jiao Tong University, 2004)—of the top 50, top 100, top 200, top 500 universities in the world. Other nations have long come—and continue to come—to the United States to find out what works, before carrying home lessons that can be integrated with home country constraints and opportunities. The world of actual university reform is a very busy place.

Researchers of changing university practice can also greatly extend the insights of inductive reasoning by pursuing case studies internationally. The time is long overdue for researchers and practitioners alike to escape nationalistic tunnel vision as fully as possible: the French, from the tunnel of unique traditional structures and practices in a national higher education system defined originally by Napoleon a century and a half ago (Christine Musselin, in her recent book, has brilliantly shown the way out—Musselin, 2004); the Russians, from their particularly rocky road of modernizing old authoritarian structures while government support collapses; the Germans, from the frozen ice of interlocked local and national interests glorified by Humboldtian ideals; and the American, most arrogant of all, from thinking the whole world must also be captivated by the grinding problem of remedial education, the never-ending debate over the fate of general/liberal education in mega-universities, and the corruption of big-time sports, all uniquely embedded in a particular U.S. combination of weak elementary-secondary education and highly differentiated, sharply competitive higher education.

Reducing our own deep disconnect between research and practice is not easy. But young scholars who put their minds and enthusiasms to it could make a difference in a decade. They need to see practitioners as their primary teachers. The mantra becomes: sit not with statisticians but with university management groups. They need to patiently pursue case studies of specific universities, forging ethnographic compromises as their narratives bracket newly identified common features amid institutional specificities. Some among them will need to pursue case studies outside their own country, by field research if possible, by document analysis alone if necessary, to reduce tunnel vision and to determine how common elements vary internationally. Researchers need to catch up with varied practice and then move on as practice moves on. Fast-moving times require adaptive research.

A good example of adaptive research operating at the cutting edge of university change comes from Canada. In a collection of papers given at a 2002 conference on "the changing role of higher education," John R. Evans reported on "the academic-commercial interface in a knowledge-driven economy," as seen specifically in "a view from MaRS"—an example of "clusters" at various stages of development across Canada, six of which have major emphasis on biotechnology (Evans, 2005). Details are reported particularly for the promising MaRS cluster (Medical and Related Sciences Discovery District) in Toronto, seen as "a great site to promote the cluster convergence of critical elements" *and* exemplifying the agglomeration effects or critical mass of having a large number of scientists, investors, and firms all in a single location. Among the practitioners at this Canadian cutting edge, *commercialization* is a highly positive term, with its financing and nurturing at the center of attention. This attitude toward university-commerce ventures contrasts sharply with the very negative connotations often assigned to the idea of commercialization by academics in the United States.

Practitioners sit at the crossroads of action. They have to make things work, to experiment and learn in compartmentalized universities, each operating in a particular societal context. What practitioners have variously been able to accomplish in recent decades provides ample ground for optimism. If you want to know how to build a great university in three or four decades, go find out how from MIT and the University of California, San Diego, and on through at least thirty universities in the American system. And go find out from the University of Toronto and the University of British Columbia in Canada; from Cambridge, Warwick, and Strathclyde universities in Great Britain; from fast-developing universities in Singapore, South Korea, Hong Kong, Taiwan, and China, in Asia; from flagship universities in Uganda, Tanzania, and Mozambique that now serve as models for university reform in African nations.

It is not university personnel who lack the grounded capacity to understand how their institutions operate and how they change (they learn it as practice) so much as it is the lagging researchers and observers whose soggy images of asserted glories of universities in simpler times lead them to exaggerate present-day deficiencies.

By invoking the status quo ante of universities during the past one hundred years or so, as is commonly done, proponents of the good old days forget that those times may have been the worst. For example, discrimination in access ran successively against Irish and Italian Catholics; Jews (in the 1920s and 1930s, Princeton had a 5 percent and Yale a 10 percent quota);[1] women (who just a few decades ago were limited to 5 percent or less of enrollment in medical and law schools); and on to the access constraints encountered in recent years by present-day minorities. And Joe College remained firmly in control of student life until the arrival of mass higher education after World War II.

What old-time colleges were like is worth perhaps half a cheer. Today we can give two cheers for modern universities and the many types of colleges that pursue productive paths of adaptive development in an age of universal access. From community colleges to research universities, from one country and one continent to another, a host of informed practitioners know how things work. What they have figured out on the spot—and go on figuring out anew in changing webs of interacting programs and practices—constitutes a largely untapped pool of resources for researchers who seriously want to explain the workings of higher education in the twenty-first century.[2]

Amid the current extensive diffusion of analytical interests and self-sustaining subfields in the sociology of higher education, a focus on the realities of successful practice, at the least, will help narrow the stubborn gap that has long persisted between the understandings of researchers and the concerns of practitioners. A more integrated pursuit of things that work should also bolster optimism and hope for the future of universities and colleges in the twenty-first century.

Notes

1. For the classic, pathbreaking work on discrimination against Jews, see Wechsler (1977); see also McCaughey (2003). Historians have a particularly fine eye for the details of documented practice.

2. My comments on pursuing practices that work flow from research that began in the mid-1990s to examine case studies of university change. I worked first in Britain and Continental Europe, then from the findings of other scholars in countries elsewhere in the world, and finally back to the United States. The results were reported in two books; the first took up five case studies (Clark, 1998), the second ranged over fourteen (Clark, 2004).

References

Clark, B. R. *Creating Entrepreneurial Universities: Organizational Pathways of Transformation.* Oxford: Pergamon-Elsevier Science, 1988.

———. *Creating Entrepreneurial Universities: Organizational Pathways of Transformation.* Oxford: Pergamon/IAU, 1998.

———. *Sustaining Change in Universities: Continuities in Case Studies and Concepts.* Maidenhead: Open University Press and Society for Research into Higher Education, 2004.

Evans, J. R. "The Academic-Commercial Interface in a Knowledge-Driven Economy: A View from MaRS." In *Creating Knowledge: Strengthening Nations: The Changing Role of Higher Education,* edited by G. A. Jones, P. L. McCarney, and M. L. Skolnick, 273–82. Toronto: University of Toronto Press, 2005.

Herbst, M., U. Hagentobler, and L. Snover. *MIT and ETH Zurich: Structures and Cultures Juxtaposed.* CEST 2002/9. Berne, Switzerland: Center for Science and Technology Studies, 2002.

Institute of Higher Education, Shanghai Jiao Tong University. "Top 500 World Universities." Available at http://ed.sjtu.edu.cn/rank/2004/2004Main.htm.2004.

Lagemann, E. C. "Report of the President." In *Spencer Foundation Annual Report. April 1, 2000–March 31, 2001,* 5–6. Chicago: Spencer Foundation, 2001.

McCaughey, R. A. "Jews at Columbia." In *Stand, Columbia: A History of Columbia University in the City of New York, 1754–2004,* 256–76. New York: Columbia University Press, 2003.

Musselin, C. *The Long March of the French University.* English ed. New York: Routledge/Falmer, 2004. (French orig. 2001.)

Stokes, D. E. *Pasteur's Quadrant: Basic Science and Technological Innovation.* Washington, D.C.: Brookings Institution, 1997.

Times Higher Education Supplement. 2004. "World University Rankings." November 5 issue.

Wechsler, H. S. *The Qualified Student: A History of Selective College Admission in America, 1870–1970.* New York: Wiley, 1977.

INTRODUCTION TO CHAPTER 33

This final brief statement is formulated from decades of research experience that began as far back as the 1950s and 1960s with my research on community colleges and distinctive liberal arts colleges. Cumulative experience has increasingly taught me that qualitative research ending in case study narratives offers major advantages over other forms of analysis. Here I summarize these advantages and place them in the larger frameworks of inquiry found in the social sciences, including education research.

CHAPTER 33

The Advantages of Case Study Narratives in Understanding Continuity and Change in Universities

ARTHUR L. STINCHCOMBE, in his basic volume *The Logic of Social Research* (2005), identifies four major methods of inquiry: experimental; quantitative regression (statistical); historical; and ethnographic. He states that the last helps "to penetrate deeply into sequences of actions and their contexts to provide evidence about action as it develops in its natural setting." Commonly, historical methods support the ethnographic in tracking what has happened in natural settings. "The context of social action is shaped by the path history has taken."[1]

When we want to know what has happened—and is happening—to universities in their "natural setting," we clearly need case studies that produce grounded understanding. We can think of such studies as an approach that has multiple and necessary advantages over other forms of analysis.

First, and most important, case study research commits to local context. It offers the opportunity to focus on mutually reinforcing interaction among both stabilizing and transforming features. Basic elements of change co-evolve; they have significant casual impact on each other's ability to persist. Thus, interaction of organizational elements plays a central role. When we lose track of this interplay in muddled analysis, we lose the crucial difference, e.g., between the emerging infrastructure of sustained change and the infrastructure of the status quo found in the traditional university. We particularly lose it when we pull "variables" out of context in order to concentrate on particular isolated components—forms of leadership, changes in faculty work, enlarged student access, and the like.

Based on unpublished writings, 2005–7.

We then make the fatal error of losing touch with the mutually engaging forces that propel a university forward.

The study of university change requires heavy use of case studies reported in rounded narratives. This form of qualitative research has made a major comeback in the social sciences in recent years. Let me point to some major viewpoints that describe the thrust and the boundaries of the ethnographic.

Anthropologist Clifford Geertz has powerfully voiced the advantages of qualitative fieldwork. He wrote about the clarity gained by "thick description" that avoids the "banalities of theory." He saw the reality of actual practice as more fundamental than either discourse or theory. The first lesson learned from Geertz is to get close to reality by anchoring research in the context being studied.[2]

Alan Wolfe and Ian Shapiro, in political science, have cogently analyzed the "flight from reality" that takes place when efforts at writing formal theory dominate the practical wisdom obtained by examining concrete cases. Better to stick with the real world, which "contains a great deal of uncertainty" but "also offers enough regularity to permit modest generalization." As an alternative to inward-looking grand theory, in which researchers lose sight of the objects of their study, we should see practitioners as "essentially pragmatists seeking to achieve what is achievable."[3] They are always knee-deep in reality.

Sociologists Charles C. Ragin and Howard S. Becker and their colleagues, in a valuable collection of focused articles, have instructively explored the qualitative foundations of all social inquiry.[4] In a contribution to their volume, Andrew Abbott argues effectively "that case/narrative explanation follows the causal action. . . . Things happen because of constellations of factors, not because of a few fundamental effects acting independently." Noting the possibilities of "narrative generalization," he concludes that "a social science expressed in terms of typical stories would provide far better access for policy intervention than the present social science of variables."[5]

Education researcher Robert E. Stake has turned to multiple case analysis to depict an analytical road where we tap "the experience of real cases operating in real situations." We can both capture local contexts and compare cases. In noting how "the case gets done," we find patterns of covariation; "things are happening together."[6] Stake even seeks to develop guidelines for balancing common issues across a group of cases with the unique features and context of each case.

Finally, Bent Flyvbjerg, a Danish professor of urban planning, in his brilliant book *Making Social Science Matter* (2001) has empirically demonstrated, as he went about his own work, the value of sustained participant-observer involvement in ongoing real-world situations. He has also drawn up a full indictment of "a social science of variables" as the key culprit in the contemporary failure of social inquiry to effectively inform public policy and the general understanding of contemporary society. The effort to imitate the physical and biological sciences leads to one dead-end after another. Pulling out all the historical stops, Flyvbjerg traces the practical approach of learning from observed practice back through Foucault, Habermas, and Nietzsche and all the way to Aristotle's conception of *phronesis*. Modern-day analysts can "empower Aristotle" by getting close to reality, by always asking how things are actually done in place-bound and time-bound concrete examples. We focus on cases and contexts, we look at practice before theory, we report observations in narratives. Asking and answering "how" means "doing narratives." Narratives have an "irreducible quality" in producing know-how knowledge.

Flyvbjerg's admirable goal is "to help restore social science to its classical position as a practical, intellectual activity aimed at clarifying the problems, risks, and possibilities we face as humans and societies, and as contributing to social and political praxis." The means to this important goal are at hand: let us empower Aristotle by concentrating on case study research and narrative reporting.

The second reason I advocate case study research, beyond the fundamental advantage of committing to local context, is that studying universities in this way also attends to the singular, crucial realities of each institution, i.e., to its own genetic imprints, its unique constraints of historic place and time, its specially evolved structures and cultures. Case narratives can then tell a fuller story of what happened locally, bridging the common and the unique.

Third, pivoting around localized accounts, case study research can identify and clarify exemplary institutions as models for others. Flyvbjerg has stressed that "a discipline without exemplars is an ineffective one. In social science, especially in those branches which find themselves to be weak, more good case studies could help remedy this situation."[7] Without doubt, the study of university change qualifies around the world as a weak branch of social science. We need to highlight some exemplary cases.

And last, a fourth benefit of this type of research is that it can probe the problems of balancing commitments in evermore complicated universities. By observing realities on the ground as I engaged in the 2000–2003 research, I was forced to take note of three balancing acts: first, among regional, national, and international aspirations and identities; then between comprehensive coverage of disciplines and subjects that offers a wide range of services *and* specialized foci that reap the rewards of selective investment; and between centralized and decentralized centers of transforming action. Here the all-university center with its interlocked top administrators and committees vies against the dean-led mid-level schools and colleges and against the base units of departments and research centers.

I am a firm believer in doing research using a combination of ethnographic and historical methods that reveals how universities, in their evolving daily actions, implement a variety of missions and purposes. The complexity involved in making a university work becomes greater with each passing decade. Contradictory actions often abound. Case narratives reveal, institution by institution, how this engagement takes place.

Notes

1. Arthur L. Stinchcombe, *The Logic of Social Research* (Chicago: University of Chicago Press, 2005), 1–9.

2. Clifford Geertz, "Empowering Aristotle," book review of Flyvbjerg's *Making Social Science Matter, Science* 53 (July 6, 2001): 293.

3. Alan Wolfe, "Reality in Political Science," *The Chronicle of Higher Education,* (November 4, 2005) Section B, 19–20. See also Alan Wolfe, "Paths of Dependence," *The New Republic* (October 14, 2002): 40–46; and Ian Shapiro, *The Flight from Reality in the Human Sciences* (Princeton: Princeton University Press, 2005).

4. Charles C. Ragin and Howard S. Becker, eds., *What Is a Case?: Exploring the Foundations of Social Inquiry* (New York: Cambridge University Press, 1992).

5. Andrew Abbott, "What Do Cases Do: Some Notes on Activity in Sociological Analysis." In Ragin and Becker, *What Is a Case?* 52–82. Quotations on pp. 68, 79.

6. Robert E. Stake, *Multiple Case Study Analysis* (New York: The Guilford Press, 2006), 2, 28.

7. Bent Flyvbjerg, *Making Social Science Matter: Why Social Inquiry Fails and How It Can Succeed Again* (New York: Cambridge University Press, 2001), 2–4, 87, 132–37.

Understanding Continuity and Change in Universities 553

Epilogue

The most important results of my research depend on the particular way I do that research. This process—*organic contextual research*—captures local interaction among organizational elements, including elements of change. Such grounded research leads to useful *narrative generalization* in the form of concepts derived from actual practice. As we reason from each institution's interconnected reality, we claim no privileged insights from ideological preference. We avoid ad hoc guessing and editorializing. We avoid deductive reasoning from bits and pieces of place and time.

As individual universities, driven by intensifying realities, grow more and more complicated, research needs to concentrate all the more on local contextualization. The research dictate becomes: stay as close as possible to concrete realities. The mantra for reform becomes: evermore complex universities operating in increasingly complex environments require complex differentiated pathways. One hundred universities require one hundred solutions.

University administrators will surely find my line of reasoning to be congenial. They grapple with complexities every day; they learn from the results of choices that have to be made. They are aware that individual universities are the main actors in higher education systems, actors that need to be grasped and weighed in their entirety. Students, journalists, policy analysts, and national commissions, in contrast, often seek simple answers to manifold problems; they reason down a narrow tunnel. Most troubling are national bodies, operating with the power of the purse, which seek comprehensive reform from a simplified posture. The Spellings Commission (2005–7), established by the U.S. Department of Education, e.g., has sought a comprehensive strategy for higher education. It has labored mightily for several years to devise the coalitions that could implement such a strategy. This *dirigiste* approach, now powerfully at work in the American setting, seeks to establish the top-down ministerial supervision that elsewhere in the world has led to massive rigidity. From such efforts come the seeds of monopoly control, planted, as always, in the name of compelling reforms. In the Spellings example, advocates of top-down, broad reform warn of "impending disaster," of "a train-wreck coming," if their twenty-five "action items" are not soon implemented.

Cross-national findings, reliably rooted in cross-national comparisons, point to an opposite approach in the United States, one that appreciates and builds upon the ingrained diversification and competitiveness of a radically decentralized national aggregation of self-propelling universities and colleges. This non-formal "system" does not respond well to central vision. Representatives of particular points of view—e.g., those who advocate the importance of the liberal arts—also repeatedly beat a dead horse about its non-responsiveness. But the system's productive strength, leading to international dominance in the last half of the twentieth century, lies in unplanned, open-ended trial and error as a thousand parts interact. These happenings are very likely to be the best way to make good use of fast-moving change.

Universities capable of adaptive change are handcrafted, not mass produced. They cannot be built a dozen at a time by state dictate—or by wandering "markets." State officials can aid their development by eliminating state-based obstacles and offering incentives that favor local initiatives. The state can *enable*. Only individual universities, however, by their efforts, can achieve a proactive character so full of initiative and adaptability that the entire institution can be seen as entrepreneurially progressive. What the state enables, the university *enacts*, thus crafting its own transformed character.

That enactment in the early twenty-first century leads to fascinating new global arrangements among universities. Since Joseph Schumpeter wrote about it in the first half of the twentieth century, innovation has been portrayed as the work of individual entrepreneurs. The entrepreneur is the driving force, the maker of new combinations, the indispensable hero. But now, increasingly, we see innovation produced by entrepreneurial groups—clusters, networks—located among universities as well as within them. We find new entrepreneurial regional clusters that interact globally with one another.

AnnaLee Saxenian, in her book *The New Argonauts: Beyond Regional Advantage in a Global Economy* (2006), has clearly revealed this exciting new world as it plays out in science and technology clusters. Her "new Argonauts"—foreign-born, technically skilled entrepreneurs—travel back and forth between Silicon Valley (where they got their training and learned the Silicon Valley system) and new centers in their home countries. They operate in two countries simultaneously. "Brain drain" becomes "brain circulation," serving the United States as well as the new regional clusters in, e.g., Israel, Taiwan, India, and mainland China. If you want to know realistically what is going on globally at a rapid pace, follow the scientific talent. You will find that talent engaged in a bottom-up process of entrepreneurial experimentation.

Although Saxenian doesn't center her analysis on universities, Stanford clearly remains a central, even iconic, player in the Silicon Valley story. Noting also that graduate students are the heart of a research university, she individually thanks over ten foreign-born graduates and undergraduates by name who helped in her research. Her accounts of the international flows of top talent notes, e.g., the selection and training of graduate students in the Tel Aviv–Jerusalem regions of Israel and in similar national elite programs in engineering and science in the countries named above. Brain circulation rotates in and out of university settings. Saxenian built this new understanding from dogged, on-the-spot interviewing after identifying important respondents from a brief questionnaire. Her findings point to an optimistic international future dominated by "brain circulation" around the world. The higher education system in the United States, through the ongoing enrichment of Silicon Valley and the comparative feedback it gets from regional partners, particularly profits. Other countries see themselves in a new win-win situation instead of being stuck under old hierarchies. The possible players depend on who pays attention and establishes enabling machinery: "Silicon Vikings" for a Swedish involvement; a Korean IT Network; a startup among Russian expatriates; a Japanese Entrepreneur Network; and even a "Silicon French" clustering.

Here is social science that matters, big time.

To conclude this volume with two brief normative notes—chapters 32 and 33—and an epilogue betrays a certain reluctance to let go. But a half-century of doing research that started with a doctoral dissertation in the early 1950s has been long enough to figure out a few things in a reliable way about the what and how of higher education at home and abroad. We hope long experience has brought a certain kind of useful understanding, one extensively displayed in this volume. We also hope this collection will encourage others, particularly graduate students and young academics, to commit to qualitative, context-defined research. As they combine research for use with research for understanding, always centered on hard realities, they can learn some dependable things.

ACKNOWLEDGMENTS

Practicing scholarship has been an inexorable force in my life for five decades. The number of individuals, institutions, and funding agencies that helped me along the way is substantial. I am deeply indebted to all of them.

The faculty and graduate students in the department of sociology at UCLA, where I earned my PhD in 1954, were very supportive. My advisors—Philip Selznick, Leonard Broom, and William S. Robinson— offered powerful views of the possibilities of sociology for further study. Selznick's institutional approach particularly caught my attention. It led me toward the analytical case study mode of research identified in part I of this volume. That mode remained basic in my research throughout a half-century of inquiry.

At Stanford Wendell Bell and Edmund Volkart helped me negotiate the vicissitudes of a one-year-at-a-time academic position. At Harvard Frank Keppel, dean of the graduate school of education, appointed me on the spot to the faculty of an administrative training program, from which I learned the value of close interaction with experienced and fledgling practitioners.

T. R. McConnell was instrumental in bringing us back to the West Coast in 1958. At Berkeley in and around his new Center for the Study of Higher Education I benefited from many opportunities to interact with Martin Trow and Neil Smelser, and later Sheldon Rothblatt. Shelly Messenger, an old friend elsewhere on campus, became an invaluable colleague. I, to this day, value the many lifelong friendships set in motion during our eight years at Berkeley.

Wendell Bell, as the new chair of the Yale Sociology Department, with the support of Kingman Brewster, a charismatic president, fashioned three new senior appointments in 1966. I was one of them. From this department base I developed a research group in Yale's new Institution for Social and Policy Studies (ISPS). I am highly indebted to the first two directors of the institute: John Perry Miller for the idea of centering my training efforts on post-docs—and for helping to fund this effort; and Charles E. Lindblom for simply being the intellectual phenomenon known as Ed Lindblom.

For the final cross-country move in 1980, I am indebted to many individuals at UCLA who fashioned a new chair—the Allan M. Cartter Chair—and convinced me to be the first occupant: Jill Cartter, Lewis Solmon, and Sandy Astin, in particular, together with members of the university's central administration. The Cartter chair helped me to develop international summer conferences, invest anew in post-docs, and prepare a steady stream of publications. It wore well up to my formal retirement in 1991—and beyond. I also want to thank Dean Aimée Dorr for her warmth, congeniality, and willingness to provide me with resources long after formal retirement.

One of the great joys of doing international comparative research was the chance to meet bright scholars in other countries, some of whom later became close friends. Three decades of cross-national involvement begun in the 1970s and extending into the twenty-first century has left a friendship trail for Adele and me that stretches throughout Europe and on to the Far East. Although we're not able to list everyone who influenced my work and our lives, we thank them all. We wish to particularly acknowledge the following scholars and friends—past and present.

IN EUROPE
Mediterranean Region
Portugal: Alberto Amaral
Spain: José Ginés-Mora
Italy: Roberto Moscati, Alberto Martinelli

Eastern Europe
Czech Republic: Ladislav Cerych, Helena Sebková

Scandinavia
Finland: Seppo Hölttä, Kyösti Pullianen, Jussi Vällimaa, Kari Hyppönen, Jouni Kekäle
Sweden: Eskil Björkland, Thorsten Nybom, Berit Askling, Olof Ruin, Rune Premfors, Björn Wittrock, Marianne Bauer

Norway: Peter Maassen, Per Olaf Aamodt, Svein Kyvik, Björn Stensaker

Central Europe
Netherlands: Frans van Vught, Jeroen Huisman, Jurgen Enders
Germany: Ulrich Teichler, Barbara Kehm
France: Christine Musselin, Jean-Claude Eicher, Thierry Chevallier
England: Tony Becher, Mary Henkel, Maurice Kogan, Michael Shattuck, A. H. Halsey, Harold J. Perkin, William Taylor, Graeme Moodie, Peter Scott
Scotland: Peter West, George Gordon, Roddy Begg
Ireland: Patrick Clancy, Ellen Hazelkorn
Switzerland: Marcel Herbst
Austria: Hans Pecher, Barbara Sporn

IN AUSTRALIA
Grant and Kay Harman, Lynn Meek, Craig McInnis, Leo Goedegeburre, David Jones, Simon Marginson

IN THE FAR EAST
Japan: Akira Arimoto, Kazuyuki Kitamura, Morikazu Ushiogi, Tatsuo Kawashima, Fumihiro Maruyama, Ikuo Amano
China: Chengxu Wang, Duanying Zhao

IN LATIN AMERICA
Mexico: Rollin Kent
Brazil: Simon Schwartzman, Marilia Morosini
Chili: José Joaquin Brunner, Andrés Bernasconi

IN THE UNITED STATES
James Perkins, Barbara Burn, Robert Berdahl; Bruce Johnstone, James Duderstadt, Philip Altbach, David Breneman; Robert Birnbaum, David Dill, Elaine El-Khawas; Richard Richardson, Ann Morey, William Tierney; Maresi Nerad, Jack Schuster, Marvin Peterson, Steven Brint, Mary Ann Sagaria

My research was supported by monetary grants from the Social Science Research Council, The Carnegie Corporation, The Carnegie Foundation for the Advancement of Teaching, The Rockefeller Foundation, The Lilly Endowment, Exxon Education Foundation, The Spencer Education Foundation, and The National Science Foundation. I am deeply indebted to private foundations that on occasion are willing to support cross-national research on higher education. Government sources of funds for this purpose have been scarce and laden with bureaucratic dictates. Private foundations typically gave me multiyear grants with sustained autonomy. I appreciated their largesse and lack of bureaucratic imposition.

My association with UCLA, Stanford, Harvard, UC Berkeley, and Yale provided me with an atmosphere of intellectual inquiry, research expectations, and the use of their valuable resources. I want to express my gratitude for having had those connections. And a thank-you list would not be complete without acknowledging the fruitful relations with four former post-docs: Roger Geiger and Daniel Levy from the Yale research group and Gary Rhoades and Patricia J. Gumport at UCLA. All have gone on to develop major research and training programs in the study of higher education.

Adding to this extensive list of supporters and friends, I cannot omit those translators who made my work more available to people in their countries: Akira Arimoto (Japanese), Chengxu Wang and Duanying Zhao (Chinese), Rollin Kent (Spanish), and Marilia Morosini (Portuguese).

My greatest intellectual and personal debts have been to my mentors and closest friends—among them, Philip Selznick at the outset; Clark Kerr, Ed Lindblom, Walter Metzger, Sheldon Rothblatt, and Neil Smelser in later relationships; and Alexander Astin and Arthur Cohen, close UCLA colleagues before and after retirement. Abroad, Guy Neave in France, Mike Shattuck in England, and Peter West in Scotland have truly been insightful, stimulating colleagues.

We also express our gratitude to Patricia J. Gumport and the editors of the Johns Hopkins University Press for suggesting that my work be made available in one place. Independently, Adele and I were musing about gathering my previously published writings into a volume; this seemed the right time to do it. It became a very felicitous coincidence when all parties decided to move forward with this project.